INVASIONS
OF THE GULF

For Donald and Jewel Leinster-Mackay, hosts in the Empire's distant outpost to refugees from Iraq's predations, observers of the rituals of rule, friends to generations of students in The University of Western Australia and Perth College.

'Masonry was like Rick's in Casablanca,' Belbo said. 'Which turns upside down the common view that it is a sercet society.'
'No, no it's a free port, a Macao. A façade. The secret is elsewhere.'
'Poor Masons.'

Umberto Eco, *Foucault's Pendulum*

THE INVASIONS OF THE GULF

Radicalism, Ritualism and the Shaikhs

Paul Rich

ALLBOROUGH PRESS
CAMBRIDGE, ENGLAND

First published in 1991 by Allborough Press,
Cambridge, England.

British Library Cataloguing in Publication Data
Rich, P. J. (Paul John)
The invasions of the Gulf: radicalism, ritualism, and the shaikhs
1. Middle East, history 2. Freemasons 3. English Public Schools
I. Title
953.04

ISBN 1-85571-009-9
ISBN 1-85571-016-1 hbk

Filmset in New Century Schoolbook
by Allborough Press.

Printed and bound in Great Britain
by Billings and Sons Ltd.

PAUL JOHN RICH

Honorary Research Fellow, The University of Western Australia

Paul John Rich is eminently qualified to comment on the collision of Eastern and Western values that the Iraqi 'annexation' of Kuwait so forcefully encapsulated. Although an American, he was a Kinsmen Scholar at Tonbridge School in England. He received his BA and EDM from Harvard and his PhD from The University of Western Australia.

His articles and reviews have appeared in the *Annals* of the American Academy of Political and Social Science, *Indo-British Review, Education Research and Perspectives, British Journal of Educational Studies* and elsewhere. He has contributed chapters to *'Benefits Bestowed?' Education and British Imperialism* (Manchester University Press 1988), *Problems in Reading for Arabic-Speaking Students* (Qatar University reprtd. 1990), and the forthcoming *Secret Texts.*

He is now writing a quintet entitled *Magicians of Arabia* about Gulf politics which will include tentatively *Viceroys of the Gulf, Tom Brown in Arabia, Stalky & Company Meet the Gulf Shaikhs,* and *Billy Bunter and the Arabs. Invasions of the Gulf,* although first to be published, will stand as the fifth and last of the completed series.

Dr. Rich has lived in the Gulf for twelve years and is a Fellow of the British Society for Middle East Studies, the Royal Asiatic Society, the Royal Society for Asian Affairs, and the Royal Geographical Society. He belongs to the Society for Arabian Studies, the Anglo-Omani Society, the Anglo-Arab Society, and other organizations with Middle Eastern concerns. He is a life governor of Manchester College, Oxford University, and an Honorary Research Fellow of The University of Western Australia.

Also by Paul John Rich:

ENGLISH PUBLIC SCHOOLS AND RITUALISTIC IMPERIALISM.

A trilogy about hegemony, education, and the Empire from Regency Press, London.

ELIXIR OF EMPIRE *English Public Schools, Ritualism, Freemasonry, and Imperialism*

CHAINS OF EMPIRE *English Public Schools, Masonic Cabalism, Historical Causality, and Imperial Clubdom*

RITUALS OF EMPIRE *English Public Schools, Imperial Baubles, Masonic Magicians, and Morphic Resonances*

CONTENTS

PLATES

FOREWORD

The Iraqi invasion of Kuwait summoned forth all kinds of instant opinions on the background to the crisis. Volumes were scanned for information on the history of frontiers, as well as on the legitimacy of the ruling family. Many questions were raised. How valid was the Iraqi claim? What rights did the Al Sabah clan have? Who had established the frontiers and when?

Numerous works were available for consultation going back to the magisterial volumes of Lorimer's *Gazetteer of the Persian Gulf* of 1908-15 and continuing with studies written both by local and Western historians. Some were sycophantic, time-serving and superficial, but many were serious attempts to understand the complex micro-histories of the area.

From the long historical viewpoint, the overwhelming factor was the British presence, beginning officially with the agreement of alliance with the Imam of Muscat in 1798. The British deeply influenced the course of events, to some extent disturbing age-old traditions, yet maintaining in power the local ruling sheikhly families. And the British brought with them the mores of a public school education, often refined through service in the Indian Empire. Paul Rich's book is a masterly, and timely, study of the effect these men had on the lives and times of those they had come to rule. It is a field he has made very much his own, and the present book is only one of a number of similar penetrating studies by him.

The Gulf was ruled from India, and those who served there constituted a unique, small foreign service of their own. They were left to themselves, working as political agents and officers, each attached cosily to one of the ruling sheikhs. At the top was the Resident, who developed into a kind of overlord; the last one proudly related that in Arabic he was referred to as the 'President of the Gulf'. He was part diplomat, part adviser, part military governor. They all imposed the *Pax Britannica* on the area and encouraged conditions which allowed the traditional industries to flourish, mainly pearl-diving, until the coming of the oil. They saw their task as efficient administration, the impartial provision of justice, the maintenance of law and order. They enjoyed their privileged lives, talking one-to-one in fluent Arabic to their Bedouin hosts, sipping coffee under the star-filled sky.

Their public school backgrounds taught them to believe in élitism and snobbery, which they passed on to their Sheikhs who became obsessed with their own positions, their wealth, rituals surrounding their *majlis* and the pompous titles of Highness and regal monarchy for simple Bedouin sheikhs and *amirs*. As Dr. Rich asks, if the British had come from grammar schools would they have thought less about élitism and more about providing good education for their charges? Would the sheikhs have bought good schools instead of thoroughbred racehorses? Would they not have treated all Indians as houseboys? The Residents did not see any incongruity between their own privileged education which they also strove to provide for their offspring, and the lack of attention they paid to often appalling local conditions. If accused of neglect, the British would often reply that without them the Arabs of the Gulf would have been even worse off.

Dr. Rich's verdict on the years of British rule is far from favourable. His conclusion is that British achievements were decidedly modest, and that a legacy was left behind which combined the worst features of Indo-British and Arab tradition. The rulers of the Gulf need to take crash courses in history, pluralism and constitutionalism if they are to survive. If the invasion of Kuwait brings the Gulf to its senses, then some good might have come from it. Perhaps the world is reaping the results of British policy which left a system in the Gulf which could not adapt, which drew frontiers which are now questioned, which created a state which has become a monster. The only nostalgia is that of a memory of stability which the century and a half of British rule provided.

In the course of his book, Dr. Rich makes an appeal for the collection and preservation of archives of all kinds relating to the Gulf. This is an appeal I warmly support, and St. Antony's has made a good start in this direction. The material on the Gulf has been understandably in great demand. A search among the H.R.P. Dickson papers recently revealed that two files had been spirited away – the two labelled 'The Iraq-Kuwait frontier'! Let us hope that they are not now lying on some desk in Baghdad. Future archivists must be more careful.

Derek Hopwood
St. Antony's College,
Oxford.
1991.

ACKNOWLEDGEMENTS

The outrageous assault by Iraq on Kuwait caught me in Western Australia on summer leave – I was scheduled to leave Perth on my way back to the Gulf on August 7 1990. An opportunity to finish this manuscript was provided by those unhappy August events. I much appreciate the encouragement of Allborough Press – not every publisher takes on a quintet and then has the last of the five volumes abruptly arrive before the first...but of course, at least in the Scriptures, the last shall or should be first!

Books are collective efforts. This is no exception. The Department of Education of The University of Western Australia did not succeed in sending me on my way after finishing the doctorate. An honorary research fellowship and subsequent visits, along with the loan of an office and chances to exchange ideas, have been of great value, and I am more than grateful. Acknowledgements are due to the Library of the University, particularly to Mr. Arthur Ellis, the University Librarian; and to specific individuals in the Department, including Dr. F.A. Haynes, Professor John Hattie, Dr. Michael Lally, and Dr. Clive Whitehead. I am also indebted to The Western Australia Computing Centre and to the Centre's Mr. Rob Van Zanten.

In preparing a chapter on Imperialism and Freemasonry for *'Benefits Bestowed?'* (Manchester University Press, 1988), I benefited from Dr. J.A. Mangan's criticisms, as I have from our correspondence through the years. A few paragraphs of the present work appeared in 'The Bahrain Public School Scheme, 1941', *Education Research and Perspectives,* December 1987. A small portion is forthcoming in 'Percy Cox's Flagpoles: Flags and Their Political Consequences in the Arabian Gulf, 1904-1920', *The Flag Bulletin,* 1991. An article considering Indo-British influences on Arabia appears in the *Indo-British Review,* May 1991.

My prosopographical studies of the Gulf began in earnest in June 1987 when I published – with the co-operation of the Media Services Department of The University of Western Australia – four booklets about the Residents and Agents in the Arabian Gulf: *Biographies of The British Residents & Agents in the Arabian Gulf, The Honours of The British Residents & Agents in the Arabian Gulf, Clubs of The British Residents & Agents in the Arabian Gulf,* and *Schools of The British Residents & Agents of the Arabian Gulf.* These were sent to retired members of the Indian Political Service and of the Foreign Service and to their families, as well as to libraries and scholars interested in the Middle East. The correspondence provoked by this exercise eventually will be placed in the India Office Library in London and St. Antony's.

Thanks are due to Alastair Campbell of Airds yr., Unicorn Pursuivant; Dame Violet Dickson and Col. H.Y.W.S. Dickson; Col. R.C. Gabriel; Mr. Tam Dalyell MP; Brother Christopher Haffner, District Grand Master of the District Grand Lodge of Hong Kong and the Far East; Dr. T.A. Heathcote, Curator, Royal Military Academy, Sandhurst; Sir Stewart Crawford KCMG; Sir Peter Moon; and H.E. P.R.M. Hinchcliffe, formerly H.M. Ambassador to Kuwait. I am grateful to Professor Rupert Wilkinson, author of *The Prefects,* for conversations and correspondence, not the least inspiring of which has been the opportunity to have a dialogue (by mail), about Freemasonry with his students at the University of Sussex. Dr. Karim Wissa of St. Antony's College, Oxford, provided a much extended version of a paper on Freemasonry in the Middle East that he delivered at the 1988 conference of the British Society for Middle East Studies. Assistance has been given me on visits to Washington by Mrs. Inge Baum, librarian of the Supreme Council, 33°, Ancient and Accepted Scottish Rite of Freemasonry, Southern Jurisdiction. At the Library of Congress I have been encouraged by the Head of the Middle Eastern Section, Dr. George Attiyeh, whose visit to Qatar in 1990 afforded an opportunity to renew our association. Appreciation also goes to the India Office Library in London and to Ms. Penelope Tuson, Dr. Steven Ashton, Dr. Richard Bingle, Mr. Anthony Farrington, and Mr. Ian Baxter. The London Library has been a splendid source and while working there I am mindful of the connection with that institution of one of the most famous of the British in the Gulf, Sir Arnold Wilson.

I am grateful to Mr. Robert Esden, Clerk to the Council, Imperial Society of Knights Bachelor; Mr. Steven Tomlinson, Deputy Keeper, Oxford University Archives; The Royal Artillery Institution Library, particularly Mr. G. Sutton; Mr. A.H.M. Kirk-Greene, St. Antony's College; Mr. R. Smith and Mr. J.E. Treble, Ministry of Defence; Ms. Janice Crichton, The Crown Agents; Emeritus Professor J.A. Roach of Sheffield University and Fellow of Corpus Christi, Cambridge; Commander G.J.T. Creedy LVO; Sir John Cotton KCMG; The Library of the United Grand Lodge of England, particularly Mrs. J.H. Hall when assistant librarian; Sir Donald Hawley, now Chairman of the Centre for British Teachers and formerly the Ambassador to Oman; The Royal Commonwealth Society Library and its then librarian, Mr. Donald Simpson; The Royal Geographical Society, particularly the archivist, Mrs. C. Kelly; Dr. G.G. Jones, Business History Unit of the London School of Economics; Dr. R.I. Lawless, Assistant Director, Centre for Middle Eastern & Islamic Studies, University of Durham; the Guildhall Library; and The Library, Palace of His Highness The Amir of Qatar. Mr. Trevor Hearl provided advice about Sandhurst; so have the librarians of the National Army Museum, London. I am indebted to Mrs. Sally Hofmann, a fellow member of the Society of Genealogists (whose library has been useful) and formerly of the India Office Library; and to Mr. John Brooke-Little, Norroy and Ulster King of Arms and Treasurer of the College of Heralds. The late Lt-Col. A.C. Galloway of the Indian Political Service and Mrs. Galloway, through letters and conversations, were extremely forthcoming.

Friends in Kuwait and Qatar, some of whom wish to remain anonymous, have been generous, especially my colleague Mr. Brian Devlin. Mrs. Jaxon Stallard, and Mr. Elgin Stallard, inadvertently, have reminded me of certain strange relationships between the 'Royal Craft' and Salt Lake City. The former secretary of the Bahrain Historical and Archaeological Society, Mr. Robert Jarman, vetted pages. My oasis in Arabia has been the Doha Club and more particularly its library, with which I have had something to do as an encourager and adviser. The librarian has transported himself to Western Australia, and I wish T. Jeyasothy well amongst the books and bits and bytes of the Antipodes. That his family served the Raj in Ceylon should give him an insight into reading about the Empire's secrets. The new librarian of the Club, Ronald Mendosa, also has been helpful.

Finally but importantly, there could be no better friend and confederate than Associate Professor Dr. Donald Leinster-Mackay of The University of Western Australia. After leaving Tonbridge for Harvard, I edited a newsletter for Old Tonbridgians in America: *Liberal Education*, namesake of a book by Vicesimus Knox, eighteenth-century Tonbridge headmaster who received a degree (presumably by mail) from the University of Pennsylvania. I never expected to meet anyone in Western Australia acquainted with Knox, who is not a household name, but Dr. Leinster-Mackay had supervised a thesis on him. Other coincidences mark our relationship – he is an Oxonian, and I am the only Governor of an Oxford college with whom he has debated academic puddings, Conan Doyle quotes, and half blues. My fortune has been to have his help and that of his wife, Jewel Leinster-Mackay. Students should be judged by what they do later (the proof of the pudding...), and I hope *Invasions*, the *English Public Schools and Ritualistic Imperialism* trilogy, and the *Magicians of the Gulf* quintet are some compensation for his hours of dialectical endurance and indulgence of syncretic ravings.

None of these well-disposed and long-suffering friends are responsible for my mistakes, prejudices, or outrages against political and jural assumptions. This is especially true of Arab friends whom I have not thanked by name. I have an affection for Qatar and anything that I write is written in friendship. I would not have spent years of my life in its service if I had not found something there to admire.

If anyone looks in vain for results of their criticisms, I plead that their patience may be rewarded in future volumes. *Honi soit qui mal y pense* writes Professor Leinster-Mackay about Thring of Uppingham's proclivities – a royalist *mea culpa* which reminds one that quotations, transcripts and translations of the Crown Records in the India Office Library and Records appear by the gracious permission of the Controller of Her Majesty's Stationery Office.

The conflict and disorder which haunts the Gulf as a result of the Iraqi *camisade* means that many of us who thought of ourselves as modern 'Gulfites' will not meet again. Perhaps this book will recall discussions and debates held in happier times. The war is over but not the consequences.

Paul Rich
Department of Education
The University of Western Australia

April 1991

PREFACE

KUWAIT, THE RAJ, AND RITUALOCRACY

The problem to consider for the moment is that in writing history one must always be conscious of how often recourse is had to generalisation, and one must always be ready to check afresh the validity of each generalisation. The success of bright ideas can quickly become a series of dim platitudes. – Arthur Marwick, *The Nature of History*, 1970.

Whether openly and visibly the hearer of suits, the righter of wrongs, collector of taxes, discerner and exacter of public duties...[i.e.] the man on the spot brought into being through unfailing attention and Norman zest for detail the regnum under which civilization could grow. – J.H. Granger, *Patriotisms*, 1986.

While it is unwise to expect historians to 'jump to' when something as dramatic as the Iraqi invasion of Kuwait occurs, it can nevertheless be argued that at such a confusing time in the Gulf there ought to be a little help forthcoming from the ivory towers. This volume, which hopefully will end its days as the fifth in a series, is based on research into a long and often unfamiliar history and (dare it be said), psychohistory of the Gulf.

Ideas spread themselves in an irritatingly untidy fashion. Trying to follow their course about the world is frustrating, but that has been my task in the books constituting the *English Public Schools and Ritualistic Imperialism* trilogy, and the task I also have set myself in the *Magicians of Arabia* quintet. I try to show that a cognitive structure (ritualism) acquired during adolescence can effect extremes of cultural and political experience (England and the Gulf, for example). This tack was perhaps suggested – if not explicitly endorsed – in Lewis Henry Morgan's classic *Ancient Society* (1877), and was pursued with distinguished success by Victor Turner in such books as *The Forest of Symbols* (1967), *The Drums of Affliction* (1967), and *The Ritual Process* (1969).

To me, chaos (in the pejorative rather than current naturo-philosophic sense), is kept outside the stockade of civilization by ritual – like Turner, I have seen ritual at work in Africa (in my case, in Uganda), and then have seen what catastrophes take its place. As the Gulf heads into the abyss, thanks to the Iraqi piracy of Kuwait, the significance of rule by ritual should be considered. Specifically in this respect, this book concerns the legitimacy of the Gulf rulers. How did they become monarchs? How do the Arabs themselves perceive the Gulf's ruling families? Why did some Arabs cheer when Iraq toppled the Kuwaiti amir? The significance of ritual to all of this is noteworthy, as are long-standing connections between Britain and each of the shaikhdoms of the Arabian Gulf.

'The centre of South-Western Asia,' wrote Sir Olaf Caroe in *Wells of Power*, 'is the Persian Gulf.' Whether the Gulf is Arabian or Persian or temporarily Iraqi, and whether it is part of the Fertile Crescent, Near East, Middle East,

Orient, the Cradle of Civilization, or South-Western Asia, its tribulations influence what temperature people set their thermostats in Omaha and the cost of a taxi ride in Osaka. If that had been somewhat forgotten, the events of 1990-91 brought the importance of the region quite quickly to mind again.

Whatever befalls Kuwait and its sister states, the main problem in all these satraps will remain the legitimacy of their regimes. Writing in 1977, Michael Hudson (*Arab Politics: The Search for Legitimacy*, Yale), noted how *vulnerable* the Gulf monarchies were. In the *American Political Science Review* (March 1990), Dr. Hossein Razi contributed an article 'Legitimacy, Religion, and Nationalism in the Middle East', in which he wrote that the boundaries of Middle Eastern states were 'created according to the needs and perceived interests of the Europeans rather than those of the local population' and that European subjugation came about 'not only overtly through imperialism but also covertly through such nominally autonomous but actually subservient élites as Nuri Said in Iraq, Sayyid Zia' Tabatabai and Muhammad Reza Shah in Iran and the shaikhs of the Gulf states.' Rather ominously, he warns that the significance of legitimacy has been neglected, and notes that economics, class structures, and foreign policies are not sufficient explanations for political stability. The shaikhdoms are ritualocracies.

It is in the monarchical Gulf that I have spent some frustrating, sometimes frightening, but always interesting years. They began for me in heady days when oil seemed to promise that everyone would have a fair chance at the distribution of life chances, and are drawing to an end in a time of disillusionment and disappointment and the promise of further turmoil even if the current Kuwait situation is resolved. The other shaikhdoms are only as quiet as gun powder. There should be no illusions about their stability. Poised around their perimeters are the flashpoints of future apocalypse.

Arguments about the sobriquet 'Arabian Gulf' and the more time-honoured 'Persian Gulf' have been avoided here. So have pedant debates about *Arab, Arabia, Arabic, and Arabian,* for which the curious can resort to Fowler's *English Usage*. In that spirit, and notwithstanding the *avant garde* currency of the term 'independent school', public schools in ensuing pages remain public schools. Possibly the changing lexiconography of Arabia and the public schools indicates the vitality of the subjects. As for 'ritualocracies' and 'ritualocracy', I claim to have devised them unless someone can show differently.

Discussion of the distinctions between *rules, customs, directives, principles, rites, rubrics, mores, and ceremonies* has been skirted. *Radicalism* is used in a peccant sense. The reader will find assistance in George Henrick von Wright's *Norms and Action,* in the works of Victor Turner, and in other books in the Bibliography. Turner writes in the Foreword to *Dramas, Fields, and Metaphors* (1974), about renewed interest in symbolism:

> Recently both the research and theoretical concerns of many anthropologists have once again been directed toward the role of symbols – religious, mythic, esthetic, political, and even economic – in social and cultural processes. Whether this revival is a belated response to developments in other disciplines (psychology, ethology, philosophy, linguistics, to name only a few), or whether it reflects a return to a central

> concern after a period of neglect, is difficult to say...Whatever may have been the causes, there is no denying a renewed curiosity about the nature of the connections between culture, cognition, and perception, as these connections are revealed in symbolic forms.

These associations in the Arabian Gulf need more exploring than they have so far received. Though far from being *meritocracies*, Kuwait and the other shaikhdoms are well qualified as *ritualocracies*. Ruritanian ritualism has been part and parcel of Gulf government. The only sultanate is not exempt. Recently Sultan Qaboos of Oman took delivery of rare matched black Friesland horses to pull his carriage on state occasions. Young Omanis have spent a year in Europe being trained in four-in-hand driving, the wearing of top hats and tails, and the general expertise required of coachmen. Gulf military bands are customers for Scottish bagpipes. The temptation to go on in this fashion, describing court life, has been resisted.

Comment about the Kuwait royal family and anecdotes about shaikhy extravagances will be viewed *cum grano salis*, for descriptions of present events and palaces and protocol would distract from this book's more enduring purposes, which include promoting interest in preserving the personal papers of the British who lived in the Gulf (no better home could be found than St. Antony's at Oxford), testifying to the need for uncensored scholarship at Gulf universities and for free expression in general, and sounding the alarm about the *immediate* need for thought about legitimate political arrangements in *all* the Gulf states.

These are the crucial concerns, and Arab preoccupations with ceremony are not incidental to them. They can be germane to the political problems. The baubles represent a ritualism which in the Gulf has been a dangerous substitute for political maturity. Obsequious bowing and scraping are signs by which we can detect what Foucault termed *assujetissement*, and by which we identify what Edward Said calls 'the subjugation of individuals...to some suprapersonal discipline or authority'. In ritual's niceties can be detected hidden strategies sustaining (in Gramsci's ubiquitous term) *hegemony*. The shaikhs have had a hidden curriculum, but in the light of the events of 1990-91 it has been dubious, and manifestly unsuccessful.

Subsequent chapters focus on four mini-states: Bahrain, Kuwait, Qatar, and the United Arab Emirates. Though small, they each have an identity. Bahrain has been called the Gulf's Curaçao, although travellers (drained by the endless parched desert of the surrounding area) have claimed upon reaching its relative greenery to detect a Mediterranean flavour. Possibly the Kuwaitis in their flamboyance of wealth have been the Italians of the Gulf. They have had a flair, and until recently have sported Gucci shoes. Their conspicuous consumption put them into a limelight which they perhaps now regret. The Qataris on the other hand are aware of Doha's dour reputation, suggestive of Scottish parsimoniousness. As for the Emirates, the federation of suspicious rivals, a drive along its coastal settlements slightly reminds Europeans of the French Riviera – with Dubai doubling as Monte Carlo.

In the end such journalistic comparisons fail. Another comparison which does not so quickly lend itself to dismissal is between the Gulf and India.

'Why, it smells like Bombay,' remarked friends whom I took on a tour of Doha's back streets. So it does, thanks to the expatriate Asian work force. Did it when the British were in charge? Ensuing discussion focuses on the significance of Indo-British influence over the years and its pertinence to present troubles. Shaikh Sultan Muhammad Al-Qasimi, the present Ruler of Sharjah in the Emirates, introduces his study *The Myth of Arab Piracy in the Gulf* (of which more anon) by remarking that British dominance of the Gulf was 'a situation which lasted for one hundred and fifty years and was certainly the major feature of the history of the Gulf until very recent times.' He could have added that the invasion, military and cultural, was of a more specific, *Indo-British* variety. This was, of course, a far less roughneck invasion than that by Saddam Hussein and much longer in duration.

Invasions remarks on the nexus of the Indian Empire, the Arabian Gulf, and old boy British administrators, and it proposes that a marked characteristic of the British Empire was the way it was ruled by public school-inspired ritual. *Ipso facto the English public school taught the Imperial rulers how to be superlative ritualists.* The liminal or threshold rites of passage of the school became the basis of the code of British rule. Turner remarks in *The Ritual Process,* 'Liminality implies that the high could not be high unless the low existed, and he who is high must experience what it is like to be low'. No doubt something of this thinking, a few years ago, lay behind Prince Philip's decision to send his son, the heir apparent to the British throne, to a bush school in Australia for a time, where he could learn how 'to rough it'. Geelong would not like to be called a bush school (although its famous Timbertops retreat offers a bush experience), but there is little doubt that the school is a *communitas* where the rituals of rule are learned.

No one in the Indian Empire derived more profit from this ritualism than did the erstwhile shaikhs, who in the Victorian era were blank slates as far as political sophistication was concerned. No one in the West should be deceived into thinking that the Kuwaiti dynasty or any of the other dynasties of the Gulf have the same claim to legitimacy within their constituencies that the royal houses of Europe or Japan do. President George Bush may have had good reasons for making one of his unnegotiable conditions for peace with Iraq the restoration of the Kuwait ruler, but he should not be under any misapprehensions about the origins, exploits, or Gulf popularity of the family.

Nor does it seem in these suddenly celebrated Middle Eastern nooks and crannies that the effects of English public school élitism belong entirely to the past. 'Dubai College', a columnist in the Gulf newspaper *Khaleej Times* reassured parents, 'is at par with renowned British schools like Eton and Harrow'. (14 April 1990.) This is a debatable proposition. Less debatable is that schooldays, at Dubai College or elsewhere, do exert a lasting influence. What better place to learn the rites of ruling than at school it might be thought – hardly a *non sequitur.* Schooling is *the* common institution in many lives, perhaps more universal even than marriage.

A Trilogy on Ritualism

Invasions applies a thesis of my trilogy *English Public Schools and Ritualistic Imperialism*, books which make a case for the connections between ritualism, schooling, and Imperialism in a general way. *Elixir of Empire* called attention to the phenomenon of school ritualism *vis-à-vis* Imperialism. *Chains of Empire* dealt with prosopography and causality. *Rituals of Empire* will consider archetypical public school traditions that found their way into Imperial ritualism.

That trilogy could only introduce the subject, which is a vast one. Future investigation was anticipated when, in *Chains*, a case was made for using prosopographical studies that emphasize school backgrounds to understanding Imperial coteries such as the Indian Civil Service, the various colonial services, the Sudanese Political Service, and *a fortiori* the Indian Political Service. An argument made in *Chains* was that the spirited biographical approach which Lytton Strachey helped to popularize in *Eminent Victorians* (1918) now has been buttressed by the advances of three generations of social historians and should be fully utilized in Imperial studies. From uninvestigated mounds of Imperial archival bones, forgotten biographical details of administrators can help recreate the Imperial ethos.

Chains further posited that the use of literature in history and political science had again become respectable. My belief in that will become evident in the other volumes of this Gulf quintet. Re-emphasizing this is a landmark essay by David Harlan: 'Intellectual History and the Return of Literature' (*The American Historical Review*, Vol.94, No.3, June 1989), summed up in his marvellous remark that 'Now, after a hundred-year absence, literature has returned to history, unfurling her circus silks of metaphor and allegory, misprision and aporia, trace and sign, demanding that historians accept her mocking presence right at the heart of what they had once insisted was their own autonomous and truly scientific discipline.' (*Anent*, in ensuing pages citations of historical accounts are often cited not to corroborate factual accounts of incidents but to document and illustrate problems.) There should be opportunities to use a literary *oeuvre* in connection with historical problems.

The one-time public school historian and now Japanese university academic Professor John Honey indicates in *Does Accent Matter? The Pygmalion Factor*, how extensive a school literature exists: 'Because of the amazing popularity of a newly-invented literary genre, the school story – read by millions of pupils who themselves had no access to real-life experience of a public school – similar institutions, expectations, and some of the language of public school life, were imported into many other different types of school.' Well and good, but these claims and those made about ritualism, prosopography, and school influence in *Elixir*, *Chains*, and *Rituals* as well as by others in other books should be applied to specific situations to see if they hold true. So extensive is the fiction written about public schools and about the Empire that there could be no excuse for not using it in reconstructing the *mentalité* of Imperialism. Such literature should be interrogated to assist in recovering Imperial intentions. The employment of public school fiction to demarcate historical boundaries reflects the view that, despite the compromises inherent in fiction and its necessarily hybrid nature, its use is highly productive.

Professor Neil McEwan, former Lecturer in English at the University of Qatar, has contributed to this discussion with *Perspective in British Historical Fiction Today*. There he considers J.G. Farrell's trilogy about the Empire, and his conclusions and mine are alike about the value of Farrell's Indian Mutiny account *The Siege of Krishnapur*: 'Farrell has taken Herbert Butterfield's idea, that the modern historian's final statement may be a piece of detailed research rather than a firm generalisation, and inverted it for his own purpose. He has explored the general history of the Indian Mutiny in order to construct his own particular case; he uses this to illustrate general truths about the British in India and about human behaviour. Farrell's "Afterword" tells us that the novel has borrowed from diaries, letters and memoirs as well as from history books.'

Historians should be free to use fiction as an example of opinion and attitude, and as a barometer of change. That is the use that I will make of Tom Brown and his friends in these books about the Gulf. As McEwan points out, *The Siege of Krishnapur* brims with ideas about the Mutiny, the East India Company, and the attitudes towards India; it is hard to see how historians concerned with the Raj could avoid considering its contribution to Indo-British historiography. The vast public school fiction offers similar opportunities.

Orientalism

Paradigms about rule by ritual developed in *English Public Schools and Ritualistic Imperialism* relate to the eloquent arguments of Professor Edward Said in *Orientalism* about the West's self-serving view of the East. Undeniably Professor Said is correct that the Western view has been distorted for a long time, as an 1812 print indicates. (See Plate 5.) In the Introduction to his *magnum opus* he observes, 'To speak of Orientalism therefore is to speak mainly, although not exclusively, of a British and French cultural enterprise, a project whose dimensions take in such disparate realms as the imagination itself, the whole of India and the Levant, the Biblical texts and the Biblical lands, the spice trade, colonial armies and a long tradition of colonial administrators.' While *Orientalism* has a secure place in literature about the Arab world, its effect has been disorienting (to use a pun of my Qatar colleague Brian Devlin). Professor Said makes such a strong argument about foibles and distortions of Western scholarship that the abysmal condition of Arab scholarship is forgotten. Its inadequacies are a prime reason why Orientalism has succeeded. In any case, Professor Said kindly wrote (24 January 1990), after reading *Elixir of Empire*:

> Of course you're absolutely right about the school ethic and the relatively small number of people who ran the Empire, along with ritual, ties, and the rest. There have been a series of intellectual convergences which you perhaps know about, but you're one of the ones who are slowly transforming the study of imperialism, to which I started to contribute in *Orientalism* and which I add another step to in my forthcoming book...called *Culture and Imperialism*. I have in mind, for example, Michael Rosenthal's *The*

> *Character Factory*, which deals with Baden-Powell...The point, as you state it so well in your marvellous book, is that it is culture – education, literature, ideology, the works – that makes the empire possible, not (in Gramsci's words), direct domination, although that was always a weapon to be used (*e.g.* 1857).

Despite such a welcome endorsement, assertions about a lasting public school influence on the Empire remain more easily made than proved. *Other theories about causality and Imperialism abound.* Professor Harlan remarks in his eminently quotable article, 'Historians are a sceptical lot. They tend to feel that one should trust one's nose, like a hunting dog. They are afraid that if they once let themselves be distracted by theory they will spend their days wandering in a cognitive labyrinth from which they will find no way to depart.' Obviously there were many influences other than the public schools on the Empire. Every time scholars view the Imperial kaleidoscope, other vistas open. All the same, *Invasions* contends that public school influence was *primus inter pares* as far as Imperial political activity in the Gulf was concerned, teaching ritualistic expertise to a future shaikhy leadership. This was not altogether positive, for ritual often proved an immobilizing glue rather than a helpful solvent.

Part of the problem in discussing ritualocracy is that although hindsight affords evidence of ritual's effects, as a subject it doesn't possess the concreteness of influences such as trade and defence; speculations about ritual's impact are precarious and have been left to specialists in such fields as heraldry and semantics. But rule by ritual does not have to be accepted *in toto* to be useful, and is starting to gain serious attention. Historians, notably Eric Hobsbawm and Terence Ranger and others in *The Invention of Tradition* have noted that the British were successful politically because they were good at *rituals of disguise*, at keeping the *forms* of institutions while changing the contents, and at creating pseudo-traditions to shore up the legitimacy of institutions. The shaikhs copy their former masters, but with difficulty.

An appreciation of ritual's numinous part in Imperialism and in post Imperial regimes should not concentrate only on describing customs, but consider *the values which were encapsulated*, a point made by John M. Mackenzie in the introduction to *Imperialism and Popular Culture*: 'In the emergence of the new nationalisms 'state, nation, and society converged', and the élite which promoted this convergence created new rituals, a whole range of invented traditions and cults through which it could be communicated to the public.' Dr. J.A. Mangan, a leading contributor to recent discussion of the public schools and the Empire, has been aware of the phenomenon of invented tradition and remarks in a contribution to *Imperialism and Popular Culture*:

> The invented traditions of late nineteenth and early twentieth-century Britain included both public school and public imperial 'traditions' which had common elements and which were related. The latter to an extent grew out of the former through the strong concern and energetic efforts of members of the upper middle classes imbued with the values and attitudes of the public school system.

Neither Doctors Hobsbawm, Mackenzie, Mangan, nor (fecklessly, alongside such eminent authorities) this author, have been left unscathed by those enamoured of the preponderantly political explanation of the effects of Imperialism; this renewed opposition to social history was a topic of *Chains of Empire*, particularly the criticism emanating from the redoubtable Gertrude Himmelfarb. Those who prefer diplomatic history will think that the ritualism of acne-afflicted adolescents provides disappointing explanations for as grand a force as Imperialism.

Others want to find causal peas under any paradigm's mattress. In *The Journal of Comparative Education*, a contumacious reviewer quoted a passage in *Elixir* about the curious habit of schools interring old boys within the school precincts, and then deflatingly remarked 'But why?'. Fair enough, and *Rituals of Empire* looks for a partial answer by exploring the *archetypes* of ritual behaviour that appeared in school and Imperial life, what they signified, and the reasons for their employment – attempting to show that the symbols employed in rituals have affinities with Platonic ideals, Jungian archetypes, Whiteheadian eternal objects, and the 'strange attractors' of the new science of *chaos*. However, it was Rupert Sheldrake's hypothesis of morphic resonance which, *Chains* and *Rituals* suggest, raised the most anodyne possibilities for social historians trying to incorporate ritualism into their work.

Chains in particular considered ritualism as the *genius loci* of the schools and Imperialism. David Newsome observed in his well-crafted *A History of Wellington College* (John Murray, 1959), 'Certainly fifty years ago there was little doubt as to what constituted the "genius loci" of Wellington...to fight for the Empire and to win renown.' Yet the idea of a trilogy about the general effects of public school ritualism was scorned by a few critics who adhere to the hoary depiction of the English public schools as citadels of gamesmanship. For them, ritualism mounted a fugacious challenge to athleticism, upset a longstanding equilibrium in educational history, and created a disturbance similar to the challenge of Darwinism to Genesis. Others have had personal reasons for unhappiness: the Masonic press does not welcome discussion of the hallucinatory *ignis fatuus* of Freemasonry – although attitudes are changing.

References to Freemasonry are frequent in my writings for several reasons. Besides seeking to demonstrate that through the lodges was one way that the schools exercised an influence on Imperial policy, I suggest that *the strength of Imperial Masonry shows that ritualism had a larger part in the Empire than has been recognized.* The Masonic membership of Imperial administrators helps to make the case for ritualism's power in the Empire, and helps to emphasize the importance of public schools, which had close ties with Masonry. The edifice of the Grand Lodge in London possibly suggests the enigmatic nature of the subject. (Plate 4.) Recent Iraqi references to Masonic plots certainly confirm the Middle Eastern paranoia about lodgedom.

Invasions and Encapsulations

Still, this may seem distant from the troops who recently lifted the lid of a Middle Eastern Pandora's box. But Tom Brown, Stalky, and Billy Bunter – although fictional heroes – encapsulate the changing character of Gulf leadership in the past. Tom Brown is at a celebrated school, part of a Victorian *Bildungsroman*, and the first important IPS Gulf Resident, Lewis Pelly, was at Rugby as a contemporary of Thomas Hughes. Stalky attends an unimportant school (United Services College), as did several of the Gulf officers, and he and his unashamedly pragmatic friends are not the lofty moralists that populate earlier novels such as *Tom Brown* and *Eric*. His adventurous attitudes have parallels with those held by early twentieth century Residents. The Greyfriars stories about Billy Bunter seem appropriate to link with the lacklustre and noisome administration of the Gulf in the 1920s and 1930s.

Despite differences between these *bahadurs*, proponents of athleticism as the *raison d'être* of public schoolism will find difficulty in making the threesome fit into a sporting mould. Rugby Chapel is central to *Tom Brown*; the very word *Stalky* implies wilyness as opposed to a sunny games ethic; and nobody confused captious Bunter with an athlete. Nor do Residents and Agents in the Gulf handily fit into an athletic image, as the girth of some testifies. This argues that the genius of public schoolism will be found outside playing fields and in a ritualism which subsumes sports, chapel, boarding house life, and other aspects of the schools.

While a paradigm can be faulted which inclusively embraces the Gulf, public schools, Imperialism, and the invasion of Kuwait, if it is regarded as an excuse for 'Raj bashing' and chuckles at the expense of Britannia, I am misunderstood. Experience shows that regardless of the sins of colonialism, worse befell countries after the West decamped. As a Harvard student working on a B.A. thesis, I spent six months at Makerere University in Uganda when the country was still a British territory. Many amongst my contemporaries there were later murdered – and, it need be emphasized, after the British left. In respects *Pax Britannica* was just that, and this should be acknowledged. There were more rights and dignities in some colonies then there are now in some so incorrectly called 'independent' countries. In the Gulf at this dark time, British suzeraincy will be recalled with nostalgia.

I think that the Gulf has suffered by not coming to terms with the consequences of British administration, although the Raj can no longer be blamed and misfortunes will have to be chalked up to the Arab account. As an example of how the past is a reference, the privatization of education has become in government circles in the 1990s an attractive solution to the Gulf's burgeoning school populations. Faced with declining oil revenues, ministries of education find the notion of encouraging private schools to be a way out of the dilemmas of indifferent quality and too large classes. Visions of Etons and Harrows have replaced sugarplums. Literature of the Hillgate Group and of the National Council for Educational Standards, two covens of public school enthusiasts, receives respectful reading. At the same time that the public school critic Correlli Barnett has lectured the Headmasters' Conference in England that they should 'thrust a stake through the living corpse of Victorian education', private schools in the Gulf have been proliferating – complete with coats of arms and sacrine mottos. Democracy is stillborn.

This is *déjà vu* to historians, who would be entitled to observe that the consequences of not having a decent state system could be similar to the situation in England. In *Education and Society* (1964), A.K.C. Ottaway pointed out that a result of the growth of the public schools was that the bulk of the population was deprived of the education that would have enabled them to take up jobs in the industrial system: 'By the turn of the century the situation was so bad that thousands of well-educated German clerks had to be employed in London offices to carry on the work of commerce.' The Gulf similarly suffers. The imported clerks today are Palestinians and Asians. The dangers of this were shown in Kuwait when the Palestinians turned on their masters and 'fingered' them to the Iraqis. Now they are persecuted in turn.

Unless something drastic is done to improve education, the *effective* native work force will continue to be as small as the endangered Arabian oryx. The wastage caused by the region's poor schools is staggering, and private schools for the 'gentility' add to the headaches. The Gulf has had more than its fill of inbred sub-cultures nurturing ill-founded assumptions of shaikhy superiority.

Tumbrels for Amirs

Public school and Imperial ritualism relates not only to historical but to present political concerns about monarchy. After a hiatus, there has been a re-appearance of criticism of 'the Royal-tribal folklore designed to keep English white-male-adult Public School chaps running things'. Tom Nairn in *The Enchanted Glass* (1988), provides that description and suggests a revival of Republicanism to exorcise the grotesqueries of Monarchy. If the Conservative Party ever lose their key to 10 Downing Street and Labour gets it, the House of Lords seems likely to go. Then? Before tumbrels roll in Britain or the Gulf, reasoned discussion of political legitimacy and its ritualism is in order.

Over the years, I have been impressed that Gulf Arabs re-enacted a past that they never had. What is sorely needed is what the Germans, with an ability to coin a word for anything and everything, call *Entideologisierung,* the dismantlement of ideologically orientated prejudices. In this light, the impermissableness of discussion is a worrisome aspect of the already disjunctive situation. In the *Financial Times* (15 March 1990), the problems of business and industry are partly attributed to heavy-handed censorship: 'Markets need and demand a free-flow of information. Local analysts point out that in the conservative Gulf states, information is tightly controlled by governments. Often releasing the sort of sensitive economic information needed by markets is against the underlying interests of administrations.' The fears that bedevil the financial community also have inhibited would-be historians. Academic freedom is unknown.

In any event, Kuwait's current troubles have prompted offering some insights I have developed over the years. *Invasions* shares that burden with other books in a projected series. Three are about the period 1858-1947: *Tom Brown in Arabia, Stalky & Stormin' Norman Meet the Gulf Shaikhs,* and *Billy Bunter and the Arabs.* The series also will include *Viceroys of the Gulf,* a long biographical and bibliographical work dealing, in addition to the IPS period, with the 'pre' and the 'post' Viceregal eras. Only provisionally titled, they should give opportunities to see if ritualism was the *élan vital,* and if old boys ruled the Arabs by ritual. At least, thanks to the events of 1990-1991, the geography of the Gulf is no longer obscure.

After comfortable months in a Saudi Arabian hotel, the disorganization of the 'dour and secretive' Kuwaiti amir and his entourage when reoccupying their pillaged country in March 1991 was ominous. Needed food rotted on relief trucks because there was no unloading equipment. Cylinders of gas for emergency cooking were useless without the necessary couplings. The first Kuwaitis to return from imprisonment in Iraq were met by the International Red Cross, not by any sympathetic shaikh. Those who had endured the Iraqi horror-drama complained that for the royal family nothing had changed; an 'old style of life, with unlimited maids, cooks and drivers' was going to be recreated. (*Guardian Weekly*, 24 March 1991.) Edward Said, doyen of Orientalism, was morose. 'Democracy in any real sense of the word is nowhere to be found in the Middle East,' he wrote in the *London Review of Books*. (7 March 1991.) 'There are either privileged oligarchies or privileged ethnic groups. The large mass of the people is crushed beneath dictatorship or unyielding, unresponsible unpopular government.' Reminding readers that the United States' part has been to side with tyranny and injustice, Professor Said decried 'a suddenly energised super-nation imbued with a fervour that can only be satisfied with subservience from sheikhs, dictators, terrorists and camel-jockeys.' He remarked about the Gulf's dynasties: 'These are monarchies which respect neither human rights nor the priorities of their own people.'

The shaikhs did not win the media battle. The 100 Hour War put a world spotlight on their activities, and future scholars will have to examine the press of many countries. 'Was Rich Kuwait Worth It?' was the headline in an Australian paper, which speculated about the amir's possible 26 wives and 4.3 billion dollar fortune. (*Sunday Times*, Perth, 10 March 1991.) Thanks to the conflict, the Gulf region was no longer a private preserve of the British and American press, or indeed the preserve of political reporters. Everyone now has an opinion about the shaikhs. The German newspaper *Süddeutsche Zeitung* called their states 'family firms with national flags'. *The Times Higher Education Supplement* concluded, 'It is hard to square public executions in societies in which most of the work is done by international migrant workers with an image of modern and progressive societies that we ought to be fighting to preserve.' (15 March 1991.)

As Western troops began flying home, the Gulf's potentates were busy ridding their domains of scared Jordanians, Mauritanians, Palestinians, Sudanese, Tunisians, Yemenis – some of whom had lived in the Gulf for thirty years, but whose governments had backed Iraq. Hospitality seemed reserved for arms salesmen, anxious to tout 'smart' bombs, Apache helicopters, Challenger tanks, Falcon jets, Maverick missiles and other weaponry that might prove useful in future confrontations. How the Gulf will fare in the post war era was the subject of a Doonesbury cartoon strip by Garry Trudeau depicting a sleazy night club patronized by those flocking to Kuwait. 'Hell,' says the proprietor, 'The city's swarming with rank, sweaty opportunists here only to feed off the detritus of this country's tragedy.'

INTRODUCTION

TALLER BOYS

In the 1870s eleven to twelve year old boys from the upper-class public schools were on average five inches taller than boys from industrial schools, and at all teen-ages three inches taller than the sons of artisans. – E.J. Hobsbawm, *Industry and Empire*, 1968.

One day soon after he started at the school he came down to breakfast to find a kipper on his plate. He sat there staring at it, not knowing where to begin. Then he cut into it, and got a mouthful of tiny bones. And after extracting them all, another mouthful, more bones. His fellow-pupils watched him suffer in silence; not one of them said, here, let me show you, you eat it in this way...the thought occurred to him that he had been taught an important lesson. – Salman Rushdie, *The Satanic Verses*, 1988.

The very meaning of the word 'travelled' has changed. It is hardly anywhere possible to travel slowly, by horse, in a sailing-boat, or on a camel, without appearing foolish or eccentric. The slow journeying, the search for the unknown, the overcoming of obstacles, the dangers and the good companionship of the road; all are gone or going. Man is sent by his masters from one capital to another like parcels by the post. – Gerald de Gaury, *Arabian Journey*, 1950.

In the summer of 1990, a mounting *qalaq* (the Arabic version of German *Angst*) in Gulf ruling circles over the region's instability was largely ignored in the West and if noticed, misunderstood. When Tariq Aziz, the Iraqi Foreign Minister, complained to the Arab League that Kuwait had no rights in the Rumaila field and 'owed' Iraq at least 2.4 billion U.S. dollars for oil already pumped, the implied threat and the reasons behind it were relegated to the back pages. Few in the West appreciated that disputes over the 129 kilometre border between Iraq and Kuwait were a legacy of British administrators and of the Indian Empire – and that relations between the two countries suffered from problems whose origins were partly the product of Imperial days. The Indian Empire's hold on the Gulf has been quickly, and some would say conveniently, forgotten. The English public schools' involvement has never even been mentioned, nor has the role of ritualism.

Since the oil boom brought a frenzy of consumerism, Gulf history has been measured more by digitals on Mercedes dashboards than by hourglasses. (However, this affluence did not go unnoticed by the neighbours. The *Wall Street Journal* noted with prescience a couple of weeks before the invasion 'increasing resentment in Iraq of the well-heeled Kuwaiti tourists who travel to the Iraqi cities of Basra and Baghdad during the summer'.)

In the shaikhdoms, two years produce a veteran expatriate who spins tales of the golden past. Five years qualify him to enter the competition for old man of the mountain. A dozen years, as in this author's case, has Old Testament connotations. 'So you were here when they first discovered oil,' a well-meaning lady told me.

Such is the lacuna created by the petro-largesse that newcomers seldom realize how strong was the former British presence, and how this modified the Gulf's character. Imperial administrators, having been immersed in ritual at school, introduced archetypes which by repetition became part of the region's humour. This was hegemony achieved by *hierophany*, the sacred manifested through objects that became symbols. Ensuing chapters examine plangent facets of Gulf history that have been neglected, and refer to the de-stabilizing dangers of indifference to ethnic and cultural pluralism. Although not intended to be useful like a car manual, *Invasions of The Gulf* suggests that those who make decisions should think more, and more seriously, than they have about the region's identity. The historiography of the Gulf argues for recognition of what is really, and always has been, a pluralistic society that is bedevilled by the conflict between Western-nurtured monarchism and illiterate radicalism.

That the Gulf is a frustrated pluralistic society, with a large underclass, is one reason why not all Arabs deplored what befell Kuwait. Those who know the Gulf know that its riches have been distributed with disgusting inequality, that its history has been grossly distorted by both Arab and Western academics who prostituted themselves for oil money, and that its rulers have displayed far more avarice than wisdom. Unsurprisingly, when those sad factors are kept in mind, the Iraqi tanks seemed to some to be the welcome resolution of an impasse. The shaikhs are 'grit in the oil'.

The Indo-British influence ('invasion' has crude connotations but the British had a *forceful* presence) divides readily into three periods. The inchoate years *before* the Indian Mutiny (1856-57) were the era of the East India Company (EIC), informally known as 'John Company'. The years with which this book are mostly concerned are between 1858 and 1947 when the epigoni were members of the vaunted Indian Political Service (IPS). The post World War II period, coming as it did *mutatis mutandis* after Indian independence in 1947, belonged to appointees of the Commonwealth and the Foreign Office (FO).

Neatly, emphasizing the distinctions between the periods in other matters, the biographies of the British before 1858, those of the IPS mysterium, and those of men serving after 1947 until the independence of Kuwait in 1961 and of the other shaikhdoms in 1971, reveal distinct educational backgrounds. The formative institutions were apprenticeship and private schools in the case of the EIC; public school for the IPS; and, after 1947, public school *and* university for the FO. Of course, the public schools mentioned in ensuing pages were not public by any sane rendering of the word. They were the élite private fee-paying Etons and Rugbys, the quasi-legendary schools of *Tom Brown's Schooldays*, then of *Stalky & Co.* and ultimately of Billy Bunter. The *Oxford English Dictionary Supplement* recorded the linguistic growth of this public schoolism in such terms as *public school accent, attitude, code, product, spirit, tie, type, schoolish, schoolishness, schooly*. Seldom does such a clear instance occur of changes in education related to changes in the body politic.

A tripartite division of Gulf history that emphasizes the influence on the region's politics of British education in public school involves assumptions about social structures and human agencies, *i.e.* about causality. My conviction, which the events of 1990-91 have strengthened, is that there is a continual oscillation between structure and agency in the Gulf. Neither is *primus*. The two forces are joined together in an endless dialectic rather than locked in an antagonistic polarity. The 1991 war exemplified that.

Gulfites

The Gulf officers in the IPS years constituted a unique foreign service of their own, a view endorsed by the veteran Political Agent (PA), and sometime Acting British Resident for the Gulf, Arnold Galloway. Before his death at the age of nearly 90 in 1988, Galloway was a helpful correspondent of mine, and commented 'Yes, I was thought of as a Gulfite, both by myself and the Government of India'.[1] He added, 'Certainly some of us regarded ourselves as Gulf specialists, which was reflected in posting to Agencies as much as possible – the knowledge of the terrain and languages was ever-widening – knowledge depending on opportunity and languages on hard work. Two first class interpreterships [often Arabic and Farsi] were no easy job to acquire with a busy day.'[2] The son of Harold Dickson, a Political Agent in Kuwait, commented about the proposal that the Gulf nurtured a distinct corps that 'Harold regarded the Gulf Service as a cadre all of its own – and certainly the best'.[3] The IPS officer and author of books about the Empire, Charles Chenevix Trench, wrote that '...the Gulf had its *aficionados* who would not willingly serve anywhere else'.[4]

Gulf Residents appeared to some to be less the aficionados of Arabia and more its patronizing *éminences grises*. Whatever their quirks, their presence meant that there was a period when rule was by a rarefied version of that famous 'heaven-born' Raj closely identified with India. His heyday was precisely the century or so when boundaries were resolved, dynasties confirmed, and other decisions made that still affect the region. To understand IPS involvement in Gulf history, an introductory explanation should compare the periods of British involvement, and the *persona* of each.

John Company Writers

The first continuous and formal representation of British interests was by East India Company officers in the period from 1763 to 1858. They appear to have been mostly self-made men who were apprenticed to the naval or commercial activities of the Company. Not everyone has agreed with the opinion that the EIC were middling in social status, and the opposite view has been expressed:

> The Writers and Cadets who sustained and supported the East India Company's administration in India generally came from 'well to do and even wealthy folk'. £3,000 was often paid *sub rosa* for a nomination to the Company's Civil Service. In India the so-called 'covenanted' servants, who were responsible for managing the Company's trade, buying and selling its goods, administering the first settlements, formed a natural élite. They

carried swords till the close of the eighteenth century, and fought or threatened to fight on points of honour.[5]

But, in contrast with the palatial headquarters which were occupied later, the early Company offices in London were rather modest. (See Plate 6.) An expansion of purpose brought a desire for more suitable surroundings, and growing pretentions were indicated by the Company's erection of a stately edifice in 1796 designed by Royal Academician, Richard Jupp, one which was considerably extended in ensuing years. (See Plate 7.) In the main, those who went in and out of the earlier building's doors were modest in social background. Few of the Company's employees came from the landed gentry, and their formal schooling was limited – petty, private, and parish schools; academies and freelance tutors. They were *not* men educated at public schools or men from families that sent boys to public schools. (See Chapter VII.)

As indicated, this case for plebeian origins could be overstated. Of late there has been a 'revisionist' opinion expressed: 'The clerks of the East India House belonged to all grades of society – from the son of a tradesman who had made himself useful to a Director in a country constituency to the son of a Vice-Chancellor. The majority, however, belonged distinctly to the well-to-do classes, and were naturally inclined to share in all the follies and extravagances of the "man about town".'[6] That description does not fit those appointed by the Company to the Gulf, whose backgrounds confirm the other view that Company staff by and large were *not* from the gentry. The question remains unresolved as to what degree the EIC was demotic.

Those who joined the Company were originally called *Factors*. The ranks of Apprentices and Writers were introduced in the mid-seventeenth century and a career ladder evolved of Writer, Factor, Junior Merchant, and Senior Merchant. The age limitations on joining this *de facto* service fluctuated. In 1784 entry was between fifteen and eighteen, or up to twenty-five for those joining the Company's Army. In 1795 the limits were extended to between age fifteen and twenty-two. Recruitment was heavily influenced by relationships between candidates and the Directors, for reasons that were both nepotistic and financial. In 1793 the price of a writership, as mentioned, was £3000.[7] The biographies of the EIC Residents in the Gulf indicate that appointments were often made on the basis of friendship or for cash.

Eidetic and Actual Differences

Things seldom change as abruptly as they appear to do; there are always antecedents. Even the invasion of Kuwait had (in the inevitable hindsight) an abundance of anticipations. Indeed, the divisive Western presence in the Gulf can be traced back to the first British appearance in India. Reaching back in time, British interest in education as a means of social control in India can be traced to East India Company days, though it was slight compared with what was to come later. The taking of the children of the Indian nationalist Tipu Sultan (1749?-1799) as hostage in 1792 almost allegorically anticipates later interest in the upbringing of the children of the native élites. (See Plate 8.) It will be recalled that Tipu sent emissaries to Arabia in his effort to find allies against the British and that the final British attack on him at Seringapatam in 1799, resulting in his death, was precipitated by fears that Napoleon's armies in Egypt might come to his defence. Curiously the character of Tipu Sultan has been a recent *cause célèbre* for the large Indian expatriate population in the Gulf, which has taken sides over a 'tele-serial' in India about him. (*The Sword of Tipu Sultan,* based on a 'novelization' by Bhagwan S. Gidwani.) Whether he was a Muslim religious bigot, or great nationalist leader whom the British traduced, occupied many columns of the Gulf press in 1990. He assuredly was a complex person. The *Edinburgh Evening Courant* (3 May 1784) records that he was made a Freemason by the French!

In any event, the preparing of British boys for service in India received more attention than did the preparing of Indian heirs for ruling. A school at Haileybury was established in 1805 by the East India Company and often figures in discussions of the British in India. To avoid confusion it must be kept in mind just which Haileybury is involved. The present school does not go quite so far as claiming to be the old Haileybury, but readers of its prospectus might be forgiven for thinking that the schools were the same: 'Four years after its closure in 1858, Haileybury opened its gates once again.' A.H. Kirk-Greene in *Biographical Dictionary of the British Colonial Governors* refers to the 'broadening of Haileybury'. Patricia James, the author of books about Malthus and someone who should know better, has annexed Malthus as one of the present school's masters or headmasters. In *The Haileyburian* (March 1985), she remarks that he was called 'the head of a great college' and adds 'Well, this great college is still here, still with a tradition of public service – *Floreat Haileyburia.*'

There actually were several antecedents of modern Haileybury represented in the Gulf. There were products of the East India Company school, Residents such as Stephen Babington and David Blane. There were representatives of the school established in 1862 which resembled Cheltenham, Clifton, and other mid-Victorian creations in its Imperial aspirations – a school attended by the Bahrain Political Agents Terence Keyes and Edward Wakefield, both IPS members. There were two schools, Imperial Service and Westward Ho!, that merged with Haileybury and which educated respectively the Trucial Coast officer Richard Bird and the Kuwait Political Agent William Grey, also IPS members. (Refer to Chapter IX for the biographies of Bird, Grey, and other IPS luminaries.) The Haileybury of today builds on all of those foundations.

The East India Company school closed in 1858; its assets were bought by a local consortium who wished to carry on. At about the time that the old college was put on the block, the EIC gave way to the IPS, a hierarchic group of Victorian gentlemen with numerous relatives serving here and there, particularly in India, and very largely from the emerging bourgeoise, *i.e.* they went to public schools, belonged to the world of London clubs and learned societies, and were united by the language of old boy obscurities and lacunae. As IPS officers they pledged particular allegiance to the Viceroy and exhibited a corporate identity which their predecessors lacked. If any group merited the title of Raj it was the IPS, who to an extent determined the geo-political dimensions of the modern Gulf. Their preoccupations were less commercial than they were political, and included phobias about Turkish 'threats' to

British ascendancy. The height of IPS power was the period of the fading opportunity for Ottoman reform during the reign of Abdulhamid II (1878-1909). More aggressive than their predecessors, along the way the IPS wrote some travel books, had some exotic adventures, and seldom disappointed when it came to fulfilling images of priapic Empire builders.

The third group, the Foreign Office appointees between 1947 and 1971, was no less distinguished and included individuals who liked their clubs, but was more socially mixed in background and dabbled in that overworked panacea, 'development'. This period gets its due in the forthcoming *Viceroys of the Gulf*. Almost everyone in the postwar period had gone to university and a sizable number specifically to Oxford. As will be seen in *Viceroys'* pages, most still attended public school but a harbinger few went to grammar school. Unfortunately for romanticism about Arabia, the era of easy travel coincided with the Foreign Office taking over from the IPS. As the Kuwait Political Agent Gerald de Gaury complained in the epigram at the start of this introduction, FO officers were 'mailed off' willy-nilly to posts whenever and wherever Whitehall wished. (Assignments after Indian independence were briefly made by the Commonwealth Relations Office, but the Foreign Office assumed responsibility on April 1, 1948.)

According to Sir Stewart Crawford (Gulf Resident from 1966 to 1970), the 'FOs' were themselves aware of a difference between themselves and the IPS:

> There was a homogeneity about the officers appointed by the India Office and Government, their schools, clubs, honours. During the Foreign Office (after 1968, Foreign and Commonwealth Office) period, they spent longer or shorter periods in the Gulf as part of their postings round the world. In consequence, their clubs became more varied (mine is the United Oxford and Cambridge University Club), and their decorations relate to different phases of their careers (my CVO was awarded in Oslo, when the Queen visited Norway).[8]

Eidetic and actual differences between the three regimes do not prevent the observation, confirmed by my reading and personal experience, that British representatives in the Middle East generally have had a knowledge of the region that exceeds that of the emissaries of other countries. The special relationship with the Gulf is not over. The traditional interest in the region continues and often a British official turns out to have had family links with the Gulf. In 1990 this author had lunch in Doha with a Foreign Office official dealing with the Middle East who had grown up in the Emirates, where his father had been a Political Agent. The 1990 British Ambassador to the United Arab Emirates was a gentleman who had served in the Gulf as a junior political agent in the early 1960s when the shaikhdoms were still betoken to the Resident. A significant number of the British academic establishment concerned with the Gulf have family ties with the region. The invasion of Kuwait particularly pained the surprisingly large number of distinguished British foreign policy buffs who belong to this Middle East cabal. One wrote to me, 'It is like someone invaded my home.'

A practical result of this cosy networking through the years is that anyone interested in the area is advised to turn to the names of the Gulf British when beginning a project and starting to search the card catalogue (or online). They and their descendants are a vital key to the history of the shaikhdoms – not the only entrées to its secrets, but crucial ones. Whether the concern is with antiquities or idiosyncrasies, the literature is assessed by knowing who the British administrators were. Be they East India Company, IPS, or Foreign Office appointees, they wrote voluminously. While much was for reports (which often were lovingly crafted), a large amount consists of somewhat obscure *belles-lettres* which, when located, have value for Gulf studies.

The Politicals

Necessarily this book, rather than introducing the Gulf, concentrates on the world of its Political Residents and Political Agents. They were called informally the 'Politicals'. One of them, Sir Olaf Caroe, wrote:

> As Macaulay showed, the term 'political' goes back to Indian practice of the time of Warren Hastings: it was a term intended to convey the sense of functions more rarefied and elusive than the steady grind of direct administration in the Indian Districts. The 'political' officer was one who had been through the administrative mill – he had been trained as a magistrate and collector of revenue, he knew where to find the law, and he had usually been tried out in a selection of the hundred and one duties of caring for the people that fell to the lot of the District Officer in an Indian Province. But he was destined for a Service where it would fall to him to represent his Government in countries beyond the Indian periphery, or in the conduct of relations with frontier tribes, or at the *darbars* [*sic*] of the Indian States, or – and not the least important – in the Persian Gulf.[9]

Politicals could be rarefied and snobbish in attitude and obfuscatory and elusive in activities, but undeniably they were veterans of the trials of experience. Their careers were not a succession of triumphs. Sir Olaf knew that well, for after being briefly the Gulf Resident in the 1930s and then head of the IPS as Foreign Secretary of the Government of India, he fell afoul of Pandit Nehru in the last days of Empire, and found himself in a distinguished but unanticipated and abrupt early retirement.

Götterdämmerung overhangs the lives of latter Politicals such as Caroe, when pensioned off. The Empire that they had served disappeared and their *raison d'être* vanished. At the same time, oil meant that the nomadic noble Arab, rare in any event, disappeared. What had been an exotic desert setting for beribboned IPS performances at durbars became a squalid urban landscape, a breeding ground for both extravagance and radical politics.

Yet the stereotypes which scores of British artists memorialized do live on. (See Plate 9.) As will be seen in Chapter II, the contradictory notions of Arabs as pious solitaries and happy brigands (see Plate 10) have been incorporated into the nascent national identities of the shaikhdoms. *Folklore* that was Victorian in origins has been enhanced and embroidered, and the British part in its creation disremembered. Trenchard Fowle, an IPS officer who was to become Resident in the 1930s, was under the spell of such images when he recorded his first visit to Kuwait just before the start of World War I:

> At Koweit I saw the Bedouin on the edge of his native desert...the Bedouin, stately, calm, and aloof, one of the last picturesque figures left to a civilised world. A long cloak hangs from his shoulders, with broad sleeves which leave full play to his sinewy wrists and well-shaped hands. Open at the front, this reveals a long garment resembling the dressing-gown of the Western world, gathered in the midst with a waist-cloth into which are stuck a couple of silver-handled daggers...From under the kerchief stares out a dark sombre face, with keen dark eyes puckered at the edges with much watching against the desert sun, and well-cut features. Over his shoulder hangs a rifle by its sling; a full bandolier crosses his chest. Such is the Bedouin, the Spirit of the Desert made manifest in flesh. Such was he that day at Koweit; such was he long centuries ago or ever Mohammed was born to Amina, wife of Abdullah, the merchant of Mecca. Not otherwise can we imagine him on the Last Day, facing the assembled nations, stately, calm, and aloof...[10]

This image contrasts with the television news footage in late 1990, of corpulent Kuwaitis fleeing their homeland in flashy late model sedans, leaving their country to impoverished Iraqi soldiers who were busy carting off the hair dryers, automatic washing machines, and other trivia of Western affluence that had replaced daggers and bandoliers. *Allan's painting thus acquires a strongly contemporary flavour* – it could be entitled *'Iraqis Dividing Spoil'*. (Plate 10.)

Ensnarled by Ritual

By lambent prose flavoured with an Imperial *nostalgie de la boue*, the Raj on a camel created myths which the West continues to believe about 'far, fair Arabia'. His metaphors about the Arabs became hackneyed, his attitudes towards them became truisms which they were not allowed to deny, and his conceits about Western superiority became reality. Well-named a labyrinth, the Middle East today remains indebted or cursed by IPS pens and enchained by its prejudices – and ensnarled by its rituals. Psychohistorical study of the period is intensely interesting, and begs questions as to who were these myth-makers. By what route did they come to Arabia?

What should be appreciated about the backgrounds of officers in the IPS and the other British Imperial services is that a great deal of their early education, formal and informal, was in ritual-making. *Not* implied by this is that societies before or since were bereft of rituals when bereft of Britons – rituals are a universal phenomenon. Notwithstanding, the Empire had a pronounced enthusiasm both for making up rituals and for elaborating on existing ones. An example chosen from many would be cornerstone layings. Cornerstone ceremonies have been around for a long time, and the nursery rhyme, *London Bridge is falling down,* refers to the practice of sealing a poor wretch in the foundations of a bridge to ensure its success. The Royal Infirmary in Edinburgh had its cornerstone laid with Masonic rites in 1737. However, it was in the Victorian era when elaborate Masonic cornerstone ceremonies for civic buildings became *de rigueur*. So it was with other rituals which may have existed previously but which were now embellished.[11]

British ritualism became intensely nationalistic, and the Victorians saw the world in terms of nations. The period was decisive for nationalism through the Middle East – and a time for the subordination of pan-Arab identity to Western imposed nationalisms. Iraq is a consequence of this, a fabrication of members of the IPS such as Percy Cox and Arnold Wilson. Regarding this making of rituals and hence of nations, Alex Callinicos calls attention to E.J. Hobsbawm's important *The Invention of Tradition* (1983):

> The way in which this occurred is an important instance of what a recent collection of brilliant historical essays call the 'invention of tradition'. Eric Hobsbawm defines an 'invented tradition' as 'a set of practices, normally governed by overtly or tacitly accepted rules, and of a ritual or symbolic nature, which seek to inculcate certain values and norms of behaviour by repetition, which automatically implies continuity with the past.' ...Hobsbawm suggests that the period between 1870 and 1924 was one in which traditions were mass-produced throughout Europe...It was in this same period at the end of the nineteenth century that much of the elaborate public ritual now regarded as time-honoured features of the British monarchy was invented as part of an effort by the rulers of the United Kingdom, faced with a growing challenge from new industrial powers such as Germany and the US, to project the state as an institution meaningful to all its subjects.[12]

The flourishing of ritualism was particularly evident in the late Victorian public school. *Elixir of Empire* cited numerous examples of this. The pancake greeze at Westminster School was one, an event which acquired renewed stature at the end of the nineteenth century. A verger bearing a silver mace was impressed into conducting the school cook and the pancake into the school's Great Hall and the pancake flipped over a bar. Boys fought ('the greeze') for the biggest piece and the winner received a guinea. (This receives additional attention in Chapter V.) A major question is whether the schools may reflect growing ritualism in a culture or *if they produce it*.

My *Rituals of Empire* discusses the work of scholars concerning the ways in which ritual influences societies. The subject is no longer the exclusive property of anthropologists. Everyone's help is needed for the daunting tasks on the agenda of identifying ritual cores or motifs which were sustained by the schools and Empire over a period. This has not been attempted for the schools so far, although obvious and more general popular examples such as Britannia and the Garter belt come to mind. When the Imperial dissemination of these motifs is considered, those who wish to sort matters out and to understand the wherefores of today's Gulf or of any other of the former Empire's possessions must look to nineteenth century education and its consequences.

When the influence of ritualism on politics is better appreciated, it will be possible to look more intelligently at Imperial history for the re-appearance of patterns from the school yard. Until then, evidence is prone to presentation anecdotally rather than in organized fashion. Dr. J.A. Mangan writes: 'It would be tedious to heap example upon example of the tendency of many historians to treat education in general histories of imperialism as of little or no consequence...odd omissions: rich opportunities for evocation missed: indifference compounded.'[13] Dr. Mangan naturally did not intend his remarks to be applied to the consequences for Kuwait of the public school education of the Gulf's Imperial administrators; how important that factor was to decision-making then or now is taken up here. Accepting the idea that the public schools taught boys how to rule with ritual, the question arises as to what the consequences were for indigenous societies. The crux of the issue is that much of what passes as Gulf tradition is a reflection of the Raj and nothing to do with Arab customs or Islam.

Neopatriarchs

Gulf society has been characterized as *neopatriarchial.* This describes a system 'neither traditional nor modern; it is unique in that it has its own particular patterns of doing and thinking, its own ways of valuing and behaving, its own manner of dealing with reality and the world.'[14] A neopatriarchal society relies on coercion rather than co-operation, on absolutist paradigms rather than pluralism, on social organization by family and tribe rather than secular and civic grouping, and on ritualism rather than creativity. In contrast, Western influence on the Middle East is thought about in terms of reason, democracy, and so on. All of this is highly debatable.

Cynics more familiar with the past Western involvement in the area and the actual status of the shaikhs have viewed the West's hurry during the Iraqi invasion of Kuwait of 1990 to help Kuwait's amir, Shaikh Jaber al-Ahmad al-Sabah in his 'hour of need' against Saddam Hussein, as offering little more than making a choice between supporting Count Dracula or Rasputin. To get at the truth of the matter, the shaping of the character of the shaikhs by the British is worth considering. The Residents' study of Plato at public schools steeped in the classics is not peripheral to this, although Gulf amirs are far from being philosopher-kings. Kuwait isn't Athens.

The suggestion made here is that the Indian Political Service officers were men who cherished and promoted myth and the metaphoric. They espoused a 'neosultanate' view of politics, and accepted and encouraged social stratification as natural. The Gulf's amirs are the result.

The corruptive factor in this relationship is not patriarchy (traditionality), as such, but a dependency whose historical cause and agency is Western imperialism. It is important, however, to stress that dependency is the product of more than just crude aggression, domination, expropriation and oppression – more, that is, than the direct economic and military overpowering of the periphery by the centre. In the Arab world, dependency presents itself in all these forms but additionally and crucially in the form of an *inner* cultural relation, one quivering in the shadow of the dominant *Other.* In this sense, besides being apolitical, economic, and military *outside*, the relation of dependency is also a cultural *inside*. This is the essential character of the socio-psychological structure called neo-patriarchy. The *usefulness* of this explanation as far as the problems of Gulf society today are concerned is striking, though admittedly it is not *always* applicable. Its utility recalls the value of *domus* for Emmanuel Le Roy Ladurie in *Montaillou*.[15]

Ideological Invasions

Invasions investigates the *mentalités* afoot in the Gulf and thus is more concerned with the incursions of ideologies than of militia. It would be foolhardy to present anything here but a survey of certain (and certainly not all) aspects of British influence, and I mention frequently that Arab patterns of thought remain largely unexplored. The way in which Iraq, nominally secularist under Saddam Hussein, successfully had cloaked in religion its bellicosity and hypocritically embraced the notion of *jihad* or holy war, illustrates how convoluted Gulf affairs have become. The Iraqi fancy footwork clearly confounded the Kuwaiti establishment, and may do the same for others unless they are wary. The Iranians play the same game.

The following chapters provide a short narrative, a digested rather than statistical biographical view, and a brief political analysis. Arguably that makes one book do for three, but *exploring the subjects together is essential.* Hopefully the approaches are integrated. Dwight Hoover has argued that narrative history is again respectable.[16] While that is true, in *Chains of Empire* the claim was made that prosopography could be applied along with 'old-fashioned chronology' in the service of psychohistory, tackling problems that confront Imperial studies such as motivation, causality, and the governing myths. Just as Ladurie looked to Inquisition ledgers for inspiration, the suggestion here is that Imperial historians should look towards English school archives.

The Viceregal ceremonialism that the Gulf officers mastered as members of the IPS, and which the shaikhs embraced, takes up Chapter I, while the growing strength in the nineteenth century of the 'Indian connection' takes up Chapter II. Old school tie associations of the IPS, and what that meant in terms of policy, concern Chapter III. Chapter IV deals with Gulf historiography. Chapter V debates the value of psychohistory for Gulf studies. Gulf Freemasonry, the schools of the IPS, and problems inherent to chronology and prosopography, are respectively the subjects of Chapters VI, VII, and VIII. Chapter IX provides IPS biographies. Chapter X and the Epilogue furnish further perspectives on events of the early 1990s.

Readers may wish to look at the two Appendices before proceeding. They are the pungent text of two speeches that Lord Curzon made when he visited the Gulf in 1903 that give the flavour of the Raj's rule over Arabia as well as anything possibly can. The IPS period was the period of confident officers who could be seen at Southampton boarding P & O steamers, India-bound: 'Their lofty situation on the upper decks seemed peculiarly suitable for the first-class passengers, for they were known to those they ruled as the "heaven-borns". They were the Raj – from the Hindustani word for rule – who were "high born": the Governors, Commissioners, Residents, Judges, all who came directly under the Viceroy.'[17] Curzon did not mention, but he could have added that the effectiveness of Imperial rule owed much to the gentlemanly manners of his high born IPS, possessed of a polish that select schools imparted. The Western officers, successfully protecting the Gulf from Iraq in the 1990s may have had more fire power at their command, but it is doubtful whether they possessed the panache that the British did in the past.

But theirs was a Janus-headed gentility, for 'strategies of politeness...may in fact also be used as strategies of social domination'.[18] In the Gulf the rituals assuredly were that, although as Rupert Wilkinson made clear in his study of the English public school *The Prefects* (1964), and Karel van Wolferen showed in *The Enigma of Japanese Power* (1989), the British civil and colonial services were not the only bureaucracies to acquire ritualistic mannerisms that helped in maintaining control. Van Wolferen observes about the Japanese: 'The bureaucracy lives in a thoroughly ritualistic world. Officials speak in code...Ritual and an emphatic demonstration of hierarchy are, furthermore, believed by the bureaucrats to be essential as a means of cultivating respect for authority and thereby the foundation of order in society.'[19]

An overseas bureaucracy illustrates this far better than a domestic one, because much behaviour overseas is exaggerated and made more obvious by the bureaucrats' relative autonomy and freedom. *Invasions* testifies to the power of men on the spot, echoing the view of Imperialism that 'the cards were always stacked against trenchant Imperial will in Whitehall',[20] and seeks to re-awaken interest in the Indian connections of the Gulf. Before the Americans and others become permanently embroiled in the intricacies of Gulf courts, they may want to do some research into just where the manners and the mannerisms originated. An observer as late as 1966 could write:

> Every New Year's morning the British Political Resident in Bahrain has a garden party. True to the Indian traditions implicit in his title, however, he calls it a durbar; and although few of his guests are aware of the fact nowadays, they are invited on this occasion not to celebrate the birth of the year, but to honour the memory of Queen Victoria, proclaimed Empress of India on this day in the year 1877...This anachronism is not altogether as absurd as it may seem, for there is a good deal of the Victorian Imperial system, as well as the Victorian Imperial flavour, still clinging to the little territories of the Persian Gulf over which the Political Resident exerts – or attempts to exert – his sway.[21]

The Resident doggedly held sway over the Gulf until the British abrogated the treaties and departed in 1971, remaining 'a very odd bird' described as 'Part diplomatist, part political adviser, part military governor'.[22] He cajoled, bullied, pleaded, awarded, commended, and complimented,[23] but never dreamed of needing the arsenals with which vertiginous shaikhs and their allies would play after independence.[24] There were more subtle quivers for his bow.[25] Through the decades his chief asset was ritual, by which he ruled and earned the title of *Viceroy of the Gulf*.

The reality is that the British 'invasion' of the Gulf, in contrast with the Iraqi one, was accomplished quietly by a few dozen select gentlemen of the IPS – in sophisticated contrast with the marauding mobs of teenage soldiers that Saddam Hussein unleashed on Kuwait in the summer of 1990. Nor during the IPS era – it should be added in the light of recent Iraqi claims – did the Ottoman predecessors of the Iraqis ever exercise a legitimate sovereignty over the Gulf. What *might* have happened has been confused with what *did* happen. *Let it always be recalled that Iraq is a British creation of the 1920s.*

The Arab historian Ahmad Mustafa Abu-Hakima comments, 'Ottoman Mesopotamia, another power bordering on the Arabian Gulf, might also have exercised strong control over affairs of the Gulf, were it not for the fact that the Governor's authority was limited to Baghdad and did not extend south as far as Basra.'[26] The *Mutasallim* or administrator of Basra was never able to extend his control to Kuwait.[27] The paramount foreign power in the Arabian Gulf before the independence of Kuwait and the other shaikhdoms was unquestionably Great Britain. Omitting this, Arab history especially these days, as offered up by radical radio and television, is often legend instead of fact.[28] The reality is that the present situation in the Middle East cannot be understood without reference to the history of Britain's Indian Empire.

Of all countries, it might be said, Arabia holds the deepest enchantment for the majority. From the time of the Romans, who sought for the mysterious land of Ophir, reputed by legend to be a stronghold of gold, rare spices and pearls, to the nineteenth century, when its arid hills and waterless dunes attracted such men as Sir Richard Burton, Charles Doughty, and the Swiss, Burckhardt, Arabia Felix and its bordering kingdoms have captured the imagination of travellers, explorers and writers. – Raymond O'Shea, *The Sand Kings of Oman*, 1947.

NOTES

Unless specified, the place of publication is London. India Office Record numbers are given for the *Persian Gulf Administrative Reports* (PGAR, see IOR discussion in the Bibliographical Essay), but the series is available in reprints produced by Archive Editions. So are the cited *Précis* by Judge J.A. Saldanha. These sources are discussed in the Bibliographical Essay.

ARS, *Ars Quatuor Coronatorum*. CUP, Cambridge University Press. Corr., file designation at RGS. GLE, Library of the United Grand Lodge of England. HMSO, H.Majesty's Stationery Office. IOR, Indian Office Library and Records. OUP, Oxford University Press. RGS, Royal Geographical Society archives. SLRCA, Sage Library, Reformed Church of America, New Brunswick (New Jersey). See for the India Office Records Martin Moir, *A General Guide to the India Office Records*, The British Library, 1988. 'That Martin Moir's *General Guide* has at last seen the light of day is a matter for rejoicing: let caparisoned elephants parade down the Blackfriars Road and kneel, trumpeting a salute, outside Orbit House.' Lesley A. Hall, review, *Archives*, Vol.XIX, No.83, April 1990, 154.

1. A.C. Galloway to P.J. Rich, 7 January 1987.
2. *Ibid.*
3. H.Y.M.R. Dickson to P.J. Rich, 6 July 1987. Dickson assuredly would be on any list of outstanding Gulf officers, but there was a prejudice about anyone like him who joined rather 'haphazardly' and had not entered the IPS through the formal recruitment channels. Galloway wrote querulously: 'Dickson might be a better example of a P.A., but he...was never I.P.S. His school was good but small and thus limited.' Arnold Galloway to P.J. Rich, 10 February 1987.
4. Charles Chenevix Trench, *Viceroy's Agent*, Jonathan Cape, 1987, 218. 'Lean and keen men for the Frontier, fat and good-natured men for the states.' *Ibid.*, 13. Trench provides a valuable

introduction to the duties of the IPS, but for someone who was (albeit briefly) an IPS officer, he is cynical about the service.

5. Samik Banerjee, *Calcutta 200 Years: A Tollygunge Club Prospective*, Tollygunge Club, Calcutta, 1981, 89. Banerjee's quote about 'well to do' comes from F.H. Skrine, 'The Voyage to India in the Eighteenth Century', *The Calcutta Review*, October 1889. This hagiography is perhaps indicative of the desire of those with EIC antecedents to believe in a more exalted social status of their forebears than would be justified by the evidence.

A useful essay on the last fifty years of East India Company rule is Robin Bidwell's introduction to *Arabian Gulf Intelligence: Selections from the Records of the Bombay Government*, New Series, No.XXIV, 1856, reptd. 1985, Oleander Press. The *Selections* were used by Kelly in *Britain and the Persian Gulf*, Bayly Winder in *Saudi Arabia in the Nineteenth Century*, Abu Hakima in *Modern History of Kuwait*, and Reginald Coupland in *East Africa and its Invaders*, and along with Saldanha's series of *précis* served Lorimer in his *Gazetteer*. 'Anyone working on the nineteenth century history of Eastern Arabia and the Gulf or East Africa comes across frequent references to the *Bombay Selections*, Volume XXIV.' *Ibid.*, i.

6. William Foster, *The East India House, Its History and Associations*, Bodley Head, 1924, 235. Lamb and the two Mills were employed in the Company's London office, as was Walter Wilson who wrote a life of Defoe, and the enterprising William Broughton who became first Bishop of Sydney, Australia.

7. Anthony Farrington, *The Records of the East India College Haileybury and Other Institutions*, HMSO, 1976, 3, 4, 5, 10.

8. Sir Stewart Crawford to P.J. Rich, 3 August 1987.

9. Olaf Caroe, *Wells of Power: The Oilfields of South-Western Asia*, Macmillan, 1951, 50. Arnold Galloway told P.J. Rich that the Gulfites found Caroe's pontifications on the Gulf wearisome, considering the fact that he had spent less than a year as the Resident.

10. T.C. Fowle, *Travels in The Middle East*, Smith, Elder, & Co., 1916, 9. Like Rupert Hay, Lewis Pelly, Arnold Wilson, and other successful IPS officers, Fowle wrote a book early in his career. Possibly this was regarded as helpful to promotion.

11. Dean F. Harwood, 'Cornerstones: Real and Symbolic', *The New Age*, Vol.XCVII, No.3, March 1989, 23-26.

12. Alex Callinicos, *Making History: Agency, Structure and Change in Social Theory*, Polity Press, 1989, 171.

13. J.A. Mangan, 'Introduction', J.A. Mangan ed., *Benefits Bestowed?: Education and British Imperialism*, Manchester University Press, 1988, 3. This collection includes contributions by a number of authors mentioned in ensuing discussion, including Professor Donald Leinster-Mackay and this author. With respect to Dr. Mangan's remarks about missed opportunities, perhaps the richest missed opportunity of all is the failure to note that the schools produced *ritual archetypes* that found their way into Imperial life. In other fields related to symbolism, identification of such archetypes has already begun, *e.g.*, Whitney Smith, 'New Flags: State of Cambodia', *The Flag Bulletin*, Vol.XXIX, No.1, January-February 1990, 3-15. Dr. Smith, who is the doyen of scholars as far as flag studies are concerned, traces the vicissitudes of vignettes of Angkor Wat as a 'core' of Cambodian vexillological and governmental symbolism. 'Manners, customs, constraints and rituals are often not so much impediments to displays of emotion or meaningful interaction as ligatures to surround such matters, scaffolding for our social arabesques. ("Nuns fret not at their convent's narrow room", wrote Wordsworth happily, from within the confines of a sonnet.)' Laurie Taylor, 'Inter-course Intercourse', *Times Literary Supplement*, 17-23 November 1989, 1286. Hence the Iraqi determination to destroy all symbols of Kuwaiti nationalism – flags, coinage, currency, *et al.* The frenzied display of Kuwaiti national emblems at international sporting contests where exiled Kuwaitis appeared in the autumn of 1990 showed the way in which symbols can become the very stuff of politics.

14. Hisham Sharabi, 'Introduction: Patriarchy and Dependency and the Future of Arab Society', Hisham Sharabi ed., *The Next Arab Decade: Alternative Futures*, Mansell, 1988, 2.

15. *Ibid.*, 3.

16. Dwight W. Hoover, 'The Return of the Narrative?', *Organization of American Historians Newsletter*, Vol.17, No.4, November 1989, 8.

17. Evelyn Battye, *Costumes and Characters of the British Raj*, Webb & Bower, Exeter, 1982, 14.

18. Ivo Strecker, *The Social Practice of Symbolization: An Anthropological Analysis*, Athlone Press, 1988, 59, and see 2. See also Donald Leinster-Mackay, *The Rise of the English Prep School*, Falmer Press, 1984, 154.

19. Karel van Wolferen, *The Enigma of Japanese Power: People and Politics in a Stateless Nation*, Macmillan, 1989, 334-35.

20. 'Imperial will was more freely exercised by those with the business in hand, all the way down from governors to district officers, by the men on the spot. Energies, action and design were local and individual. One has only to consider the activity of Sir Harry Smith, Sir Bartle Frere, Lord Lytton, Sir John Pope-Hennessey, Captain Lugard, Sir Charles Eliot, Lord Milner, Lord Curzon – or that of Joyce Cary's Mr Rudbeck or Cock Jarvis. 'We leave', wrote G.P. Gooch, 'the government of India to the officials in the serene assurance that our administrators must by this time have learned all the secrets of statecraft...'. Indian Civil Service and Colonial Service constituted special missions of something more than English middle-class virtue overseas. Whether working through prince, khedive, emir or chiet or directly ruling acephalous peoples, whether the hand was hidden or open, the alien official classes considered themselves to be the state, the effective operating, improving agency.' J.H. Granger, *Patriotisms: Britain 1900-1939*, Routledge & Kegan Paul, 1986, 135.

21. David Holden, *Farewell to Arabia*, Faber and Faber, 1966, 141.

22. *Ibid.*, 142.

23. Many of these skills were, no matter how *singular*, learned *collectively* at school. 'Each of us plies the trade learned with other apprentices and creates forms by using the repertory of a culturally accepted style in a unique manner. Some aspects of our actions, procedures and results receive our singular marks better than others. As the cultural is included in the human, so the singular is included in the cultural. Human, cultural, and singular are related to each other as Russian dolls, by inclusion. This also entails, in most cases, a process of restriction. Regarding the foods available in my society, I express my uniqueness by preferring some and abstaining from others and rarely by inventing a new recipe. Similarly, I dress in a unique manner by choosing a few items among those considered appropriate in our society at a certain time and rarely by designing an original outfit or having one designed for my exclusive use.' Jacques Maquet, *The Aesthetic Experience: An Anthropologist Looks at the Visual Arts*, Yale University Press, New Haven, 1986, 177.

24. In 1971 Bahrain, Qatar, and the Emirates had virtually no expenditures on military forces, and Kuwait (already independent) only spent 185 million United States dollars. In 1981 Bahrain spent 135 million dollars, Kuwait spent 1,300 million dollars, Qatar spent 893 million dollars, and the Emirates spent 1,700 million dollars. Bahgat Korany, 'Unwelcome Guests: The Political Economy of Arab Relations with the Superpowers', Hisham Sharabi ed., *The Next Arab Decade: Alternative Futures*, Mansell, 1988, 85. Although the shaikhdoms spent increasing sums on armaments during the 1980s, they were never able to recruit large ground forces. When Iraq invaded Kuwait, the Kuwaiti army had less than 20,000 soldiers.

25. At least one Political Agent was a *real* archer equipped with *real* arrows. See the biography of Percy Gordon Loch in Chapter IX, with the anecdote about his membership in the Royal Company of Archers. For an example of the abandonment of some ceremonies of the common life and the embracing of more royal rites, see Elizabeth Wirth Marvick, review of Ralph E. Giesey's *Ceremonial et puissance souveraine: France XV-XVII siècles, American Historical Review*, Vol.95, No.2, April 1990, 506-507.

26. Ahmad Mustafa Abu-Hakima, *The Modern History of Kuwait, 1750-1965*, Luzac, 1983, 11. 'The recorded history of British relations with Kuwait,' says Lorimer, 'opens in 1775, when on the investment of Basrah by the Persians, the British desert mail from the Gulf to Aleppo began to be dispatched from Kuwait instead of Subair [a town west of Basra]. The latter town was not occupied by the Persians until 1778.' *Ibid.*, 27.

27. *Ibid.*, 12. 'Kuwait seems to have offered a solution to the difficulties of the English East India Company in exporting goods to the markets of the Middle East.' *Ibid.*, 27.

28. No one was more conscious of history's use than was Saddam Hussein, who proclaimed that he was a descendant of the Prophet Mohammed and the heir to the Babylonian King Nebuchednezzar. Indeed, before launching the invasion of Kuwait he had made a further bid for legitimacy by refurbishing the tombs of the British-sponsored Hashemite dynasty of Iraqi kings that he as a young man had helped overthrow. This piety for the past contrasted with the loss of the 20,000 items spanning 14 centuries that his troops ransacked from the Kuwait National Museum. *The Economist*, 16 March 1991. Nor in the aftermath of the war did Saddam's shelling of his opponents in the holy Shiite centres of Karbala and Najaf, cities spared by the Americans during the war, indicate that he revered antiquity.

PART I

RITUALS OF RULE

*If the Town of Grain [*Kuwait*] is suffered to remain neuter, Caravans may be made no doubt to and from thence to this Place, for as long War will probably be caused by the Loss of Bussora, that City will be deserted unless Merchants can find some Method of carrying on Trade near it. Grain seems to be well situated to serve as a Substitute...but that can only be whilst it remains independent for should the Persians take Possession of it, it will be dangerous for Merchants to bring Goods from thence...* – British Consul at Aleppo to Mr. Latouche of the East India Company at Basra, 11 June 1776, *Factory Records*, India Office Records.

The life of the British in India, even in 1939, was still Victorian. Clothes had changed, some customs a little, but the framework of life had been settled in the last years of the old Queen. And since it was a country ruled by an official hierarchy, it was socially conservative. Seniority played a big part in promotion and senior officials do not usually undervalue the wisdom that experience has brought them. In social matters they are likely to prefer the standards of their youth and long before the young men of their day have become old enough to change things they too have accepted the standards of their seniors...And again, the time-lag was greater with the ICS and the Indian Army than with officers of the British service, who were often more aware of modifications in the social climate in England – but then they seldom stayed in India long enough to have much influence. – Charles Allen, *Plain Tales From the Raj*, 1975.

*We know that they [*the Saudis*] go over the causeway to drink in Bahrain. Everyone knows that they are hypocrites, so why won't they at least let us have a beer when we are fighting, and maybe dying, to defend their country?* – Corporal Stephen Quairby, British Gulf Forces, *The Australian*, 6 February 1991.

Applaud your victory, my dear citizens, and the honour and dignity of all Iraqis. You have faced 30 countries and the evil they have brought here. You have faced the whole world...You have won. – Saddam Hussein, radio address announcing withdrawal from Kuwait, 26 February 1991.

I

VICEREGAL RITUALISM

When we think of symbolic strategies, we must often think of the use of symbols to manipulate persons and groups, and most often for deceitful self-serving purposes. – James W. Fernandez, *Persuasions and Performances*, 1986.

The limited political institutionalization as well as the limited political legitimacy of all but a few Middle Eastern states stand out as significant characteristics. – L. Carl Brown, *International Politics and the Middle East*, 1984.

It is rather difficult for the student of history to follow Kuwait's relations with the British in the official records of the English East India Company...Lorimer, who made extensive use of these records, states that the mention of Kuwait during the forty years that followed the Company Factory's withdrawal from there in 1795 is scanty. During Shaikh 'Abd Allah's rule [and Sabah Ibn Jabir's, 1815-1866], relations with the British were on a cordial basis. Therefore, the question arises: could it be that Kuwait lost its independence and became a larger country in the neighbourhood? – Ahmad Mustafa Abu-Hakima, *The Modern History of Kuwait*, 1983.

'Far and fair Arabia' conjures up such distinctive images that the Indian, or more precisely the Indo-British, contributions to its ethos came as a surprise. Valentinoesque fancies of camel milk and palm dates afford little room for the curries of swarthy sepoys and Sikhs. The Raj has firmly belonged in imagination to Bombay, Calcutta, and Delhi; not to Bushire, Kuwait, and Dubai. Western notions of Arabia and of India remain tied to geographic boundaries. In actual fact, the story is much more complicated.

The compass exerts strong historiographic force over the popular stereotypes of countries – but geography can mislead and in this case has. The influence exercised by the Raj was not confined to the Indian subcontinent, and the consequence is that the shaikhs of the Gulf have much in common with the now deposed maharajahs of India. Hence there is an element of justification in the denouncements by the Iraqis of the Gulf rulers, and at least an iota of truth to the claim that their deposition has popular Arab support.

Chutney and *Kim* found their way to St. Helena and China, and topees were nowhere better displayed than in the Gulf, where the fabled Indian Political Service (IPS) held durbars amongst the dunes as effectively as it did in Hyderabad and Rajastan. The culprit in the tale, the IPS, had its origins in the days of the East India Company – but came into its own after Parliament imposed direct rule on India in 1858.[1] Recruited primarily from the Indian Civil Service and the Indian Army, the IPS grew into a cosseted diplomatic corps of the Viceroy, exerting considerable effect on all of India's affairs.

The Gulf did not escape the consequences of India's becoming the jewel in the crown. Lewis Pelly, whose post-Indian Mutiny regime as the Gulf's Political Resident (1862-72) was marked by the growth of British authority, wrote: 'Our interests in these regions being mainly British Indian, and the bulk of British subjects here trading or residing being British Indian or connected with India, I am of opinion that the officials of this residence should remain wholly subordinate [to] the Indian Government.'[2] They did.

Iraq, Iran, Saudi Arabia, and (to an extent) Oman may be littorally part of the Gulf, but belong to other worlds as well. (Oman should not be confused with Trucial Oman, a name applied to what are now the Emirates.) The Iraqi invasion of 1990 is hardly the first or only example of conflict between states of the region. A snarl often has interrupted the lip service given to supposedly amiable relations between the shaikhdoms and the bordering 'big brothers'.

In fact, the Iraqi invasion was not even 1990's only example of inharmonious relations. An instance occurred during the football matches for the Gulf Cup, when Saudi Arabia angrily pulled its team out of the games on the grounds that the 'logo' that host Kuwait had selected for the tournament featured the revered horse *Ebyan* that had helped in Kuwait's post World War I defence against Saudi marauders. Kuwaiti suspicions were that the Saudis were less troubled with stallions and history than with the risk of hostile crowds in Kuwait that would vocally express views about Saudis' parentage. Of course, subsequent more serious events in August 1990 put that sort of feuding into perspective, and may do so again.

Relationships between the shaikhdoms themselves have never been particularly harmonious. As early as 1809, the Kuwaitis were volunteering to help the East India Company in an expedition against the shaikhdom of Ras al-Khayma in the lower Gulf – the Kuwaiti ruler of the day, Shaikh Abd Allah offered pilots to guide the British war vessels. Nevertheless, Bahrain, Kuwait, Qatar, and the United Arab Emirates are distinctively *Gulf,* and the present-day Arabs of those shaikhdoms claim a common identity when they are not making snide remarks about each other. Although they would be loath to admit it, this identity owes much to the British and to India. The longtime Adviser (1926-1957) to Bahrain's shaikhs, Sir Charles Belgrave, wrote: 'The Gulf Arabs had closer connections with India than with the countries of the Middle East, for most of the Gulf trade was with Bombay.'[3] Understandably, the 'camel cantons' emphasize in press releases the pan-Arab and Muslim aspects of their past, but among less publicized similarities are many that can be attributed to the British and Indian presence in the Gulf, felt the more keenly because of sparse population and the longstanding and now justified fears of being gobbled up by their larger neighbours.[4]

For these well-heeled satraps, statehood owes much to their entanglement with the Raj; not all of the Imperial influence was harmful. Plagued by arbitrary boundaries, of which the bitterly-contested border between Iraq and Kuwait is only one example,[5] they faced long odds in becoming nation-states.[6] Surprisingly, instead of ending in political oblivion as they might have, or relegated to being obscure provinces of one of their large neighbours, the shaikhdoms became proudly independent members of the United Nations – with *per capita* incomes that for a time were the highest in the world and which remain, despite fluctuations in the price of oil, far the largest in the Arab world. The British Empire had much to do with this, but Indo-British contributions do not fit into an Arab patriotic historiography and are not acknowledged.

Since independence, the Gulf states have re-fashioned their pasts in hopes of stabilizing their futures. A major example is the way in which ties with India have been expunged from the record. The employment of large numbers of Indians in menial jobs also changed Arab perceptions of the status of things Indian. Rather than being officious surrogates for the British, Indians today in the Gulf are the gas station attendants and supermarket bag boys. So numerous are they that the Indian weekly *National Herald* (6 September 1990) lamented that 'the Iraqi tanks rolled not into Kuwait but to the heart of Kerala.' There is more to it than that. Indian dishes such as keema, daal, and biryani have long been part of the Gulf diet, and the lasting influence extends beyond food to the Gulf's *mentalité*.

Swan-necked Spurs

The induced historical amnesia has some justification, because the story of the Raj in the Gulf does not run to good fellows well met. Relations between British India and Arabia were never easy. A case can be made that the secretariats in Calcutta, and later Delhi, were on the lookout for any *casus belli* that advantageously might become a *casus fortuitus*. In the course of the nineteenth century, enough fancied slights occurred to force treaty concessions that effectively turned the Gulf into a British lake. Frequently incidents were of no more real gravity than the flimsy pretext of a 'popular uprising' that Saddam Hussein seized upon to enter Kuwait, albeit less effectively.

Usually in Gulf history when Western powers have needed an excuse for intervention, an excuse has been found. Today the Americans have *more* of an excuse for their presence, but the relationship between the United States and the Arabs is not any more altruistic than was the one that existed for so long between Britain and the shaikhs. Nor are the long-term effects likely to be any more happy. If the Americans want to stay, they will.

Indo-British influence helped to prevent absorption by the surrounding powers, it also postponed the development of national identity.[7] Intentions proved as cross-purposed as in India, but whatever the ultimate verdict on Imperial adventures in the Middle East, for nearly a century (1858-1947), the Gulf was as much at the mercy of the Indian Political Service as was India, betoken to an old boy Raj whose beaver cocked hat and swan-necked spurs denoted that – albeit while stationed nearer to Mecca than Madras – he was part of the Viceroy's entourage. The incongruous rituals that the IPS introduced illustrate the Indo-British idiom working its way to the furthest corners of Imperial society, spread by 'occidentotics' who displayed that bias by 'so much gaud and gook, that enough goods to stock a haberdashery hang from their chests'.8

While hardly the only cultural force at work, the Indo-British one was considerable. Recalling Antonio Gramsci's assertions about rule involving the hegemonics of culture, the astute readers will not be surprised that the Gulf performed to Indo-British tunes.[9] Many East India Company officers stationed there, and the majority of the IPS officers, had family ties with the subcontinent: fathers, grandfathers, and in-laws with Indian service. Not only were some IPS officers born in India, but most of them spent more time in India than in Britain until their retirement:

> The Service was not recruited directly in England and India, as were the Indian Civil Service and the Indian Army. In early years many soldiers of the British or Company's Service entered its ranks: John Malcolm, Henry Lawrence and John Nicholson are renowned examples. Curzon did much to strengthen and reorganize it, and, in the half-century that has since passed, its recruits have been drawn from the Indian Army and the Indian Civil Service roughly in the proportion of two to one. The work of the Service was little known to the British public, or even to Parliament, but its activities covered a great stretch of territory far wider than India herself, and its unobtrusiveness is some measure of its success throughout more than a century and a half of British dominion in Asia.[10]

The Company and The Mutiny

Just as 1990 will be regarded in years to come as a critical year in Gulf history, 1858 was a turning point – although a less obvious one at the time. The Mutiny of 1857-58 and the transfer of control of India from the East India Company to a Government of India brought important changes in the Gulf. Just before the Mutiny, in 1856-57, the East India Company had a last military fling, a comic opera sortie that involved Indian troops engaging the Persians at Bushire, Khoosh-ab, and Mohammerah. Yet it was in the wake of the Mutiny that there was a notable political restructure, and a dramatic transformation in attitude. The monuments of resistance, massacre, and reprisal coloured the outlook of post-Mutiny Imperial leadership. (See Plate 11.) Residents for years to come would be men with personal experience of the catastrophe, and suspicions based on that debacle.

During the Mutiny, the surprising loyalty had been noted of many of the Indian princes. Afterwards claims were made that India would have been lost without their support. This had its effects on a new breed of Imperial administrators who were unequivocally political in orientation and it contributed to their stance towards the shaikhdoms. A distinctive style of leadership amongst the Arabs was encouraged by IPS tutelage, and it was not a populist one.[11] A shaikhy class began to emerge, with authority marked by salutory if not salutary differences from that of a hoydenish past. Its gingerbread and ginger beer Indo-Britishness largely has been ignored by historians.[12] It reflected the impact of the IPS and of the Viceroy on Gulf social structure, which even today partly recalls a process similar to that which went on between the IPS and the erstwhile Indian ruling houses. Not the least of these resemblances lies in royal excesses: 'Much of the blame lay with the British, who made tools of them, then pets of them, and finally scapegoats of them.'[13] *Mene, mene, tekel, upharsin.*

One of the great problems arising out of the British influence has been that monarchies such as those in the Gulf establish and hang on to legitimacy by an emphasis on an invented past. That bondage to tradition or at least to what is *perceived* to be the tradition makes the acceptance of modernity difficult.

A radical state such as Iraq, which brutally murdered the members of the royal dynasty that Britain imposed, has the opposite problem – it must scratch the ground to find a legitimate past. This can become a literal archaeological scratching as in the case of Saddam Hussein's farcical efforts to rebuild the Hanging Gardens of Babylon. The differences between the two political systems, both of which are multi-flawed and highly imperfect, could not be more productive of misunderstanding.

Origins of the tradition-modernity divide in the Middle East, a division which authorities such as Michael Hudson were astute enough to perceive as fraught with possible troubles, existed long before the present confrontations and can be traced back to EIC years. The Imperial impact on the Arabs may have been Victorian and Edwardian, but its origins were just barely Elizabethan, and assuredly Jacobean. The East India Company came into the region in the seventeenth century and had a trading post at Shiraz by 1617, at Bandar Abbas (Gombroon) in 1623, and at Basra in 1635. A post was opened at Mocha in Yemen in 1618. While the Company maintained Gulf representatives in the seventeenth and eighteenth centuries, interests continued through the years to be overwhelmingly commercial and the involvement in local affairs appears limited, though still unresearched.

The Company became over the years increasingly more political and more imposing in its purposes and pose, as shown by comparing its successive headquarters. The early building mentioned in the Introduction looked a little like a comfortable coffee house. (Plate 6.) As is often the case, architecture kept pace with ambition. In the early nineteenth century pretentiousness prevailed – but the imposing enough Leadenhall Street building would in turn be demolished in 1862 for something grander still. The buildings became Viceregal at the same time that the political system did. (Plate 12.)

The harbinger of change can be seen in the men who now filled the post of Gulf Resident. The last East India Company Resident, Captain Felix Jones, was appointed in 1855. When the Company was involuntarily dissolved in the wake of the Mutiny in 1859, Jones became by default the representative of the new Government of India, to be followed by officers whose establishment backgrounds and social aspirations contrast strikingly with the picaresque careers of those appointed by the EIC. The enormous consequences for India of the Mutiny (including the rise of the cult of the Queen-Empress) will not be fully argued here, but the uprising was a *coup de foudre* as far as the Gulf was concerned. *Because the Residents proceeded to impose a political ritualism different from anything previously seen, the Mutiny can be described as a coup de théâtre as well.* The Gulf was 'Indianized' and 'ritualized'.

The Indian rupee became the Gulf's currency.[14] The stamps were Indian issues. An Indian post office opened in Bahrain in 1884 and only in 1933 did the British trouble to overprint Indian stamps with 'Bahrain'. Dubai's post office opened in 1909, but no Dubai stamps were produced until 1961.[15] As an example, a letter from the author's collection that was sent from Kuwait to

Bombay in 1942 uses a George V sixpence issue. The envelope is appropriately addressed, because the boat schedules and telegraph linked the ports to Bombay.[16] Essentials such as cloth and food came from India.[17] The Resident's guard and his fifer too were Indians.[18] The highest of honours awarded was named the Star of India. Most books and journals came from India,[19] and that was where the majority of exports went.[20] Some Arabs carried ties further, leaving the Gulf to settle permanently in India at Ponnani and Bhaktal.[21]

The Indo-British cultural onslaught included inroads on the Arabic language itself, which absorbed or suffered, depending on a linguist's pluralism or puritanism, from a rank harras of Hindustani words and pejorative 'barracks' English. For good or ill, Gulf Arabic is considerably different from *fusha*, the pure Arabic much admired and considered the true tongue for literary purposes. G. Rex Smith comments:

> I have long been of the opinion that the linguistic interference of the English colonial languages (in particular English and French) in Arabic dialects is in itself an important research desideratum. Leaving French aside, perhaps the strongest such interference took place in and around Aden...One wonders too how Arabic is changing in this regard in the Gulf and Southern Arabia. Are the Anglicisms still there, firmly set within the local language and in effect no longer Anglicisms at all?...One hears of, rather than hears, a quadriliteral verb *damfal*, 'curse', 'insult', from the Indian English 'damned fellow'. At any rate the use of genuine Indian/Persian words...and quaint Indian English is significant. One too is reminded of the Egyptian Delta Arabic *yishtaghil shit*, 'he works as a sweeper in a British Army camp and one of his jobs is to clean out the latrines!'[22]

The lasting semantic and cultural effects of this invasion are indicated in the remarks of an American visiting Bahrain in 1946 about the 'colonial-Indian class-conscious flavour of the place – a lot of Indians and Indian vocab – *dhobi, coolie*...Americans who went over there [from Dhahran in Saudi Arabia] would come back and have the natives calling them *Sahib* – "You call me *Sahib* boy." '[23] Elderly Arabs in 1990 could recall that Indians, as *de facto* representatives of the British, were automatically addressed as 'sir'. A Doha merchant recounted to this writer that his father used to hitch rides from Indians who drove for the oil company in Qatar, and lived long enough to employ an Indian driver for his half dozen seldom-used Bentleys. Alas, 'easy come, easy go', and many Kuwaiti-owned Bentleys are now in Baghdad.

Post War Shaikhy Identities

Thus the Gulf in many ways laboured or benefited under the yoke of Calcutta and Delhi as much as did Hyderabad or the Punjab. Imperial authority relied on the 'susceptibility' of natives to a contrived ritualism[24] and made ingenious use of baubles and bangles to achieve this: 'Lord Curzon's view was that though these questions might appear to be trifling, and interference might even be thought to be vexatious, they were really of no small importance.'[25] In India a plentiful supply of servants helped to make ceremonialism more practical than in the shaikhdoms.[26] Deference, as Bagehot and others have often noted, is the other side of the ritualistic coin...and servants are the essence of deference.

While Bushire lacked the resources of Bombay, the Residents copied as much as they could the Viceregal iconography.[27] 'Indianization' contributed to a growing if superficial homogeneity in what had been a heterogeneous Gulf. This received extra impetus from Lord Curzon's Viceroyalty. Curzon is an inexhaustible font of examples of Imperial hauteur, and his involvement with the Gulf is the proof of the pudding as far as the proposition that the British ruled there by ritual. A Gulf Resident wrote, 'Perhaps Curzon's greatest achievement was to put the Gulf once more upon the map: for it was mainly under his hand that interest in this region revived before the discovery of oil around these shores, and before man had learned to fly. It seems almost as if his vision had been illumined by some spark of prophetic fire.'[28]

Thus favoured by the Viceregal eye and flavoured by Bombay, the shaikhdoms should never be dismissed as they sometimes are as appendages of Saudi Arabia, a country of far different antecedents which in its present boundaries did not exist until 1932.[29] Saudi never felt the Indo-Britishness being discussed here. In contrast with Egyptian, Ottoman, Yemeni, and other contributions to the Saudi stockpot, the present identity of the Gulf and the resemblances between its mini-states owes much to the Indian Empire.[30] What identity and boundaries would have been achieved without the ministrations of the IPS is problematical, but the populations living along the coast of Arabia retain these special affinities despite being part of a greater Middle East being described variously and recently with considerable truth as an 'interface', 'maelstrom', 'shatterbelt', 'rimland', or 'marginal crescent'.

Despite their denials of the fact, the Gulf states are characterized by a cultural pluralism enhanced by maritime connections, a blending of Indian and African motifs that is found nowhere else in the Middle East. Had this been openly admitted and respected, the world's perception of the shaikhdoms today would be kinder. Those who are uneasy at the West defending feudalism during the recent Kuwait fracas would have less of an argument: the refusal to acknowledge the variety of races and persuasions that actually have gone to make up the Gulf states has deprived those states of a telling argument for their independence. To enjoy a future, the shaikhdoms will have to realize that their pluralism is a virtue rather than a shame, and will have to find ways to include everyone in their political structure. If the West grows weary of protecting the Gulf, one reason will be the continued disenfranchisement of most of its citizens.

As will be seen in Chapter IV, the Gulf's historiography suffers today at the hands of historians scratching for a past to bolster (if a pun be permitted) shaky monarchical identities. Expatriates have been enlisted in the effort. An example of how the cheque book hopes to accomplish what footnotes cannot is Sharjah's employment of the aptly named and prolific American painter Edward Miracle to churn out canvases that depict a romantic and fictitious history of the emirate. A highlight of Mr. Miracle's 1990 exhibition in Sharjah was a colourful but fanciful depiction 'The British Massacre of Arabs at Ras Al

Khaimah'. Paintings do not have footnotes and so Mr. Miracle was relieved of the necessity of mentioning that the Kuwaitis were happy to help out and that the British 'raids' were part of a much more involved scenario.

The level of Gulf historical discourse has been ultra simplistic, outdoing in excesses the nation-building histrionics in nineteenth century America with the patriotic emphasis on George Washington's chopping down the cherry tree. Heroes are in demand, especially if they are members of the ruling families. The history and art has had echoes of the Soviet Union in Stalin's prime. Newspapers have not been exempt and reality has never been a strong suit of Gulf journalists. Unable to present actual news for fear of offending the rulers, the Gulf papers concentrate on nonsense. Hundreds of column inches chronicle a national going around the world on a camel, and the Gulf press embraces him as a substitute for the British explorers of an earlier era. No Burton, he poses with his can of Pepsi and flies home to recuperate between segments of his journey. Western newspapers were the first to report the Iraqi invasion.

The officially-scripted Gulf opéra bouffé concocted by Arab historians suffers from the 'Sinbad syndrome', an enthusiasm for the whitewashed personalities of swashbuckling days when Arab dhows smuggled treasure to India's Malabar Coast from what was then the 'Pirate Coast'.[31] Reconstructed dhows race on holidays, and murals depict fierce and highly legendary sailor ancestors. The interest somewhat resembles that which the Australians acquired for convict ancestors on the 'First Ships', only the Arabs are less likely than the Australians to 'call a spade a spade'. Possibly neither Arabs nor Australians would find their ancestors agreeable company in the flesh, but like the Australians, the Arabs have decided that a rogue or two does not blot the escutcheon. At least he's our rogue, and he can be cleaned up.

This would be vaguely amusing if it had not prevented the more serious business of developing the Gulf's historical and political sciences. There have been enough material resources in the last few decades to do so, and in the long run the interests of the shaikhdoms would have been served by letting the scholarly chips fall where they may – such has not been the case. Now, when desperately in need of serious friends who could argue for the continued existence of their enclaves, the amirs find that they have paid for sycophants only rather than scholars.

Siblings?

Despite resemblances between the shaikhdoms, and a patent eagerness for inventing a shared historical background as a prelude to further economic and political integration, differences persist between Bahrain, the Emirates, Kuwait, and Qatar. An epitome of this will have to do.

Bahrain has the strongest ties with Persia. The United Arab Emirates, ironically the least united state, constitute a confusing federation of seven city-states (Abu Dhabi, Ajman, Dubai, Sharjah, Ras al Khamiah, Fujairah, Umm al Qaiwain) that were treated individually during British days. Kuwait, far the wealthiest, was particularly close to the Ottomans, and as a result of that legacy has had to fight off Iraqi threats to its independence. Qatar was stubbornly defiant of British interference and the most enigmatic – and to some, such as this author, the most interesting (or curious) shaikhdom.

Nonetheless, these feuding siblings have, like Scandinavia or Central America, enough of a shared identity to justify being considered together. There are uniting factors other than the Indo-British one, especially the maritime interest.[32] This encouraged other similarities: an aptitude for trade and, despite incessant ballyhooing about the gentil nomadic bedouin, the concentration of populations in towns.[33] These prosaic facts get scant notice in Ministry of Information press kits, which dote on desert-dwellers.

Considerable evidence suggests how prevalent was an urban maritime culture, and more instructive than looking at tents is a visit to Zubara in northern Qatar, which in the eighteenth century was a bustling entrepôt and whose surviving foundations bespeak a sophisticated commercial centre. The failure to emphasize the merchant and trading heritage misses an opportunity, since early urban sophistication could be as fully a source of pride as herding. Authorities have, in the face of contrary evidence, insisted that the bucolic was pre-eminent and that town-dwellers sent sons to live with the bedouin 'much as the British gentry would send their sons to Eton'.[34]

The British encouraged trading by inveterate mapmaking, so much so that it can be said that the East India Company outlook reflected cartography as well as ideology. Cartographic hegemony is a key to the earliest British influence, and anyone interested in the East India Company's success should consider a seminal article by Jane E.A. Dawson – 'William Cecil and the British Dimension of Early Elizabethan Foreign Policy' (*History*, Vol.74, No.241, June 1989). Dawson claims that Cecil's passion for maps was an important ingredient in his career, that he 'thought in a cartographical idiom'. Precisely the same thesis about a 'cartographic mind' seems applicable to the EIC officers. The Dawson hypothesis deserves to be applied to the extraordinary history of Gulf mapmaking, for no part of the Empire derived more political benefit from the cartographers.

The maps through the years show clearly that the settled population lived in small ports. One, in the author's possession, of Ras Al Khaimah, issued by the Chief Engineer's Office in Bombay in 1855, depicts what was almost the standard Gulf settlement of fortress, storehouses, and fortified enclave. Other maps equally testify to the thoroughness of this EIC cartography, a thoroughness which gave the navy a considerable advantage.

Urban settlement, seafaring, fishing, and pearling – all these interests reflected an outward-looking attitude that has struck observers as a deliberate defiance of the desert.[35] Be that as it may, discussion here focuses on contributions to Gulf identity palpably stemming from the shaikhdoms' administration as part of the Indian Empire. Ultimately (an example of *negative causality*, a force discussed in my book *Chains of Empire*), the Gulf peoples were further united by a resistance to the same Indo-British traditions which helped to give an initial unity to the region. Such cacophonous resistance to their own origins led to historical fantasizing about a distinguished, but wholly unsubstantiated, *Arab* rather than *pluralistic* past.

In this respect, a distinction should be maintained in examining the differences between *tradition* and *custom* in the Middle East. Custom is often simply routine which a simple society endures as part of the drudgery of earning a living. Tradition, albeit a contentious word, includes the paraphernalia and ritual surrounding an activity, much of it decidedly non-utilitarian. Customs evolve more readily and unobtrusively than ritual, which derives strength from not appearing to change. *Faute de mieux*, customs become traditional – and traditions have often in Arabia sunk back into being customs.[36]

Cosseting the Haut Monde

Mention of the IPS in the midst of the discussion occasioned by the present Middle Eastern turmoil can draw the response that the subject has limited interest to anyone interested in the contemporary situation, and *inter alia* Kuwait's problems. After all, today's grave political crisis in the Arab world usually is seen to relate more to oil, OPEC, and Islamic fundamentalism. In actuality, understanding the Gulf today requires understanding the confrontation between monarchicalism and radicalism and thus requires the understanding of the long-lasting consequences of the IPS administration, the nurturing of a shaikhy class by the British, the suppression by both British and Arabs of the inherent cultural pluralism, and the jockeying of innumerable competing factions with roots in Viceregal days that still goes on.

No issue in the Middle East begins *de novo*. The Iraqi scorn for the shaikhs has hoary origins. Presiding over what were the beginnings of many of the present problems were British officers who were members of a stylish service that made a speciality of guiding the rulers of the princely Indian states.[37] Their uniforms were unforgettable, replete with chest decorations reminiscent of a charlotte fancied with arabesques of glazed fruit.[38] The attitudes that they imparted were equally distinctive. Steeped in Indian administrative history, the IPS often treated the shaikhdoms simply as Indian states, and initially regarded their real purpose as being the gatekeepers to India. Paranoia and Russophobia stoked this. As Aaron Friedberg has observed, Russia confronted British planners with a dilemma. Abandoning India or a portion of India was unthinkable, but the prospects of all-out war with Russia were almost as depressing. The place of India in the Imperial scheme was extraordinary:

> The English historians Ronald Robinson and John Gallagher have written that 'to all Victorian statesmen, India and the British Isles were the twin centres of their wealth and strength in the world as a whole.' Max Beloff, in his book *Imperial Sunset*, goes further. 'Britain without India would not have been the world power that at the time of the Diamond Jubilee [1897] she seemed to be. At that time it could well be argued that she had as much right as Austria-Hungary to be styled a dual monarchy or dual empire.'
>
> The importance that British statesmen attached to India is reflected in the pattern of their imperial and diplomatic strategies during most of the period separating the Napoleonic Wars and World War I. Indeed, the whole of Britain's external policy during this period is absolutely incomprehensible without some understanding of the centrality of its eastern empire...The

Persian Gulf, Persia, and Afghanistan were important almost exclusively because of their proximity to India.[39]

The IPS were proudly a part (and from *their* perspective, the most important part) of the fabled Indian civil services, the so-called 'heaven-born', and were steeped in the doctrine of India's pre-eminence in the Empire. Not only did the IPS share the political concern of all the Indian services for protecting India against Russian and other threats ('The Great Game'), but radiated the tremendous personal presence and force of character which was part of the Raj's ruling mystique.

It would have been extraordinary if this had not had an influence on the Arabs, although its influence has gone largely unnoticed. As with the IPS in princely India, the Gulf IPS kept the upper hand by stagecraft as much as by statecraft, employing a theatrical sense of decorum and studied insouciance rather than force of arms. Of course, gunboats were *most* helpful, although they were not available as much as Gulf Residents would have liked and the British in the Empire displayed considerable experience in using ritual rather than force as a means of control *because they had to do so.*[40] Throughout the nineteenth and twentieth centuries, military means of enforcing decisions were not as adequate as might be thought, and the Residents on occasion complained bitterly about the lack of support.

Contributing to ritual expertise, and perhaps the single most significant factor, was schooling. Indo-British ritualism during the nineteenth century was spread by boy-men, public school old boys whose policies in adult life reflected their adolescence, displaying a prefect's interest in the smallest matters of form and ritual.[41] These misnamed schools were the antithesis of public, being fee-paying establishments for the emerging middle classes. The Gulf passed into British hands at a time when Tom Brown was acquiring a pith helmet and booking his ticket to East of Suez. He took with him a liking for the ceremonies of the schoolyard. Roundabout as a means of control rituals may have been, but success sometimes is achieved *prendre le chemin des écoliers*. The Empire perpetuated schoolboy enthusiasms for juvenile social gradations, reinforced as at school by soigné sartorial splendours.[42] Armed with plume boxes from Horton & Sons (the plumes went through holes in the separately-boxed topee and were then screwed on), IPS officers were striking, if occasionally moulting, apparitions.

An example of growing preoccupations in the later nineteenth century with an elaborate political etiquette, was the appointment of an IPS officer as Aide-de-Camp to the Secretary of State for India. He was stationed in London starting in 1872 to oversee the increasingly strict protocol of visits and to chaperon and direct the affairs of Indian students.[43] This is far from the only instance of the IPS comforting and cosseting the *haut monde*. The ritualistic and administrative duties of the IPS officers overlapped. This would not have been difficult to manage, for ritual and the routine of daily life had been intermingled for IPS officers ever since traumatic experiences at school.

While not all the British loved their schools, and while definitely some ranted against them and hated every moment spent in them, the public school was undeniably part of Britain's indigenous culture. While they were hardly indigenous or natural to India or Arabia, the use of reiterated rituals that owed much to Eton and Rugby contributed to the shaping of the Arab mind (as well as to that of the Indian mind). *The Gulf found itself coping not only with an alien government but with an alien and quasi-religious ritualism.* In the later years it became difficult to honour the former without embracing the latter.[44] Thus the shaikhs have a credibility problem with democratically-minded Arabs, no matter how much they profess their oneness with the masses. They are perceived as quislings who long anticipated Quisling.

Viceregal Ritualism and Lord Lytton

In summary, the closing years of the nineteenth century saw the rise of a politically useful variety of Imperial ritualism that was distinctly *Indian Viceregal*: '...the pomp and protocol surrounding the Viceroy grew more complex: all designed to dazzle the ruled and maintain the authority of the rulers.'[45] Every Viceroy played his part in the growth of this Imperial ritology, but the advent of Lord Lytton as Viceroy (1876-1880) was notable in this respect. (He was an Old Harrovian. It is needless to add that *every* Viceroy was a public school product.) Lytton firmly believed that the Indian allegiance would be assured by exploiting a 'susceptibility to the influence of symbolism'.[46] He wrote to Disraeli:

> I find evidence that small favours and marks of honour bestowed from time to time by the British Government on the head of the family (such as an additional gun to his salute, the right to a return visit from the Viceroy, or a more honourable place in Durbar, etc.) are quite as highly prized and appreciated as the more substantial benefits (of augmented territory or revenue)...I believe that at the present moment an Indian Maharaja would do anything, or pay anything, to obtain an additional gun to his salute.[47]

Lytton was both an expert and experienced ritualist, but the miniver-clad apogee of elaborate Viceregal ceremonialism came during Lord Curzon's regime (1898-1905). Although 'not quite the Roi Soleil', he exacted 'a traditional deference that gave every function, at least in part, the character of a charade...architecture, robes, sound and silence, the dignity of the principals, the immobility of the acolytes, combined to reaffirm the permanence and nobility...'.[48] (The *annus mirabilis imperii* was the Queen's Jubilee Year, 1897.)

While in the Gulf the effects were always more modest because of limited treasuries and personnel, the political results were equally significant. That affairs in Arabia could not be conducted on the vast and magnificent scale of government in India did not prevent the growth of a salute and honours system, but the Residents meanly *charged* for some of their ritualism, making the reluctant and parsimonious shaikhs *pay* for gun salutes. The Shaikh of Kuwait begrudgingly spent £69 in 1932 for a replacement saluting cannon, although eventually he was able to get a small refund as the Admiralty upon reconsideration sent him a bill for only £67.3.1. Bahrain's shaikh was promised a discount on his salute bills if the spent shell cases were 'returned empty with lids'.[49]

Despite being forced to pay for some of the pomp, the shaikhs[50] became as entranced by the honours game and the idea of *L'état, c'est moi* as did any of the Indian maharajahs. Such obvious pretentiousness was contrary to Islamic teachings[51] and in any event rather ostentatious in the setting of the simple fishing villages which passed as the Gulf's metropolises. Doha after all was never Delhi, and Kuwait was never Karachi. Nevertheless, the durbars of the Residents as they travelled about reflected the romantic fantasizing surrounding the India Office and its mission. By this time, as noted, the bureaucrats back home had moved again, into an awesomely splendid building which truly was a palace. (See Plate 12.) Imperially housed, the Indian Empire had a finesse that the Bourbons would have envied.

Kuwait's Victoria

Preoccupations with appearances began to prevail even in such a backwater as Kuwait. At the turn of the century, Shaikh Mubarak of Kuwait acquired a handsome but impractical victoria and forbade anyone else to keep one,[52] although such a dainty carriage seemed slightly inappropriate for a burly man who had gained power by murdering his family. An India Office file on Gulf salutes eventually grew to 295 pages and included correspondence over the proper number of salutes with dignitaries such as George V, Austen Chamberlain, the Secretaries of State for Foreign Affairs and the Colonies, and the Admiralty. Honours were taken *very* seriously, and they gave a significant boost to the Residents' success in winning – and keeping – control.[53]

What the Arabs were witnessing in the way of ceremonial improvisations were a small part of a growing Empire-wide preoccupation with ritual in which the public schools played a leading role and the Viceroy performed an exemplary one. In Britain and overseas the tradition-makers were assiduously at work. India was particularly involved, yet the Methodist valleys of Wales were not immune to the onslaught of myth-making. The energetic Augusta Addington (1802-1896) helped to establish a Welsh public school, Llandovery College, to further her bizarre but successful notions of what constituted a distinctive Welsh ceremonialism. (Her husband, Benjamin Hall, was the minister in Palmerston's government who was responsible for finishing the new Palace of Westminster – and it is he for whom Big Ben is named.) Adopting the bardic name of Gwenynen Gwent, the Bee of Monmouthshire, she evangelized for the Welsh Mother Goose stereotype with red cloak and tall black hat, and her Llandovery boys were given a thorough dose of Druidism and leeks along with mundane subjects.[54] Meanwhile, Englishmen joined Welshmen and Scots in donning traditional costume and Morris dancers proliferated. (See Plate 13.) Shaikhs acquired thrones.

Elsewhere in the Empire, others of unquestioned abilities but rather peculiar inclinations were trying on equally improbable costumes. Although identified with theosophy, Annie Besant's contributions in India included starting a public school, founding various Masonic orders, and being the chief promoter of scouting. She was accepted despite her peculiarities by the British Imperial establishment, although with reservations, and the Prince of Wales (George V) visited her school on his 1906 visit to India, as he did Aligarh and other educational foundations. Besant was exceptionally varied in her activities, but only one of a number of prominent British who became involved in Indian public schools and Freemasonry simultaneously. Cecil Tyndale-Biscoe of Kashmir and V.A.S. Stow of Rajkumar and Mayo Colleges are others who were both active Masons and educationists.

Indian boys received a full dose of ritual as a public school education became *de rigueur* for the children of India's élite. Some Indian public schools anteceded the Mutiny. Symbolically, the boys of La Martinière, one of the first and most famous, helped defend the Residency at Lucknow during the Mutiny, and a handsome scholarship annuity providing free education at Martinière was settled on them and their descendants.[55] Kim attends Martinière in Kipling's famous novel. Bishop Corrie in Madras was established in 1813, later merging with a Doveton school to become Bishop Cotton. A number of schools such as Lawrence Memorial at Abu were originally open only to British children but later liberalized their admissions policy. Some of the Indian public schools opportuned the supposed Gulf élite to send their sons, and a few boys made their way to them. However, the primary effect of the public schools was through the British who came, rather than through the Arabs who went away.

Thus the Government of India Act of 2 August 1858 must be regarded as a watershed not only for India but for the whole Empire. An emerging Indo-British etiquette of subordination had profound consequences not only in India but everywhere. *The British reply to the Mutiny was a redefinition of the entire Imperial role, one that was extended and formalized by a unique ritualism and theatricalism that drew many of its motifs from the expanding English public schools.*[56] The years immediately after the Mutiny were the *kairos* of modern Gulf history, as they were for other of Victoria's domains.

None of the outposts were more theatrical than Viceregal Simla, the hoity toity hill station to which the Viceroy escaped from the hoi polloi and which almost all the Gulfites visited at one time or another:

> The British penchant for dressing up and guying both themselves and 'the natives' was given its head at the popular Fancy Dress Balls. At one of the first to be held in the new Viceregal Lodge, the Commissioner of Assam appeared as a Manipur chieftain, an aide-de-camp's sister came as a Brilliant Gadfly, Lord William, recovered from his fall, but 'hobbling on a stick and coughing painfully', was 'the most perfect Chelsea pensioner', and D. [Lord Dufferin, the Marquess of Dufferin and Ava and Viceroy 1884-1886] himself was so cleverly disguised as 'an Arab gentleman' that even his wife did not recognize him.[57]

In summary, the Gulf's history in so far as the British era is concerned reflects the mores of a public school-dominated Viceregal establishment.[58] This was thanks largely to the old boys of the Indian Political Service, impresarios who drew on images from schooldays to introduce a liminal symbolism which arguably still persists.[59] More important, because of their attitudes the IPS slighted the merchant oligarchies and allowed in each shaikhdom a family to become *primus inter impares*.

As Frank Stoakes has noted, a family, patronized by the British (albeit often unenthusiastically), came to regard the estate as theirs, particularly the oil for which there was no precedence as far as scope of customary rights. Other families might be consulted and their decline in status was neither uniform nor accepted without objection. Kuwait is an outstanding example of this:

> In Kuwait the aristocratic families tried to participate in the selection of a new ruler in 1921, and in the same year insisted on the formation of an (in fact ineffective) advisory council, while the constitutional movement of 1937-9 was provoked largely by the autocratic attitude of Ahmad Jabir to the other families, following the example of Mubarak Sabah; on this occasion, before the access of oil revenues, the aristocrats commanded material force.[60]

Much political tension in the Gulf has related to the efforts of these large 'aristocratic' or merchant families to regain a semblance of the power they feel they lost to what are now reigning families. A visitor to Qatar from the Research Department of the Foreign and Commonwealth Office suggested to this author that there was during the British administration a quite deliberate and agreed-upon division of authority between the prominent families of the shaikhdoms, and that the merchants of the Gulf originally acquiesced at the division of responsibility. They could not have anticipated that along with the then irritating minor duties of government ceded to their cohorts would go the use of the oil revenues.

Disturbances in Qatar in 1963 appear to have been an indication of this friction between the royal dynasties and the business community. At that time a National Unity Front made demands on the Al Thani family for changes such as the election of a municipal council and the drawing up of a budget. As with other protests, the demonstrations died out.[61] More recently, 1990 disturbances in Kuwait demanding parliamentary elections involved a group of upper crust protesters who drove to rallies in Rolls Royces. Modest demands by these well-heeled discontents for enlightened medievalism were unacceptable to the Al-Sabah dynasty. This was forgotten in the turmoil of later months, with efforts to return Kuwait's freedom.

At the time, the reporting about such incidents in Kuwait was without reference to the historical background. The *Financial Times* (10 May 1990) commented:

> Conflict between Kuwait's ruling al-Sabah family and pro-democracy activists came to a head yesterday when the Government announced the arrest of eight Kuwaitis who have been campaigning for the restoration of parliament...Among the eight arrested were Dr Ahmed al-Khatib, a nationalist ex-MP who warned earlier this year: 'We hope for a peaceful change, but if people are frustrated violence cannot be ruled out.'...Opposition activists said the eight were arrested when security forces

> stormed the *diwaniya* of Mr. Abdul-Mohsen al-Farhan and assaulted some of the 200 people attending the meeting...In an embarrassing coincidence for the Kuwaiti authorities, an Amnesty International delegation was on its way to Kuwait from London yesterday to monitor the trial on May 12 of a group of Shia Moslems accused of subversion.[62]

The election that finally was held was not for a legislature but for an *in camera* committee to discuss the possibility of a legislature. The ruling family must wish now that they had buttressed their case for legitimacy while they had the opportunity, for much of the criticism over Western support for Kuwait in its *contretemps* with Iraq arose over the control of an arrogant ruling dynasty, openly contemptuous of civil rights.

Almost as regrettable as the inhibiting of political freedoms in the shaikhdoms is the tolerance or blatant assistance given by Gulf governments in years past for the bulldozing away of the region's history. An infinitesimal portion of the oil money went for preserving heritage and ecology. Now there is more consciousness of the destruction, but there are fewer resources to cope. The indifference to the historical heritage of the region may have had some purpose, for as seen, history does not support the claims of ruling families with the obsequiousness which they expect.

The lack of freedom to criticize is what may ultimately be the Gulf's undoing. J.A. Hobson wrote in *Imperialism* (1902):

> Great Britain would be incapable of this policy if she realized in clear consciousness the actual play of motives and their results. Most of the men who have misled her have first been obliged to mislead themselves.[63]

An irony is that the same words could be written about the current Gulf crisis. The West has allowed itself to be misled about the perception that many Arabs have of the ruling shaikhs. Foolhardy is the way to describe the head-in-the-sand attitude to these signs of unhappiness – but in Arabia there has been plenty of sand in which to hide. Those from the West who would pin hopes for the region on political continuity should reflect on the results of the Micawberish approach to mounting problems. If the present situation is saved by Western intervention, it is about time lessons were learned by the shaikhs about political maturity. The spectacle of Kuwait's claims to the world for legitimacy relying 'almost exclusively on the ruling al-Sabah dynasty' may be followed after the invasion's mess is 'sorted out' by the rulers facing the wrath of the masses who bitterly opposed the 'invitations' they extended to the 'imperialist forces'.[64]

> *There is a vast standardization of taste in the region, symbolized not only by transistors, blue jeans, and Coca-Cola but also by cultural images of the Orient supplied by American mass media and consumed unthinkingly by the mass television audience. The paradox of an Arab regarding himself as an 'Arab' of the sort put out by Hollywood is but the simplest result of what I am referring to...if all told there is an intellectual acquiescence in the images and doctrines of Orientalism, there is also a very powerful reinforcement of*

this in economic, political, and social exchange: the modern Orient, in short, participates in its own Orientalizing. – Edward W. Said, *Orientalism*, 1978.

NOTES

1. Caroe, *Wells of Power,* 1951, 50-51.

2. Lewis Pelly to Bombay Government, 11 March 1871, qtd. J.A. Saldanha, *Précis of the Affairs of the Persian Coast and Islands, 1854-1905,* Government Printer, Simla, 1906, 94. See Pelly to Bombay Government, 2 May 1871, *Ibid.*, 92. Pelly rightly gets considerable credit for the extension of British rule in the Gulf, but David Robertson (Dubai Political Agent in the 1960s) suggested that the creation of the Gulf's present identity should be dated from Curzon's Vice-Royalty. David Roberts, 'The Exclusive Treaties – A British View', B.R. Pridham ed., *The Arab Gulf and the West,* Croom Helm, 1985, 10-11. *Cf.* n.28 of Introduction *supra.* Also *cf.* Philip Marlowe, *The Persian Gulf in the Twentieth Century,* Cresset Press, 1962, 27, 137. *N.B.* J.A. Saldanha, 'Preface', *Précis of Bahrein Affairs, 1854-1904,* Government Printer, Simla, 1904, 2. See Indian Office Records (hereafter IOR) L/P&S/12/3760, Enclosure to East Indies Letter No.1879, 7 August 1936. Consider Fahim I. Qubain, 'Social Classes and Tensions in Bahrain', *Middle East Journal,* Vol.9, No.3, Summer 1955, 276-77. *Cf.* Herbert J. Liebesny, 'Administration and Legal Development in Arabia: The Persian Gulf Principalities', *Middle East Journal,* Vol.X, No.1, Winter 1956, 33-42. Also *cf.* Fuad I. Khuri, *Tribe and State in Bahrain: The Transformation of Social and Political Authority in an Arab State,* University of Chicago Press, 1980, 5, 8. Khuri hopelessly confuses the 'Bahrain Administrative Reports' with the *Persian Gulf Residency Reports* and *vice versa.*

3. Charles Belgrave, *The Pirate Coast,* Librarie du Liban, Beirut, 1972, 191.

4. 'Previous writers have covered the whole area under a general title of "India used in the Persian Gulf "; but I am convinced that this is too large a field to cover in great detail. There are three distinct areas – Eastern Arabia, Persia and Iraq – all of which had Indian Postal Agencies at one time or another and for very differing reasons; and I believe that they should all be considered separately. Moreover it was only the first of these three areas which later had British Postal Agencies.' Neil Donaldson, *The Postal Agencies in Eastern Arabia and the Gulf,* Harry Hayes, Batley (West Yorkshire), 1975, 8. Contrasted with the diminutive size of the Gulf states was the huge size of their neighbours. Iran has an area of 636,296 square miles; Iraq has 168,927 square miles; Saudi Arabia has 865,000 square miles. Only in income do the four countries compete in stature, which makes them all the more vulnerable. In 1984 Bahrain claimed 231 square miles in area, had 400,000 people, and a per capita income of $9300. Kuwait was 9375 square miles, had 1,600,000 people, and a per capita income of $19,900. Qatar's area was 4000 square miles, its population was 200,000, and there was a per capita income of $21,900. The Emirates were 36,193 square miles, claimed 1,500,000 in population, and had a per capita of $23,770. Variations in figures in various sources are partly accounted for by conflicting boundary claims, *e.g.* the Bahrain-Qatar dispute over the Hawar Islands and other small islands, and by population figures Gulf states produce to serve specific political ends, *e.g.* to increase the size of their vote in international bodies. The maritime nature of the four states is indicated by their disproportionate land areas in relation to their coasts, *e.g.* Bahrain has only 2.9 square miles of land for every mile of coast. See Alasdair Drysdale and Gerald H. Blake, *The Middle East and North Africa: A Political Geography,* OUP, 1985, esp.15. *Despite or because of the states' tiny populations, visitors (there are understandably few tourists) notice that the Indian military garrisons supporting the British left a genetic legacy, as did the slave trade.*

5. A point well if exhaustively, illustrated by the *twenty-five volumes* of Richard Schofield and Gerald Blake, *Arabian Boundaries: Primary Documents 1853-1957,* Archive Editions, Slough, 1988. See especially Sir Rupert Hay, 'The Persian Gulf States and Their Boundary Problems', *Geographic Journal,* Vol.CXX, Part 4, December 1954, 433-45. Also Husain M. Albaharna, *The Arabian Gulf States: Their Legal and Political Status and Their International Problems,* 2nd rev. ed. 1975 [1968], Manchester, np. See Zamil Muhammad Al-Rashid, *Saudi Relations With Eastern Arabia and Uman (1800-1871),* Luzac, 1981, esp.7-14 for sources, and for bibliography 133-46. For maps and discussion, Anthony H. Cordesman, *The Gulf and the Search for Strategic Stability: Saudi Arabia, the Military Balance in the Gulf, and Trends in the Arab-Israeli Military Balance,* Mansell, 1984, 402-422. See also Arnold J. Toynbee ed., *Survey of International Affairs 1934,* OUP, 1935, 221-25. Majid Khadduri, 'Iran's Claim to the Sovereignty of Bahrayn' [*sic*], *American Journal of International Law,* Vol. 45, 1951, 631-47. *Cf.* Ahmad Mustafa Abu Haikima, *History of Eastern Arabia, 1750-1800,* Khayats, Beirut, 1965, *passim.*

However, despite resemblances, each of the four possesses a cultural discreteness which is partly attributable to geography. Qatar is a peninsula cut off from the mainland. The Emirates' capital, Abu Dhabi, is an island. Bahrain is an island. Kuwait includes island possessions. The Emirates as a whole are separated from lands further east by mountains and west by the Rub'Al-Khali.'...conquerors are stopped by the sea; and the islanders, being outside the reach of their arms, more easily preserve their own laws.' Montesquieu, *The Spirit of the Laws*, Chapter 5, Book XVIII. See John Duke Anthony, 'The Gulf States and Iraq', *The Political Economy of the Middle East: 1973-78*, A Compendium of Papers submitted to the Joint Economic Committee, Congress of the United States, Government Printing Office, Washington, 1980, 211-12. Mordechai Abir, *Oil, Power and Politics: Conflict in Arabia, the Red Sea and the Gulf*, Frank Cass, 1974, 206. Consider Robert David Sack, *Human Territoriality: Its Theory and History*, CUP, 1986, 19-27, esp. 26.

6. One reason that the achievement of national consciousness is noteworthy is that, when the British assumed control the populations were so extraordinarily heterogeneous. Moreover, there were *indeterminable* disputes, both between factions in each shaikhdom and between the shaikhdoms, *e.g.* see IOR:L/P&S/12/3767, 'Intelligence Summary of the Political Agent, Bahrain, for the period 15th May to 15th June 1938'.

7. A caveat is that remarks about Gulf nationalism must be considered against a countervailing pan-Arabism. '...Arabist ideology has encouraged the belief that a nation-state can be fully legitimate only if it includes all Arabs. The strength of confessional ties, the interests and aspirations of classes...all reinforce the feeling that the existing states are only temporary and so reduce the force of allegiance to them.' Maxime Rodinson, *The Arabs*, University of Chicago Press, 1981, 156-57. Another warning should be about the ambiguities of the word 'development' and the phrase 'political development'. 'So many were the attempts at interpreting desirable political change stemming from the grand socio-economic transition from agraria to industria, and so shifting the variety of theoretical models that there had to come a final statement putting all the hypotheses into *the* theory of *political development*. It would mean to political science what economic growth theory meant to economics. We all know that this was not what happened. The theme fell apart, rejected as methodologically flawed due to its unrecognized Western-value biases.' J.E. Lane and S. Ersson, 'Unpacking the Political Development Concept', *Political Geography Quarterly*, Vol.8, No.2, April 1989, 141-42.

8. Jalal Al-i Ahmad, *Occidentosis: A Plague From the West*, Mizan Press, Berkeley (California), 1984, 97.

9. In ways it still strongly does, reinforced now by the vast numbers of workers brought from the subcontinent during the oil boom. The 'odour' of India can be detected, as well as 'infiltrations' in the Arabic language. Darwish Mostafa Al Far (Director, Qatar National Museum), 'Qatar: An Historical Review', *This is Qatar*, December 1987, 44. See Richard E. Littlefield, 'Bahrain as a Persian Gulf State: With References to Its Relations with Great Britain and the Province of Al-Hasa', M.A. thesis, American University of Beirut, 1964, 46. Bibliographically, the Gulf crops up in Indian book lists, *e.g.* Arabia was included as Vol.8 in the Botanical Survey of India's *Flora* series. Another reason for the strength of ties with India was the Arab interest in British treatment of Muslims in India. See esp. P. Hardy, *The Muslims of British India*, CUP, 1972, 103-104.

10. Caroe, *Wells of Power*, 49. Numerous memoirs testify to how generations of the same British family would have careers in India. See, *e.g.* John Christie, *Morning Drum*, British Association for Cemeteries in South Asia, 1983, 7. Despite the Association's rather specific name, BACSA is a pillar of Indo-British scholarship and publishing.

11. See Peter Lienhardt, 'The Authority of Shaykhs in the Gulf: An Essay in Nineteenth-Century History', R.B. Serjeant and R.L. Bidwell eds., *Arabian Studies, II*, C. Hurst, for The Middle East Centre of Cambridge University, 1975, 61-75.

12. In fairness, it must be noted that another view commonly held is at odds with these claims about the Indo-British influence, namely that the British did *not* interfere in Gulf domestic affairs: 'This resulted in a great measure of autonomy for the individual emirates; but it also contributed to the delay in political and economic development.' Ali Mohammed Khalifa, *The United Arab Emirates: Unity in Fragmentation*, Croom Helm, 1979, 9, 23. The argument here (and made at much more length in the author's doctoral dissertation *The Rule of Ritual*) is that the British *did* interfere and that because of administrative attitudes that were shaped in Viceregal India, the IPS magnified the position of a 'shaikhly clientele' which exhibited far more interest in its own prerogatives than social development. See Khalifa, *Ibid.*, 128-29.

13. James Cameron, *An Indian Summer*, Penguin, Harmondsworth, 1987 [1974], 115. In the forthcoming series by me, the origins of IPS influence in Arabia are traced back as far as the influence of the Secret and Political Department of the East India Company, which was established in 1783 and became the Foreign Department in May 1843. But the Department's functions changed immensely after 1858. In 1914 it was renamed the Foreign and Political Department. The reputation of the IPS

as an élite cadre dates to after the Mutiny. See S.R. Ashton, *British Policy Towards the Indian States, 1905-1939*, Curzon Press, 1982, 4. Also IOR:L/P&S/10/888, T. Keyes to Earl of Reading, 13 August 1921. See the illustration from the 'Currie and Rice' series, showing the slovenly dress of the EIC era, in P.J. Rich, *Elixir of Empire*, Regency Press, 1989. This famous series of prints depicts the 'Tom Jones' style of the British in India that vanished with the end of 'John Company' and was replaced by the 'Tom Brown' style. Sartorially, the IPS were the Viceroy's own and much more smartly turned out than their EIC predecessors. Because of 'spit and polish', IPS officers were conscripted for state visits and other ceremonials, and the ornateness of uniforms reflected its ceremonial participations. See *Dress Regulations for Officers of the Indian Political Service*, Government of India Press, New Delhi, 1937. *Cf.* Humphrey Trevelyan, *The India We Left*, Macmillan, 1972, 158. IPS uniforms were in three classes based on length of service, and in six categories that were based on the demands of the occasion. The basic garment was a 'coatee', a close-fitting jacket with tails, embroidered in gold. For 'undress' there was a double-breasted blue frock coat trimmed in black mohair braid. The attention to sartorial details was reminiscent of school obsessions with dress discussed in *Elixir* and *Rituals*.

Ritualism was embodied in the very title of Viceroy. The title did *not* replace that of Governor-General. It was *added* to the Governor-General's dignities, and indicated additional functions, not the least of which were ritualistic ones. When the Sovereign came to India, the Viceroy reverted to being Governor-General. Imperial India was aware of the distinctions between the two offices, despite the fact that one man was holding both. The Viceroys spent much of their time planning ritual occasions – and were emphatically public school in outlook. Mark Bence-Jones, *The Viceroys of India*, Constable, 1982, 2, 98-100, 112, 178-79, 222, 252-53, 272-73. Also M.S. Tyagi, *British Administrative Policy in India (June 1895-September 1903)*, S.S. Publishers, Delhi, 1982, 4, 62-63.

Although the celebrated trip of a Viceroy to the Gulf was Curzon's in 1903, other Viceroys also visited, *e.g.* Lord Hardinge of Penshurst came in 1915, and conferred the KCSI on the shaikh of Kuwait and the CIE on the shaikh of Bahrain. IOR:R/15/6/515, *PGAR1915*, 'Administration Report for the Kuwait Political Agency for the Year 1915', 53.

14. G.F. Walford, *Arabian Locust Hunter*, Robert Hale, 1963, 52. Notwithstanding the arcane title, Walford offers interesting material about Gulf domestic affairs.

15. See IOR:R/15/6/531, *PGAR1913*, 'Administration Report for the Kuwait Agency for the Year 1913', 127. Also Donaldson, *The Postal Agencies in Eastern Arabia and the Gulf*, 57, 76, 139. 'Many other Indian Postal Agency Offices had been opened from the mid-19th century onwards on the Persian Coast and in Iraq; but they had all been closed by 1923, and do not form part of the present story.' *Ibid.*, 17.

16. S.M. Zwemer, *Arabia: The Cradle of Islam*, 2nd ed., Fleming H. Revell, New York, 1900, 225-26. The telegraph to Bombay had considerably more importance to communications than today attaches to telex and telephone, which face competitors such as DHL, air-speeded post, and computer links. The staff of the Indo-European Telegraph performed political duties in the Gulf in addition to their normal work. Indian Police from Bombay were seconded to the Gulf. See IOR:R/15/6/513, *PGAR1913*, 'The Arms Traffic in the Persian Gulf during 1913', 11.

17. IOR:R/15/6/478, *PGAR1878-79*, 'Report on Trade for the Persian Gulf for 1878', 29, 41, 45, 48. See 'Gulf-Lanka Pearl Links Found', *Khaleej Times*, 6 February 1988, 5. Also Michael Field, *The Merchants: The Big Business Families of Saudi Arabia and the Gulf States*, Overlook Press, Woodstock (New York), 1985, 21-22, 24.

18. See Saldanha, *Précis of the Affairs of the Persian Coast and Islands*, 79-80.

19. IOR:R/15/6/501, *PGAR1901-2*, 'Table 2', 23.

20. *Ibid.*, 'Abstract Statement Showing the Total Value of Principal Articles Exported', 61.

21. *Gulf Times*, 10 April 1987, 9. *Khaleej Times*, 12 April 1987, 3. This little known aspect to Gulf-Indian ties would make a first rate dissertation or book.

22. G. Rex Smith, review of Ian Richard Netton ed. *Arabia and the Gulf: From Traditional Society to Modern States, Journal of the Royal Asiatic Society*, No.1, 1988, 181-82. See Zwemer, *Arabia: The Cradle of Islam*, 109.

23. qtd. Field, *The Merchants*, 209.

24. Ashton, *British Policy Towards the Indian States*, 23.

25. *Summary of the Proceedings of the Government of India in the Foreign Department during the Viceroyalty of Lord Curzon, January 1899 – November 1905: Native States*, Superintendent of Government Printing, Calcutta, 1908, ctd. *Ibid.*, 7. See Edward Farley Oaten, *My Memories of India*, Janaki Prakashan, Patna (India), 1984, 12-13. Oaten was head of the Indian Educational Service, an enthusiastic Freemason, and an Old Tonbridgian.

26. See Leonore Davidoff, *The Best Circles: Social Etiquette and the Season*, Cresset, 1986 [1973], 69, 88-89. Etiquette is described as *ritual with a moral imperative*.

27. Possibly dependence on Indo-British icons postponed development of Arab ones: patriotic shrines, national anthems, and the other trappings of national mythology are post 1971 inventions – *e.g.* the Al-Thanis have been making a park out of a site near Doha where an ancestor bested the Turks, and each shaikhdom confers orders and medals designed by London jewellers.

28. Caroe, *Wells of Power,* xv. See *supra* n.1. Peter Mansfield claims that 'Indianization' was deliberate, and that IPS officials such as Arnold Wilson (Gulf Resident in 1920): '...even considered "Indianitizing" Iraq by settling thousands of Indians in the country.' Peter Mansfield, *The Arabs,* Allen Lane, 1977, 216.

29. George Linabury, 'The Creation of Saudi Arabia and the Erosion of Wahhabi Conservatism', Michael Curtis ed., *Religion and Politics in the Middle East,* Westview Press, Boulder, Colorado, 1981, 280. The population centres of what is now Saudi Arabia were far removed from the British sphere in the Gulf. See Donald Powell Cole, *Nomad of the Nomads: The Al Murrah Bedouin of the Empty Quarter,* AHM Publishing, Arlington Heights (Illinois), 1975, 141.

30. Oman was a responsibility of the Gulf Resident, but was on a different political footing. Husain M. Al-Baharana, 'The Consequences of Britain's Exclusive Treaties: A Gulf View', Pridham, *Arab Gulf and the West,* 19. Also J.A. Saldanha, *Précis of Maskat Affairs, 1892-1905,* Government Printer, Simla, 1906. There was an Agent in Muscat from 1800 to 1810. The post was abolished in 1810, and Muscat affairs handled by the Resident at Bushire. A Muscat agent was reappointed for 1840-1843. In 1843, when the Ruler moved his court to Zanzibar, the Agent accompanied him and Muscat business was conducted for the Resident by a native agent. An Agent was again appointed in 1861. From 1861 until 1947 the following served in Muscat who also served in the Gulf proper and appear in the biographies in Chapter IX: Disbrowe (1863-66, 1869-70), Ross (1871-72), Miles (1872-77, 1878-79, 1880-81, 1883-86, 1886-87), Sadler (1892-95), Cox (1899-1904), Shakespear (1906), Trevor (1910-11), Knox (1911-14), Hugh Stewart (1915-16), Haworth (1916-19), Crosthwaite (1924-26), Alban (1925, 1931, 1933, 1942), Barrett (1926), Fowle (1930-32), Watts (1935-39), Hickinbotham (1939-41), Howes (1941-42), Pelly (1942-43), Bird (1943), Metcalfe (1943-44), Galloway (1944-45), Andrew Stewart (1946-47). The situation of Muscat was ambiguous – when Disbrowe was Muscat Agent, he argued with Pelly over having to report through Bushire rather than directly to India. Later a scheme was proposed unsuccessfully to put Muscat under Aden rather than the Gulf.

The Sultan of Muscat ruled as well *Gwadar* on the southern coast of Baluchistan, where an Agency was established in 1863 under both the Agent at Muscat and the Agent at Kalat (where some Gulf officers served). In 1877 the Gwadar Agent was made Assistant to the Gulf Resident, and in that respect was responsible for the country between Gwadar and Jask – but remained Assistant to the Agent at Muscat for Gwadar and took on the post of Assistant to the Agent to the Governor-General (AGG) in Baluchistan for Kalat. Gwadar continued as a Muscat possession after Indian independence, and was sold to Pakistan by the Sultan in 1958. See J.E. Peterson, *Oman in the Twentieth Century,* Croom Helm, 1978, *passim.*

31. 'Pirate Coast' is not 'slang', although the term is disliked by Gulf Arabs. It appears in official documents. See Belgrave, *The Pirate Coast,* 1. Also J.E.H. Boustead, 'Abu Dhabi, 1761-1963', *JRCAS,* Vol.L, Parts III & IV, July/Oct 1963, 273-78.

32. H. Dodgeon and A.M. Findlay, *Ports of the Arabian Peninsula: A Guide to the Literature,* Centre for Middle Eastern and Islamic Studies, University of Durham, Occasional Papers Series No.7, nd. I am grateful to the late Arnold Galloway, drawing on his experiences as the Political Agent in Bahrain and Kuwait and from his perspective as last surviving Gulf IPS Resident, for emphasizing that the strongest link between the countries of the Gulf was and is the *maritime* one. A.C. Galloway to P.J. Rich, 17 August 1987. See J.B. Kelly, *Britain and the Persian Gulf,* OUP, 1968, 1. Also and *cf.* Peter Boxhall, 'Arabian Seafarers in the Indian Ocean', *Asian Affairs,* Vol.XX, Part III, October 1989, 287-95.

33. *Too much is made in the Gulf of an idyllic bedouin culture.* The genuine bedouins were about as significant as the Beefeaters. (On reading this, the antiquarian of Bahrain, Robert Jarman, remarked that the Beefeaters were more numerous – but that is an exaggeration.) The engraving of 'A Warrior At Prayer' used as an illustration (Plate 9) is an example of romanticism about the nomad. Put bluntly, the British were besotted with the ideal of the noble Arab, and as taken with fancied bedouin customs as they were at home with pseudo-English ritualism. In actual fact, 'A town Arab often uses the word "bedu" as an insult.' Walford, *Arabian Locust Hunter,* 47. For other minorities and for tribalism in the Gulf, see Levon H. Melikian, *Jassim: A Study in the Psychosocial Development of a Young Man in Qatar,* Longman, 1981, esp. 20-21. Brian Devlin, an Arabist who has lived in the Gulf for many years, noted on reading this 'Odd indeed that Dickson was so mesmerised by the desert Arabs but spent his life in the town.'

34. Raphael Pati, *The Arab Mind,* rev. ed., Charles Scribner's Sons, 1983 [1973], 74.

35. John Morehead, *In Defiance of The Elements: A Personal View of Qatar,* Quartet, 1977, 117, 160.

36. See Eric Hobsbawm, 'Introduction: Inventing Traditions', Eric Hobsbawm and Terence Ranger eds., *The Invention of Tradition,* CUP, 1985, 2-3. The archaeological evidence of a common tradition has not been described here because of limited space. As for the oil discoveries, the consequences were postponed by World War II - in Qatar the first well had just been drilled at the start of the war and was summarily capped for the duration. Delay also can be attributed to the British emphasis on the exploitation of the Iraqi and Persian fields, although part of the procrastination was caused by the indeterminable negotiations between the shaikhs and the companies seeking concessions. See Anthony Sampson, The Seven Sisters: The Great Oil Companies and the World They Made, Hodder and Stoughton, 1975, 70-71, 108-09. The failure to exploit petroleum sources is a further example of indirect British influence on internal development, but even without such evidence control over external affairs would obviously have domestic implications, e.g. it was considered 'most desirable' that youths going overseas to study should consult the British Political Agent. IOR:R/15/2/838, 'Bahrain schools', 201. Cf. IOR:R/15/2/208, 'Education', 60, 119.

37. An *alleged* difference was that Residents in India did not have the varied responsibilities that those in the Gulf did, although this is open to debate. Sir Anton Bertram, *The Colonial Service,* CUP, 1930, 72.

38. See and consider Roland Barthes, *Mythologies,* Paladin Grafton, 1987 [1973], 78.

39. Aaron L. Friedberg, *The Weary Titan: Britain and the Experience of Relative Decline, 1895-1905,* Princeton University Press, 1988, 218-19. See H.F.B. Lynch, 'The Persian Gulf', *The Imperial and Asiatic Quarterly Review and Oriental and Colonial Record,* Third Series, Vol.XIII, Nos. 25 & 26, January/April 1902, 225-34. A number of the Gulf officers as young men served in the fabled passes of the North-West Frontier. See service records in Chapter IX.

40. Friedberg, *The Weary Titan,* esp. his tables 'The Diffusion of Sea Power, 1896-1906', 153; 'The Naval Balance in Asia, 1901', 177; 'Distribution of British Regular Army', 277. See also map 'British Naval facilities, 1900', 136.

41. They were afflicted with what can be called the 'Peter Pan syndrome', to the perpetuation of which Freemasonry contributed. See Oaten, *Memories of India,* 11. 'I do not wish to exaggerate, but I regard Freemasonry as one of the three agencies among others which helped to bring Indians and Englishmen into friendly social intercourse, the other two being within their respective spheres cricket and polo.' *Ibid.* As already mentioned, Oaten was a member of the Indian Educational Service, 1909-1930, and the Director of Public Instruction of the Government of India, 1924-1928. He was Master of the Old Tonbridgian Lodge No.4145, either its secretary or treasurer for twenty years, and Assistant Grand Registrar of the Grand Lodge of England. His autobiography is prima facie evidence of the widespread public school Freemasonic influence in the Indian Empire. See *Ibid.,* 9-11, 55-56, 73, 89, 96, 125.

42. See Hugh Trevor-Roper, 'The Invention of Tradition: The Highland Tradition of Scotland', Hobsbawm ed., *The Invention of Tradition,* 41. The trend in the nineteenth century towards ritocracy can be tracked in India Office records, *e.g.* through the proliferation of material on gun-salutes in the Gulf. See IOR:L/P&S/12/3760. Also see discussions of armorial bearings in IOR:L/P&S/10/636 and IOR:L/P&S/3/352. *Cf.* H.G. Rawlinson, *The British Achievement in India,* Prabha Publications, New Delhi, 1985 (1948), 107. Also Ashton, *British Policy Towards the Indian States,* 17, 21.

43. 'He was specifically ordered (1) to take a personal interest in the studies and general well being of the sons of "native Noblemen and Gentlemen" sent to England for the "purposes of education".' Ian Moir, 'A Study of the History and Organization of the Political and Secret Department of the East India Company, the Board of Control, and the India Office, 1784-1919, With a Summary List of Records', University of London Diploma in Archive Administration thesis, 1966, 135. Rozina Visram, *Ayahs, Lascars and Princes: Indians in Britain 1700-1947,* Pluto Press, 1986, 172. In June 1909 some of his duties were transferred to an *Educational Adviser to Indian Students. Ibid.,* 138.

44. See, convincingly, IOR:L/P&S/12/3725, 'Decipher of Telegram, Political Resident to Secretary of State for India', regarding Bahrain's National Anthem. Also see IOR:L/P&S/12/3862 and IOR:L/P&S/12/3927.

45. Visram, *Ayahs, Lascars and Princes,* 8. See Tom Nairn, *The Enchanted Glass: Britain and Its Monarchy,* Hutchinson Radius, 1988, 282-85.

46. Ashton, *British Policy Towards the Indian States,* 21.

47. Lytton to Disraeli, 30 April 1876, qtd. *Ibid.* Many of the Indian rulers became Freemasons, another illustration of the desire for Western honours. See the table of salutes for officers in one of the Masonic orders: Grand Master, 11; Great Seneschal, 9; Right Eminent Knights, 7; Very Eminent Knights, 5; in *Statutes of The Great Priory of the United Religious, Military and Masonic Orders of the Temple and of St. John of Jerusalem, Palestine, Rhodes and Malta of England and Wales and its*

Provinces Overseas, Grand Priory, 1986, 3. Also *Constitution and Regulations for the Government of The Order of Mark Master Masons and The Degree of Royal Ark Mariner*, Grand Lodge of Mark Master Masons, 1955, 105.

48. Nigel Nicolson, *Mary Curzon*, Harper & Row, 1977, 116. (Nicolson's father served on Curzon's staff when Curzon was British Foreign Secretary.) Curzon is notorious for his fascination with and emphasis on ritualism – and for his demanding nature. The view expressed in the foregoing quotation that ritualism sought to exact *deference* is particularly appropriate in connection with Curzon. Although his preoccupation with ritual would appear to 'clinch' this proposition about Viceregal ritocracy, there has been considerable discussion of 'the deference theory'. See Dennis Kavanagh, *Political Culture*, Macmillan, 1972, 55-56. However: 'The Viceroy's establishment numbered an unbelievable 5000! No wonder Edward VIII, as Prince of Wales, on his first visit to India when staying with the Viceroy, was reputed to have said, "Now I know how a King should live." ' E.W. Robinson-Horley, *Last Post: An Indian Army Memoir*, Secker & Warburg, 1985, 82. (See Plate 41.)

49. IOR:L/P&S/12/2186, H.V. Biscoe, Political Resident, to Foreign Secretary, GoI, 28 February 1932. *Ibid.*, 'Repayment Voucher Form', 19 December 1934. *Ibid.*, Director of Navy Accounts to Under Secretary of State for India, 2 May 1933.

50. Brian Devlin, Arabist and longtime teacher in Qatar, points out with humour that 'The term "shaikh" is primarily a reference to old age and the wisdom, experience, and leadership expected of old men. Only recently has the term been applied to ten-year-olds.' *Cf.* Ann Morrow, *Highness: The Maharajahs of India*, Grafton, 1986, *passim*.

51. 'The shaikh who in the time of the peasant's father or grandfather had been the honoured elder, the generous host who dared not inflict the most trifling punishment on the poorest man in the tribe, had become an absolute master...'. William R. Polk, *The Arab World*, Harvard University Press, Cambridge (Massachusetts), 1980, 126. 'Remember, these Princes weren't a bunch of oil-well Arabs with a garage full of Cadillacs and a kitchen full of chorus girls.' Gavin Lyall, *The Wrong Side of the Sky*, Pan, 1983 [1961], 27.

52. See, in the Sage Library and Archives of the Reformed Church of America, New Brunswick (New Jersey), hereafter SLRCA: Stanley G. Mylrea, 'Kuwait Before Oil: Memoirs of Dr. C. Stanley G. Mylrea, Pioneer Medical Missionary of The Arabian Mission, Reformed Church in America', written between 1945 and 1951, bound typescript, 'produced privately by Mrs. John Van Ess and Mrs. A.L. Warnshuis', 38.

53. The Gulf Resident and his Political Agents were also Foreign Office consuls-general and consuls in Persia, but they did not have the moral or political authority in Persia (or Iraq) that they had over the Arab territories. The dispensing of British honours and the display of British pomp in Persia and Iraq was limited and largely unwelcome.

54. Prys Morgan, 'From a Death to a View: The Hunt for the Welsh Past in the Romantic Period', Hobsbawm, *Inventing Tradition*, 80-81.

55. Gloria Jean Moore, *The Anglo-Indian Vision*, Australasian Education [*sic*] Press, Melbourne, 1986, 80. 'If he was not Anglo-Indian, generations of Anglo-Indian parents and students would remember with affection the name of Major General Claud Martin, who began life as a common soldier...Attached to the court of the Nawab of Oudh as surveyor, commander of artillery, he became influential and wealthy. He cast cannon, minted his own coins, sailed the first balloons to float in the Indian air. Martin left a huge estate, the interest of which was to be distributed to the poor...but the bulk of his fortune went to found, in his mansion, Constantia at Lucknow, the famous College – La Martinière. Knowing the Nawab meant to appropriate Constantia, Martin arranged to be buried there – a Muslim would not inhabit a tomb. It is said he won the land for the college in a cock fight, and that he first offered it to the Catholic church, who, surprised at his Muslim customs (four wives!) discreetly declined the offer. The Anglicans did not demur – and La Martinière has been Anglican ever since...There are sister schools at Calcutta and at Lyons in France, Martin's birthplace.' *Ibid.*, 151. 'The people who to this day write of Anglo-Indians "mimicking" the British are unenlightened. Anglo-Indians and Indians were educated in schools which were models of schools such as Rugby and Harrow; their products were not "mimicking", but were genuine products of their system of education and culture handed down through generations.' *Ibid.*, 154-56.

56. Bernard S. Cohn, 'Representing Authority in Victorian India', Hobsbawm, *Inventing Tradition*, 172-73, and *cf.* Shirley Pollitt McGreal, 'A History of Mayo College, Ajmer, India, 1875-1971', Ph.D. dissertation, University of Cincinnati, 1971, 1-10.

57. Pat Barr, *The Memsahibs: In Praise of the Women of Victorian India*, Century, 1976, 196. Lord William was Lord William Beresford, the Viceroy's chief-of-staff. He limped from the effects of a spirited Victoria Cross Race, a game in which the contestants on horseback and hurdling obstacles seized life-size dolls representing sympathetic figures such as an Ayah and a Special Correspondent. See *Ibid.*, 196. 'If Dufferin did not spend as much time at his desk as he ought to have done – in fact

he seldom did any work after dinner – he certainly did not neglect the social and ceremonial side of the Viceroyalty...He enjoyed Durbars, receptions and Viceregal progresses; he enjoyed sitting enthroned under a canopy of State surrounded by scarlet-clad attendants bearing the peacock fans and the other emblems of royalty.' Bence-Jones, *The Viceroys of India*, 142.

58. 'One can see how ritual can thus be used as an analytical indicator which allows an insight into the inner differentiation or anatomy of a social system. But at the same time there are serious analytical limitations. Ritual belongs, after all, to what has come to be called since Marx the superstructure (*Uberbau*) of society. *Ritual is ideology in action.* Any anthropological description which does not take this into account and uncritically bases its generalizations on observations from the realms of ritual is bound to present not the true but the ideological form of society.' Strecker, *The Social Practice of Symbolization*, 15.

59. 'Liminal periods, times out of structure, are periods in which cultural symbols are generated, times during which a society speculates on its ultimate values through the fruitful alienation of the total individual from the partial person.' Sherry Roxanne Turkle, 'Symbol and Festival in the French Student Uprising (May-June 1968)', Sally Falk Moore and Barbara G. Myerhoff, *Symbol and Politics in Communal Ideology*, Cornell University Press, Ithaca, 1975, 91.

60. Frank Stoakes, 'Social and Political Change in the Third World: Some Peculiarities of Oil-Producing Principalities...', Derek Hopwood ed., *The Arabian Peninsula: Society and Politics*, George Allen and Unwin, 1972, 196.

61. *Ibid.*, 197.

62. Victor Mallet, 'Eight Kuwaiti Pro-Democracy Activists Arrested', *Financial Times*, 10 May 1990, 5. Kuwait had been a partial exception to tight control, with the Sabah dynasty willing to tolerate some dissent – albeit with hesitation. The cabinet composition was relatively (for the Gulf) cosmopolitan, *e.g.* of 75 ministers who served between 1962 and 1986, 18 men or 24 per cent have been members of the ruling family. The other 57 men or 76 per cent had other origins. However, 69.3 per cent of ministerial positions were held by members or associates of nine families. Abdul-Reda Assiri and Kamal Al-Monoufi, 'Kuwait's Political Élite: The Cabinet', *Middle East Journal*, Vol.42, No.1, Winter 1988, 48-58.

63. J.A. Hobson, *Imperialism: A Study*, George Allen & Unwin, 3rd ed., 1961 [1902], 211.

64. Douglas Davis, 'Kuwait a Well-Placed Pawn', *The Australian*, 11 September 1990, 8. Matters were not helped by fears of pro-democracy Kuwaitis that the Al-Sabahs were planning to murder opposition leaders. Abdul Aziz Sultan (chairman of the country's second largest bank, Gulf Bank of Kuwait) asserted there was 'strong reason to believe that some members of the al-Sabah family are setting up some assassination task force here in Kuwait.' *Financial Review*, 6 March 1991, 10. 'They have talked publicly about how to liquidate their opponents, and we know they have contacted various terrorist organisations with this in mind.' Ahmed al-Khatib, former member of the National Assembly and leader of the Kuwait Democratic Party, qtd. *The Australian*, 7 March 1991, 6. It was recalled that the suspension of the 1962 Constitution in 1986 by the Al-Sabahs seemed as much an effort to head off investigations of the ruling family's part in the collapse of the Kuwait stock exchange as it did an effort at maintaining order. Professor Fred Halliday of the London School of Economics wrote: 'The political emergency has been compounded by the dispute over control and management of Kuwaiti assets...The removal recently of four senior officials, including Fahad al-Rashid, the director-general of the Kuwait Investment Authority, the London-based body meant to exercise control over Kuwaiti overseas investment, highlights this. The KIA personnel reflected the views of the merchant families of Kuwait, and their anxiety at the ruling family's practices.' Fred Halliday, 'Is the Lesser of Two Evils Good Enough for Kuwait?', *The Australian*, 27 February 1991, 13. The Al-Sabahs had lost some of whatever trust they had previously enjoyed. Remonstrated Issa Ibrahim, a Kuwaiti critic who endured the occupation, 'We have suffered through seven months of hell here while they left the moment the Iraqis crossed the border in the middle of the night.' Another opponent, Nasser Jabar, commented, 'I think we have to ask hard questions of the defence minister who left this country vulnerable to invasion even though the Iraqis had been menacing us for a month and a half before they came in.' *Financial Review*, 5 March 1991, 12.

II

INDIAN CONNECTIONS

I suppose 'something in India' was always a possibility for me. My father had been Principal of a school near Amritsar where the sons of Indian Christians were educated. It was housed in an old shooting lodge which had belonged to Maharaja Ranjit Singh, the Lion of the Punjab. – Sir Conrad Corfield, last head of the Indian Political Service, *The Princely India I Knew*, 1975.

Aden and Nairobi are no substitutes for Karachi and Quetta as bases from which to control the Gulf. – Maurice and Taya Zinkin, *Britain and India*, 1964.

Bahrain's recorded postal history begins on August 1st, 1884, when a Post Office was opened in Manama, the capital and port of the island. It was a sub-office of the Indian Post Office at Bushire, under the administration of the Bombay Circle, and it remained Bahrain's only post office for 62 years. Indian Queen Victoria stamps and postal stationery were placed on sale. – Neil Donaldson, *The Postal Agencies in Eastern Arabia and The Gulf*, 1975.

Any lingering Arab doubts about the long-term intentions of the British died with the opening of the Suez Canal in 1869 and the purchase of the Khedive's shares of canal stock in 1876. (See Plate 14.) These events underscored the Gulf's importance to the route to India. For Imperial strategists at pains to secure the key to the East, strengthening the outposts along the way became essential.

Moreover in the last part of the century a heightened interest in the Empire meant that the British became more intrusive in 'situations' like the Gulf, where they previously were content to keep only a low profile. In the case of India, this increasing interference did not go unremarked at the time. There were contemporary critics who thought that what was being replaced in Indian political life had had considerable merits, and sought to link the vanishing political structures with a romantic tradition of political democracy. In particular, H.M. Hyndman in *The Bankruptcy of India* (1886) saw disappearing Indian village life as having a continuity with early Aryan civilization, while Sir Henry Maine in *Village Communities in East and West* (1896) compared Indian communities with his idyllic vision of democratic Teutonic villages and Swiss cantons. The historian J.E. Woolacott has poured scorn on the claims that there was a wonderful India that was blighted by the British occupation:

> The legend of a Golden Age of India which ended with the advent of the British has no foundation. Nor is there any basis in fact for the assertion that an idyllic system of village government existed until it was destroyed by the newcomers from Europe. The evidence available regarding the lot of the people of India during the centuries which preceded the rise of British

power shows that the masses were steeped in misery. There was splendour in the palace of the ruler and hopeless poverty in the hut of the peasant.[1]

As Arabs have begun to rethink their own political heritage, they have asserted that what was left after British rule was a political infra-structure that was inferior to an earlier and glorious era. Problematical is whether there was such a golden age, or whether the Gulf ever enjoyed a sort of rudimentary or participatory democracy – or indeed whether the simple society in the nineteenth century, if it had remained unmolested, offered any more chance of evolving into a Swiss canton than did the Indian princely states. Such speculation will be left to those who admire the *faux-naïf* character of bedouin campfire gatherings as seen on television. Sometimes naïveté was simply naïveté. Tributes to Arab resourcefulness should be balanced with less flattering accounts. Not *all* British visitors to the region found the scene picturesque. An RAF officer at the end of World War II wrote:

> The villages have no drainage or sanitation; garbage and offal are thrown on a heap outside the houses, or on the sea-shore, there to be removed in time by those voracious scavengers, the vultures and kites. It is a common experience to see the carcases of donkeys and other livestock lying on the shore, swollen and covered with flies, decaying under the hot sun. The stench within half a mile of an Arab village is simply appalling; one would be truthful if unkind to describe the Arab as having no prejudices against filth...Another serious cause of infection are the flies, which breed in that climate on a scale to be observed nowhere else in the world. I have seen a plate of fresh dates carried a few yards from one room to another across an open courtyard. By the time it reached the second room it would be covered with a mass of flies at least two inches deep. Incredible to the insect-free European, this must be seen to be believed. Yet the Arab would not think of cleansing food that had been thus contaminated. He nonchalantly sweeps away the flies with his sleeve and proceeds to masticate the polluted mess with relish.
>
> Apart from the piles of offal and refuse which are a feature of every village, another inducement to flies are the windowless shops in which dried fish, raw meat, ghee butter and other foodstuffs are openly displayed. These goods are always black with flies and as one drives through the narrow streets of the shopping centre a black, buzzing cloud obscures the windscreen. In summer it is much worse. The Arabs are curiously indifferent to this plague of dirt, bad odour and insects, and will sit for hours outside the shops, idly gossiping, while flies settle on their beards and faces, fall into their Turkish tea, or get mixed up with their rice.[2]

No reason exists to disbelieve this description, but fixing blame for the conditions is not easy. What *can* be concluded is that the proponents of an idealistic past have pragmatic objections to overcome before they can convince anyone that the flies were solely British imports.

Nevertheless, India's influence on the Gulf was magnified because so much of what happened in the shaikhdoms depended on individual IPS officers.

There was never a great Gulf bureaucracy, and the few who served there were compelled to perform myriad tasks. The prosaic-sounding titles of 'Resident' and 'Agent' do not convey the dimensions of their authority and autonomy. Their portrayal as benign referees, clamping down on brigandry but leaving the Arabs alone to settle domestic affairs, does not stand up when India Office archives are thoroughly examined, while describing the IPS as a *corps diplomatique* only partly indicates the extent of its activities.

The activities of the IPS as educationists afford a case in point. The IPS brief included responsibility for the Princes' Colleges, the Indian schools for rulers' families and other sons of the privileged. Sir Conrad Corfield, the last head of the IPS before it wound up in 1947, described them:

> The Rajkumar College at Rajkot was a place which particularly interested me. It was one of the five Chief Colleges which Lord Curzon was responsible for founding. They were for the sons and relations of the Rulers. There was another one at Ajmer, the Mayo College, which I came to know even more intimately later. Each college was run on the lines of a public school at home, though there had to be some special arrangements for heirs apparent in the way of hereditary servants and religious teachers. The value of these schools for the future generations of Rulers was proved by imitation, the sincerest form of flattery. When leading Indians of British India were thinking later of the future of their country, they realised how important it was to train future leaders. Their conclusion was that a first class public school was required, and in due course the Doon School was established at Dehra Dun.[3]

The Gulfites certainly knew India and knew its schools. Of the sixty-six Gulf Residents and Agents between 1858 and 1947, at least twenty-four had fathers who spent part of their careers in India. These were Barrett, Bird, Birdwood, Biscoe, Bray, Cole, Crawford, Crosthwaite, Dixon, Fowle, Gastrell, Keyes, Knox, Loch, Meade, Miles, F. Prideaux, Prior, Shakespear, Tandy, Trevor, Watts, F. Wilson, and Worth. (See Chapter IX.) At least twenty more had close relatives who served there, such as a brother or uncle. Many of the remainder had fathers or relatives who served overseas in the military or other services but whose possible service in India is unknown.

A number of the Gulfites had family ties with the IPS public schools. The father of Percy Loch (Bahrain Political Agent 1916-18, 1932-37) was the principal (1878-1903) of a celebrated one, Mayo College. When Loch was casting about for places to send boys, he naturally corresponded with one of his father's successors, the then headmaster of Mayo, V.A.S. Stow, one of the most celebrated of the Indian public school headmasters. He had been at Mayo only a few years when Loch contacted him, having been headmaster of Rajkumar from 1912 to 1931.

This was not the only connection between the IPS and the Indian public schools. For example, the father-in-law of Robert Hamilton (Kuwait Political Agent in 1916-18) was Governor of Lahore College. The top offices at these colleges were carried as 'Miscellaneous Appointments' of the IPS in the *India Office Lists* and deliberately placed under the Political Service rather than the

Indian Educational Service. The IPS had a long history of involvement with education and inherited a responsibility for the EIC's Fort William College ('Oxbridge-on-the-Hooghly') – which after a brave start changed into a quasi-Indian version of the College of Preceptors in England, concentrating on examinations and foregoing classroom instruction. Gulf officers served on its Board of Examiners.[4]

The IPS did not always welcome educational duties enthusiastically. When a public school for the Gulf was mooted in the early 1940s, C.G. Prior (Gulf Resident 1939-46) wrote testily to H. Weightman (Bahrain Political Agent 1937-40), then Deputy Secretary to the Government of India: 'This [Political] Department has a lamentable record in fathering ill-conceived colleges and I should be very reluctant to add to them.'[5] Still, and regardless of how individual officers felt about it, the IPS was definitely in the 'school business', and besides worrying about the education of shaikhs, officers kept an eye on Gulf schools conducted for the non-Arab populations such as the Indians. This group was present in the Gulf long before the 'invasion' of labourers during the oil-boom, and at one time petitioned the Resident for an 'English public school system' for Indians that came to nothing because of finances.[6] (When the number of Indian workers swelled during the oil boom, schools for Indians based on an Indo-British public school model were established in considerable numbers. The result was that the invasion of Kuwait in 1990 meant that tens of thousands of youngsters had their educations terminated as their parents fled the Gulf. Their prospects on returning to India and Pakistan were gloomy, as placement in good schools even if their families had the money was by no means easy.)

An Indian Excuse for Intervention

The presence of an Indian population in the Gulf gave the Political Residents a useful lever for enlarging the British position. Any 'outrage' against Indians provided a convenient excuse for righteous indignation and attacking the rudimentary sovereignty of the local enclaves. Typically, in 1882 when Shaikh Jasim of Qatar tried to expel Indians from the country, he instead was forced by the British to apologize abjectly to them. He then had to indemnify them and let them triumphantly return. Shaikh Jasim was a persistent man, and there was a rematch when in July 1887 with his connivance the Indian shopkeepers in Doha, the principal town in Qatar, had their stalls 'plundered'. Then, in August, two Indian traders were beaten up. This provided sufficient excuse for the Resident, Edward Ross, to have Bahrain's shaikh sequester money and pearls belonging to Shaikh Jasim until compensation was forthcoming. This was not done reluctantly.

Early on the IPS became more involved with internal affairs than has been appreciated. The commercial interest displayed in matters such as fixing customs duty, vital to the Indian traders, or the right of Indians to conduct local business, does not surprise as much as the British interest in matters like education – but Empire-wide activities of the IPS officers' former headmasters are a reminder that English public schools were keenly interested in the Empire's schools. In the case of the Gulf, British involvement in education was selective, but though sporadic it contravenes notions of non-intervention in domestic affairs.[7]

The Victorian and Edwardian eras were not times when education *per se* was an academic discipline. In fact, the public schools deliberately avoided pedagogical professionalism when hiring masters, preferring gifted amateurs. The Raj would not have felt any embarrassment of background in dealing with education, any more than he did in dealing with a myriad of other matters as *factum factorum*. He had *connections*. They were a way in which Victorians validated their expertise. Public school associations of the Gulfites are intriguing. A Resident, Lewis Pelly, was at Rugby when Dr. Arnold was headmaster and with Cotton, the 'grave young master' in *Tom Brown* who became Marlborough's headmaster (1852-1858), and then Bishop of Calcutta. Cotton was the person to whom Dean Farrar dedicated the famous school novel *Eric, or, Little by Little*. An Old Marlburian IPS officer in the Gulf such as Arthur Trevor, the Resident from 1920 to 1924, would have known about that – when Cotton died in India, the caps worn by Marlborough boys had their red stripes changed to black, and so they remained in Trevor's own schooldays.[8] The patrician Harrovian Percy Cox (Resident 1904-20), who was acclaimed by Curzon as 'Uncrowned King of the Gulf' and was the decision-maker when it came to setting Kuwait's boundary with Saudi Arabia, would have been aware of his old headmaster, J.E.C. Welldon's, misadventures as Metropolitan of India during Curzon's viceroyalty – especially given Cox's warm friendship with Curzon. A glance at the biographies in Chapter IX will reveal other connections between the IPS officers and leading figures in the public schools.

British success relied on a handful of 'Politicals' such as Pelly, Trevor, and Cox whose school loyalties are so strong and lifelong that such ties must be considered for the effects they had on administration. It would be appropriate to suggest that alongside a patriarchy or an oligarchy there can be a *scholarchy*.

Peculiar Flavours and Silurian Rocks

Had the IPS officers considered themselves as rather the best of the Empire's rulers, it would not have been surprising. There was a distinction to a career in India that careers in other parts of the Empire did not enjoy. The IPS learned as boys in their Imperially-flavoured public schools that India meant kudos, and that those who joined the Indian cadres were considered a special credit to *alma mater* – the *Tonbridge School Register* enshrined those serving in India on the same page as International Rugby selections.

The selectivity of the IPS was enhanced by the apprenticeship required of those who joined it. They either had to join the Indian Army or the Indian Civil Service and only then could they apply to the IPS. This had implications for the Gulf, for if few served there without a public school education, no one served there without the IPS initiation into the social rituals of Viceregal India. The novitiate in an Indian district and the study of a rather antiquarian reading list was part of this. Furthermore, many candidates were personally interviewed by the Viceroy before acceptance. Sometimes membership in the

Plate 1: Lord Curzon of Kedleston, 1859–1925. Viceroy of India 1898–1905. Foreign Secretary 1919–1924.

Plate 2: (left) Master's Chair of Britannic Lodge, a London lodge much patronized by British royalty.

Plate 3: (below) Map of Arabia.

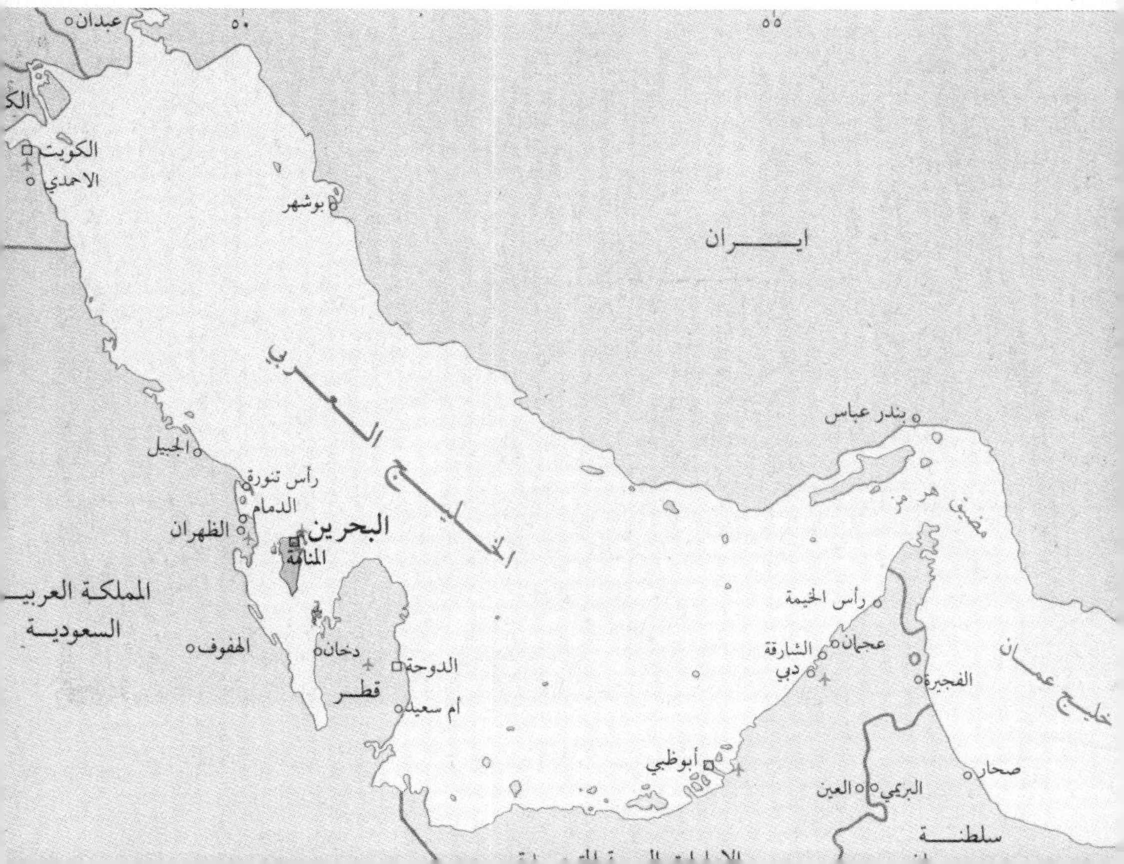

Plate 4: Freemason's Hall, London. Cornerstone laid 14 July 1927 by His Royal Highness The Duke of Connaught, Grand Master 1901–1939, Queen Victoria's third son.

Plate 5: (left) 'Mahometan Woman and Son' – an 1812 print showing a Western view of the East highly distorted by Orientalism. Note the pigtails.

Plate 6: (below) View of the early East India Company offices, London. Chartered by Queen Elizabeth I in 1600, the EIC was organized on a stockholder basis in 1612.

Plate 7: (above) East India House, 1810. Parliamentary action in 1813 ended the EIC's trade monopoly.

Plate 8: (below)Tipu's two sons given up as hostages, 1792. He was killed by the British in 1799.

Plate 9: (above) F. Pierdon's 'A Warrior at Prayers' from *Artists and Arabs* by Henry Blackburn, 1868.

Plate 10: (opposite) An engraving of Sir W. Allan's sentimentalized but popular painting 'Arabs Dividing Spoil'.

Plate 11: (above) The Residency, Lucknow. The ruins were preserved as an Indian Mutiny memorial of the siege of 1857.

Plate 12: (below) The India Office – view from St. James's Park, London. Sir Walter Scott's grand scheme of 1868–1873 had to suit Palmerston's Italian Renaissance taste.

IPS was associated with an actual initiation: of those in the Gulf known to have been Freemasons, *every one* received his initiatory degrees in India. (See Chapter VII.) Freemasonry contributed to IPS clannishness. The Indian lodges were not large, and frequently several IPS officers belonged to the same one. For example, the lodge at Quetta had only 63 members when Lionel Haworth (Resident 1927-8) was initiated in 1904, but they included the head of the IPS, Sir Henry McMahon, and two other high ranking IPS officers, J. Ramsay and F. MacDonald. Since the 'Gulfites' depended for career and Masonic advancement on relationships with superiors in India, old school, regimental, and lodge ties were helpful.

Masonic and school affiliations were more pronounced and more significant in India than they were in many of the other Imperial possessions. They had become a distinguishing hallmark of the Indo-British and Raj tradition. (Typifying the public schools' Indian involvement is *Oakfield; or Fellowship in the East,* a two-volume *Tom Brown in India* autobiographical novel written by William Arnold, Thomas Arnold's son and a pioneer of education in the Punjab.) British social life in India owed much to old boy rituals, conscientiously and sometimes exuberantly carried out. The annals of men's clubs in India reveal, rather than debauchery, the not-always-refined antics of public school reunions, the midnight cricket games in the dining room. Assured that this sort of manic activity was *done,* as inane as middle-aged men posing as boys might appear, Indian rulers sent sons to public schools for instruction in the Imperial establishment's bewildering rites. This princely patronage of education meant that a need for teachers and tutors gave some old boys their original way East. Before entering the IPS, Daniel McCullum (Kuwait Political Agent 1918-20) taught at an Indian school. The Bahrain Political Agent Harold Dickson was tutor in the household of the Maharajah of Bikaner. Hugh Stewart, Bahrain PA in 1916, was a tutor to the Raja of Dawas. Another Bahrain PA (1909-10), Charles Mackenzie, tutored the Raj Kumar Hari Singh.

Increasing IPS influence coincided with the expansion and growing ritualization of the public schools, with an emphasis on a legitimatizing tradition that had been lacking in the early nineteenth century. Attitudes nurtured by the schools helped shape thinking about India. The old boy outlook can be seen in Imperial outlook.[9] There was no sense of incongruity about the transportation of adolescent school customs to the far corners of the world. The headmaster of at least one Indian public school used to read *Tom Brown* to his charges.[10] With the patronage of the Raj – and, it should be added, contrary to snide asides that Indian schools were 'a smudgy copy of the English public school'[11] – the Indian public school tradition acquired considerable stature and influence of its own.[12] At end-of-term the Indian railways ran trains taking pupils home, decorated with school shields and reminiscent of the custom of the Southern Railway in Britain naming locomotives after schools.[13]

In token of aspirations to exert an influence similar to the schools of England, Indian schools tried to recruit boys from the Middle East. The Gulf IPS did attempt to send Arab boys to India. Again a reminder is necessary that the Gulf was not possessed of the human or material resources that India had, and these efforts had only limited success. Nevertheless, the IPS officers there duly corresponded with Indian public schools in what were the usually unsuccessful hopes of sending off the sons of shaikhs.[14] The Indian schools were more than willing to co-operate. To an inquiry in 1906, Girassia School replied that 'In the case of boys in poor circumstances one servant is considered enough'. Rajkumar College hopefully sent blueprints of all of its buildings, and Mayo College proudly mentioned that Lord Kitchener had just inspected its Cadet Corps, adding that on Speech Day the Agent to the Governor-General had presided. Mayo also forwarded a leaving examination for 1905 which might have raised parental concern about the appropriateness of the curriculum had any Arabs seen it, as students were asked to write on St. Cuthbert's Isle and Dunedin's Cross. Geography at Mayo was strictly British geography.[15]

Possibly the lack of money to send boys abroad was partially a blessing in disguise for the Arabs. Not everyone in the Empire was sure that imposing English education on 'natives' was an unqualified success. The diffusionists or filtrationists who thought that the benefits of élite schooling would somehow trickle down to the masses were opposed by Lord Mayo (Viceroy 1869-72), who wrote distastefully to Sir W.W. Hunter:

> I dislike this filtration theory...If you wait till the bad English, which the four hundred Babus learn in Calcutta, filters down into the forty millions of Bengal, you will ultimately be a Silurian rock instead of a retired judge.[16]

An Indian Cantonment in the Gulf

Although the strenuous efforts to emulate Indian administration often were constrained by the realities of such small and poor populations, the Indian ethos that was achieved in the Gulf is substantiated by accounts of how Indian in style was the Residency headquarters in Bushire. As has been mentioned, the Residency was there on the Persian side of the Gulf by default, and this was awkward since most responsibilities of the Resident were on the Arab side. Ideas of moving it were frequently debated through the years. Locations in India itself were proposed, confirming that the IPS saw the shaikhdoms as an adjunct of IPS responsibility for the Indian states. Illustrative of this are the yearnings of Frederick Johnson (Gulf Resident 1928-29) to relocate in Karachi because it was the 'London of the Persian Gulf'. Another Resident (Hugh Biscoe, 1929-32) urged that the Residency could be put in Karachi, or at least a summer station built, so that he could obtain a spell in 'civilization'. Delhi was unmoved by appeals, and the Residents were compelled to remove themselves to Shiraz each summer, which did not come up to the standards of Indian hill stations. (See Plate 42.)

Proposals for relocation being frustrated, Bushire remained as the Residents' seat. Its cantonment atmosphere emphasized Indian connections. Despite difficulties, the Residency attempted to replicate the standard Residency in India.[17] Lord Curzon noted after a visit:

> The Union Jack fluttering from the summit of the Residency flag-staff is no vain symbol of British ascendancy in Bushire...the goods that crowd the

> stalls in the bazaar are British or Indian goods; the rupee is as readily, nay more readily, accepted than the *kram*...In appearance and structure the English quarter of the town is not unlike an Indian station; while the friendly sentiments of the populace were unmistakably shown by the manner in which was celebrated at Bushire the Jubilee of the British Queen.[18]

Bushire's amenities were crucial to the handful of British who lived there, but its physical layout was not as critical as was the Anglo-Indian mentality of the officers. When trying to discern the IPS outlook, reminders frequently come to light of how much they were quintessential old boys – albeit further distinguished by a certain Indo-British style. The peculiarities of the public schools' influence on India had significance in Arabia *because the Gulf was part of India.* How much it was a part of India has been forgotten. On a 1923 visit to Bahrain, the Lebanese traveller Ameen Rihani wrote:

> Bahrain, one would think, belongs to British India; for as soon as the steamer anchors, a motor launch – a giant launch or a small yacht, as you please – comes out, with the British Political Agent and his distinguished household on board, for no other purpose, perhaps, than a little cruise. He sat on deck in a wicker chair...and he seemed to be surveying the traffic and watching the passengers, particularly those who travel first class or appear of any importance. But no one was of more importance that morning than himself; for besides the ladies and the yacht, there stood near the helm, with hands folded across their breasts, two slaves in uniforms of red and gold – the Indian flunky uniform of officialdom. Which brings [one] back to the first impression – Bahrain belongs to British India.[19]

Policy Implications of Gulf 'Indianness'

That the Gulf was ruled from India remained a bone of contention through the years with the British Foreign Office, which never accepted the idea that the Indian Political Service should be determining strategy there or that policy arguments going on in India affected the Gulf more than London's concerns. Many instances will be offered.

To take education again as an example, the history of educational policy in India was relevant to Gulf educational developments. It was difficult in India for Muslims to win sympathy for mosque education. The British resistance to Muslim schools in India was for reasons, which good or bad, were missing in Arabia. Views of native education in India found their way to the shaikhdoms although the conditions which had given rise to them were different. Educational policy in India, the lodestone of which was Macaulay's famous minute, unsympathetically viewed indigenous education. The Raj's attitudes to native Indian schools were highly critical, although there was ample evidence of Indian support for education that could have been encouraged. In fact, students given scholarships donated by Indians had been favourably compared with 'the foundation Scholars of the Public Schools of England',[20] and such endowments were an argument for the British adding their own tithe. Macaulay, however, wanted schools on the English model, and he turned arguments about indigenous education around, ingeniously (and ingenuously) claiming that scholarships were evidence that Indians had to be paid to study. An opponent replied: 'As well might it be assumed from the fact that there are foundation scholars at Eton...that no body would learn Latin and Greek if it were not for these stipendiary advantages.'[21] (See Plate 15.)

Given their continual comings and goings between India and the Gulf,[22] and the thorough indoctrination IPS officers received in Indian policies, the Residents must have been familiar with these arguments and aware of Macaulay's 'victory' over advocates of native schools. Macaulay's pronouncements had lasting effects.[23] Considering the Gulf's ties with India, the fortunes of Muslim education in the subcontinent are relevant to the history of Gulf education.[24] Curzon when he was Viceroy remarked: 'Ever since the cold breath of Macaulay's rhetoric passed over the field of the Indian languages and Indian text-books, the elementary education of the people in their own tongue has shrivelled and pined.'[25] In any event, British support for mosque schools in the Gulf was non-existent. Their resilient interest in any sort of general educational initiative was minimal. When the British withdrew in 1971, they left an appallingly ill-educated society.

Neither Fish Nor Fowl

The Indo-British flavour to the Gulf does not contradict the fact that the region had as well its own character.[26] This was accentuated by the British feelings about the Arabs being 'different' from other peoples of the Empire. 'Arabs are more generous and hospitable than the men of any other race,' wrote a Kuwait Political Agent (1936-39), Gerald de Gaury.[27] Ironically, partly because of this romanticism, the *actual* political status of the Gulf *vis-à-vis* India was never resolved. The Gulf remained neither fish nor fowl, although understandably this was not the way the Residents saw it. Regardless of the optimistic official view, in actuality the British role was a confused and confusing one that was complicated by competing British bureaucracies.[28] The Gulf might have fared better in terms of facilities and aid had the region been either fully incorporated into India or completely separate with its own colonial administration.

However, in the case of the Gulf the effects of the cultural invasion cannot be viewed simplistically. L. Carl Brown enterprisingly put forward a theory of what he contended *really* did happen:

> In other areas, the outside impact was at one time more intensive than what the Middle East endured, but such confrontation was not sustained. In these cases, the Western presence challenged and often largely destroyed the indigenous political systems, but later the West departed or at least slackened its pressure. This...is not the same as penetration.
>
> A penetrated political system is one that is neither effectively absorbed by the outside challenger nor later released from the outsider's smothering embrace. A penetrated system exists in continuous confrontation with a dominant outside political system...the politics of a thoroughly penetrated

> society is not adequately explained – even at the local level – without reference to the influence of the intrusive outside system.
> The Middle Eastern political culture has not just been shaped by intrusive Western influences in modern times. That is a trivial truth since the same can be said about any part of the world. Rather, the Middle East has been so continuously interlocked politically with the West as to have become almost an appendage of the Western power system...[29]

Professor Brown's comments are intended to apply to the present, but can be applied equally to when the Gulf was part of the Empire. *The Gulf cannot be understood without discussing the influence of India, either in times past or now.* In 1979, years after the Indian Political Service had been disbanded, the authoress Molly Izzard visited the widow of Harold Dickson, the Political Agent in Bahrain from 1929 to 1936. Dame Violet Dickson was still resident in Kuwait and living in the same house that she had shared with her husband during his days as the Agent:

> The delicious plain food conjured up an awareness of the generations of Victorian Englishwomen who had imposed their standards of housekeeping on the alien Indian scene, and taught the secrets of treacle tart and plum pudding, featherlight scones and perfectly fried fish, to men who in turn passed their acquired skills to their descendants, ensuring a continuity of culture whose last evidences I was perhaps experiencing...The Indian note thus struck, with its insistent reminders of my own childhood, was to recur constantly in my travel down the Gulf...As in the upcountry bungalows of the India of my parents' generation, a certain Edwardian practicality in the furnishings was joined to a plenitude of Persian rugs, of game trophies, of Oriental bric-a-brac and framed photographs and watercolours and bowls of flowers to produce the characteristic domestic interiors of the Raj. Here the unexpected arrival would be taken in and put up with cheerful helpfulness, the novice guided, the sportsman welcomed, and oh, the delight of a fourth for bridge![30]

Remarkably, Violet Dickson was in her house in Kuwait *still* when the Iraqis invaded in August 1990, and only reluctantly was evacuated. If the influences mentioned here seem as elusive as Dame Violet's pudding, it is partly because few physical monuments of Indo-British influence or indigenous Arab tradition were allowed to remain when petro-dollars permitted the bulldozing of the past and the slapdash erection of a garish version of Arabia that owes more architecturally to Hollywood than to antiquity.[31] Only occasionally authentic remains survive, ideological or architectural. For years the author lived in Wakrah, to the mystification of colleagues who prefer the antiseptic blockhouses of Doha. Wakrah is one of the few places in Qatar where out of a window can be seen a smidgen of the old. Admittedly most old buildings have gone, but the town retains an interest because of the remaining ruins. Lytton Strachey in his sketch of Cardinal Manning in *Eminent Victorians* recounted that the Metaphysical Society meeting which Manning always remembered was on 'Wherein consists the special beauty of imperfection and decay? Are not ruins recognized and felt to be more beautiful than perfect structures?'

Thus the Gulf of the Raj has become something which future-shocked Arabs look back upon with affection, because in ways it was a *more Arab* era than today. British misunderstandings and mistakes should not obscure the fact that, in his fashion, the IPS officer displayed a greater (if selective) interest in Arab customs than did the Arabs, who (to be candid) often were commercially-motivated buccaneers.[32]

There is truth to the double-edged remarks by John Strachey that the Raj had admirable characteristics and a circle of appreciative Arab friends: 'But the Arabs whom this kind of Englishman knows and loves may prove the least likely and the least suited to guide the development of their countries.'[33]

The Indian maharajahs who were such loyal supporters of the British come to mind. Reality was kept without their gates. At one of the schools that the IPS helped to establish for them, Mayo College, the statutes ordered that 'the police guard and the gatekeepers must see that no beggars, fakirs, dervishes, improper characters, mountebanks or other vagrants remain in the College grounds.'[34] Modernity was eschewed. Lewis Pelly, one of the most famous of the Gulf Residents, cautioned about hiring staff for Mayo: 'One of two conscientious experienced Hindu gentlemen of what is called the old school who might not even have thrown off their own religion, would be preferable to many of the clever young Indians that may be found in polished boots and a thin veneering of Civilization.'[35] In the end, the Raj's supporters came to curse the style in which they had been educated for leaving them unprepared for the demands of independence, and as suspect traitors in the eyes of fellow countrymen.

Manipulation and Circumspection

An appreciation of Viceregal ritualism in the Gulf involves an understanding of the British attitude towards what appeared to be trifles and incidentals. 'Natives' in the Empire generally were judged by how they manipulated rituals, and not their own but ones whose genesis was in the schools of the administrators. Ritual competence brought natives social acceptance in the Empire. The dilemma for the ambitious was that because the subject of ritualism was the most taciturn part of the Empire's hidden curriculum, it was hard for anyone who had not gone to public school to achieve an expertise in the nuances. Circumspection surrounded the topic. An example of this was Freemasonry, discussed in Chapter VI. Another was the almost clandestine role of architecture, an appreciation of which was more likely to be *absorbed* than learned in formal sessions. The effects of sitting in chapel have been suggested as one way in which such spatial and symbolic lessons were learnt, *e.g.* when Cyril Barrett (Bahrain Political Agent 1926-1929) was a boy at King William's in 1896 he could not have avoided noticing the installation that year of a window memorializing an IPS officer who had been murdered at Manipur. Given the nature of sermons and the wandering eyes of boys, such chapel embellishments may have been more effective teachers than the preachers' homilies.

Despite being riddled with incongruities and stitched together partly from a gallimaufry of half truths, Imperial traditions were a case of *credo quia absurdum est*. It did not matter that their origins were fanciful inventions, anymore than it mattered if Alfred burned the cakes or the Duke of Clarence drowned in a butt of malmsey. The Gulf Arabs were kept distant from the machinery that produced this, thus enhancing the effect of the results. In resisting the IPS cultural onslaught, the Arabs were severely handicapped. They were encased in a cocoon, with panegyrics constantly enforcing a British 'positional superiority'. After India gained independence, the alien nature of this hegemony was shown when old boys repatriated, to their old schools, the statues of their alumni. Similarly, Masonic lodges sent their regalia back to England. The ritual trappings were considered important enough to be carted home. Left behind in the Gulf was a lack of confidence amongst the population in its abilities, and the problem of how to make city-shaikhdoms into nations.

After the British departed there was also a shaikh-sized educational problem, not only with building schools but with deciding what to teach. As mentioned, sending Gulf boys to schools overseas had not been unknown in the Residency period. A local solution would have been preferred but few schools, and none which could be called models of the English public school, were established in the Gulf. This was surprising, because although establishing overseas schools anywhere was never easy, the IPS was prominent in starting many. The IPS involvement with schools in India has already been mentioned. The Principal of Edwardes College in Peshawar, for example, was appointed by the IPS officer serving as Governor of the North-West Frontier Province, and the British did manage to establish similar schools in the Middle East – but not in the Gulf. Egypt's Victoria College in Alexandria was pre-eminent. Gulf policy required boys going overseas to consult the British and when they did, Victoria was preferred. It was nationalized after the Suez war and renamed *Victory* College. Old boys never regarded the renamed school (which continues and has made much use of the fact that the film star Omar Sharif is a graduate) as their own, and they purchased an estate in Surrey. A 'proper' Victoria College reopened, but in England. It had been there in spirit anyway.

Indian Backgrounds to the Fore

In summary, the backgrounds of the Gulf Residents came to the fore in their expressions of interest in educating what they considered to be a native élite, and in not giving a tinker's damn for the education of anyone else. Little attention was given to the general population, while discussions with the shaikhs about their sons were diligently reported to Delhi. The interest was in education for potential and would-be royal houses rather than literacy for the masses. Although it was not considered desirable to have many boys together, at one time there were seven Bahrainis at Millfield alone. (This inspired Kuwaitis to ask whether or not Millfield might be the school for them as well.) Lists were kept of the sons of the rulers who could be prospects for schooling. School prospectuses were diligently collected by the IPS for reference.

Through the years IPS attempts to educate the young shaikhs involved considerable frustration, one reason being that the necessary preparatory education was unavailable and they could not meet the standards of public schools. Fees were also a problem. Rulers were pennypinching even in the matter of their sons' education. Another reason was the reluctance of the boys themselves to be away from home. An example was the heir to the shaikhdom of Kalba, a principality now 'absorbed' by its neighbours in the Emirates. There was an extra reason for sending him abroad because there were suspected plots to murder him by other claimants to the throne:

> At one time the British Resident in Bushire had the idea of sending him to the Princes' School...an academy run on English public school lines, to which the sons of the Indian princes were sent. It was considered that not only would such a step be prudent from a political point of view, but that it was advisable for the young future ruler to have a sound education. Young Ali, however, would have none of this, and he ran away after the first term.[36]

Schools in Aden were also considered as a solution because a Resident (Trenchard Fowle, 1932-39) had been involved with Aden College during a previous posting. The atmosphere was Arab and the connections between Aden and the Gulf were numerous. Despite turmoil in South Yemen, the College continued well into the post-war era, but it never succeeded in attracting many Gulf students. That no comparable college was built in the Gulf was largely because of a lack of money. When the Gulf received its independence, the oil revenue made it possible to opt for universal free education, but by that time social patterns and shaikhy privileges had been confirmed.

If neither Aden College nor the Indian public schools developed Gulf alumni constituencies, that does not mean that public school mannerisms went unemulated in the Gulf. To the contrary, they were *diktat*.

Hierarchicalism and obsequiousness were part and parcel of this as they were for the Indian maharajahs. Those who know the Gulf of late will confirm the fondness for pomp at endless ceremonial comings and goings, the *folie de grandeur* of airport arrivals and departures, and will recognize the affinities with the rituals attending the reception of petty Indian officials:

> The reception committee, dozens strong, will have long assembled at the airport, the garlands ready, the phrases prepared. The politician will appear, a small furtive man, or a large glossy man some distance behind his own stomach; in either case he knows his power. The disciples surround him, pressing their palms in greeting; everyone smiles with a sort of desperation; he does not. He acknowledges the scene through lifeless eyes, pacing through the press of acolytes without pause into the eagerly opened door of his car; the wildly bobbing faces against the window.[37]

Gulf television carries hours every week of similar useless rites. The dignitaries come and go, but not talking of Michelangelo.

NOTES

1. J.E. Woolacott, *British Rule in India*, Anmol Publications, Dehli, reptd. 1986, 1.

2. Raymond O'Shea, *The Sand Kings of Oman, being the experiences of an R.A.F. Officer in the little known regions of Trucial Oman Arabia*, Methuen, 1947, 14. O'Shea completed this controversial book about Sharjah and the Trucial Coast in 1944-1945 when he was safely back in Bristol in November 1945. He laid the blame for conditions squarely on the shaikhs: 'It is to be regretted that out of his large income the average shaikh contributes very little indeed to the welfare and enlightenment of his people. There are no schools to speak of, except in the large shaikhdoms, such as Bahrein; roads are an unheard-of-luxury; there is no system of sanitation, drainage or water supply; graft and chicanery amongst the shaikh's ministers are rife, so that large profits are made by the ruling families and merchants out of the silver rupee exchange and, by a cunning system of cornering the markets in wheat and other essential produce, the people are frequently kept short of food or obliged to buy at exorbitant prices. In other words, it suits the convenience and the pockets of the shaikhs to retain an ignorant and illiterate peasantry, living in conditions of extreme poverty and intolerable squalor. Unfortunately the British Government, through its system of treaty-relations with the shaikhs, unwittingly fosters this undemocratic form of rule.' *Ibid.*, 17. O'Shea recorded that the longtime British Residency Agent in the Emirates, Khan Bahadur, was contemptuous of the 'meanness and extravagance of the shaikhs, and was often driven to vitriolic outbursts of scorn at their neglect of their subjects.' *Ibid.*, 71.

3. Sir Conrad Corfield, *The Princely India I Knew: From Reading to Mountbatten*, Indo-British Historical Society, Madras, 1975, 34-35. See Ashton, *British Policy*, 46-47. Assumptions that the chiefs' colleges were *only* for the sons of rulers have no basis in analysis of old boys lists. Evidence suggests that the schools took other boys: 'There is nothing so far as I am aware to prevent British-Indians from entering any of the Chiefs' Colleges, and there have been several sons of British-Indian Zemindars at the Mayo College.' IOR:L/P&S/302. 'Chiefs' Colleges, Enquiries', P.J. Patrick, India Office, to Sir Philip Hartog, 13 November 1936.

4. Part of the college's library and archives found its way to the Asiatic Society in Calcutta. A history of the college in the light of recent scholarship about the development of the ICS would make a first class study.

5. IOR:R/15/2/210, C.G. Prior to H. Weightman, 1 May 1941.

6. See IOR:15/2/1565 16/54, 'School for Indian Children in Bahrain'.

7. Robert Jarman suggests that boredom was a factor in the pattern of sporadic intervention: the Residents were active men who at times could not stand to 'just sit'. See Sir Malcolm C.C. Seton, *The India Office*, G.P. Putnam, 1926, 143. Also see H.J.K. Usher, *An Angel Without Wings: The History of University College School*, Chancebest, Harrow, 1981, 63.

8. F.B. Malim, *Almae Matres: Recollections of Some Schools at Home and Abroad*, CUP, 1948, 12. See Simon Brett, *Marlborough College*, Essex Reprographics, Brentwood, 1971, 30-31. *Cf.* J.W. Mangan, 'Athleticism: A Case Study of the Evolution of an Educational Ideology', B. Simon and I. Bradley eds., *Victorian Public Schools*, Gill & Macmillan, Dublin, 1975, 177.

9. See *e.g.* W.H. Sleeman, *Rambles and Recollections of an Indian Official*, rev. ed. (Vincent A. Smith ed.), OUP, 1915, 255-56.

10. This zealot was Chester Macnaughten (1843-1896), the 'forgotten pioneer of the public-school education of the fudatory chiefs' and headmaster of Rajkumar College in Kathiawar, who displayed the 'pragmatism of G.E.L. Cotton of Marlborough together with the idealism of ...Almond of Loretto'. J.A. Mangan, 'Eton in India: The Imperial Diffusion of a Victorian Educational Ethic', *History of Education*, 1978, Vol. 7, No. 2, 112-13. A remarkable article about Macnaughten and the elaborate awards system that he promoted at Rajkumar is by Robert P. Puddester, 'Rajkumar College and Its Medals', *Coin and Medal News*, July 1988, 27-30.

11. Correlli Barnett, *The Collapse of British Power*, Alan Sutton, Gloucester, 1984, 140. See the discussion of Barnett's views of the public schools in *Chains of Empire* and in *Rituals of Empire*.

12. Philip Mason, *The Men Who Ruled India*, Jonathan Cape, 1985, 106-07. Also David C. Potter, *India's Political Administrators, 1919-1983*, OUP, 1986, 233. The rise of the public schools in India took place *after* the debate over 'English vs. indigenous education' in which Macaulay '...triumphed over his adversaries, and obtained the recognition of the principle that Indians should be taught European science and civilisation, and through the medium of the English language.' Z.H. Kour, *The History of Aden*, Frank Cass, 1981, 100-01. As far as Indian *Muslim* public schools are concerned, the example invariably cited concerns Sayyid Ahmad Khan (1817-98), who wrote *Loyal Muhammadans of India* to show that the Muslims were devoted to the Crown and founded the Muslim Anglo-Oriental

College with an English headmaster at Aligarh in 1878. In 1886 he established the Muhammadan Educational Conference to encourage interest in English education. He was made KCSI in 1888, partly because he consistently advocated Muslims obtaining a traditional English education. S.A.A. Rizvi, 'Muslim India', in Bernard Lewis ed. *The World of Islam*, Thames and Hudson, 1976, 312.

13. Denise Coelho, *Orchids and Algebra: The Story of Dow Hill School*, Maidstone Publications, Maidstone (Kent), 1986, 65, 70.

14. See IOR:R/20/A/1730, 'School for Sons of Arab Chiefs', Col. R.I. Scallon, Acting Political Resident Aden to Principals of Mayo College, Raj Kumar College, Girassia School, Scott College, 6 August 1905.

15. IOR:R/20/A/1730. There were also (though the subject has not received the attention it deserves) *American* boarding schools in India. The American Mission in the Gulf particularly showed an interest in sending children to Kodaikanal near Madurai. See in the Reformed Church of America Archives: 'Minutes of the Annual Meeting of the American Mission', November 1912, manuscript. This author visited Kodaikanal in 1975. The school had not completely Americanized the town. There remained a few British who drove up from Madurai to escape the heat, including my host J.C. Minns. The old hotel had strayed from Eastbourne. There was a sports day in progress with American-style cheerleaders waving pompoms and exhorting a puzzled Indian audience. A booming amplifying system announced the results of the competitions to the bemused countryside.

16. qtd. Michael Edwardes, *British India, 1772-1947*, Taplinger Publishing, 1968, 237.

17. Kenneth Ross, *Curzon: A Most Superior Person*, Macmillan, 1985, 227.

18. George N. Curzon, *Persia and the Persian Question*, Vol. II, Longmans Green, 1892, 233-36.

19. Ameen Rihani, *Around the Coasts of Arabia*, Caravan, Delmar (New York), 1983 [1930], 258. The officer was Clive Daly, Bahrain PA 1921-26.

20. *Note by H.T. Prinsep*, H. Sharp ed., *Selections from Education Records*, Part I, Bureau of Education, India, Superintendent of Government Printing, Calcutta, 1920, 123.

21. *Ibid.*, 123.

22. See H.H. The Nawab Sultan Jahan Begam, GCIE, *The Story of a Pilgrimage to Hijaz*, Thacker, Spink & Co., Calcutta, 1913, *passim*. This book's uniqueness rests in what the Nawab thought would interest her public. Not one excruciating detail of the trip is omitted. The Nizam of Hyderabad maintained a school in Medina ('Madrasa Nizamiah'), aided other schools in Arabia, and wrote to the IPS about such matters as the lighting of the Prophet Mohammad's tomb at Medina, presumably because the IPS were as involved in such affairs as anyone in the Empire could be. See IOR:L/P&S/12/2148, 'Institutions in Arabia receiving financial support from HEH The Nizam of Hyderabad'. Also H.St. J.B. Philby, *Arabia of the Wahhabis*, Frank Cass, 1977 [1928], 42.

23. For the Macaulay-Prinsep debate see Sharp, *Selections*, v-vii. Also *Minute by the Hon'ble T.B. Macaulay*, dated the 2nd February 1835, Ibid., 107-117, *Cf.* W.H. Carey, *The Good Old Days of Honourable John Company, being Reminiscences Illustrating Manners and Customs of the British in India During the Rule of the East India Company from 1600 to 1856*, Vol. I, R. Cambray, Calcutta, 1906, esp. 396-97, 403, 410-13. Jane Millgate, *Macaulay*, Routledge & Kegan Paul, 1973, 62. Millgate cites Gerald and Natalie Robinson Sirkin in the 'Battle of Indian Education: Macaulay's Opening Salvo Newly Discovered', *Victorian Studies*, Vol. 14, June 1971, 407-28, but that article must itself be examined. Emphasis on Macaulay has prematurely led to the conclusion that Westernization of Imperial education followed on his lead, whereas antecedents such as James Mill's *History of British India* (1818) were important. The Eurasian Henry Derozio at Hindu College and Alexander Duff at Scottish Church College were early proponents of Anglicization. Nihar Nandan Singh, *British Historiography on British Rule in India: The Life and Writings of Sir John William Kayes, 1814-1876*, Janaki Prakashan, New Dehli, 1986, 108. Also see *Note, dated the 15th February 1835*, by H.T. Prinsep (with marginal notes by Macaulay), Sharp ed., *Selections*, 117-121. *Cf.* D.P. Sinha, *The Educational Policy of the East India Company in Benghal to 1854*, Punthi Pustak, Calcutta, 1964, 167-209. *Cf. Macaulay's Minute*, Sharp ed., *Selections*, 107, 109-10, 116-17. Also *cf. Note by H.T. Prinsep, Ibid.*, 118. See Garry Leiser, 'Notes on the Madrasa in Medieval Islamic Society', *Muslim World*, Vol. LXXVI, No. 1, January 1986, 16-23. *Cf.* Sharp ed., *Selections*, 119-21, 123-24. Exchanges between Macaulay and Prinsep, with extracts from Prinsep's diary and Macaulay's notes on Prinsep's memoranda, are reproduced in Sharp. Consider also S.R. Ashton, 'The Indian National Congress 1888-1985', British Library notes for an exhibition to mark the centenary of the first meeting of the Indian National Congress at Bombay in December 1985, 30 November 1985 to February 1986. Finally, see R.P. Singh, *Education in an Imperial Colony*, National, New Dehli, 1979, 4-7, 46-58, 90-91, 114-17, 130-33.

24. An introduction to Muslim schooling in India: M.K.A. Siddiqui, *Educating a Backward Minority*, Abadi Publications, Calcutta, 1984 esp. 31-2, 64-66, 126-29. *Cf.* a sympathetic account by Asim Roy, 'The Politics of Education: The British Raj and Bengal Education, 1871-1884', *History of*

Education Review, Vol. 17, No. 1, 56-69. *Cf.* Iqtidar Hushin Siddiqi, 'Writings on Muslim Educational Movements in Modern India', *Studies in Islam*, Vol. IX, No. 2, January 1972, 86-131. And *Cf.* 76.

25. qtd. Lovat Fraser, *India Under Curzon & After*, William Heinemann, 1912, 187. But *cf.* 199.

26. The late Arnold Galloway stressed this in correspondence with this author, cautioning that the Gulf displayed a special *variety* of the Indo-British tradition.

27. Gerald de Gaury, *The Grand Captain: Gonzalo de Cordoba*, Longmans, Green, 1955, 4. See Sir Reader Bullard, *Britain and the Middle East: From the Earliest Times to 1950*, Hutchinson, 1951, 163. Bullard was Minister and then Ambassador at Tehran, 1939-46.

28. Aaron Klieman described intra-mural feuding in the 1920s: '...the several departments possessed different sensitivities. The Foreign Office sought to meet the susceptibilities of Britain's allies (France, Greece, Italy, and the United States), to punish the Turks, and to devise a comprehensive foreign policy of which the Arab provinces were but one element. Conversely, in its capacity as spokesman for the government of India, the India Office was more concerned with the sensitivities of millions of Indian Muslims. The Arab Bureau in Cairo came to support the sharifians as the instrument most suitable to British interests and Arab aspirations, whereas officials in the India Office urged support for the Saudis as the rising power in Arabia...Any efforts at co-ordination, such as the Interdepartmental Conference on Middle Eastern Affairs, proved too slow and cumbersome.' Aaron S. Klieman, *Foundations of British Policy in the Arab World: The Cairo Conference of 1921*, John Hopkins Press, Baltimore, 1970, 30-31.

29. L. Carl Brown, *International Politics and the Middle East: Old Rules, Dangerous Game*, I.B. Tauris, 1984, 5.

30. Molly Izzard, *The Gulf: Arabia's Western Approaches*, John Murray, 1979, 52.

31. 'In many ways, the Arabia of the *Arabian Nights* lived on...it was in the cinema that the exoticism of the Near East had its apotheosis...Genii were released – in Technicolor – from their bottles, and magic carpets still have an appeal...the cinema itself was sometimes decorated to resemble a Moorish palace – the final meeting, perhaps, of the dream with the dream.' Michael Edwardes, *East-West Passage: The Travel of Ideas, Arts and Inventions between Asia and the Western World*, Taplinger, New York, 1971, 145.

32. Sometimes the Arabs shared these feelings of affinity. Of the Kuwait Political Agent (1916-1918), Robert Hamilton, his son wrote: 'This pride, carried as if it were a thing apart from him like a banner, he guarded with unreasoning fury...to the desert Arab, its source unknown, it was admirable and matched the stern gallantry of a great fighting *sheikh*.' Lord Belhaven, *The Uneven Road*, John Murray, 1955, 24.

33. John Strachey, *The End of Empire*, Victor Gollancz, 1959, 172-73. Apportioning blame for Gulf backwardness sometimes seems to depend somewhat on the nationality of the observer: 'Any reforms of communal life, such as the provision of schools, courts of law based on Western procedure, good roads, efficient water supply and sanitation, the provision of hospitals and pre-natal centres, municipal medical services, and a proper supervision over food supplies and control of prices, all of which are long-standing necessities, should be undertaken by the paramount rulers, the sheikhs, but they, for obvious reasons, are not anxious to diminish their personal incomes by such "extravagances".' O'Shea, *Sand Kings of Oman*, 18. (1947).

34. Herbert Sherring, *History of Mayo College*, Vol. 1, Thacker, Spink & Co., Calcutta, 1897, 165. qtd. McGreal, 'A History of Mayo College', 59.

35. Lewis Pelly, Officiating Agent to the Governor-General in Rajputana, to C.V. Aitchison, Secretary to the Government of India Foreign Department, 28 July 1873, qtd. McGreal, 'A History of Mayo College', 60.

36. O'Shea, *Sand Kings of Oman*, 24.

37. Cameron, *An Indian Summer*, 138. The slavishness of the minions surrounding the Gulf shaikhs cannot be exaggerated. Shame and honour are what motivates everyone, and the political and military consequences of this must be constantly kept in mind: 'Westerners habitually and ignorantly misconceive the responses they are likely to encounter from the Arabs, unsuitably and even laughably projecting their own political and moral attitudes where these cannot apply. Since the Suez campaign of 1956, there have been several Western expeditionary forces in the Middle East, for instance in the attempt to free American embassy personnel held hostage in Tehran in 1979, in Lebanon in 1983, and in the Gulf in 1987. Depending on the interests at stake, either such entry into the Middle East should be avoided altogether for the sake of the shame-based hostility it will trigger, or it must be undertaken with inflexible determination to use whatever degree of force is required for supreme arbitration. David Pryce-Jones, *The Closed Circle: An Interpretation of the Arabs*, Paladin/Grafton, 1991, 405.

III

OLD BOY PANACHE

Participation in bedouin life was in some respects like a prolongation of adolescence, a period of life at which many Englishmen of that time and class appear to have been permanently fixated. – Kathryn Tidrick, *Heart-beguiling Araby*, 1981.

School life becomes the reality, and home life the illusion. – Robert Graves, *Goodbye to All That*, 1929.

Indeed, if one looks beyond Eton and Clifton to the whole formidable corpus of late Victorian public schools, however considerable the differences between them in style or background, the resemblances seem even greater. – Mark Girouard, *The Return to Camelot*, 1981.

Gulf visitors encounter an operatic atmosphere, with tedious protocol pursued meticulously and with as much melodrama as can be found in any Gilbert and Sullivan production.[1] Can such an obsequious social pageantry be the indigenous tradition of the famously egalitarian Arabs, doughty democrats of the desert who bowed the knee to none? The court life of the Gulf rulers, strikingly resembling that of the German principalities before Bismarck and carried on in palaces whose bad taste Ludwig II would have envied, owes much to the IPS and thus indirectly to the Victorian and Edwardian English public schools. (See Plate 16.) This has been grist to Arab radicalism and Iraqi propaganda. It enabled Saddam Hussein to be a populist.

Kuwait's Al-Sabahs recently have had to worry more about people hurling bombs than rose petals. They surely must reflect that part of the settlement of the Gulf's troubles must be less ostentation and more democracy. Yet if the shaikhs appear to have cornered the market in red carpets, the excesses are not entirely their fault. Their mentors in palace construction and in ways to command quivering subservience were the Residents and Agents. Although the extremes are now curbed, British society to foreign observers still appears strongly deferential, whereas – for example – American society does not. The English public schools have contributed mightily to that difference in national culture. British rule relied on deferential rituals that originated at school. As James Morris said of the overseas Englishman: 'The pound sterling in his pocket, the Royal Navy at his back, the rules the old school taught him: that was *his* ideology.'[2]

Common to the lives of the British in the Gulf was membership in the ritualistic Imperial élites: the public schools, the gentlemen's club, the learned societies, the Masonic lodges. Although worlds of their own, the club, the learned societies, and the lodges were closely identified with the public school milieu. More attention to these institutions as a unifying network supporting Imperial administration and as a source of the Imperial rubrics has been overdue. The lack of comment about these connections in standard histories makes one wonder if the network was simply accepted – like the British Royal Family.[3]

While the Imperial system has similarities with the convoluted prefect, fagging, and honours system of the public schools, books about the Empire have not focused on those schools as the incubators of administrators. A resulting lack of comment about public school influence on the Gulf is understandable.

The pertinence of this becomes evident when the school experiences of the Gulfites are juxtaposed with events in their careers. This represents a considerable departure from past efforts to explain Victorian and Edwardian Imperial policies and skates close to being psychohistory, has the merit of raising questions about uninvestigated matters,[4] and suggests the answers to puzzles about the making of Gulf policy.

The motives of the Residents were not entirely directed by their superiors, and sprang from other sources. The heroes of the Empire displayed personality traits which were unusual by any standards, and carried on in ways which in retrospect appear *peculiar*.[5] Dr. J.A. Mangan, a historian of the public schools, observes that so far nobody has gone beyond acknowledging that there was a public school influence on Imperialism to actually demonstrating that it was a principal one and explaining what that means. Dr. Mangan has made significant contributions to discussion of the Empire and the public schools in such books as *Athleticism in the Victorian and Edwardian Public School*, 1981, and *The Games Ethic and Imperialism*, 1986.[6]

Nevertheless, neither he nor any of the other recent writers about the public schools have emphasized sufficiently the connection between the schools' ceremonialism and the ritualism of the Empire, or the public school syndrome as a political factor. It is interesting that in searching for explanations of the Gulf in crisis, authorities the world over in the autumn of 1990 found themselves trying to explain to the general public about the system of Residents and Agents. Glenn Frankel in an article entitled 'Britain's Legacy Will Keep Gulf in Limbo' (*The West Australian*, 3 September 1990), asserted that 'To make sense of Iraqi President Saddam Hussein's claims that Kuwait is really part of Iraq, it helps to go back nearly 70 years to a meeting in a tent in the Arabian desert. It was there that a British high commissioner named Sir Percy Cox drew what became the Kuwait-Iraq border.' Frankel goes on to quote Harold Dickson, then an attaché and later the longtime Kuwait PA: 'It was astonishing to see Ibn Saud being reprimanded like a naughty schoolboy by His Majesty's High Commissioner and being told sharply that he, Sir Percy Cox, would himself decide on the type and general line of the frontier.' Frankel concludes by warning that 'By invoking the colonial past, Saddam Hussein has raised a much deeper issue of legitimacy. For if, as he claims, Kuwait is not really a country, then neither are the other British creations in the Gulf – Oman, Qatar, the United Arab Emirates, Bahrain and Saudi Arabia itself.' That is a rather broad-ranging opinion, but it does touch on the real confrontation in the Gulf which is between manipulated populism, a pseudo-radicalism, élitism and monarchicalism.

Elixir of Empire

The Imperial elixir remains an enigma, although arousing admiration from those who have surveyed the pageantry of the Empire. Jan Morris writes with perceptiveness in *Pax Britannica* about the British overseas:

> They were the children of a unique culture, that of the English public schools, with its deliberate discipline, its classical loyalties, its emphasis on self-reliance, team spirit, delegated responsibility, Christian duty and stoic control. One did not cry when one said good-bye to Mama at Paddington station. One did not, as a general rule, wish to appear too clever, or too enthusiastic. One loyally upheld the prefectorial system, while realizing that certain rules were made to be broken. The public schools, greatly expanded in the second half of the century, and ever more dedicated to their own code of conduct, lay somewhere near the heart of the imperial ethic.[7]

Others too have been curious about the schools' influence. There has been no more astute critic of the relations between the East and West than Edward Said, himself a product of Victoria College, the English-style public school in Egypt. In his magisterial book on the Western view of the East, *Orientalism*, Said suggests that the study of the institutional links between the West and the Middle East is neglected, and that the relations between pedagogy, administration, culture, and imperialism are in great need of examination.[8] Simply put, just who the Imperial leaders were has much to do with what they did, and questions about their motives lead back to the *ethos* of their schools: 'In order to move beyond the false notion that schools are merely sites that impose dominant hegemonic meanings and values upon relatively passive students and teachers, a notion of ideology has to be developed that provides an analysis of *how* schools sustain and produce ideologies as well as *how* individuals and groups in concrete relationships negotiate, resist, or accept them.'[9]

Premature generalizations about the psychohistory of the Gulf are ruled out by the scarcity of scholarship on the subject, but at least it should be possible to fuel the debate about 'the mind of the Gulf'. The assertion made here is that the administrators at least sometimes saw themselves as rather grand schoolmasters and treated the Arabs as members of the lower Fifth.

There was a public school mythology influencing British life that had an existence of its own, quite separate from the actual conditions in any school at any particular moment. In a preface written for the Puffin edition of Thomas Hughes' *Tom Brown's Schooldays* (Penguin, 1988), Naomi Lewis remarks, 'It is a great mistake to think that books copy life, and that's all there is to that. They do, of course, but life does a good deal more of copying from books.' That the mythical English public school depicted in hundreds of novels was the origin of a political mythology which the Empire reflected, and that the maharajahs and shaikhs in a sense were pupils in the mythical school, is a proposition worth examining – the orientalist, Joseph Chailley, in his Gallic examination of the Raj, *Administrative Problems of British India,* rhetorically asked: 'To what extent is the conqueror to turn schoolmaster? Is he to endeavour to influence the mass of the subject race...?' The answer is that the

Imperialists *did* play at schoolmaster; they were not only Viceroys of the Gulf, but schoolmasters of the Gulf.

Although the flat statement has been made that the British did not interfere in day-to-day affairs, that appears untrue. Nothing could illustrate this better than a letter sent in 1940 from the Resident, Charles Prior, to the India Office. (See Plate 17.) The Residents were anxious to give the *appearance* of not interfering. In the same Political and Secret file as this letter in which Prior admits obstructing the shaikh as much as possible, reposes his letter of August 20th 1941 to O.K. Caroe, head of the External Affairs Department in India and (briefly) Gulf Resident. After admitting that the treaty does not permit interference ('...it would require more straining than the words are capable of to construe this in such a way that we could, as a matter of right, prevent the Ruler from employing anyone he wished'), Prior breezily writes:

> So much for the Treaty position. Our position in these waters depends, however, not so much on our Treaties as upon the good-will of the Arab Rulers and prestige and power of our Political Officers. Daly, for example, was able in a few years to turn Bahrain into more of a British protectorate than the average Indian State without much assistance from the Treaty position or the Residency or any one else. Similarly, an incompetent officer ignorant of Arab ways and mentality could lose us our position with almost equal rapidity. In fact, I have very often wondered how far we should be able to maintain our position if it was seriously challenged by any State which desired, for example, an anschluss with Saudi Arabia or Iraq.

A rule of thumb is that when something *interested* the British, they found a reason for interfering. The attitude supporting their interference was one of monumental cultural self-confidence. The Bahrain Political Agent in 1939 wrote to the British Adviser to Bahrain: '...to suggest that Bahrain should be taught that it is "on an absolute equality with other nations" and that Bahrainis are "sovereign people able to hold their own as regards antiquity and race integrity with any nation in the world" can only lead to misunderstanding and unhappiness of everyone in the future.'[10] The failure to appreciate the degree of interference goes hand-in-glove with the often-made assertions that 'nothing happened' before the oil bonanza. This belief in a historical vacuum in 'third world' and 'undeveloped' countries is common but it would be difficult to find a better instance in historiography of armchair over-generalization than is such a view of the Gulf before oil.

The shaikhdoms may lack indigenous scholars but they have had far more than their share of flippant expatriate *jeu d'esprit* journalistic historians. James Lunt in his popular but egregiously inept version of Imperial soldiering, *Imperial Sunset* (Macdonald, 1981), remarks, 'It is a curious commentary on British relations with the Trucial States that even during the two world wars little attempt was made to improve the miserable lot of their Arab inhabitants...The shaikhs maintained their own bodyguards, mostly of African slave origin, but these existed solely for their own protection in a land where murder was as common as traffic accidents in Britain.' Would that things were so exciting. Reality had scant resemblance to accounts such as Mr. Lunt's, but pearls, piracy and slavery are beguiling.

Cultural Hegemony

Whether it is an English public school or an Arab school, such as the *kuttab*, the experiences of youth do shape the man and his decisions. So do the idealized experiences. The idealized Arab school contrasts with the Raj's pretentious beau ideal of colonial education. (See Plates 18 and 19.) The neighbourhood school of Sooltan Hassan, small and friendly, has an altogether different atmosphere from an Indian public school like Rajkumar with its ostentatious architecture. When the aspirations behind such images are ignored, misunderstandings of a culture become inevitable. Being an old boy or a member of the Athenaeum is in its way an affiliation similar to tribe or religion.

While in the British case many schools and other institutions have survived the Empire's passing and prosper, the school of Sooltan Hassan is no more. Such kuttabs have vanished, but Eton celebrated its 550th anniversary in 1990. Once a society's institutions and the identities it produced have been lost, reconstitution is artificial. The efforts in the shaikhdoms to reconstruct old buildings or folk customs are painful. Only a boor would excuse the Gulf's losses on the grounds that what vanished was humble, simple, or 'only' on a small scale.

Cultural hegemony, an overworked phrase, nevertheless remains a useful one to describe the problems presented by Western penetration. Imperialism made itself felt not just in education but in the arts, and in language. Failing to mention Antonio Gramsci's work in a book about the Middle East would be difficult. Professor Said in discussing the phenomenon of Orientalism commented: '...certain cultural forms predominate over others, just as certain ideas are more influential than others; the form of this cultural leadership is what Gramsci has identified as *hegemony*, an indispensable concept for any understanding of cultural life in the industrial West.'[11] Gramsci's pertinence to Imperial studies lies in the single-minded and persistent way the British pursued hegemony, and in how – as far as the Gulf was concerned – tacit consent was obtained.

Hegemonic forces in a Gramscian sense are subtle. So was the Raj's touch. The Empire's success was not achieved by brute force. This means that studies purely of Imperialism in the Gulf in which political matters dominate are impossibly passé. Gramsci gave notice that prevailing views of Gulf society which may be universally accepted will probably *not* be sufficient in the future. In his time, strictly political analysis was already outdated. He emphasizes society's pluralistic and social nature, to which *all* education and affiliations contribute.

Let it be reiterated that the subject of hegemony in the Gulf cannot be viewed solely in terms of the lives of the Arabs and the British officials. Those involved in the power struggle are more numerous. I hope to resurrect some more of these forgotten players in projected further Gulf investigations, and do some justice to the Germans, Americans, and others who were on the scene. Their adventures have not received due notice.

Moreover, the very act of thinking of a Gulf state as an entity presupposes unities and homogeneities which require discussion. British cultural hegemony changed the Gulf through endorsement of a system of Gulf nation-states, a concept taken for granted by Western thinkers but which was antithetical to Arab nomadic and tribal structure. This was not because nation-states are the ultimate in sophistication and that the Arab lacked sophistication, but because administrators thought in a 'nation-state way'. Gramsci's writings emphasize indirect causation, insisting that unintended results come about as a result of activity aimed at other goals. 'Nation-state thinking' provides an instance of how British prestige encouraged the growth of Western-style institutions and the diminishing of traditional systems, contributing to new power centres and unforeseen developments. Even as that was happening, time moved on. Nowadays there is an irony to the fact that while the West is pursuing regional groups, the less politically advanced part of the world is pursuing a particularly strident and radical variety of nationalism. Eritrea, Quebec, Tamil Eelam and assorted Arab states are waving flags at exactly the same time that provincialism is being phased out elsewhere. At least the flag makers are happy. In respects Saddam Hussein was swimming against the tide when he assailed the small Gulf states, because in them nationalism is much more popular and much more in vogue than in some other parts of the world. His pan-Arabism was curiously dated.

Class, Tribe, Enforcement

Arab tribal and theocratic structure lacked the class structure of Western society. British society relished class distinctions and had all manner of rituals to preserve them. (To what extent the current social distinctions between tribes in the Gulf are of recent origin is controversial.) The Residents' political power on occasion was serving and subserving rather than creating and subsuming cultural hegemony. The case put here is that the schooling and memberships of the British caused them to pursue cultural goals that had little relationship to goals such as the safety of the route to India or to other overt political concerns, but that they had an immense effect on the creation of dynasties and social classes.

If it is accepted that English public school traditionalism is an outstanding example of education-for-hegemony, and that thanks to the Imperial civil services it became a force throughout the Empire, it is not surprising that it influenced Gulfite thinking. The visiting British Council representative in 1941 wrote to the cantankerous Gulf Resident, Charles Prior:

> I believe it is essential for sons of sheikhs and important people to be able to continue their education...until Bahrein [*sic*] becomes much more socialist in structure, the sons of notables (irrespective of their ability to pass examinations) will hold most of the positions of importance...I feel it is dangerous to run an educational system on purely selective lines, particularly in a Sheikhdom.[12]

Enforcement of British rule relied on the subtle use of rituals. Gramsci emphasized how people used symbolism to create their reality and to rationalize the irrational. The Imperial institutions were awash in ritualism, and the Gulf despite poverty and isolation was treated to a full measure of Victorian plumes and pomp. The inculcation of obeisance by ritual was at the heart of the Residents' power. They did not have to make much of a studied effort, for they themselves enjoyed a profound love of the hocus-pocus that was a phenomenon of Victorian society and nurtured by the schools. The Residents were old boys through and through. They appreciated prize day. Not only did they have them for adults, when they awarded assorted Imperial orders and medals, but they had actual school prize days. There is an irony to the Resident presenting prizes to schools which were devoid of equipment and lacking in rudiments such as writing paper. One surviving file is full of deliberations over the Resident's prize-giving efforts at Kuwait schools.

The British liked baubles and bunting, partly because the adornments they cherished were reminiscent of school. Figuratively the old school tie flew right under the Union Jack on Gulf flagpoles. The flags themselves, which I have written about in vexillological publications, played a part in British strategy. Rosemarie Said Zahlan in *The Making of the Modern Gulf States* (Unwin Hyman, 1989) points out how the requirement that each of the small shaikhdoms displays a flag 'increased the separateness, and played a part in establishing the difference between, say, Dubai and Sharjah, and between Qatar and Abu Dhabi.' As she agreed when we discussed the subject, the ritualism encouraged by the Resident was also important in the way it helped in the introduction of a harmful social duality to the Gulf.

There is little sign that there was an awareness of this at the time, let alone opposition, and no sign of sensitivity to the growth of social distinctions. Only now in light of Iraq's Kuwait claims can it be fully appreciated that the Gulf was not exempt from what Gramsci noted about how dualism between egalitarian notions and instilled respect for 'traditional conventions' kept the under class in a subordinate position – and worse yet, fashioning their own long-lasting restraints.

This self-imposed inferiority was true in Britain itself, and so strong was Western hegemony that it is impossible to discuss the history of former Western possessions without becoming involved in discussion of the internal history of the Western countries involved. The peculiarity is highlighted if one considers having to discuss Britain by going into details of Nigerian clan initiations, or America by examining Filipino religious festivals. Much of what was set up by colonial administrators was not the result of diabolical schemes to usurp local customs but because the only course of action was to emulate what was known at home. In the British case, as the lives of the Residents demonstrate, schools produced an attitude that cowed the local inhabitants.

Unhappily for the Gulf Arabs, the increased British interest in their affairs came at the same time in the nineteenth century as when the middle classes had captured the public schools. Some of the schools had been the redoubts of the aristocracy, which now had to share its social institutions with the middle classes. The recently enfranchised bourgeoisie gladly used the schools to shore up their new standing. This was a popular development, but there were

Englishmen who saw what was happening and fought against the emerging class stratification and the shutting out of the poor from education. For example, Donald Leinster-Mackay has discussed the under-appreciated Edmond Holmes (1850-1936) in *Cross-Pollinators of English Education: Case Studies of Three Victorian School Inspectors*. If the last assumption about 'shutting out' is accepted, Holmes lost his job partly because he criticized the debilitating ways that the middle class was using education as a bludgeon to subdue the lower class.

Hegemonic tensions over educational élitism continue to exist in British society. However, there is considerably more awareness of what the problem is. The 'brainwashing' in the past was so effective that the working class had contradictory emotions about its lack of education and displayed confused emotions about whether they had been denied educational opportunities or rather had failed to use those that had been available.

The public schools, and the surrogate supporters of public school ideology such as clubs and lodges, created inhibitions on the part of the 'natives' that were extraordinarily controlling, far more so than physical or legal constraints. This advanced the Empire without a need for unpleasant confrontation. Protest was absent because the changes produced were gradual. When there was opposition it was over narrowly-conceived and immediate political issues, and not over the far more lasting cultural impositions. The old school tie prevailed silently. The *rapports* it encouraged were almost infinite and the *Zusammenhang* that were fostered were innumerable. The Repton School letter to old boys for October 1989 carried an interesting example of these myriad interconnections: 'Peter Neil (Priory House '75) writes that he and his brother Charles (Priory House '65) were exploring the deserts of Dubai recently when they became hopelessly stuck in thick mud in a wadi. After several hours, with the heat beginning to take its toll, they saw two vehicles coming their way out of the shimmering haze. Their rescuers turned out to be S.J. Ali Khan (Priory House '47) and a Repton parent, Iqbal Alam.' Similar stirring stories of rescue may come out of Kuwait during the period of the Iraqi occupation.

That the Residents all were subjected to one highly distinctive kind of schooling should at least raise questions about whether this had anything to do with the attitudes they displayed in later life.[13] The Raj, pundits noted, was an 'amiable bargee'[14] who clung to his school as a sheet-anchor throughout adult life, the 'survivor' of a distinctive education that was the equivalent to the voyage in the belly of Jonah's whale. The schools excelled in producing an homogeneous Imperially-minded product.

While comments about the public school boy's strange world might lead to the conclusion that the Residents were divorced from reality and other-worldliness, that only would be the case if the 'real world' had not been under old boy control. With an asylum big enough, the behaviour of the inmates becomes the norm. Since the old boys created the Imperial reality, they did not find the connection between school experiences and Imperial experiences out of place. Within the Gulf's small world, they succeeded in converting general values into *their* values. Physical courage and mental fortitude deserve praise, but it should be remembered about their success that it was they who made the rules and were the referees.

The public schools' speciality was the inculcation of lifelong ways of behaviour; and the leaders produced by the public schools had as much a style of life as any Benedictines ever did. This phenomenon of public school oligarchy was widespread. If the Gulf was run by public school men, so was Malaysia and so was Ceylon, and – most important – so was Britain. Britain arguably still is. Like Pooh-Bah's imaginary execution, the old boys' demise has been much anticipated, yet they flourish still. There are several reasons for this longevity: because superiors 'talked the same language', out of loyalty to one's own, or (one dares to suggest), because of merit arising out of the schools' excellence. Despite criticisms of the attitudes that they fostered, that the schools' influence has been in inverse proportion to the numbers of students enrolled remains undeniable. During the Gulfite years not only the great majority of the Indian Civil Service and Indian Political Service had attended public school, but the staffs of the Foreign Office and Diplomatic Service, most Bishops, and most directors of banks and railways were old boys. The preferment of old boys and the espirit de corps in which they luxuriated spanned many years of British history.

Questions historians might ask about the origins of Attlee's Haileyburian and Baldwin's Harrovian school loyalties can also be asked about Macmillan's Etonians. They are not asked about a Cabinet in the United States. The lifelong preoccupation with schooling by otherwise mature and sophisticated men was quintessentially English and originated in the singular effects of the boarding experience on pubescent children, the emotive qualities of buildings and tradition, the charisma of teachers, and, transcendentally, an assertive public school ethos combining religion, patriotism, aestheticism and athleticism. The topic has not been raised before about the IPS and the public schools, although a few perceptive writers have fastened onto the public school as an ingredient in the Middle East cauldron. Dame Freya Stark wrote that '...the differences between the feudalism of the East and that of our public schools...was not so great as one might think.'[15] Another shrewd observer, Briton Cooper Busch, in his outstanding review of British diplomatic policy in the Gulf, *Britain and the Persian Gulf, 1894-1914*, concluded that 'In the final analysis, without such men Britain could never have taken a strong Gulf position in the 1890s and, despite, or perhaps because of, every challenge emerged in 1914 with one which was all the stronger.'[16]

Putting Away Childish Things

The uninitiated will find it singular that schooldays at Clifton or Winchester, reinforced by membership in the United Services Club or a Masonic lodge, influenced Gulf decisions. It should be recalled that rather than being carefully thought out policy, most decisions were 'fire brigade' responses by the man on the spot to sudden crises. When day-to-day decisions are made, there lurk hidden persuaders that influence the process. The Residents relied on their general knowledge, not on specific instructions from India. There was too much variety in what they faced for long-considered response and any other than an eclectic approach. Sir Arnold Wilson, the son of a headmaster of Clifton and one of the most renowned Residents, described the various demands made on his intellectual resources when he was a junior officer:

> A little geology and a little botany, a little astronomy and a little more surveying; some Hindustani, Persian and Arabic, some Pushtu and Punjabi (to talk to my surveyors and Indian cavalrymen), some French for the Belgians and Russians I meet, some German for the Germans. I can still bandy the classics with an occasional Consul, such as Capt. Lorimer or his brother J.G. Lorimer, I.C.S. or Crown at Basrah; and I have learned enough Christian and Islamic theology to enjoy a good sermon and to exchange ideas with Islamic priests, missionaries and chaplains.[17]

Although eclecticism has an admirable side, the versatility displayed had a juvenile strain. Like the writer of Ecclesiastes, an onlooker could feel that there is a time and place and that men should put away childish things. The whole topic is approached reluctantly by historians, for somehow to admit that political ends were shaped by adolescence represents an acknowledgement as well that much of life remains happenstance or irrational despite a scientific and administrative veneer. In *Tom Brown's Schooldays*, Mrs. Arnold remarked of Rugby old boys, 'Many is the brave heart now doing its work and bearing its load under the Indian sun and in Australian farms and clearings.' *Pari passu* and *par excellence* were the British in the shaikhdoms: 'Knights-errant tended to be drawn to Arab countries, or to countries relatively untouched by Western civilization, partly because they could get away on their own there, partly because they found such traditional ways of life preferable (in short spells, at any rate) to modern civilization.'[18]

The Arabs may have been regarded affectionately, but there should be no illusions about the social limits that circumscribed Philo-Arabism. Old boys had from an early age expected deference. They had passed through a school system which thrived on deference and they ran an Empire which expected deference. Allusions to the Roman Empire, perhaps partly induced by the public school classical curriculum, abounded in Imperial literature. (Not, unsurprisingly, were there references as well to Greek mythology.) Lord James Bryce took a cultural view of Imperial problems:

> Bryce's thinking on the relations of 'superior' and 'subject' races was probably especially shaped by the model of imperial rule in India, which he likened closely to the Roman Empire. In an essay in 1901, he justified the British Raj as a Roman-style despotism because 'no other sort of government would suit a vast population of different races and tongues, divided by religious animosities of Hindus and Mussulmans, and with no sort of experience of self-government on a scale larger than a Village Council'...Nevertheless, the relationships between the 'conquering' and 'conquered' races in the Roman and British Indian examples were, he admitted, different in that the Roman case led to a 'fusion of the peoples' while the Raj made such a fusion impossible...The allusion to Rome was a

convenient ideological ploy in late Victorian imperial thought for it was 'made to serve as a heuristic reinforcement, a magnificent historical reference in a historically conscious age.'[19]

The IPS era provides a prototypical instance of the confrontation of one culture with another, a classic example of the imposition upon one people by another of a different notion of the relationships between appearance and meaning. The British inevitably perceived experience in terms of referents, while the Arabs were inclined to accept images *per se* and not to move from signifier to signified. The idea of ritual representations – symbols or icons – went against Islamic proscriptions. Without falling prey to monocausality, it can be asserted that, far more than has been realized, having old boys in charge was one of the experiences that gives Bahrain, Kuwait, Qatar, and the United Arab Emirates a similar history.

The School Novel and the Schoolboy's Gulf

While the whole period 1858 through 1947 was the Viceregal and public school era as far as the Gulf was concerned, there were differences between the school experiences of men who served in the early and later periods. In his monumental *Public Schools and British Opinion Since 1860,* Edward C. Mack writes:

> ...the school novel, which, used intermittently to praise or criticize education as early as the eighteenth century, was given a tremendous new lease on life by the publication of *Tom Brown's Schooldays* in 1857. Though in the early 'sixties and, indeed as late as the 'nineties, the full tide of novel writing about adolescents, particularly writing which was realistic and critical, had not arrived, writers were by this time already beginning to see the intrinsic interest in novelized pictures of youthful days, as well as the opportunity which such pictures gave them of expressing their ideas about education. In October, 1860, the *Quarterly Review* found school novels of enough importance to warrant a long review of three of them, all directly or indirectly hostile to schools. Two of these, Monro's *Basil The Schoolboy,* which dealt with a school 'neither private nor public, but uniting the faults of both,' and Heygate's *Godfrey Davenant,* a plea for a church school with ritual, dogma, and confession, need not concern us. But F.W. Farrar's *Eric,* which was followed shortly afterward by *St. Winifred's* and *Julian Home,* deserves a consideration second only to that accorded Hughes's *Tom Brown's Schooldays* and Kipling's *Stalky and Co.*[20]

Disagreement can be recorded with some of Mack's opinions about individual novels (especially his views on *Godfrey Davenant* which will be considered in the projected *Tom Brown in Arabia*), but he was right that the school novel provides insights into the changing mind of the public schoolboy through the Victorian and Edwardian era. This idea is why school fiction has been adopted as a measuring rod to be used in the entire series of books about the Gulf of which *Invasions* is the harbinger.

There were striking changes between the Rugby of *Tom Brown* and the Imperial Service College of *Stalky*. Robin Gilmour writes:

> Although Farrar's 'pure-minded boy' is a running joke throughout the book, *Eric* is something of a dead letter by 1899, and Kipling's deeper purpose is revealed in the indifference Number Five study shows towards the house cricket-match on the 'blazing July afternoon'. This is a declaration of their (and their creator's) scarcely concealed contempt for two of the most zealously promoted values of the Victorian school – the socially cohesive force of house spirit, and the morally educative power of team games, especially cricket. The target here is not *Eric* but the more recent school novels of Talbot Baines Reed (1852-93), author of *The Fifth Form at St. Dominics* (1887), and behind these the father of the genre, *Tom Brown's Schooldays* (1857). Neither Reed nor Hughes is mentioned in *Stalky*, although there is one remark by Beetle about 'what they do at all schools accordin' to the B.O.P.' – a reference to the *Boy's Own Paper* founded in 1879, in which Reed published his school stories. And at one level *Stalky* can be seen as a kind of *Fifth Form at Westward Ho!*, a tale of fifth-form boys and their troubled relation to authority in the shape of prefects and masters. But the more rewarding comparison is with *Tom Brown's Schooldays*. Reed's novels codified an ethic of school life which Hughes pioneered: he created the essential elements of the myth on which the later novelists fed. Whereas their novels present school as an enclosed system, *Tom Brown* and *Stalky* make links with a larger world beyond the school, setting the values learned there in a wider context of national culture and, in Kipling's case, imperial destiny.[21]

Developments in this relationship between the schools and Imperialism parallel developments in IPS administration, and the entire era is characterized by the fascination with ritualism that the schools and the IPS officers displayed.

How pervasive the interest in ritual was can be illustrated from the experiences of a Bahrain Political Agent, Edward Wakefield, when he was Secretary to the Punjab Resident, Sir Harold Wilberforce-Bell. Wakefield had to enforce Bell's armorialisms, which 'suffered no encroachments'. Sir Harold's nemesis was crowns:

> In his view it amounted almost to high treason since it 'impinged upon the Royal prerogative'. How often did I use these words when writing to offending Durbars...rulers compromised by using a crown that was semi-arched, or even three-quarters arched. Sir Harold would study such coats of arms with a magnifying glass to see whether they transgressed his strictly enforced rule. Only the Maharaja of Kapurthala got the better of him. Acknowledging a stern letter from Sir Harold on this prickly topic he sent a courteous reply from the George V Hotel in Paris. At the top of the hotel notepaper was a gigantic arched crown...[22]

Wakefield, an Old Haileyburian, suffered much from Sir Harold's social idiosyncrasies and tartly noted that his superior 'had not been educated at one of the major public schools [*he went to Ellesmere College*] and felt that this constituted a chink in his social armour. To compensate for this deprivation he would keep a copy of the *Eton College Chronicle* lying about the house.'[22]

Another instance of the attention to detail is the apparel of the Residents, which suggests that the public schools produced a sedate Beau Brummellism – and indeed the real Brummell was an Old Etonian.[23] An interest in the details of dress became a public school fetish[24] that markedly increased in fervour as the nineteenth century wore on.[25] The parallel sartorial concern of the Empire gives added meaning to the velvet glove rather than the mailed fist in Imperial affairs. Questions of dress absorbed immense Imperial energies.[26] Harold Dickson while the Kuwait Political Agent in 1929-1936 'would not have dreamed of ordering a suit except from Savile Row, or of wearing shoes that were not bespoke'.[27] His Jermyn Street interest was unexceptional because the school and Empire required elaborate costumes. The writer Philip Oakes recalled being told at school by his headmaster, 'I have, on occasion, heard boys criticize the uniform. But it is the badge of your school, just as surely as the badge which you wear on the blazer pocket. Boys here have worn it for nearly one hundred years. It is living history...it is a vital part of your education. It is the best we have to offer. It is a lesson which goes beyond the classroom.'[28]

Faute de mieux would never have been an excuse of Gulf officers, who had *gorgeous* uniforms. Lord Lytton, Viceroy in 1876-1880, had redesigned the IPS uniform and mandated a variety of changes of costume to fit various occasions.[29] As boys at school they had grown up with corps uniforms gleaming with brass, resplendent sportswear, and colourful blazers. 'Pop' at Eton with dazzling multi-coloured waistcoats were not the only ones with distinctive clothing. Christ's Hospital Old Blues would find dressing up to visit the shaikhs reminiscent of putting on the school's Tudor uniforms of blue cassock, yellow stockings, white bands and buckled shoes. A stock Imperial cliché was about wearing formal wear for dinner in incongruous surroundings. The Kuwait PA from 1920 to 1929, James More, always did so. Dame Violet Dickson recorded how he even donned evening clothes when dining alone.[30] Edward Wakefield wrote, 'One always changed for dinner, of course. That was taken for granted...and no more out of the ordinary than brushing one's teeth or shaving.'[31]

Putting It All Together

Costumes and medals do not make a ritualistically-oriented society. They are accoutrements that contribute to the effect and which even gain impact from being displayed in incongruous settings. Dressing for dinner becomes doubly effective when the temperature hovers at 50° centigrade. Maximum impact is achieved when the rituals are choreographed into a life style, as they were in the case of the public schools. Moreover, the participants in the pageant must *believe* in its efficacy. As Erich Fromm points out, 'The little boy in the story of the emperor's clothes who sees that the emperor is naked, is, after all, no more intelligent than the adults, but he is not yet so eager to conform.'[32] The public schools produced the *belief* in the emperor's clothes that was essential to the success of the Gulfites. To conduct ritualism effectively during the course of a career in the IPS required the old boy impassiveness. In this, Dame Freya Stark found one of the more celebrated Kuwait Agents, Gerald de Gaury, a formidable success:

> I dreamed the other night that he was telling me, rather apologetically, that it is no longer *fashionable* to smile. 'What can I do?' I said in my dream. 'I can't *help* smiling.' 'Well,' he said, 'of course...if you must...but perhaps you could smile *very* slightly...not as much as you do.' I have just read *The English: Are They Human?*, an amusing and subtle study, attributing our inhumanity to the public school. I wonder what all the muddle is going to end in.[33]

The schools produced more than a fascination for nominals, medals and miniatures. Their graduates were the Admirable Crichtons of ritual. When they did something, it was done with flair. In Kuwait in 1913, the Political Agent, Captain Shakespear, reported:

> On the 29th July a large portrait in oils of His Majesty the King-Emperor, George V, presented by Government, was formally unveiled in the Shaikh's palace. The day was treated as a holiday and marked by the dressing of the Shaikh's flagstaff and by all boats in harbour flying their flags. In the afternoon a gathering of all local notables took place at the Shaikh's palace, attended also by the European community. The Political Agent briefly addressed the gathering and then unveiled His Majesty's portrait. After this the local poet-laureate read an Arabic ode in eulogy of His Majesty...The Shaikh took great personal interest in the preliminary arrangements and the proceedings and expressed in the warmest terms his thanks and appreciation in being honoured with so signal a mark of His Majesty's favour.[34]

If Captain Shakespear and his comrades believed that a judicious application of abracadabra was part of their job, they were not mistaken. Imperial manifestations of that belief were innumerable. One illustration to be taken up in Chapter VI has been neglected by Middle East historians – Freemasonry. In 1875, the same year he went up to Eton, the precocious M.R. James composed a story in which the Freemasons 'took off their jackets and waistcoats and toggery and they made the Demons light a fire in the midst of the room and they danced round it.'[35] There was as well an Imperial dance, an Imperial ceremonialism, an Imperial coxcombry.

The IPS officers had been to a school of etiquette, an unexcelled school in ritualism, the English public school.[36] Their style confirms Aldous Huxley's remarks about ceremony: 'People will accept certain theological statements about life and the world, will elect to perform certain rites and to follow certain rules of conduct, not because they imagine the statements to be true or the rules and rites to be divinely dictated, but simply because they have discovered experimentally that to live in a certain ritual rhythm, under certain ethical restraints, and as if certain metaphysical doctrines were true, is to live nobly, with style.'[37] This *partly* was true of the world that the Gulf Residents created. Not everyone accepted the rhythm or the restraints, or liked the rituals, as we were so abruptly reminded by the Iraqi invasion of 1990.[38]

British support for a ruler was conveyed in many different ways, even in the number of gun salutes he was accorded. In 1929, for example, the rulers of Kuwait, Bahrain and Qatar were the recipients of seven-gun salutes; the ruler of Abu Dhabi received a five-gun salute; and the ruler of Dubai, only a humble three. That year, an attempt was made by the family of Shaikh Said of Dubai to depose him. The Political Resident stepped in to uphold the ruler: he warned that any move to depose Shaikh Said would incur the strong disapproval of the British government. To reconfirm this support, a public and audible gesture to Shaikh Said followed: he was granted a five-gun salute. – Rosemary Said Zahlan, *The Making of the Modern Gulf States,* 1989.

NOTES

1. Indeed, Freemasonry too found its way into opera, notably in Mozart's *Magic Flute.* See also William Wynn Westcott, *The Magical Masons: Forgotten Hermetic Writings of William Wynn Westcott, Physician and Magus,* Aquarian Press, Wellingborough, 1983, 114, 269-86.
2. James Morris, *Pax Britannica,* Faber & Faber, 1986, 512. Commenting on *Elixir of Empire,* Morris has been good enough to write to me that the notion of rule by ritual is 'surely right'.
3. See Brian Simon's review of J.R. de S. Honey, *Tom Brown's Universe: The Development of the Public School in the 19th Century,* in *History of Education,* June 1978, 160.
4. Consider Rosemary Said Zahlan, 'Hegemony, Dependence and Development in the Gulf', Tim Willock ed., *Social and Economic Development in the Arab Gulf,* Croom Helm, 1980, 73.
5. See *e.g.* John E. Mack, 'T.E. Lawrence and the Use of Psychology in the Biography of Historical Figures', L. Carl Brown and Norman Itzkowtiz eds., *Psychological Dimensions of Near East Studies,* Darwin Press, Princeton (New Jersey), 1977, esp. 52.
6. However, as noted elsewhere, many of his comments seem to have been anticipated by Bruce Haley, *The Healthy Body and Victorian Culture,* Harvard University Press, 1978. Evidently this book has gone unnoticed by Dr. Mangan, and it does not appear to be cited in any of his work.
7. *Pax Britannica,* 220.
8. Edward Said, *Orientalism,* Routledge & Kegan Paul, 1978.
9. Henry A. Giroux, *Ideology, Culture, and the Process of Schooling,* Temple University Press, 1981, 22.
10. IOR:R/15/208 4/16 1, 'Education', H. Weightman to Charles Belgrave, 6 December 1939.
11. Said, *Orientalism,* 6-7.
12. IOR:R/15/2/210, 'Report on Mr. Dundas's Visit to the Persian Gulf from 19th February to 5th March, 1941', 56-57.
13. See Robert Heussler, *Yesterday's Rulers: The Making of the British Colonial Service,* Syracuse University Press, Syrcause (New York), 1982, 82.
14. An Etonism for someone who 'makes sport on the water'.
15. Freya Stark, *The Journey's Echo,* John Murray, 1963, 27.
16. Briton Cooper Busch, *Britain and the Persian Gulf, 1894-1914,* University of California Press, Berkeley, 1967, 388.
17. Arnold Wilson, *S.W. Persia: Letters and Diary of a Young Political Officer, 1907-1914,* Reader's Union, 1942, 173.
18. Mark Girouard, *The Return to Camelot: Chivalry and the English Gentleman,* Yale University Press, New Haven and London, 1981, 271.

19. Paul B. Rich, *Race and Empire in British Politics*, CUP, 1986, 22-23. Rich quotes from James Bryce, 'The Roman Empire and the British Empire in India', in *Studies in History and Jurisprudence*, Vol.I, Clarendon Press, Oxford, 1901, and from Raymond Betts, 'The Allusion to Rome in British Imperialist Thought of the Late Nineteenth and Early Twentieth Centuries', *Victorian Studies*, Vol.15, No.2, December 1971, 156.

20. Edward C. Mack, *Public Schools and British Opinion Since 1860: The Relationship Between Contemporary Ideas and the Evolution of an English Institution*, Greenwood Press, Westport (Connecticut), 1971 [1941], 15.

21. Robin Gilmour, '*Stalky & Co.: Revising the Code*', Phillip Mallett ed., *Kipling Considered*, Macmillan, 1989, 20-21.

22. Edward Wakefield, *Past Imperative: My Life in India, 1927-1947*, Chatto & Windus, 1966, 157.

23. *Ibid.*, 158. *Cf.*, Trench, *Viceroy's Agent*, 169-70.

23. See Mary Ellen Roach and Joanne Bubolz Eicher, 'The Language of Personal Adornment', Justine M.Cordwell and Ronald A.Schwarz eds., *The Fabrics of Culture: The Anthropology of Clothing and Adornment*, Mouton, The Hague, 1979, 11.

24. See W.K. McClure, 'Memories', H.R. Pyatt ed., *Fifty Years of Fettes: Memories of Old Fettesians, 1870-1920*, T. & A. Constable, Edinburgh, 1931, 132-33.

25. See A.K. Cook, 'Hills, Meads, and Games', Earl of Selborne, *et al*, *Winchester College, 1393-1893*, Edward Arnold, 1893, 131 n.3.

26. Oaten, *Memories of India*, 73.

27. H.V.F. Winstone and Zahra Freeth, *Kuwait: Prospect and Reality*, George Allen & Unwin, 1972, 105.

28. Philip Oakes, *From Middle England*, André Deutsch, 1980, 26.

29. A photograph of IPS officers in stunning full dress appears in T.A. Heathcote, *The Afghan Wars: 1839-1919*, Osprey, 1980, after 114.

30. Violet Dickson, *Forty Years in Kuwait*, George Allen & Unwin, 1971, 75. Winston and Freeth, *Kuwait*, 78.

31. Wakefield, *Past Imperative*, 7.

32. Eric Fromm, *Beyond the Chains of Illusion: My Encounter With Marx and Freud*, Abacus, 1980, 146.

33. Freya Stark to Venetia Buddicom, 22 August 1933, Lucy Moorhead ed., *Letters: The Open Door, 1930-35*, Vol.II, Compton Russell, 1975.

34. IOR:R/15/6/513, PGAR1913, 'Administrative Report for the Kuwait Agency for the Year 1913', 130-31.

35. Michael Cox, *M.R. James: An Informal Portrait*, OUP, 1983, 17-18.

36. The ceremonial gauchery of today's Gulf leaders is no less than that of most public leaders in the West, whose public appearances are often dismal. 'When they eat at a public meeting, they are asked to "honour their head table," as the "chairperson" (such people have no discernible sex on public occasions) asks each head table guest to stand, strictly in order of precedence; applause must be 'withheld' until all are standing, or at least crouched in a jack-knife posture above their chairs. When a patriotic air is played or sung, such people may be seen placing the right hand upon the left breast, markedly higher than the real position of the heart...But it is unkind to jeer at them, for they are reaching, however ineptly, toward ceremonial, without which public life cannot be carried on.' Robertson Davies, 'Nobility and Style', *Parabola*, Vol.VII, No.3, August 1982, 15.

37. In *Texts and Pretexts*, 1932, qtd. *Ibid.*

38. 'For all his bombast and apparent style, Mr. Hussein is a hick, a political thug, an assassin, and – especially this – naïve.' Wilson, *'Truth is Still the First Casualty'*, 65. But Saddam was at least a quasi-Western Arab. The vacuum his defeat has created will probably not be filled by quasi-Western political liberalism but by a variety of Islamic fundamentalism. 'It will be remembered that Saddam belonged to a party founded by a Christian; that he executed prominent Islamic scholars; that under his rule alcohol was freely sold; above all that he waged war for eight years against Iran's Islamic revolution and eventually prevailed only with massive help both from non-Muslim "imperialist" powers and from corrupt Arabian sheikhs (including the Emir of Kuwait), whose interests that war was seen to serve. The pendulum will swing back away from nationalism and in favour of militant, xenophobic Islam.' Edward Mortimer, 'After Saddam, What Next?', *The Spectator*, 26 January 1991, 12.

IV

GULF HISTORIOGRAPHY

In foreign propaganda, British influence in the Persian Gulf is pictured as a kind of cold storage in which the backwardness of these areas is artificially perpetuated. I must admit that the British somewhat play into the hands of these authors by an exaggerated secretiveness where anything connected with the Gulf is concerned. As a jealous sheikh veils his favourite wife, so the British authorities shroud conditions in the Arab states in such thick mystery that ill-disposed propagandists might almost be excused for thinking that something dreadful is going on there. – A.R. Lindt, *Lecture to the Royal Central Asian Society,* 1939.

I searched for mention of Raunkiaer's visit to Kuwait in the Records of the Agency. Nearly all the records were destroyed or removed at the outbreak of the first Great War and there was nothing about him in what little remained. – Gerald de Gaury, former Kuwait Political Agent, preface to *Through Wahhabiland on Camelback,* 1969.

The word 'historiography' can be confusing. Running through the English language there is a distinction between 'logys' and 'graphys': 'biology' (the science of life) and 'biography' (the description of lives); 'geology' (the science of the earth) and 'geography' (the description of the earth), etc. The once respectable word 'historiology' has dropped out of just about everybody's vocabulary, and 'historiography' has had to do double duty for both 'historical science' and descriptive accounts of historical writing. – Peter Novak, *That Noble Dream,* 1988.

At the Exeter University conference on the Gulf held in the summer of 1989, the only seer to predict accurately the future of the region after the Iran-Iraq war was a historian. Edward O'Ballance remarked, 'The unspoken fear is that either of the combatants may pick off Arab Gulf states one by one.' Others at the meeting were less successful in crystal-ball gazing, praising Iraq's new moderate attitude, and its desire for friendship with surrounding countries. Reviewing the report of the proceedings (Charles Davies ed., *After the War: Iran, Iraq and the Gulf,* Carden) – which was published the day before the Iraqis occupied Kuwait on August 2, 1990 – *The Economist* mused with commendable hindsight, 'For two big reasons Iraq's invasion of Kuwait came as a nasty surprise, not least to the Kuwaitis. Iraq was expected to squeeze everything it wanted from them (cuts in oil production, border revisions and new subsidies) through intimidation. Second, the received wisdom was that the war with Iran had so transformed once-radical Iraq that an invasion of its most supportive Arab ally was unthinkable.' (18 August 1990.)

The nearly universal misjudgement of Iraqi intentions can partly be attributed to the sorry prostitution of Gulf studies. Scholars have all too often spiked cannons in the interest of a grant or two from the Arabs. British universities, which like to think they are not as venal as their American counterparts, have been fully involved in vanity publications that have abandoned scholarly judgement. They have also been happy to confer degrees on the flimsiest pretence. An example is Exeter's giving of a Ph.D. to Qatar's Minister of Information, a lurid episode which found its way into the tabloids and of which even a Yankee degree mill would have found shameful.

The Gulf has a fuller history than is usually recognized. Evidences of a Greek and Roman presence have come to light, Christian bishoprics existed, and there are enough mysteries to keep archaeologists employed for years to come. (See Plate 20.) Unlike Ottoman studies, enlivened by Paul Wittek's *ghazi*-theory as well as the 'Austrian tradition' and Colin Heywood's mordant contributions, the Gulf has not attracted enough historians, Arab or Western, to provide a basis for a historiography as such. No Arab Ladurie has found a Gulf Montaillou. Sultan Muhammad Al-Qasimi, discussed below, constitutes an exception to the local lack of concern about history.

Enormous amounts of undigested archival material repose in the India Office Library and Records (IOR) in London. So much remains to be explored there, that it appears redundant to look elsewhere, which in itself has produced a bias in what *kinds* of history have been written. Day after day in the reading room a request can bring forward an amazing variety of yet unplumbed files. Why indeed look elsewhere? The Library solicits the papers of anyone with Gulf associations, so that its manuscript resources grow year by year. Moreover, and although materials representing the Arab viewpoint undoubtedly do repose on the library's miles of shelves, *most* of what is available clearly represents an Imperial 'establishment' viewpoint.

In the case of the donated family papers that the IOR safeguards, the suspicion is that material often has been held back. Uncle Harry's escapades may have been burnt or kept in the attic. Inside information about scandals is not the kind of donation that hagiological relatives, acting out of filial nepotism or piety, customarily make. Official letters and reports are unlikely to give the peep behind the curtain that historical voyeurs would enjoy. The danger, therefore, is that by concentrating on the treasures that the India Office collection has in abundance, a one-sided historiography emerges and is perpetuated. A useful reminder of how narrow such a view can be is the Qatar National Museum's depiction of cultural influences. (See Plate 21.) Archives in Turkey, Iran, Iraq and India would have relevant Gulf material.

Another reminder of how many places need searching, and of the need to encourage those who have family papers to place them in a secure library, comes in Gillian Grant's *Middle Eastern Photographic Collections in the United Kingdom* (Middle East Libraries Committee, Durham, 1989). There is no surprise to learn that the Middle East Centre at St Antony's College, Oxford and the Royal Geographical Society have significant collections of photography. Less anticipated are the holdings on Kuwait of the Royal Electrical and Mechanical Engineers Museum in Arborfield, the pictures taken by Sir Arnold Wilson that are deposited with the Royal Photographic Society in Bath, postcards in the Cambridge University Library, and photographs kept by the Royal Engineer Corps Library in Chatham. Equally intriguing are the photographs of Gulf boats in the Exeter Maritime Museum, the Bahrain 'anti-riot operations' photographs in the Hereford Light Infantry Museum, the Sharjah collection of the Liverpool Scottish Museum Trust, and the Gulf pictures collected by the Britain/Israel Public Affairs Committee in London. The National Maritime Museum reports having a 1903 album of Admiral Sir O. Backhouse taken during Curzon's Gulf visit, as well as pictures from the late 1920s and early 1930s taken by a Captain A. Villiers. The United Africa Company, just down Blackfriars Road from the India Office Library, lists among other treasures pictures of pearl dealers in Bahrain, date harvesting in Kuwait, the *suqs* (markets) in Qatar, and street scenes in Dubai. The Kent Archives Office has three albums of photographs taken in 1915 during Lord Hardinge's visit to the Gulf.

American intelligence archives offer opportunities. The Navy Department's intelligence operations were widespread and there is a large quantity of so far still classified reports relating to the Gulf. Examples that have been declassified include the observations of agents at Basra, and at Aden. One wonders if the quality of the American intelligence about the situation in Kuwait was any better in 1990 than it was in the 1940s – judging by the surprise over Iraq's incursion, it may not have been. The unfortunate fact is that even if the information were good, it may not have found its way to the right people...as those who have observed the American intelligence operations in the Middle East will have to acknowledge.

State Department archives are extensive, although they can illustrate the misinformation that policy-makers in Washington received. When a Defence Intelligence Agency officer who had served in North Yemen in 1979 testified *in camera* to a House of Representatives committee, he indicated that the ambassador and CIA station chief sought to edit his reports to indicate clashes with South Yemen were more serious than they really were, thus making a case for military assistance. It is almost needless to add that using intelligence archives or drawing on a personal knowledge of current operations requires tact. The recent Iraq-Kuwait war is another example.

Notwithstanding reservations about ignoring other sources and disappearing into the India Office building never to emerge, records on a bewildering number of subjects are there in such abundance that the building at Blackfriars is the first stop for any Gulf scholar. An indispensable introduction to these holdings remains Penelope Tuson's *Records of the British Residency and Agencies in the Persian Gulf* (1979). Judge Saldanha's many-volumed précis, published by the Government of India at the beginning of the twentieth century and listed in the Bibliography, is essential. Precisely because he was careful to call the series a précis and to make clear that the documents represented selections, doubts arise about papers not included. What is unclear is how his selectivity influenced what was reproduced. Judge Saldanha collated material that was then accessible in Indian archives. As far as historiography is concerned, looking at what he preserved and at what has now become available, it is obvious that much of the official correspondence was produced by officials with no background in history – but their output reflects the prejudices of their backgrounds and so, to the extent that these attitudes can be extrapolated from the documents, the archival material suggests a nascent historiography.

Gulfites were not all hapless 'duffers' when it came to history – *i.e.* in 1937, the Kuwait Political Agent Gerald de Gaury wrote to the Resident, Trenchard Fowle, that he intended to use his leave for research in libraries.[1] This necessity of locating an incipient historiography in unpublished sources such as the papers of those like de Gaury who were in the field, rather than in printed works of those who *interpreted* the sources and published, would seem likely to be a necessity for some time to come. There are apparently no Gulf Arab historians of stature from the pre-British period who are waiting to be discovered, although authorities such as Paul Radin have stressed that abstract thinking about experience is not confined to literate societies.

Regardless of Radin's injunction, thought about the past in a relatively unschooled society could not be expected to display the systematic approach of the West. Not only did the environment discourage any such efforts, but the IPS was uncongenial to the few requests for research help that did come from academics. In 1931, the Agent at Bahrain wrote to the Resident that he had received 'impudent' letters from American scholars requesting information. He added suspiciously 'I expect the same inquiries are going on right round Arabia, but I doubt if the writers are really students.'[2]

Reflections about history *per se* do occur in the magazine of The Arabian Mission, *Neglected Arabia*. The American missionaries in the Gulf represented the American Dutch Reformed denomination, which was an upper middle class sect known for well-educated clergy. They wrote a number of books, a large number of articles that appeared not only in *Neglected Arabia* but elsewhere, and approached the Gulf with a different perspective from the Residents – with whom they tangled on occasion. The comparisons that they were prone to make between Islam and Christianity are useful, if prejudiced.

Indian Historiography

Another comparison that suggests itself is between the poverty of indigenous Gulf historiography and the considerable historiography produced by Indians, which even in the nineteenth century included interesting interpretative work. An account of this would include the *Derozians*, the native humanist scholars in the 1840s who organized and then published through the Society for the Acquisition of General Knowledge. Sayyid Ahmad Kahn, founder of the famous Aligarh public school that evolved into the Aligarh movement, was also a historian who thought about historiography. (His contributions should not be confused with the modern Aligarh School of historical studies, which has a Marxist tint.) Ram Krishna Gopal Bhandarkar's *A Peep Into the Early History of India* (1890) displayed his debt to Ranke; he can be regarded as one of the founders of indigenous Deccan studies.

In the twentieth century, the Harvard graduate Damodar Dharmanand Kosambi (1907-1966), made original contributions with such books as *An Introduction to the Study of Indian History* (1956) and *Myth and Reality: Studies in the Formation of Indian Culture* (1962). He was intrigued by 'the primitive roots of some Indian myths and ritual that survived the beginning of civilization and indeed survive to this day'.[3] More recently, the so-called subaltern school under the leadership of Ranajit Guha has agnostically advocated 'history from below' and provided a series of works that complement such Western poststructuralists as Michel Foucault while displaying a debt to Gramsci. The unpredictable consequences have been that Gandhi's saintliness sometimes becomes more a calculated pose to gain national leadership, and jute mill workers turn out to be as unpleasant as mill owners.

Whilst lacking in Arab historians to provide such historiographical excitements, the subject does not lack bountiful archives – although as has been seen, most papers are not located in the Gulf. The documents in the IOLR include East India Company papers such as seventy-one volumes of original correspondence received by the Company in the period 1602-1712, and letter books containing copies of outgoing communications from the Company to its agents. For the early EIC period, Shafaat Ahmad Khan's book *Sources for the History of British India in the Seventeenth Century* of 1926 remains valuable and appears in a Curzon Press reprint of 1975. As with many bureaucracies, the material produced by the Company inexorably multiplied and by the nineteenth century had become voluminous. After the Mutiny, with the increased reporting required by the Government of India, the quantity that has survived becomes overwhelming. The Government of India's Foreign Department, which was the 'home office' of the IPS, was constantly involved with its counterpart in London, the Political and Secret Department of the Secretary of State for India. (In 1914, the Foreign Department was renamed the Foreign and Political Department.) Much correspondence which ensued between the two departments was considered secret, and ironically that may have assisted its survival.[4]

Because of extensive inter-departmental correspondence and the penchant for copying everything, papers relating to the Gulf which may have been destroyed by one authority can be found elsewhere. This was a favourite idea of Mrs. Christina Harris, an American University of Beirut scholar, who at one time was assembling material for a never-completed study of Sir Lewis Pelly. Her research, concentrating on material surviving in the British Foreign Office archives series FO/248, is in the now inaccessible Beirut collection and unfortunately not microfilmed. She located commercial correspondence sent to the Resident which apparently was not retained in Bushire but of which copies went to Whitehall.

Reports and manuscripts are not the India Office's entire contribution, for in addition to becoming the depository for official pedantry on a grand scale, the Library had a statutory right to every book in every language published in India. It was said that the library represented more knowledge about India than any office of government, anywhere, had ever known about another country. (The map collection illustrates this encyclopaedic inclusiveness superbly.) Anyone who has toured the stacks at Blackfriars will agree that hegemony can be achieved by archival might.

Unfortunately the housing of this magnificent accumulation has not been ideal. Since 1982 the IOLR has been part of the Humanities and Social Sciences Division of the British Library. This allies it with the Library's Oriental Collections, part of the Division and the most complete collection of oriental material in the world. The staff are well aware of obligations to the public as well as to academics, although sorely overworked and poorly housed. The proposed move over the river to the new British Library would help, but only if accompanied by additional funding for personnel. Of late the IOLR has developed an educational programme for teachers and students, promoting the use of original sources in secondary schools and encouraging the students' ability to collate information and use it in relation to a topic.

The exemplary desire to broaden the IOLR's constituency of users does not change the fact that the records are in *London*, and that London is where history of the Gulf must be seriously pursued, which says much about the end results of British Gulf hegemony. Gulf history remains largely the property of the West and not of Arabs, a *tabula rasa* for Oxbridge professors. When the British withdrew from India in 1947, in the House of Lords there was a discussion about the fate of the Indian archives. The Earl of Listowel, Secretary of State for India and Burma, assured the peers that it was 'obvious' that the records should be repatriated to England.[5] He might have added that this applied only to some records, because at the time of British departure, deliberate destruction of crucial documents occurred.[6] This was not the first time that the records of the British in India had been 'sanitized'. In 1912, after the Viceroy's removal to Delhi from Calcutta, there was a massive jettisoning of records.[7]

Most records in the India Office Library collections represent official views of an ICS and IPS élite, but the opinion has been offered that, because they are so wide-ranging, they also can be used to research the attitudes of other strata of British society who encountered the Arabs.[8] Penelope Tuson has demonstrated this with a paper concerning the Bombay Marine and a naval lieutenant's visit to the Gulf.[9] In resurrecting the writings of those in the Bombay Marine, Ms. Tuson sought to meet criticisms of the aprioristic prejudices inherent in official materials.

The collective sympathy which developed in the minds of the English ruling classes for the 'Arab of the desert' was contributory, in Tidrick's words, to the creation 'of the notion that Englishmen possessed an intuitive understanding of Arabs which gave them a special right, even an obligation, to interfere in their affairs'.[10] It is the absence of these prejudices which makes the naval officers' accounts informative, as she has shown.

There are plentiful opportunities for revisionism in Gulf studies. A striking example is the way longstanding views of Bahrain history have been upset by the 1989-90 London-Bahrain Archaeological Expedition, which seems to have overthrown the idea that the hundred thousand burial mounds on the island indicate that bodies were transported there in ancient times from Iraq or Saudi Arabia. By uncovering substantial settlements on Bahrain, the archaeologists have demonstrated that the settlements on the island were large enough to fill the ancient cemeteries. Bahrain's significance as a commercial centre is thus enhanced, but its mytho-religious significance as ancient Dilmun has been challenged. No doubt other cherished ideas can be disputed, and none more so than the antiquity of shaikhy rule.

Obsessions

Historians of the Gulf should consider the consequences of almost obsessional record keeping by the Residents and Agents. Contributing to why their view is so dominant is the fact that a remarkable preoccupation with writing characterized the British in the Indian Empire.[11] The efforts reflect a fixation for memorialization, and the result was so voluminous and inclusive that, as noted, the objection that it represented strictly the Raj's point of view is partly mitigated by the eclecticism of what was written about and kept. It may well be that 'the common people leave only postholes, almost imperceptible shadows in the soil where once a wooden pile rotted away',[12] but ironically much evidence of the 'non-establishment' Gulf has found its way to Blackfriars thanks to this thoroughness.

How fair it is to attribute this zeal for writing everything down to a public school education remains for educational historians to debate. By teaching the fundamentals of good prose and demanding countless written assignments, the public schools at least were encouragers of the diarist letter-writing syndrome that fortunately characterized the Raj. This should not give the official and private India Office records a sacrosanct and definitive aura that they do not deserve, and regardless of volume they do represent generally one view, the British bureaucrat's version of what he wanted his superiors and posterity to know. Gayatri Chakravorty Spivak brilliantly examines this process in an essay 'The Rani of Sirmur: An Essay in Reading the Archives', showing that the administrators of the East India Company constructed representations that became the reality of India. The fiction they produced became 'India'.[13]

But while bearing in mind all the re-constructing and culling that went on before material ended up in the archives, the surviving records *can* be employed to provide a critical gloss, as they do for Bradford Spangenberg in *British Bureaucracy in India: Status, Policy and the I.C.S. in the Late 19th Century.*[14] His use of India Office records produces a picture contradictory to the standard version extolling the virtues of the Indian services. An ongoing debate in Imperial historiography is between revisionists such as Spangenberg and Imperial enthusiasts such as Philip Mason. Mason in his books depicts the dashing emissaries of the Crown, while Spangenberg describes vain careerists. (Mason perhaps confirms suspicions about his romanticism by having changed his surname from Woodruff. The desire to have a euphonious name is not confined to writers – as seen in Chapter IX, one of the Residents [Loch], changed his name by deed poll to the more impressive *Dalyell of the Binns*, albeit in pursuit of a castle as well as a title.)

Tom Brown and the Empire on the Shelf

There exists an enormous literature on the public schools. Much is sheer hagiography. It is understandable that a school historian would not want to subtitle his *magnum opus* 'One Hundred Years of Fumbling Mediocrity'. School histories are 'written from the perspective of the moulders, with a little local colour here and there supplied by the mouldees'.[15] In addition to this source, any compendium of references about the schools must mention the portions relating to youth of the biographies and autobiographies of almost everyone of prominence of the Imperial period. The total amount written about public schools staggers the imagination.[16] Every public school had a magazine, and that provides hundreds of running feet of original sources material.[17] (See Plate 22.) Schools have developed their own archives, sometimes with fulltime employees.[18] Public school fiction is a well-developed category of its own, attracting no less a critic than George Orwell,[19] and surveyed with flair by Isabel Quigly in *The Heirs of Tom Brown.*[20] In short, the material about the schools is so extensive that it is, in its bulk alone, a persuasive argument for their social and political impact.

Any advice proffered as to what to read is sure to be faulted. Notable in an earlier period is Dr. Gray's *Public Schools and the Empire,* because Gray was assistant master at Westminster and later headmaster of Bradfield. He wrote the book at the insistence of L.P. Jacks, Unitarian cleric and Principal of Manchester College, Oxford, who insisted it was needed 'at a time critical for English education, and still more critical for the Empire'. No one immediately took up Gray's Imperial public school interests, but a few authors have started exploring the *consequences* of public schools hegemony for British and Imperial nineteenth and twentieth-century history. Ground-breaking was E.C. Mack's two volume *Public Schools and British Opinion, 1760 to 1860* and *since 1860,* which appeared respectively in 1938 and in 1941. Mack remains the starting point for any understanding of the schools. However, his failure to mention the Taunton Commission is one of several serious lapses.

After what seems a hiatus in efforts at in-depth interpretation, Rupert Wilkinson's *The Prefects* carried investigation significantly further in 1964 by raising questions about the schools' effects on the British bureaucracy. There was nothing strikingly original about T.W. Bamford's *The Rise of the Public Schools* in 1967, but it was a balanced and superbly crafted book which remains the best recent survey of the schools. Scholarship then took a turn away from the broad picture with J.R. de S. Honey's *Tom Brown's Universe* in 1979, and with J.A. Mangan's books which have already been mentioned, *Athleticism in the Victorian and Edwardian Public School* and *The Games Ethic and Imperialism.* Dr. Honey and, to an extent, Dr. Mangan, became enamoured of statistics and were interested in ranking the schools by social standing.

While this succession of authors at least demonstrates the continuing importance of the public schools, none investigated the *consequences* for policy development in a *specific* situation. It fell to an Old Westminster anthropologist, Colin Turnbull, to revive discussion of the socio-political consequences of the schools in *The Human Cycle* (1985).

Like the public schools, the British Empire's history is awash in a vast sea of books. As a starting point, perhaps James Morris' triptych with its succession of brilliant anecdotes is as good as any, frequently making reference to the public schools' role.[21] Another triptych are the volumes of reminiscences by British Imperial administrators edited by Charles Allan: *Plain Tales From the Raj, Tales From the Dark Continent,* and *Tales From the South China Seas.* Because of the Gulf's connections with India, two books by L.S.S. O'Malley, *Modern India and The West,* and *The Indian Civil Service: 1601-1930* are important, as is *The I.C.S.: The Indian Civil Service* by Sir Edward Blunt and Aparna Basu's *Essays in the History of Indian Education*.

Correlli Barnett's *The Collapse of British Power* is less a history and more a study of why the Empire declined, a debacle that he blames partly on the public schools.[22] This is offset by the optimism of J.M. Roberts' *The Triumph of the West*, which concludes that the history of Western civilization has become the history of humankind, with so diffuse and successful an influence that concepts such as Orientalism are largely meaningless.[23] Roberts signals another way in which the growth of Western imperialism may be viewed, but in the midst of making sweeping historiological statements he finds occasion to pay tribute to the public schools' contribution to the creation of the Empire.

Surveys and Introductions

The Gulf comes well-introduced in the massive *The Persian Gulf: A General Survey*, edited by Alvin J. Cottrell. A critical summary of its bibliography occurs in an *Asian Affairs* review of the same book, and places in perspective the standard works on the area such as J.B. Kelly's *Britain and the Persian Gulf* and two seminal works by IPS Officers, Sir Arnold Wilson's *Persian Gulf* and J.G. Lorimer's *Gazetteer of the Persian Gulf*.[24] Lorimer's *Gazetteer* and other important works have been reprinted in an astonishingly ambitious and astonishingly highly-priced series from Archive Editions. Starting with J.A. Saldanha's *Persian Gulf Précis* and the *Persian Gulf Administration Reports 1873-1947*, Archive has gone on to issue such block-busters as a 25 volume and 13,500 page collection entitled *Arabian Boundaries: Primary Documents 1853-1957*. Some sets from Archive are virtually indispensable: *e.g. The Bahrain Government Annual Reports 1924-1970* which were initiated by Charles Belgrave, British adviser to the Bahrain amir and which are available in eight volumes. Other reprints include *The Persian Gulf Trade Reports 1905-1940*, Aitchison's *Treaties and Engagements Relating to Arabia and the Persian Gulf*, and *The Persian Gulf Gazette and Supplements 1953-1972*. Despite the prices and lack of editorial guidance, Archive has made an outstanding contribution to Middle East studies.

In less official vein, and while social history as such has not attracted Gulf historians, something has been written from sociological and psychological viewpoints about the British interaction with the Arabs. Sometimes this probing of the British psyche *vis-à-vis* the East is by individuals not normally associated with the Orient – Disraeli in *Tancred* is an example. Suggestions that Arabia had entered subliminally into the Western mind began appearing in nineteenth-century narratives, interweaving Proustian reminiscences of English public school life with Middle Eastern vignettes. Old Etonian Alexander Kinglake's celebrated *Eothen* written in 1840 did that memorably:

> As for me and my comrade...in this part of our journey we often forgot Stamboul, forgot all the Ottoman Empire, and only remembered old times. We went back, loitering on the banks of the Thames,...Thames, the 'old Eton fellow' that wrestled with us in our boyhood till he taught us to be stronger

than he. We bullied Keate [the Eton headmaster 1809-34], and scoffed at Larrey Miller, and Okes; we rode along loudly laughing...

Two landmarks in a genre involving the interchange between East and West which have widened the discussion of the ties between the Middle East and the West, and which tantalizingly refer in passing to the public schools' role in Arabia, are Edward Said's *Orientalism* and Kathryn Tidrick's *Heart-beguiling Araby.*[25] That these astute commentators on the relationship between the Occident and Arabia – neither with any specific interest in educational history – noticed the importance of the public schools, lends weight to the idea that the English public schools are part of the history of the Middle East, esoteric as the idea first appears. (As for the interest of the English public schools in Arabia as a region, there is no doubt that romantic depictions of military exploits in the Middle East were firmly a part of the reading of nineteenth-century schoolboys.[26])

Because of the way in which the public schools manipulated tradition, a fine introduction to the whole subject is *Tradition* by Edward Shils, with its consideration of tradition's centrality in culture and education and its acknowledgement of Islamic traditions. Shils' remarks are pertinent to the British Residents and Agents. Also useful is David I. Kertser's *Rituals, Politics, and Power,* which begins with the powerful statement that 'Through ritual aspiring political leaders struggle to assert their right to rule, incumbent power holders seek to bolster their authority, and revolutionaries try to carve out a new basis of political allegiance.'

The story of Islam and its divisions is fully as complex as that of Western Christianity. Although obviously no discussion of any Gulf topic is complete without reference to Muslim history, it is surprising how often the subject is left out. Philip K. Hitti's standard *History of the Arabs* provides an introduction and bibliographical advice. Byron G. Massialas and Samir Ahmed Jarrar's *Education in the Arab World* is essential, but only for lack of a really full exposition. Rao H. Lindsay's unpublished doctoral thesis, *Nineteenth Century American Schools in the Levant: A Study of Purposes* effectively explores the Arab interaction with the Western nations. *The Cambridge History of Islam,* despite Said's criticisms of its 'Orientalism', remains a resource. Majid Khadduri's *Arab Contemporaries* is a rich study of Arab intellectuals (and their schooling) in the last hundred years.

These titles are initial suggestions out of thousands that could be cited. The Gulf offers opportunities for research because of the converging traditions – British, Indian, Ottoman, Arab – and the unsynthesized nature of its bibliography. There should be an explosion of historical activity in the next decades as these possibilities are appreciated.

Historiographical Opportunities

Among the avenues that could be pursued, prosopography offers unique opportunities because of the public school backgrounds of the IPS group. A determined antiquarianism preserved material about the alumni of the leading schools and holds out the prospect that diaries, letters, and commentaries which would otherwise be lost can be located. This is not to give complete pride of place to the archival discoveries, because prosopography is not only a technique based on such sources, but an outlook:

> ...those who dismiss 'high-political history' as restricted to what Sir Stafford Northcote wrote or did not write to Lord Cranbrook on a certain date, miss the real significance of the bracing air and light let in by the sceptical excavations of tomblike Victorian archives begun twenty-odd years ago. The frame of reference within which modern British political historiography operates was created not only by the meticulous landscaping of Gash, Hanham and Pelling, but also by the slashing billhook of Namier – whose interests, more than anyone's saw political history as comprehended by the study of psychology, intellect and culture.[27]

Dr. J.A. Mangan suggested what could be accomplished when he employed prosopographical techniques on a limited scale (and reaped the criticism that reviewers reserve for social science terminology) with his study of recruits to the Sudan Political Service (SPS) in *The Games Ethic and Imperialism*. Mangan focused on the public schools, and did not examine the Sudan Civil Service as far as family origins, club and fraternal affiliations, *et cetera*. He confirmed that the British Sudanese administrators uniformly attended such schools, and he discussed which ones. As to what that *meant* in terms of government in the Sudan, he offered no opinion.

This book reaches similar conclusions about the IPS as Dr. Mangan did about the SPS – that British Gulf administration was dominated by old boys. The difference in approach is that the current effort suggests the implications, and claims that the social and political consequences stemmed from a sensitivity to ritualism inculcated by the schools.

This has not meant abandoning chronology. Dates of the regimes of individual Residents and Agents enumerated in Chapter VII provide a framework for further research. In coming to grips with Gulf history, periodization comes easily by reference to the incumbent Resident, much as American presidents or British monarchs are used to identify the period. While the terms of British prime ministers or Indian viceroys are not entirely a suitable framework for studying the Gulf, the years of Residents are.

Writing about the Lewis Pelly or Percy Cox eras has validity, partly as has already been emphasized because the population was small compared with Western states and the effect of individual Residents because of this was pronounced. In this connection the period 1858 to 1947 has as much unity as any period in Gulf history.

The reader will probably agree on looking at the evidence in Chapter IX that British officials in Arabia were a homogenous group, but another implication of this might be overlooked: all were men. That is not a truism. Such a fact can no longer be taken for granted when it comes to historical influences. Male domination of the political structure means that the history has been the history of men ordered by male values. These men were educated at schools that excluded women and sometimes by teachers who were women-haters. Not only the quintessential masculinity of the public schools is a factor. Various insights into Gulf historiography might also flow from the relative social standing of the schools the IPS attended, if that could be agreed upon. This topic, which has somewhat preoccupied public school studies in the last twenty or more years, is discussed in Chapter VII.

On the other hand, the similarities between schools were many and the similar background of Gulf IPS officers encourages prosopographical questions about what schools either had, or lacked, in common. The fact that only one officer in this study went to Eton while frequently their superiors in India did go there, seems to support the proposition that the aristocracy did not join the Imperial services. If that view is subject to reservations, it remains that the Gulf British were a peg below the Viceroy's innermost circle, and their public schools reflected that.

Prosopography and the Royal Touch

When Gulf studies are approached prosopographically, there are inherent biases – notably, emphasis on biography supports the belief that men make history. It is fashionable to ascribe historical development to impersonal forces, but the British success in the Gulf illustrated that individuals could determine historical development. An instance was the initial decision as to which of the shaikhs in each Gulf state with whom to open negotiations, thus determining the ruling dynasty from amongst competing clans. Equally important Arab families who were ignored by the Resident vanished into political oblivion.

Not all of the British who influenced the Arabs were in the IPS. The importance of the adviser ostensibly employed by the amir of Bahrain, Sir Charles Belgrave (1894-1969; Bedford School; Adviser 1926-1957), provides perhaps the most prominent example of influence exerted by someone who was neither Resident nor Agent. His *Bahrain Government Annual Reports* have already been mentioned. He was a complex character who had a profound influence, and possibly not wholly a good influence. Of his significance there can be no doubt. He was Bahrain's Euhemerus.

Whether IPS or not, what is remarkable is that expatriates could ensconce themselves and blatantly intervene for so many years in the affairs of a culture vastly different from their own without being brought up short. Significant credit or blame can be given to a number of British worthies. Any such list, in addition to luminaries such as Belgrave, Cox, Pelly, and Arnold Wilson would include Harold Dickson, Kuwait Agent, 1929-1936, 1941; and Trenchard Fowle, Resident, 1932-1939.

The power of this small intelligentsia recalls Croce's study of the Neopolitan political intelligentsia, and both of these élites bear testimony to the processual character of human reality. At its worst, the IPS was a procession of Mrs. Grundys. But the study of individual officers makes Gulf history that of men rather than of inert, environmentally bound and monolithic impersonal forces. Such a biographical emphasis is needed to redress the long-standing over-emphasis in Gulf studies on diplomatic history alone.

Those familiar with the *Annales* school might wonder if a stress on biography was in respects contradictory to an emphasis on social history, and thus out of place in a book calling for more emphasis on social history. While the *Annales* school sought to correct an undue emphasis on chronology and great men, it did not repudiate biography:

> While it is true that the revival of biography is part of a certain reaction against *Annales*-type history, it would be wrong to see the founding fathers of the first two generations of *Annales* as sworn enemies of biography or of 'great men', as they were of political history and old-style historical narrative. Lucien Febvre wrote a biography of Luther, and chose to illustrate the religious universe of the sixteenth century through the individual consciousness of Rabelais. As his great disciple Braudel was to do forty years later, Febvre took as a point of reference for his doctoral thesis a 'great historical figure', Philip II of Spain.[28]

Marc Bloch, whose *The Royal Touch* must be included in any bibliography of ritualism, did move away from biography. Yet he deserves to be known as a pioneer of collective psychology,[29] which as seen in the next chapter has much to do with prosopography. Neither he nor any other historian could approach *mentalités* without reference to individual lives. Surely the need is not to oust one approach and bring another, but to use *all* the ammunition that has been made available. Any other attitude is presumptuous. Any departure from standardized diplomatic history about the Gulf is welcome. Moreover, a single historian, whether his equipment is statistical, economic or political, cannot fully explain a historical situation.

Nevertheless, a prosopographical overview of the IPS provides important facts about policy in Arabia. So would a prosopographical overview of the Arab leadership. This makes it doubly frustrating to note how impoverished historical studies are in the Gulf. This is an example of a field where the journal articles that are the building blocks for larger studies are lacking, and where a dearth of native social scientists handicaps scholarship. This seems all the more regrettable because of how essential history is to a nation's identity. National self-images, the 'structures of significance' closely involved with national myth-making, are 'not merely derived *from* the past but are regarded as essentially *of* the past.'[30] Kuwaitis now appreciate this.

Neither *force majeure* nor platitudinous references to a vague golden past are substitutes for solid historical research. If a fear of the shaikhdoms is that too much dirty linen would come out in the historical wash, the reassuring reality is that all history, good and bad, helps to establish a national identity. The lack of real Arab contributions leaves a historically dysfunctional Western historiography as the *only* viable historiography alongside Arab flummery.

This is painfully embarrassing because a purpose of history is to deal with the relationship between change and continuity;[31] the Gulf must come to terms with that relationship. The problem facing the shaikhdoms is to find political order in an era critical of authoritarianism. Writes J.D.Y. Pell, 'The past is intensely relevant to politics, modern as well as traditional...'. He adds: 'Making history is really a single process with two strands: the practice of fashioning a future social order entails a constant revaluation of the past. Consequently the historical – supposedly factual accounts of what has happened –

can never be entirely separated from the mythical-persuasive elaborations of what exists eternally and what might be.'[32] The prostitution of Gulf academics in the service of political goals makes the excesses of Orientalism seem minor.[33]

Pirates of the Pirate Coast

Middle East historiography – such as it is and as practised by Western and crypto-Western scholars – has enjoyed its share of controversies. (As an example, and for a demonstration of sheer antagonism, the war over interpretation of the Husayn-McMahon correspondence between J.B. Kelly and Briton Cooper Busch, involving as well Elie Kedourie and George Antonius, affords a classic instance of how four scholars can produce five opinions. If nothing else, it confirms Busch's remark that 'I remain an unregenerate quibbler.' His comment perhaps applies to others in the field.[34])

Disagreement and recrimination about what the record means are not new. A bone of contention has been over what portion of the record has been allowed to survive; there is no doubt that there has been fiddling with documents. The IPS were not above adjusting history to expediency. In June 1939, the Resident (Trenchard Fowle) wrote to Arnold Galloway, who had just become Political Agent in Kuwait, about publication of history books to be used in schools: 'Both the Histories of Bahrain and Kuwait will have to be vetted by us before being issued...In addition to the above two Histories there should certainly in my opinion be a third one: that of our beneficent connection with the Arab States...Copies should also be sent to the Trucial Coast, which is now taking an interest in education.'[35]

Censorship remains a Gulf tradition. The consequence is that, since reality is forbidden, desperate editors fill pages with the bizarre. Readers of the *Khaleej Times* of Dubai in the spring of 1990 were denied most information about political disturbances over the franchise in Kuwait but could update themselves about an amorous ram killing a 100-year-old Cretan farmer, a spontaneously-igniting Chinese boy, and a man-hunting snake that coiled itself around a rifle and shot a Cypriot hunter. Disturbances in Colombia are reported in detail, the implication being that the Gulf is an oasis of calm in a mad world. The initial reaction in the press in Saudi Arabia and in the other Gulf states to the invasion of Kuwait supports this. *The papers for the first day or two made no comment at all.* The Gulf had to rely entirely on Western sources for information during subsequent events.

In a sense, all history has been 'vetted'. There are no value-free histories, but since Arab schoolmen embrace the past as a refuge from 'modernity', *anything* which contradicts that is unacceptable.[36] The work of Gulf academics fails to accept that the day when 'third world history' was 'good old-fashioned imperial history writ large' has been so long gone that the fight against such parochialism is also outmoded. Thirty years ago points could be scored by simply castigating Western bias. That is a feeble excuse today.

It is now accepted that there are subtle dependencies and relationships which are just beginning to be explored. Unfortunately in the Middle East secrecy is endemic, and information on almost any subject is considered by *someone* to be politically sensitive. Because of this, much information is not available because it deliberately has been suppressed. Not only the Arabs have played that game. The British produced their share of sweeping historical generalizations that remain waiting to be debunked, as indeed to justify intervention they probably exaggerated the problem of piracy. A most persistent canard in Gulf history has been the accusation that 'The Persian Gulf was the haunt of pirates until almost the end of the nineteenth century, and the waters around Sharjah and Dubai were infested with these cruel and bloodthirsty sea-brigands, most of whom belonged to the Quasimi clan, of which the Shaikh of Sharjah is the titular head.'[37] A breath of fresh air in this respect is a one man campaign by Sultan Muhammad Al-Qasimi, present Ruler of Sharjah, whose book *The Myth of Arab Piracy in the Gulf* disputes prevailing views. The Shaikh has protested against the stereotype:

> For three-quarters of a century, since J.G. Lorimer compiled his *magnum opus,* his deliberate misrepresentation of the history of the Arabian Peninsula and the Gulf has prevailed, and has never been challenged. The fact that his work was commissioned by Lord Curzon, the Viceroy of India, as an apologia for the long history of British colonialism in the Gulf has been forgotten. As a civil servant in the Government of India, Lorimer could not be expected to be an impartial student of the affairs of his government. The prominence of his *Gazetteer* is due to the fact that he had access to all the relevant documents, but the flaw in his work is that he did not use this advantage properly. Indeed, with the authority derived from his access to the documents, he was able to present falsehoods and rumours as irrefutable facts. His method of compilation was highly selective and so designed to serve his purpose as to render his work apocryphal. It is not difficult to understand the effort put into translating it into Arabic because this effort has helped to propagate the British imperial point of view.[38]

Shaikh Muhammad's lance was aimed at the claims that his ancestors were pirates, but he would have found more of a target had he suggested that distortions are not limited to those introduced by British bias. The duplicity about the extent of the cultural and economic contributions of various nationalities in the Gulf states is an example – the number of nationals is inflated because expatriates so outnumber the locals. He also could have remarked with justice that Gulf history has been characterized by a relative lack of attention to topics such as commerce, architecture, naval history, coinage, and linguistics. The specialized organizations that might contribute to the region's historical process, so ubiquitous in the West and dealing with a vast spectrum of topics, are unknown and forbidden in the Middle East.

Gulf states view scholarly societies with suspicion. They suspect simple gathering of people for any reason whatever, let alone for debate or discussion. They suspect the printed word. In an information age they suspect information. In short, the acute paranoia of the shaikhdoms has rendered them incapable of understanding themselves. Notwithstanding the contributions of Shaikh Muhammad, nothing recently has arisen to challenge the appraisal offered here of the long dominance of British scholars and of the

IOLR, or the estimate of Professor A.J. Arberry, who wrote in 1938 that 'The Library of the India Office is the oldest, and also the largest, specialist oriental library in existence.'[39] So it remains.

This author can testify to a dozen years of having the most innocent books confiscated by Gulf authorities. Book dealers grow wary of dealing with anyone with a Gulf address. London is a better place than the Gulf to find books about the Gulf. The India Office Library is only one of a dozen libraries in London that are resources for the study of the Middle East. It should not be used to the exclusion of the others. Those of the School of Oriental and Africa Studies, Chatham House, the Royal Asiatic Society, the Royal Society for Asian Affairs, the London Library, and the Royal Commonwealth Society come immediately to mind. The Arabs should be chagrined at the Gulf's lack.

The situation as far as Gulf scholarship is concerned is depressing. The fact is that in a country such as Australia that does not have strong connections with the Middle East, there are libraries with better collections on it than can be found in the Middle East itself.[40] The Reid Library of The University of Western Australia has a better collection on the Gulf than that of Qatar University. Arab librarianship like most Arab scholarship looks back at accomplishments in the ninth and tenth centuries, which is of little use to current students.[41] Given the climate of censorship in the area, it is not inappropriate that the most famous library in the region was the lost one of Alexandria. If it is revived, as is now proposed, will the shelves be censored?

> Those radicals who seek to expunge from Arab society all evidence of external influences have gained ground in recent years. Those Arab intellectuals who support this view write extensively to defend it. Although they do not all necessarily agree with each other....The visions of the past that underlie these paradigms are mostly romanticized, but this does not make them less appealing, as they are considered to be at the roots of Arab culture, where genuine cultural authenticity resided and gave the Arabs their historic power and greatness...This traditionalist view of Arab culture and the heritage is static. It does not take into consideration the historical factors that went into the formation of the cultural heritage in the first place. If it concedes change, it does not relate it to the continuous influence of historical factors in society, but rather to the perversion of human wilfulness and to evil external factors with nefarious anti-Islamic intentions of undermining the heritage.[42]

The shaikhs' best ally, if they only knew it, is unfettered scholarship. Their words pale besides the deficiencies of the renegade radicalism of a man like Saddam Hussein. He has used history as a weapon.

Apart from the consequences of sanitizing history to conform to the rulers' whims, pragmatic nuts-and-bolts decisions made over the last two decades have also adversely affected scholarship. The advantage of the oil money was largely squandered as far as libraries and information services were concerned, and research funded by the revenues has been discouragingly small. Central planning regarding libraries was a failure. Missed opportunities include the frustrated efforts to set up an effective inter-library loan system, the refusal to share responsibility for collection development, the lack of union catalogues, and the inability to agree on computer standards. Virtually no Gulf nationals have been adequately trained in librarianship and the libraries are largely staffed by non-nationals. Another problem is the blatant ignoring of copyright laws which has made the old Pirate Coast a world centre for the pirating of texts.

To have a historiography, it is necessary to develop historians, and to encourage freedom of thought. The Middle East today does not have universities that support serious scholarship in Middle Eastern topics. To use the word 'university' to describe institutions using that name in the Gulf states is to take great liberties. Too often it can be remarked about the expatriate Westerners familiar with this truth about higher education in the Arab world that, 'Anxious (quite rightly) to avoid the superiority myths of colonial times, they gloss over deficiencies and play down the inherent conditions...'.[43] The size of library collections is only one indication of just how difficult research would be. The Egyptian National Library, when the holdings of its myriad branches, multiple copies, and holdings of fiction are included, has 250,000 volumes.[44] Of course, a million volumes today are barely adequate to support programmes of any depth, especially when a library claims to 'cover the waterfront'.

Ironically, the American Library of Congress maintains an office in Cairo which purchases for the Library of Congress and for about seventy universities – none of them in the Middle East. A representative of the Cairo office travels throughout the region and acquires material that otherwise would not be obtainable. The Middle East Division of the Library publishes various bibliographical guides. The Washington collection and those of the co-operating institutions that are supporting the Cairo operation have many titles which cannot be found in the region where they were published. The Lebanese civil war has meant that collections in Beirut are unusable. In the Arabian peninsula itself, two collections often mentioned are those of King Saud University in Riyadh and of King Abulaziz University in Jeddah – but neither are what would be considered research libraries.

Sources and Suggestions for Research

There are a number of inviting directions that anyone striving to make contributions to Gulf history can pursue. The holdings relating to the Middle East of institutions in India are somewhat ignored. Through the foresight of previous generations there are several dozen historically significant collections and there are approximately fifty Indian journals published in English that carry articles of interest to a historian of the Middle East.[45] An excellent thesis or dissertation could be based on a review of Indian resources for the study of the Middle East.

The lives of the Residents and Agents in the Gulf can be researched with the confidence that the effort will produce more titles for a Gulf bibliography. This will add to the unbalanced Western nature of the area's historiography, but the fact is that the Imperial administrators produced a large number of articles and books. One of the best research opportunities open to those whose primary language is English is in the biographical study of those who served in the Gulf.[46]

Numerous sources are waiting to be examined that may not be as ethnocentric as the writings of the Residents. Shaikh Muhammad's challenge was based on his investigations in Bombay:

> By far the most important documentary sources for this study are the Bombay Archives. It comes as a surprise to learn that, though they were opened in 1954, to our knowledge they have never been used by Western scholars interested in this subject: indeed, their existence is hardly known. The overwhelming reputation of the documents preserved in the India Office Library has completely overshadowed the documents in the Bombay Archives. Admittedly the Bombay documents are in a sad state of repair and organization, and, indeed in some cases are falling apart, which makes them sometimes difficult to use. But the fact remains that they are richer and more complete than those of the India Office Library...[47]

Not only are there *sources* such as Bombay waiting to be explored; many *subjects* are untouched. The Pilgrimage is an instance. Piety sent Gulf citizens to the holy cities in Iraq and Iran to study, and brought others from far off to Holy Mecca. This created a 'pilgrimage literature', part of which is in English. There is no history in English of the colleges or study centres at Mecca which attracted pilgrims. Conversely, because the longtime influence of India means that Gulf Arabs studied there, Indian educational and social history needs investigation. Military history in the Gulf is complicated and requires a grounding in regimental history to make headway, but the growth of regimental museums in Britain means that their newsletters and archives will be increasingly consulted for Imperial studies.[48] The correspondence between a Resident or Agent who published profusely, such as Arnold Wilson, and his publisher or agent, might provide insights. It is a source that has not been investigated with respect to any Gulfite.

As another suggestion for study, a singular and unnoted public school relationship with Arabia and publishing, is that of Haileybury and Stephen Austin of Caxton Hill, which started with associations between the firm and the 'old' Haileybury and was strengthened when a descendant of the firm's founder canvassed the local gentry to support the reopening of Haileybury in 1862. Stephen Austin has always made a speciality of printing in exotic languages, which is how the company forged a connection with Haileybury and the East India Company; the firm has a two-centuries-old history of publishing in difficult scripts, including Arabic.[49]

Possible sources such as these which may illuminate the way in which cultural hegemony was achieved, deserve exploration all the more because of how overwhelmingly the historiography of the Gulf so far has concentrated on political topics. Edward Said wrote in *Orientalism*: 'My contention is that without examining Orientalism as a discourse one cannot possibly understand the enormously systematic discipline by which European culture was able to manage – and even produce – the Orient politically, sociologically, militarily, ideologically, scientifically, and imaginatively during the post-Enlightenment period. Moreover, so authoritative a position did Orientalism have that I believe no one writing, thinking or acting on the Orient could do so without taking account of the limitations on thought and action imposed by Orientalism.' [50] It should be added that Professor Said is *not* optimistic about the prospects of indigenous scholarship correcting this.

Middle East Studies in the Middle East

Does a dearth of indigenous scholarship imply there are no advantages to doing Middle East research in the Middle East? The answer is not as easily given as it might seem, and a conclusion became even harder when the region became, albeit briefly, the potential site of the world's first all-out biological and chemical war. Westerners can find quieter sabbatical locations.

The opportunity to talk with people who are familiar with the local situation and have access to ephemeral material that never finds its way to Western libraries are compensations. Among the disadvantages is the fear that the police or social upheavals like the present one may destroy notes and personal libraries, something which has happened on occasion. Most Kuwait academics lost their libraries and their work in process because of the Iraqi invasion. Fears of retribution have had their effect on the large numbers of Gulf students studying for higher degrees in Britain and the United States who have produced dissertations on Gulf subjects, resulting in largely bland tomes which lack the first-hand insights that would be expected.

Most of this dissertation work done by Gulf Arabs is unpublished. A few doctorates finally have been turned into books, notably Fuad I. Khuri's *Tribe and State in Bahrain*, and Morsy Abdullah's *The United Arab Emirates*. Gulf Arabs in general have not made very good students, or been particularly rigorous in the pursuit of learning. The *Guardian Weekly* commented when considering the ability of the Kuwaitis to stand against Iraq, 'Young Kuwaitis, babies of the world's most lavish welfare state, have never known hardship, war or life without air conditioning. Like any other Gulf citizen, their government was there to enrich and protect them from the turbulence of the rest of the Arab world.' (12 August 1990.) The soft life of the Gulf has not produced strong individuals, either in statecraft or academia.

While approaches to Gulf history being too 'Western' has been long noted, little has been done to redress the deficiency. Remarks by Colin Heywood about Ottoman historiography are apposite to the problem: '...if we approach the earliest literary sources not as repositories of "hard" data, more or less susceptible to *Quellenkritik,* but manifestations of *mentalités* – the unconscious formative attitudes and collective defence mechanisms of an existentially primitive society, they may reveal more valuable "soft" insights to a historian, less fettered by strict methodology.'[51] This is good advice, but there are no shaikhy expiations or Gulf Arab confessions, fictional or otherwise. Fortunately the scarcity of material becomes less of a problem when the Gulf's place in the Indian sphere of influence is considered. Britain's Indian Empire has spawned whole libraries. Such resources are praiseworthy, but Orientalism is thus made almost inevitable.

For understanding the *British* psyche at work in the Gulf, the literary sources are *par excellence* the unending shelves of public school novels – hence the plan to link books in this quintet with the figures of Tom Brown, Stalky, and Billy Bunter. Admittedly there is a touch of *Verstehen* to this, a notion that history has to be inferred from subjective materials. After all, that was a contribution that Wittek made to Ottoman studies. His writings are as accomplished as literature as they are as history. This has its perils and German historians of romantic disposition have been accused of fancifulness, but the readability is most welcome. Wittek and other historians of the Ottomans have had considerably more to discuss in the way of published work than Gulf historians do. Gulf historiography will be denied the luxury of debate over which approach best serves the subject until there is enough written to criticize and until criticism is allowed.[52]

Commentators have shrugged off the Gulf's past as scarcely worth more than a few lines. The small shaikhdoms were despotically ruled, mused Stephen Longrigg in *The Middle East*, and 'had little history in the first half of this century other than *inter se* boundary quarrels, fears of Saudi acquisitiveness, and hopes of oil discovery.'[53] He adds, 'There has been hitherto no administration in the states other than that, strictly patriarchical, of the rulers themselves.'[54]

Were that really the sum truth, there would be no point in discussing the historiography of the Gulf. It would be similar to trying to discuss the historiography of one of the asteroids.[55] There is *some* truth to pessimism about the future of the topic, because of the lack of Arab scholarship resulting and because of the resulting absence of the building blocks of general history, *e.g.* of local historical society journals, of monographs about lesser worthies, of sets of collected papers. Professor L. Carl Brown remarks about the region:

> Giving the Middle East the full treatment it deserves thus remains difficult. Anyone, for example, with access to a good library could uncover a wealth of fact and interpretation on, say, Gladstone and the Eastern Question. One could obtain a reasonably good sense of not only what Mr. Gladstone did but how he felt about the issues. What if one tried to do the same for someone whose role in Eastern Question history was equally central – Sultan Abdul Hamid II? The available books and articles would provide a very sketchy picture, indeed, largely tendentious as to his deeds and almost nothing about his ideas.[56]

By the use of ingenuity, more can be uncovered than first appears – yet far from as much as could be wished. 'As a jealous sheikh veils his favourite wife,' A.R. Lindt told the Royal Central Asiatic Society in 1939, 'so the British authorities shroud conditions in the Arab states of the Gulf in such thick mystery that ill-disposed propagandists might almost be excused for thinking that something dreadful is going on there.'[57] Still, notwithstanding warnings about the obstacles to Gulf research, there does exist an intriguing psycho-historical dimension to the Gulf, as seen in the next chapter.

Petty tribal wars continued throughout the century. They were never on a large scale or serious enough to interfere with British interests in the Gulf, because the sheikhs were so jealous of one another that to combine was out of the question. The political game was played at its wiliest, and the practice of a sheikh was to play one ally off on another. If they had only acquired sufficient wisdom to settle their disputes amicably, co-operate on such matters as land reform, agriculture and water supply, the Oman Coast today might be a flourishing centre of Arab life. Instead of this, the major part of it is uncultivated desert, because the people have no incentive to irrigate the land and plant cereals and vegetables; that this can be done with considerable success is evidenced by the flourishing gardens at Sheikh's Wells and at Ras-al-Khaimah. It has never been the policy of the sheikhs to better the lot of their subjects... – Raymond O'Shea, *The Sand Kings of Oman*, 1947.

NOTES

1. IOR:R/15/1/529: Gerald de Gaury to Trenchard Fowle, 19 February 1937. The material in this file illustrates the blurring of the dividing line between research out of simple curiosity and for intelligence gathering.

2. IOR:'Kuwait Miscellaneous, 1/1/29 to 3/5/34', R/15/1/505, H.R. Dickson to Hugh Biscoe, 5 January 1931.

3. Subodh Kumar Mukhopadhyay, *Evolution of Historiography in Modern India: 1900-1960*, K.P. Bagchi, Calcutta, 1981, 125. 'By contrast [with the Middle East], one finds that area studies focusing on Latin America, Sub-Saharan Africa, and South Asia have been far more productive in generating findings and paradigms of relevance to their disciplines as a whole...One should note also that comparison among cultural and linguistic segments of the Middle East itself has not been very frequent.' John Waterbury, 'Social Science Research and Arab Studies', Sharabi ed., *The Next Arab Decade*, 294.

4. For a discussion of records, see Moir, 'A Study of the History and Organization of the Political and Secret Department of the East India Company, the Board of Control and the India Office', esp.107-109, and see 127-304.

5. *Hansard*, 22 July 1947, qtd. Nicholas Mansergh, *India: The Transfer of Power, 1942-1947*, Vol.XII, HMSO, 1983, 400.

6. Penelope Tuson, *The Records of the British Residency and Agencies in the Persian Gulf*, India Office Library, 1979, 48, 136.

7. S.A. Tirmizi, 'Record Management in British India', *The Indian Archives*, Vol.XXIX, No.2, 1980, 4-5.

8. D.J. Hastings RINVR ed., *Bombay Buccaneers: Memories and Remembrances of the Royal Indian Navy*, British Association for Cemeteries in South Asia, 1986, 6, 20-23.

9. Penelope Tuson, 'Lieutenant Wyburd's Journal of an Excursion Into Arabia', R.B. Sergeant and R.L. Bidwell, eds., *Arabian Studies*, Vol.IX, C.Hurst, 1979, 21-37. Arnold Galloway (see biography in Chapter IX) had a relative in the Bombay Marine and so took exception to Tuson's conclusion that the officers were not of the same social standing as those in other Indian services: 'I question P. Tuson's distinction between the I.P.S. and the I.N. and doubt very much if the officers of the Bombay Marine were ill educated. Considering the conditions in which they served they were in fact less rough than one might expect...'. A.C. Galloway to P.J. Rich, 10 February 1987.

10. Penelope Tuson, *'Some British Views of Bahrain: The Work of the Bombay Marine and Indian Navy, 1785-1863'*, typescript provided by author, 15.

11. Basudeb Datta-Ray, *Assam Secretariat, 1874-1947: An Administrative History of North-East India*, K.P. Bagghi, Calcutta, 1978, 221-26.

12. Neal Ascherson, 'Dracula Lives and Thrives in Britain', *The Observer*, 31 August 1986, 7.

13. Gayatri Chakravorty Spivak, 'The Rani of Sirmur: An Essay in Reading the Archives', *History and Theory*, Vol.XXIV, No.3, 1985, 247-73. The paper was presented at the 1984 Essex Conference,

'Europe and Its Others', University of Essex. See, quizzically, Isabel Quigly, *The Heirs of Tom Brown: The English School Story*, OUP, 1984, 284.

14. Bradford Spangenberg, *British Bureaucracy in India: Status, Policy and the I.C.S., in the Late 19th Century*, South Asia Books, Columbia (Missouri), 1986. This was the first major *documented* attack on the 'heaven born' reputation of the Indian services, placing everyone on the *qui vive* as far as generalizations about the calibre of Imperial corps.

15. Andrew Davies, 'Primary and Secondary Sources', *Times Educational Supplement*, 30 December 1988, 21.

16. See F.B. Malim, *Almae Matres: Recollections of Some Schools at Home and Abroad*, CUP, 1948, 58-59. Malim, sometime headmaster of Wellington College, is one of the headmasters *cum* educational theorists who is overdue for reappraisal. See *simplex munditis* Leinster-Mackay, *Rise of the English Prep School*, 227. Dr. Leinster-Mackay points out, amongst other things, that Malim invoked Whitehead!

17. J.A. Mangan, 'The School Magazine as a Primary Source', Appendix III, *Athleticism in the Victorian and Edwardian Public School: The Emergence and Consolidation of an Educational Ideology*, CUP, 1981, 243-50.

18. See Sheila Himsworth, compiler, *Winchester College Muniments*, Vol.I, Warden and Fellows of Winchester College, 1976.

19. George Orwell, 'Boys' Weeklies', *George Orwell*, collected ed., Vol.II, Secker & Warburg, 1980, 477-94.

20. Less successful is Peter Musgrave's *From Brown to Bunter*, Routledge, 1985. See Gillian Avery, 'New Realists for Old', *Times Literary Supplement*, 11 April 1986, 386. Some books were not only for youngsters, targeting too an adult audience, *e.g. Stalky and Co.* and *The Loom of Youth*. A.L. Le Quesne, 'Educational Aspects', *Times Educational Supplement*, 11 April 1986, 386.

21. During the writing of the trilogy, James Morris completed a change of sexual role, becoming Jan Morris.

22. Barnett, *The Collapse of British Power, passim*. Barnett has been an invited speaker to the Headmasters' Conference, the premier group for heads of public schools, urging it to 'bury the ghosts of Victorian public schoolism'. For an antidote to pessimism see J.M. Roberts, *The Triumph of the West*, British Broadcasting Corporation, 1985, esp. 305, 431. *Cf.* Anthony Wood, *Nineteenth Century Britain, 1815-1914*, 2nd ed., Longman, 1982, 223.

23. Roberts, *The Triumph of the West, passim*.

24. In respects, a successor to Lorimer's two volumes for those seeking an introduction to the region is the tome produced by Alvin J. Cottrell ed., *The Persian Gulf States: A General Survey*, Johns Hopkins University Press, Baltimore, 1980. Scholarship moves on – in 695 pages of Cottrell, there is only one reference to Lorimer!

25. See John Julius Norwich, 'The Englishman and the Sons of the Desert', review of Tidrick in *UR: The International Magazine of Arab Culture*, No.1, 1982, 74.

26. See Ronald Blythe, 'That Men Died for an Ethos Does Not Mean That the Ethos Was Worth Dying For', *The Listener*, 12 March 1987, 23. The young boys conscripted into Saddam Hussein's Kuwait army of occupation might have found Mr. Blythe's title appropriate.

27. Roy Foster, 'What is Political History?', Juliet Gardiner ed., *What is History Today....?*, Macmillan, 1988, 24.

28. Jacques Le Goff, 'After *Annales*: The Life as History', *Times Literary Supplement*, 14 April 1989, 394.

29. Marc Bloch, *The Royal Touch: Sacred Monarchy and Scrofula in England and France*, Routledge & Kegan Paul, 1973 [1961]. 'In Bloch's hands, old anecdotes about "the king's touch" turned into a history of the origins, meanings, and demise of ritual kingship. Of his books, *Les rois thaumaturges*, which anticipates current work on political ceremonial, has stayed the freshest in its entirety.' Natalie Zemon David, 'A Modern Hero', review of Carole Fink's *Marc Bloch: A Life in History, New York Review of Books*, Vol.XXXVII, No.7, 26 April 1990, 27. See Theda Skocpol, 'Sociology's Historical Imagination', Theda Skocpol ed., *Vision and Method in Historical Sociology*, CUP, 1984, 1-21.

30. J.D.Y. Peel, 'Making History: The Past in the Ijesha Present', *Man*, Vol.19, No.1, March 1984, 111.

31. *Ibid.*, 127.

32. *Ibid.*, 128-29.

33. See Said, *Orientalism*, 13-14.

34. See the correspondence in *Middle East Journal*, Vol.32, No.1, Winter 1978, 139-40. Also Elie Kedourie, *In the Anglo-Arab Labyrinth: The McMahon-Husayn Correspondence and Its Interpretations, 1914-1939*, CUP, 1976. À propos of archives and historiography, Professor Kedourie

writes: 'The Anglo-Sharifian transactions generated in time a large quantity of records which accumulated in Cairo and London. Detailed records are indispensable to successful diplomacy. But archives themselves are useless unless officials master their contents and acquire a precise and detailed knowledge of past transactions. Here, knowledge is indeed power. The evidence reviewed in this book shows that the records of the negotiations with Jusayn were imperfectly grasped, and that from first to last faulty and sometimes fanciful conclusions were derived from them....The officials, in their role as historiographers, are thus shown to have been simply out of their depth, neglecting the evidence in their files, asking anachronistic questions and coming up with implausible answers.' *Ibid.*, 310-11. Little has changed!

35. IOR:R/15/1/545.

36. 'When the present offers nothing and the future appears aborted, only the past, with its *real* achievements, becomes capable of offering the security of promise and the promise of security as well as the promise of achievement in the present by emulating its modes of feeling, thinking, and operating. And the past in Arab consciousness exists only in one form: as a *religious* experience and modes of political, social, and culture organizations. This fact in itself testifies to the failure of the efforts made by modern Arab writers, thinkers, and artists alike to reinterpret Arabic history in terms other than those of the dominant traditional culture.' Kamal Abu-Deeb, 'Cultural Creation in a Fragmented Society', Sharabi, *The Next Arab Decade*, 169. See Ronald Charles Benge, *Cultural Crisis and Libraries in the Third World*, Clive Bingley, 1979, 27-30. The almost total state dominance of culture and education in the Arab world does not encourage independent scholarship. There is no highly organized world of private scholarly societies and universities. He who pays the piper...'My own impression is that in general the political constraints on social science research have never been stronger...I tend to think that Arab social science research that attracts favourable attention will continue to be done "offshore".' Waterbury, 'Social Science Research and Arab Studies', 298.

37. O'Shea, *Sand Kings of Oman*, 105-106. 'Piracy in the Persian Gulf has as ancient a history as pearl fishing and, like pearling, most of the able-bodied men of the coastal towns and villages were engaged in it.' *Ibid.* 113. 'Piracy is dead in the Persian Gulf, although isolated attacks on dhows still occur. As recently as 1944 a large Arab dhow, containing food supplies on its way to Dubai, was attacked by a native sailing ship and the crew murdered. The matter was immediately reported to the Political Officer, Captain Bird, who ascertained that the pirates came from a village on the Persian side of the Gulf, near Jask. Representations were made to the Iran Government, and it is believed that the culprits were apprehended and hanged, suitable compensation being paid to the dependents of the victims.' *Ibid.*, 116. For the lingering effects of the grand old Imperial history, see Gordon Johnson, 'What is Third World History?', Gardiner, *What is History Today...?*, esp. 163.

38. Sultan Muhammad Al-Qasimi, *The Myth of Arab Piracy in the Gulf*, Croom Helm, 1986, xiii. See and consider Benge, *Cultural Crisis*, 200.

39. A.J. Arberry, *The India Office Library: A Historical Sketch*, Commonwealth Office 1967 [1938], v. Kuwait's destruction makes one glad the records are in London.

40. See Richard Stone, *Information Resources in Australia on the Middle East*, National Library of Australia, Canberra, 1986.

41. See Leslie W. Dunlap, *Readings in Library History*, R.R. Bowker, New York, 1972, 51-63.

42. Issa J. Boullata, 'Challenges to Arab Cultural Authenticity', Sharabi ed., *The Next Arab Decade*, 150-51. It is precisely this restraint on scholarship that has made those interested in Middle Eastern bibliography sceptical of the Alexandria library plan. Can a *real* library be built in a Muslim country where there are so many restrictions on which books may be collected? Yet the resurrection of the Alexandrian idea, currently somewhat smothered by café society patronage for the building, might provide a useful symbol of the need for a new leaf *vis-à-vis* freedom of information. A counterbalance to the disastrous public relations of the Rushdie *Satanic Verses* affair is sorely needed. For the Alexandrian legend, see Edward Alexander Parsons, *The Alexandrian Library: Glory of the Hellenic World*, Cleaver-Hume, 1952.

43. Benge, *Cultural Crisis*, 234.

44. Abdulaziz Mohamed Al-Nahari, *The Role of National Libraries in Developing Countries: With Special Reference to Saudi Arabia*, Mansell, 1984, 29.

45. B.S. Kesavan and C.R. Banerji, 'Library Resources in Oriental Studies in India', J.D. Pearson ed., *Papers on Oriental Library Collections*, Inter Documentation, Zug (Switzerland), 1971, 14-24. For background information see A.K. Ohdedar, *The Growth of the Library in Modern India: 1498-1836*, World Press, Calcutta, 1966.

46. For an example of how a search of archives can produce new material see Derek Hopwood, 'Servants of Empire: Sidelights on the British in Egypt', B.C. Bloomfield ed., *Middle East Studies and Libraries: A Felicitation Volume for Professor J.D. Pearson*, Mansell, 1980, 69-84.

47. Al-Qasimi, *The Myth of Arab Piracy*, xvii. See Michael W. Suleiman, 'Survey Research in the Islamic World: Challenges and Rewards', *MESTAB*, Vol.19, No.2, December 1985, 173-182.

48. See Ian D. Grosvenor, 'Review', *Archives*, Vol.XVII, No.74, October 1985, 120.

49. See 'Stephen Austin', *The Haileyburian and I.S.C. Chronicle*, November 1957, 591-92.

50. Said, *Orientalism*, 3. 'One ought never to assume that the structure of Orientalism is nothing more than a structure of lies or of myths which, were the truth about them to be told, would simply blow away. I myself believe that Orientalism is more particularly valuable as a sign of European-Atlantic power over the Orient than it is as a veridic discourse about the Orient (which is what, in its academic or scholarly form, it claims to be). Nevertheless, what we must respect and try to grasp is the sheer knitted-together strength of Orientalist discourse, its very close ties to the enabling socio-economic and political institutions, and its redoubtable durability.' *Ibid.*, 6.

51. Colin Heywood, 'Wittek and the Austrian Tradition', *Journal of the Royal Asiatic Society*, No.1, 1988, 19.

52. Leeds University now has 276 *miles* of videotape of the Iraq-Iran war, representing the four main British channels, plus Sky, CNN, and overseas stations. *Times Higher Education Supplement*, 15 March 1991, 7.

53. Stephen H. Longrigg, *The Middle East: A Social Geography*, 2nd ed. incorporating new material by James Janowski, Gerald Duckworth, 1970, 87.

54. *Ibid.*, 167.

55. 'What has been written previously has been largely impressionistic travel literature (but often of a more than transitory value), professional journalism or political memoirs. Historians are only now starting to work in the field – by a historian I mean one who searches for and then investigates the patterns of past human life and by choosing those patterns which seem significant writes his history. The lack of historical works of this nature on nineteenth century and twentieth century Arabia is clear...'. Derek Hopwood, 'Some Western Studies of Saudi Arabia, Yemen and Aden', Hopwood ed., *The Arabian Peninsula*, 13.

56. Brown, *International Politics and the Middle East*, 280. *Cf.* 292.

57. A.R. Lindt, 'Politics in the Persian Gulf', *Journal of the Royal Central Asian Society*, XXVI, 1939, 179. The veil simile, frequently used in describing the Gulf shaikhdoms ('the veiled protectorates', 'the veiled shaikhdoms') conveys a double entendre: 'If no amount of veiling can conceal the veiling itself, the issue is how far we will go in our seriousness at self-veiling, and how far we will go to have others act in complicity with us.' James P. Carse, *Finite and Infinite Games*, Ballantine, New York, 1987, 17. 'It is hard to judge just how the war is going because each side is lying (Iraq) or economical with the truth (us).' Wilson, 'Truth is Still the First Casualty', 64.

V

PSYCHOHISTORY AND THE ARABS

He [the Resident] may with a greater truth than phrase sometimes conveys, be entitled the uncrowned king of the Persian Gulf. – George Curzon, *Persia and the Persian Question*, 1892.

Studies of tribal Arab societies have tended either to concentrate on the tribes and to set aside the question of leaders, or to deal with the leaders and to set to one side the tribes themselves. – P. Dresch, *Man*, 1984.

A report from Jordan suggests that ordinary people support Saddam, that they are jubilant even...It was, Arab commentators freely admitted, a yardstick of the abysmal sense of despair and impotence into which Arabs everywhere have sunk. What stake does the Arab man in the street really have in a persisting Arab order which, they always used to be told, should have been swept away long ago. The new era which the Arab world has entered with Saddam's invasion of Kuwait can hardly be worse than the last. In the Arab people's state of mind, any change might seem more appealing than none at all – even if it requires a Saddam to wreak it. – David Hirst, 'A Hungry Lion Among the Frightened Gazelles', *Guardian Weekly*, 12 August 1990.

Psychohistory often deals with *homo fictus* rather than *homo sapiens*. The urbanity of a Terence is needed in applying psychohistory to the Gulf, and for the moment the subject offers more speculations than conclusions. The technique must be used cautiously.

Indeed, this is more a chapter on 'metapsychohistory' than psychohistory, because the subject has already shown signs of outgrowing itself. Psychobiological, psychohistorical, psychoanalytical, or psychopolitical approaches may be frustrating, but the theatricality of British administration is pronounced enough to encourage psychohistorical speculations. The Residents were hardly pedestrian in taste or pursuits, and some of them were far from being what the Arabs call *al-bashar al-sawiiy*, the harmonious or balanced man.

The Raj's personality has been described simplistically in terms of duty and honour, cautiously in terms of self-control and restraint, and severely in terms of public school hypocrisy and anti-intellectualism. To be Imperially-minded was to embrace a religion of sorts: 'At some point the British attachment to India seems to have transcended reason and to have become an article of faith that most concerned citizens shared. To ties of national and self-interest were added over the years personal, cultural, and religious connections that struck deeply into both societies. If the empire was anything large and noble it was India.'[1]

This rings true, but generalizations as to a *Gulfite psyche*, as with much else about the IPS, depend on which closet door is opened. What brought them to

Arabia can be considered in light of the effects of childhood, schooling, relationships with parents, and manifold other influences. Further complicating the scenario, some Residents and Agents found Arabia a place to live out fantasies. The Victorians, as Lytton Strachey pointed out about Cardinal Newman, wished that they could believe that the *Arabian Nights* were true – and when they reached manhood sometimes found the wish granted. (See Plate 23.)

Katherine Tidrick showed how productive psychohistory could be in *Heart-beguiling Araby* (1981), where she provided highly original insights into the lives of individual Arabophiles such as Wilfrid Blunt (1840-1922), whose antecedents were seemingly already well researched. In the case of Blunt, she suggests that the anxiety of being sent to Stonyhurst for school and then removed to Oscott had a connection with his religiosity and his 'singularity'. In the instance of St. John Philby, Tidrick drew parallels between his 'reign' as head boy at Westminster School when he aimed to restore 'vigour and discipline' and his support of Ibn Saud's reforms in Arabia. In Tidrick's judgement, school experiences are part of what created Arabophiles. The record of them sometimes shows a man before he 'lowers the shutters' and conceals his emotions.

Like Blunt and Philby, almost all IPS officers endured the traumas of public school life. Libby Purves has pointed out in *The Times* ('And Why Can't the Little Hero Swoon, Too?', 20 June 1990) that the children's literature of the time was as damaging as were the actual experiences. Boys were seldom allowed in fiction to show emotion: 'Although in earlier novels like *Tom Brown's Schooldays* they were free to weep and embrace, the upper lip stiffened some time around 1880 and never unfroze again. There is a wonderful item in the advice column of *Boy's Own Paper*, 1892, replying to a poor youth who complained of a tendency to blush. The paper advises him to practise "blanching with rage" instead, thus replacing a natural, humble, human response to embarrassment with an aggressive and furious one.' As she mentions, G.A. Henty was never able to work Lord Nelson into a novel because he was 'Latin' and too fond of Lady Hamilton. Henty's heroes were supposed to give a manly thrashing to dacoits and not display emotional subtlety.

Whether the epizootic experiences encouraged either through fiction or by actual schooldays were life-expanding or destructive depended on a boy's resilience. The public school literature has examples of those whose suffering had lifelong consequences. Robert Graves described the sad effects of Charterhouse:

> Let me begin my account of Charterhouse School by recalling the day that I left, a week before the outbreak of war. I discussed my feelings with Nevill Barbour, then Head of the School. First, we agreed that there were perhaps even more typical public schools than Charterhouse in existence, but that we preferred not to believe it. Next, that no possible remedy could be found, because tradition was so strong that to break it one would have to dismiss the whole school and staff, and start all over again. However, even this would not be enough, the school buildings being so impregnated with what passed as the public school spirit, but what we felt as fundamental evil, that

they would have to be demolished and the school rebuilt elsewhere under a different name.[2]

Discussion of the psychological effects of public schools has concentrated on traumatizing consequences, particularly those caused by competitive sports. The rigours of the playing field were a part of public school education, but arguments that athleticism was the principal factor in shaping the old boy mentality seem strained. Surely a host of influences were at work and are reflected in the Imperial personality. A cartoon is apropos of embracing athleticism as *the* paradigm of the public school influence on the Empire. A man prepares to jump off a cliff, wearing a beak and pointed cap. His friend remarks 'Are you sure about this, Stanley? It seems odd that a pointy head and long beak is what makes them fly.'[3] The point, to pun, is that there were other distinctive experiences than sports in a public school education, and some were even more unique to the public schools than were games. Pancake greezes at Westminster School are an instance. I have taken the greeze as a touchstone in my books, not only because of the metaphors it involves but because of its long history. The pancake is thrown over a bar in the Westminster schoolroom or great hall and boys scrimmage for the biggest piece, which entitles the winner to a guinea reward. (See Plate 24.) That sort of experience would be recalled by Philby, or another Old Westminster such as the Gulfite, Robert Hamilton. *Arguably this peculiar ritualism was what was distinctive about public schools*, not games. Of course, in the case of games such as Eton fives, the game itself was largely confined to public schools and was more a ritual than it was a sport.

The schools exerted enormous influence on personality. Not surprisingly, comparisons between being a new boy and a young officer thrust into an alien milieu have been made, as well as analogies between school and tribal rituals. A biographer of Anthony Blunt, the spy and art historian (whose father Wilfrid Blunt was named for the Arabian explorer, a cousin), described his youth:

> Recalled the poet Louis MacNeice, Anthony's contemporary, 'physical discomfort and futile ritual – those were the first things I noticed.'...The shock of incongruous tribal rituals did not hold much terror for the fourteen-year old Anthony Blunt when he arrived at Marlborough in January 1921. He had learned about the school's peculiar customs from his older brothers. But no amount of foreknowledge could have spared him from the humiliating duty of 'fagging' for senior boys. Bullying was also institutionalized and tolerated by the masters as a necessary part of the hardening-up process in the Junior House, where the length of stay depended on sexual development rather than educational accomplishment. Junior housemasters made periodic bathroom inspections to watch for the sprouting pubic hair, the signal for a boy's promotion to Upper School. Most Junior House boys faced the prospect of their promotion with considerable apprehension. It meant that in two years before they became members of the sixth form, they ran the constant risk of beatings and sadistic rituals.[4]

Ritualistic Personalities in the Gulf

What psychological defences were necessary to survive as a newcomer in an English public school or, later, in the Gulf? An individual coped through ritual. The heat was defied by putting on costumes whose elaborateness flouted the sun. Threatening locals could be put in their place by hoisting the flag each morning. Perhaps the Imperial personality has never been so fully described before as a *ritualistic personality* shaped by schooldays, but ritualism enabled individuals to be integrated into the Imperial system.

Future study should be assisted by the recent welcome emergence of a constructionist school of emotion studies that embraces historians as well as social psychologists and sociologists, and argues that emotions should be examined in terms of their functions in the society that they serve. The insistence that an understanding of emotions is essential to historical understanding overlaps with the demand for an emphasis on historical empathy. Yet which of the emotions? Albeit each and every Resident and Agent was a bundle of impulses and passions and influences, but it can be argued that the feelings which the school cultivated in boys were the ones that the job of representing the Crown to the Arabs called upon, and which scholars interested in the political evolution of the Gulf need to examine. In other words, the audience the Gulf provided was one for whom the public school education particularly, if by chance, prepared men. Roland Barthes writes:

> Yet 'private life' changes according to the *Doxa* [popular opinion] one addresses: if it is a *Doxa* of the right (bourgeois, petit bourgeois: institutions, laws, press), it is the sexual private life which exposes most. But if it is a *Doxa* of the left, the sexual exposition transgresses nothing: here 'private life' is trivial actions, the traces of bourgeois ideology confessed by the subject: confronting this *Doxa*, I am less exposed in declaring a perversion than in uttering a taste: passion, friendship, tenderness, sentimentality, delight in writing, then become, by simple structural displacement, *unspeakable* terms: contradicting what can be said, what it is expected that you would say, but which precisely – the very voice of the image-system – you would like to be able to say *immediately* (without mediation).[5]

Ritual was essential to the larger-than-life requirements of Imperial role playing.[6] Incorporated into this ritualism and integral to the Imperial *persona* was a lifelong identification with the public schools; affiliation with a school was part of a man's personality. Amplifications and standardizations of Imperial character invoke public school images. There was a 'prefect-style'[7] which evolved from the public schools. The changes in this style through the years are mirrored by changes in the public school novel:

> In place of the evolutionary optimism of *Tom Brown's Schooldays*, Kipling affirms the continuing validity of more primitive, less socialised skills – 'stalking' rather than cricket. In place of the smooth progress and fluent moralism of the Victorian *Bildungsroman*, he offers a series of what seem arbitrary chosen episodes, with no connecting principle of development and

> an oblique, questioning relationship to the social morality of the day...*Stalky* stands in relation to the Hughes tradition as a training manual to a prospectus: it celebrates the qualities necessary to make an existing Empire work, not the qualities it might be nice to encourage if life obeyed the rules of a cricket-match.[8]

Stalky's emphasis on the practical does not contradict another characteristic of old boy Imperialists: an inclination to reject objective scientism in favour of the irrational, *masquerading as common sense.*[9] Bertrand Russell, who put the responsibility for moulding the Imperial psyche on the experiences of schooldays, claimed that when the old boy became ensconced as a district officer: 'Instinctively he looks about for opportunities of similar enjoyments in later life: he desires people to govern, people to whom he will seem a god-like being...he becomes an empire-builder, an outpost of culture, a man whose mission it is to bring Western enlightenment into dark places. If the "natives" regard him as the small boys did during his last years at school, all goes well: he is kind and gracious, upright and hard-working, stoical about the loneliness and discomfort, which are no worse than what he endured in his first years at school.'[10] Observers have been similarly unkind to the Raj in Arabia, and psychobabble about the mystique of the desert gets short shrift from Jan Morris when she reviews Wilfred Thesiger's *The Life of My Choice*: 'He is anything but a desert mystic. For years he enthusiastically shot almost any animal that came within range (he liked "the sound of the bullet striking home"), and his fondness for tradition by no means excludes traditional brutality. After telling us in horrible details about ritual beatings at Eton...he concludes that the school taught him the decencies of life and standards of civilised behaviour. After describing with approval the Bedu custom of revenge by blood-feud, he observes that he has "no belief in the sanctity of life".'[11]

The relevance of the public school to psychohistorical aspects of Gulf historiography emerges in at least three ways whereby Gulfites participated in initiatory rituals. They were those of school, of secret societies, and of the quasi-mystical Imperial vocation.[12] Indeed, the impact of the oxymoronic initiations through which the IPS officers had passed during school was enhanced by the vacuum left when an unmysterious post-Darwin Anglicanism dispensed with initiatory cultic values. After allowing for the exception of the growing ritualism of the Oxford Movement, the impression is of an increasing lack in the nineteenth century of a secret corpus of doctrines and rituals in religion that was partly compensated for by the esoterica of public schoolism, Freemasonry, and Imperialism. The glory of the schools, lodge, and Empire replaced the church's *gloria*. Imperialism became a homeopathic cure for extreme Protestantism, as did Puseyism and High Church ritualism.[13] The number of Anglican churches in England employing vestments increased from 336 in 1882 to 2158 in 1901, and the number that used incense grew from 9 to 393.[14]

All the same, in psychohistorical considerations of Imperialism, ritualism cannot be considered as synonymous with mysticism. Despite affinities with Anglo-Catholicism and Freemasonry, Imperial ceremonialism could be the opposite of mysticism and at times was embarrassingly literal. The practical

'Stalkiness' of the later Imperialists is not incompatible with the ritualistic aspects of their behaviour and proved to be long-lived:

> The optimistic Victorian moralism of 'fair play' expunged in Kipling's revision of the Hughes code is not replaced by anything of comparable largeness and decency, but by something narrower, more efficient, more 'realistic'. The historical irony fifty years after Kipling's death is that, while the Empire his schoolboys trained for is now indeed at one with Nineveh and Tyre, an Indian cricket team can still tour England playing a game not very different from that played by Tom Brown. The code so vigorously revised in *Stalky & Co.* clearly has some life in it yet.[15]

Creative Tensions

Opportunities exist in dealing with *British* biographical subjects to move back and forth between the particular and the general, but Gulf studies have lacked a similar appreciation of the tension between *Arab* biography and the socio-cultural systems which are a creative part of psychohistory. In an Arab context, appreciation of the interplay between individual and tribe, and in a British context the interplay between the Resident and the social system which begat him, suggest dimensions which plain vanilla political studies do not. The lack of biographies of Arabs challenges the abilities of indigenous academics with newly-minted doctorates provided by the oil bonanza. The ruling families are replete with larger-than-life figures whose biographies would beggar the imagination as far as conspicuous consumption and huge appetites of the flesh are concerned. (See Plate 25.) This helps explain why the reaction of the average Arab to the plunder of Kuwait has been far from the indignation of Washington. 'Yes, the Kuwaitis are demonstrating. They are demonstrating in the Riviera and in European capitals,' a Jordanian professor told the journalist Nora Boustany. (*Guardian Weekly*, 12 August 1990.) He added that the Kuwaiti money spent on the high life would have been better spent to 'feed the starving Sudanese'.

It is unlikely that *any* professor in the Gulf will dare to explore the psyches of the reigning families. In any event, Gulf studies will not be left to the Arabs even if they do get their scholarly act together, as Western academics have more than enough to do concerning the region within their own English language bound preserves. The scarcity of biographies about Residents illustrates how much remains to be done by those at home with Western archives. Lewis Pelly, Edward Ross, the Lorimer brothers, and Gerald de Gaury are priority cases for biographers. Percy Cox and Arnold Wilson have had biographers, but not critical ones. They are candidates for a joint biography, a psychohistorical study describing how Wilson progressed in Cox's life from being *amanuensis* to *alter ego* and then fell from grace. The same approach would be suitable for the relationship between Cox and Curzon. Another instance is Pelly's lifelong relationship with Bartle Frere, whom he regarded as a father. (See Plate 26.) Arguably Curzon and Frere from afar, through Cox and Pelly, had as much influence on the Gulf as did many who actually lived there. When biographies do appear about the Gulfites, such geneo-psychological factors should not be ignored.

More than a paragraph is required to explain the motivations and expectations of anyone who left home, spent years overseas, dominated large numbers of foreign peoples, and claimed a moral superiority over those of other societies. What went into being a Sahib, a Nabob, or a Raj (or later a Stormin' Norman) was not sugar, sunshine and rum. Ambition was part of the brew. At times the deference that was expected and exacted as part of this epigrammatic equation verged on the psychopathic; just what part attitudes towards colour played in Imperial dominance remains controversial.[16]

Graven Images

Equally controversial aetiologically is the Gulf's iconography and how much of it is African thanks to slavery, how much is Indian, and how much is Persian. The making of graven images may have been biblically proscribed, but it has continued unrelentingly in political cultures of all sorts, with surprisingly little interest on the part of historians to 'descend some distance into these speculative caverns'.[17] A nagging suspicion recurs in looking back at the Empire that although appearances can be reconstructed, *e.g.* the Tussaud exhibit at Windsor railway station of Queen Victoria receiving foreign guests, the origins and meanings remain elusive. The archetypal factors have escaped notice, despite Jung's warning that 'the psychology of modern man depends upon its historical roots, and can only be judged by its ethnological variants.'[18] Gulf historians need to be oneirocritics.

Notions that at least some of the ritualism of the Gulf and its iconography can be traced to the English public schools partly depends on the extent to which the adolescence of the Residents and Agents exerted permanent psychological effects. This can be debated but unquestionably existed, for adolescence is when a personality is most pliable. The last lines of T.E. Lawrence's *Seven Pillars of Wisdom* acknowledge that: 'I had dreamed, at the City School in Oxford, of hustling into form, while I lived, the new Asia which time was inexorably bringing upon us. Mecca was to lead to Damascus, Damascus to Anatolia, and afterwards to Baghdad; and then there was Yemen. Fantasies, these will seem, to such as are able to call my beginning an ordinary effort.'[19] Psychohistory has a long way to go before becoming acceptable in some historical circles, but days have passed when Imperial motives could be completely laid at the door of tariff policy or naval strategy.

The Raj enjoyed a luxuriantly ritualistic and ceremoniously colourful life, albeit with hardships as a price. *He was commissioned as a symbol, the representative of the Queen-Empress or King-Emperor.* Surely this involved a psychological fulfilment of deferred ambitions for certain of the IPS, the opportunity finally to be head boy. That can be in turn dismissed as an ego trip, a taste for aggrandizement and power. On the other hand, the Raj had a flair sorely missed in modern political life, or for that matter everywhere on the contemporary stage. Nor were the personal consequences altogether bad. Imperial *savoir vivre* was useful in coping with the psychological pressures of living in the Gulf, where Europeans could go 'around the bend':

> The symptoms of this affliction are extreme pessimism about life in general, loss of appetite, a penchant for excessive drinking, loss of memory, and the liability to unreasoned fits of temper over the slightest thing. The only remedy is to return the patient without delay to England or, if this is impracticable, send him on leave to a hill station in India...Some men find a deep inner enjoyment in living in lonely places, and occupy their minds by taking a creative interest in the country, the people and their language, and the flora and fauna...To others the mere sight of the desert is anathema and they quickly tire of the strange sights and the romance provided by the Arabian mode of life. They detest the sun and the heat, complain of the food and the discomfort and try to maintain exactly the same sort of life they enjoyed in suburbia. Behaving as they would on holiday in Brighton, they expose themselves to the dangerous tropical sun, drink far more than is good for them even in a European climate and, when they begin to feel unwell, sink into an incurable melancholia for which the only cure is a ship home.[20]

The isolation of the posts contributed to ectopic conduct. Residents and Agents constitute a striking assemblage of unreconstructed individualists, a self-appointed pantheon of father figures. A disproportionate number of this small coterie published and achieved fame. On the other hand, several committed suicide or met bizarre deaths, confirming Sir Ronald Wingate's view that appointment to the Gulf was 'a form of punishment or exile or the reward of eccentricity'. John Lorimer died in a suspicious gun accident. Captain Shakespear courted suicide by staying by a field gun in the face of several hundred advancing tribesmen. Such demises recall that Lawrence's death in a motorcycle accident still stirs controversy.

The fascination Arabia exerted had psychohistorical implications. Thackeray (himself an Old Carthusian and the son of an East India Company official) wrote in *Notes of a Journey from Cornhill to Grand Cairo*: 'Walk into the bazaar, and the East is unveiled to you; how often and often have you tried to fancy this, lying out on a summer holiday at school! It is wonderful, too, how like it is; you may imagine that you have been in the place before, you seem to know it so well!' Parallels between school and later postings in the Imperial services are several. Partly because of the prefect-fag relationship that was part of their schooling, the British had a proprietary feeling about 'their Arabs' and savoured what they felt was a unique relationship.[21] This affection may have been counter-productive for the Arabs, the British wanted them to be romantic swashbuckling sons of the desert, a part incompatible with economic and educational progress. Arabs admired by the Residents would be unlikely to embrace Western technology and democracy, or to challenge British feelings of superiority. Deference and rusticity, not 'radical' democracy, were the way to friendship.

Role and Rehearsals

Self-confidence was essential to Imperial hegemony. Public schools made the Residents the self-assured men they were, and provided them with their ideology. School was an adolescent rehearsing for adult roles. Whether parents, religion, and other forces were equally or more significant psychologically than the schools has to be considered – evidence suggests that at the very least, schooling was important.

The men singled out in this study exerted control over a vast area of the Middle East and that took considerable *chutzpah.* A major contribution to this confidence was their education. The ability of the public schools to engender an overweening *presence* was central to the IPS success in the Gulf. Freemasonry's contribution to this confidence is noted in Chapter VI, although its psychological impact on initiates remains unexplored. There has been nothing written about influences that longtime lodge membership had on personality. Perhaps the lodge experience can be regarded like the public school experience as a rehearsal for Imperial roles. Professor David Stevenson of the University of Aberdeen has put forward the more complicated thesis that Masonry relates to the *art of memory.* He explains:

> The art of memory was a technique for improving the capacity of one's memory which developed in ancient Greece but is mainly known through Roman writers...The Greek mnemonic technique was based on a building. The student of the art was instructed to study some large and complex building, memorising its rooms and layout, and particular features or places in it. In doing this he should establish a specific order in which he visited the individual rooms and places. When memorising a speech, he should then imagine himself to be walking through this building on his set route, and in each of the *loci* or places he had memorised he should establish *imagines* or images which were to be attached to each argument or point in his speech.[22]

The *genius loci* again! Should Freemasonry be found to be related to such a psychologically fundamental topic as memory, there would be consequences for the personality development of members.[23] Masonry's claim to be a resurrection of ancient wisdom about the memory implies that the Imperial leadership who were Freemasons were possessed of a particular mind-set that lodge membership gave them, one linking 'the powers of imagination with moral activity'.[24] Recurring motifs in Masonic rituals – the Babylonian captivity, Jerusalem, restoring the temple – may have become part of the Imperial outlook.

Such speculations are engaging, yet the Raj's personality remains largely uncharted, having been contradictorily characterized as disciplined, austere, hedonistic, and ostentatious. Something of a consensus exists about the ubiquity of a few characteristics. Imperial rulers were depressingly punctilious and so are the shaikhs – an indication of the importance of ritualistic behaviour. There is plenty of apocryphal and anecdotal evidence of this. In *The Perfect Victorian Hero,* Michael Brander describes the domestic life of Sir Samuel Baker (1821-1893): 'The clocks all chimed together. There was no indulgence for lateness. When the gong boomed for dinner up got Sam and if no Number One lady was present he would latch on to Number Two and walk off with her to the dining room. When at last the poor breathless defaulter rustled in he would bow her to her seat with rather awesome ceremony.'[25]

Ritualism could verge on obsessional-compulsive-disorder. There were closet Lady Macbeths, and there may have been victims of what is a little understood physical affliction, an obscure disease with ritualistic symptoms as physical in origin as Parkinson's and Tourette's Syndrome. Curiously, some 'natives' who suffered from the Imperial social meticulousness acquired a perverse affection for its precision, 'down to the last crease in the damask napkins at their dinner-table'.[26] In India after the British departed, the Raj's style has been perpetuated by an imitative colonialism, whose guardians are an upper class infected by 'Raj-mania'.

The Gulf, thanks to remoteness rather than precept, received less of a dose of Viceregal pretentiousness. That did not prevent the Arabs from succumbing to its blandishments as had the Indians. Reality was replaced by affection for the pavilion etiquette of the Imperials. More sinisterly, along with the stylish sartorial symbolism (warned the Government of India *Dress Regulations* in 1931, 'With butcher boots, field boots and ankle boots, hunting spurs of sealed pattern will be worn; with butcher boots, steel chains and black strap; with black ankle boots, black straps and shield (no chains); with brown field and ankle boots, brown straps and shield (no chains); with Wellington boots, box spurs with plain rowels') – a sartorialism which appeared more ludicrous in Arabia than in Rajastan – came a touch of racism. Racism is supposedly anathema to Islam, and the religion's claimed colour blindness has been a reason for its spread. Despite this, the shaikhdoms were not exempted from racial tension. The IPS record on race there is chequered and the present situation is little better; blacks are poorly represented in positions of authority. Palestinians and Indians have no legal existence.

Racist attitudes were an unplanned consequence of the overwhelming cultural apartheid that ritualism enforced, but much racism was also deliberate. A barometer of its extent and degree was the membership of clubs. The Gulfites were virtually all members of clubs in London, as well as of the club in the particular place where they were assigned for the moment. The story of how the Willingdon Club in Bombay was founded indicates how racist the Empire could be. Lord Willingdon, at the time Governor of Bombay, invited several Maharajas to dinner at the Yacht Club. When they didn't appear, he asked where they were and was informed that they were waiting outside because Indians were not allowed: 'And he then and there wrote his resignation from the Yacht Club. He collected whatever food he could – he was Governor after all – and they went to Government House and had dinner. And that day they sat down and decided to form a club. Lord Willingdon said: "Yes, for Indians only." And all the Maharajas, who gave a lot of money, said: "No, we're not vindictive. It's for everybody." And that's how it was called the Willingdon Club.'[27]

Exclusion and blackballing are part of club life, but there are other psychological aspects to club (and lodge) membership. The severely male atmosphere was not encouraging to natives who might be tempted to allow their wives to enter into society. Nor did discrimination levied at even high born native leaders set a good precedent for social integration between them and their own people. One wonders how much racism and reflexive radicalism today reflects British behaviour in the years when clubs were opinion makers.

Black skins are absent in the high councils of business and government, marriages between those of fair and darker complexions are few, and perhaps unconsciously the most visible part assigned to the black Gulf Arab is of entertainer and music maker – much as was the fate of blacks in a segregated United States of America. Lots of really black faces appear only when a bit of folk culture is required by ministries of information. (See Plate 27.)

While the Gulf did not have the money in pre-petroleum days to maintain the social divisions that were nurtured in India, the consequences of the Raj mentality may have been the same. Education certainly was a prerogative of the shaikhs. Throughout the Empire not only clubs but schools reinforced the racist ego-building that made the Raj what it was:

> Along with Christian ethics went an often incongruous imitation of the secular ceremonial of the great British public schools – neo-Gothic cloisters and quadrangles, prefects and monitors clad in ties and blazers, and fish fingers and jam roll for dinner. Even a day school like the Cathedral was divided up into 'Houses', each with its own colours, to encourage the competitive team-spirit at games and exams; and its school song was set to the music of Harrow's 'Forty Years On'. Like their British models, the schools of the Raj laid great store by patriotism. But the patriotism they celebrated was British; and for Indians under British rule that could be confusing.[28]

Once the Residents and Agents felt that they had become the uncontestable masters of the Gulf, they willingly became role models for an admiring local leadership. Part of the Imperialist mentality was a fiction that the 'locals' *enjoyed* being dominated.[29] There are toadies in every society, and there is no reason to doubt that the affection for Imperial mannerisms that pervaded the Indian ruling class lacked a Gulf counterpart. Leadership was fluid and there would have been a natural desire to secure it and shore it up by securing British patronage.[30] In any event, whether by emulation or by rejection, the Arabs were compelled to respond to the Imperial centripetal force. If the views of one authority are accepted, the role model was not altogether an easy one for the IPS to provide, and recalls Anthony Sampson's phrase 'the public school proletariat':

> The disparity between the public school product oriented for leadership and the bureaucratic subordinate positions available to him led to admonitions against the outmoded practices of the public school. Not only was the system itself outdated, said critics, but the sort of man that it sustained was outmoded as well. There were not enough positions of authority left to justify the mass production of English gentlemen of the Empire...Victorian hyper-patriots and gentlemen were succeeded by the more conventional gentleman of the early twentieth century who was still urbane, snobbish, and well-mannered, but perhaps also more petty.[31]

Psychological changes did take place, as is indicated in the possible titles of the books in this series: *Tom Brown in Arabia, Stalky & Stormin' Norman*

Meet the Gulf Shaikhs, and *Billy Bunter and the Arabs*. An effort will be made to show that in the Gulf the hyper-patriots of Tom Brown's day ultimately were succeeded by more petty-minded gentlemen of a Billy Bunter cachet. Not coincidentally, the first significant Resident of the IPS era, Lewis Pelly, was a contemporary at Rugby of Thomas Hughes, the author of *Tom Brown's Schooldays*. The characters in the book, in so far as Hughes modelled them on his schoolfellows, are the schoolmates and lifelong friends of Pelly.

Group Psychohistory

Psychobiography and psychohistory face enough challenges when used in considering one life; hardly ever does documentation survive to give conclusive answers to questions about group-mentality or *Massenpsychologie*. When prosopography takes on a psychohistorical slant, the problems of sources are multiplied many times over. Every individual has to be examined with attention to the detail that usually is associated with a full length biography. Further confusing the issue is that group psychohistory when associated with prosopography involves psychopolitics, a term now popular to differentiate psychoanalytic approaches to politics from general psychohistory and from academic psychology. The justification made for separating psychopolitical studies from psychohistory is a need to emphasize the effects of personality on decision-making. Conceivably this reflects a distaste over past misuse of psychohistory in group-mentality studies:

> ...this branch of psychology tended to concentrate its attention on extreme forms of group behaviour such as the outbreaks of mass-hysteria in the Middle Ages, or Le Bon's classic studies of the French Revolution (which Freud and others took as their text). This tendency to focus attention on the dramatic manifestations of mass-psychology made them overlook the more general principles underlying group mentality and its dominant influence on human history, past and present. For one thing, a person need not be physically present in a crowd to be affected by the group-mind; emotive identification with a nation, Church or political movement can be quite effective without physical contact. One can be a victim of group-fanaticism even in the privacy of one's bathroom.[32]

Psychopolitical studies can be encompassed in a psychohistorical approach, but when actions and emotions are considered as the shared patterns of a group, 'their comprehension seems almost beyond imagination'.[33] The bulk of studies being made of the psyche of groups are of now existing groups and appear as current research in sociological literature; far less common are investigations of groups from the past. Study of group mentality of now vanished cadres is not quite as difficult as this implies. When group psychohistory is attempted, it first has to take into account the group's self-image. This can be determined by attention to the full spectrum of surviving evidence – even the tailors' bills are relevant, as the subjects may have covered their tracks. The official posture held out to the world by the IPS was of poise, ability, and power. Only occasionally do the official records permit a behind-the-scenes view of the Service's foibles and fallibility.

The Gulfites themselves expressed doubts about just how select and how motivated they were. In 1938, Tom Hickinbotham, sometime Bahrain Agent and Secretary to the Resident, and at the time of his writing the Civil secretary in Aden, wrote a memorandum about recruitment in which he complained about the reluctance of IPS officers to come to the Gulf: 'He is averse to being appointed, as he is afraid that when he is appointed he can never leave it. There are, however, a few eccentrics who prefer the Gulf to India and like living with and dealing with the Arabs.'[34] Hickinbotham thought the answer might be to separate the Gulf administration from the IPS and create a Department of Arab Affairs, warning that 'Careful handling of the personnel of the "Department of Arab Affairs" will be necessary since those that serve the country in Arabia are unusual people. They become scarcely normal about Arab affairs in their own part of Arabia.' An anonymous hand has added a marginal note to the file reading 'They aren't *all* Philbys'.[35] A departmental minute notes Hickinbotham's suggestion 'the present system in the Persian Gulf, if it does not provide for continuity as sufficiently as one could wish, at least calls for introduction of fresh blood and a change of work for the officers concerned. That is better than a self-contained cadre of cranks whom Captain Hickinbotham seems to envisage suggesting that their crankiness may be mitigated by circulating them around the different posts in Arabia.'[36]

There were others who questioned the intentions of *all* of those who joined the IPS. Edward Oaten, the head of the Indian Educational Service, recalled a conversation with Richard Maconachie, a fellow Old Tonbridgian who had joined the IPS and at the time was a deputy commissioner:

> When I called on him, I found him whiling away his loneliness by reading through Gibbon's history of the 'Decline and Fall of the Roman Empire'. We discussed the political situation in India. He told me that he had chosen the Political Department of the Civil Service because he foresaw that freedom must come to British India, sooner or later, and that the Political Service would be Indianized last. He illustrated his argument by quoting a conversation which he had had with one of the semi-independent Maharajahs, Patila, I think. Patila had said to him: 'Maconachie, British India must become, in due course, Indian. But can you imagine an *Indian* coming to me with the orders of the Central Government? Why, I'd kick him downstairs.'[37]

The Arabs had role models who were closer to home than IPS officers with views like those of Maconachie, albeit mythologized. As has been pointed out, they admired (but did not practise) a centrifugal ideology of nomad heroes. The Gulf was always a more urban place than the prevailing mythology of today admits. All the same the idealized way of life was much freer of constraints than that which the Victorians cultivated. Without applying too psychological an interpretation to why these dreams of freedom have never been realized in the Gulf, it can be observed that the effect of the Imperial presence was repressive for political life and an invitation to radical dissent.

Little is written about the consequences of British martinetism, while there had been until recently an abundance of comment about the effects of the East on Westerners. Professor Edward Said changed that situation.

What surprised the perceptive readers about Edward Said's *Orientalism* was that he tried to come to terms with the effect of the West's East on the real East. *Orientalism* was really about *Occidentalism*. Seldom in the Middle East does one hear about the 'East'. Incessantly the harping goes on about the West, and for excellent reasons:

> ...the critique of orientalism leaves us open to a peculiar form of indigenous conservatism posing as progressive anti-westernism. In some Arab intellectual circles, Foucault has been virtually stood on his head. The argument goes like this. If the critique of orientalism is true, then all western observations are a distortion of the real nature of Islam. Therefore, our own version of ourselves is true. While it is clear that what Muslims say about themselves, 'must have a central role in the enquiry' into Islam, the 'internal' evidence cannot have an exclusively privileged position. We do not want to exchange an outdated Orientalism for an equally prejudicial Occidentalism.[38]

Incumbent rulers gain by perpetuating ignorance about this IPS involvement in sustaining regimes, because legitimacy is bolstered by invoking the indigenous rather than the imported. The desire to conceal British participation gives the current Gulf leadership something in common with the anonymity sought by the Imperial myth-makers themselves such as Maconachie and his IPS ilk. The danger is that the successors to the British in power are in danger of being perceived as time-warped surrogates of the Raj, and thus as unconvincingly Arab nationalists. They sorely need better advisers in dealing with such problems.

Their life style has attracted far too much comment and fuelled radical criticism, as the following quotation describing a visit to camel racing in Dubai from *The Hindu* (23 September 1989) demonstrates – the truth of which this author can fully endorse:

> There were four or five temporary huts, where some people were engaged in feeding camels. In one of the huts, there were seven or eight children who had injuries and even fractures sustained after riding the camels in the race. Both were told by some Indians and Pakistanis already residing in the Omalkhand area, about 200 km from Dubai, that the children were tied to the camel's back and forced to ride the animal in the race. To speed up the camels, electric shocks and whips were used. Worse, the wailing of children riding them also made the animals run faster. But the sadistic shaikhs would not bother about the injuries the children sustained. If the child died in the race, he would be buried on the spot...They pleaded with the shaikh, who was organising the camel race, to release the children. But the shaikh would not listen and reportedly said that he had purchased the five.

Anyone who has left his luxury hotel and poked about the dirty byways of a Gulf city knows that slavery is alive in the shaikhdoms. It can be called contract labour, but in essentials it is slavery. The hypocrisy is that the Western Christian expatriate is treated far better by the Arabs than the Muslim brethren who are bought as cheap labour. Having paid agents and corrupt Gulf Arabs for the jobs, they often work two or three years before they have paid off those debts and can begin to accumulate anything for themselves. The public relations chief of this author's department in the Ministry of Education in Qatar extracted every year a month's salary from each of the Indian Muslims he had brought to Qatar. He felt no obligation to find them a job or otherwise help them – they paid, shifted for themselves, or were deported. He also badgered them to find (illegal) liquor for him; few are the veterans of Gulf service who have not been asked to locate booze for their Muslim colleagues. The utter depravity of many of the shaikhs has not been fully reported, and that is why the Iraq-Kuwait situation appears in such stark black-and-white terms.

In the Gulf and elsewhere Professor Said's Orientalism has become an excuse that apologists use for the graft and repression that he abhors. Criticism is now dismissed as Orientalism:

> In order to cope with their profound economic and social problems, Arabs must first consider some equally profound political changes. Sounds obvious? Not, alas, to erudite Arabists in western universities, who caution against applying western tests of democracy in an Arab context. The Arabs, they say, are primed by Islam to accept or even to relish authoritarian government...Those are indeed views to which Arab rulers find it convenient to subscribe. But ordinary Arabs have little trouble understanding what the West, and now increasingly the East, mean by democracy. Arabs are as keen as Indians, Americans, Poles and Rumanians to see their rulers' autocratic power constrained by checks and balances. They would like the chance to remove unpopular leaders through the ballot box instead of uprisings or coups. And they are denied that right by rulers who cling ruthlessly to power, not by some ineffable cultural handicap it takes a professional Arabist to understand.[39]

An attempt at group psychohistory involves considering the Arab as well as British psyche. The part the shaikhs played when parleying with the British was turned around when they stood in a relationship to their own subjects – but despite emulation of the Residents' tactics it was hard to acquire the self-confidence that made the strategy workable. The mystique of the Raj involved the native being cast as impulsive and lacking discipline, whether he was a shaikh or commoner. The legacy includes a lack of self-confidence, both in rulers and ruled. This insecurity hides behind a cultural smokescreen which often depicts the West as a sink of depravity and uses modesty to excuse treating the female half of the population with amazingly boyish immaturity. As would-be father figures, the leadership shore up egos by recourse to force rather than reason, attested by the mushrooming amounts spent on internal security.

The shaikhs' nauseating self-imaging that has accompanied the purchase of armaments recalls the Raj's cultivation of an image as the magnanimous but strong-willed ruler who took care of his children: 'The task of looking after the child, in an age moulded by the public-school spirit, could not be performed without the help of the rod...'.[40] By twist of fate, the wholesale acquisition by the shaikhs of armaments, which may amount to nearly half the total income they have derived from oil since 1930, has proved futile. The Imperialists have been invited back. The American Marines, the British 'Desert Rats', and the French Foreign Legion returned when the Iraqis threatened. This is after the endless talk about the abilities of the Gulf *mujaahid* or holy warrior, the references to the inherent martial virtues that supposedly were part of the *al-qiyamor* value system of the Gulf Arabs, and the drivel about the virtues of the Gulf's *ri'aasa* or shaikhy leadership.

Dark Things

In summary, psychohistorical approaches to Imperial cadres and to the shaikhs can be profitable, especially when reinforced by social history and by recourse to Max Weber, the *Annales* school, and Braudel. Unearthed are unattractive aspects to the character of those studied, evidence of immaturity and self-centredness – and worse. At times little subtlety hid the pleasures derived from being head prefect of a school or a colony.

In *The Guardian* (30 May 1990), an old girl comments concerning the difference between girls' and boys' public schools: 'Boys have sex with each other at school; girls don't. [*A questionable assumption.*] No wonder they have these bonds.' The article, *The Best Years of a Girl's Life?* claims about girls' schools that 'The power and the clout, the paraphernalia of belonging isn't there', but the reader has the feeling that girls leave school to get married while boys leave school to a life of old boy networking. Whether this had a strong homosexual side and whether the public schools were responsible or not for creating homosexual Imperialists, there seems to be much more research required to show the relevance of the *flagrante delicto* of deviant sexual aspects to the Imperial joy in dominance. Suspicions frequently have been mooted, for the essence of Imperial dedication seemed to be not regard or love but an emotion verging on the sado-masochistic. This impulse relates to homo-eroticism – but does not *necessarily* produce overt homosexuality. The temptation of linking the public school and Arab interests in homosexuality has to be resisted. Nevertheless Gulf homosexuality is ubiquitous.

Opportunities for heterosexual activity were severely limited. The lack of comment about this may have been thanks to 'old-fashioned delicacy'; more plausibly there was sublimation involved. In the writings of the IPS officers, 'There is seldom a reference to the most commonplace of biological facts, and one feels that, beneath the busy beards and thick-lensed sun-glasses, there bubbled a veritable volcano of repressions.'[41] The public schools produced sado-masochists and homo-erotics, and turned out their share of homosexuals. Robert Graves remarks:

> Rendall, the then Headmaster of Charterhouse, is reported to have innocently said at a Headmasters' Conference: 'My boys are amorous, but seldom erotic'...I agree with Rendall's distinction between 'amorousness' (by which he meant a sentimental falling in love with younger boys) and eroticism, or adolescent lust. The intimacy that frequently took place was very seldom between an elder boy and the object of his affection – that would have spoiled the romantic illusion – but almost always between boys of the same age who were not in love, and used each other as convenient sex-instruments. So the atmosphere was always heavy with romance of a conventional early-Victorian type, complicated by cynicism and foulness.[42]

The Gulf was a stressful environment, and an end result could be homosexuality or sublimation in paperwork. The employment of young native boys as assistants or *farash* was common and the Hindi word has entered Gulf Arabic. (Nineteenth-century scandals in the Punjab involving the British and their young helpers will be recalled.)

Freud does not have to be invoked to note the implications to Victoria as *Regina et Imperatrix,* and how she took on mother-figure aspects in old age. The Imperial leadership shared other images too: 'Shared feelings and fantasies in the group are communicated unconsciously and indirectly. They are embedded in other ideas subliminally, to slip them past the conscious mind of group members. The subliminal element is a linguistic pattern or style of unconscious communication that the leader seems somehow to have an unconscious aptitude for. The subliminal style says what the group wants indirectly but quite powerfully; it speaks directly to the unconscious.'[43] Therein lies some of the not-so-latent power of Freemasonry.

Masonic Archetypes and the Gulf

Doubts as to whether a ration of psychohistory can help, and whether a 'nefarious' side exists, are allied when confronted with the murky involvement of the IPS with Freemasonry. The Imperial and Victorian prosperity of Freemasonry involved a revival of archetypes which had vanished from the humdrum world of commerce and the routine of government bureaucracy. Spengler has much to say about the loss of the world outlook of the Middle Ages which appreciated an invisible world that existed side by side with the tangible world. There were demons rather than neuroses, and guardian angels rather than luck. Religion had a hundred ambiguous gods and there was poetry and wonder. This living in what Spengler called a quivering cavern-light was going missing in the nineteenth century. Masonry restored it.[44] Masonic ties of the IPS are *prima facie* evidence of a *mentalité* involving the love of secrecy:

> Masonry and the Establishment support one another, and Freemasonry is the more easily ridiculed with its self-important air of secrecy, its rituals, and special sign language. In fact, the highly prized secrets of Freemasonry are not the rituals but the secret grips and signs these ceremonies teach. These are provided, along with Masonry's protection against personal

feelings of insecurity and insignificance, so that Masons anywhere can recognize each other and begin to behave towards each other in a special way...The Mason belongs to a society which professes universal brotherhood, but is exclusive; the movement condemns patronage, but is capable of conferring it; and, while it maintains it is not a religion, it apes religious ceremonies. Freemasonry exploits deeply rooted desires for true brotherhood and religion, yet offers neither. Its continued existence as a sad shadow across our national life is an advertisement of the fact that many men have stopped searching for true brotherhood and religion and appear to have lost the vision of what these might be.[45]

These are hard words, and deserve investigation. While Masonry seems to have been important to IPS officers, the question arises why this was. One of the brotherhood, R.L. Kennion, points out in *Diversions of an Indian Political* that the IPS were 'rolling stones'.[46] Masonic lodges provided a stability missed in moving from post to post. Membership meant that there would be friends wherever the officer would be sent. In addition, Masonic rituals provided a training in oratorical technique rather like the worldwide Toastmasters' International luncheon club offers today for businessmen. Arabs would have been susceptible to manipulation at the hands of someone versed in abracadabra. Some Arabs according to an observer were of 'dark mind which sees deep motive in all objective existence and even in inanimate things.' They peopled their world 'with forms that are mere chimera to the Westerner.' The mention of a unicorn did not make them laugh.[47]

Regardless of this and of the pragmatic reasons underlying membership, including the charities that provided a form of insurance for a man's family in the event of death, lodge cabalism suggests psychohistorical forces at work that merit study. A text for this is *Kim*, and it is surprising that such polymaths as Edward Said have missed its abundance of Masonic allusions.[48]

Not only can Masonry be approached through its own literature and historiography; it can be considered in terms of psychohistory. A lodge affiliation indicates certain emotional and aesthetic propensities and recalls claims about psychohistory: '...history and psychohistory are clearly different. History, though interpretative, is essentially concerned with representing historical reality as best the scholar is able. Psychohistory, on the other hand, reverses this emphasis, being almost totally concerned with interpretation and slightly concerned with the representation and description of historical reality...Psychohistorians emphasize the importance of emotion and fantasy in their explanations.'[49] This would be a Rankean interpretation; E.H. Carr would not approve! Substitute 'Masonry' for 'psychohistory' in the quotation and the result is a quite adequate explanation of the movement.

To perhaps overdo the *mot juste*, the stumbling block to responding to a *cri de coeur* for the use of psychohistory or *pari passu* Masonic historiography is that no matter what inner thoughts are at work, much of what shapes an individual remains external. A simple example is that Masonry has been declining in numbers as entertainment such as television expands. With a hundred channels to watch, the lodge brothers have temptations to stay at home that they did not have in the Victorian era. 'Try as we might, we are all creatures of fashion and prisoners of the *zeitgeist*.'[50] The steadying influence of mainstream history is always needed, despite the arresting interest of byways such as psychohistory – or Masonry.

What could be put down to clandestine secret movements may well be explained by more widespread, if unglamorous causes such as the daily newspaper or radio broadcasts. And when psychohistory and collective biography are employed in understanding the policies of the Empire, a prosopographical *pandect* must balance between speculation about 'mind-sets' and pragmatism reflecting 'facts'. The facts, after all, can explain the *culture* of a group more coherently than can psychohistorical speculation. Still in all, having made that admission, there persist benefits to combining prosopographical analysis with psychohistorical insights.

The public school ethos involves archetypes repeated in the Imperial tapestry. *The prefect-fag relationship would be high on a list of recurrent motifs.* Relationships based on subservience that were created and cherished by Imperialism have provided an opportunity for the novelist; E.M. Forster's *A Passage to India* has as much insight into the psychohistory of Imperialism as does non-fiction. The relationship of prefect and fag can be compared to that of colonial master and subject, and of Resident and Gulf Arab. Did it not also *inspire* such relationships? Imperial ritualism contributed to the charged and often erotic relationships that existed. Dominance and submission are a recurring theme. They are what passes for Gulf politics today.

The prefect-fag relationship can mask the insecurities that the supposed master feels, which D.K. Fieldhouse perceptively noted in *Colonialism 1870-1945:*

> The system made no provision for those indigenous people who acquired education, emancipated themselves from traditional forms of deference and expected to obtain work and respect related to their achievements, not their social origins. Such men found themselves frustrated in most colonies because Europeans monopolized top posts, but it was worst for them in places where archaic social and political systems were bolstered against change by the colonial authorities. Men of this kind received little sympathy from most white officials, who seem to have felt empathy with African chiefs and Indian princes rather than with those educated Africans or Indians who more closely resembled themselves. This may have been partly due to the tendency for officials of middle or lower middle-class origin to respect men who bore some resemblance to those European landed gentry on whom they often seem to have modelled themselves...The British were right to believe that the easiest way to run their colonial empire was to act as the allies of established conservative élites wherever these could be found. With such people the imperialists could make a mutually rewarding deal.

Masonry made the same sort of Imperial deal, initiating the native élite. This was the ultimate compromising of loyalty for an Indian or an Arab, because he became oath-bound to support the brethren over his own. Public school Freemasonry went one better, for it combined two total and greedy institutions that delighted in symbolism and in making consuming demands on loyalty.

School and Masonic symbols fused together in the school lodges played upon subliminal if not unconscious associations. None knew the usefulness of sophisticated symbolic manipulation better than the products of public schools and the Masonic lodges, nor appreciated more the contribution that ritualism could make to hegemonic continuities. The genius of ritualism is that it does not need a strong personal leader to perpetuate its influence. The totem provides a sense of union: thus the regimental flag which soldiers in battle carried even at the price of their lives.

Too much said about the current Masonic affiliations of Gulf Arabs in relation to these psychohistorical themes would be grist to the radical mill. There is more profit in considering the possible contributions of Masonic fantasy to the lives of the IPS officers, as well as pondering Masonry's part in Orientalism and to maintaining illusions about Arabia. That takes up the ensuing chapter.

East Europe's Leninists collapse, tyranny ends in Romania. This reminds Arabs mainly that their own Ceausescus are still riding high...Not one ruler in today's Arab League got his job through a free election. Whatever legitimacy these regimes enjoy derives mainly from tradition, fear, or an unwritten contract between ruler and ruled: in return for your loyalty I will meet your basic economic and social needs. That may be a splendid contract in times of plenty. But a bursting population is already making it hard for governments to keep their side of the bargain. – *The Economist*, 18 May 1990.

NOTES

1. Friedberg, *The Weary Titan*, 221. The 'Imperial public school personality' was not always attractive. 'The customary middle-class and public school anti-intellectualism – a mixture of fear and disdain for ratiocinative or imaginative faculties – led to the ostensibly hypocritical ability to think one thing and do another – not an unusual trait, but an important one, especially since it was an inevitable part of British upper-class education.' John R. Reed, *Old School Ties: The Public Schools in British Literature*, Syracuse University Press, Syracuse (New York), 1964, 124.

2. Robert Graves, *Goodbye to All That*, Penguin, Harmondsworth, 1986 [1929], 36.

3. *Science*, 2 September 1989, 1399.

4. John Costello, *Mask of Treachery*, Pan Books, rev. ed. 1989 [1988], 46-47. School was '...a cruel society, especially and deliberately to the newcomer; but whether this was so or not, the boy found the new culture, all its ways, habits of thought and action, its esoteric language, its basic attitudes to life and to the individual all quite different from those to which he was used at home...[overseas] he adapts, like the schoolboy he will behave somewhat differently when he goes to live in the new culture; the difference between his home behaviour and abroad behaviour may be the measure of his adaptation to life abroad.' Norman Daniel, *The Cultural Barrier: Problems in the Exchange of Ideas*, Edinburgh University Press, 1975, 60.

5. Roland Barthes, *Roland Barthes*, Macmillan, 1977 [1975], 82-83. Of course, Barthes as a social commentator considered emotion, but: 'Sociological scholarship on emotion easily dwarfs explicit historical inquiry into the same subject. There are to be sure welcome signs of growing interest among social historians, often as an outgrowth of mentalities research, many decades after Lucien Febvre's cogent first appeal...a key reason for calling attention to the sociologists' initiative is to bolster and inform the band of historians intrigued by the same general subject. Social historians who have not saddled up this particular hobby horse may also profit from interchange with the emotions

sociologists, most obviously in the various reaches of family history but also in studies of work and professional settings and potentially in dealing with the history of leisure as well.' Peter N. Stearns, 'Social History Update: Sociology of Emotion', Journal of Social History, Vol.22, No.3, Spring 1989, 594. See sub modo Strecker, The Social Practice of Symbolization, 14. Emotionology and psychohistory are contentious subjects, as is psychohistory itself: 'Beginning, however, with David Stannard's work, *Shrinking History*, which was first published in 1980, there have appeared a variety of works which have posed serious challenges both to psychoanalysis proper and to psychohistory. In several essays, seemingly rather well-received, Frederick Crews, who had utilized aspects of psychoanalysis in a most stimulating analytical work on Hawthorne, now turned on psychoanalysis with an almost gleeful vehemence. Like one released from a variety of diabolical enchantments, Crews declared that the scales had fallen from his eyes, and that he now saw Freud and psychoanalysis in general for what they were – mystifying frauds...Jeffrey Masson published a work, Assault on Truth, in which he accused Freud, not of incompetence, but of dishonesty...Probably the most serious challenge to psychoanalysis, and thus, necessarily, to psychohistory as well, has been raised by Adolph Grunbaum. In a series of articles which, in 1984, were brought together in the book, The Foundations of Psychoanalysis: A Philosophical Critique, Professor Grunbaum offered a variety of criticisms centred around the guiding idea that psychoanalysis did not – in fact, constitutionally, could not – offer any variety of proof acceptable to any sort of scientifically informed skepticism.' Robert A. Pois, 'The Case for Clinical Training and Challenges to Psychohistory', The Psychohistory Review, Vol.18, No.2, Winter 1990, 180. See Christopher Portal, 'Empathy', Teaching History, No.58, January 1990, 36-38.

6. 'In societies where multiplex face-to-face relations prevail, the question of who at a certain moment in time is acting in which of his many roles may often need an immediate answer if social conflict or, at least, insecurity is to be avoided. Therefore, the identity of an actor is often defined by way of ritual, the ritual acting as a means of orientation which prevents the different roles of a person from being mixed up.' *Ibid.*, 16.

7. 'Whatever the interest aroused by such remarkable figures as the eccentric Gordon or the entrepreneurial Rhodes, the brand of heroism offered for public consumption was bound up with a conformist racial identity, with "Britishness" in the abstract, and stressed public school 'initiative' rather than eccentricity. The stereotype wears regulation pith helmet, spurred boots, and takes upon himself, in the name of the Empress, a vigorous, prefect-style dispensation of "justice".' Mark Paffard, *Kipling's Indian Fiction*, Macmillan, 1989, 29.

8. Robin Gilmour, '*Stalky & Co.*: Revising the Code', Mallett ed., *Kipling Considered*, 27.

9. See David Icenogle, 'The Romantic Adventurer As Explorer? The Case of Charles Chaille-Long', *Terrae Incognitae*, Vol.20, 1988, 21, 23, 25, 27.

10. Bertrand Russell, *Education and the Social Order*, Unwin, 1977, 51-53.

11. Jan Morris, 'Explorer Who Couldn't Change a Wheel', *The Independent*, 7 May 1987, 15.

12. As Mircea Eliade suggests, '...modern man is still capable of being moved by initiatory scenarios or messages.' 'A Conversation with Mircea Eliade', *Parabola*, Vol.1, No.3, Spring 1976, reptd. 1988, 76.

13. See Nigel Yates, *The Oxford Movement and Anglican Ritualism*, The Historical Association, 1984, esp. 30-31. There is a vast literature on the subject.

14. *Ibid.*, 32.

15. Gilmour, '*Stalky & Co.*', Mallett ed., *Kipling Considered*, 31.

16. 'The British imperial experience from the heyday of Victorian expansionism to the withdrawal from the colonial arena in the 1950s and 1960s left an indelible mark on British attitudes towards race and colour. While much of the Victorian thinking on race was shaped by the debate on liberal manhood, it is a limited view of the nature of imperialism and the governance of black "subject races" to suggest...that this was not linked in any causal way with Victorian doctrines of race. The lurch into popular imperialism and jingoism in the late nineteenth century acted as a crucial vehicle for the reinforcement and bolstering-up of racial notions which had already taken hold of a considerable section of middle-class and informed opinion by the middle years of the century.' Rich, *Race and Empire in British Politics*, 201. Berkeley psychologists who produced *The Authoritarian Personality* (T. Adorono, *et al*, Harper, New York, 1950) felt that there was a personality syndrome related to ethnic and racial prejudice. 'They expected, as a result of both theory and experience, that this syndrome would be composed of nine variables: (1) a rigid adherence to "conventional middle-class values"; (2) an uncritical submission to ingroup authority; (3) a punitive aggressiveness toward those who violate the conventional norms of bourgeois society; (4) a distrust of subjectivity and imagination; (5) a superstitious belief in mystical fate over which people have little control; (6) a preoccupation with symbols of strength and toughness; (7) a negative conception of human nature; (8) a disposition to fear conspiracy and external threat; and (9) a punitive attitude toward violators of

MERRIE ENGLAND ONCE MORE!

Plate 13: (left) 'Merrie England Once More!' celebrated the Morris dancing revival – a cartoon from *Punch*.

Plate 14: (below) 'Key to India' marked the acquiring of the Suez Canal shares – *Punch*, 1876.

Plate 15: (left) Thomas Babington Macaula
1800–1859, Supreme Council of India, 1834–1838.

Plate 16: (below) His Highness the Amir Shaikh Jaber Al Ahmad Al-Sabah of Kuwait processes as children throw rose petals, 1990.

Confidential.

Office of the Political Resident
in the Persian Gulf,
Camp, Shiraz.

D.O.No.C/338.

Dated the 12th September, 1940.

My dear Peel,

There have recently been indications that Shaikh Abdullah bin Qasim al Thani of Qatar is trying to obtain an Iraqi to be his adviser on foreign affairs. Last April, Ibrahim Helmi al Omar, Press Director, Bagdad, was offered employment as "Oil Specialist" in Qatar, but was unable to accept, and his request for further details, with a view to finding some one else, was apparently not answered. At the end of August, however, the Shaikh's son Hamad asked Howes in Bahrain to arrange for him to go to Iraq in his own launch. The reason given was that he needed medical treatment, but it is probable that this is merely an excuse to continue the search for an Iraqi adviser.

2. It is clearly most undesirable that an Iraqi should hold this position in Qatar, but I do not think that the Treaty position entitles us to forbid it. We are, however, obstructing the Shaikh as much as possible, and are delaying Hamad's trip to Iraq by pointing out the difficulties of entering the Shatt-al-Arab under war conditions, and by suggesting a visit to India instead. Unfortunately Hamad now seems very keen to visit Iraq, and it will scarcely be possible to refuse him a visa if he should persist.

3. I am sending a copy* of this letter to Caroe.

Yours sincerely,

R.T.Peel Esquire, C.B.E.,M.C.,
The India Office,
London.

*sent under Printed letter No.C/339 of 12th September 1940.

Plate 17: Letter from Charles Prior to R.T. Peel, External Secretary of the India Office, 1940 (IOR:L/P&S/12/3943).

Plate 18: (above) The School of Sooltan Hassan. The scholar Hasan Al-Basri, 642–728, lived in Basra at the head of the Gulf and was forced into hiding (705–714) by the dictatorial ruler Al Hajjaj.

Plate 19: (below) Main building (1894–1915) of Rajkumar College, famous Indian public school.

Plate 20: (left) A sample of rock drawings found near Fuwayrit, Northern Qatar, variously attributed to Phoenician, Sumerian, Portuguese and Indian sailors.

Plate 21: (below) Cultural influences on the Gulf region.

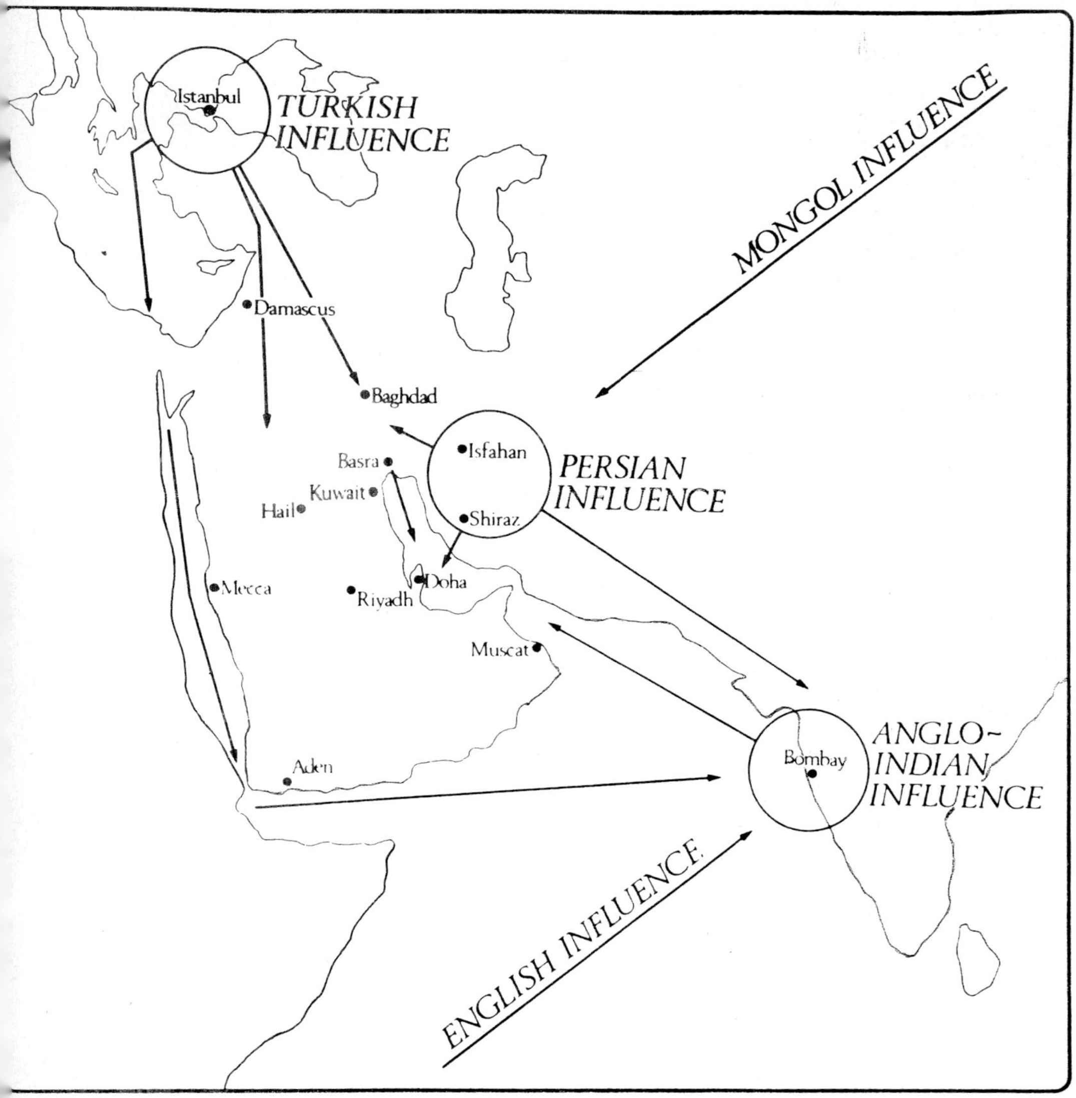

Plate 22: The *Haileybury Observer*. Published 1839–1857. This impish design by John Doyle, father of Richard Doyle (designer of the original *Punch*), appeared first in 1846.

Plate 23: (above) The Prince and Princess of Wales (George V and Queen Mary) enter Gwalior, on the Agra–Bombay road, December 1905.

Plate 24: (below) The traditional 'pancake greeze', Westminster School. (Photograph c.1905 by Sir Benjamin Stone M.P., official photographer for the 1911 Coronation.)

Plate 25: (above) The Al-Thani ruling family, Qatar, 1985. Third from right, His Highness Am Shaikh Kalifa; fourth from right, His Highness The Heir Apparent Shaikh Hamad.

Plate 26: (left) Sir Bartle Frere, 1815–1884. Old Haileyburian. Chief Commissioner of Sind 1850. Governor of Bombay 1862–1867.

sexual mores.' Thomas Lewis, 'Authoritarian Attitudes and Personalities: A Psychohistorical Perspective', *The Psychohistory Review*, Vol.18, No.2, Winter 1990, 144.

17. Patrick Collinson, 'Fundamental Objections', *Times Literary Supplement*, 17 February 1989, 155.

18. C.G. Jung, 'Foreword', Frieda Fordham, *An Introduction to Jung's Psychology*, Penguin, Harmondsworth, 1987 [1953], 11. 'This tendency, one might say this necessity, to apprehend and experience life in a manner conditioned by the past history of mankind Jung calls archetypal...we become aware of them through certain typical images which recur in the psyche.' Fordham, *An Introduction to Jung's Psychology*, 24. 'Every culture is its own mental prison, from which few can escape for long and none escape altogether.' Daniel, *The Cultural Barrier*, 88.

19. E.M. Forster remarked about T.E. Lawrence: '...if when the schoolboy grows up he takes to archaeology seriously, he seldom loses this primitive excitement, this thrill of adventure, reinforcing the thrill of research. The trespassing-spirit persists, the angry farmer becomes an Arab with a gun, the clergyman and the policeman coalesce into a foreign government, which it is a pleasure to fool and a duty to spy on.' qtd. Michael Haag, 'Preface', T.E. Lawrence, *Crusader Castles*, Michael Haag Press, 1986 [1936], 9. Lawrence inevitably springs to mind when the British and Arabia are mentioned, but his cult found few enthusiasts in the IPS or the Gulf. Arabists took up the cudgels for the Residents as neglected but as important as Lawrence. Graves deplored the belief that Lawrence had a monopoly of knowledge about Arabs; Bertram Thomas explained that Lawrence was a meteor beside the major planet that was Percy Cox.

20. O'Shea, *Sand Kings of Oman*, 87. Surely the ritualistic and theatrical side of the IPS officer's personality that a public school education developed should enter into consideration of his ability to handle the rigours of the Gulf, or of his failures. 'As a playgoer of fifty years' experience, I have grown weary of productions of Shakespeare and other classical drama, in which ceremonial is not given its due. The fall of a tragic figure is not especially terrible if he has been represented for four of the five acts as simply one of the boys. If Hamlet is not a prince, why is his predicament especially impressive.' Robertson Davies, 'Nobility and Style', *Parabola*, Vol.VII, No.3, August 1982, 21.

21. There are comparative educationalists who have seized on national *psyche* as an explanation of educational development, *e.g.* Mallinson maintained that national character was a fixed mental disposition that produced common behaviour. The notion of a national spirit, which the British *à la Lawrence* claimed to understand and empathize with in the case of the Arabs and have an empathy for, seems a dubious foundation for political development. Nevertheless, it has had such adherents as Jose Ortega y Gasset, Salvador de Madriago, and André Siegfried.

22. David Stevenson, *The Origins of Freemasonry: Scotland's Century, 1590-1710*, CUP, 1988, 87.

23. Of assistance in understanding this is Dr. Michael Perlman's consideration of memory in *The Psychohistory Review*. He believes that 'Memory itself – from the mythic remembrances of Hesiod (who envisioned the Muses as daughter of Memory) and the philosophical recollecting (*anamnesis*) of Plato to the explorations of Freud, Jung, and others of the psychological depths of memory – is a key theme of our cultural imagination.' Michael Perlman, 'Memory, Soul, and the Place of Hiroshima', *The Psychohistory Review*, Vol.16, No.1, Fall 1987, 67-68. He concludes that memory provides the key to 'opening up hidden depths of historical and psychological life. The wounds remembered open into deepening and widening engagements with archetypal images of life and death.' *Ibid.*, 92.

24. *Ibid.*, 94.

25. Michael Brander, *The Perfect Victorian Hero*, Mainstream, Edinburgh, 1982, 166. See and *cf.* Zareer Masanie, *Indian Tales of the Raj*, BBC Books, 1987, 3.

26. *Ibid.*

27. *Ibid.*, 52.

28. *Ibid.*, 82. 'Colonial ritual might be a harmless and colourful evocation of past traditions if it were not so alien and oppressive to students from less privileged backgrounds.' *Ibid.* 157.

29. Paffard, *Kipling's Indian Fiction*, 53. 'As Edward Said points out, every writer on the subject "saw the Orient as a local requiring Western attention, reconstruction, even redemption"...'. *Ibid.*

30. *Cf.* P. Dresch, 'The Position of Shaykhs Among the Northern Tribes of Yemen, *Man*, Vol.19, No.1, March 1984, 31-49.

31. Reed, *Old School Ties*, 11.

32. Arthur Koestler, *Janus: A Summing Up*, Picador, 1983, 80. See Elizabeth W. Marvick, 'Introduction', 'Case Studies in Psychopolitics' issue of *International Political Science Review*, Vol.10, No.1, January 1989, 5. *Cf.* Henry Lawton, *The Psychohistorian's Handbook*, The Psychohistory Press, 1988, 177.

33. *Ibid.*

34. IOR:L/PS/10/1273, 'Memorandum', T. Hickinbotham, 3 May 1938.

35. *Ibid.*

36. IOR:L/PS/10/1273, Minutes Paper, PZ45/39.

37. Oaten, *My Memories of India*, 57. Maconachie became Sir Roy Maconachie, Ambassador in Kabul.

38. Bryan S. Turner, 'From Orientalism to Global Sociology', *Sociology*, Vol.23, No.4, November 1989, 636.

39. 'The Arab World', *The Economist*, 12 May 1990, Survey, p. 4.

40. Shamsul Islam, *Chronicles of the Raj: A Study of Literary Reaction to the Imperial Idea*, Macmillan, 1979, 5. 'It is clear that banal recommendations to scrutinize our own value positions when conducting empirical research on alternative cultures are pointless. The critique of orientalism leaves us open to two dangers. The first is a naïve trust in the "native" or the pre-modern as a form of humanity which is not corrupted by westernization or modernization. Basically there are *a priori* no privileged moral positions...we also have to take note of the problem of excessive anthropological charity when understanding alien beliefs in their context.' Turner, 'From Orientalism to Global Sociology', 636.

41. O'Shea, *Sand Kings of Oman*, 89. 'There is no doubt that the man who decides to spend part of his life in the desert must be prepared to overcome normal desires by sublimating them in some way.' *Ibid.*

42. Graves, *Goodbye to All That*, 39.

43. Lawton, *Psychohistorian's Handbook*, 185. 'The "infernal dialectic" of this process is reflected on every level of the various social holarchies. Patriotism is the noble virtue of subordinating individual interests to the interests of the nation; yet it gives rise to chauvinism, the militant expression of those higher interests. Loyalty to the clan produces clannishness; *esprit de corps* blossoms into arrogant cliquishness; religious fervour into zealotry; the Sermon on the Mount into the Church militant.' Koestler, *Janus*, 83.

44. Robertson Davies, *World of Wonders, The Deptford Trilogy*, Penguin, Harmondsworth, 1983 [1975], 835.

45. James Dewar, *The Unlocked Secret: Freemasonry Examined*, William Kimber, 1986, 257.

46. R.L. Kennion, *Diversions of an Indian Political*, William Blackwood & Sons, Edinburgh, 1932, 21-22. An Old Reptonian, Kennion offers a number of insights into the IPS (he was consul at Mohammerah in the Gulf, 1915-1916). 'The fact is that every Political billeted in India is *sui generis* and every officer of the Department is supposed to be capable of dealing with "any old" situation as it comes along, a faculty which seems to have been imbibed with their mother's milk by Englishmen generally.' *Ibid.* He notes differences between IPS men recruited from the ICS and from the Army. The Civilians had 'blunt, sporting, so-called "soldierly" qualities', and the Military Politicals were credited with a 'fraction of the brains of their civilian brethren'. *Ibid.*, 22.

47. O'Shea, *Sand Kings of Oman*, 104.

48. 'Assuming that he is the son of a Mason, the sooner he goes to the Masonic Orphanage the better.' Rudyard Kipling, *Kim*, Macmillan, 1978 [1901], 100.

49. Lawton, *Psychohistorian's Handbook*, 83-84.

50. Gavin Stamp (architectural historian), qtd. *Time*, 31 August 1986. 'There is something humiliating in the notion of the zeitgeist – that invisible hand which, acting invisibly behind our backs, fixes the direction of our thoughts and so produces a "spirit of the age," or, more modestly, a trend or mere fad. We have, each of us, a pride of authorship in our thoughts, and we do not like the idea that at the very moment some clever notion is crystallizing in our minds as we sip our morning coffee it is also crystallizing in the minds of several thousand other people as they sip their morning coffee.' 'The Talk of the Town', *The New Yorker*, 18 August 1986, 17. Is this any more humiliating than the notion that our actions are determined not by our will but by our unconscious? *Is this Rupert Sheldrake's morphic resonance under another guise?*

VI

ORIENTALIST FREEMASONRY

Rituals are places in the social process where groups become adjusted to internal change and adapted to their external environment. Thus, the ritual symbol becomes a factor in social action, a positive force in an activity field, a dynamic entity. – Victor Turner, *The Forest of Symbols*, 1967.

Taking things as we find them, it seems that the bond [Freemasonry] at present is mainly drawing its Indian candidates from the Civil Service Department. Too much vigilance cannot be exercised to exclude those who join from purely sordid motives. And it goes without saying that unless a candidate is thoroughly conversant with the English language, he cannot be accepted. A smattering of English in this country should be an inexcusable bar to the portals of our Order. – T.L. Erasmus, *The Indian Freemason*, December 1902.

Seven Freemasons, viz. six Entered Apprentices and one Master Mason, acting under a charter or dispensation from some Grand Lodge, is the requisite number to constitute a Lodge of Masons, and to initiate a candidate to the First Degree of Masonry. – Duncan's Ritual and Monitor of Freemasonry, 1903.

Tom Brown's greatest tomfoolery was Freemasonry. Being an old boy and being a Mason were highly compatible. So there is nothing surprising about the movement's involvement with the Gulf Residents and Agents. Moreover, the Middle East loves conspiracy theories – and no organization more lends itself to accusations of conspiracy than Freemasonry. The rhetoric used by Saddam Hussein made much of the dirty plots of Westerners to fragment the Arab nation into small states. 'Malicious Westerners partitioned the Arab homeland and intentionally multiplied the number of countries,' he told the press shortly after the invasion. 'They intentionally distanced the majority of the population and areas of cultural depth from riches and their sources.' (*Financial Review*, 9 August 1990.) The Arab conviction is deeply rooted that events march along to a hidden agenda, which feeds fears about Freemasonry in the Middle East which are unappreciated by Westerners.

Imperial Freemasonry was dominated largely by public school old boys. The movement roosted in the Empire's attic, where those who could not resist the blandishments of symbolism rummaged about and became besotted with rites and ceremonies, trying on *isms* of the past that had long since become '*wasms*'. Perhaps least pellucid of all societies, Masonry has enjoyed long-time associations with the Middle East and because of its deliberate obscurity became a favourite whipping boy for those who thought history was largely a plot and conspiracy. Imperialist Freemasons took on Roscian proportions.

The increased xenophobia that the Iraqi invasion of Kuwait unchained has been accompanied by considerable rhetoric about 'Zionist-Masonic designs' but despite such attacks, Masonry is a part of the Arab world and not just a Western intrusion. The Middle East exercised an influence on the development of nineteenth century Masonic ritual. Just how much of an influence remains a challenge for scholars. The movement's complicated genesis resists understanding, and visits to its archives produce more of a feeling of *in partibus infidelium* than do visits to bedouin camps.

The subject presents unique difficulties because it requires research into a secret society which has zealously protected the confidentiality of its records. Masonic journals and newspapers in the past were issued on the understanding that they would only be pursued by members. *The Indian Freemason* put matters succinctly (15 January 1901): 'In this issue we publish an account of the installation of Bro. H.E. North Northcote, Governor of Bombay, as Grand Master of all Scottish Freemasonry in India, which took place at the Masonic Hall, Bombay on the 17th December. We are indebted to a friend who forwarded the account, which is taken verbatim from the *Times of India*. The fact of our accepting Masonic news from a secular source can by no means be taken as indicating our approval of the publicity given to a Masonic Ceremonial in such organs. On the contrary we add to our frequently expressed opinion on this point a deep regret that the brother who furnished the news is so wanting in the spirit of Freemasonry.'

Nineteenth-Century Ragbag

Masonry flourished in the nineteenth century as never before, adding not only members but a ragbag of newly-coined symbolism of fake antiquity that 'crowned the Masonic edifice'. Why did the lodges enjoy such a vogue in the *belle époque* of Imperialism? A reason was that the order provided a catharsis achieved through immersion in mumbo jumbo for those who felt a loss of ritualistic fulfilment in religion. It afforded as well a career opportunity for those who sought advancement through association with highly placed Imperial officials. Similar to the way in which nineteenth-century antiquarians fabricated myths surrounded the Black Prince's Ruby, the Kho-i-noor Diamond and Edward the Confessor's Sapphire in the Crown of State (none of which gems had clear claim to the pedigree attached to them), magpie Masonic antiquarians busily invented histories for the order's degrees which had little resemblance to truth.

Nonetheless, scepticism about Freemasonry's significance could be misleading. Not all its claims to antiquity were false, and not all its seers were inept and fatuous. Masonry found its way to Arabia surprisingly early in the Imperial period. In 1846 the Scottish grand lodge felt the need to extend the jurisdiction of its Provincial Grand Master of Western India to Arabia.[1] Officers in Indian Navy ships that visited the region participated in meetings of Lodge Felix in Aden in the 1850s.[2] Lodges met in Gulf ports such as Basra, Kuwait, and Sharjah. The fate of the temple in Kuwait during the events of 1991 seemed highly problematical, but when this author visited it in 1981 it was immaculately maintained.

Brother Mahmoud Churchward

Individual reports on Masonry in Arabia in Victorian and Edwardian times are few. Hedley (Mahmoud Mobarek) Churchward, who converted to Islam as a young man, claimed after a pilgrimage to Mecca in 1910, although many aspects of Western culture were forbidden, that:

> One world-renowned cult is, however, familiar to the Meccans, namely Freemasonry. I am an old member of the craft, with fairly advanced degrees, so it was easy for me to discover unmistakable evidence that numerous Arabs belonged to the brotherhood. No meetings take place within the city but hundreds of local men have been initiated.
>
> The spirit of Freemasonry conforms with the teachings of Islam, and the great numbers of lodges throughout the Muslim world might surprise the stay-at-home member. Cairo, in fact all Egypt, possesses many brethren; so too, India and, to a considerable extent, Arabia. At Mecca I met a great variety. Some were learned scholars, others belonged to lowly professions. Most of them had no acquaintance with Occidental conditions, and felt delighted to meet a colleague from the West.[3]

Like much else that has been written about the lodges, Churchward's account of Mecca Masonry should be viewed with scepticism. Churchward, after all, also recounts a supposed encounter in East Africa between a Johannesburg Mason and a Swahili headman who '...made a perfectly obvious masonic sign, then another and finally a few which the white lodge member did not then understand, but which, during his subsequent advancement, he found to be the prerogative of brethren holding high degrees.'[4] The extravagance of Churchward's personality means that his claims have to be received with a pinch of salt.

A similar exchange of Masonic recognition signs excited Lewis Pelly, one of the Gulf Residents, when he visited Riyadh in 1865. Whether or not he was correct that he was greeted with Masonic passes and tokens, and whether any Arabs of the period were involved in Masonry, the real significance of IPS officers' belonging to Masonic orders rests with what membership indicates about their attitudes. For some Gulfites who were manic Masons, it appears to have been a neurosis, *e.g.* they pursued in the lodge what an outsider could regard as *fabricated honours* and were motivated in joining and serving by the promise of *achieving control over others*.

On the other hand, the high-minded fraternal obligations that Masonic oaths imposed on members contained much that was internationalist and ecumenical in dimension. That these promises made of fraternity and brotherhood were taken seriously should not be discounted. *The Indian Freemason* in July 1902 reported that:

> Lieutenant-General Sir George Wolseley's installation as Master of Lodge Faith, Hope and Charity, took place at Ootacamund on Tuesday night. A feature of the ceremonial was the presence of five Boer Officers from the Kaity Camp, who are Masons, and were invited by the Lodge to the installation and banquet. Sixty-five Masons and guests were present. Lord

Ampthill, the District Grand Master, in the course of a long speech, referred to the presence of the Boer brethren, and paid a high tribute to the courage and endurance of their countrymen. One of the Boer Officers, in reply, thanked the District Grand Master for his speech and the members for their hospitality, which, he assured them, would never be forgotten by him or his fellow-prisoners. In conclusion, he asked all present to drink the health of the two greatest fighting men in the world – Briton and Boer.

The incident illustrates as well that the existence of a formally organized lodge conferring the degrees, or of pretentious buildings, does not matter as much as the 'networking' that membership made possible. As Arthur Koestler remarks in *Janus*, '...the metamorphosis of individual minds into the group-mind does not necessarily require the individual's physical presence in a group or crowd, only an act of identification with the group – its beliefs, traditions, leadership, and/or its emotion-rousing symbols.'[5] In any case, a chartered lodge and a well-furnished lodge room would not have been necessary for meetings. An evening of Masonry would not need a permanent home; after all, the organization flourished in such unlikely places as prison ships during the Napoleonic wars and German concentration camps. *Its importance in the Gulf rests more with the networking that went on amongst members and with their attitudes as shaped by membership, rather than with the conferring of degrees.*

What was the influence of the lodge on colonial administrators? Characterizing Masonic attitudes is a precarious exercise. Such a secret movement might be thought to be the original home of the *arrière-pensée*, but at the least membership points towards an inordinate interest in ceremony. To claim that one man was motivated by careerism and another by a love of ritual is a judgement in dire need of supporting evidence. Since Masonic ritualism usually could not be satisfied in the Gulf by formal gatherings, there would be more reason for energy to go into the official Residency and Agency rituals. There was little chance for Gulf Masons to put on the formal pageantry of the lodge. Still a Resident or Agent who was active in Freemasonry can be assumed to have a certain insight into ritualism, building or no building.

The actual staging of the degrees could, and indeed did, go on in India and England. Individual lodges in England formed close associations with India and with the Arab world. The Marquis of Dalhousie Lodge No.1159 in London provides one example, honouring in its name a Governor-General of India and including in its membership a Viceroy, the Earl of Ripon. A number of blue-blooded Indian students in England were initiated by Dalhousie, and the lodge had connections with Freemasonry in Persia and Zanzibar. Buckingham and Chandos Lodge No.1150, another London lodge, maintained close associations with Iraq Lodge No.4471 and with Babylonian Lodge No.4326. Buckingham's name commemorated a Governor of Madras. The first master was Henry Creed of the East India Company, whose brother Richard Creed was killed in the Gulf when storming Kujjuck in February 1841 – and who is commemorated by a tablet in Westminster Abbey.[6]

Not to be overlooked in considering Gulf Masonry are all the arabesque developments in Masonic ritual that occurred in the nineteenth century, improvisations inspired by a generally heightened interest in the East. Lodge rooms around the world incorporated Middle Eastern motifs. Masonic halls had their supporting pillars painted to resemble palm trees. Ritual changes reflected an enthusiasm for the mysterious Orient. The Freemasons' Hall in Dublin acquired two enormous sphinxes. The Great Eastern Hotel at London's Liverpool Street station inaugurated an Egyptian Temple to attract lodge meetings. This Oriental enthusiasm was not limited to Masonry – even Leicester Square was to have its minarets. (See Plate 28.)

Battista Belzoni

A number of travelling Masons helped to spread the idea of Masonic links with the Arabs. The mountebank adventurer Giovanni Battista Belzoni (1778-1823), who had joined in Cairo and affiliated with lodges in Cambridge and Norwich, told credulous lodge brethren in England that he had discovered a pharonic Masonic temple at Thebes in which the wall murals showed Osiris being intitiated. The erection of a genuine obelisk, 'Cleopatra's Needle', on Victoria Embankment in London in 1878 by English Masons was emulated elsewhere; a veritable forest of exported Egyptian obelisks and imitations rose in squares around the world, joining in the Imperial architectural ensemble the ubiquitous bandstands, cricket pavilions, clock towers, and other architectural embodiments of hegemony.

Much of modern Masonic ritual preserves nineteenth-century improvisations and reflects an Occidental and Victorian susceptibility for things exotically Islamic and Arab. Freemasons shared with antiquarians a mania for an Oriental vaudevillism in the arts and literature:

> Even Middle Eastern monarchs who came in person to Europe were liable to be incorporated themselves into its theatrical events. When the Khedive of Egypt visited Paris to attend an earlier Exposition Universelle in 1867, he found that the Egyptian exhibit had been built to simulate medieval Cairo in the form of a royal palace. The Khedive stayed in the imitation palace during his visit and became a part of the exhibition, receiving visitors with medieval hospitality.[7]

The bewildering resultant smorgasbord of odd Masonic degrees included a number of gauche improvisations based on the 'evidence' provided by the penny dreadful school of Orientalism. This is harsh and perhaps charity should be exercised. Such non-Masonic historical speculations are in the same vein as the assertion that the origins of Imperialism owed much to the twelfth century English invasion of Ireland – so licence must be given to the Masons' claims that the Pharaohs were members of the order. In *The Indian Freemason* (May 1902), a correspondent congratulated brothers on the introduction of the Order of the Eastern Star: 'I was very glad to see that a Chapter of the Order of the Eastern Star had been organised in your city. I certainly hope that the Masons of Calcutta will give this their hearty support...'. In September of the same year, readers learned about the degrees of another order that doted on camels and dunes, the Mystic Shrine: 'Their Imperial Sheik lives in Mecca or

Medina, according to circumstances, and some of their most noted men are Egyptians...Members wear the Turkish fez, their emblem is the crescent moon and scimitar and when they go mounted, they must have Arab steeds.' This pseudo-history was of course completely false. There were no Egyptian members of the Shrine, and the leaders, who called themselves Imperial Potentates rather than shaikhs, would have had a fatal reception if they had ever appeared in Mecca or Medina.

Masonic history offers amusements such as this which no connoisseur of historiological confusion should overlook. Internecine warfare between ritual systems, fictional but stoutly-held claims to historical reality, and deliberate blurring of origins provide a rich feast. Admittedly similar claims to authenticity are made for other secret and esoteric organizations. A familiar newspaper of today in the Gulf, *The Offshore Adviser* (May 1989), protests about the Order of Malta that 'Freemasonry is nothing but a pipsqueak copycat compared with the intrigue associated with the Order. Indeed, in some esoteric circles it is rumoured that the Order of Malta is officially "at war" with the Ancient & Accepted Freemason's Rite, the notorious 33rd Degree.' Such a claim is rash, given how complex and bitterly sectarian are the disputes within Masonry. No other society jealously preserves the gradations and distinctions that the 'Royal Craft' boasts. (See Plate 29.) If various branches of the Knights of Malta (there is a Masonic version) indeed do have their reputations for intrigue, it remains more likely that they have been the catspaws or copycats of Masonry rather than *vice versa*.

The unashamed theatricality of Masonry and of Imperialism recalls Dr. J.A. Mangan's references to the 'mass-producing' of traditions, and even more notably Raymond Williams' comments in *The Long Revolution* (remarks that Martin Weiner approvingly quoted in *English Culture and the Decline of the Industrial Spirit*) that, 'It is with the discovery of patterns of a characteristic kind that any useful cultural analysis begins'. Dr. Mangan associates himself with Hobsbawm, asserting that the assiduous creation of tradition that went on in the Victorian era reflected the need for 'new devices to establish or express social cohesion and corporate identity and to create new social relationships.'[8] Masonry was an excellent example of this, a pre-existing system which, like the public schools, rallied to the Imperial cause.

There were Masons who did not admit to Masonry being organic or evolving, and who adhered to the view that it rested firmly on actual historical events and was unchanging. This view was widespread. IPS and Arab Freemasons who understood the rituals as depicting real occurrences – as historically as well as metaphysically 'true' – could claim a perspective about the Middle East that the uninitiated lacked. Many of the so-called 'higher' degrees concerned *supposed* events in the region. The case for these degrees, which proliferated in the later nineteenth century, was put by a correspondent in *The Indian Freemason*, 31 January 1901: 'Suppose that a minister of the gospel, of the most eloquent and impressive kind, should prepare three sermons treating on the leading tenets...and should then read them to his congregation...when all had been delivered suppose he began over again and continued to repeat them, how long would that congregation be satisfied?' The argument ingeniously promotes candidates taking more degrees since it treats the initiatory three or 'blue' lodge degrees as insufficient or tedious.

However, another correspondent (September 1902, after the journal became monthly) complained, 'We have lately been informed, through the medium of the local Masonic press, that the 360th degree (why not the 365th?) is the apex of oriental and continental Masonry. I do not know. I cannot tell.' The conflict over these views of Freemasonry and its associated movements, a dispute over the actual historical basis for Masonic Rosicrucianism, Templarism, Numerology, Gnosticism, and the other bizarre strains that were incorporated into the movement, has never been resolved.

Undeniably many degrees purported to present authentic historical insights about the Middle East, the secret details of events which outsiders could never possess. Gulf Freemasons could claim authority that came from possession of privileged historical insights, authority similar to that which scholars were claiming by virtue of the learning and the exercise of learning which Said has identified as at the heart of Orientalism.

When considered as commentaries on actual historical events, several of the favourite degrees appear part of the West's elaboration of Orientalism that Said has exhaustively documented:

> By the end of the nineteenth century, as Said has shown, knowledge of the Orient had become an expertise institutionalised in the centres of colonial administration, in government ministries, and in universities. This expertise, combined with images of the Orient in popular writing, entertainment, the press, government reports, guide books, travelogues and the memoirs of colonial officials, came to form a broad discursive field, a vast theatre or exhibition of the real. Within this theatrical machinery, elaborate representations of the 'objects' of colonial authority could be produced.[9]

Whatever the debate over its origins, Masonry by the end of the nineteenth century had firmly become a part of the dramaturgical machinery of Empire. Its symbolism was part of the representation of authority upon which the Raj depended. Timothy Mitchell writes in *Colonising Egypt* that colonialism was marked by its ability 'to reproduce theatres of its order and truth. Colonialism was distinguished by its power of representation...The order and certainty of colonialism was the order of the exhibition, the certainty of representation itself.'[10] *Imperial Masonry was a private pelmanism of the ruling ritualism, a green room for officials where they could rehearse the rituals by which they ruled.* The lodge room was an effective schoolroom in ritual. (See Plate 30.)

Indian Lodges and the Gulf

In India, several of the more renowned lodges counted Gulf IPS officers as members, including the most distinguished of all, Himalayan Brotherhood No.459 – a lodge which was frequented by Lord Roberts and to which Bishop Welldon, headmaster of Harrow, Old Etonian friend of Curzon, and Metropolitan of India, belonged. He became a member in 1900 in India, while he was still Grand Chaplain of the District Grand Lodge of Middlesex. In 1904 an evening meeting to install the lodge's master included as participants Lord Ampthill, the Viceroy, and Lord Kitchener, the Commander-in-Chief. Another meeting in 1914 saw the initiation of the Maharaja of Patila and the 'raising' (taking of the third degree) of the Chinese ambassador. Lodges were connected by reciprocal relationships just as clubs were (discussed in *Chains of Empire*), and Himalayan Brotherhood reciprocated with Fortitude No.229 in Calcutta. Members could attend either without paying additional fees.[11]

The Gulf Residents and Agents include at least fourteen men who have been identified as Freemasons, and four whose background indicates a strong possibility of membership. At least three officers – Robert Hamilton, Frederick Johnston, and Terence Keyes – held extremely high Masonic offices. Hamilton became Grand Master of Scotland and one of his successors was the Duke of York (George VI). Equally significant, Keyes was the brother-in-law of the highest ranking Freemason in the Empire who was not a member of the Royal Family, Sir A.H. MacMahon, sometime head of the IPS.

Probably more Gulf officers belonged than are represented on the present list. There are difficulties in tracing the Masonic affiliations of men who served in the Gulf. Not the least is that several national or grand lodges were involved and that the libraries of those grand lodges are not as comprehensive as could be wished. For example, the Grand Lodge of Scotland established Pioneer Lodge in 1920 at Abadan, which was sponsored by Lodge Forman of Western India and Lodge Caledonia of Bombay. Pioneer in turn sponsored Lodge Masjid-i-Suleman at Maidan-i-Nafton in Mohammarah at the head of the Gulf in 1924. Little reference to the activities of any of these lodges occurs in the vast library of the United Grand Lodge of England; filling out the story of Scottish Masonry in the Gulf requires recourse to the archives in Edinburgh.

Notwithstanding the difficulties of research, enough lodge affiliations are known to raise the question whether affiliation with a specific rite or a lodge such as Himalayan Brotherhood conferred greater prestige than membership in other Masonic affiliates. Thus lodge attendance might, like public school attendance, offer a way in which to advance the individual's social standing: '...as I understand, some of the British residents who joined the lodges, and who were educated in public schools, used the lodges as a means of social climbing in the administration of the areas you are studying...[but] if they used the old-boy network, and the masonic lodge was its clearest expression, this was quite true for most of the other *clubs à l'Anglaise* that existed in the British Empire.'[12] In this vein, James Dewar in an *exposé* of lodgedom, *The Unlocked Secret*, suggested that the two World Wars provided a social motive for the growth of the public schools and the lodges. Men who were not from the officer class but obtained a commission wanted to keep their new status, and so they and their families patronized the public schools and Masonry. Dewar substantiates the proposal about lodges and status by citing the fact that 'lesser public schools' acquired lodges 'to take their place alongside the older and more eminent ones'.

While acknowledging validity to such observations, the meaning of Masonic membership does *not* rest in determining IPS status based on which lodge was joined. *Similar to arguments in Chapter VIII about the weight to give the relative social status of schools attended by the IPS are the arguments that can be made that the generic fact of belonging to the Craft remains more significant than particular lodge affiliations.* Undeniably there were countless Masonic distinctions and titles and honours – which in the case of someone like Kuwait PA Robert Hamilton take lengthy explanations. Nevertheless, the essence is membership rather than the minute distinctions between the specific Masonic orders and the dignities that they conferred.

Chancing on the Lodge

Generally, lodges made returns listing members to the English, Scottish, Irish, or other grand lodge secretaries. These returns permit the identification of members *if* the right lodge is chanced upon – with the emphasis on 'chance' because a Mason could attend a lodge for years while keeping his membership in another lodge, often in another country. (By no means did the grand lodges initiate only their own nationalities. Many Englishmen overseas joined Scottish lodges and *vice versa*.) The minute books remained with the lodge secretary unless the lodge dissolved. If the lodge did wind up there was no guarantee that the records would be given to a grand lodge. The United Grand Lodge of England has few records of defunct lodges, and its staff believe that many records remained with the former officers. The assumption is that much evidence for the membership of Gulfites is with descendants of the secretary or other officers of the lodge to which they belonged, complicated by the lodge's movements. Pioneer Lodge of the Scottish jurisdiction moved from Abadan to Aden in 1955 and then reopened in Linlithgowshire in Scotland in 1986, and of course its records followed it around. Grecian Lodge No.1105, which began in Cairo in 1866, now meets in London. Kitchener was master in 1892; Reginald Wingate was master in 1897; and Sir Lee Stack was a member until his assassination in 1924.[13]

Masons are chary of divulging information to brother Masons of different rites and jurisdictions, let alone to inquisitive interlopers. Therefore the membership and the extent of the activities of lodges in the Empire remains mysterious, partly hidden in records which are inaccessible and which were at the time considered highly secret. However, despite injunctions to secrecy, there exist published examples of Masonic affairs involving the IPS. There is a case in point involving the IPS. In the matter of the initiation of Habibollah Khan, the Amir of Afghanistan, General George Macmunn (himself an active Mason) wrote:

> His new Highness came down to India in 1906 and was well pleased. And then it was that Sir Henry McMahon, aided and abetted by the Grand Master of all the Freemasons in the Punjab, no less a person than Lord Kitchener, by triple dispensation passed His Highness to the High and Sublime Degree of Master Mason in one night. Staunch masons looked askance one with another, but when a commander-in-chief is also Grand Master of Freemasons in the Frontier Province and the Foreign Secretary to the Government of India, who was also in the Masonic World Lord High

> Everything Else combined together, it does not much matter who does sniff at them. As it happened these two high masons builded better than they knew, better even than Solomon on Mount Tabor...[14]

The Sir Henry McMahon of the story is the brother-in-law of the Gulf Political Agent Terence Keyes, and a lodge brother (in Studholme Lodge No.1591) of Winston Churchill. He was a boon companion of Brother Kitchener, who himself held numerous Masonic offices and had lodges named after him. (See Plate 31.) The tale of the Amir's initiation has been told by several others who were present at the ceremonies. The rites accomplished the purpose of binding the Afghan leader to the British cause, and Macmunn recounts that Habibullah kept his Masonic vow: 'When the Sultan of Turkey joined the war, and proceeded to proclaim a *Jihad,* a world *Jihad,* and to cry from all the mosques and *minars* in Islam that the faith was in danger, then the frontier fat was in the fire. But Habibullah, the "beloved of God", master mason in the English Constitution, was mindful of his obligation "Of the badge of friendship and the bond of peace," and he sat very tight in Kabul.'[15] The Holy Koran on which the Afghan King took his Masonic obligations is preserved by the Grand Lodge of England. Unfortunately lodge membership and professed affections for the British did not protect him from assassination in 1919, nor is it likely protection for any present day shaikhs.

The Man Who Would Be King

Masonry today *may* be guileless and its penalties allegorical, but for Victorians and Edwardians the obligations were taken most seriously and references to the use of recognition signs referring to dire penalties for turncoats – as skull cleaving and throat and belly slitting – provide part of the plot in several of Rudyard Kipling's stories. The most notable is *The Man Who Would Be King,* a classic tale of Masonic adventures.

Since the IPS was a small service with its total force usually 140 or less in number, the secret bond between even a few men has significance. What were the commitments made on joining? The oath taken in the third degree included the undertaking recorded in the numerous editions of *Duncan's Masonic Ritual and Monitor*:

> I will keep a worthy brother Master Mason's secrets inviolable, when communicated to and received by me as such, murder and treason excepted...Further, that I will not give the Grand Hailing Sign of Distress except in case of the most imminent danger, in a just and lawful Lodge, or for the benefit of instruction; and if ever I should see it given, or hear the words accompanying it, by a worthy brother in distress, I will fly to his relief, if there is a greater probability of saving his life than losing my own. All this I most solemnly, sincerely promise and swear, with a firm and steady resolution to perform the same, without any hesitation, mental reservation, or secret evasion of mind whatever, binding myself, under no less a penalty than that of having my body severed in two, my bowels taken from thence and burned to ashes, the ashes scattered before the four winds

of heaven, that no more remembrance might be had of so vile and wicked a wretch as I would be, should I ever, knowingly, violate this my Master Mason's obligation.

In addition to the gravity of such oaths, Freemasonry's connections with the public schools invoked ties that existed between old boys. Grand lodges supported school lodges which included in membership both old boys and masters. Addressing the Grand Lodge of Scotland in reference to one such lodge, Edinburgh Academy Centenary No.1327, Lord Clyde remarked:

> To what sentiment is the appeal made in our case? Not exactly to local patriotism, but to a patriotism of another kind which is at least as capable of being woven into the fabric of Masonic unity as local patriotism is, namely the common loyalty of old school-fellows for their *alma mater*. It is in school that the serious impulses of our youth are first brought into active contact with the instinct of *esprit de corps*, the sentiment of loyalty to something bigger and more important than ourselves [exclamations of 'hear, hear'] – a place for which, just as truly as for the place of home or the place of birth, we keep in our hearts a warm corner of affection...[16]

In the audience in 1924 when Lord Clyde made those remarks was Robert Hamilton. Hamilton (Lord Belhaven) seems, on returning to Scotland from Kuwait where he was Agent, to have put the energies into Masonry which he had been putting into the Gulf until he broke with Percy Cox and left the service. Kuwait's loss was Masonry's gain.

The case for the connections between British education and Masonry is strengthened by the fact that there were opportunities for someone like Hamilton to practise Masonry not only overseas or in school lodges, but through university lodges with school associations. There was an Oxford lodge as early as 1730 and a number of lodges initiating undergraduates flourished at Oxford and Cambridge. The Oxford and Cambridge University Lodge No.1118 promoted friendship between the universities and had a 'Godfather Fund' which paid the initiation fees of men joining the Oxford Union and other Oxford and Cambridge clubs and university lodges such as Apollo and Isaac Newton lodges. The lodge sponsored 'Camis', another lodge which was maintained to promote ritual proficiency among varsity men. Although the majority of Camis members also were in the Oxford and Cambridge lodge, it included non-varsity Old Wykehamist and Old Etonian Lodge members and was itself included as a member of the Public School Lodges Council.

The school lodge spirit was spread by headmasters who were Masonic enthusiasts. A good example already mentioned is the feverish Masonic activity of J.E.C. Welldon, headmaster of Harrow and then Metropolitan of India. *The Indian Freemason* (15 January 1901) approvingly reported the Masonic Service Welldon conducted in the cathedral in Calcutta in December 1900: 'Bro. the Lord Bishop placed a room in the palace at the disposal of the Brethren, and Grand Lodge was opened therein by R. Wor. Bro. Sir H.T. Prinsep, the District Grand Master of Bengal...The Service was conducted by Bro. the Rev. W. Luckman assisted by the Venerable the Archdeacon of

Calcutta. Bro. Welldon, Bishop of Calcutta preached the Sermon.' Welldon's enthusiasm for Masonry begs the question as to why an ecclesiastic like himself found that the lodge was (apparently) more satisfying than the church. In his sermon to the Masons on that occasion, he remarked: 'Brethren, I value the charities of Freemasonry. I value them not the less, but all the more, because they are done not with display and ostentation, not by advertisement, but modestly and secretly...And now how frequent in this land of India is the need for the solace of the fatherless and the widows, how many the missions of love which Freemasonry is permitted to render.' He also may have enjoyed the honours aspect to Masonry. Masonic recognition was prized. *The Indian Freemason* of 15 August 1901 noted that 'Past Rank has been lavishly conferred on eminent Brethren, and we find India has not been neglected. Bro. Lord Bishop Welldon receives the high and fitting dignity of *Past Grand Chaplain*...Bro. Lord Kitchener, whom it is likely will ere long throw in his lot among Indian Freemasons, has received the rank of *Past District Grand Master* of Egypt and the Soudan.'

The suggestion thus is not being made that the school lodges were the sole way in which a man like Welldon became involved. (Nevertheless, the school lodges do show that the schools were involved in the Masonic movement. Although there were many lodges for special interests, lodges for men working in a specific occupation or with an interest in art or music or literature, school and university lodges were particularly strong and they are as active or more active today as in the past.) Convinced that he was acquiring all manner of distinctions and prestige, a Masonic zealot would join not just a school lodge but every Masonic body in sight. Ian Gordon, an Old Carthusian, records a not untypical Masonic career in his 'exposé' *The Craft and the Cross*, which he wrote after he had left the lodges and taken up evangelical Christianity: 'I held the positions of Assistant Sojourner in the Royal Arch, Raphael in the Rose Croix, and Captain of Guards in the Knights Templar. I had also become acquainted with Mark Masonry, which is one of the oldest grades...I joined its appendant Order, the Royal Ark Mariners...I was installed as a Knight of the Red Cross of Constantine...I was admitted to the Order of the Knights of the Holy Sepulchre, and during the same year I joined, by invitation, two other Craft lodges, one being my old school lodge, Charterhouse, and the other, one of the Stewards', or Red Apron, lodges.'

> I was a completely dedicated and totally committed Freemason and I loved it! I loved the whole thing – the camaraderie, the exclusivity, the wining and dining after each meeting, *but most of all I loved the ritual*. The more I had to learn, the better I liked it. I loved the rather quaint formality of the language used in the Craft ceremonies...[17]

What the IPS involvement in Masonry illustrates is the influence of the British love of ritual rather than support of school lodges. This is not an influence which completely disappeared when the British government withdrew from the region. Associations between the grand lodges of England, Scotland, and Ireland and the Middle East have continued long after the end of the IPS, though subject to vicissitudes. In contrast with Iraq or Iran,

Freemasonry has been tolerated in the Gulf states as long as it has not been too conspicuous. In 1967 the Grand Master Mason of Scotland visited Kuwait and Lodge Kuwait Caledonia 1570. A delegation was present from Basra in Iraq, where at the time the Scottish jurisdiction's Lodge Faiha was not being permitted to meet openly.[18] Masonic meetings that do take place in the modern Gulf are often like this, organized on the spur-of-the-moment to fête visitors. A source of recruits has been Arabs who have attended university in the West and been initiated during varsity careers. Their participation in the Gulf's future presents intriguing questions, but the subject has become increasingly dangerous to Arab members because of the events of 1990 and 1991. Yet Freemasons in Dhahran, Saudi Arabia, openly operated a fleet of some hundred vehicles for nightly deliveries of books and personal items to Allied military personnel in February 1991. (*New Jersey Freemason*, March 1991.)

In considering Gulfite membership in Masonic lodges, it should be emphasized how such memberships support the thesis that India was the nonpareil Imperial Masonic territory. The fraternity was well established there by the end of the eighteenth century and subsequently received particular impetus during the Governor-Generalship (1813-22) of the Earl of Moira. (See Plate 32.) Masonry achieved a popularity in India that was perhaps unmatched elsewhere in the Empire. Most nineteenth and twentieth-century Governors-General and Viceroys were members, with the great exception of the Marquess of Ripon (1880-85). He had been Grand Master of the Grand Lodge of England but withdrew from Masonry in 1874 on becoming a Roman Catholic. Contrary to the belief that Roman Catholics never were Freemasons, some did join – but Lord Ripon felt unable to reconcile the commitments. When he resigned *The Times* (5 September 1874) was scathing:

> What should induce the Marquess of Ripon thus to withdraw, without apparent reason, from a position of dignity and influence, if not of real importance? How many of our readers have surmised the answer? Lord Ripon has become a Roman Catholic! It is notorious that the Freemasons are under the especial ban of the Church of Rome. That Church tolerates no secret society, except that of the Jesuits; and the first sacrifice that would be demanded of a convert like Lord Ripon would be his withdrawal from the Craft. As the first pledge of his new obedience he has to abandon his honourable position in the Brotherhood, and to renounce a harmless and kindly association in which he might for years have held the foremost place...To become a Roman Catholic and remain a thorough Englishman are – it cannot be disguised – almost incompatible conditions...

It was not Freemasonry that excluded Catholics so much as it was the Church of Rome that forbade its members to join. Imperial Masonry prided itself on being ecumenical, although the evidence for the truth of that is mixed. In India during the nineteenth century numbers of Hindus and Muslims became Freemasons.

While lodges existed in many Indian towns, outside Bombay and Calcutta there is one place that seems to recur in Masonic records more than most, that of Quetta.[19] Furthermore, Quetta frequently surfaces in the records as a Masonic centre that involved IPS members. This is noteworthy because, although a strategic priority, Quetta was a relatively small city – but by all accounts a beehive of Masonic activity. The lodge activities complemented the gentlemanly ambience of Quetta, which had a hunt and the inevitable club, as well as a population of *ayahs* (nursemaids) to look after the children who populated its pleasant bungalows. A pack of one-horse *tongas* resembling pony carts were the approved way in which to go calling.[20] Attendance at lodge was something that 'one did' according to Arnold Galloway, and it provided a way to meet visitors and newcomers in what was a transitory society. Galloway recalled to this author his surprised pleasure when a Colonel Lancaster came to Bahrain that he had known socially from attending McMahon Lodge in Quetta.[21] (See Plate 33.)

With the exception of Quetta lodges, there is no pattern of concentration of Gulfite membership in one place or one lodge. This can be attributed to frequent changes in posting. The following lodges are known to have had more than one Gulf Resident or Agent as a member:

Industry in Lahore No.1485: Hamilton, McCollum. The lodge moved to Delhi after Partition and brought with it sister organizations giving other degrees, including Royal Arch Chapter Progress, No.1485 E.C. (English Constitution); Mark Lodge Fidelity, No.98 E.C.; and Royal Ark Mariners (RAM) Lodge Mount Ararat, No.98 E.C. Eventually the lodge ceased activities.

Khyber No.582: Lorimer, Stewart. Khyber removed from India and now meets at 10 Duke St., St. James's, London. It is a relatively old lodge, having been formed in Peshawar in 1850.

Kitchener No.2998: Edmund (not his brother Cecil) Gabriel, Lorimer. Kitchener was founded in 1903. After partition in 1947 its membership, which was then entirely European, declined and left Quetta. Kitchener now meets at Freemasons' Hall, Janpath, New Delhi. Other Masonic bodies that depended on Kitchener for members also moved, including Royal Arch Chapel Simla No.2998 E.C., and the Blackham Conclave.

Mesopotamia No.3820: Hamilton, McCollum, Stewart. Mesopotamia was one of the lodges that prospered because of the British troops in the Middle East during World War I. The lodge met in Basra and has now ceased activities. A Scottish lodge was formed much later in Basra, Lodge Basra in 1929.

McMahon No.3262: Keyes, McCollum. This represents another Quetta lodge which 'emigrated' to England and now meets at 86 St. James's St., London – one street away from Khyber No.582.

Rajputana No.2800: Edmund Gabriel, Hamilton, Francis Prideaux. This lodge has ceased activities and surrendered its charter.

The lodges listed above are 'blue' lodges, which means they are lodges working the initial three degrees of *Entered Apprentice, Fellowcraft,* and *Master Mason.* These blue lodges were by far the most common in Masonry, and there were far more of them than those working 'higher' or 'side' degrees. Blue lodge Masons took exception to the idea that taking further degrees made anyone more a Mason. The public school lodges in England were mostly blue lodges, conferring the initial three degrees.

Several ladders beckoned after the blue lodge initiation, one of which was composed of the *Supreme Council of the Empire Degrees.* The Supreme Council worked (and today works) degrees from the fourth to the thirty-third whose origins in their complexity would have confounded Hermes Trismegistus. Johnson and Keyes achieved high office in this system, which includes chivalric degrees with affinities to Templarism and the Knights of Malta. In *Foucault's Pendulum,* Umberto Eco mentions one of the legends concerning the establishment of these 'Scottish' degrees: 'These knights supposedly escaped, took refuge in Scotland, and joined a Masonic lodge in Kilwinning. According to the legend, they became part of the society of Freemasons, who serve as guardians of the secrets of the Temple of Solomon.'[22]

In achieving the eighteenth degree, the Rose-Croix of Heredom, they first took the first three degrees in the blue lodge and then passed through the ceremonies of the following degrees:[23]

4° Secret Master
5° Perfect Master
6° Perfect English Master
7° Provost and Judge
8° Intendant of the Building
9° Perfect Master Elect
10° Grand Elect
11° Sublime Prince Elect
12° Grand Master Architect
13° Royal Arch of Enoch
14° Scotch Knight of Perfection
15° Knight of the East
16° Prince of Jerusalem
17° Knight of the West

When Johnson and Keyes finally were allowed to continue on the Masonic road to the thirtieth degree of Knight Kadosh, they were required to endure the rites or the equivalents of the following degrees:

19° Grand Commander of the Temple
20° Grand Master of Symbolic Lodges
21° Prussian Knight
22° Knight of the Royal Axe
23° Chief of the Tabernacle
24° Prince of the Tabernacle
25° Knight of the Brazen Serpent

26° Prince of Mercy
27° Sovereign Commander of the Temple
28° Knight of the Sun
29° Grand Scottish Knight of St Andrew, sometimes called Grand Patriarch of the Crusades

While much more could be written about Supreme Council degrees and their Middle Eastern and Arabian connections, as well as about other Masonic degree systems claiming Middle Eastern associations, attention now must pass to short sketches of the Masonic careers and connections of the IPS Residents and Agents.

Masonic Backgrounds of Gulf Officers

BARRETT, CYRIL His brother-in-law, Lionel Haworth *qv,* was a Freemason. Barrett's membership has not been established.

BIRDWOOD, RICHARD An F.W.L. Birdwood belonged in India to Lodge Bolan of the Scottish Constitution. He died in August 1884. The connection with Richard is unknown – but Richard's brother, Christopher Birdwood, was initiated 11 July 1892, passed 8 August 1892, and raised 10 October 1892 in Himalayan Brotherhood Lodge No.459. He resigned when his regiment moved, 27 June 1893. Christopher died at Ambala 1894.

DALY, CLIVE In the United Grand Lodge of England library (NJE160PUN *Proceedings of the District Grand Lodge of the Punjab, 1869-82*), G.H. Daly is listed as a member of the Masonic Board of General Purpose and Worshipful Master of Wahab or Benevolent Lodge No.988. This lodge still exists in Lahore, but is inactive. His relationship to Clive Daly is not established.

GABRIEL, CECIL He was what the Masons call a 'Martin', the brother of a Mason. His brother Edmund belonged to Rajputana No.2800, transferring to Kitchener No.2998 in 1902. Rajputana only had been warranted in 1899, and Francis Prideaux *qv* was one of its first candidates. In 1901, Hamilton *qv* joined Rajputana from Industry in Lahore No.1485. So these three IPS officers were associated together in the beginnings of Rajputana Freemasonry. When contacted, Cecil Gabriel's son when queried lacked any information about the Masonic membership of his father.

GALLOWAY, ARTHUR Initiated, passed, and raised 1921, in Glittering Star No.322 I.C. (Irish Constitution), the Lodge of the 1st Battalion Worcestershire Regiment. His wife's father was a Freemason. In retirement Galloway attended Yeovil Lodge in England.[24] When visited by this author, he proudly displayed his Glittering Star member's medal.

HAMILTON, ROBERT A school lodge was consecrated January 20, 1888, while Hamilton was at Westminster. As Lord Belhaven, he was The Grand Master Mason of Scotland in 1931-33.[25] In 1933, King Gustav V of Sweden invited him to Stockholm, where Gustav presided over various rites of the Swedish grand lodge. In the course of the celebrations he gave Hamilton the highest Swedish order, which is reserved exclusively for Freemasons: *Knight of the Order of Charles XII of Sweden.* In 1934, when presented by Scottish Masons with a decoration commemorating his Grand Mastership, Belhaven replied, '...I thank you, brethren, from the bottom of my heart as the donors of this most beautiful jewel, which I shall treasure as much as any decoration given me by the King...For thirty-six years I have joined in the grand march of Freemasons of the world, and hope I will still "go marching on".'[26] Belhaven's son, the 12th baron, was a Grand Lodge member as proxy for an Indian lodge during much of his father's holding of high offices, and was himself a political officer in Aden. Hamilton was initiated 9 November 1898, passed 20 June 1898, raised 18 July 1898, all in Lodge Industry in Lahore No.1485. He joined Rajputana No.2800 in 1901 from Lodge Industry. Rejoined Rajputana No.2800, 2 May 1912. He joined Mesopotamia No.3820 in Basra in 1918, from Rajputana Lodge. Other Mesopotamia members were Hugh Stewart *qv* and Daniel McCollum *qv*. Hamilton's involvement in English lodges did not handicap his Scottish Masonic career.

HAWORTH, LIONEL Initiated 15 October 1902, passed 18 April 1904, and raised 16 May 1904, all in Quetta No.2333. Haworth was one of ten initiates in 1904. The lodge that year had 63 members. Sir Henry McMahon was a member. The Worshipful Master was Major J. Ramsay CIE of the IPS.[27] Quetta Lodge still exists, meeting at Sanobar Colony, Tarbela Dam, Hazara, Pakistan. In 1984 it was one of two remaining lodges of the English Constitution that were active in Pakistan.[28]

HICKINBOTHAM, TOM His membership was identified in Grand Lodge records as 'raised in India, demitted to Aden'. According to the *Masonic Year Book of the Punjab, 1927-28* he was a member of McMahon No.3262 in 1927-28. Keyes was master of this lodge in 1924-25. Member Light of the North 1308 at Dalhousie, 1931-37.

JOHNSTON, FREDERICK WILLIAM No record has been found of his blue lodges, but in 1923 Johnston was listed as holding the 18th degree as a Sovereign Prince of Rose Croix de Herodem and Knight of the Eagle and Pelican. This was in McMahon Chapter No.161, and was the same rank achieved by Terence Keyes *qv.*[29] He does not appear in the 1922 edition. In 1925 he became Most Wise Sovereign (presiding officer). He was again Most Wise Sovereign and 'IMS' in 1929. He received the 30th degree of Grand Elect Knight Kadosh or Knight of the White and Black Eagle in 1926. In 1931 he was raised to the 31° of Grand Inspector Inquisitor Commander. In 1933 and subsequent *Rules and Regulations* of the Supreme Council, Johnston's name appears but with no indication of where he belonged or whether he was on 'special assignment'.

KEMBALL, CHARLES Kemball entered Charterhouse with Francis Dames, subsequently Charterhouse housemaster, Masonic enthusiast, founder of the

Carthusian lodge *Deo Dante Dedi* in 1901, and its Master in 1907. Another school contemporary was Charles Hampson, Grand Secretary of the Grand Lodge of Mark Master Masons. No record of Masonic membership has been found of Kemball or of his uncle, who was also a Gulf Resident.

KEYES, TERENCE HUMPHREY He joined McMahon Lodge No.3262 in Quetta, 1908. Entered Apprentice 19 November 1908. Fellowcraft 10 December 1908. Master Mason 13 May 1909. He left McMahon and then rejoined 16 June 1910, left again for No.1066, 1921, but in 1924 was McMahon's Worshipful Master. He received the 18th degree (Sovereign Prince of Rose Croix de Herodem and Knight of the Eagle and Pelican) in McMahon Chapter No.161, 1923. His brother-in-law, A.H. McMahon, was elected to the Supreme Council for the Empire in 1917 and served as Lt.Grand Commander, Supreme Council 1929-1948, and then became Grand Commander of the Supreme Council. In 1930 Keyes transferred to Golcunda Chapter No.51, Secunderabad, Deccan. He joined Golcunda No.3249 (craft lodge) at Secunderabad on 8 August 1930, resigning on 31 May 1934. In 1931 Keyes is shown in records as District Grand Warden and Past District Grand Pursuivant of the District Grand Lodge of Madras. In 1932 he was elected Senior Grand Deacon of the United Grand Lodge of England. He became a member of Rock of Gwalior No.1066 (craft lodge) on 16 January 1934, resigning on 20 September 1935. In 1933 he was Most Wise Sovereign of Golcunda and received the 30th degree (Grand Elect Knight Kadosh or Knight of the White and Black Eagle). He died 26 February 1939 at Bexhill. His executor was Sir A.H. McMahon, not only his brother-in-law and Masonic superior, but fellow Old Haileyburian.

LOCH, PERCY GORDON 'My father was a Free Mason because he thought it political and helpful to be so in India and the Gulf.' Tam Dalyell to P.J. Rich, 5 October 1987. (As the son of a Freemason, Dalyell is 'Lewis' and would have received special consideration had he elected to petition to join.)

LORIMER, JOHN GORDON Initiated 20 August 1896, passed 17 September 1896, raised 15 October 1896, in Khyber Lodge No.582. Rejoined Khyber Lodge No.582 on 15 April 1897. Joined Himalayan Brotherhood No.459 from Khyber 13 November 1899. This was a lodge to which McMahon belonged and which initiated a number of Viceregal figures, including the Earl of Suffolk. On 19 January 1909 he rejoined Lodge Industry & Perseverance No.109, Calcutta, from Khyber 582. Resigned 31 March 1909. He joined Kitchener No.2998, 13 April 1903. No record has been found of Lorimer's brother David as a Mason, although he like Gabriel was a Martin and was the Political Agent in Bahrain.

McCOLLUM, DANIEL VINCENT Curiously, no record has been uncovered of his initiation. He joined Mesopotamia Lodge, Basra, 1919, from Lodge Industry in Lahore No.1485 – which seems to have no record of him. The members of Industry were largely Indians. He also belonged to Quetta Lodge No.3262. His membership seems to contradict suppositions that he was a Catholic.

PELLY, LEWIS Pelly appears as a member of Lodge St.George No.549 in the *'Alphabetical List of Members of Lodges'* in both the 1870 and 1872 editions of *The Masonic Register* for Bombay.[30] In the membership list of St. George's that was maintained by the United Grand Lodge of England, there is no record of his taking the Entered Apprentice degree, but there is in Isaac M. Shields, *A History of Lodge 'St.George' of Bombay*, Times of India Press, 1898, copy in GLL:NTE166(549)Shi. There he is recorded as being made Entered Apprentice on 18 January 1870. He is shown in the register as passed to the Fellowcraft degree on 1 February 1870 and raised to Master Mason on 7 February 1870. Immediately below Pelly's name in the register is an entry for another IPS officer, Lewis Penn, joining St. George's from Lodge No.514 of the Scottish jurisdiction. Lord Willingdon, when Viceroy, belonged to St. George's. Pelly's Masonic adventures will be related in the forthcoming *Tom Brown in Arabia*.

PRIDEAUX, FRANCIS BELVIEW Initiated in Rajputana Lodge No.2800 16 June 1900; passed to Fellowcraft Degree 25 April 1912. Rajputana was only warranted (founded) a year before, in 1899. A mystery about Prideaux's Masonic career is that he was raised to the Master Mason degree only on 25 April 1912 in No.3554, an unusually long period between the second and third degrees. (This author met an Entered Apprentice in Qatar who was hoping to take the second and third degrees after a period of more than fifteen years – so apparently when men move about, such gaps can occur.) Hamilton *qv* joined Rajputana in 1901. Cecil Gabriel's *qv* brother was a member at the same time. No record has been found of Prideaux's father as a Mason, although he was a Gulf Resident.

STEWART, HUGH Joined Roos-Keppel Lodge No.3374 (Dunga Gali, Punjab) from Khyber No.582, 20 July 1910. No record found so far of his membership in Khyber. Resigned 31 May 1912. Joined Mesopotamia Lodge No.3820 in Basra in 1919 from Roos-Keppel Lodge. Hamilton *qv* and McCollum *qv* belonged to Mesopotamia.

WILSON, ARNOLD Favourable references to Freemasonry occur in his writings, but no record of membership has been found. He appears to go out of his way to use various Royal Arch Mason's identification phrases such as *the headstone of the corner* in his book *Thoughts and Talks*. As chairman of the Industrial Health Research Board, Wilson strongly advocated a Masonic section in the welfare departments of private companies.[31]

Governmental consequences of the memberships of these gentlemen should be viewed sceptically. A grand and malevolent Masonic design at work in the Gulf can be discounted, but Masonry did offer a treasure house of piebald rituals which could be used to impress and manipulate. Eco in *Foucault's Pendulum* suggests that it could be 'a pastime for provincial politicians and professional men' and 'the caricature of a caricature. Except that those gentlemen take it extremely seriously.'[32] If it is accepted that part of the Gulf's current problem is that the British indoctrinated the shaikhs in a highly divisive élitism, then the Masonic membership of the IPS does have significance. If the reader wonders why the IPS bothered with Masonry, it may be helpful to view the Craft as a chamber crammed with useful symbols that could be redeployed in the service of the Empire. More than that, and no matter what the denials, Masonry for some was a religion:

> Although today Masons do not call their Craft a religion, it has nevertheless a religious origin...and it does religious work in helping its initiates and through them the rest of the world. To many of the Brn. it is the only real religion they have ever had, and certainly many of them put its principles nobly into practice: for masculine Masonry is a stupendous charitable organization as well as a 'system of morality', and it offers a splendid training in practical kindliness and fraternity.[33]

It was also a form of escapism. Regardless of kindnesses or benevolences, the fraternity's cultivated anachronisms were an opportunity to transcend boredom and enter a world of princes and knights and the ultimate wish-fulfilment of becoming Cyrus or Solomon. Moreover, Masonry dispensed the most coveted coinage of Imperialism, *royal ritualistic recognition.* The Monarch was either patron, in the case of Victoria, or Grand Master, as in the case of Edward VII. The 'Royal Craft' definitely had a political outlook and it was an autocratic and monarchical one. The grovelling that went on behind the lodge doors was more feudal than that associated with any monarchy.

Boyhood and Brotherhood

'The connection between the public schools and the attitude of the British raj is substantiated by the involvement of the schools in Imperial masonry. Quite plainly, along with carefully cultivated connections with aristocracy and royalty, the lodges enjoyed connections with the public schools.'[34] Welldon was not the only head to enjoy lodge life. Grand Lodge records show that headmasters who were involved included:

> P.J.A. Attenborough (Sedbergh), A.P. Boissier (Harrow), E.F. Bonhote (Haileybury), W.V. Cavill (Hymer's), H.G.M. Clark (Repton), James Cobban (Abingdon), Harold Costley-White (Bradfield, Westminster), A.A. David (Clifton, Rugby), C.A. Elliott (Eton), W.A. Fearon (Durham, Westminster), G.G. Fisher (Repton), F. Fletcher (Chigwell, St. Paul's, Harrow), Clifton Jekings (Clifton), J.E. King (Clifton), Richard Lee (Christ's Hospital), Spencer Leeson (Merchant Taylors', Winchester), F.B. Malim (Sedbergh, Haileybury, Wellington), J.A. Nairn (Merchant Taylors'), Cyril Norwood (Marlborough, Harrow), Brian Reeves (Merchant Taylors'), M.J. Rendall (Winchester), Douglas Lee Scott (Mercers), H.W.P. Sloman (Sydney Grammar, Tonbridge), J. Talbot (Haileybury), T.W.H. Smith-Pearse (Epsom), R. Waterfield (Cheltenham), and Jack Wolfenden (Uppingham, Shrewsbury). *This is only a sampling.*

Again, a caveat or two is in order to avoid the impression that too much is being claimed. Although public schools provided the majority of Grand Lodge officers, the stratified nature of Masonry never became total social ossification.

Kipling made much in his poetry of the cross-class nature of the movement, and asserted that the brotherhood encompassed men from various strata of life. The usual script could be departed from, just as elsewhere in society there were surprising instances of unprecedented forms arising in what appeared to be the most rigid circumstances:

> This is not because of the inveterate tendency of man's 'free will' to resist manifest good and manifest reasonableness, as Dostoevsky, Beryawev, Shestov, and other 'alienated' Russians would have it, but because of the processual structure of social action itself. Van Gennep made a striking discovery when he demonstrated, in his comparative work on rites of passage, that human culture had become cognizant of a tripartite movement in space-time. His focus was restricted to ritual, but his paradigm covers many extra-ritual processes. He insisted that in all ritualized movement there was at least a moment when those being moved in accordance with a cultural script were liberated from normative demands, when they were, indeed, betwixt and between successive lodgments in jural political systems. In this gap between ordered worlds almost anything may happen.[35]

What simply is claimed here is that the subject of Freemasonry in the Middle East deserves more attention than it has received, and that the study should not be left to Freemasons alone: '...are we really to leave the history of astrology, so influential on so many of the most sophisticated minds of the Renaissance, to be written by gypsy ladies in tents?'[36] Aspects will seem to have more of a relationship to Alice in Wonderland than history, at least as some of the Masons present the topic, and the Orientalism which exercised a hyperbolic influence on the Craft's ritual development in the nineteenth century will strike modern-day Arabs as amusing. After all, despite *Haji Baba* and the *Arabian Nights,* Doha and Dubai are to their inhabitants no more exotic than Carlisle and Coventry.

As seen, a number of the Gulf Residents and Agents invested their treasure and time in pursuit of Masonic titles. No evidence suggests that they took the obligations other than to heart. That they *willingly* took the blood-curdling oaths confirms a suspicion that ritualism was not only part and parcel of the Imperial baggage but exerted real influence. (This author personally knows of a modern American instance, when a politician who was in line for his party's nomination for governor of an American state stood aside in return for help in becoming the grand master of the state's Masonry.)

When the subject of rule by ritual is raised, not to be discounted in any study of the Imperial civil services is the effect on individuals of the drama and ceremonial of Masonic degrees.[37] While all initiation rites have a theatrical side – the better to cement the newcomer to the group – the Masonic rituals had a singular solemnity and laboured mightily to present an aura of age.[38] In Drama and Craft, Rev. Neville Cryer, the 1974 Prestonian Lecturer (the lecture is the most prestigious endowed lecture of the United Grand Lodge of England), devoted himself to ways in which lodges contrived to carry on the histrionic tradition of the medieval miracle plays:

> What I hope that I have sufficiently shown is that what we now possess in contemporary freemasonry is a dramatic practice which has links with, and echoes of, the past of a much more persistent nature than we might previously have been aware...a refashioned esoteric experience that bears the marks of almost every age through which it has passed from the time of the first Masonic Constitutions until now. We have, I become more and more convinced, a ritual procedure that carries within it dramatic emphases that are the lasting imprints of an earlier masonic age which no amount of refining and resigning in the eighteen and nineteenth centuries could erase, because this is the very stuff the masonry is made of – a system of moral instruction and practical fellowship, framed in given allegorical forms and enlightened by deep, folk-laden symbols...For those who have eyes to see and ears to hear with, not least those who continue to wonder what is meant by this or that facet of our ceremonies and who ask in our study circles, 'Why do we do or say these things?', I can only close with one word from one who, if never a member of the Craft, at least was alive to drama: There are more things in heaven and earth, Horatio, than are dreamt of in your philosophy.[39]

The Reverend Cryer could have added that Masons in the past were not embarrassed with adding to or changing William Shakespeare's writings. When a lodge attended the theatre, it was common for a prologue or epilogue to be tacked on 'extolling the excellence of Freemasonry, and the virtues of the Brethren', or even to rework a scene to allow for the introduction of a Masonic song in which the attending members 'join'd in the Chorus to the entire Satisfaction of the whole Audience.'[40] Times change, and it is unlikely today that a West End audience would welcome such revisions!

What has not changed is the remarkable Masonic dedication to ritual *per se*. The Craft is a monument to the enthusiasm for ritual that runs through human history. Another Prestonian Lecturer, George Draffen in 1956, told *his* audience that, 'The function of ritual is to enshrine the teachings or dogma of the society to which it applies, in such a way as to be recognizable only by the initiated...A man who accustoms himself to ritual will end up loving it. He familiarizes himself with the movements, the sounds and the words. Under their influence he becomes elevated...Ritual always acts in a conservative fashion. It is, *par excellence* the guardian of tradition and the principal means by which the historical aspect is safeguarded and perpetuated.'[41] The fascinating old boy lodges have a similar custodial function.

Masonry, Gulf Politics, and Future Research

As the guardians of the Gulf, presumably the Residents and Agents would have found informal exchanges of information with brethren who had been travelling in the Middle East to be politically useful. An indication that they were earnest in their Masonry is the trouble they took to reaffiliate when they reached a new post. This involved paperwork, fees, and an interview. The capsule summaries of their Masonic careers in this chapter illustrate this pattern of loyally and repeatedly affiliating when re-posted.

As mentioned, by no means is it an easy matter to state to which lodges a man belonged. *The Indian Freemason* (March 1902) gives one reason for this: 'In India, as we know, most Lodge Bye-Laws have a provision for absent members. This class of Brethren are allowed to retain their connection with the Lodge by paying – say one Rupee per mensem. A Brother on being transferred to this list disappears from official returns, for, were his name to remain thereon Grand Lodge dues would be payable in the same ratio as for ordinary members.' In other words, lodges had 'unofficial' members, men who had belonged but who because of transfer maintained later only a loose connection.

This is not the only obstacle that exists to further efforts in determining membership. The various difficulties mean that it may be found that an IPS officer affiliated with a lodge without any evidence appearing in the reports sent back to Grand Lodge in England. *Nor does mere membership indicate the degree of commitment.* Thus the ultimate consequences of membership for IPS attitudes are debatable, but surely such lifelong affiliations indicate *some* interest in ritualism.

Did Freemasonry in the Gulf reinforce conservative or liberal views? Would a Britisher or Arab who affiliated be more likely to be radical or conservative? Hamilton after serving as head (Grand Mason) of Scottish Freemasonry became involved with the small Scottish fascist movement of the 1930s. Keyes when he was the Resident in Hyderabad, one of the choicest of IPS posts, staunchly defended native royalty and opposed the 'dangers of democracy' in the directly British-administered part of India. In 1930 he complained to Sir Denis Bray, the Foreign Secretary of the Government of India, 'To me this is the madness that the gods send before destruction...what Butler calls British India is just that part of India that is trying to repudiate all that is British...what he calls Indian India is the part that wants to retain the British connection.'[42] He was more IPS than he was British.

Keyes was an arch Mason and arch conservative. On the other hand, Freemasons were denounced as encouraging revolution and anarchy and in Turkey were linked with the Young Turks. The deposition of Shah Muhammad Ali in 1909 has been laid at their door:

> In these events too, the influence of Freemasonry if not of Zionism was suspected by some who observed them closely. The Masonic lodges of Salonika and Turkey proper had close connections with the Grand Lodges of India, and Indian Freemasonry was fraternally allied to the lodges of Basra, which had existed since 1839. The most influential of all the Masons of the Middle East was probably Shaikh Khazal of Muhammerah, the tiny principality on the Persian side of the Shatt-al-Arab. Khazal was the almost inseparable companion of the Shaikh of Kuwait, guardian of the oil installations of southern Persia, a loyal ally of Britain from the turn of the century, and Grand Master of all Freemasonry in Mesopotamia.[43]

In Egypt, where both French and British Masonry were widespread, the implications have been studied by Oxford's Karim Wissa, now of the Egyptian foreign service, who concludes that lodges provided a way that the élite could 'seclude itself', and that the interest of most was more in politics than in spiritual and symbolic instruction. The French-influenced lodges, he contends, were more liberal-secular than were the British-influenced lodges. The wealthy cotton merchants and propertied class tended to join the British lodges. Names from the political establishment such as Sa'd Zaghlul, Mustafa Kamil, Butrus Ghali, and Yusuf Wahba were identified with the French *Kawkab al-Sharq* lodge. Wealthy conservatives such as Fahmi Wisa, George Khayyat, and Isma'il Abaza were on the rolls of British lodges.[44] Wissa is probably correct that lodges provided a ready-made structure for anyone with political notions, although he adds that the social club side to Masonry was equally important. This is true in today's Gulf.

The subject will always present wonderful opportunities for diving off the deep end and disappearing forever in a world of cabalism and conspiracy theories, as bewildered readers of Umberto Eco's *Foucault's Pendulum* will appreciate: 'And finally their moment comes; on the tide of Islamic irredentism they stick their heads out again. Putting Hitler in the Plan, we found a good reason for the Second World War. Now, putting in the Assassins of Alamut, we explain what has been happening for years in the Persian Gulf. And this is where we find a place for our Tres, *Templie Resurgentes Equites Synarchici*. A society whose aim is to heal the rift, at least, between the spiritual knighthoods of different faiths.'[45] Given the irrational nature of much of human behaviour, the desire to impose order becomes irresistible. In the case of Masonry, the order achieved is incomprehensible to outsiders.

The tone of this consideration has been critical of the brethren, and it would be churlish to depart the topic without acknowledging that Masonry's aspirations, if not its realities, were often lofty. Kipling wrote in *Mother Lodge*:

We'd Bola Nath, Accountant,
An' Sauil, the Aden Jew,
An' Din Mohammed, draftsman
Of the Survey Office, too;
There was Babu Chuckerbutty,
An' Amir Singh the Sikh,
An' Castro from the fittin'-sheds,
The Roman Catholic.

We 'adn't good regalia,
An' our Lodge was old and bare,
But we knew the Ancient Landmarks,
An' we kept them to a hair;
An' lookin' on it backwards
It often strikes me thus,
There ain't such things as infidels,
Excep', perhaps, it's us.

This can be viewed as pure condescension on Kipling's part, but the author will state from personal experience that there is truth to his lines. That praise of the fraternity's good side must be balanced with serious and substantial criticism. In the 1880s Ambrose Bierce wrote that the Freemasons claimed, 'The order was founded at different times by Charlemagne, Julius Caesar, Cyrus, Solomon, Zoroaster, Confucius, Thothmes, and Buddha. Its emblems and symbols have been found in the Catacombs of Paris and Rome, on the stones of the Parthenon and the Chinese Great Wall, among the temples of Karnak and Palmyra and in the Egyptian Pyramids – always by a Freemason.'[46] The morass of myth and of accretions of legend which make Masonry so confusing a subject are precisely why it was useful whenever ritual-making was afoot. It served the Jacobeans, assisted the American and French Revolutions, and was useful to Imperialism. No conspiracy theory is necessary to accept that it was an ingredient in Victorian *fakelore*. Regrettably, the tenuous connections with Rosicrucianism, Templarism, *et al* that have received so much attention are not half as promising to scholars as are topics such as the little understood role the Craft played in Imperialism and education, or in Middle Eastern affairs.

Advice to Masons and Their Critics

The subject of Masonic influence in history will continue to raise tempers. The debate in years past which went on over political consequences in the Middle East has not died down, and as long as the movement insists on deep secrecy (sometimes ingenuously excused as a simple demand for privacy), it will be suspect. Apologies that the secret recognition signs are merely an old-fashioned version of the plastic membership cards carried by the members of less esoteric societies seem contrived, as does Masonic hair-splitting about the fact that the pass words are in the public domain while their use in context is private. Granted that all secret passwords would be in the dictionary, but that is not what makes them secret passwords. The matter of secrecy cannot be dismissed quite so easily as it is by Christopher Haffner, the widely-respected District Grand Master for Hong Kong and the Far East: 'Masonic secrets – which are simply recognition signs – are trivial in comparison with State secrets, industrial secrets, or even the shared secret hopes of a husband and wife.'[47]

The Masons themselves may want, out of self-interest if for no other reason, to display openness not only to historians but to the public. The present Grand Master in England, the Duke of Kent, has indicated that he has misgivings about whether the stubborn silence of the lodges was an effective policy. In 1984 he commented:

> Brethren, you will be aware that the Craft has recently been the subject of another 'exposure', this time by an author [Stephen Knight in *The Brotherhood*] who seems to make it a speciality to attack Freemasonry...Our response was, in the traditional manner, to be largely unresponsive. This may have temporarily dampened the delight which the media seem to take in Mason-bashing – and it is remarkable how resolute but courteous refusal to comment dampens debate – but I am beginning to wonder whether our stonewalling attitude is necessarily the best for the interests of the Craft.[48]

In keeping with this concern, the Duke approved the creation of an exhibition at Grand Lodge headquarters in London to which the public would be admitted. *Inside the Brotherhood,* Martin Short's sequel to Stephen Knight's *The Brotherhood,* was unimpressed by this, complaining that the offensive artefacts had been kept locked in the closet: 'There was no tyler's sword to fend off intruders. There was no hoodwink to blindfold initiates, no poniard or dagger to thrust against their breasts, and no rope or cable-tow to loop round their necks, all symbols of the traditional fate awaiting any Mason who betrays the brotherhood.' Nor, he noted, was there the human skull used in one of the rituals or plaque with the mysterious names of God, the titles of three deities with 'satanic overtones'. He was unmoved by a videotape in which one Mason said the Craft gave the feeling of fellowship that was had from 'being with the boys'. Masonic *glasnost* came in vain.[49]

Students of the Middle East can feel confident that, prosopographically speaking, Masonic membership indicates a more than passing acquaintance with symbolism and ritualism. It may also indicate a secular mentality, no matter how overtly religious the individual Mason professes himself to be. It is important to re-emphasize the observation that the lodge seems to receive added impetus when the prevailing religion lacks ritual: 'Hence the sparse Presbyterianism of Scotland and Northern Ireland has produced a masonic population of something like one tenth of the adult males, whilst the various counties of England have generally been stronger in masonry where the influence of the liturgical Anglican church is less.'[50] Dr. David Steel, a former moderator of the Church of Scotland and father of the Liberal Party leader, has echoed this, remarking that the kirk's lack of imagery meant that Scots found in Masonry the ritual 'which articulates deep feelings which they may have, not in any rational sense, but in an imaginative way.'[51] (In similar vein, it may be that Imperial civil servants sought out Masonry with more frequency than civil servants in the home government, and that this was because the lodges were a refuge in an alien environment – but to substantiate that conclusion would require an enormous study of affiliations of government officers at home and abroad.)

'There are elements in Freemasonry which bring out the worst in some men,' remarks an opponent of the order, adding, 'Whether they are "possessed" by evil spirits or just mentally destabilized by occult mumbo-jumbo, they are a danger to society and themselves.'[52] Be that concern paranoia or prudence, the widespread existence of Masonry shows *something* about need in life for ritual and the yearning to be part of an élite. It points to man's ritualistic nature and to the fact that he seeks it elsewhere than in church.[53]

Study of the relationship between Masonry and the Middle East has been complicated by the borrowing of Islamic and Arab motifs to give the Masonic rituals more of a mysterious flavour, and, appositely, the invention of so-called higher degrees with their claims to carry on the traditions of the Crusades. This contradiction, with certain of the degrees indicating a respect for Muslim society and others stirring up memories of war between Christians and infidels, is one that scholars will want to investigate. Commenting on Masonic knighthoods, Short rails:

> This ritual fills me with ignoble thoughts. There are some 13,000 Masonic Knights in England and Wales...They must all be Master Masons of the good old Craft which, as Grand Lodge tells us, took Christ out of its rituals 'to enable men of different faith to join in prayer (to God as each sees Him)'. Yet here such men enter an order which is not only exclusively Christian: it is bigoted, militant and commemorates the Crusaders who pillaged and slaughtered their way round the Eastern Mediterranean for centuries. When the ritual talks of 'infidels' it means Muslims; people who are allegedly welcome in Freemasonry, 'which is open to men of all religious faiths'. Perhaps British Muslim Masons (a few exist, I understand) should form themselves into the Knights of Saladin, in order to revere a Muslim leader with more humanity than any Crusader king. There are times when the whole of Freemasonry seems like an overgrown schoolboy's morbid fantasy, with war-games thrown in.[54]

Discussion of this would go far beyond the limits of this book. An object has been to demonstrate that problems for historians and political scientists presented by the influence of Masonry in the Gulf are numerous.[55] However whether lodges were the resort of reactionaries or the nursery of revolutionaries, the Gulfites' involvement suggests a commitment that could be as significant as was the commitment to the old school.

Even the sophisticated Westerner finds Masonry and the English public school to be confusing institutions, so it can be appreciated that when the Arabs complain about the bewildering intrusions of the West into the Gulf that they have a valid point. The old school tie evoked emotions similar to the affection felt for the mother lodge, and is the ensuing subject. Not by accident was the 'freemasonry of the public schools' frequently noted, although many who used the description did so as a synonym for comradeship and missed the double meaning that it could and often did carry.

To conclude, it is clear that masonry has, and always will have, a double function to perform for humanity, a function whose philosophy is illustrated by its activity. This function is to reflect upon the relationships of men in society, which we call speculation; and to act in accordance with the results of such speculation, which we call reciprocity. – William Sanderson, *Two Hundred Years of Freemasonry: A History of the Britannic Lodge No.33*, 1930.

NOTES

1. A. Finan, *History of the Grand Lodge of All Scottish Freemasonry in India, 1837-1924*, Thacker, Bombay, 1928, 121. Few scholars are working on topics relating to the Arabs and Freemasonry. 'Lastly, answering your question about other writers on freemasonry in the area [of the Middle East], I can only cite off the top of my head a very few, if not the only ones: Professor Jacob Landau of the Hebrew University in Israel, Professor Bruno Etienne of the University of Aix-en-Provence, and Professor Paul Dumont of the Centre National de Recherche Scientifique in Paris – both I know very well. Unfortunately, this topic has not received due attention from scholars because of the sensitive aspect of it in our part of the world.' Karim Wissa (St Antony's College, Oxford), to P.J. Rich, 25 October 1988. See Karim Wissa, 'Freemasonry in Egypt 1798-1921: A Study in

Cultural and Political Encounters', *British Society for Middle Eastern Studies Bulletin*, Vol.16, No.2, 1989, 143-61. Mr. Wissa has since joined the Egyptian Foreign Service.

2. Finan, *History of the Grand Lodge*, 161-63.

3. As told to Eric Rosenthal, *From Drury Lane to Mecca*, Sampson, Low & Co., 1931, 198.

4. *Ibid.*, 199.

5. Arthur Koestler, *Janus: A Summing Up*, Picador, 1983, 90.

6. GLE/BE166(1159): *The Marquis of Dalhousie Lodge No.1159, 1867-1967*, 2-4. GLE/BE166(1150): Charles H. Monckton, *The Buckingham and Chandos Lodge No.1150, 1867-1967*, 24.

7. Timothy Mitchell, *Colonising Egypt*, CUP, 1988, 4.

8. J.A. Mangan, ' "The Grit of Our Forefathers": Invented Traditions, Propaganda and Imperialism', John M. Mackenzie ed., *Imperialism and Popular Culture*, Manchester University Press, 1986, 116-17.

9. Mitchell, *Colonising Egypt*, 168.

10. *Ibid.*, 171.

11. GLE/BE166(459)WIL: E.O.W. Wilsen, 're-edited and extended' by G. Reeves-Brown, *Lodge 'Himalayan Brotherhood' No.459 E.C. Being Extracts from the Minutes Books and Correspondence From the Foundation of the Lodge on May 19th, 1838 to the 30th May 1927*, 62, 67.

12. Karim Wissa to P.J. Rich, 25 October 1988. The correspondence was an aftermath to Dr. Wissa's presentation of a paper on Middle Eastern Freemasonry at the 1988 British Society for Middle East Studies meetings.

13. GLE/BE166(1105)GRE: *Grecian Lodge No.1105, 1866-1966*. Grecian was originally called Hellas Lodge.

14. George Macmunn, *The Romance of the Indian Frontiers*, Jonathan Cape, 1931, 254. An altogether different perspective on the visit is given by Idries Shah, whose father at the time was an Afghan student at the Indian public school Aligarh. (See the illustration of Aligarh used for the endpapers of *Chains of Empire*.) Not knowing the Afghan national anthem, the British chose a German march, which the papers dutifully hailed as 'weirdly beautiful Oriental strains'. The King visited Aligarh and presented the Shah's father with a bag of gold for his Koranic recitation. Idries Shah, *The Natives are Restless*, Octagon Press, 1988, 178-80.

15. Shah, *The Natives are Restless*, 256.

16. This was delivered at the meeting of Grand Lodge on 3 December 1924, *Proceedings of the Grand Lodge of Ancient Free and Accepted Masons of Scotland from February 1924 to January 1925*, Edinburgh, 1925.

17. Ian Gordon, *The Craft and the Cross*, Kingsway, Eastbourne, 1989, 91-92. Mr. Gordon claimed that he suffered an appropriate punishment when he abjured Masonry: his business deteriorated, his family life was threatened, *and he had to send his son to a grammar school*: 'But it was...the realization that I could not now afford to send him to the public school I had chosen for him which hit me hardest.' *Ibid.*, 114. The number of lodges to which he belonged was not unusual; they exist for every conceivable interest. For an excellent history of a 'private' academic lodge, *i.e.* a lodge limited to members sharing a common school or college affiliation, see GLE/BE166(1118)PET: E.W.R. Peterson, *The History of the Oxford and Cambridge University Lodge No.1118, 1866-1966*, Oxford and Cambridge University Lodge, 1966, 4, 9, 11.

18. George Dratten ed., *Yearbook of the Grand Lodge of Ancient Free and Accepted Masons of Scotland*, Edinburgh, 1968, 98.

19. See GLE/NJE60 Jam Rai Bahadur Jamiat Rai, *A Brief History of Freemasonry in Quetta, with a Preface by The Honourable Sir Henry McMahon, KCIE, GSI*, The Times Press, Bombay, 1908.

20. Dickson, *Forty Years in Kuwait*, 57.

21. Arnold Galloway to P.J. Rich, 11 December 1987.

22. Eco, *Foucault's Pendulum*, 67. 'The whole Templar mystique, from the trial on, was focused on the plan to avenge Jacques de Molay. I don't think much of the Masonic rite – a mere bourgeois caricature of Templar knighthood – but nevertheless it's a reflection, however pale, of Templar practices. And one of the degrees of Scottish Masonry was kadosch knight, the knight of revenge.' *Ibid.*, 116. 'The Scottish rite was a Franco-German invention. London Masonry had established three degrees: apprentice, fellow craft, and master. Scottish Masonry multiplied the degrees because doing so meant multiplying the levels of initiation and secrecy. The French, congenitally foolish, love secrecy....' *Ibid.*, 356.

23. See esp. A.C.F. Jackson, *Rose Croix: The History of the Ancient and Accepted Rite for England and Wales*, rev. ed., Lewis Masonic, 1987, 228-44. 'As for the influence of the original Rosy Cross on Christianity, Bramanti pointed out, for those who hadn't got their bearings, that it was no accident that Jesus had died on a cross. The sages of the Great White Fraternity were also the founders of the first Masonic lodge, back in the days of King Solomon. It was clear, from his works, that Dante had

been a Rosicrucian and a Mason – as had Saint Thomas, incidentally. In cantos XXIV and XXV of the "Paradiso" one finds the triple kiss of Prince Rosicrux, the pelican, white tunics (the same as those worn by the old men of the Apocalypse), and the three theological virtues of Masonic chapters (Faith, Hope, and Charity).' Eco, *Foucault's Pendulum*, 170-71. Eco is clearly having fun here at the reader's expense! Because of the difficulties in dramatizing the degrees, for some of them sometimes only the passwords and a description were communicated. One Supreme Council body in Western Australia known to the author kept a collection of the costumes and showed them to the initiate, surely a lazy way to communicate 'esoteric wisdom'!

24. Arnold Galloway to P.J. Rich, 3 May 1987.

25. See GLE/BS140Sco.: 'Succeeds to the Throne of the Grand Lodge', *Proceedings of the Grand Lodge of Scotland from February 1931 to January 1932,* 301.

26. GLE/BS140 Sco.: *Proceedings of the Grand Lodge of Scotland, February 1934 to January 1935*, 157.

27. See GLE/NJE60 Rai, *A Brief History of Freemasonry in Quetta.*

28. See K.W. Henderson, *Masonic World Guide*, Lewis Masonic, 1984, 106.

29. See *Rules and Regulations for the Government of Degrees From the 4° to 32° Inclusive Under the Supreme Council 33° of the Ancient Accepted Scottish Rite in England, Wales, the Dominions and Dependencies of the British Crown,* January 1923.

30. GLE/NJE16.Mas.: Education Society's Press, Byculla, India.

31. Arnold Wilson, *Thoughts and Talks*, Right Book Club, 1938, 35. A number of other Residents and Agents make use of illusions in their writings that could be taken as hints at Masonic affiliations, but this could simply be the picking up of Masonic terms from the works of acknowledgedly Masonic authors such as Kipling, rather than an indication of membership.

32. Eco, *Foucault's Pendulum*, 295. *NB.* the quotation from Eco which prefaces this book.

33. John Marlowe, *Late Victorian*, Cresset Press, 1967, 283.

34. C.W. Leadbeater, *The Hidden Life in Freemasonry*, Theosophical Publishing House, Madras (India), 1926, 237. 'The whole subject of Masonic history is one of exceeding interest; but owing to the fact that Masonry is after all a secret society it is often almost impossible to trace the line of its descent by means of any documents which are now available, and consequently there is great confusion and contradiction among the various accounts.' *Ibid.* '...chambers filled with a bewildering variety of artefacts – bewildering not only in their profusion but in their respective ages.' Peter Ackroyd, *First Light*, Hamish Hamilton, 1989, 187.

35. Lodges primarily catering to public school constituencies can be divided into several groups. The greatest number are those that started as general town or city lodges, were physically near to a public school, and hence attracted masters and old boys. Then there were lodges expressly started for old boys and for masters and governors of a school, of which at least 170 can be identified. Finally, amongst those 170 there are lodges which belong to the élitist Public Schools Lodge's Council. In 1987, Council lodges and the dates of founding were as follows: Westminster, 1887; Charterhouse, 1901; Cheltenham, 1907; Sherborne, 1908; Clifton, 1908; Wellington, 1908; Marlborough, 1911; Winchester, 1911; Bradfield, 1911; Felsted, 1913; Repton, 1914; Haileybury, 1918; St.Paul's, 1919; Tonbridge, 1920; Dulwich, 1920; Uppingham, 1920; Malvern, 1921; Eton, 1922; The Leys, 1923; Harrow, 1924; Lancing, 1924; Bedford, 1925; Shrewsbury, 1925; Merchant Taylors', 1879 (only joined Council later); Rossall, 1928; Radley, 1930; St.Edward's, 1930; Oundle, 1937; Gresham's, 1939; Ardingly, 1922 (only joined Council later); Taunton, 1938; Stowe, 1980. A lodge of social consequence might decide not to apply to join the Council, or join at a later date as Merchant Taylors' and Ardingly did. See GLE/BE166(2233)OLD: *Fifty-Fourth Festival of the Public School Lodge's Council at Westminster School on Saturday, 6th June 1987*, 21.

36. Victor Turner, *Dramas, Fields, and Metaphors: Symbolic Action in Human Society,* Cornell University Press, Ithaca (New York), 1987 [1974], 13.

37. Stefan Collini, 'What is Intellectual History...?', Gardiner, *What is History Today?*, 109.

38. In respects, the lodges replaced the bardic orders and the guilds. See Raymond Williams, *Culture*, Fontana Press, 1986 [1981], 59.

39. N. Barker Cryer, 'Drama and Craft', Cyril N. Batham ed., *The Collected Prestonian Lectures 1961-1974*, Lewis Masonic, 1983, 240-41. 'Obviously the masons' method of life was its own reference. Struck by its antiquity, attracted by its mystery...antiquarians and scholars sought to examine their manuscripts and, interestingly enough, they were not withheld. "Can we be masons?" they asked; to be answered, "We cannot admit you as masons because you are *not* masons, but although you are not, we will *accept* you though you were." ' Rev. Keith Bennett in *Scottish Grand Lodge Year Book* for 1968, qtd. *Ibid.*, 239.

40. F.C.C.M. Fighiera, 'Freemasonry and Contemplative Art', H.Carr ed., *The Collected Prestonian Lectures 1925-1960,* Lewis Masonic, rev. ed. 1984 [1965], 201.

41. George Draffen, 'The Making of a Mason', Carr ed., *The Collected Prestonian Lectures 1925-1960*, 416-17. 'One might conceive an aversion to the whole idea of ritual and consider it of little importance – even superfluous. Such an idea would be wrong because it is based on a wrong theory of spirituality and wrong understanding of the place of ceremonialism in man's life. It is a mistake to think of ritual as merely an outward action or ornamental ceremonial. It is an error to think of ritual as a list of prescribed words and actions by which our ancient Craft admits its aspirants.' *Ibid.*, 417.

42. Keyes to Sir Denis Bray, 21 July 1930, qtd. Ashton, *British Policy*, 132. Keyes was important enough for the Viceroy, Lord Willington, to write that he ought 'to be watched pretty closely'. qtd. *Ibid.*, 133. In connection with the idea that Freemasonry was a conservative force – and since in Keyes' judgement the ICS, in contrast with the IPS, was dangerously liberal – it would be helpful to determine prosopographically the relative proportions of ICS and IPS officers who were Freemasons.

43. H.V.F. Winstone, *The Illicit Adventure: The Story of Political and Military Intelligence in the Middle East from 1898 to 1926*, Jonathan Cape, 1982, 11. On Middle Eastern *Masonic* influences, Winstone has the following note: '...from Sir Percy Sykes, *History of Persia*, it seems that Prince Malkom Khan, sometime Persian Ambassador in London, founded the country's first Masonic lodge in the 1860s, *Faramush Khana* or the house of Forgetfulness. The Prince was dismissed as Ambassador following the visit of the Shah to London in 1889...From then on Malkom Khan edited the influential *Kanun* in London. He was joined in 1896 by a fellow Freemason, who was the father of the Persian constitutional movement, Sayid Jamal ad Din...*Thacker's Indian Directory* and the *Bengal Freemason's Almanac* show the District Grand Master for all the east from 1873 to be Stephen Scouloudi, resident in Turkey.' *Ibid.*, 390 n.10.

44. Wissa, 'Freemasonry in Egypt 1798-1921', 157. 'Because the lodges were filled with foreigners, the Egyptian members sought to join these lodges in order to gain the favour and protection of such foreigners. In fact, just as during the regime of the Capitulations members of the Egyptian aristocracy became *consuls honoraires* of different foreign countries so as to enjoy foreign protection (or diplomatic immunity), so also for the same reason they sought representation of foreign lodges: Idris Ragheb represented the Grand Orient of Greece, Italy, Mexico, and New Zealand; Michael Saleh (Salih) Bey represented the Grand Orient of Belgium, Portugal, and Hungary; Ahmed Zaki Bey represented the Grand Orient of Albania; and Mohammed Farid Pasha was a delegate of the Constantinople Grand Orient in Tantah (Tanta).' *Ibid.*, 156.

45. Eco, *Foucault's Pendulum*, 426-33. Ian Gordon recalled his brother raising the 'international conspiracy' theory with him: '"What would you say," Graham began, when the two of us were finally sitting alone over a drink, "if you found that the world was actually being run by people who were no part whatsoever of the official governments." I assumed that this question was rhetorical and waited for him to continue. What he said aroused my interest still further. It appeared that Graham, too, was involved in the search for a personal truth, and his browsings had led him into a so-called Christian bookshop where he had discovered some, as he put it, "pretty amazing stuff ". He showed me some of the books he had bought: two by Nesta Webster, published in the 1920's and called *World Revolution* and *Secret Societies and Subversive Movements*, one by Dan Smoot, published in 1962, entitled *The Invisible Government*, a large volume called *Occult Theocracy* by Lady Queensborough, first published in 1933, [one] written by Gary Allen, with the title *None Dare Call It Conspiracy*.' Gordon, *The Craft and the Cross*, 70.

46. Christopher Haffner, *Workman Unashamed: The Testimony of a Christian Freemason*, Lewis Masonic, Shepperton, 1989, 57.

47. *Ibid.*, 83.

48. Address by the M.W. Grand Master, 25 April 1984, qtd. David W.M. Vaughan, *The Diary of a Freed Mason*, Sovereign World, Chichester, n.d., 125-26. This is one of many books written by former Masons who left the lodge to embrace Roman Catholicism, evangelical Christianity, secular humanism, or other panaceas.

49. Martin Short, *Inside the Brotherhood: Further Secrets of the Freemasons*, Grafton, 1989, 9.

50. Haffner, *Workman Unashamed*, 113.

51. Qtd. James Dewar, *The Unlocked Secret*, William Kimber, 1966, in Short, *Inside the Brotherhood*, 45. Anti-Masonic 'authorities' tend to be incestuous in their citations.

52. Short, *Inside the Brotherhood*, 104.

53. Dewar, *The Unlocked Secret*, 45.

54. Short, *Inside the Brotherhood*, 106.

55. 'The Masonic fraternity is also active in Saudi Arabia even though Masonry is not well received in the Arab Nations. There are reports from the American-Canadian Grand Lodge [there] who have been in communication with a Masonic Lodge in Dhahran, Saudi Arabia...'. *New Jersey Freemason*, Vol.12, No.3, March 1991, 1.

VII

SCHOOL TAROT

We know which are the Major Public Schools even if we don't like them. But spiralling down are the Minor Major Public Schools, Major Minor Public Schools, Minor Public Schools and Schools Which Make You Pay Them Money. – Charles Jennings.

'Is Harrow or Eton better?' I am asked. It is the matter of his son's education. The Shaikh listens. I suppress a sigh as I embark on this difficult subject...in the end he was sent to a school in Chicago. – Gerald de Gaury, *Traces of Travel*, 1983.

We must...establish an Eton in India. We require a college on an extensive scale, with ample accommodation within its walls for a large number of pupils and the followers (few in number of course) who would accompany them. – Col. C.K.M. Walter IPS, *Rajputana Administration Report*, 1869.

Identifying an individual as having attended an English public school truly puts the biographer in clover when it comes to sources about the subject's adolescence. The schools are so documented that it is possible to find out what a boy was doing at Rugby in 1839 on a Wednesday at 8 pm (preparing the first lesson of the next day) or what he was studying if he were taking fifth form French (*Pensées de Pascal*).[1] This becomes important biographically if one agrees with Karl Mannheim and others who have suggested that each generation was distinctively imprinted by the events of its youth, and that generational formation ended at about the age of 25.[2]

Not everyone accepts generational approaches as valid. Assertions that *generation* can be employed to explain behaviour have been challenged on the grounds that there is not enough evidence to show that early experiences have permanent ideological effects, and that when attitudes can be attributed to a particular period of formation, the connection is found with an entire population rather than with a specific group (school, race, religion, *etc.*).[3] A reply is that while in the case of single traumatic events such as an assassination, there would exist a collective memory uniting an inter-generational group – but such influence is not contradictory of influences on generations.[4] Thus the proposition that the development of the Gulf owes something to the fact that the Indian Political Service officers attended public schools does not exclude other influences.

As I indicated in *Chains of Empire*, the other influences in the lives of administrators were in turn subject to public school influence: *'The tone was set by the reformed English public schools.'*[5] Even the material culture of Imperialism was considerably affected, a proposition I put forward in both *Chains* and *Rituals of Empire*. Schooling affected not only individual attitudes but the models of political life that the Empire considered appropriate.[6]

The search for information about the schools of Gulfites requires deciphering school lists and registers. This is a genre of its own, one that offers amazing detail: so much so that the Society of Genealogists in London felt warranted in conducting a seminar in their use. Solomonic decisions were forced on the compilers of the registers when a boy upset careful designs by going to two schools, entering in midterm, or engaging in other unorthodox statistical behaviour. Among annoyances, the use of bank and club addresses complicates geographic analysis. Another discomfiture that will affect prosopographical studies of more recent times but that seems minimal in such a properly Victorian and Edwardian group arises because of an increase in concealed illegitimacy, *in vitro* fertilization, surrogate motherhood, artificial insemination and state-mandated concealment of adoption. Future historians may be in the invidious position of tracing lineages back to ancestors who in actuality were unrelated to an individual. Whether social niceties in the past concealed the origins of any Residents remains a mystery, as it would with any group of similar social standing in that period.

The premise here of course is that digging into school records is worthwhile because schooling tells an enormous amount about a person.[7] In contrast, most Arabs during the period of the IPS administration received an education, if they received an education at all, light years removed from what the British had enjoyed and which is largely undocumented as far as who the teachers were or what was taught.[8]

Attendance at public school immediately confirms upper middle class aspirations if not antecedents, and is a strong indication of a man's basic cultural background. The English public schools were, as Rupert Wilkinson suggests in *The Prefects*, 'an awe-inspiring and complex institution whose details had to be learned by rote if the individual wished to fit in'.[9] In school the importance of ritual was inculcated, energies were channelled into ritual, and boys encountered the ritual magic behind government – and the ways in which maces, wands, and batons supported rule.[10]

Before interpreting any compilation of the Gulfites' schools, a warning should be repeated about giving too much weight to a specific school's supposed status. What is important is that the IPS officers in the Gulf all went to public schools. As Wilkinson emphasizes, the differences 'were dwarfed by a fundamental uniformity between the schools.'[11]

The schooling of East India Company officers (1763-1858), and of Foreign Service officers in the Gulf (1947-1971), has been included in this analysis for completeness sake, but the focus is on the schools of the IPS. And, interesting as information is about the schools attended, there are limits to what can be inferred. Classifying schools by social standing hinges on the idea that reputations remain constant, which is *not* the case. Oakham, which educated one Resident, was obscure when he attended. With aggressive leadership the school became prominent in the 1980s. Conversely, St. Edward's reputation was higher when the famous Kuwait Agent Harold Dickson attended, rather than subsequently. Socially categorizing schools is an exercise fraught with problems – some Clarendon schools, for example, are no more prestigious than certain non-Clarendon schools.

Brian Gardner in *The Public Schools: An Historical Survey*, identified 'The Seven' (based on an 1881 survey) that, by his including Marlborough, differed from the Clarendon list: Eton, Harrow, Winchester, Rugby, Westminster, Marlborough, Charterhouse. He cites as well 38 schools appearing in the first *Public Schools Year Book* (1889). All the Seven are represented on the Gulf list. The subjectivity of such a process is shown by the first *Year Book* including in its 38 the names of Hereford, Portsmouth Grammar School (which one Agent, William Shakespear, attended prior to going to King William's), and Wyggeston, and omitting Sedbergh, Christ's Hospital, Repton, and Felsted.

Not until 1899 did the *Year Book* abandon its system and use the Headmasters' Conference membership list. *Whitaker's Almanack* kept its own list of public schools for years until deciding to use the Conference's. Another rating was that of 'The Ten' in the 1893 volume *The Great Public Schools*: Eton, Harrow, Charterhouse, Cheltenham, Rugby, Clifton, Westminster, Marlborough, Haileybury, and Winchester. The Ten are all represented on the Gulf list. The Residents also attended schools that by any reckoning were not renowned, and which recall a passage in James Hilton's *Goodbye Mr. Chips*:

> It was, nevertheless, a good school of the second rank. Several notable families supported it; it supplied fair samples of the history-making men of the age – judges, Members of Parliament, colonial administrators, a few peers and bishops. Mostly, however, it turned out merchants, manufacturers, and professional men, with a good sprinkling of country squires and parsons. It was the sort of school which, when mentioned, would sometimes make snobbish people confess that they rather thought they had heard of it.[12]

In 1900, A.H.H. Maclean in *Where We Get Our Best Men* surveyed biographical sources in order to resolve the dilemma of school standing, including *The Times* obituaries. The list he compiled of 3068 prominent men produced twenty leading schools. The Victorian foundations were missing except for Marlborough, which also appears on Gardner's list. Twelve of Maclean's twenty are represented on the Gulf list. Maclean made another effort and ranked schools by the number of officers serving in the Boer War (*Public Schools and the War in South Africa*, Edward Stanford, 1903), which produced a different leading twenty, of which sixteen appear on the Gulf list. (He completed his trilogy with *Public Schools and the Great War, 1914-19*, 1923.) Maclean's attempts not only anticipated the efforts of Drs. Honey and Mangan mentioned previously, but were based on more evidence. Another indication of a school's status was whether it had direct-grant standing. While this generally was not as prestigious as being independent, it indicated a stature that was superior to being state-maintained. Direct grant schools on the Gulf list include Hymer's, King's (Worcester), and Oakham.

Social rankings of schools are distorted by the selection of criteria, and there is no end to the criteria that could be employed or in fact have been suggested (possession of a beagle pack, quality of the chapel organ, old boys in the Athenaeum). Ranking the schools has been a virtually endless avocation. *The truth is that similarities in public school culture outweigh what differences existed.* This is not to say that the appearance of schools on the Gulf list is entirely coincidental. The evidence indicates that the *size* of a school does have a relationship to whether it appears on the following list. *The nine largest public schools in 1866 all appear.* In order of numbers enrolled, they were Eton, Harrow, Marlborough, Rugby, Haileybury, Cheltenham, Rossall, Wellington, and Winchester.

This author has argued vigorously in several books that more important than the status of individual schools is the common public school background of a group, especially in a case like the Gulf when two important men who served in one service or in one region were at the same school. That Arnold Wilson and Trenchard Fowle were at Clifton in the same house at the same time is more significant than whether Clifton 'rates' higher or lower on a subjective scale than Shrewsbury. Percy Cox's friendship with Harcourt Butler when Cox was Resident and Butler was India's Foreign Secretary was strengthened by the two men being contemporaries at Harrow. The effects of this old boy network were no desert mirage, but the stuff of power.

As for the consequences for the Gulf, the old school affinities encouraged an élitist approach to politics and education. Speaking to a conference on the Chiefs' Colleges in Calcutta, Lord Curzon warned against increasing enrolment: 'I would not unduly democratize them. I would frankly admit that Rajkumar College relies, as its name implies, on class distinction, and if anyone is found to deprecate such a basis, I would reply that it is neither an ignoble nor a strange distinction, that it is familiar in all countries, that it is founded upon sentiments inherent in human nature, that it is compatible with the finest fruits of enlightenment and civilization.'[13]

The same conference heard from Colonel Loch, headmaster of Mayo College from 1878 to 1903. This was the Colonel Loch whose son Percy Gordon Loch would have such a long term of service that he would be called 'the Grand Old Man of the Gulf'. Loch not only agreed with Curzon, but he opposed the suggestion of scholarships on the grounds that the 'social level of the College might, I fear, be lowered'.[14]

The British preoccupation with schooling as an *open sesame* to the glittering prizes of political life rubbed off. In Kipling's *Kim*, the old lama who is Kim's mentor inquires of the Catholic priest about an education for the boy: 'Well,' said Father Victor in English, when Kim had translated, 'that depends. The Regiment would pay for you all the time you are at the Military Orphanage; or you might go on the Punjab Masonic Orphanage's list (not that he or you 'ud understand what that means); but the best schooling a boy can get in India is, of course, at St. Xavier's in Partibus at Lucknow.'[15] As indicated in Chapter II, the public school influence in the Gulf was primarily through the attitudes that the shaikhs absorbed from the Residents; few Gulf Arabs actually made their way to the IPS schools in India.

Perhaps that was best for all concerned. When the heir to the throne of Muscat did enrol in Mayo College, he made a poor impression with his 'rash wild nature' and was noted for 'bad temper, intolerance, flashing knife and negro slave'. This same prince, Syed Bin Taimur, became ruler and was deposed in 1970 by his son, the present ruler Sultan Qaboos. Syed is recalled for forbidding the wearing of trousers and spectacles – and for not building a single school in Muscat during thirty-eight years of rule.[16] So much for a public school education!

Firm Believers Learning Ritual Skills

Among reasons why studies of 'the mind of the Gulf' merit an emphasis on the peculiar education of the British is that school experiences included an initiation into clan rituals. The Arabs, with their own complex adolescent rites of passage, sensed this. Although the influence of school sports spread through the Empire, emulation and admiration for the school ritualism was more widespread still. The impetus for establishing public schools in the Empire was partly a desire for the knowledge of ritualism. Sports were *not* emphasized to acquire an expertise in cricket *per se*. Until recently, cricket was rarely played in the Gulf; now it is played on a professional basis only in one emirate, Sharjah. Any expertise in games that the Arabs acquired was more often than not, as a ritual skill. Pseudo-traditions were another matter, created by overseas schools and then by the IPS in hopes that this would aid in turning out leaders. Other kinds of schools might offer athletics, but they lacked the ritualism that is the hallmark of public school education.

With the schools apparently so important in boyhood, the consequences should appear in Gulf careers and writings. That will be the burden of the other books in this series already mentioned. From Lewis Pelly's account of his trip to Riyadh in the 1860s, to Hay's descriptive work of the region after World War II, there was an old boy version of Imperial (and specifically *Gulf*) history. The public school pen of the Residents described a Gulf with more shaikhs and palaces than fishermen. And as far as Gulf educational policy was concerned, the British equated any good education with their own. The son of Harold Dickson, the Kuwait Political Agent in the 1930's, wrote to this author: '...he didn't particularly enjoy life at St. Edward's, but, like myself, was a firm believer in such education...'.

With their loyalties concentrated on the school, Empire, and lodge, it is no wonder that the British in the Gulf ignored Arab customs and imposed their own. They intruded on areas that Arabs considered private, and this led to the formalizing of events that the Arabs had never treated ceremoniously. But to substantiate claims about public school Freemasonry, about the spread of school rituals, and about the specific influence on the Gulf, it is mandatory to identify the schools that were attended and the other circumstances of individual Gulfite educations.

Not Vice Versa

The need for an emphasis in the biography of the British in the Gulf on what happened at public school is supported by the way that the Gulfites tampered with native customs but considered *vice versa* taboo. The Imperial punctilio was sacrosanct, whereas in reality – like school traditions – it had been invested with a pseudo-antiquity in much the same way as a designer sprays fake cobwebs around a film set. Arabs were not enlightened by the residents about this Victorian 'crêche-ification', which amounted to a hijacking of history. Fakery was endemic in the period. While Whitehall and the schools grew moss and affected medievalism, Freemasonry buried its origins in a mythical past. The schools' and Freemasonry's rise coincided with and influenced the growth of bogus ritualism throughout Imperial life. Customs were cooked-up out of thin air, or warmed up from ritualistic leftovers. On several occasions I have mentioned as an example how Westminster resuscitated pancake greezing. The school cook, superintended by a beadle bearing the mace (how many state schools had maces?), tossed a pancake and boys scrambled for the largest piece and a prize. The reason the ceremony has particular interest is that it provides a telling metaphor for Imperial honours. After the greeze, Old Westminsters overseas would not have lacked the confidence for their own ceremonies. The difference was that shaikhs competed for gun salutes instead of a pancake.

The honours in the Gulf besides gun salutes ranged downwards from knighthoods to bronze medals. The 'gongs' of recognition epitomized hierarchicalism. The shaikhs became part of a mad greeze to win awards. These honours demonstrate how to extract a deference from the recipients while enhancing the ego of the donors. Too often honours are thought about in terms of recipients, when as in the Gulf it really is the British donors who gain the most status. Perhaps the worst excesses were the mini-coronations when the Resident proclaimed the succession of a Gulf ruler. The shaikhs, who started with the prestige of a JP, metamorphosed if they behaved, into Arabian versions of lord-lieutenants, a transformation achieved by baubles from Spinks & Co., St. James' Street, London, W.1.

The lasting results should not be minimized. The Arabs are not ritualistically illiterate but their religion is deliberately and forcefully anti-ritualistic. The ceremony surrounding the Gulf shaikhs nauseates many of them. Ritualism and élitism are not peripheral to Gulf politics. Ataturk had understood the significance of totems when abolishing the fez in Turkey. The Scottish nationalists understood it when they stole the Stone of Scone. Walpole was aware of it when the kilt was embargoed in the Hanoverian era. Talismans from the British era in the Gulf are the substratum of present ideology. The monarchist ideology of the present ruling families could not endure without being celebrated and sustained by ritual.

The antecedents can partly be found in school rewards, including scholarships, prefectorial privileges, prizes, and colours. The idea behind this system carried over into the Gulf. Most Residents garnered knighthoods. Percy Cox (Gulf Resident 1904-20) became sequentially CIE, CSI, KCIE, KCMG, KCSI, GCIE, and GCMG. His deputy, Arnold Wilson, acquired the CMG, CIE, CSI, KStJ, and KCIE. Every Resident and Agent who served in the Gulf had at least one nominal after his name. No less than 35 became CIE and 10 became KCIE. Another 15 were CSI. The Arabs were incorporated into this system and they too became Companions and Knights in *Christian* chivalric orders.

The continued listing of school awards well into old age in a man's potted autobiographies written for directories points to a system which was considered highly important. As with the Imperial orders bestowed on the shaikhs, scholarships and prizes often involved awarding archaic-looking costumes or other talismans identifying the holder. Public school scholarships became accolades for an élite at the same time Imperial nominals were proliferating, and were similarly exclusive. They by and large were not scholarships for the poor. To flesh out the school honours programme, besides these scholarships, public schools had a vast number of endowed prizes.

In their way, public school scholarships were the KCIEs and prizes were the CIEs. Premonitions of Sir Arnold Wilson's Gulf career can be seen in the prizes he won at Clifton. (The awards were often books on an Imperial theme.) A prize dispute at Eton was suggested as being behind Curzon's resignation as Viceroy – the cause of the enmity that St. John Broderick held for him when he became Secretary of State for India. School prizes covered every conceivable achievement.

Equally diverse were the decorations distributed about the Gulf. The wives of Residents hoped for a Kaisar-i-Hind. Rarely someone in the IPS got a CVO (Gabriel), or a CB (Sadler), and six were foisted off with an OBE (the 'Order for Britain's Everybody'). There were awards for everybody, IPS and shaikhs and even telegraph operators, recalling Lord Melbourne's remark: 'I like the Garter; there's no damned merit in it.'

A fascination amongst the Gulf ruling families with giving and receiving symbolic awards distinctly suggests the public school prize days, and there were several aspects in which the Gulf honours system was reminiscent of public school awards. In fact, the durbars at which the honours were given were compared with prize days. Once awards were created, they had to be properly conferred. The Gulf Residents expended considerable energy in publicly rewarding their shaikhs with ribands, incongruous for Muslims considering that the mythology of British orders was based on Templar motifs of the Crusades. Nor were actual school prizes for the Arabs forgotten. They, too, seemed out of place when what miserable schools there were sometimes lacked textbooks and had to beg for writing paper. This concern for the 'gongs', whether school or Imperial, was common to Residents and shaikhs and created protocol problems that equalled any at the Court of St. James. IPS officers were uniquely equipped to settle the difficulties, and in India they were often assigned to supervise ceremonial events. These tours of ceremonial duty appear in a number of the biographies in Chapter IX.

Schools of the IPS

The sixty-six men of the IPS Service who served as Residents or Agents in the Gulf between 1858 and 1947 attended a number of different schools, but *all* of those attended were public schools. Only five public schools claimed as many as three officers: Cheltenham, Clifton, King William's, Marlborough and Winchester. King William's provides the only 'surprise' amongst these – and not only did it educate three Gulfites, but it had strong connections with Arnold Wilson's family, whose grandfather was headmaster. The Scottish schools are represented by Dundee Institution, Edinburgh Academy, and Kelvinside; Ireland by Clongowes; the Isle of Man by King William's; and Guernsey by Elizabeth's. At least one man was privately educated (Daly), and then went to Woolwich at a young age. In Sadler's case (consult his entry) he possibly was educated privately and accompanied his father on his frequent moves as a diplomat. The schools of three (de Gaury, More and McCollum) are unknown.

If Haileybury's amalgamation with Westward Ho! permitted counting of old boys as from one institution, Haileybury would have the most men on the list, four. Before 1858, the old Haileybury of East India Company fame, with some claim to resemblance of a public school (Philip Mason called it in *The Men Who Ruled India* 'a mixture of verdant green and Tom Brown'), educated several Residents. (See Plate 34.) Imogen Thomas of the Haileybury library has expressed surprise in reviewing the following that there were not more names from either the old or modern Haileybury. However, as far as the leading individuals amongst the Residents, it produced as many as any school did. No one school educated more than one or two of the dozen men of the group that would be considered principal figures. The staying power of *all* of the schools has been remarkable, indicated by the fact that only one school (Charsley Hall), and of course Addiscombe (consider Jones' biography in Chapter IX), have not survived to this day.

The schools represent several traditions. There are old grammar school foundations that metamorphosed like Aldenham and Repton, new foundations of Victorian England such as Cheltenham and Marlborough, and the perennially great schools such as Eton and Harrow. Schools with military associations such as Wellington do not predominate, nor do schools with religious emphasis such as the 'high church' Woodard schools.

The reason that a Resident attended one school rather than another may be a small one. Robert Graves wrote in *Goodbye to All That* that he went to Charterhouse because its scholarship examination did not have a Greek grammar paper and he could not conjugate two of the most frequently used verbs: 'But for these two verbs, I should almost certainly have gone to the very different atmosphere of Winchester.'[17]

For the reader's convenience, Indian Political Service officers serving between 1858 and 1947 appear in upper case in the following summary. For comparative purposes, those serving before 1858 or after 1947 appear in upper and lower case. The change in officers' educational backgrounds after the Mutiny, and to a lesser extent after 1947, is self-evident.

The list of preparatory schools remains regrettably incomplete, but available information confirms the view of Professor Donald Leinster-Mackay that '...the English preparatory school was essentially a Victorian institution which developed in tandem with, if originating differently from, the English Public School.'[18] The preparatory schools deserve more attention than they usually get. If public school influences are not noted enough, preparatory school influences are virtually unnoted. Some of the preparatory schools attended by Gulfites have as notable histories as do public schools, and their sudden nineteenth-century appearance in the backgrounds of Imperial officers bears out Professor Leinster-Mackay's thesis about the metamorphosis of the prep school at that time.

Introducing a new edition of Trollope's *Dr. Wortle's School,* Dr. John Rae, former headmaster of Westminster, writes, 'A small school founded by a clergyman and accommodating a wide age range was not that unusual in the nineteenth century. Many of today's private preparatory schools have their origin in the initiative of country clergymen, such as Dr Wortle, whose parochial duties matched neither their energy nor their ambition. At first these schools appear to have taken boys of almost any age; Dr Wortle's seventeen year old in a school for children is not a figment of Trollope's imagination. In 1855, when the headmaster of Cheam preparatory school decided to weed out the older boys, it is recorded that some were twenty years of age.'[19]

EIC Tutors & Academies

India Office records show that many applicants to the Company were educated by individuals who took boys for tutoring. Apparently only one IPS officer, Clive Daly, was tutored privately for the whole of his education. Thus the Gulf illustrates sea changes in education in the mid-nineteenth century: the abandonment of private schools and tutors for the public school. The first named below is the tutor or private school proprietor. This is followed by the name of the EIC officer.

James Comber, Richmond, Surrey: *William Bowyear*
P. Kelly, Finsbury Square: *Stephen Babington*
J. Le Middleton, The Academy, Bishopsgate St.: *Benjamin Jervis*
James Robertson, schoolmaster, Kirkmichael, Perthshire: *James Dow*
J. Scardfield, 'my Academy', Twyford near Winchester: *Nicholas Smith*
Mr. Stoton's, Wimbleton: *Arnold Kemball*
James Smith: *John Beaumont*
Mr. William's, Edmonton: *Samuel Hennell*
John Willis, Foster Lane: *James Morley*

Preparatory Schools

For this study, the public schools of Residents and Agents were written to and specifically asked about the preparatory schools of their old boys. Unfortunately, and somewhat surprisingly to the author, the majority of schools did not have any record of the preparatory school from which a boy entered. Consequently only 19 of the 66 IPS officers' preparatory schools are so far known. In the case of a few such as Talbot, who entered Eton at the age of 7 and left when he was 17, the years in lower school have been treated as preparatory. There were no prep schools represented in the educations of the EIC group. When known, the prep schools of the post 1947 officers are also included.

Bedford School: John Tripp
Berkhamsted School: REGINALD HADOW 1925-30
Cathedral School, Salisbury: Patrick Stobart
Cheltenham, a dame school: RICHARD BIRDWOOD
Cheam School: Hugh Bolstead
Cherry Orchard Preparatory School: GORDON JACKSON 1921-26.
Clifton College: EVERALD GASTRELL 1910-11
Cordwalles Preparatory School (St. Piran's since 1919): PERCY COX

Dulwich College Preparatory: LIONEL HAWORTH 1881-86
Eton College: ADELBERT TALBOT 1852-57
Elizabeth College, Guernsey: STUART KNOX 1880-83.
Elstree Preparatory School: SAMUEL MILES 'c.1852'.
Hymer's College: ANDREW STEWART
Kersal Glen Preparatory School: CECIL GABRIEL 'c.1887'.
Kikeel: A.S. Carey's: Charles Gault
Marlborough Junior School: FRANCIS PRIDEAUX 'c.1884'.
Mostyn House Preparatory School: ARNOLD WILSON 1897.
Paris, Mr. Demmler's: HERBERT DISBROWE
Portsmouth, Misses Lacell: WILLIAM SHAKESPEAR 'about 1893'.
Sevenoaks School: ARNOLD GALLOWAY
Summer Fields: Gawain Bell 1922-27. OLAF CAROE 1903-06.
Temple Grove Preparatory School: ROBERT HAMILTON. Hamilton was a close friend of H.W. Waterfield, who became Temple Grove headmaster. His son also went to Temple Grove and gives an account of the school in his book *The Uneven Road.*
Westward Ho! Junior School: E.H. GASTRELL '4 yrs'.

Public Schools of Gulf Officers

A few of these schools have not been considered as 'public' by all authorities. Without getting into a lengthy debate about their individual histories, it can be stated that they are all schools which displayed the *characteristics* of the public school.

Ashby de la Zouche School: Geoffrey Arthur
Aldenham School: WILLIAM PRIDEAUX 1852-58.
Berkhamsted School: REGINALD ALBAN 1912-17, RICHARD HADOW 1925-1934.
Bradfield College: WILLIAM HAY 1907-13.
Bryanston: Julian Walker
Charterhouse School: CHARLES KEMBALL 1874-81.
Charsley Hall: HUGH STEWART 1886-92.
Cheltenham College: EVERALD GASTRELL 1912-14, PERCY LOCH 1901-1904, MALCOLM MEADE 1867-1871.
Christ's Hospital: HUGH RANCE
City of London School: ARTHUR GALLOWAY, Philip McKearney
Cleveland House School, Salisbury: Patrick Stobart
Clifton College: RICHARD BIRDWOOD 1893-97, TRENCHARD FOWLE 1898-1902, Edward Henderson 1931-36, ARNOLD WILSON 1898-1902.
Clongowes Wood College: CORNELIUS PELLY
Dover College: RAYMOND MURPHY
Dundee Institution: DAVID LORIMER, JOHN LORIMER
Dunfermline High School: Michael Weir
Elizabeth College: LIONEL HAWORTH 1887-1889.
Edinburgh Academy: EDWARD ROSS 1845-51.
Epsom College: TOM HICKINBOTHAM 1916-17.

Eton College: Bernard Burrows, ADELBERT TALBOT 1852-1862.
Gresham's School: Stewart Crawford
Haileybury College: Stephen Babington 1806 EIC, David Blane 1818-1819 EIC, TERENCE KEYES 1891-94, EDWARD WAKEFIELD 1917-22.
Harrow School: PERCY COX 1878-1882, Charles Gault, SAMUEL MILES 1853-1855, Christopher Pirie-Gordon
Hereford Cathedral School: David Roberts
Highgate School: ROY METCALFE 1922-1927.
Hymers College: HUGH WEIGHTMAN
Imperial Service College/Westward Ho!: RICHARD BIRD, WILLIAM GREY
Kelvinside School: FREDERICK JOHNSTON
King Edward's School, Birmingham: Aubrey Halford-Macleod
King William's College: CYRIL BARRETT 1894-1896, WILLIAM SHAKESPEAR 1894-1896, FREDERICK WILSON 1854-1858.
King's School, Canterbury: Anthony Parsons
King's School, Worcester: GORDON JACKSON 1927-1931.
Lancing College: John Blake
Liverpool Institute: Albert Craig
Malvern College: CHARLES MACKENZIE 1895-1897, GEORGE MALLAM 1910-1913.
Marlborough College: MICHAEL DIXON 1923-1929, FRANCIS PRIDEAUX 1885-1886, ARTHUR TREVOR 1886-1889.
Montrose Academy: Alan Rothnie
Oakham School: HERBERT DISBROWE 1841-1845.
Radley: Donald Hawley
Repton School: STUART KNOX 1883-1886, MEREDITH WORTH 1920-.
Rossall School: JOHN HOWES 1921-1927.
RNC, Osborne: Hugh Bolstead 1907.
Rugby School: Julian Bullard, JAMES CRAWFORD 1869-1874, LEWIS PELLY 1838-1841.
St. Edward's School: HAROLD DICKSON 1894-1900.
St. Lawrence College: George Middleton
Scarborough College: ANDREW STEWART
Sedbergh: Hugh Balfour-Paul
Shrewsbury School: CHARLES CROSTHWAITE 1891-1894, CHARLES PRIOR 1912-1914.
Stamford School: CECIL GABRIEL 1892-1895.
Stonyhurst College: GEORGE COLE
Stowe School: Martin Buckminster
Sutton Valance: John Tripp
Swansea Grammar School: Albert Lamb
Taunton School: RALPH WATTS
Victoria College, Guernsey: Sam Falle
Wanstead School: Arthur Wilton
Wellington College: JOHN BILL 1891-1895, NORMAN BRAY 1898-1903.
Wellington College, New Zealand: Charles Treadwell
Westminster School: STUART GODFREY 1875-79, ROBERT HAMILTON 1885-88.

Winchester College: Gawain Bell, HUGH BISCOE 1894-, OLAF CAROE 1906-, John Moberley, MAURICE TANDY 1928-30.

A legitimate reaction to reading such a list could be *What of it?* By now perhaps the reader will have some idea of the reply. The education that was imparted was so distinctive that the fact that a man attended such a school represents one of the most important facts about him. Sometimes this unique public school indoctrination is described as 'character training', but often what public schools *called* 'character training' was training in ritual. On occasion a boy's reputation for good character was in reality based on facility in society's proscribed rituals. Moreover, this ritualism was not an epiphenomenon of power – it was *fundamental*. To be successful, authority and its accompanying ritualism required – as Durkheim suggested – tangible artifacts such as names, books, flags – *totems*. A nation's political culture can become a giant metaphor reinforced by such apparent trivia. In the case of the British Empire, the metaphors often can be traced back to the schools. *School ritualism constantly reappeared as an Imperial idiom.* The resemblances between school and Imperial ritualism are not so unusual when it is considered that schoolboys were immersed in ritualism. Ritualism was the way in which the school transformed boys into a cohesive group. The Residents' sometimes irrational ideas could represent the resonances of school influences that went unquestioned but *not* untaught.

What a public school education produced was not just a code of manners, but an expertise in manipulating and ruling. Rituals similar to those of public school enabled Gulf officers to exert authority beyond that which their Indian sepoys could exact by arms.

Although Imperial ritualism in the Gulf was a means of control, it was not always employed for the sake of power, but because it was appreciated for itself. It persisted when sounder counsel would have been to keep a lower profile. There was an appetite for ritual that flourished independently of political machinations. However, ritualism had considerable political usefulness – Imperialism relied as much on baubles as it did on dreadnoughts. Possibly this was part of successful earlier empires as well. Byzantium and its church come to mind, and indeed schools resembled churches in their use of ceremony to create deference. In any event, as opportunities overseas beckoned, the schools rushed to provide boys. Headmasters had no reservations about the relationship. From before the Clarendon Report in 1864, until after the Education Act of 1944, the schools incubated 'The Guardians'. The self-assumed stewardship was likened to building the Roman Empire – an analogy suggested when Rossall called its old boy secretaries 'Consuls'. Neo-Roman or public school, this hierarchical approach to education became widespread.

For those who attended public schools, adolescent years afforded an opportunity to dream about prospects of consulships. The visits of old boys, chapel memorials to the fallen, and the commemorative names of the buildings anticipated kudos to come. The behaviour patterns that were instilled resulted in Imperial administration becoming a replay of school. Old boys stationed overseas did *not* look at it in the way that others might. For example, it was asserted that a public school and a bedouin camp had things in common. Fancied affinities of duty with schooldays led Olaf Caroe to compare postings with Winchester, and Arnold Wilson to pronounce that Clifton was *his* Mecca. Indeed, the Gulf Residents did resemble prefects, and the stagecraft that school had taught them was reflected in their daily activities.

Biographers often miss the opportunity which the school registers and archives offer.[20] Almost every school inspired at least one master or old boy to devote his life to amassing details about those who had attended.[21] This material deserves incorporation into studies of the various Imperial services. A pioneer in this respect has been A.H.M. Kirk-Greene, who in the privately printed *The Sudan Political Service* identified the schools of 351 SPS officers from between 1902 and 1952, and noted that 105 went to Clarendon schools (although he mistakenly includes Marlborough as one of the Clarendon group). Winchester had the biggest representation, followed by Eton, Rugby, and Marlborough. Edinburgh Academy was the leading Scottish school. The background of the remainder included private schools and schooling abroad. In *A Biographical Dictionary of the British Colonial Governor*, Mr. Kirk-Greene reported that out of 169 African governors whose education he could determine, 39 went to Clarendon Schools (Charterhouse 9, Eton 8, Winchester 7, Rugby 6, Harrow and St Paul's 3 each, Shrewsbury 2, and Westminster 1). Another 80 went to one of 42 Public Schools in the Headmasters' Conference (Cheltenham 10, Clifton, Marlborough, and Tonbridge 6 each), and 32 came from 28 minor schools. Similar analyses of other groups will enable important comparisons to be made.

Dewey in his analysis of the schools of ICS members in 1900 concluded that the typical school attended by an ICS recruit was a 'second-rank public school'. Philip Mason was more sanguine about the success of the minor schools: '...it was exceptional for any school to provide more than one or two successful candidates in any one year. In earlier years the larger Public Schools produced a high proportion, but even in the 'seventies a fair number of the smaller Grammar Schools and High Schools were represented. In 1929, by which time competitive examinations were held both in London and India, supplemented by a limited number of nominations, the 52 successful candidates came from 48 different schools, including 16 in India and at least as many small Grammar Schools, High Schools or Secondary Schools in England, Scotland or Ireland.'[22] A difference in schools attended between the ICS and the IPS as far as any Indian public schools would be expected as Indians and Anglo-Indians were rare in the IPS. The few IPS Indians were not posted to the Gulf.

The mention here of school backgrounds is not unprecedented in prosopographical and political history, *but the emphasis is*. While interpretation presents problems, in the case of the Gulf the study of the school ties affords a unique opportunity to observe the results of an educational system in one country and political system in other countries many years after the perpetrators have left the scene.[23] The rise of the shaikhs and the rise of the public schools coincided with the 'palmy' days of the IPS in the Gulf. This was the time, as the historian of Queen Elizabeth's Grammar School of Blackburn sourly notes, that 'The rich or even the middle classes were beginning to send their children to boarding schools like

Sedburgh or Giggleswick. While one source of pupils was thus stopped, another was blocked by the establishment of charity schools for the poor, so two major sources of supply dried up, with a consequent reduction of numbers.'[24] The 91 pupils at Elizabeth's in 1860 were reduced to 58 by 1900.[25]

None of the Gulfites between 1857 and 1947 went to a grammar school. The significance of public school dominance of British administration for the social progress of the Gulf cannot be overstated. I have argued that throughout the Empire it had a profound effect on what the British thought necessary or appropriate in social development.[26] The Gulf suffered no differently than did Britain or elsewhere in the Empire.[27] Public school-educated administrators simply were no more sympathetic to universal education or egalitarianism overseas than they were at home.[28]

All learned their places in the rigidly ordered hierarchical mini-society of the school. Those who completed the top form were ready to assume leadership in the larger sceiety, and to continue playing the same awesome and threatening role that they had learned to play so well at school. The leader ruled by awe, and, when that failed, by beating his inferiors. Awe, though, was often insufficient. – James S. Masters, Review of *Elixir of Empire, The Journal of Psychohistory*, Autumn 1990.

NOTES

1. Michael McCrum, *Thomas Arnold, Headmaster: A Reassessment*, OUP, 1989, 20, 127. See David Newsome's review in *Conference & Common Room*, Vol.27, No.2, Summer 1990, 40. 'McCrum may be right in saying that Arnold fell short of being a great headmaster. If so, has there ever been a headmaster worthy of that accolade?' *Ibid.*

2. Mannheim claimed that adolescence and early adulthood was when a 'distinctive personal outlook on politics emerges'. Howard Schuman and Jacqueline Scott, 'Generations and Collective Memories', *American Sociological Review*, Vol.54, No.3, June 1989, 359. An interesting article about Schuman and Scott's research into generational concepts is 'Generational Memories', n.a., *Institute for Social Research Newsletter*, The University of Michigan, Vol.16, No.3, 1989/90, 4-7.

3. Schuman, 'Generations and Collective Memories', 360.

4. 'Societies which are not undergoing rapid economic transformation are likely to generate similar experiences and thus a similar ideological perspective for its inhabitants. Thus the game of assurance is relevant, enforcement costs are negligible, and the theory of induced institutional innovation is relevant. Alternatively, as economic growth and transformation begin to occur the process of specialization will also begin to take place leading to the development of divergent ideologies.' Richard Grabowski, 'The Theory of Induced Institutional Innovation: A Critique', *World Development*, Vol.16, No.3, March 1988, 389.

5. 'In the late Victorian age, the structure of bourgeois careers took on a new stability, which crystallized around the organized professions, university qualifications, and competitive examinations. *The tone was set by the reformed English public schools.*' Robert Anderson, 'A Higher and Wider Road', *Times Higher Education Supplement*, 3 February 1989, 17.

6. 'Modelled on the processes of schooling, the new politics was to acquire an individual hold upon both the body and the mind. The need for a hold upon the mind was explained by Lord Cromer in terms of the very process of constructing a colonial authority. The problem for the British colonial regime in Egypt, he explained, was that the traditional communal bonds between a ruler and those who were ruled – the "community of race, religion, language and habits of thought" did not exist. It was therefore necessary for the government to forge what he called "artificial bonds" in their place.' Mitchell, *Colonising Egypt*, 104.

7. J. Gould has provided an excellent and unusual example of schooling as a character determinant in his seminal study of Isaac Emmerton and Thomas Hogg, early nineteenth-century florists who disagreed over compost. As Gould remarks, 'Few people who have given thought to the

various composts used by florists can fail to have heard of Isaac Emmerton growing auriculas in very rich but nauseating composts at the beginning of the last century.' Emmerton's nemesis was Thomas Hogg, a sceptic about Emmerton's use of goose dung, bullocks' blood and sugar-bakers' scum in composting. He preferred a more conventional mixture based on horse manure. Their rivalry, as Gould suggests, may partly be attributable to Hogg's superior education. Jim Gould, 'Isaac Emmerton, Thomas Hogg and Their Composts', *Garden History*, Vol.17, No.2, Autumn 1989, 181-87.

8. See Stephen Cook, *Empire Born*, Hodder & Stoughton, 1986, 42.

9. Rupert Wilkinson, *The Prefects: Ritual Leadership and the Public School Tradition, A Comparative Study in the Making of Rulers*, OUP, 1964, 41.

10. See *Ibid.*, 54-55.

11. *Ibid.*, 22.

12. James Hilton, *Goodbye Mr. Chips*, Hodder and Stoughton, 1986 [1934], 24. Former direct grant schools place high in a poll of headmasters, academics and examiners in autumn 1990. Asked for the 'best' schools in terms of academic excellence, they listed King Edward's Birmingham, Manchester Grammar, St. Paul's, Winchester, Eton, Westminster, Haberdashers' Aske's, Bradford Grammar, Royal Grammar Newcastle and Leeds Grammar. *Financial Times*, 17 November 1990. So *perhaps* attitudes in Britain are changing.

13. Speech delivered by Lord Curzon, 27 January 1902, Mayo College Archives, Basta 50-785, qtd. McGreal, 'A History of Mayo College', 86.

14. Comments by Colonel Loch, 27 January 1902, *Ibid.*

15. Kipling, *Kim*, 10. St. Xavier is a real school, La Martinière, thinly disguised.'It is written in the books of St. Xavier's in Partibus that a report of Kim's progress was forwarded at the end of each term to Colonel Creighton and to Father Victor, from whose hands duly came the money for his schooling. It is further recorded in the same books that he showed a great aptitude for mathematical studies as well as map-making, and carried away a prize (*The Life of Lord Lawrence*, calf, two vols., nine rupees, eight annas) for proficiency therein; and the same term played in St. Xavier's eleven against the Alighar Mohammedan College, his age being fourteen years and ten months.' *Ibid.*, 180.

16. Pollitt, 'A History of Mayo College', 131-32.

17. Graves, *Goodbye to All That*, 25.

18. Donald Leinster-Mackay, 'The Changing Fortunes and Functions of the English Preparatory Boarding School', Vincent Alan McClelland ed., *Private and Independent Education, Aspects of Education Journal*, The University of Hull, No.35, 1986, 15.

19. John Rae, 'Introduction', Anthony Trollope, *Dr. Wortle's School*, The Trollope Society, 1989 [1881], xii. 'Some of them have been run by the same family for decades having been handed down from father to son. Until very recently, Twyford (1809) – probably the oldest preparatory school in the country – was run by a Mr David Wickham, of the fifth generation of schoolmasters, the family's connection with the school stretching back to 1834. The Maldens of Windlesham House; the Chittendens of Hoddesdon Grange (Hertfordshire) and now of Newlands in Sussex; the Grenfells of Mostyn House, the Radcliffes of Fonthill and the Sandersons of Elstree have been families – and there are many more – which have all kept their same schools over a very long period of time. This family dynasticism stems very largely from the original "private venture" nature of these schools, and is a characteristic almost totally lacking in the public schools.' Donald Leinster-Mackay, 'The Changing Fortunes', 13.

20. See Wilfrid Blunt, *Slow on the Feather: Further Autobiography, 1939-1959*, Michael Russell, 1986, 4.

21. The editor of *Downside School Entries, 1967-1982, First Supplement to the List of Boys at St Gregory's From 1614* (Downside Abbey, Bath, 1983), faced co-education with a disarming remark about girls: '...although, at first they were not included in the school lists, they were definitely part of the school. They are included in the present list without any special mark...'. Presumably from an old girl limbo he resurrected a Downside girl who had inexplicably attended *before* co-education. He also considered problems caused by a house for small boys: 'Plunkett boys are listed under the term when they first arrived at Downside, but in the "House" column their house is followed by the year of entering the upper school; September is to be implied unless the year is followed by "j" for January or "e" for Easter (April). Thus, R80 means entered upper school form Plunkett (Roberts, but normally Junior House at first) in September 1980.' (Except for one troublesome new boy, 'killed in a motor accident on his way to join the school' and therefore separately memorialized.)

22. Phillip Mason, *The Men Who Ruled India: Vol.II, The Guardians*, Jonathan Cape, 1954, 366.

23. See Brian Gardner, *The Public Schools: An Historical Survey*, Hamish Hamilton, 1973, 202-203, 226.

24. G.F. Eastwood, *Queen Elizabeth's: A New History of the Ancient Grammar School of Blackburn*, Published by the Governors of the School, 1967, 59.

25. *Ibid.*, 127. Elizabeth's had 50 pupils in 1800, so a century later it was almost in the same position. As Eastwood notes about this 'wilting' in the face of the public school competition, 'Curiously enough, at this moment of decline, the grammar schools were just beginning to justify themselves.' *Ibid.*, 59. Some Gulfites are representative of the rising middle class rather than the upper middle or upper class, and the suggestion is that parents sent them to public school rather than grammar school because of the belief that public school was becoming a necessity. For others in this situation, including a few aggressive working class fathers who sought 'something better' for their sons, the public school, 'went with a turning away from the immediate life around him, and a reaching for figures and images which seemed more richly charged with life...Grammar school seemed such a *practical* disengagement from the sheer mass and density of working-class life around.' Brian Jackson and Dennis Marsden, *Education and the Working Class*, Monthly Review Press, 1962, 71. Scepticism about grammar schools continued through the decades: 'I've often said in the past that I wouldn't send my children to public school, but when I think of the lack of self-confidence in myself I think that perhaps I will...They're born to rule, and all the way through it's drummed into them and they come to believe it.' A parent qtd. *Ibid.*, 182. There was another, historically neglected, class of school that might be described as 'very minor public school' or even 'hoping to be mistaken for a very minor public school' and founded by occupational groups such as the warehousemen – including such nineteenth-century foundations as Cheadle Hulme and Royal Russell that are now fully public schools. None of these are represented in the Gulf lists. See S. Hopewell, *Royal Russell School*, Hutchinson Benham, 1978, esp. 21, 42. Royal Russell did produce Imperial mandarins, notably Sir Norman Edgeley, onetime Under-secretary of the Political Department and later Legal Remembrancer to the Bengal government and Judge of the High Court at Calcutta. He became President of the Royal Asiatic Society. *Ibid.*, 91.

27. P.J. Rich, 'The Bahrain Public School Scheme, 1941', *Educational Research and Perspectives*, Vol.14, No.2, December 1947, 76-84. See also P.J. Rich, 'The Rule of Ritual in the Arabian Gulf, 1858-1947: The Influence of English Public Schools', Vols.I and II, Ph.D. thesis, The University of Western Australia, 1988, available from University Microfilms, 300 N.Zeeb Road, Ann Arbor, Michigan, USA.

28. 'The very wealthy stratum of the planter class sent their children to school in England. The handful of local secondary high schools catered to the progeny of the "poor" rich, including some of the middle class....in 1930 only one student in fifty attended secondary school.' Aggrey Brown, *Colour, Class, and Politics in Jamaica*, Transaction Books, New Brunswick (New Jersey), 1979, 85. 'Jamaica College in Kingston, founded in 1885, eptitomizes the historical élitist tradition of secondary schooling in the island. It was until recently an all-male boarding school...In 1911 (the school year consisting of three terms), the fees at Jamaica College for a boarding pupil ranged from £13.6.8 if under age twelve, and £15 if over age twelve per term. For nonboarding pupils the fees were £3.6.8 and £4 for the respective age groups. By themselves, these figures are quite meaningless, but the prohibitive cost of secondary schooling for all but the wealthy is appreciated more when it is also pointed out that the assistant principal of the school (an Oxford M.A. and a rarity in those days) was paid a salary of £240 per year. If he had one son of secondary school age, it would have cost him over 20 per cent of his salary to send him to boarding school. He could not have sent three at the same time.' *Ibid.*

Saddam Hussein's childhood and schooling, far from privileged and arguably a reflection of the lack of attention to education during the period of British domination of Iraq, came in for close scrutiny during the events of winter 1990-1991 and were repeatedly contrasted with the patrician upbringing of George Bush, who came as close as an American could to having the secure and élitist public school background of the Residents. Saddam's stepfather 'was a brutal and illiterate man' who prevented him from getting an educations. When he did manage to go to school, his experiences at the Karch secondary school in Baghdad and at Wasr al-Nile sixth form college in Cairo seem to have been more political than pedagogic. Darwish and Alexander, *Unholy Babylon*, 198-200. What will the repercussions and insecurities be thirty years on resulting from the disruptive effects of 1991 on the schooling and homes of hundreds of thousands of children in Iraq and Kuwait? *Palestine Refugees Today*, UNRWA Newsletter No.128, November 1990, 8-9.

PART II

RULE BY RITE

After the invasion, the Kuwaiti Government first stationed itself at Khafji, a small town just across the Saudi border. But within days they had moved to two hotels in Taif on the Red Sea coast, well away from any possible military action. Their comfortable existence there has led to persistent rumours that few, if any, of the ruling 1000-member al-Sabah family had actually volunteered to fight to retake their country. Such feelings were not helped when a senior Gulf official was quoted in a United States newspaper as saying: 'You think I want my teenage sons to die for Kuwait? We have our white slaves from America for that.' – The Australian, 7 January 1991.

While Saddam is an aggressor who ought to be punished, what is the prognosis for those sandbox sheikhdoms we are defending, after the firestorm that is to come? When the Amir of Kuwait is returned to his ruined capital and the people he abandoned, will those who lived through the hell of the occupation welcome back the white-robed rulers who spent the war sipping coffee in Taif? – Patrick Buchanan, 'Alone in the Gulf', 1991.

The British and the French, the victors of the war against Nasser, who had dominated the region for a century, were wiped out without a trace...A similar fate awaits the Americans – especially if they win a military victory. For Saddam the Martyr (even more than Saddam the Conqueror) will ignite a revolution in Arab hearts that will set fire to the citadels of the very Sheikhdoms that the Americans are so determined to protect. – National Herald, New Delhi, 21 February 1991.

US leverage in Kuwait could not be greater. US troops are on the ground. US civil administration teams are establishing the structures of Kuwait's government. US corporations are poised to garner the lion's share of reconstruction contracts. And yet the Bush administration is watching helplessly as the Emir's regime re-establishes its autocracy in the form of martial law. – Guardian Weekly, 10 March 1991.

VIII

SQUARE PEGS, ROUND HOLES

The toad beneath the harrow knows
Exactly where each tooth point goes...
– Rudyard Kipling, *Departmental Ditties*, 1886.

For a study of any degree of sophistication, categories will fluctuate as data is acquired and previous categorizations are found to be too simplistic or too fine-grained. Even so, the prosopographer is frustrated daily by the problem not of fitting square pegs into round holes, but of selecting from amongst an indefinite number of roundish holes the one which produces the tightest fit for the square peg. – Philip Rehbock, *Ideas and Production*, 1987.

These terrible sociologists, who are the astrologers and alchemists of our twentieth century. – Miguel de Unamuno, *Fanatical Scepticism*, 1914.

The shaikhdoms are ideal for the use of prosopography in studying history and policy because the cast of characters is fairly small. Prosopographical pontifications require a well-defined homogeneous group, which explains why the Gulfites make good subjects. If *attitude* and *opinion* can be effectively studied by this technique anywhere, they can be studied in regard to the Westerners and shaikhs in Bahrain, Kuwait, Qatar, and the Emirates.

Collective biography and the conclusions it supports came into its own during the nineteenth century when biographical compendiums led to historians considering what such data 'proved'. Publication of the *Dictionary of National Biography* in 1885 comes immediately to mind, augured by appointment as editor of Leslie Stephens in 1882. The genre's precursors included Samuel Smiles's *Lives of the Engineers* (1861-62) and John Morley's series about English authors, which began in 1878 with publication of Stephen's *The Life of Johnson*. The pedigree of the approach extends back to Plutarch, but as a scholarly tactic it lately has been put on the defensive by sociobiology and other fledgling sub-disciplines in search of recognition.

Disparagers argue that prosopography and biography are burdened by chronology and lack action-explanations.[1] Impatient with the *impedimenta* of facts, they find the whole business old-fashioned. This disdain is not new. *Blackwood's* (February 1887) painted an unappealing scene: 'It is to the outside spectator a goodly and inspiring sight to behold Mr. Stephen and his merry men gathering in the Reading-room of the British Museum, pouring over catalogues with a zeal and enthusiasm which do equal honour to their heads and hearts, and wrestling with mighty tomes even until evening. The fare provided by these literary bees is no doubt nourishing food but it is not always appetising.' However, the discussion of psychohistory in Chapter V possibly shows that prosopography is not incompatible with recent developments.

Much was made in Chapter IV of the inadequacy of Gulf libraries. This particularly affects prosopography. Prosopographical studies make intensive use of library resources and for that reason they cannot be adequately carried out in the Gulf. Not coincidental to late Victorian projects such as the *DNB*, libraries at the time were undergoing transformation. Sir Anthony Panizzi's reorganization of the British Museum Libary while its principal librarian (1856-66) emphasized its research potential for prosopographical work.

With Sir Lewis Namier's *The Structure of Politics at the Accession of George III* (1929), the prosopographical technique reached maturity. Even so, what constitutes prosopography has continued to be controversial:

> To place prosopography in historiographic perspective, imagine a spectrum in which traditional biography is at the far right, siding into dual, family, and comparative biographies toward the centre, and arriving at prosopography at the far left. The choice of 'right' and 'left' is politically symbolic, as it reflects the fact that traditional biographies have most often chronicled the lives of single, heroic individuals, whereas the more 'radical' prosopography seeks to define the character of larger, less distinguished groups of historical actors. Such a spectrum also reflects a range of historiographic attitudes as well: on the right is the historian-biographer's intimate concern with the unique events and character traits of a single life – the ideographic approach; while on the left is the social scientist's need to submerge the lives of individuals into collectives, to induce laws from particulars, as Bacon would have it – the nomothetic approach.[2]

Chronology and prosopography go together like the proverbial horse and carriage. Obviously prosopography requires selecting and defining a group and *that involves selecting dates*, recalling the discussion in earlier chapters of eras in the Gulf. As far as the Gulf's chronology is concerned, Professor L. Carl Brown has given considerable thought to the significance of Middle Eastern dates in *International Politics and the Middle East*. He begins in 1606 with the Treaty of Sitvatorok between the Ottomans and Austria, which in a sense represents the start of concessions that led to Western penetration of the East. He considers the importance of 1774 when the Treaty of Kucuk Kaynarca ended the Ottomans' war with Russia, and of Napoleon's 1798 invasion of Egypt. He then discusses the rise of Muhammad Ali's dynasty in Egypt, and the possibility that his innovations launched 'the Eastern question', the Western powers' serious interjection into Middle Eastern politics:

> This approach to periodization would pinpoint the Greek War of Independence (in which Muhammad Ali was involved) and its attendant international complications covering the years 1821-1829.
>
> The argument for beginning the Eastern Question in the 1820s is as follows: A persistent power imbalance to the disadvantage of the Ottomans in facing Europe was present by 1774. European manoeuvres to strike well behind the conventional lines of Ottoman-European military confrontation were dramatically inaugurated by Napoleon in 1798. His action also brought Britain seriously onto the scene, making the Eastern Mediterranean an arena of multipolar great power confrontation.
>
> The Greek War of Independence added the remaining elements. For the

first time the approach to international politics that was to set the tone for European diplomacy from the Congress of Vienna to the First World War was brought fully to bear on the Eastern Question (the very term, Eastern Question, came into use at this time).[3]

No doubt 1990 and 1991 are destined to be two of the most important dates in Gulf history, but whether they will be regarded as the end of one era (the monarchical period or the years of the shaikhdoms), or the start of one (the democratization of the shaikhdoms), remains to be seen. However dates may be employed, criteria applied in their selection must be explicitly stated. Commenting on Karl Mannheim's rejection of Mentre and on Mannheim's interest in Dilthey's romantic-historical *Zeitgeist,* Goertzel warned, 'Generational location is particularly important because of the openness and sensitivity of individuals in certain age groups to current social trends.'[4] *Thus any date used as a starting-point is itself a statement.* Starting in 1858 gives significance to the Mutiny. Starting with another date such as the opening of the Suez Canal in 1869 shifts the emphasis. Moreover, when dealing with Muslim societies in the Middle East, the use of a dating system relying on the birth of Christ is perhaps an example of what Edward Said labelled as Orientalism. While acknowledging difficulties in treating any subject *seriatim,* the period beginning with the Mutiny and lasting until 1947 displayed considerable unity as the heyday of the Empire, of the public schools, of British cultural hegemony, and, concomitantly, of the invention of *believable* rituals. The era propitiously began with such highlights as publication in 1862 of James Bryce's *The Holy Roman Empire* and George Rawlinson's *The Five Great Monarchies of the Ancient Eastern World,* and the building of Gilbert Scott's Albert Memorial – monuments in their way to an Imperial attitude. It ended just as dramatically in 1947, not only with Indian independence but with such challenges to the self-satisfied mind as Guido Ruggiero's *Existentialism* and Karl Jaspers' *The Question of Guilt.*

None of the dates that could be adopted as a framework would turn out to be those that were highlighted on everyone's calendar. The public schools for example had their own chronological sense or cycle, as do most academic institutions. To school historians, headmasterships often rang the changes. On the other hand some public school historians have rather arbitrarily selected one or another years for starting an account of the schools. Edward Mack began his massive two-volume consideration *Public Schools and British Opinion* in 1780. John Chandos selected 1800-1864 for the provocative *Boys Together.*

Lunar Chronology

Alongside familiar chronological approaches determined by reigns or treaties or the publication of germinal works, there were and are other chronological schemes. Significantly, Ladurie devoted a chapter in *Montaillou* to 'Concepts of Time and Space'. Particularly relevant to a discussion of Gulf chronology is the stubborn and understandable loyalty of Muslims to their lunar calendar, affording an example of a society that has kept its tradition in the face of the West.

Having cast aspersions on other Gulf traditions as inauthentically contrived, it is refreshing to point to this authentic survival. The Islamic calendar begins on 16 July 622 of the Christian era, which was the first day of Muhammad's flight to Medina. The months are marked by phases of the moon, and the moon itself must be sighted by reliable witnesses. This explains why the fasting month of Ramadan sometimes starts on a different day in different Gulf countries.

Day does not begin at midnight for Muslims but at dawn, and is punctuated by the times of obligatory prayers: *fajr* (dawn), *zuhr* (noon), *asr* (afternoon), *maghreb* (sunset), and *isha* (night). The twenty-four hour Western clock was a novelty in the Gulf when first introduced, and the installation by the American Mission of a clock on its building in Bahrain in 1905 created a sensation:

> This clock was a public educator since it was kept on European time, of which the man in the street then knew nothing. He kept Arabic time, and to a large extent did so for many years. In Arabia the new day begins at sunset when everyone sets his clock or watch at 12 o'clock, a very simple arrangement when one lives in a country which is generally cloudless...At the equinoxes, when the sun sets approximately at 6 o'clock European time, one has only to add six to know the Arabic time, but for many months in the year, to translate European time into Arabic time involves some troublesome arithmetic.[5]

A chronology's arrangements are not only subjective but can be highly political. This was recognized during the French Revolution when it was proposed that Year 1 should begin on 22 September 1792, the day the Republic was proclaimed. The revolutionaries' attempts to rename months and create new weeks of ten days each showed how controversial chronology could be. The Islamic, or for that matter the Avestan, Hebrew, Hopi, Mayan, or other calendars, may not be defensible on utilitarian grounds, but the imposition of Western chronology is as hegemonic as other cultural impositions. (See Plate 35.) When the traditional calendar at best is only used for festivals and ceases to be used day-to-day, the regularization to a Western routine deprives a society of part of its heritage. Time becomes an artifact on display, admired but discarded along with costumes, camel saddles, and coffee pots. Elias Canetti comments, 'The way such objects are put side by side in museums robs them of the best of the time and patience that went into producing them. So many things, such different things, lie close together; order deprives objects of their history.'[6] (See Plate 35.)

Ceteris paribus, cultural disruption inevitably ensues from arranging the dates of a non-Western society according to the West's calendar. In the face of the aggressive imposition of Western dating, most cultures have abandoned their own system. The Arabs have struggled to retain their lunar calendar for business and everyday life, which is a comment on their tenacity. If positions were reversed and Western historians were asked to transcribe Christian Era dates that they employed to fit the Muslim calendar, the implications of imposing Western hegemonic ideas of time would be more appreciated.

The use of calendars frequently has ritualistic connotations. In Masonic calendars, of which there were several and some of which were lunar, 'the function of dating codes was either to express their actual or wishful ties to specific traditions or their dissimilarity from other masonic groups'.[7] Indeed, a few lodges still follow the lunar calendar. A more commonly recognized example in which the calendar's symbolic importance outweighs other considerations is the Queen's Birthday celebrations, which do not occur on the real date but on a date more convenient for ceremonial.

Saldanha and the V/12 Series

An effort at a Gulf chronology highlighted J.A. Saldanha's preface to *Selections from State Papers, Bombay* (Superintendent of Government Printing, Calcutta, 1908). He attempted to describe British involvement by eras and to relate this to his celebrated *Précis*. He was concerned with dates relating to the British administration, as is the following effort (with acknowledgements to Penelope Tuson of the India Office Library and Records) devoted to the Residents – hardly dates that the Arabs would include in their chronology. The dates of the Residents focus attention entirely on the past, whereas a more exciting chronology would include dates such as the projected future exhaustion of oil resources. There is no reason why a chronology must deal entirely with *auld lang syne*.[8] Predicative chronologies are useful.

There were East India Company representatives in the Gulf prior to the establishment of a headquarters in Bushire in 1763. The following list (based largely on Saldanha) of Agents prior to 1763, and of dates when they are known to have served, will be of interest:

> Edward Connock 1616-17, Thomas Barker 1617, Edward Monox, William Burt 1627-30, Mr Gibson 1635-37, William Weale 1650-56, Mr Foster 1661, Mr Buckerdig, Richard Craddock 1662-64, Thomas Rolt 1671-77, Mr Petit, Mr Gladman, Capt. Brangwin 1695-96, Edward Owen 1697, Mr Barnwell 1697, Mr Oliver 1700, Mr Prescott 1704-5, Mr Prescott 1705, Mr Lock 1706, John Eaton Dodsworth 1708, Mr Waters 1727, W.H. Draper 1727, J. Harne 1732, Mr Cockell 1733, Mr Cordeaux 1733, Mr Waters 1734, J. Geekie 1734, Mr Pierson, D. Graves 1748, Francis Wood 1750, Alexander Douglas 1753, Martin French 1728-37, Nathaniel Whitwell 1737, Thomas Dorrill 1739, Thomas Grendon 1746, Brabazon Ellis 1750, William Shaw 1753-61, James Stuart 1762, Dymock Lyster 1762. In 1763 the Company appointed its first specifically Gulf agent, William Price.

The years of service for early EIC Residents are often approximate. Then as the nineteenth century unfolds, it becomes easier and easier to uncover biographical material. The IPS officer may have been a reticent gentleman, but, *malgré lui*, has more of an identity than his EIC predecessors. The task of finding information is made easier because the schools and organizations to which the men belonged were not large in membership. Rugby School when

Lewis Pelly was a student in the late 1830s had about 300 students, and an annual intake of about 100.[9]

While, as emphasized in Chapter IV, Gulf biography must be based first on records in the India Office Library and Records, *after* the India Office records have been considered the choice of where to look broadens out to include the Public Record Office (Kew), the Library of the United Grand Lodge, the Society of Genealogists, Somerset House, and many other possibilities. Moreover, the old secondary workhorses remain essential: *Debrett's, Kelly's, The Times, Who's Who* and *Who Was Who, Dictionary of National Biography,* Army Lists, College of Heraldry and Heraldry Society collections, club histories, and school registers. These references can be biased and sometimes depended on the biographees alone for information.

Additional problems arise when trying to reconcile disparate sources. The 1953 *corrigenda* to the *DNB* was 46 pages long and noted 2800 errors. Space limitations present another dilemma. Simply four or five pages devoted to each of the 66 IPS officers who served between 1858 and 1947 can produce a book, but one without any detailed consideration of aspects such as schools or clubs. Add biographies of the EIC officers and FO officers along with comments, and the result could have a price that would discourage all but the most dedicated Gulf enthusiasts. Nevertheless, *Viceroys of the Gulf* will have biographies for the entire three hundred years.

Attention is called to the postings of Residents and Agents outlined in the India Office Library's 'Histories of Services Foreign and Political Series', the IOR:V/12 files. The V/12 files begin in 1886 and are indispensable since men were often given special duty (escorting royalty, arranging durbars), took extensive leaves, and during wars had unusual postings. Details about the duties of the positions, including those that IPS men filled *in India, e.g.* in Rajputana, Central India, Gwalior, Baroda, Gujerat, the Punjab, Jammu and Kashmir, Baluchistan, and Waziristan, are provided in Trench's *Viceroy's Agent*. To avoid pitfalls, this should be consulted before examining the V/12 series. Sometimes the title of Resident was honorary and the IPS officer actually was an Agent, sometimes the Secretary to a Resident was also an Agent of a Native State, and some states shared an Agent or Resident with others. In Trench an idea is obtained of the problems of interpreting IPS service records. While it would not be possible to provide a reference to every India Office file containing information about an officer, the V/12 files are as follows:

Alban, V/12/34, 7-8; Barrett, V/12/31, 11-12; Bill, V/12/15, 161-2; Birdwood, V/12/13, 205-6; Bird, V/12/34, 28-29; Biscoe, V/12/31, 17-19; Bray, V/12/17, 144; Caroe, V/12/34, 41-43; Cole, V/12/34, 51-53; Cox, V/12/16, 188-90; J.A. Crawford, V/12/7, 140-42; Crosthwaite, V/12/31, 44-47; Daly, V/12/32; 51, 9; De Gaury, V/12/32, 80; Dickson, V/12/31, 48; Dixon, V/12/34, 72-73; Fowle, V/12/32, 69-71; Gabriel, V/12/31, 75-77; Galloway, V/12/34, 97-99; Gastrell, V/12/34, 100-102; Godfrey, V/12/13, 278-281; Grey, V/12/18, 175-76; Hadow, V/12/34, 113; Hamilton (Belhaven), V/12/17, 306-309; Haworth, V/12/21, 155-57; Hay, V/12/34, 126-28; Hickinbotham, V/12/34, 130-32; Howes, V/12/34, 136-38; Jackson, V/12/34, 140-41; Johnston, V/12/30, 117-19; C.A.

Kemball, V/12/13, 307-9; Keyes, V/12/31, 114-17; Knox, V/12/18, 210-12; Loch, V/12/32, 133-35; D.L.R. Lorimer, V/12/20, 220-21; J.G. Lorimer, V/12/12, 318-19; Mackenzie, V/12/18, 226-27; Mallam, V/12/34, 164-66; McCollum, V/12/15, 275; Meade, V/12/10, 294-6; Metcalfe, V/12/34, 171-2; Miles, V/12/28, 52 & V/12/2, 181-2; More, V/12/30, 131; Murphy, V/12/34, 176-7; C.J. Pelly, V/12/34, 187-8; F.B. Prideaux, V/12/20, 253-6; W.F. Prideaux, V/12/28, 66-7, & V/12/3, 228-30; Prior, V/12/34, 194-6; Rance, V/12/34, 198-9; Ross, V/12/28, 75-6, & V/12/1, 203; Sadler, V/12/4, 314-6; A.C. Stewart, V/12/34, 231-3; H. Stewart, V/12/20, 278-80; Talbot, V/12/6, 312-4; Tandy, V/12/34, 234-6; Trevor, V/12/18, 286-288; Wakefield, V/12/34, 245-7; Watts, V/12/33; Weightman, V/12/34, 248-50; A.T. Wilson, V/12/17; 323-4; F.A. Wilson, V/12/4, 337-8; Worth, V/12/34, 258-60.

Postings

Postings were numerous and arbitrary – weeks or months here and there, and periods with no duty. One reason for the changing about was the effect of accumulated leave, sometimes two years or longer, and anticipated with the glee of 'a schoolboy at the approach of holidays'.[10] In 1909, David Lorimer *qv* went on leave on April 1, 1909. He took subsidiary leave, privilege leave, and a furlough, before returning to duty on March 11, 1911. Charles Mackenzie *qv* went on leave November 19, 1910 and returned on November 23, 1912. Absences necessitated shuffling around to plug the gaps. Leave mounted up during wars when men seldom left posts. In 1947 the combination of leave and half-leave enabled the officers taking early retirement to stay nominally on the rolls until as late as 1949. Richard Bird *qv* went on average pay for eight months and on half average pay for nineteen months and twenty-three days from August 15, 1947.[11]

Mesopotamia and Iraq

A reason for gaps in the service records in 1914-1922 is the complicated IPS involvement in Mesopotamia, most of which is now incorporated in the state of Iraq. Over 570,000 Indian troops served in World War I, and they were concentrated in the Middle East. The Indian Expeditionary Force began operations in the Shatt al-Arab in October 1914. Recent television footage about the importance of that waterway and its outlet into the Gulf near the Kuwait border would not surprise the Residents – the February 1991 ground war was conducted on ground much travelled by the IPS.

Until February 1916, the Government of India Military Department managed the campaign. Then operations became the responsibility of the War Office, while political administration remained with the Government of India. With the capture of Baghdad in March 1917, administration was transferred from the Government of India to the India Office. In 1921 Iraq became the responsibility of the Colonial Office. As noted in Chapter IX, the IPS provided men for all of these operations and their years of service during the period are understandably hard to summarize.

This was not the only case of disruption because of war. The majority of IPS officers had commissions and so were called to duty when crises arose.[12] The effect on tenures was again marked in World War II, when there were two million Indian troops requiring officers. An observation arising out of the wide variety in postings is that those men who did spend a long time in the Gulf (noted in Chapter III) had their relative influence enhanced by the short postings of their colleagues.

Further Prosopographical Possibilities

A biographical dictionary of the entire Indian Political Service from its inception to its demise is not beyond possibility, given the material available. The idea is attractive. If attempted, it should go beyond self-evident sources. Regimental histories containing anecdotal material about ICS and IPS officers have not been investigated. Another untapped source is the War Diaries that units of battalion size or greater kept, indexed in WO95/5494 in the Public Record Office. For those who saw combat in World War I, the Diaries *might* be psychologically insightful. Hopefully, this book suggests neglected possibilities such as parish church records, London club archives, and provincial newspapers.[13]

The starting place for research remains the V/12 files,[14] or in the case of those who served under the East India Company, the India Office 'Index of Applications for East India Company Cadetships, 1775-1860'.[15] The pension records (the IOR:L/AG/23 series) also should be consulted. They reveal divorces (Loch, Bray) that go unreported anywhere else and suggest family sources that could be pursued and family lines that lead to manuscripts accumulated by the India Office Library and elsewhere. As far as research into the family papers of the IPS Gulfites, it should be kept in mind that Indian Army officers were not considered for IPS appointment if they had completed seven years' service or attained the age of twenty-seven. Nor could they be married, *ergo* they married late after joining the IPS, and a number of their children were still alive in 1991, and watching Gulf events with keen interest.

Dates become useful in pursuing another suggestion for what would make a good project, one which arises from there being no history of photography in the Gulf. Pauline Rohatgi's *Portraits in the India Office Library and Records* (British Library, 1983) is an introduction to the Library's Prints and Drawings section. Cited are pictures of Biscoe, Caroe, Cox, Hadow, Hay, Kemball, Pelly, Prior and Weightman. The British embassies in Bahrain, Kuwait, and Muscat have uncatalogued collections of photographs and lithographs. The History Section of the Royal Photographic Society has been publishing studies of local photographers in Britain which could be correlated with the dates and locations of leave and retirement residences of officers who lived in the Gulf, hopefully with the prospect of finding negatives or prints that Gulfites handed over for processing. As a matter of fact, the wills of David Lorimer *qv* and Gerald de Gaury *qv* show that they were enthusiastic photographers. A book of photographs taken by the Residents and Agents would be fascinating.

In examining military sources, no concentration stands out of IPS officers in particular regiments, although sometimes it has been shown that individual public schools enjoyed special ties with one or another British or Indian Army unit.[16] The necessity of having a private income for belonging to a crack regiment means that membership in a specific regiment may indicate a family's finances, just as joining the Indian Army rather than the British Army may indicate a lack of means. Robert Hamilton, who was Bahrain Political Agent, described the membership of the 4th Gurkhas to which he belonged as 'of good family [but] forced to live on their pay'.[17] The extra-regimental postings were sometimes the opening gambit in an officer's campaign to gain admission to the IPS. (Again, chronology gains importance thanks to the consolidations of regiments and the necessity of knowing dates when locating regimental records.)

Some military records found their way into the IOLR files. Often superior officers would write revealing letters about candidates. The application files of Army and ICS aspirants to the IPS reveal useful information, but as in other areas there is no consistency in what was kept and what was discarded. Personal files that have been located are sometimes cited as *IOR:Personal File* because of being recorded on a separate typed handlist in the India Office Library and Records in the 1980s. A discussion is necessary with the IOR staff before using them. These files often have other identity numbers acquired through the years.

Personal files include many remarks made by colleagues on the performance of individuals. This is why the Library is circumspect about access. Despite the passage of years, unabridged airing would prove embarrassing to families. About one officer's wife, who died recently (1987), and whose children (of considerable prominence and helpfulness) are alive, a note reads: 'Mrs.***** cannot, I fear, be looked on as one of *****'s assets. Her behaviour was in fact at times so peculiar as to make one wonder whether she was entirely sane.' Another reason the material is sensitive is that it is mostly recent. More personal information from the 1930s and 1940s has survived than from earlier times, and the extent of the India Office's eclectic collections means that there is probably much of this personal material which awaits discovery.

Who's Who on the Kuwait-Iraq Border

There are a number of directories and compendiums where the Gulfites appear or do not appear in sufficient numbers to permit generalizations, *i.e.* that they were prominent enough to gain entry to *Who's Who* but not prominent enough to be listed in the *Dictionary of National Biography*. Knowledge of the service origins of IPS applicants helps in this 'paper chase' when it comes to more obscure directories. Of the sixty-six Gulfites who served between 1858 and 1947 and whose biographies appear in Chapter IX, eleven entered the IPS from the ICS (Bill, Biscoe, Caroe, Crawford, Hadow, Johnston, John Lorimer, Cornelius Pelly, Wakefield, Weightman, Worth). A further forty-nine entered from the Indian Army, including nine who were seconded to the IPS but never 'fully IPS', *i.e.* they kept their primary military connection. Another six entered otherwise. One each came from the police and from the Bombay Political Service (Jackson, Barrett). Three were originally in the East

India Company (Disbrowe, Jones, Pelly). James More came from the Mesopotamian civil service.

The majority of the Gulf IPS were in *Who's Who*, but in using that series and in using the public school registers, the biography appearing closest to date of death may *not* contain data found in previous editions. It is necessary to check not only *Who Was Who* or the latest school register, but also the *previous* editions. Imogen Thomas underscores this in discussing the *Haileybury Register, 1862-1983*: '...the new *Register* should be used in conjunction with the earlier editions. Indeed, by following entries through four or five editions, a great deal of information can be gleaned...to add to the basic facts. The most splendid edition...was that of 1910, edited by L.S. Milford. It comprised 844 pages for a school of 48 years standing, compared with this edition's 582 pages covering 121 years.'[18]

The biographies in *Who's Who* and the school registers are often based on what the individual submitted rather than an editor's view. For example, if a child died the entry sometimes (understandably) showed only the survivors and omitted any record of the child. Charles Kemball's *qv Who's Who* entry is an instance. His eldest son, Arnold Lewis (b.4 Sept 1897, d.14 Dec 1911), is omitted and his entries show only one son. In the course of research for this book, the author inadvertently informed a son of a previous marriage and divorce of his father, a first marriage unreported in any *Who's Who* or school registers and unknown to the family of the second marriage. (Interestingly the family had a tradition that the first wife was the gentleman's mistress, which leads to speculation that possibly that was more acceptable with Edwardians than was divorce.) Only Arnold Kemball, Percy Cox, and Lewis Pelly are in *DNB*, but of 66 IPS Residents and Agents, 42 were in *Who's Who* and a further six died before the start of the series or at an age before they merited listing.

Listing in *Who's Who* has limited status value, although in one case the innocent fun of fifty years ago takes on an importance that the participants never could have imagined. Everyone by now has read of the demands of the Iraqis for the Kuwaiti islands that dominate the approaches to Iraq's limited Gulf access. Edward Wakefield, the Bahrain Political Agent in 1943-44, amusingly recounted how he and Tom Hickinbotham achieved their *Who's Who* fame:

> Hickinbotham and I discovered Warbah [*sic*] Island when we visited Umm Qasr in connection with the Kuwait-Iraq boundary dispute. The tide was high, the area of island temporarily unsubmerged was small, and we took advantage of these conditions to sail round the island in our launch. At that time neither of us had his name included in *Who's Who*. As we sat in the launch we had a friendly argument about which of us would achieve this distinction first. We settled the argument, as arguments between friends should always be settled, by compromise. We made a pact that the one of us who first had his name included in *Who's Who* would ensure simultaneous inclusion of the other's name by recording our joint circumnavigation of Warbah Island. Hickinbotham reached *Who's Who* status before I did. For twenty years now the names of Hickinbotham, Wakefield and Warbah Island have been linked together in its pages.[19]

Warbah is one of the islands which the Iraqis view as 'theirs'. If ultimately the award of Warbah Island or the non award of Warbah Island to Iraq has anything to do with the destabilization of the Middle East that the Kuwait crisis of 1990-91 has produced, 'two men in a boat' with their casual boundary investigations should be recalled.

The biographee's recollections and his *Who's Who* and other entries are sometimes contradicted by the true particulars. Vanity or brevity enters into the picture. An Acting Resident would describe himself as Resident. An officer who attended first one school and than another would list the more distinguished. In resolving such discrepancies another helpful source is the Probate Registers maintained by the Accountant's General Department of the IOL, which include balances owed to officers' estates. They provide an accurate date and place of death, probate dates, letters of administration, executors and solicitors.[20]

Family Trees, Tenures, Revisions

Often more relationships are uncovered in a prosopographical investigation than can be pursued. Nevertheless, the ones that have been are suggestive. In 1896 the daughter of Adelbert Talbot (Resident 1891-3) married Stuart Godfrey, the Resident 'in charge' in 1893 when Talbot was on leave. There is a father-and-son combination, the two Prideaux. The son of one agent (Wakefield) became the right-wing head of the Standing Council on the Baronetage, while the son of another (Loch) became a left-wing Labour MP (Tam Dalyell). Three sisters married two Residents: Cyril Barrett married Mabel Geddes; her two sisters in turn married Lionel Haworth. An EIC Resident, Arnold Kemball, was Charles Kemball's uncle. The father of one Resident (Wilson) was Headmaster of Clifton and the uncle of another (Caroe) was headmaster of Winchester. Further family analysis can be suggested, but the temptation had to be resisted. The careers of ancestors or descendants would fill volumes. The same restrictions apply to schools. Many school archives have the daybooks of individual houses with minutes of noteworthy occurrences. Some schools have the diaries and manuscript memoirs of masters. These could profitably be searched for information about individual IPS men.

The tenures provided in this chapter will help to locate the Residents and Agents by either their years in office or the places where they served, and to juxtapose their service with that of their predecessors and successors. This is followed in Chapter IX by the biographies.[21] No distinction has been made between *acting, officiating,* and *being in charge*. Penelope Tuson in her excellent *The Records of the British Residency and Agencies in the Persian Gulf,* did not differentiate between the terms.[22] The distinctions seem to have been small.

Revisions have been made in this book's lists to previous lists of Residents made by others. These corrections include dates, spelling and the additional names of interim officers. Part of any disagreement over dates can be attributed to arbitrary decisions that must be made in allocating travel and leave time between postings. Arnold Galloway called attention to the names that the men preferred, such as Geoffrey rather than Charles Prior, and Rupert rather than William Hay, or the use of a single Christian name or several. When a man was knighted, as many were, he could designate which of his Christian names would be used.

Because of short staffing, it was occasionally necessary to fill posts with a clerk, surgeon, or telegraph operator.[23] No evidence has been uncovered that they got involved in policy, but they are listed when they did a turn so researchers will not be mystified by the appearance of names in documents and think that a Resident or Agent has been omitted. However, men are omitted who were appointed but never took up posts.[24] Undoubtedly the anonymous native staff of the posts achieved influence, especially when they were long tenured. Their part in the story has been left as a separate project for investigation.

Another clarification that needs making is that, during Percy Cox's long administration, a three-tiered system developed to accommodate Cox's other responsibilities throughout the Middle East. Arnold Wilson was for much of the time the Deputy, and his overall importance is not indicated by the short time he was the full Resident. Others served as Deputy Residents under Cox and Wilson.[25]

A brief spell in the Gulf and then a complete disappearance from that scene can indicate a dedication to a career in India and being sent to the Gulf under duress, but the short terms sometimes conceal a long-time connection with Arabia expressed in other than Gulf service. An example was Caroe, who showed continuing interest in the Gulf as Foreign Secretary of the Government of India and wrote extensively about the region, but only served briefly as Resident. The names of those who were assistants to the Resident and never became Political Agents can be found in the *Persian Gulf Administration Reports* (IOR:R/15/6/473-541). Years in Aden, the Hadhramaut, Muscat, Mesopotamia and Persia mean that a man spent more time in the Middle East than a short stint in the Gulf indicates. Similar strictures apply to those who were only briefly Agents.

The Resident supervised men in several Persian and Mesopotamian postings, and the history of Iraq itself cannot be written without substantial references to the IPS. Cursory examination of those who served on the Persian side and were not primarily Arab enthusiasts does not indicate whether there was a complementary cadre to the Gulfites of 'Persianites', but the question will be taken up in my projected series. The activities in those posts created considerable Foreign Office records because they were dual appointments. Although they were part of the Residency's mandate, there is a case to be made that their inclusion in a review of Britain's policy towards the shaikhdoms would be more confusing than clarifying. While there is a strong argument for including the Muscat records in any prosopography of the Gulf, there are also arguments for the history of Muscat being quite different from that of Bahrain, the Emirates, Kuwait, and Qatar. Indeed, that there is such a separate identity to the four mini-states is part of what the entire Iraq-Kuwait confrontation was all about. They are regarded as satraps by many Arabs.

The Residency and the Agencies in the Gulf proper have an historical unity of their own. There the matter has been allowed to rest for the moment, while acknowledging the case for an inclusive Gulf *dramatis personae* that would give detailed biographies of all who served in the 'British lake', including Company and Foreign Office appointees, and Muscat officers, those in the Persian postings, Arab rulers, assorted freebooters such as St. John Philby, American missionaries, naval officers – and others.

P.D. Coates, a former member of H.M. Consular Service in China, has done what amounts to a prosopographical study of that service. In a talk given to the Royal Society for Asian Affairs in 1989 he described some of the difficulties. His remarks apply to the Gulfites: 'All over the globe there were bodies of British officials, some of course weaker vessels, odd ones crooked or otherwise scandalous, but speaking generally actuated by a belief in duty and in public service, whose story has not been recorded and deserved to be recorded.'[26] A regret he expresses will be shared by anyone who has done similar research: 'When I came on information, I did not know whether or not related information was waiting for me in later documents and would build up into a picture.' He found that he accumulated masses of notes that proved of no use, but 'In other cases I failed to appreciate in time the significance of some bricks. An abnormally high proportion of entrants to the Victorian service were fatherless, evidently because the service offered a respectable career without requiring the university education which fatherless men could often not afford, but I realised the significance of this trend too late to make a statistical count of fatherless entrants.'[27]

In the case of the Gulfites, the interest in cremation by one Resident, Sir Arnold Wilson, led him to write a booklet advocating the custom. This suggests an intriguing line of inquiry. Since cremation was initially controversial and was only legalized in England in 1884, the disposition of the remains of Gulf Residents and Agents might be an index of progressive sentiments. Cremationists were not revolutionaries, but funeral customs were a way in which identity and status were declared. The subject would be a legitimate one for a prosopographer, and is being pursued by this author.

Evidently prosopographers have much in common, for Coates had similar difficulties to this author in seeking to bring to attention the wives of the officials, as well as regrets over lacking time to chase down obscure leads about family papers in shoe-boxes. At times he was delighted at what school records could provide, and at other times he was sorely disappointed:

> In 1875 a young consular officer named Margary was murdered while travelling officially, with Chinese official agreement, near the Burma border. The resulting diplomatic row was so great that Margary was given a place in the Dictionary of National Biography and was commemorated on the Shanghai bund by a memorial 37 feet high, described as a neat and graceful structure after the Gothic style. In the twentieth century, however, the published register of Brighton College, where Margary and his brothers had been educated, included some biographical information about the unremarkable brothers and none about the consular officer, whose posthumous celebrity had apparently escaped the college's memory.[28]

Coates suffered from another familiar quandary: what to omit to avoid pain to descendants or libel actions. He agonized over an inability to document assertions made by others, either in conversation or in questionable writings. There were 'other stories which had to be forgone because what Gibbon, I think, called the decent obscurity of a learned language is no longer available to authors.' A prosopographer passing up a good story should be comforted by Virgil – *carpent tua poma nepotes*. Perhaps though, there is no harm in hinting!

A provisional list of the Gulf Residents and Agents which would include the East India, Indian Political Service, and Foreign Office eras would total 132 men. (The forthcoming studies will deal in more detail with this subject.) The East India Company officers are only 25 in number. The Indian Political Service constitutes the majority with sixty-six:

Alban, Barrett, Bill, Bird, Birdwood, Biscoe, Bray, Caroe, Cole, Cox, Crawford (James), Crosthwaite, Daly, De Gaury, Dickson, Disbrowe, Dixon, Fowle, Gabriel, Galloway, Gastrell, Godfrey, Grey, Hadow, Hamilton, Haworth, Hay, Hickinbotham, Howes, Jackson, Johnston, Jones, Kemball (Charles), Keyes, Knox, Loch, Lorimer (David), Lorimer (John), McCollum, Mackenzie, Mallam, Meade, Metcalfe, Miles, More, Murphy, Pelly (Cornelius), Pelly (Lewis), Prideaux (Francis), Prideaux (William), Prior, Rance, Ross, Sadler, Shakespear, Stewart (Andrew), Stewart (Hugh), Talbot, Tandy, Trevor, Wakefield, Watts, Weightman, Wilson (Arnold), Wilson (Frederick), Worth.

The Commonwealth and Foreign Office accounts for the remaining forty-one.

Gulf Residents 1763-1971

BENJAMIN JARVIS: April 1763 – July 1766
WILLIAM BOWYEAR: July 1766 – November 1767
JAMES MORLEY: November 1767 – February 1769
The post was not filled between 1769–1775
JOHN BEAUMONT: May 1775 – January 1781
EDWARD GALLEY: January 1781 – June 1787
CHARLES WATKINS: June 1787 – October 1792 (Not listed in Farrington.)
NICHOLAS HANKEY SMITH: October 1792 – October 1798
MEHDI ALI KHAN: April 1803 – January 1804
JONATHAN HENRY LOVETT: April 1803 – January 1804
SAMUEL MANESTY: February 1804 – March 1804
WILLIAM BRUCE: March 1804 – May 1807
NICHOLAS HANKEY SMITH: May 1807 – July 1808
Capt PASLEY: July 1808 – September 1808
WILLIAM BRUCE: September 1808 – July 1822. Temporary only:
Surgeon Andrew Jukes: December 1808 – May 1809; Stephen Babington: September 1810; Robert Taylor: April 1812 – November 1812; Assistant-Surgeon James Orton: August 1813 – April 1814; James Dow:

November 1819 – January 1820, May 1820 – January 1822, May 1820 – January 1822; Assistant-Surgeon John Tod: January 1822 – March 1822, July – December 1822 (Broker and Linguist i/c).
JOHN MACLEOD: December 1822 – September 1823
HENRY HARDY: October 1823 – December 1823
EPHRAIM GERRISH STANNUS: December 1823 – January 1827
DAVID WILSON: January 1827 – March 1831
SAMUEL HENNELL: March 1831 – January 1832
DAVID ANDERSON BLANE: January 1832 – June 1834
SAMUEL HENNELL: June 1834 – July 1835
Surgeon Thomas Mackenzie: July 1835
JAMES MORISON: October 1835 – October 1837
THOMAS MACKENZIE: October 1837 – April 1838
SAMUEL HENNELL: May 1838 – March 1852
Henry Dundas Robertson: January 1842 – April 1843; Arnold Burrowes Kemball: April 1843 – December 1843.
ARNOLD BURROWES KEMBALL: March 1852 – July 1855

IPS Residents 1858-1947

The principal school attended follows the date.

JAMES FELIX JONES: October 1855 – April 1862 *Addiscombe* (Not in Farrington.)
HERBERT DISBROWE: April 1862 – November 1862 *Oakham*
LEWIS PELLY: November 1862 – October 1872 *Rugby*
EDWARD ROSS: October 1872 – March 1891 *Edinburgh Academy*
WILLIAM PRIDEAUX: *Acting* May 1876 – August 1877 *Aldenham*
SAMUEL MILES: *Acting* 1885 – October 1886 *Harrow*
ADELBERT TALBOT: 1891 – May 1893 *Eton*
STUART GODFREY: *i/c* May 1893 – June 1893 *Westminster*
JAMES HAYES SADLER: *Acting* June 1893 – July 1893
JAMES CRAWFORD: *i/c* July 1893 – December 1893 *Rugby*
JAMES HAYES SADLER: *Acting* December 1893 – January 1894
FREDERICK ALEXANDER WILSON: January 1894 – June 1897 *King William's*
MALCOLM MEADE: June 1897 – April 1900 *Cheltenham*
CHARLES KEMBALL: *Acting* April 1900 – April 1904 *Charterhouse*
PERCY COX: April 1904 – October 1920 *Harrow*
ARTHUR TREVOR: *i/c* August 1909 – May 1910 *Marlborough*
JOHN LORIMER: December 1913 – February 1914 *Dundee Institution*
RICHARD BIRDWOOD: *i/c* February 1914 – March 1914 *Clifton*
STUART KNOX: *i/c* March 1914 – November 1914 *Repton*
STUART KNOX: *Special Duty* January 1915 – April 1915 *Repton*
ARTHUR TREVOR *Deputy PR* April 1915 – November 1917 *Marlborough*
JOHN BILL: *Deputy PR* December 1917 – September 1919 *Wellington College*
CECIL GABRIEL: *Deputy PR* September 1919 – November 1919 *Stamford*
ARTHUR TREVOR: *Deputy PR* November 1919 – October 1920 *Marlborough*

ARNOLD WILSON: *Officiating* October 1920 – November 1920 *Clifton*
ARTHUR PRESCOTT TREVOR: November 1920 – April 1924 *Marlborough*
STUART KNOX: *Acting* April 1923 – October 1923 *Repton*
FRANCIS PRIDEAUX: April 1924 – January 1927 *Marlborough*
CHARLES CROSTHWAITE: *Acting* June 1925 – October 1925 *Shrewsbury*
LIONEL HAWORTH: January 1927 – November 1928 *Elizabeth's*
FREDERICK JOHNSTON: November 1928 – April 1929 *Kelvinside*
CYRIL BARRETT: April 1929 – November 1929 *King William's*
HUGH BISCOE: November 1929 – July 1932 *Winchester*
TRENCHARD FOWLE: May 1931 – August 1939 *Clifton*
PERCY LOCH: *Acting* April 1933 – May 1933, July 1933 – October 1933, July 1934 – October 1934, July 1935 – October 1935, July 1936 – October 1936 *Cheltenham*
OLAF CAROE: *Acting* August 1937 – November 1937 *Winchester*
HUGH WEIGHTMAN: *Acting* March – May 1938, August 1938 – September 1938 *Hymer's*
GEOFFREY PRIOR: September 1939 – May 1946 *Shrewsbury*
RUPERT HAY: *Officiating* October 1941 – September 1942 *Bradfield*
TOM HICKINBOTHAM: *Officiating* October 1944 – November 1944 *Epsom*
ARNOLD GALLOWAY: *Acting* May 1945 – November 1945 *City of London*
RUPERT HAY: *Bradfield* May 1946 – 1953
ARNOLD GALLOWAY: *Officiating* June 1947 – October 1947 *City of London*

Foreign Office Appointments

HAY was the last IPS appointment and he carried on for the Foreign Office.
BERNARD BURROWS: 1953-1958
GEORGE MIDDLETON: 1959-1961
W.H.T. LUCE: 1962-1966
STEWART CRAWFORD: 1967-1972
GEOFFREY ARTHUR: 1970-72

Bahrain Agents

JOHN GASKIN: *Uncovenanted Assistant* February 1900 – October 1904
FRANCIS PRIDEAUX: October 1904 – May 1909 *Marlborough*
CHARLES MACKENZIE: May 1909 – November 1910 *Malvern*
STUART KNOX: November 1910 – April 1911 *Repton*
DAVID LORIMER: April 1911 – November 1912 *Dundee High*
ARTHUR TREVOR: November 1912 – May 1914 *Marlborough*
TERENCE KEYES: May 1914 – March 1916 *Haileybury*
HUGH STEWART: March 1916 – May 1916 *Charsley Hall*
J.M. DA COSTA: *Head Clerk* May 1916 – June 1916
TRENCHARD FOWLE: *Acting* July 1916 – November 1916 *Clifton*
PERCY LOCH: November 1916 – February 1918 *Cheltenham*
GEORGE MUNGAVIN: *Telegraph Operator* March 1918 – December 1918
NORMAN BRAY: December 1918 – June 1919 *Wellington*
SAIYID SIDDIQ HASAN: *Indian Assistant* June 1919 – November 1919

HAROLD DICKSON: November 1919 – November 1920 *St. Edward's*
SAIYID SIDDIQ HASAN: *i/c* November 1920 – January 1921
CLIVE DALY: January 1921 – September 1926
GEORGE MALLAM: *Acting* May 1925 – November 1925 *Malvern*
CYRIL BARRETT: September 1926 – April 1929 *King William's*
REGINALD ALBAN: April 1927 – November 1927 *Berkhamsted*
GEOFFREY PRIOR: April 1929 – November 1932 *Shrewsbury*
PERCY LOCH: November 1932 – April 1937 *Cheltenham*
KHAN BAHADUR ABDUL HAIYAL-HASHIMI: *Officiating* April 1933 – May 1933
EVERALD GASTRELL: *Officiating* July 1933 – November 1933 *Cheltenham*
MEREDITH WORTH: *Officiating* July 1934 – October 1934 *Repton*
GEORGE COLE: *Officiating* March 1935 – October 1935 *Stonyhurst*
TOM HICKINBOTHAM: April 1937 – October 1937 *Epsom*
HUGH WEIGHTMAN: October 1937 – October 1940 *Hymer's*
JOHN HOWES: *Acting* August 1938 – September 1938 *Rossall*
REGINALD ALBAN: October 1940 – January 1942 *Berkhamsted*
EDWARD WAKEFIELD: January 1942 – October 1943 *Haileybury*
MICHAEL DIXON: *Acting* August 1943 – October 1943 *Marlborough*
TOM HICKINBOTHAM: October 1943 – March 1945 *Epsom*
CORNELIUS PELLY: March 1945 – October 1945 *Clongowes Wood*
ARNOLD GALLOWAY: October 1945 – March 1947 *City of London*
HUGH RANCE: *Acting* July 1946 – November 1946 *Christ's Hospital*
CORNELIUS PELLY: March 1947-1954 *Clongowes Wood*
HUGH RANCE: July 1947 – August 1947 *Christ's Hospital*
GORDON JACKSON: August 1947 – November 1947 *King's Worcester*

Bahrain Foreign Office Appointments

PELLY was the last Indian Political Service appointment, and carried on for the Foreign Office.
CHARLES GAULT: 1955-1959
EDWARD WILTSHIRE: 1960-1963
JOHN TRIPP: 1964-66
A.D. PARSONS: 1966-1969
J.C. PHILIP: 1969
ALEXANDER STIRLING: 1970-1971

Trucial Coast (Sharjah) Officers

JOHN HOWES: October 1939 – October 1940 *Rossall*
ROY METCALFE: October 1940 – April 1941 *Highgate*
CORNELIUS PELLY: March 1941 – April 1942 *Clongowes Wood*
MAURICE TANDY: March 1943 – August 1943, October 1943 – April 1944 *Winchester*
REGINALD HADOW: May 1944 – October 1944 *Berkhamsted*
RICHARD BIRD: October 1944 – April 1945 *Imperial Service College*
RAYMOND MURPHY: April 1945 – April 1946 *Dover College*

HUGH RANCE: May 1946 – January 1947 *Christ's Hospital*
GORDON JACKSON: January 1947 – May 1947 *King's Worcester*
HUGH RANCE: May 1947 – June 1947 *Christ's Hospital*
CORNELIUS PELLY: June 1947 – July 1947 *Clongowes Wood*
GORDON JACKSON: July 1947 – August 1947 *King's, Worcester*

Trucial Foreign Office Appointments

Gordon Jackson was the last IPS appointment.
J.E. HUDSON: 1947
P.D. STOBART: 1948
A.J. WILTON: 1951
M.S. WEIR: 1952
On 20 May 1953, the post became a Political Agency.
JOHN WALL: 1952-1955
C.M. PIRIE-GORDON: 1955
JOHN PETER TRIPP: 1956-1958
D.F. HAWLEY: 1958-61

Dubai (PA for all emirates except Abu Dhabi.)

ALBERT CRAIG: 1962-64
HUGH BALFOUR-PAUL: 1965-66
DAVID ROBERTS: 1967-1968
JULIAN BULLARD: 1969-1971
JULIAN WALKER: 1972

Abu Dhabi

MARTIN BUCKMASTER: 1957-1958
E.R. WORSNOP: 1958-1959
EDWARD HENDERSON: 1960
O.R. MILES: 1961 *Acting*
In 1961 the title was changed from PO to PA.
J.E.N. BOUSTEAD: 1963-1965
ALBERT LAMB: 1966-1968
CHARLES TREADWELL: 1969-1972

Qatar

ARTHUR WILTON: 1950-54
MICHAEL WEIR: 1954
H.G. JAKINS: 1954
W.B.M. JOHNSTON: 1955
DERRICK CARDEN: 1956-58
D.S.R. DUNCAN: 1959
JOHN MOBERLEY: 1960-1962
PHILIP McKEARNEY: 1963-1965

R.H.M. BOYLE: 1966-1969
EDWARD HENDERSON: 1970-1971
Qatar became independent in 1971.

Kuwait Agents

STUART KNOX: August 1904 – April 1909 *Repton*
DA'UD AL-RAHMAN: *Assistant-Surgeon i/c* May 1905 – October 1905
WILLIAM SHAKESPEAR: April 1909 – January 1914 *King William's*
WILLIAM GREY: January 1914 – June 1916 *Westward Ho!*
ROBERT HAMILTON: June 1916 – March 1918 *Westminster*
PERCY LOCH: March 1918 – September 1918 *Cheltenham*
DANIEL McCOLLUM: September 1918 – February 1920
L.M.D. MELLO: *Agency Clerk* June 1919 – June 1920, February 1920 – May 1920
JAMES MORE: May 1920 – May 1929
CYRIL BARRETT: *Acting* April 1927 – October 1927 *King William's*
HAROLD DICKSON: May 1929 – February 1936 *St. Edward's*
ALLEN GREENWAY: *Assistant-Surgeon, Acting*
May 1931 – September 1931
RALPH WATTS: *Acting* June 1934 – October 1934 *Taunton*
GERALD DE GAURY: February 1936 – May 1939
ANDREW STEWART: *Acting* April 1937 – May 1937 *Hymer's*
ALLEN GREENWAY: *Acting* May 1937 – June 1937
ARNOLD GALLOWAY: May 1939 – May 1941 *City of London*
HAROLD DICKSON: May 1941 – August 1941 *St. Edward's*
TOM HICKINBOTHAM: August 1941 – September 1943 *Epsom*
GORDON JACKSON: *Acting* June 1943 – August 1943 *King's, Worcester*
CORNELIUS PELLY: October 1943 – June 1944 *Clongowes Wood*
GORDON JACKSON: June 1944 – August 1943 *King's, Worcester*
CORNELIUS PELLY: October 1943 – June 1944 *Clongowes Wood*
GORDON JACKSON: June 1944 – April 1945 *King's, Worcester*
MAURICE TANDY: April 1945 – March 1946 *Winchester*
RICHARD BIRD: March 1946 – May 1946 *Imperial Service College*
MAURICE TANDY: May 1946 – April 1948 *Winchester*

Kuwait Foreign Office Appointments

Tandy was the last IPS appointment.
H.G. JAKINS: 1948-1952
F.L.C. CHAUNCY: 1953
H.G. JAKINS: 1954
CORNELIUS PELLY: 1955
G.W. BELL: 1955-1957
AUBREY HALFORD: 1957-1959
J.C. RICHMOND: 1959-1961
J.L. CHRISTIE: 1961
Kuwait received independence in 1961.

To summarize, the long duration of British rule does not necessarily 'prove' the existence of a chain of causation going back to the English public schools, but certainly the presumption is that such a continuity had effects. There is great bibliographical value in having readily available the names of these stalwarts. Through them is a logical way to begin searching for information about specific places in the Gulf, specific issues, and specific eras.

Having introduced – and the emphasis is only on introducing rather than giving any definitive statement – the history of the IPS influence in the Gulf and presented a list of the officers, the time has arrived to offer capsule biographies of the 'Viceroys of the Gulf'. These descriptions will bear out the contention that although the Residents and Agents were a varied group, the notion that there was a *protypical Gulfite* is not illusory.[29]

It is not by the direct method of a scrupulous narration that the explorer of the past can hope to depict that singular epoch. If he is wise, he will adopt a subtler strategy. He will attack his subject in unexpected places; he will fall upon the flank, or the rear; he will shoot a sudden, revealing searchlight into obscure recesses, hitherto undivined. He will row out over that great ocean of material, and lower down into it, here and there, a little bucket, which will bring up to the light of day some characteristic specimen, from those far depths, to be examined with a careful curiosity. – Lytton Strachey, *Eminent Victorians*, 1918.

NOTES

1. For the title of this chapter, see Edward Wakefield's biography in Chapter IX. 'Intentional explanations of human action, invoking beliefs and desires as reasons for acting, are necessary because of the peculiar kind of living organisms human beings are – in particular, because of the especial capacities they possess for consciously reflecting on and altering not merely their actions, but also their thoughts. Action-explanations contain a hidden premise referring to the agent's power to perform the action in question.' Callinicos, *Making History*, 235. This is the 'why' of sociobiology. However, 'A word of explanation is needed on the use of the term "sociobiology". The word is used very inconsistently among those who call themselves, or are called, sociobiologists, by those who are critical of a school of thought or an intellectual camp identified "as" sociobiology, and not least by journalists and other communicators. For some, but not for others, the term has a built-in human reference. Some use it very broadly to connote the entire domain of behavioural science within the neo-Darwinian tradition, thus including the established territories of ethology, primatology, ecology and population genetics. Others use it more narrowly, to refer to a set of concepts for accounting for social behaviour as an outcome of the mathematics of genetic transmission; they may then contrast this mode of explanation with that attributed to (say) "classical ethology". For some, notoriously, the use of the term becomes itself a predatory act: a call for the incorporation of the other life-sciences, the social sciences and humanities, and their relegation to the status of component or antecedent sub-disciplines in a "new synthesis". It is not unknown for writers to use the term in all these senses on the same or different occasions.' Hilary Callan, 'The Imagery of Choice in Sociobiology', *Man*, Vol.19, No.3, September 1984, 405.

There seems much in common between a prosopography, limited in goals and modest in assertions, and what Richard Dawkins calls 'hierarchical reductionism': 'The non-existent reductionist – the sort that everybody is against, but who exists only in their imaginations – tries to explain complicated things *directly* in terms of the smallest parts, even, in some extreme versions of the myth, as the *sum* of the parts! The hierarchical reductionists, on the other hand, explain a complex entity at any particular level in the hierarchy of organization, in terms of entities only one level down the hierarchy; entities which, themselves, are likely to be complex enough to need further reducing to their own component parts; and so on. It goes without saying – although the mythical, baby-eating reductionist is reputed to deny this – that the kinds of explanations which are suitable at high levels in the hierarchy are quite different from the kinds of explanations which are suitable at lower levels.' Richard Dawkins, *The Blind Watchmaker*, Penguin, Harmondsworth, 1988 [1986], 13.

2. Philip F. Rehbock, 'Prosopography?', *Ideas and Production*, Issue VI, 1987, 117. See P.J. Rich, review of Christine Heward's *Making a Man of Him: Parents and Their Sons' Education at an English Public School, 1929-50*, *British Journal of Education Studies*, Vol.XXXVIII, No.1, February 1990, 96-97.

3. L. Carl Brown, *International Politics and the Middle East: Old Rules, Dangerous Game*, I.B. Tauris, 1984, 28. When enlivening his book with a table showing 'Western Colonial Rule in the Middle East', Brown felt unable to include the shaikhdoms: 'The British control in Kuwait, Bahrain, the Trucial Coast and Oman, while substantively equivalent to protectorates, involved such informal, and often imprecise, arrangements that these cases do not accurately fit into the above table.' *Ibid.*, 91. The problem of dates is not confined to the Gulf: 'We start at 1789, and English Jacobinism appears as a by-product of the French Revolution. Or we start in 1819 and with Peterloo, and English Radicalism appears to be a spontaneous generation of the French Revolution.' Thompson, *English Working Class*, 24, qtd. David B. Tyack, 'Foreword', Harold Silver, *Education as History: Interpreting Nineteenth and Twentieth Century Education*, Methuen, 1983, 2.

4. Ted George Goertzel, *Political Society*, Rand McNally, 1976, 174-76.

5. SLRCA: Mylrea, 'Kuwait Before Oil', 18-19. *NB.* that a subsidiary problem is the introduction of Western *numbers*, ironically termed *Arabic* numbers, on clocks, watches, and elsewhere. Almost all Gulf Arabs are familiar with and use Western numbers, but a number system is itself symbolic, *e.g.* Latin numerals are used in the West for 'impressive' purposes such as on diplomas and cornerstones. See Paul Keyster, 'The Origin of the Latin Numerals 1 to 1000', *American Journal of Archaeology*, Vol.92, No.4, October 1988, 529-46.

6. Elias Canetti, *The Human Province*, Picador, 1986 [1973], 112. See 'The Year They Lost Ten Days', *Horizons*, n.a. Vol.2, No.2, 9 January 1987, 8-9.

7. Alain Bernheim, 'The Dating of Masonic Records', *AQC*, Vol.99, 1986, 9.

8. Relevant is Boulding's remark that 'In tracing the effect of images on the course of history, peculiar attention must be paid to the images of time and especially the images of the future...The spectacular rise of Islam in its first two centuries is a striking tribute to the creative power of a charismatic image of the future.' Kenneth E. Boulding, *The Image: Knowledge in Life and Society*, University of Michigan Press, Ann Arbor, 1961 [1956], 126.

9. See McCrum, *Thomas Arnold*, 19. However, see also the further discussion in my forthcoming *Tom Brown In Arabia.*

10. Bence-Jones, *Viceroys*, 158.

11. IOR:V/12/34.

12. Arnold P. Kaminsky, *The India Office, 1880-1910*, Mansell, 1986, 110-11.

13. 'The traditional sources...do little more than suggest the informal lines of influence that flow from close personal friendships or from intimate professional collaboration; conversations occurring in corridors or over the telephone, or at cocktail parties, corporate board meetings, even college reunions, can at times shape events more decisively than whole stacks of the official memoranda that find their way into the archives.' John Lewis Gaddis, 'A Time of Confrontation and Confusion', *Times Literary Supplement*, 8 May 1987, 479.

14. See also 'Rules Regulating the Admission of Junior Military Officers to the Political Department of the Government of India' and a sample application form in IOR:L/PS/10/849.

15. IOR:L/MIL/9/107-254.

16. '...the Indian Army has always been a Fettesian stronghold...mainly as members of the 27th, Meerut, and Lahore Divisions.' J.H. Brett, 'Fettes and the Great War', Pyatt ed., *Fettes*, 263.

17. V.E.O. Stevenson-Hamilton, *Yes, Your Excellency*, Thomas Harmsworth, 1985, 13. NB. Stevenson-Hamilton's brother-in-law was Lord Birdwood, Commander-in-Chief in India, and brother of Richard Lockington Birdwood, a Gulfite.

18. *The Haileyburian*, Vol.XLIV, March 1985, 63. Michael Stenton in his preface to *Who's Who of British Members of Parliament* (Michael Stenton and Stephen Leas, Vol.I-IV, Harvester Press, Sussex, 1976-81), which is based on Dodd's *Parliamentary Companion*, claims that the *DNB* and *WW* are often wrong.

19. Wakefield, *Past Imperative*, 186.

20. See esp.IOR:L/AG/33.

21. See the individual biographies – the list of tenures in Chapter VIII is a simplification.

22. Tuson, *Records of the British Residency*, 184.

23. Some lists in Gulf histories are seriously faulted, *e.g.* among many mistakes Rumahihi lists G. Gaskin as PA Bahrain, 1900-4. In actuality, he was *political assistant*, and the British replaced him

with an Agent because they felt that having a junior official was not making enough of an impression. C.F. Mackenzie served as PA Bahrain from 1909-10 and Stuart Knox in 1910-11, not the dates as given by Rumahihi. The dates for Lorimer, Trevor, and Keyes are wrong. Stewart and Fowle are inexplicably omitted. Loch's dates are wrong. He lists 'G.A.G. Hungavin' as the PA Bahrain in 1919. This is George Alexander Mungavin, a telegraph operator who filled in during March to December *1918*. He lists A.G. Philips as PA Bahrain in 1920, but Harold Dickson was PA until November 1920 and was succeeded by Clive Daly in January 1921, with a brief interim filled by an Indian clerical as 'in charge'. He lists Cyril Barrett as PA Bahrain 1927-29 but Barrett was PA from September 1926 to April 1929. He lists Geoffrey Prior as PA Bahrain, 1930-2, but Prior was PA from April 1929 to November 1932. He lists 'W. Weightman' as PA Bahrain 1938-40. The PA Bahrain from October 1937 until October 1940 was Hugh Weightman. See M.G.Rumahihi, *Bahrain: Social and Political Changes Since the First World War*, Bowker, 1976, *passim*.

24. *E.g.* John MacNeil in 1830. Tuson, *Records of the British Residency*, 184.

25. See IOR:R/15/6/518, *PGAR1918*, 'Administration Report for Fars and Bushire for the Year 1918', 1.

26. P.D. Coates, 'The China Consuls', *Asian Affairs*, Vol.XXI, Part I, February 1990, 44.

27. *Ibid.*, 47.

28. *Ibid.*, 51.

29. Related to the notion developed here of a protypical Gulfite is the question of whether the Middle East, as a stark backdrop, brought out similar traits in other nationalities who found themselves involved in its history. When a dramatist wants the audience to concentrate on his characters, he dispenses with sets and props and uses an austere and barren stage. General Norman Schwarzkopf certainly came to the fore from obscurity when given a part to play, and it was intriguing to see the various roles he was cast in: closet liberal or New Deal Democrat, rogue general like Douglas MacArthur, scion of a tradition (his father was chief of the New Jersey State Police), self image builder like Lawrence (given to collecting 'mountains of press clippings about himself'), humorist (on Saddam, 'He is neither a strategist, nor is he schooled in the operational arts, nor is he a tactician, nor is he a general, nor is he a soldier. Other than that, he's a great military man.'), prospective university president ('Eisenhower was head of Columbia University before running for president'), or even 'America's Sexiest Man' to whom Madonna, the pop star, sings, 'Talk to me Norman Schwarzkopf.' John Cassidy, 'Stormin' Norman could blow Bush away, if he wants', *The Australian*, 3 April 1991, 11.

IX

BIOGRAPHIES

Having passed all his examinations, undergone Secretariat training, passed a departmental exam on the history and background of the states, and learned the art of rapid encyphering and de-cyphering, the probationer found himself at the end of about three years a full-fledged member of the service. His next move was to buy a very expensive uniform, consisting of the mess-kit, an evening tail-coat with dark blue cuffs and facing; and the day-time full dress, which was not unlike that of the commissionaire of the Ritz Hotel, surmounted by a white topee with a silver spike. In the Dress Regulations of the service he might be surprised to read: 'Trousers will not be worn when ladies are present.' One was supposed then to wear white kerseymere breeches. – Charles Chenevix Trench, *Viceroy's Agent*, 1987.

Readers of the biographies in this chapter, short as they are, will know more about the Residents and Agents than the Arabs were permitted. There are numerous ways in which the lives of the IPS can direct the researcher towards material on a Gulf topic. If they wish to concentrate on a particular place such as Kuwait, they can refer to the tenures in the previous chapter and look at the biographies of the men who served there. The same holds true of investigating a period such as World War II.

Although the sketches represent only a brief beginning compared with what might be uncovered, they provide a dimension that was altogether absent in the public *persona* presented by the Residents to those they ruled. Victorian circumspection partly accounts for this, but there may have been other reasons. Biographical disclosure would have spoiled the hoped-for theatrical effect. Making Arabs privy to information about the officers' families and schooling, much less any *louche* side, would have taken away from the aloofness that was assiduously cultivated. *Boulevardiers do not make effective priests*. Despite his many years in the Gulf, the personal side of an IPS officer (with a few exceptions such as Dickson) remained *vita umbratilis*, a life in the shade.

The picture presented of the IPS in the Gulf remains a pastiche when it comes to conclusions about collective mentality; wariness should be a necessary companion in reading prosopographical collective tea leaves concerning a group as small in numbers as the Gulf Residents and Agents. The limited number of Gulfites limits the conclusions that can be reached about patterns. For example, there undoubtedly was meaning to the given names that each man received from his parents, but for whom the men were named or why for the moment remains a mystery. A summary of the few names involved seems meaningless: Four each were christened *Hugh*, *James*, and *Charles*. Three each were dubbed *William*. Otherwise, the only consistency appears to be variety, including an *Adelbert*, an *Olaf*, and a *Trenchard*.

Almost as many approaches exist for would-be prosopographers as there are people who could be the subject of biographies. A life can be described tersely in terms of dates, or pursued through endless byways. Biographies can stress psychohistory or medical history or one period of life or the enveloping family, *e.g.* a prosopographer with medical interests could attempt to resurrect the medical crises in a life, and interpret their effects. The collective criteria that can be emphasized are as various as the lives of the individuals. A compendium of biographies can be based on membership in the Lily Society, Rotary Clubs, or Charterhouse. When and if the learned societies of London are studied prosopographically, a large number of ICS and IPS names will be represented. Many in the Imperial services were Fellows of the Royal Geographical Society or entitled to the nominals of other royal learned societies. Colonel Creighton, the otherwise reserved IPS officer and spymaster in Kipling's *Kim*, reveals a rare emotion with his hopes to become FRS:

> No money and no preferment would have drawn Creighton from his work on the Indian Survey, but deep in his heart also lay the ambition to write 'F.R.S.' after his name. Honours of a sort he knew could be obtained by ingenuity and the help of friends, but, to the best of his belief, nothing save work – papers representing a life of it – took a man into the Society which he had bombarded for years with monographs on strange Asiatic cults and unknown customs. Nine men out of ten would flee from a Royal Society soirée in extremity of boredom; but Creighton was the tenth, and at times his soul yearned for the crowded rooms in easy London where silver-haired, bald-headed gentlemen who know nothing of the Army move among spectroscopic experiments, the lesser plants of the frozen tundras, electric flight-measuring machines, and apparatus for slicing into fractional millimetres the left eye of the female mosquito. By all right and reason, it was the Royal Geographical that should have appealed to him, but men are as chancy as children in their choice of playthings.[1]

In detail and design of approach, the spectrum of biographical strategies extends from the relatively leisurely pace of the classic full and would-be 'definitive' biography such as Trevelyan's *Macaulay*, through variations in a growing group of comparative studies that contrast the lives of two or three individuals such as William Irvine's *Apes, Angels and Victorians* did for Darwin and Huxley, to the full scale prosopographical panorama such as the portrayal of parliamentarians in Namier's *...at the Accession of George III* – and beyond that into a world of jargon in which the individuals rather than being explained, disappear, absorbed by statistical tables.[2]

Prosopography offers no guarantee that the result will be lively reading.[3] To keep the interest of both the author and the reader there has to be a rapprochement between the demands of precision and the limits of curiosity; it would be naïve to think that there was an altogether happy compromise. Occasionally here, and in other books in the series, an incident has been included in a biography much as a raisin enlivens a muffin, *i.e.* not every aside offered has momentous Freudian implications. While restraint largely has prevailed as to detail, additional volumes may satisfy those who enjoy a more detailed approach.

The Mutiny and After

In looking over the biographies, unifying factors that emerge in the lives of the IPS officers in the Gulf such as their public school education stand out, but one traumatic commonality might be overlooked: *the careers were post Mutiny*. The Mutiny was a horrific event whose bloody episodes affected the British attitude towards the entire Empire. In the short run, the uprising's part in bringing about the end of the East India Company gave the IPS a golden opportunity. In the long run, the suspicions engendered poisoned the attitudes of the Raj towards co-operation rather than rule. Nor was the winding up of the Company as foregone a conclusion as is often assumed. No less a person than John Stuart Mill, a longtime EIC employee, argued forcefully against rash action: 'Defending the East India Company in 1858 against the threat of dissolution by Parliament, Mill, the opponent of monopoly, put forward anew the argument for the Company's exclusive rule. He claimed that the rule was in the interests of India, and that British government rule would entail the opposite.'[4]

A few post-Mutiny Gulfites began their careers in the EIC. The social status of such Indian appointments in the last days of the Company has been challenged, particularly in several articles and in a book by Bradford Spangenberg. He writes:

> Most historians have accepted the notion that Indian careers were highly popular among University students in Great Britain, and that, as a consequence, the competitive examination system, inaugurated as a replacement for the patronage of the East India Company in 1855, guaranteed a superior body of highly efficient administrators for British India. The fact is, however, that the Civil Service Commissioners themselves had voiced dissatisfaction with the calibre of recruits as early as 1858, only four years after the establishment of the competitive system...the maximum limit in 1859 [was reduced] from 23 to 22: men in their twenty-third year who had already graduated would not likely 'be much tempted by the prospect of an appointment which will withdraw him at once from the distinction...he looks for at home.' By lowering the limit, it might be possible to lure men into the I.C.S., just prior to or immediately after graduation before they were drawn away by more attractive careers at home.[5]

What was significant about post-EIC recruiting was that after an initial flurry of university applicants, the number of entrants applying directly from public school rose precipitously. From a high of 62% in 1858, the Oxford and Cambridge candidates fell to 8.2% in 1874.[6] Trying to account for this, Dr. Spangenberg remarks that '...many pragmatic, thrifty middle class people doubtlessly questioned the merit of spending a great amount for a son's university education when a shorter, less expensive education at the crammers proved sufficient to gain success at the examination.'[7]

A second but less emotional winding up faced those who experienced the post-colonial era in the Middle East after the loss of India in 1947. They were deprived by Whitehall of purpose or direction, and faced an ever diminishing status. Appropriately, since the opening of the Suez Canal had given such an impetus to Imperial expansion, Eden's Suez debâcle ended the British hegemony in the Middle East. There would no longer be a British *eminence grise* on whom the Arabs could blame disorder, although for many years they have appreciatively found Imperialism an excuse for post-Imperial failures. The quickness with which the Iraqi invasion of Kuwait of 1990 was turned into a fight against Western Imperialism should be noted. The West continues to be the great excuse for everything and anything in the Middle East.

Military Backgrounds

Another aspect to the changes wrought by Indian independence was that the military background which was typical of many IPS officers became less noticeable in post-1947 dossiers. Few Commonwealth or Foreign Office appointees were professional soldiers, whereas a majority of the IPS entered the service from the Indian Army (IA), where they had been required to have at least passed the examination for Captain. Thus they were able to log military experience before 'passing over' to the IPS, and this was a permanent asset. 'The Game,' Geoffrey Moorhouse remarked in reviewing Peter Hopkirk's book *The Great Game: On Secret Service in High Asia,* 'was a good thing to have on your record, like First XI Colours won at school.' (*The Guardian,* 10 May 1990.) Some entering from the ICS had army experience, but they were expected to have passed the ICS departmental examinations with distinction rather than have military qualifications.

Army entrants to the IPS were given time to study for the ICS examinations in the Indian legal codes which ICS men had already passed. This was often done while working in a district as Assistant Commissioner. Much of the work a man did when a junior was concerned with the IPS land settlement programme, which involved registering property claims and assessing taxes. Arguably the IPS system of short assignments merged the IA and ICS recruits into one cadre, but the experiences of the IA entrants certainly had more of a touch of Great Game glamour.

Aspects of the Army service of the Raj have been considered by Philip Mason, Correlli Barnett, and others. Keeping up appearances in the Indian Army cost an officer much less than in the British Army. David Thomson relates rather typically in his autobiographical *Nairn in Darkness and Light* (Arena 1988) how his father was gazetted to the British Army after Sandhurst but found that the cost of uniforms and mess bills was beyond him. To avoid embarrassment he transferred to the Indian Army, which paid for uniforms and where infantry officers were mounted and hence could pursue polo. Whether for economic reasons or a desire to join the IPS (which many stated was their reason), the regular Army experience of IPS officers was usually a brief prelude to a short period of Indian Army service. While after the Cardwell reforms (named for Edward Cardwell, Gladstone's secretary of state for war between 1868 and 1874) there was more emphasis on the colonies undertaking their own defence, the expansion of the Empire still required a disproportionate deployment of regular Army battalions overseas. Aaron Friedberg in *The Weary Titan* reported that in 1897 according to Public Record

Office files there were 77 battalions on duty in India and elsewhere overseas, and only 64 stationed in the British Isles. Colonel John Dunlop in *The Development of the British Army, 1899-1914* (Methuen 1938) offers similar figures: 71 home battalions and 52 in India in 1899; 81 home battalions and 52 in India in 1906. Some of the IPS found themselves first in India via that Army route and then joined the Indian Army to get into the IPS, but there were numerous other ways in which military experience was obtained.

World War I, as the biographies indicate, saw many IPS officers in active service. Keeping track of regimental service at that time presents problems. The expansion of the Indian Army in World War I was achieved by raising second and further battalions of existing regiments, the raising of new regiments that took spare numbers in the existing roll, and with new regiments (numbered from 131 on).[8] The Indian Army presence in the Middle East was on an immense scale. (See Plate 36.) A number of these regiments had ties through their officers with specific public schools in England. Joining the Army from public school, usually via Sandhurst, was assisted by the establishment of special Army classes in the schools.

A majority of the ex-Indian Army IPS officers do not appear to have been in the special side at school. The Army class did not have a high reputation with headmasters. The Winchester head wrote to a boy's father in 1896, 'I regret to see you are sending your son to the Army Class, and I hasten to assure you this desperate step is not necessary, as I believe your son has sufficient ability to make his way in other walks of life.' The boy did do the Army course at Winchester and became Field-Marshal the Earl Wavell PC GCB GCSI GCIE CMG MC, Commander-in-Chief in the Middle East (1939-41) and Viceroy of India (1943-47).[9]

Assignments and Clubs

IPS assignments varied enormously because of the geographical extent of the service's Viceregal mandate. The North-West Frontier Province was a principal responsibility, and had six districts. Skirmishes there were likely as a part of the Great Game and assignments had, partly thanks to Kipling, a considerable mystique. Relatively more salubrious as a posting was Baluchistan, whose centres such as Quetta and Ziarat were quite civilized in comparison with the Frontier. Quetta became a principal garrison and few Gulfites escaped a spell there, as has been noted in Chapter VI. Rajputana also offered several postings; its small kingdom employed a number of Politicals as tutors and ministers to native rulers. Central India's states were numerous and so were grouped under one agent, the AGG or Agent to the Governor-General. The Bhopal Agency included ten states; the Bundelkhand Agency had thirty-three. The three large states of Gwalior, Baroda, and Gujerat invariably had their own agent. Hyderabad, which was almost as big as France, was another significant assignment. So was Jammu and Kashmir, partly because of having borders with Tibet, China, and Afghanistan.

Although postings in the IPS were supposedly on merit, there are hints that the old school tie helped. Sir Conrad Corfield, the head of Indian Political Service mentioned in Chapter II, said as much in his autobiography *The*

Princely India I Knew. In his case, when he wanted to join up he sought out George Ogilvie, the Political Department official who handled the selection of candidates, and then 'started to pull strings'.

Careers of IPS officers could be researched by looking into the literature about the places where they served, since in many instances the histories of districts and states have been written. This could involve as much work for each man as researching a full length biography, which isn't practical. The numerous assignments that an officer was given are one reason why membership in overseas clubs is not given here, while membership in London clubs is. The same stricture applies to learned societies. There were over 200 gentlemen's clubs in Edwardian London. Undoubtedly some have escaped notice as far as the Gulfites are concerned, and more can be done to ascertain which ones they belonged to. The London association of club managers was contacted and individual clubs were visited, but that only turned up more research leads. My monograph of 1987, *Clubs of the British Residents and Agents,* elicited feedback about IPS preferences for clubs.

Chains of Empire includes two chapters discussing Imperialism and clubdom. There I take the position that the clubs were steeped in public school tradition – and that they were consistently discriminatory as far as admitting natives. With that comment about discrimination no less an authority than Charles Chenevix Trench took issue, claiming that only a couple of Indian clubs in the 1930s barred Indians. I remain unconvinced. Recently Hugh Tinker, an ex-Indian Army officer, has recorded in his reminiscences that, 'I stayed at the Allahadbad Club [*in 1946*] (which had long before blackballed both the Nehrus, father and son; this has been denied, but I saw the Minute Book).' [10] On the other hand, one club's anniversary history (*Hundred Years of Chittagong Club,* Chittagong Club, 1979), records the reminiscences of a European member:

> There is a general belief that up to independence in 1947 natives of this country could not become members...but records show that this is not correct. Going through the old papers I found from the list of members attached to the Annual Report from 1916 onwards for a few years the name of Mr B.K. Mullick, I.C.S. later on described as Hon'ble Mr B.K. Mullick among the absentee members. If he was an absentee member in 1916 one wonders when did he join! From some senior employees I have learned that several Indian doctors in Government service were also members before 1947. Incidentally, Mr K.C. Dey became a member in 1916 and before leaving Chittagong he was a member of the General Committee of the Club.

At any rate, more Gulfites belonged to the United Service in London than to any other club anywhere. (See Plate 38.) The Service (nicknamed 'The Senior'), had an influence on clubs throughout the Empire: when the Bengal Club was organized in Calcutta in 1826, the inaugural meeting was told that: 'A plan is under consideration for the establishment of a club in Calcutta similar to those instituted in London such as the United Service Club and others which have proved there so successful. It can scarcely be necessary to observe that if such associations have been found beneficial in London, where so many and such various resources offer themselves, they will be infinitely more serviceable in Calcutta, where nothing like a respectable hotel or coffee-house has ever existed.'[11] In the case of India, it can safely be concluded that an officer was *ipso facto* a member of the club where he was assigned. Whether he invariably joined the local historical or antiquarian society has not been established, but a large number of the Gulfites belonged to the Royal Geographical Society. Others belonged to the Royal Asiatic and Royal Central Asian Societies. A search of the RGS records provided interesting information about who proposed whom for membership. Possibly the Royal Society for Asian Affairs records would be equally enlightening. The treasurer for 36 years (1939-1975), Major Edward Ainger, was a close friend of Sir Olaf Caroe (biography *infra*) at Winchester and later.

The subject of IPS memberships in Indian clubs deserves investigation, and would be made easier by the way that clubs have flourished there in post-Independence, 'a tropical blend of Pall Mall and palace leather sofas, marble floors, gin and tonics, but served by turbanned bearers.'[12] The edifices frequented by the IPS still exist and presumably so do records of their affiliations. Almost all the towns in India where the IPS served maintain their clubs. The grand ones such as the Saturday, Tollygunge and Turf in Calcutta carry on, 'ossified in splendour'.[13] The minutes of whom was blackballed, Indian or British, and of whom didn't pay his chits, await social historians.

Orders and Decorations

Another category of entries requires explanation, the orders and decorations listed for each man. These are considered in detail in *Stalky and Stormin' Norman meet the Shaikhs*. Two common errors are to confuse orders with medals and decorations and to confuse the order in which orders were worn with the precedence conferred by statutes on the members. The two rankings are not co-terminous. The order in which orders were worn, according to the Government of India's *Dress Regulations (1931)* was:

> Victoria Cross, Order of the Garter, Order of the Thistle, Order of St. Patrick, Order of the Bath, Order of Merit (immediately after Knights Grand Cross of the Order of Bath), Order of the Star of India, Order of St. Michael and St. George, Order of the Indian Empire, Order of the Crown of India, Royal Victorian Order (Classes I, II and III), Order of the British Empire (Classes I, II and III), Order of the Companions of Honour (immediately after Knights and Dames Grand Cross of the Order of the British Empire), Distinguished Service Order, Royal Victorian Order (Class IV), Order of the British Empire (Class IV), Imperial Service Order, Royal Victorian Order (Class V), and Order of the British Empire (Class V).

This was followed by Baronets' Badges, Knights Bachelors' Badges, and then certain *decorations*, some confusingly called orders but *not* orders – the Order of British India, the Indian Order of Merit. Orders also had medals or decorations, *i.e.* the Royal Victorian Medal, the Imperial Service Medal, and the Medal of the Order of the British Empire.

The subject, though complex, provides an entry to interesting archival materials. Forms were necessary to claim various medals, *e.g.* the India Mutiny Medal, and are preserved by the IOR. Timothy Ash has written an extremely useful article in *Medal News and Military Chest* on how to use medal records, 'Research Notes From the India Office Military Department Records'.[14] In the case of the orders, each has an extensive history and the award could carry significant implications to a career. The India Office Records preserve files relating to why such awards were made. Sometimes awards will crop up in a medal dealer's catalogue, as did one set with Gulf associations in August 1989:

> SIX. Major C.H. Lincoln, Indian Medical Dept & Political Dept. OBE (1st type) (Civil); 1914-15 Star (Asst Sugn, IMD); BWM & VM (Political Dept); Delhi Durbar 1911 (unnamed); Jubilee 1935 (unnamed). Mounted as worn. EF. Cecil Henning Lincoln OBE; born 1883, joined IMD as Asst Surgeon 1904, Lieut 1927, Major 1934, retd 1938. Served in the Persian Gulf with Political Dept 1910-36 as Vice-Consul then Consul at Bunder Abbas and Mohammerah; award MBE 8/1/19 and promoted to OBE 30/12/19, both awards for services in connection with the Great War in the Persian Gulf.

This notice of an extra fine set of six medals (priced at £195) appeared in the catalogue of Norman W. Collett, a London dealer, and illustrates the usefulness of what could be regarded as an ephemeral subject. Lincoln does not figure prominently in accounts of the Gulf, but his medals show that he was there and that his life deserves being investigated – his medals are the clue to his possible significance. The weight that officers attached to these awards cannot from a distance be fully appreciated. Sir Conrad Corfield recounted an anecdote about an agent and his wife who displayed considerable anxiety as the 1st of January New Year's Honours List was about to be published. The gentleman was suffering from being 'overdue', having passed the usual number of years which entitled him to the accolade, and he and his wife had lost their usual good humour. A colleague when asked why they looked so downcast replied, 'I think they are suffering from knight starvation.'[15]

Coveted orders although old in origins at times went through vicissitudes on their way to being incorporated into the Imperial system. The Most Honourable Order of the Bath was created in 1725, but reorganized in 1815. It was a military order until 1847, when a civil division was implemented. The numbers in each class have varied. There are currently limits of seventy-eight military and twenty-five civil for Knight Grand Cross, of 191 military and 100 civil for Knight Commander, and for Companion of 1055 military and 650 civil. The Most Distinguished Order of St. Michael and St. George was founded in 1818 and limits awards to 99 Grand Crosses, 412 Knights Commander, and 1686 Companions. The Most Excellent Order of the British Empire was established in 1917. There are 32 military and 79 civil Knights Grand Cross, 257 military and 580 Knights Commander, and 1622 military and 6055 civil Commanders – but no limit to the numbers of Officers and Members.[16]

The reasons for the decision as to who got what varied through the years. Recent awards policy will help to put in perspective the ranks of Grand Cross, Knight, Commander, *et al.* Those at the top such as Admirals of the Fleet and the highest posts in the Civil Service receive a Grand Cross. Lieutenant-Generalships get knighthoods. Major Generals receive a CBE on retirement. A shelved Brigadier hopes for a CBE, and Ambassadors in one of the top two grades are made KCMG after posting. The GCMG goes with Washington or Paris, or with the Governor-General of the larger Commonwealth nations which have not jettisoned British decorations.[17]

A number of Gulfites received St. John decorations that were not strictly part of the honours ladder. The Most Venerable Order of St. John of Jerusalem was based on a long tradition but only chartered by Queen Victoria in 1888. It appears in the order of precedence but because of its unique standing it is not part of the honours system as such.

Several Gulfites won awards for military gallantry, which are different from the orders mentioned above. The Distinguished Service Order was inaugurated in 1886. Members are styled 'Companions'. It has not always been given for bravery, and many a DSO given during World War I was for administrative or staff work rather than combat. The Military Cross, which for example Gerald de Gaury was awarded, was only instituted in 1914 and it was only for officers of the rank of Captain or below. (In 1953, Majors were included.)[18] Arnold Galloway made the point to this writer in an interview that MID – 'mentions in despatches' – had a significance somewhat like a decoration. There were about 150,000 mentions in despatches in World War I. There was a bronze oak-branch emblem awarded for mentions in despatches which was to be worn on the ribbon of the Victory Medal.

The significance of Imperial honours has been put down to a craving by the middle class for upper class status, akin to one reason suggested for the success of Freemasonry. Bradford Spangenberg takes that tack:

> An overpowering deference for aristocratic authority existed in the mentality of the most middle class civilian officials. Accompanying this was the craving to attain the title of a 'gentleman' through assuming 'the trappings of gentility'. Companionships or the Knight Commanderships in the Star of India titles were cherished as appropriate symbols of a gentlemanly status. These honours came almost automatically to those who gained appointment to the Viceroy's Council or to Lieutenant-Governorships. Yet the struggle to achieve such exalted status was so arduous, relentless, and enervating that the final achievement often seemed hollow or devoid of its anticipated glamour. Higher officials suffered various degrees of disillusionment, serious illness, or unsatiated desire for further recognition in England...As promotion and status dominated the motivations of men at the top of the hierarchy, so deference and caution characterized their actions throughout much of their careers. They were tragically paradoxical figures in the sense that their obsequious mentality had resulted from deference to an aristocracy who then turned on them over and over again, most notably [when] Curzon had condemned them for lack of initiative, backbone, creativity and character.[19]

Compromises

In trying to present a summary of each officer's career there have been compromises that *multum in parvo,* will be greeted by some with relief and by others with annoyance, but the suggested sources in the India Office Records such as the pension records and references to sources elsewhere may mollify those who would wish for more.

Companion volumes in the quintet, which has the overall title of *Magicians of Arabia,* will include the results of additional investigations. Detailed tables will include all EIC and FO appointments and list subordinates such as Major Lincoln, and will provide fuller details than found here of postings and family backgrounds. It would of course be useful to include an appreciation of the significance of the postings in India, because the fact that a man was stationed somewhere conveys little about his duties. Nor are the titles themselves always easily understood. An instance is that although men serving in Jaipur, Jodhpur and Udapiur in Rajputana usually appear in biographical data as Residents, the title of Resident in those states was only a courtesy one and in actual fact the incumbent was only a Political Agent.

Just how full and complete will be the detail in various other books in this project is yet to be decided. T.W. Bamford in *Rise of the Public Schools* introduced the idea of depicting in a genealogical tree the linkages of a family with the Imperial services and public schools. In illustration, Bamford enables a reader to *see* via a family tree if a Harrovian viceroy is related to a Wykehamist governor-general.

The Indians who faithfully served the Residents would be another topic that would be rewarding. However, adding genealogies and the lives of assistants adds greatly to the number of pages. At any rate, information and corrections about the biographies, and biographies that could be added to the list, should be addressed to the author at the Department of Education, The University of Western Australia, Nedlands, Western Australia.

Biographies of the Gulf Residents and Agents

ALBAN, REGINALD GEORGE EVELIN WILLIAM Political Agent Bahrain 1927, 1940-42. b. 21 August 1899. Raised in Alexandria, Egypt, where his father was the Consul-General. BERKHAMSTED SCHOOL 1912-17. Joined 7th Gurkhas. Military employ to 1925. 'Temporarily' IPS 1925. Acting PA Muscat 1925. Reverted to Military Department. Entered 1927. Acting Political Agent Bahrain 1927. Probationer in Multan, Lyallpur, Dharamsala, Montgomery 1927-28. Vice-Consul Duzdap, 1929. Undersecretary to Gulf Resident 1930-31. Acting Political Agent Muscat 1931. Undersecretary to Gulf Resident 1931-32. Acting Political Agent Muscat 1932, 1933. Served Indore, Kalat, Sibi 1934-36. British Legation Kabul 1939-1940. Acting Political Agent Bahrain 1940-42. Acting Political Agent Muscat 1942. Political Agent Punjab Hill States 1942-44. Commissioner Mardan 1945. Secretary to NWFP Government Home Department 1945. Consul Kerman 1945-47. Retired 1950. OBE 1939.

BARRETT, CYRIL CHARLES JOHNSON Political Agent Bahrain, 1926-29. b. 26 May 1884. Son of E.C. Barrett, Castletown, Isle of Man; Superintendent Survey of India. KING WILLIAM'S COLLEGE 1894-1900. Cricket XI 1895-96. Football XV 1896. Day boy and then Hemingway's House. Sandhurst 1901. 2nd Lt.1902. Indian Army (IA) 1904. Married 1908 Mabel Ada Geddes, daughter of Col. A.D. Geddes, Royal Enniskillin Fusiliers. Her two sisters both married Lionel Haworth *qv*, and her brother Edwin Cyril Geddes, CMG, was Malaysian Civil Service and had a son Edwin Cyril Geddes Barrett CMG, also in Malaysian Civil Service. Joined Bombay Political Service 1907. Savantvadi, Kathiawar 1907-10. Assistant Resident Aden 1910-1913. Mesopotamian Expeditionary Force (despatches twice)

1915-19. 1st Assistant to Resident Aden 1919-1925. Transferred to IPS 1924. Political Agent Muscat 1926. Political Agent Bahrain 1926-1929. Acting Gulf Resident 1929. Consul-General Meshed 1930-32. CIE 1918. CSI 1922. East India Club. d. 12 July 1933. Cancer diagnosed June 1932. Left Meshed for X-ray therapy in London. J.G. Laithwaite wrote Undersecretary of State, 17 July 1933: 'As you will remember he would have had the Gulf Residency had it not been for a breakdown in his health. The Secretary of State might perhaps be willing to send a letter of sympathy to Mrs Barrett (who is a sister-in-law of Sir Lionel Haworth).' She replied in a letter written from Haworth's house. See IOR:Political Postings 1931-35, P/PS12/11 (PZ831/31) and L/P&S/12/7-12, 831.

BILL, JOHN HUGO HEPBURN Deputy Gulf Resident, 1917-19. Son of Charles Horsfall Bill, who was at Wellington College 1866-68. WELLINGTON COLLEGE 1891-95. Benson Scholarship. School Prefect. Entering Michaelmas 1891 with him were John Brind (Gen. Sir John Brind KCB KBE CMG), Commander in Chief India 1937-41, and Henry Chilton (Sir Henry Chilton GCMG) Ambassador to Chile, Spain, and Argentina. Lionel Portman's novel *Hugh Rendal*, set at Wellington in 1888-92, offers an unpleasant picture of hazing and brutality. BA New College Oxford. Exhibitioner. Taylorian Scholar in Russian. Entered ICS 1900. In charge Multan Jail 1901. Plague Duty 1902-1903. Served Hazara, Nowshera, Bannu 1904-1906. Assistant to Gulf Resident 1906-1908. Assistant Secretary Foreign Department Government of India 1908. Consul Shiraz 1908-10. Assistant to Gulf Resident 1911-1912. Served Peshawar, Bannu, Kobat, Miranshah 1912-17. Deputy Gulf Resident 22 December 1917 – September 1919. CIE 1911. d. 1919. Murdered by Kurdish insurrectionists in Iraq.

BELHAVEN – Peerage of Robert Hamilton, *qv*.

BIRD, RICHARD ERNEST Political Officer Trucial Coast 1944-45. b. 5 March 1912. Son of Lt-Col. W.F. Bird. Relative in India: Capt. R. Bird. IMPERIAL SERVICE COLLEGE. Haileybury and ISC amalgamated in May 1942. Sandhurst. Entered IPS 1938. Assistant Political Agent Bahrain 1938. Assistant Magistrate and Collector Moradabad and Meerut 1938-39. War service 1939-43. Assistant Political Agent Muscat 1943-44. Political Officer Trucial Coast 1944-45. Assistant Political Agent Bahrain 1945-46. Political Agent Kuwait 1946. Undersecretary External Affairs Department 1946-47. Undersecretary Foreign Department 1947. 'A sahib to the core.' IOR: Personal File, R/1/4/1366, F.S. Poynder to N.S. Alington, 14 May 1936. Retired 1949. IPS pension. Joined Anglo-Petroleum Company. d. 29 December 1986 at Ascot.

BIRDWOOD, RICHARD LOCKINGTON Acting Gulf Resident 1914. b. 7 September 1879. Son of Herbert Birdwood, Undersecretary Government of Bombay, and of Edith Impey who '...also came of a family whose roots went into the annals of British India.' *Khaki and Gown*, 25. Daughter of Elijah Impey, Surgeon-Major Bombay Horse Artillery and Postmaster-General Bombay. Dame school, Cheltenham. CLIFTON COLLEGE 1893-97. Four Clifton brothers: Field Marshal Lord Birdwood of Anzaz and Totnes GCB GCMG (Commander in Chief India and President of Clifton College), Brig-Gen. Halhed Birdwood (Persian campaigns 1911-13), Lt-Col. Gordon Birdwood (Indian Medical Service), and Christopher Birdwood (Royal Engineers, d. Ambala 1894). Entering with him in September 1893: George Barne, headmaster of Lawrence School India 1912-32; subsequently Bishop of Lahore. In Oakley's House. Sandhurst, Queen's India Cadet. IA 1898. lst Gurkhas. Tibet 1903-1904. Assistant to Gulf Resident 1912. Field Marshal Birdwood wrote two books that include family and Clifton memories: *Khaki and Gown: An Autobiography*, 1941; and *In My Time*, 1946. *Khaki* recounts the Field Marshal's Gulf visit when he stayed at Residency with his brother, who was Percy Cox's assistant. d. 17 November 1914 in first action of the war in the Gulf, an attack on Turkish forces near Fao at mouth of the Shat-el-Arab. His death created the opening for Arnold Wilson *qv* which led to his becoming Cox's *alter ego*.

BISCOE, HUGH VINCENT Gulf Resident, 1929-32. b. 27 June 1881. Son of Lt-Gen William W. Biscoe CB, educated Winchester, Commander 19th Bengal Lancers. WINCHESTER COLLEGE 1894-97. In Bramston's House (Colver's Close). Sandhurst. IA 1901. Biscoe joined the Army *after* joining the ICS – the 9th Lancers (Fane's Horse) in 1901. Married 1908 Dorothy Eva, daughter of C.J. Tisdall. They had two daughters and one son. Entered ICS 1900. IA 1901. Served Ambala, Rawalpindi, Mianwali 1903-1906. Entered IPS 1906. Served Quetta 1907-1910. Assistant Resident and Consul, Bunder Abbas, 1910-15. Undersecretary and Deputy Secretary. Foreign Department 1915-16. War service, primarily France 1917-19. Served Haraoti, Tonk, Indore, Quetta, Dungarpur 1919-26. Consul General and Agent Khorasan 1926-29. Gulf Resident 1929-32. Legion of Honour 1918. Medaille de la Reconnaissance Française 1918. KBE 1932. United Service Club. d. 19 July 1932 of heart-attack on gunboat HMS *Lupin* off Sharjah. Treaty negotiations with Shaikh of Sharjah were in process and

Biscoe's assistant, Leslie Chauncey, wrote that he tried unsuccessfully to contact Lady Biscoe: 'So back to sea we went, and the burial took place. I then had the idea that if I returned to Sharjah and told the Shaikh that he had killed the Resident with his arguing, he might out of remorse complete the agreement.' He did. Trench, *Viceroy's Agent* .

BRAY, NORMAN NAPIER EVELYN Political Agent Bahrain, 1918-19. b. 17 August 1885, Belfast. Son of Capt. Norman Aiton Bray, who died in Upper Burmah. 'I was born in Belfast, but my parents soon after removed to India and were never again quartered there....My mother was born in Australia.' IOR:L/MIL/9/304, Sandhurst application, 24 August 1903. WELLINGTON COLLEGE 1898-1903. XV 1903. In 1898 the Prince of Wales distributed speech day prizes. Sandhurst IA. 18th KGO Lancers. War service: Military Cross 1918. Lawrence in *Seven Pillars of Wisdom* mentions being helped in the raid on the Yarmuk bridges by 'Captain Bray's Indian volunteers'. Married 1913 Dorothy Gertrude Lynden Bell and had sons. Divorced 1926. See IOR:L/AG/23/16/17, No.3032. Married 1926 at Copenhagen, Ebba Sofie Marianne Nielsen. Political Agent Bahrain 1918-19. Special duty under Civil Commissioner Mesopotamia Expeditionary Force 1919. Employed India Office 1920-21. Attached Political Department India Office 1921-22. Retired 1923. IA pension. An 'ardent disciple' of Lt-Col. Gerard Leachman after working with him in Mesopotamia, having also worked with Lorimer in the Hijaz and formed of him 'the poorest opinion'. Winstone, *Leachman*, viii. Winstone criticizes Bray's biography of Gerard Leachman, *Shifting Sands*, noting that he gets Leachman's first name wrong. OBE. d. 1 May 1962.

CAROE, OLAF KIRKPATRICK Acting Gulf Resident 1937. b. 15 November 1892. Son of William Douglas Caroe, architect, whose commissions included buildings for Wycombe Abbey and Sherborne schools. And of Grace Desborough Rendall. Her brother was 2nd master at Harrow and his son, her nephew and Olaf's cousin, was head of Charterhouse. Caroe believed that Montague Rendall, relative and headmaster of Winchester, was 'sweet' on his mother. See 'Five Autobiographical Narratives of Sir Olaf Caroe', IOR:MSS Eur C.273/1-5, 2. Summer Fields Preparatory School, 1903-1906. Football XI 1905. At Summer Fields, Caroe began a lifelong friendship with Harold Macmillan, whom he credited with getting his books published. Caroe was a loyal old boy and contributed reminiscences to *A Century of Summer Fields.* WINCHESTER COLLEGE 1906. In Morhead's House. At Winchester Caroe became friends with Arnold Toynbee. Magdalen Oxford (Demy). Army 1914. Queen's Royal West Surrey Regiment, 2nd Lt. Temporary Lt. 1915. Substantive Captain 1916. Mohmand Blockade Force and Wazirstan Field Force. Demobilized 1919. Married 1920 Frances Marion; daughter of A.G. Rawstorne, Bishop of Whalley. She received Gold Kaisar-i-Hind 1947. Two sons. ICS 1920. Entered IPS 1924. He had considerable trouble getting ICS permission to join the IPS. Assistant Commissioner, Lahore, Amritsar 1920-23. Magistrate, Peshawar, Kohat, Mardan, 1924. Deputy Commissioner Peshawar 1925. Assistant Commissioner Mardan 1925-27. Confirmed in Political Department 1927. Assistant Commissioner Manshera 1927-28. Deputy Commissioner Kohat 1928-29. Secretary to Agent to the Governor-General NWFP 1929-33. Chief Secretary NWFP 1933-34. Deputy Secretary Foreign Department 1934-36. Recalled from leave 1937 to be Acting Gulf Resident 19 August 1937 – 22 November 1937. Resident Baluchistan 1937-38. Revenue and Judicial Commissioner Baluchistan 1938. Resident Waziristan 1938. Secretary External Affairs Department (renamed Foreign Department) 1939-45.

Governor NWFP 1946-47. '...not as imperturbable a man for the day when heaven was falling'. Trench, *Viceroy's Agent*. 'Caroe was a victim of the pressures of his office – terribly tired and strained', Ismay found him when he visited Peshawar in April [1947] ...Caroe went – ill-health being the formal reason, and 'on extended leave' rather than dismissed. Dismissed he had been, however, and the fact caused him lasting distress and transitory bitterness. Any grievance he might have had against the Viceroy quickly passed, however; in later life he freely conceded that his departure was necessary for the future of the province. Mountbatten for his part paid tribute to Caroe's gallant acceptance of the inevitable: 'if you had not behaved as a very great gentleman', he said, 'it would have been impossible...'. Caroe returned the compliment. 'I can only say,' he summed up, 'that to me personally, then and later, Mountbatten behaved with honour and sincerity, and an attitude that I can only describe as royal.' Philip Ziegler, *Mountbatten: The Official Biography*, Fontana/Collins, 1986, 376-77.

Vice Chairman, Overseas League 1951. Visited USA for British Information Services 1952. 1st president Tibet Society, 1959-77. CIE 1932. CSI 1941. KCIE 1944. KCSI 1946. FRSL 1959. D.Lit. Oxford 1960. FRCA (Lawrence of Arabia Medal 1973). Lansdowne Club. Overseas League. United Service Club (Simla). See his papers in 12 boxes IOL. A few papers are in the Winchester College Archives. Author *Wells of Power, Soviet Empire, The Pathans, From Nile to Indus, Englishmen in Tibet from Bogle to Gould, Poems of Khushal Khan Khatak,* 'Introduction' to ed. Mountstuart Elphinstone's

Canbul, articles in *Round Table* and *Asian Affairs*. See George Chowdharay-Best, 'Sir Olaf Caroe: An Annotated Bibliography', *Central Asian Review*, Vol.6, No.1, 1987, 141-49. d. 23 November 1981.

COLE, GEORGE ASHMEAD Acting Political Agent Bahrain, 1935. b. 1 February 1902, Travancore, South India. Heir presumptive to Earldom of Enniskillen. In 1918 the third son of the fourth Earl had issue who succeeded to title. Son of Robert Hymore College, tea planter. Great-grandfather was Lt.Gen Galbraith Lowry Cole. STONYHURST. 11 colours. Boxing: 'Broke some bones in my right hand and arm in the open boxing which prevented me winning distinctions there.' Personal File, IOR:R/1/4. 'Losing his mother when he was very young and being mostly separated from his father, who worked in India, he grew up with a sturdy independence of character and opinions which helped him to succeed as a schoolboy in debating...George's three years at Stonyhurst ended in *Poetry*. "Poetry" is the Stonyhurst name for the Lower Sixth.' Rev. F.J. Turner, Librarian & Archivist, Stonyhurst College, to P.J. Rich, 23 July 1987. Sandhurst. IA 1921. Cameronians (Scottish Rifles). Learned Arabic at SOAS while being treated for dysentery. Played Rugby for London Scottish. Baluch Regiment. War service. DCO. Married 1933 Elsie, daughter of Major-Gen. Bowle-Evans. Six children. Entered IPS 1928. Assistant Political Agent North Waziristan 1928-29. Probationer Rawalpindi 1929-30. Lyallpore 1930. Gurdaspur 1930-31. Assistant Commissioner Kohat 1931. Peshawar 1931-32. Special Duty Beshwar 1932-33. Assistant Commissioner Peshawar 1933-35. Assistant Political Agent and Officiating Political Agent Bahrain 17 March 1935 – 27 October 1935. Assistant Political Agent Bahrain 28 October 1935 – 5 April 1936. Assistant to Political Agent Kalat and Chagai, 1936-37. Political Agent Chagai 1937-39. Assistant Political Agent Zhob 1939-40. Political Agent Zhob 1940-41. Assistant Commissioner Charsadda 1941. Deputy Commissioner D.I. Khan 1941-43. Political Agent Khyber 1943-44. Director Agricultural Production NWFP 1944. Political Agent Khyber 1945. Political Agent Kurram 1946. Personal file in the R/1/4 series has a note by Denys Bray (Foreign Secretary, Government of India), 17 January 1929, 'I understand from him that he apprehends difficulty in getting into an Indian regiment if it is known that he is using it as a stepping stone to the Political Department', and stating that Cole expressed a 'desire to work with Arabs'. Also a note by Percy Gordon Loch, 26 April 1936, that Cole had a 'strong tendency to think that people and conditions are against him' and could be 'inaccurate and almost incoherent', concluding that he was 'unsuited to political work in the Persian Gulf'. T.C. Fowle wrote, 14 July 1936, that he was 'jumpy'. Retired 11 November 1948. IA Pension. Farmed 1000 acres near East London, South Africa, raising Jerseys and Herefords. Established a native school for 100 children. FRGS 1930. Resigned 1934. Himalayan Club. d. 2 January 1969.

COX, PERCY ZACHARIAH Gulf Resident 1904-20 b. 20 November 1864. Youngest son of Arthur Z. Cox, landowner of Herongate, near Brentwood, and of Julienne Emily Saunders. Cordwalles Preparatory School (called St. Piran's since 1919). Situated in Maidenhead from 1873 when it was refounded by Rev. T.J. Nunns, who was a private schoolmaster at Blackheath before going to Maidenhead in 1873. Cordwalles' masters may have included Jack the Ripper, since J. Druitt, a suspect, taught at its progenitor. Disraeli is reputed to have been a student. H.A.L. Fisher, a pupil at about the same time as Cox, claimed that Nunns vetted all books that boys read on Sundays and compelled the reading of Keble's *Christian Year* at the rate of one poem a week. Fisher commented about Cordwalles: 'I cannot say that I was ever really happy at my preparatory school. Indeed I vividly remember thinking during my first term that all joys were at an end and that I should never know what happiness was again.' Fisher, *An Unfinished Autobiography*, 35. HARROW 1878-82. Headmaster's House. Monitor. Sandhurst 1882. IA 1884. 2nd Scottish Rifles (Cameronian) until 1889. Staff Corps, 1889. Assistant to Political Agent Jhelum 1890. Kolhapur 1892. Savantvadi 1892. Married 1889 Louisa Belle (DBE 1923); youngest daughter of Surgeon-General J. Butler Hamilton, who served in India. One son Derek, Old Harrovian, killed in World War I. Entered IPS 1892. To enter he resigned from his British regiment and joined an Indian one, the 29th Punjabis. Vice-Consul Somalia Coast 1893. Berbera 1894-95 as well as Assistant Resident Aden 1892-1895. Baroda 1895-1897. Political Agent Muscat 1899-1903. Gulf Resident 1904-1920. Secretary Foreign Department 1914. High Commissioner Mesopotamia 1920-23. Tuson correctly divides Cox's Gulf terms because of his 1914 assignments, but the IOR Service Records show continuous tenure broken by special assignments. CIE 1902. CSI 1909. KCIE 1911. KCMG 1920. KCSI 1915. GCIE 1917. GCMG 1922. LLD Oxford 1925. LLD Manchester 1929. DL Bedfordshire. FRGS 1895. Council 1925. President 1933-36. Proposed by George Curzon. Lady Cox a member (1933). FZS. Member British Ornithologists' Union. Vice President 1927. Hakluyt Society. Vice President 1931. DNB. Athenaeum. Carlton Club. Hurlingham Club. Marlborough Club. Naval and Military Club. Raneleagh Club. United Service Club.'...his genius shone calm and steady, come wind, come water. He was tall and slender with a face like a Roman senator. His outstanding feature was a very large nose which had a decided "list" to starboard. I always felt that nothing could get past that nose and it is quite certain that very little did.' SLRCA: Stanley Mylrea, 'Kuwait Before Oil: Memoirs of Dr. C. Stanley G. Mylrea, Pioneer Medical Missionary of The Arabian Mission', typescript, 79. The Philip Graves biography *Life of Sir Percy Cox* (1942), compiled with the help of the Cox family, is not a critical study. Some papers are at St. Antony's, Oxford. The RGS has his *Journal*, Somaliland, 1894; *Journal*, Somaliland, 1898; *Journal*, Gulf, 1902-1907; letters, 1933-1936. He was interested in genealogy and compiled family trees of the Ansa and Gadabursi tribes of Somalia. Contributor to *Encyclopaedia Britannica*. Wrote for *Journal of the Bombay Natural History Society*. Collected for the South Kensington Museum. See Cox and Ticehurst, 'Birds of the Persian Gulf Island', *Journal of the Bombay Natural History Society*, Vol.XXX, 725. d. 20 February 1937 while foxhunting, the same way his father had died. Tablet, Anglican Church, Baghdad. Buried, family vault at Upminster church.

CRAWFORD, JAMES ADAIR Gulf Resident i/c 1893. b. 1857. Son of Arthur Travers Crawford CMG 1887, Old Rugbeian 1847, Bombay Civil Service 1854-85 – for whom the Arthur Market in Bombay is named. Grandfather, James H. Crawford ICS, Bengal. The Crawford family as well as having many Indian connections provided a Berkhamsted headmaster (1850-64), James R. Crawford, who was at Rugby under Arnold. RUGBY SCHOOL 1869-1874. In B. Smith House. Passed 8th in ICS exam 1876. ICS 1878. Assistant Collector Ratnagiri 1878. Poona, Khandeish, Ahmadedabad, Hyderabad 1879-82. Entered IPS 1881. Attache Foreign Department 1882-84. Ajmere 1884-85. Assistant Secretary Foreign Department 1885-87. Junior Undersecretary 1887-89. Political Agent Quetta, Jacobabad, Coorg, Hyderabad, 1889-92. Deputy Secretary Foreign Department 1892. Special Duty with Archduke of Austria during tour of India 1892-1893. Undersecretary Foreign Department 1893. Gulf Resident i/c 21 July 1893 – 19 December 1893. Resident Quetta, Amraoti, Hyderabad, 1894-1900. Resident Mysore 1900-1902. East India Club.

CROSTHWAITE, CHARLES GILBERT Acting Gulf Resident 1925. b. 3 June 1878. Second son of Sir Robert Crosthwaite KCSI, who served chiefly on the North-West Frontier. Nephew of Sir Charles Crosthwaite KCSI, member Council of India and author *Notes on the N.W. Provinces of India.* SHREWSBURY SCHOOL 1891-94. Sandhurst. IA 1897. Attached to 1st S. Wales Borderers. Quartermaster 13th Rajputs 1898. Married 1907 Joan, daughter of Maj-Gen. A.C. Becher CBE, who served in the Afghan War 1879-80. One daughter and two sons. Entered IPS 1903. Served Indore, Bannu, Dera Ismail (Commandant, Border Military Police), Shirani, Peshawar, Nowshera, Kohat Hangu 1903-10. District Judge Peshawar 1912-17. Agent Peshawar 1921-23. Political Agent Muscat 1924-26. Acting Gulf Resident, 3 June 1925 – 3 October 1925. Political Agent Muscat 1925-26. Agent Eastern Rajputana 1926-27. Resident Gwalior 1927. Agent to Governor-General Madras 1928-29. Resident Baroda 1931-33. Retired 1933. OBE. d. 30 July 1940.

DALY, CLIVE KIRKPATRICK Political Agent Bahrain 1921-26. b. 3 April 1888 Woolwich. Son of Edward Dermot Hamilton Daly (1853-1933), who was educated at Winchester, as were Edward's brothers (Clive's uncles): Arthur, Inspector General (1925-27), Ministry of Defence, Iraq; Hugh, CSI, Deputy-Secretary Foreign Department Government of India and author *Memoirs of General Sir Henry Dermot Daly GCB CIE* (John Murray, 1905); and Henry, who like Edward served in 15th Hussars but became captain and fought in the Afghan and Boer Wars. Edward was Queen's India Cadet, Sandhurst, 1873. His father (Clive's grandfather) was Gen. Sir Henry Dermot Daly KCB CIE (1821-95), Bombay Staff Corps, commander Hodson's Horse. See IOR:L/MIL/9/298. Two Gulfites Frederick Wilson *qv* and Malcolm Meade *qv* served under General Daly when young agents in Central India. Meade's father was General Daly's predecessor as Agent to the Governor-General Central India. General Daly encouraged the Chiefs' Colleges and Daly College was named after him. Clive was privately educated and at Woolwich. The Woolwich cadet magazine reported Daly as educated privately but since his father went to Winchester, this raises questions. Sir Henry Daly had eight children by two marriages and in his will (Somerset House N.1233) omits only Edward. Clive Daly's grandmother left an estate of £12,000 but his mother left only £500. IOR:L/AG/33/5 and Somerset House 1920 No.1183. Edward had a lacklustre career compared with his brothers. He was only a lieutenant and one possibility is he was disinherited and unable to pay for a public school education for his children. Army 1907. 2nd Lt. 1907, RGS. Lt. 1911. Transferred Indian Army 1911. War service. Bt.Major 1919. Lt.Colonel 1933. Married Bridget Julia. Four children. Married 2nd Dorothy, daughter of Col. P. Allen. Entered IPS 1920. Exempted from training and Department exams. IOR:R/1/4/1221. 'I joined the Department while serving as a major in Political employ in Iraq...I was appointed as a special case...On joining, however, I found I had been placed below young officers, many years my junior, some of whom had trained under me in Iraq.' IOR:L/PS/11/303 P35/1929. Political Agent Bahrain 1921-26. In 1926 Daly asked to leave the Gulf for Meshed: 'for which post my qualifications and experiences of Shiah Divines and their politics, acquired in Iraq and Bahrein [are relevant]...I had the matter of the Shiah classes and their intimate relations to deal with.' He took long leave and in 1929 accepted Seistan 'with alacrity'. Consul Seistan and Kain 1929-32. Consul-General Khorasan 1932-36. Political Agent Rajkot 1938-39. Resident Baroda and Gujarat 1939-43. National Savings Commissioner of India 1943-45. *Times* obituary 23 September 1966 notes 'During the Second World War he was selected to organise and develop the Savings Movement in India, which he conducted with conspicuous success and for which services he was knighted'. Retired for pension purposes 1943 but given extension. IA pension. CIE 1925. CSI 1943. Kt. 1946. d. 17 September 1966.

DE GAURY, GERALD SIMPSON HILLAIRET RUTLAND VERE Political Agent Kuwait 1936-39. b. 1 April 1897. Only son of Hubert Stanley Buchanan de Gaury, stockbroker; and of Christine Simpson, only daughter of Pindar Simpson, land agent and member of a firm of surveyors established for over 150 years in Old Burlington Street, London. Huguenot stock. Army 1914. Joined from Oxford University OTC. Temporary 2nd Lt. Hampshire Regiment 1914-15. Lt. Essex Rifles 1916. Acting Captain 1916-19. Wounded Gallipoli, Somme, Arras. Intelligence, Iraq. Military Cross 1917. Iraqi Levies 1924-27. Captain 1926. Air Ministry 1927-28, 1930. Retired from Army 1936. Honorary Lt-Colonel 1948. In 1934 made a solo journey to Riyadh. Returned in 1935 accompanying Sir Andrew Ryan, 1st British Minister to Saudi Arabia. Probationer IPS 1936 on ten year contract. Political Agent Kuwait 1936-39. De Gaury had difficulties in Kuwait and was offered the chance to resign on health grounds, did not, and was dropped from the service. Given six months notice 22 March 1940. Attached Legation, Tehran, possibly for Intelligence work. 22 April 1940. Thought at fault in dispute with Kuwait ruling family. See IOR:R/1/4/987. 'We can see that friction in Koweit rendered it difficult to employ him further there, while lack of administrative experience precluded employment elsewhere in the Gulf; at the same time, he is a distinguished Arabist with wide knowledge of Arab Rulers...'. Olaf Caroe *qv*, Government of India External Affairs Department, to Secretary of State for India, 1 April 1940. IOR:L/P&S/12/3599. 'Mr de Gaury must have realized...that the Gulf hadn't room for both him & Col. Prior.' IOR:Minute Paper PZ/332/40, 23 January 1940, L/P&S/12/35/3599. See also IOR:R/1/4/987. First Secretary Tehran 1940. Raised Druse camel detachment for Syrian campaign against Vichy. Under him were Gawain Bell and Wilfred Thesiger. Gold Staff at Queen Elizabeth II's coronation. Visited Imam's cave fortresses during Yemeni civil war 1962.
FRGS 1927-1950. Rejoined 1979. FRSAF 1923. FRSAF has a painting of de Gaury and Ibn Saud, de Gaury's bequest. Founder member Anglo-Iraqi Society. Council Anglo-Arab Association. Anglo-Yemeni Committee. Member Travellers' and possibly Garrick and Army and Navy: G.P. Anderson to P.J. Rich, 5 April 1990. Contributor to *Spectator, London Magazine, Journal of Royal Central Asian Society.* Wrote *Arabian Phoenix, Arabian Journey, The Rulers of Mecca, The Grand Captain, Gonzalo de Cordoba, Three Kings in Baghdad, Faisal: King of Saudi Arabia, Travelling Gent: A Life of Alexander Kingslake* (his own favourite). Edited *Through Wahhabiland on Camelback, The Road to Kabul.* The original of *Wahabiland* was written in Danish by Barclay Raunkiaser and translated for the Admiralty War Staff, Cairo, 1916. See IOL:V3605. In the preface, de Gaury acknowledged help in re-translation from Prince George of Denmark and the Princess Eugenie of Greece. His will at Somerset House left papers to Princess Eugenie of Greece. In codicil he left books to Wilfred Thesinger. The RGS now has twelve of his albums and fourteen notebooks. There is a pressing need for a biography of de Gaury that addresses some of the anomalies in his career, *e.g. The Geographical Journal* obituary implies that he resigned from Kuwait when war broke out, but it appears that he was sacked. See Vol.150, Part 2, July 1984, 298-9. Molly Izzard's obituary in *Asian Affairs* asserts that he spied in the Balkans in 1939. Vol.15, O.S. 71, No.2, 1984, 227-28. In checking for his papers, his surname is sometimes found under De and sometimes G, as in IOR:V/12/32. d. 13 January 1984, Brighton. 'With his passing goes yet another of that small and dwindling band of Englishmen who shared in the creation of the Arab states which emerged between the wars.' *Times,* 14 January 1984. Estate probated at £69,699. Bequeathed presentation swords from Ibn Saud and Shaikh of Bahrain, a silver box with the bullets from his war wounds, drawings and other memorabilia, to HRH Princess Eugenie of Greece and Denmark.

DICKSON, HAROLD RICHARD PATRICK Political Agent Kuwait 1929-36, 1941. b. 4 February 1881. Son of John Dickson, Consul-General Jerusalem. ST. EDWARD'S SCHOOL 1894-1900. In MacNamara's House and Apsley House. Prefect. Rugby XV. Cricket XI. '...like myself, [he] was a firm believer in such education for the son of an English gentleman. I was accordingly sent to Wellington, and in due course sent both my sons to public school!' H.Y.W.R. Dickson to P.J. Rich, 6 July 1987. Wadham, Oxford. Army 1903. Connaught Rangers. 'He never really enjoyed the somewhat dull life of a British Infantry Regt. Mess and in 1908 transferred to the Indian Army – 29th Lancers [Deccan Horse]. But his interests lay more in the political field.' HYWSD. War service. Mesopotamia with 33rd

QVO Light Cavalry. Married 1920 Violet Penelope Lindley MBE 1942 CBE 1964 DBE 1976, daughter of Neville Lucas-Calcraft. One daughter Irene Zahra. One son Hanmer Yorke Warrington Saud. Tutor Maharaj Kumar of Bikander 1912-13. Guardian Maharaj Kumar 1913-14. Mesopotamian Campaign. Transferred to IPS 1915. Political Agent Bahrain 1919-20. Private Secretary to Maharaja of Bikaner 1927. 'Selected to officiate' in IPS 1928 'Through the good offices of the Maharajah.' HYWSD to PJR. Secretary to Gulf Resident 1928-29. A shortage of IPS officers created an opening for Dickson. No. F.1-E/30. From Foreign Secretary, Government of India, to Under Secretary of State for India, 7 January 1930, IOR:L/P&S/12/3599. Political Agent Kuwait 1929-36. Retired 1936. IA Pension. Recalled as Political Agent Kuwait 1941. CIE 1916. FRGS 1922. Proposed by P.M. Sykes. At the time studying surveying at the Society. RCAS. United Service Club. '...being proposed I believe by Sir Percy Cox – my godfather, as it was "the thing to do"...In India the various Gymkhana Clubs attracted Harold for the sporting facilities they offered.' HYWSD to PJR. Freemasonry: 'Harold was never a Freemason – its ritual ceremonies were repugnant to him.' HYWSD to PJR. Dickson wrote *The Arab of the Desert* and *Kuwait and Her Neighbours.* The suspicion is that his talented wife was more than a small help. Arnold Wilson *qv* remarked to him once 'You're a very good Political Officer, but you can't write a damn.' Dame Violet, and their daughter Zahra Freeth, wrote extensively. Dame Violet wrote *Wild Flowers of Kuwait and Bahrain*, and *Forty Years in Kuwait.* See 'My Early Years in the Persian Gulf', *Journal of the Royal Central Asiatic Society*, Vol.XLIX, Part 1, January 1962, 23-32. Zahra co-authored with H.V.F. Winston. *Kuwait: Prospect and Reality*, and *Explorers of Arabia: From the Renaissance to the End of the Victorian Era.* Papers at St. Antony's, Oxford. d. 14 June 1959. *Times* obituary 15 June 1959.

DISBROWE, HERBERT FREDERICK Officiating Resident 1862. b. 1826. Third son of Rev. Henry Disbrowe, Rector of Welbourn in Lincolnshire and Fellow, All Souls, Oxford. Mr Demmler's School, Rue de Courcelles No.12, Paris. OAKHAM SCHOOL 1841-45. Mr. Miller's, Woolwich. Wadham, Oxford 1845-46. Nominated by Lord Ripon. IOR:L/MIL/9213. Disbrowe was assistant to Felix Jones *qv* from whom according to Robin Bidwell, in the introduction to *Arabian Gulf Intelligence*, 'he absorbed the old Gulf tradition of minimal interference on land as long as the peace was kept at sea'. Appointed as Political Agent in Muscat in 1863, which unfortunately for him coincided with start of the Residency of Lewis Pelly *qv* who favoured interventionism. Bidwell comments 'In addition to this political difference, he and Disbrowe seem to have conceived a personal antipathy towards each other, quarrelling with gusto for seven years. Disbrowe refused to regard himself as Pelly's subordinate and continued to correspond directly with Bombay despite a stream of angry orders that he should report only through Bushire.' In 1869 Disbrowe broke relations with the Imam, Azzan ibn Qays, whom he regarded as a religious fanatic. Pelly ordered ties restored, but Disbrowe pestered India with letters about Pelly's ignorance and rudeness. The Viceroy removed Disbrowe, January 1870.

DIXON, MICHAEL GRAY Acting Political Agent Bahrain, 1943. b. 24 June 1910 in India. Son of Rev. T.H. Dixon. MARLBOROUGH COLLEGE 1923-29. Jesus, Cambridge. Army 1931. IA 1934. Entered IPS 1935. Probationer Indore and New Delhi 1935-36. Undersecretary to AGG Gujerat 1936. Probationer Rawalpindi, Murree, Lahore 1936-37. Assistant Political Agent Punjab Hill States 1938. Special duty Kahmir 1939-40. Undersecretary Punjab Hill States 1940-42. Assistant Political Agent Bahrain 1942 and Acting Political Agent 1943. Public Relations Officer Gulf 1943. Vice-Consul Kabul 1944. City Magistrate Peshawar 1944-45. Deputy Commissioner Mardan 1945-46. Assistant Commissioner Peshawar 1946. Undersecretary and Deputy Secretary External Department 1946-47. Opted for Pakistan 1947.

FOWLE, TRENCHARD CRAVEN WILLIAM Resident 1932-38. b. 28 November 1884. Son of Col. T. Fowle CB, Inspector General of Indian Ordinance. CLIFTON COLLEGE 1898-1902. Brown's House with Arnold Wilson *qv*. Fowle joined Clifton in April 1898 and Wilson in September 1898. They left 1902. Army 1904. Royal Munster Fusiliers. IA 1907. 40th Pathans. Travelled Turkish Arabia and Syria 1910, and Persia 1912-13 (language leave). Journeys are the basis of his book *Travels in the Middle East*, a *success d'estime*. Married 1923 Honor Cowell Williams. One daughter and one son. Entered IPS 1914. Special Duty in Gulf 1915. Acting Political Agent Bahrain 1916. Assistant Political Officer Baghdad 1916-18. Assistant to Consul-General Meshed 1919. Consul-General Khorasan 1919-20. Consul Sistan and Kain 1921. Assistant Political Agent Loralai 1921-22. Superintendent of Census Baluchistan 1922. Assistant Political Agent Zhob 1922-23. Assistant Magistrate Moradabad 1923. Political Agent Chagai 1923-24. Consul Kerman and Assistant to Gulf Resident, 1924. Assistant Resident Aden 1926-28. Secretary to Gulf Resident 1929-30. Political Agent Muscat 1930-31. Gulf Resident 1932-38: 'After the death of Colonel Biscoe, it was felt that a comparatively young officer would be required...'. Memo, 9 December 1936, IOR:R/1/4/975. Retired 1939. His offer to stay on indefinitely was 'to his indignation' refused. Trench, Viceroy's Agent. Employed British Council, London 1940. CBE 1929. KCIE 1937. FRGS 1910. Army and Navy Club. East India Club. According to Galloway qv Fowle had an appetite for Agatha Christie mysteries. A.C. Galloway to P.J. Rich, Interview. Trench writes that Fowle was Resident for seventeen years, and applies to him the same nickname that Prior gave Loch qv of 'Grand Old Man of the Gulf'. d. 23 February 1940.

GABRIEL, CECIL HAMILTON Deputy Gulf Resident, 1919. b. 16 February 1879 at Gunnersbury. Son of Edmund William Gabriel, Conservative Party Agent and manufacturer's representative, of Cranmore House, Co. Carlow and Babbacombe Glen, Torquay, S. Devon. And of Ellen Anne Pike. An elder brother: Sir Edmund Vivian Gabriel, IPS, 37th Lancers (Baluch Horse). Kersal Glen Preparatory School, Higher Broughton near Manchester. Punctual Attendance Prize Xmas Term 1887. Edmund also attended Kersal 1886-88, and then Manchester Grammar School 1889-93; and Emmanuel, Cambridge; entering ICS 1897 and IPS 1913. But Cecil was at STAMFORD SCHOOL 1892-95, winning Divinity, Drawing, Maths, and Chemistry Prizes. See *Register of Stamford School, 1553-1960*, Old Stamfordian Club, 1961. (Scarce, copy in Institute of Historical Research, London. This apparently was the first published register of the school, based on a register kept by Joseph Phillips O.S. 1835-40, who founded the Old Stamfordian Club in 1889.) Aldershot. 2nd Lt. from Militia, Army Service Corps 1901. Woolwich. York and Lancashires 1902. Sent to South Africa but hostilities had ended. Re-despatched to India. Information supplied by Col. Robert Gabriel. The 1st Battalion York and Lancs relieved 2nd Battalion in India 1902. Lt. 1903. IA 1903. 37th Baluch Lancers, Bombay Cavalry. Served Mhow, Indore, Fort Sandeman. Major 1916. Captain 1932. Lt-Col. Married 1913 Harriet Mabel, only surviving daughter of Col. George Blakiston Renny. One son: Col. Robert Cecil Gabriel, b. 1917 and served Royal Engineers. Entered IPS 1904. Assistant to Gulf Resident 1905-1906. Consul Bandar Abbas 1906-1908. Served Hyderabad, then Chilas 1908-11. Special Duty Coronation Durbar 1911. Ladakha 1913-14. Srinagar 1914-18. First Assistant to Gulf Resident 1919. District Judge Kohat 1920-21. Deputy Secretary Foreign Department 1921-22. Secretary to AGG Central India 1924-25. Political Agent Bhopal 1925-26. Resident Western Rajputana States 1928-29. Resident Gwalior 1929-32. Retired 1932. CVO 1922. FRGS 1905. Proposed by Percy Cox. Gabriel assisted Saldanha in assembling the Précis used by Lorimer as a basis for his Gazetteer. Authored the *Précis on Arms Trade in the Persian Gulf*, Simla 1904. d. 25 February 1947.

GALLOWAY, ARNOLD CRAWSHAW Political Agent Kuwait 1939-41. Political Agent Bahrain, 1945-47. Acting Gulf Resident 1945, 1947. b. 5 January 1901. Only son of Percy Christopher Galloway. Cowford Prep Sussex 1908-12. Sevenoaks School 1911-16. Headmaster's House. CITY OF LONDON 1916-17. '...at Sevenoaks for 4 or more years but at C.L.S. for only a short time to catch up for Sandhurst entrance exam extra subjects...left school to volunteer for war.' A.C. Galloway to P.J. Rich, 10 April 1987. Sandhurst. IA 1920. 2/10 Gurkha Rifles. Married 1946 Mary (MA *Oxon*, India Office employee), daughter of Arthur William Odgers. She had ancestors in EIC and an uncle in ICS. Three sons: two ed. Rossall and one at Westminster. IPS 1928. Unable to secure permission to leave the Gurkhas until a family friend, Field Marshal Lord Birdwood (see Richard Birdwood), interceded. A.C. Galloway to P.J. Rich, Interview. For the refusal by commanding officer to approve his application see IOR:R/1/4/1244. Assistant Collector, Meerut, Aligarh, Moradabad 1928-29. Undersecretary to AGG Rajastan 1929-30. First Assistant to Resident Baroda 1930. Vice-Consul Ahwaz 1930-33. Vice-Consul Zahidan 1933-34. Undersecretary to Gulf Resident 1934. Secretary to Gulf Resident 1934. Secretary British Legation Kabul 1934-36. Secretary to Gulf Resident 1937. Assistant Political Agent Bahrain 1937-38. Secretary to Gulf Resident 1938-39. Political Agent Kuwait 1939-41. Military Service (despatches) 1941-43. Consul-General Khuzistan 1943-44. Political Agent Muscat 1944-45. Acting Gulf Resident 1945. Political Agent Bahrain 1945-47. Acting Gulf Resident 1947. Political Agent Kuwait 1948-49. Retired 1949. IPS pension. UK Representative, Bahrain Petroleum, 1950-68. Chairman, Middle East Navigation Board 1958-68. OBE 1941. CIE 1946. FRGS. Council of RCA. East India Club. Flyfishers. Royal Thames Yacht. Freemason. d. August 1988.

GASTRELL, EVERALD HUDDLESTON Officiating Political Agent Bahrain 1933. b. 30 April 1898 (Cheltenham Register has April 31!). Son of Col. Everald T. Gastrell IA. His uncle was an IA captain and awarded CIE. Westward Ho! Junior School 1907-10. Clifton College 1910-11. CHELTENHAM COLLEGE 1912-1914. In Hazelwell House. Joined Military Side. RMC Wellington India. IA 1916. Sistan's Levy Corps. 9th Hodson's Horse. Palestine 1918. Married 1927 Delicia Crampton. One daughter and one son. IPS 1922. He gave Trenchard Fowle *qv* and Francis Prideaux *qv* as references. Consul Mohammerah 1922. Vice Consul Ahqaz 1922-24. Probationer Rawalpindi 1926. Settlement training Campbellpur 1926-27. Assistant Resident Kolhapur 1927-30. Vice-Consul Duzdap 1930-31. Secretary to Gulf Resident 1931-33. Officiating Political Agent Bahrain 1933. Secretary to Gulf

Resident 1933-34. Consul-General Khorasan 1934. Earthquake Claims Officer Quetta 1935-35. See Robert Jackson, *Thirty Seconds at Quetta*, Evans Brothers 1960. Political Agent Quetta 1936-37. Agent Kalat and i/c Bolan Pass 1937-38. Secretary to Resident Central India 1939. Census Superintendent Quetta 1939-41. Consul-General in French Establishments in India, Pondicherry 1941-44. Counsellor Legation Tehran 1944-46. Retired 1949. IPS pension. OBE 1937. Royal Overseas League. d. 21 September 1960.

GODFREY, STUART HILL Gulf Resident i/c 1893. b. 2 June 1861. Son of John R.R. Godfrey of Surbiton, Surrey; and of Jane Mary Hill of Exeter. One brother Raymond, also at Westminster, became a coffee planter in Ceylon. WESTMINSTER SCHOOL 1875-79. Queen's Scholar. Sandhurst 1880. IA 1881. 2nd Lt, 2nd Foot, Queen's Royal West Surrey Regiment. Served Sabathu, Belgaum, Karachi, Bombay 1883-86. Language study Russia 1887. 24th Bombay Infantry. Unpaid Attache, Intelligence Simla 1888. Paid Attache Intelligence, serving Simla, Palanpur, Aden, Apozai 1888-90. Wing Officer 24th Baluch Regiment Quetta 1892. Married 1896 Gwendolen, daughter of Lt-Col. Sir Adelbert Talbot *qv*. Two daughters and two sons. IPS 1892. First Assistant to Gulf Resident 1892 and temporary Gulf Resident 1893. Served Leh, Kashmir, Gilgit, Ladekh 1893-1900. Political Agent Zahob 1901-1902. Malakand 1902-1903. Toehi 1903-1904. Malakand 1904-10. PA D.I. Khan 1910-11. Satna 1911-13. Retired 1916. United Service Club 1907. United Services Institution of India. CIE 1908. FRGS 1912. Translated Pushkin's *Kapitanskaya Dockada* and wrote reports on Gilgit and Wazarat (Superintendent, Government Printing, Calcutta, 1898). Also *Narrative of Maskat Affairs, 1889-1892*, Foreign Office Press. 'Notes on Snow Passes', *Journal of United Services Institution of India*. Article on Kohistan in July 1912 *Geographic Journal*. IOL: Papers, 13 boxes, including material on Talbot. RGS: manuscripts; also 'Papers' and Corr. 1911-20. d. 29 November 1941, E.Hastings, Hants.

GREY, WILLIAM GEORGE Political Agent Kuwait, 1914-16. b. 12 October 1866, Wellington, New Zealand. Son of Major W.R. Grey. WESTWARD HO! 1880-83. In Green's (later Willes'), House. Army 1886. Prince of Wales's Volunteers (South Lancashire). IA 1889-1902. Madras Staff Corps. 3rd Madras Light Infantry. Plague duty 1898. Lt.Colonel 1912. Married 1909 Mary Evelynd Aymer Ainslie. One son. Entered IPS 1902. The Haileybury Register mistakenly has 1889. Permanent Appointment 1906. Vice-Consul Bundar Abbas 1902-1904. Political Agent Muscat 1904-1908. First Assistant to Resident Bangalore 1910. Secretary to Board of Examiners Calcutta 1910-11. Assistant Political Agent Loralai, Chagai 1911-12. Political Agent Quetta 1912-13. Political Agent Kuwait 1914-16. Consul-General Khorassan 1916-20. Consul-General Meshed 1921. Retired 1921. Urdu Lecturer Caius College Cambridge 1929-40. Hon. MA Cambridge. United Service Club 1922. Army and Navy Club. d. 6 April 1953. Last address: The White House, Cartmel, Grange-over-Sands, Lancs.

HADOW, REGINALD MICHAEL Trucial Coast Officer 1944. b. 17 August 1915. Son of Malcolm McGregor Hadow, solicitor; and of Constance Mary Lund. Numerous relatives in the Indian services. BERKHAMSTED SCHOOL 1925-34. BA King's Cambridge. For first marriage note below. Married 2nd 1976 Hon. Mrs. Daphne Sieff. ICS 1938. IPS 1942. Assistant Private Secretary to British Ambassador Moscow 1942. Vice-Consul Meshed 1942-43. Assistant Political Agent Bahrain 1943-44. Political Officer Trucial Coast 1944. Assistant Political Agent Bahrain 1944. Vice-Consul Bushire 1944-45. Consul Bandar Abbas 1945-46. Undersecretary External Affairs 1946-47. '...he has apparently broken his thigh pigsticking.' IOR:Personal File, nd. 'Avoids taking the examination in Arabic (he speaks it quite well) as he does not wish to serve on the Arab side.' Geoffrey Prior, 13 March 1945. 'Unfortunately he is married to a Pole...I do not believe that anyone who speaks broken English is a suitable chatelaine for a British Community.' Geoffrey Prior, 15 May 1946. Retired 1948. ICS pension. Ambassador Israel, 1965-69. Ambassador Argentina, 1969-72. CMG 1962. KCMG 1971. Travellers. Norfolk (Norwich).

HAMILTON, ROBERT EDWARD Political Agent Kuwait, 1916-18. Became The Master of Belhaven and then 11th Lord Belhaven and Stenton. Added surname Udny, 1934. b. 8 April 1871. Eldest son of Lt. Archibald William Hamilton RN. Temple Grove Preparatory School. Hamilton and H.W. Waterfield were boys together at Temple Grove. Waterfield was headmaster when Hamilton sent his son. Hamilton distributed prizes there. GLE/BS140Sco. *Proceedings of the Grand Lodge of Scotland from February 1931 to January 1932*, 315. WESTMINSTER SCHOOL 1885-88. Queen's Scholar. In the O.W. register for 1883-1960 the editors claimed 1883 as 'the dividing line between ancient and modern Westminster...the house system was firmly established; teaching had been transferred to classrooms; modern subjects had taken their place in the curriculum; and from about that time several other institutions and customs now taken for granted, among them the library, the commemoration service, and the school prayer book'. A school Masonic lodge was consecrated while Hamilton was there – Old

Westminsters' Lodge, on 20 January 1888. Sandhurst. Army 1890. Royal Scots Fusiliers. Probationer ICS 1893. 2-4th Gurkhas 1893. East Africa campaigns 1895-96. Tirah Campaign 1897-98. Mesopotamian Expeditionary Force 1915-18. Hon. Col. 52nd Lowland Divisional Engineers. Married 1898 Kathleen Gonville; daughter of Col. Sir B.P. Bromhead CB (4th Baronet), who was Governor of an Indian public school, Lahore Chiefs' College. His house in England was filled with Indian memorabilia. *Uneven Road,* 13. One daughter and one son, who succeeded to title Lord Belhaven. Married 2nd 1938 Sheila de Haunteville, only daughter of Maj. A.G. Pearson DSO. His son by first marriage, who became the Master of Belhaven and 12th Lord Belhaven, was educated at Eton and Sandhurst (Sword of Honour), was a political officer in Aden, and wrote *The Arabian Carpet and Other Verses, The Uneven Road* (autobiography), and *The Kingdom of Melchior* about Agent's life in Arabia. When at Eton, the 12th Lord Belhaven knew Ralph, the heir to 10th baron and at the time Master of Belhaven – who predicted he would be killed in World War I and was. The 12th Belhaven's daughter married the 4th Baron Raglan, a political officer in Palestine and author. The 12th's son, the 13th Lord Belhaven, also educated at Eton, is a Company Director, and *his* son and the 14th baron presumptive is the present Master of Belhaven, educated at Eton.
Hamilton entered the IPS in 1901. Served Mount Abu, Udaipur 1901-1905. Kashmir 1905-1909. Tutor to Maharaja Holkar of Indore 1910-11. Hamilton was unable to continue for financial reasons: the Maharaja stayed at the best hotels and went to the best restaurants. IOR:R/1/4/872, Hamilton to Political Aide de Camp, India Office, 6 March 1911. Special Duty at Delhi Durbar 1911-12. Foreign Service as Political Officer with Maharaja Holkar of Indore 1913. Served Mount Abu, Udaipur 1913-15. First Assistant to Gulf Resident 1915-16. Political Agent Kuwait 1916-18. First Assistant AGG Rajputana 1918-19. Financial Member State Council Jodhpur 1919-20. Gold Kaisar-i-Hind 1905. CIE 1918. Succeeded uncle to baronage 1920. Scottish Representative Peer 1922-45. In 1930s active in the Scottish Fascists, whom his son called: '...a society of loud-voiced old fellows, who regarded Mussolini as their champion against Bolshevism'. Belhaven, *Uneven Road,* 177. Freemason: The Grand Master Mason of Scotland 1931-33. United Service Club 1915. Royal Northern Club. Publications of the Grand Lodge of Scotland during Hamilton's rise to Masonic prominence in the 1920s and during his grand mastership (the grand master in Scotland is called the Grand Mason) have many references to him. d. 26 October 1950.

HAWORTH, LIONEL BERKELEY Gulf Resident 1927-28. b. 30 September 1873, Sydenham. Son of J.H. Haworth, Old Falinge, Lancs. Dulwich College 1881-86. ELIZABETH COLLEGE 1887-89. Haworth entered Elizabeth in the same year as his older brother, Cyril Henry Haworth (Dulwich, 1881-83), who was b. India 1871 and killed playing polo at Poona, June 1896. An Army Class was established in 1885. Fifth Formers were given instruction for the Army Preliminary Examination and when they passed, they proceeded to a Woolwich and Sandhurst Class in the Sixth Form where they studied for the Army Entrance Examination. Sandhurst. IA 1893. King's Own Yorkshire Light Infantry. 2nd Bombay Lancers. 9th Bombay Infantry. 21st Bombay Lancers. Married 1st 1901 Lilian Maude, daughter of Col. A.D. Geddes, commander Enniskillin Fusiliers. Two sons. Married 2nd 1912 Gwendoline Olivia; also daughter of Col. A.D. Geddes. One daughter. His wives were sisters of Mabel Ada Geddes, who married Cyril Barrett *qv.* IPS 1902. Consul for Arabistan, Mohammerah, and Assistant to Gulf Resident 1911-14. Political Agent Muscat 1916-19 and Intelligence Officer 1916-19. Assistant to Gulf Resident 1925-26. Gulf Resident 1927-28. Retired 1929. Kaisar-i-Hind 1900. KBE 1928. Active in RCAS. Freemason. d. 11 September 1951 in Jersey.

HAY, WILLIAM RUPERT Gulf Resident 1946-55. b. 16 December 1893. Son of William A.E. Hay, physician; and Louisa Tucker. BRADFIELD COLLEGE 1907-13. Herbert Gray head 1880-1910. Harold Costley-White head 1910-1915. Gray's departure was followed by crises which culminated in Costley-White's resignation. Hay gave White, by then headmaster of Westminster, as a reference when he applied to IPS, as well as the Viceroy, Lord Chelmsford. Foundation Scholar. Upper Sixth 1909-13. Wilder Divinity Prize 1911, 1912, 1913. Denny English Prize 1911, 1912, 1913. Stevens Scholar 1911, 1913. Head Prefect. Hay played Cleomestra in school's Greek production 1913. University College Oxford 1913-14. Heron Exhibitioner. IA 1914. Special Duty, Civil Administration of Mesopotamia 1917-19. He served under Arnold Wilson *qv.* Married 1925 Sybil Ethel, daughter of Sir Stewart Abram, Mayor of Reading. IPS 1920. Assistant Political Agent Chitral 1921-22. Assistant Commissioner Bannu, 1922-23. Superintendent of Jail Bannu 1923. Political Officer Moradabad 1923-24. Assistant Commissioner Tank 1924. Political Agent Wana 1924-25. Political Agent S. Waziristan 1925-28. Deputy Commissioner Peshawar 1930-31. Special Magistrate D.I. Khan Riots 1931. Political Agent Swat 1931-32. Chief Secretary NWFP 1932-33. Counsellor Kabul 1933-36. Deputy Secretary Foreign Department 1936. Continuing on change to External Affairs 1937-40. Temporary Resident Waziristan 1940-41. Officiating Gulf Resident 1941-42. Resident Baluchistan

1942-46. Gulf Resident 1946-47. Retired 1948 on IPS pension, but Gulf Resident as FO appointee to 1955. CIE 1932 (The Indian Army Register of Officers & Bradfield Register have 1934). CSI 1943. KCIE 1947. KCMG 1952. FRGS 1924. FRCA. FRA. East India Club. Challoner Club. (A Roman Catholic club.) Wrote *Two Years in Kurdistan* and *The Persian Gulf States*. Papers at St. Antony's, Oxford. d. 3 April 1962.

HICKINBOTHAM, TOM Political Agent Bahrain, 1943-45. b. 27 April 1903, Colchester. Second son of Dr. J.R. Hickinbotham and Beatrice Elliot, daughter of Rev. Theophilus Sharp. EPSOM COLLEGE 1916-17. Higginbotham left in 1917 for Colchester Royal Grammar School. (Humorists claimed that Epsom was a school for third-class sons of first-class doctors and first-class sons of third-class doctors.) Sandhurst. IA 1923. 5-10th Baluch Regiment. NWF 1924 (medal). Entered IPS 1930. Probationer Gardaspur 1930-31. Assistant to Resident, later Political Secretary Aden 1931-32 and 1933-35. Undersecretary to AGG Punjab 1932-33. Assistant Political Agent Mirnashah 1935-36. Assistant Political Agent Bahrain 1936. Political Agent Bahrain 1937. Secretary to Gulf Resident 1937-38. Secretary Aden 1938-39. Undersecretary to Gulf Resident 1939. Political Agent Muscat 1939-41. Political Agent Kuwait 1941-43. Political Agent Bahrain 1943-44. Acting Gulf Resident 1944. Political Agent Bahrain 1944-45. Passed interpretership test, Bushire, 1945. Political Agent Kalat 1945-47. Retired 1949. IPS pension. Governor Aden, 1951-56. Director Eastern Bank OBE 1939. CIE 1944. CMG 1951. KCMG 1953. KCVO 1954. FRGS 1936. Resigned 1953. Proposed by Harcourt Butler. Freemason. Wrote *Aden*. d. 14 October 1983.

HOWES, JOHN BARON Acting PA Bahrain, 1938. POTC, 1939-40. b. 17 December 1907. ROSSALL SCHOOL 1921-27. In Pelican House. Scholar. Ainsworth Exhibitioner. School Monitor. Leaving Exhibition. 'The big events of this period in the School's history were the completion of the War Memorial Chapel [1925] and the building of a new Headmaster's house.' W. Furness, *The Centenary History of Rossall School*, Gale & Polden, Aldershot, 1945, 140. Keble College Oxford 1926-27. Classical Scholar. 2nd class honours. IA 1931. Royal Warwick Regiment. Entered IPS 1935. Assistant to Gulf Resident 1935-36. Assistant Political Agent Bahrain 1936. Probationer Agra and Meerut 1937-38. Acting and Assistant Political Agent Bahrain 1938-39. Political Officer Trucial Coast 1939-40. Political Agent Muscat 1940. Political Agent Trucial Coast 1940. Publicity Officer Gulf 1940-41. Political Agent Muscat 1941-42. Secretary to Gulf Resident 1942-43. Consul Bushire 1943-44. Undersecretary and Deputy Secretary External Department 1944-46. Secretary to Resident Kolhapur and Deccan 1946-47. 'He wishes to transfer to the Indian Army so as to marry as he cannot afford to live as a married man in a British Regiment.' IOR:Personal File, F.G. Spring, Brigadier, 21 August 1934. 'I recommended him for an OBE, but amended this under advice to an MBE which he eventually got in the Birthday Honours, but I still consider he should have received the former decoration.' *Ibid.*, Geoffrey Prior, nd. 'He is in danger now of being fascinated by the "Deserta" facet of Arabia...' *Ibid.*, H. Weightman, 30 October 1940. '...his wife, who has acquired much more aplomb and shed her early gaucheries, made an excellent chatelaine at Bushire.' *Ibid.*, Geoffrey Prior, 19 August 1942. Retired 1949. IPS pension. MBE 1941.

JACKSON, GORDON NOEL Acting Political Agent Kuwait 1943. Political Agent Kuwait 1944-5. Political Officer Trucial Coast 1947. b. 25 December 1913 at East Langton near Market Harborough, Leics. Son of Thomas Herbert Jackson, landowner and farmer; and of Louise Harris. Cherry Orchard Preparatory School, Blackheath, London, 1921-26. Col. C.J.T. Robertson, headmaster. KING'S SCHOOL, WORCESTER 1927-31. Rev. C. Creighton, headmaster. His IPS application includes a testimonial from Creighton. School Monitor. Captain Football. Captain Boats. Sergeant OTC. Married 1959 Mary April Nettlefold, oldest daughter of Frederick John Nettlefold and Mrs Albert Coates. Two daughters and one son. Assistant Master Sunnydown School, Guildford 1931-32 under S. How, headmaster. Assistant Master, Cherry Orchard 1932-33 under Col. Robertson. Entered the Indian Police Open Competition 1933 for IPS, coming 5th of 13. 'Appointed to the Indian Political Service substantively on probation with effect from the date of joining.' IOL:V/12/34. Entered IPS 1933. 'As an alternative to an I.C.S. candidate if we are unable to obtain what we want.' Note in IOR:Personal File. '...his brain is not as impressive as his bulk.' *Ibid.*, by Charles Prior, 8 November 1941. Probationer: Lahore, Phillaur, Simla, Ferozepore 1934-5. Assistant District Officer Peshawar, Tank, Darazinda 1936-38. Assistant Political Agent S. Waziristan, Wana 1938. Assistant to Resident Rajputana 1939-40. Air Raid Officer Quetta 1940-41. Political Agent Bahrain 1941-42. Acting Political Agent Muscat 1942-43. Undersecretary to Gulf Resident 1943. Acting Political Agent Kuwait 20 June 1943 – 15 February 1944. Tuson gives June 1943 to August 1943 and then Cornelius Pelly *qv* October 1943 – June 1944. Vice-Consul Bushire 1944. Political Agent Kuwait 1944-45. Political Officer Trucial Coast 1947. Secretary to Gulf Resident 1947. Again Political Officer Trucial Coast 1947 and Acting Political

Agent Bahrain to 14 August 1947. Retired 1949. Indian civil pension. Transferred to Foreign Office 1950. Consul St. Louis 1953. Consul-General Basra 1955-57. Lourenco Marques 1957-60. Benghazi 1960-63. Ambassador Kuwait 1963-67. Ambassador Ecuador 1967-70. CMG 1962. MBE. Travellers. Wrote *Effective Horsemanship* and *The Encyclopedia of the Horse.*

JOHNSTON, FREDERICK WILLIAM Gulf Resident 1928-29. b. 2 Nov. 1872. Son of Rev. A. Orrock Johnston DD. KELVINSIDE. BA 1894 Trinity Hall Cambridge. Married 1905 Gertrude Young, daughter of Lt-Col. J. Young. Entered ICS 1896. Appointments as Officer of Political Department, 'time-scale' 1910 and 1919. Deputy Secretary Government of India Finance Department 1911-13. Special Duty Foreign Department 1920. Resident Baluchistan 1922-27. Gulf Resident 1928-29. Johnston's brief time as Resident was marked by efforts to end the impasse with Persia over claims to Bushire and Bahrain. He viewed Persian demands 'with feverish anxiety and obstinacy, clearly influenced by recent Persian aggressiveness towards Arab dhows, whose owners were under British protection...He suggested that the Indian Government should inform the Persian Government that the Gulf lay within the area of a kind of British Monroe Doctrine.' Talks between Johnson and Teymortache, the Minister of the Persian Court, failed to resolve the problems. Abdullah, *The United Arab Emirates*, 251-52. CIE 1911. CSI 1913. KCIE 1927. Royal & Ancient St. Andrews. d. 1 May 1947.

JONES, JAMES FELIX Gulf Resident 1855-62. Buckland's Dictionary of Indian Biography has 'John' Felix. b. 5 September 1813. Son of John Jones, merchant's clerk, & Elizabeth. ADDISCOMBE. Nominated to HEIC by James Pattison. Appointed 8 February 1828. Midshipman on *Palinurus*, EIC Navy 1828. Some sources give 1827 but IOR and *Annals of the Oriental Club* confirm 1828. Lt. 1837. Commander 1847, Captain 1858. Married 8 December 1853 Safee Takoor Murad, b. 10 July 1834 and d. 1 January 1927. Two daughters and two sons. Steamer Captain. Surveyed Tigris and Euphrates Rivers 1843-44. Mapped Gulf. Agent Baghdad and Consul-General Turkish Arabia 1853. Gulf Resident 1855-62. Kept order during Indian Mutiny but Sir Bartle Frere, Governor of Bombay, replaced him with his protégé, Lewis Pelly *qv*: 'Jones was harshly and unfairly treated, unable to reply when Frere referred to his "numerous petty squabbles", some of them never reported, his "petty meddling and querulous interference" and "the humiliation of being represented by him". Jones received only derisory compensation after an abrupt termination of 35 years service.' Bidwell, 'Introduction', *Arabian Gulf Intelligence*, vii-viii. FRGS 1864. Oriental Club 1853. Author *Extracts from a report on the harbour of Grane (or Kuwait) and the island of Pheleechi, in the Persian Gulf.* Prepared November 1839. In *Bombay Selections*, Vol.XXIV, Bombay, 1856. Memoirs in *Bombay Selections*, 1857, IOR:V/23/225. RGS: Crr. Block 1871-80; script; referee's reports. d. 3 September 1878 Norwood.

KEMBALL, CHARLES ARNOLD Gulf Resident 1900-1904. b. 27 June 1860. 2nd son of Charles Gordon Kemball JP; grandson of Vero Clark Kemball and nephew of Arnold Burrowes Kemball, EIC Gulf Resident 1852-55. CHARTERHOUSE 1874-81. Charterhouse Registers have 1874-77. Robinites House. Robert Baden-Powell entered 1872. Kemball entered with Francis Dames, later Charterhouse housemaster and founder of Carthusian masonic lodge *Deo Dante Dedi* 1901, lodge master 1907. Another contemporary was Charles Hampson, Grand Secretary, Grand Lodge of Mark Master Masons. Sandhurst. Army 1881. Subaltern 2nd E.York Regiment. 17th N.Infantry 1882. 21st Bombay Infantry 1884. On duty in Russia for study 1888-1889. Married 1895 Mary Antoinette daughter of Joseph Askew Turner of Lindfield. Two sons. Entered IPS 1890. Assistant Agent Rajputana, 1890. 1st Assistant to Gulf Resident 1891-92; Assistant Political Agent Quetta 1892-93. Political Agent Thal Chotiali 1893-94. South Baluchistan 1894-95. Perso-Beluch Frontier Commission 1895-96. Political Agent Bhopal 1896. Neemuch 1896-98. Jhalwar 1898-99. Gulf Resident 1900-1904. Kemball asserted British interest in various islands in the Gulf, backing the claims of Sharjah against Persia. Abdulla, *The United Arab Emirates*, 244. He was a an observer of the shift of trade from Lingah to Dubai, and predicted correctly Dubai's future role as a major port: 'When I visited Arab Coast I saw one of the steamers of the Bombay Persia Company at Dubai, and I was told that steamers of the British India Navigation Company make Dubai a port of call. It may be taken for granted that the trade which has now been diverted from Lingah will not return there...'. *Ibid.*, 232. Political Agent Loralai 1905-10. Resident Gwalior 1910-12. Retired 1914. JP Norfolk. CIE 1903. United Service Club 1904. d. 25 January 1943, Harleston, Norfolk.

KEYES, TERENCE HUMPHREY Political Agent Bahrain 1914-16. b. 28 May 1877. Son of Gen. Sir Charles Keyes GCB, commander Punjab Frontier Force. HAILEYBURY COLLEGE 1891-94. Colvin House. School Prefect. O.H. Society formed 1893. Top hats abolished 1896. Sandhurst. IA 1897. 2nd.Lt. 1897. Rawalpindi and Tirah Field Force. 38th Dogras. Served Siakot, Malakand Field Force,

Ferozepore. Action of Chagree Kotal, wounded, despatches, medal and two clasps. Special duty Russia 1901-1902. Special Duty Coronation Durbar 1902-1903. Military Mission South Russia 1917-20. Married 1909 Edith (Kaisar-i-Hind Medal), daughter of Lt-Gen. C.A. McMahon FRS, Commissioner of Lahore who spent 30 years in Punjab. Her brother Gen. Arthur Henry McMahon, Sovereign Grand Commander, Ancient and Accepted Rite of Masonry in the British Empire, controlling 4th through 33rd degrees. Two daughters and three sons. Entered IPS 1903. Haileybury Register has 1902. Served Rawalpindi, Jhelum, Seistan 1903-1906. Assistant and Consul Turbat-i-Haidari 1906-1908. Assistant to AGG Baluchistan 1908-12. Undersecretary Foreign Department 1912. Assistant Political Agent Mekran and Commandant Mekran Levy Corps 1912-13. Political Agent Bahrain 1914-16. Special Duty Mekran Border 1916-1917. Special Duty War Office 1917-19. Special Duty Foreign Office 1919-20. Served Sibi, Mastung (in-charge Bolan Pass), 1921-1927. Political Agent Kalat 1927-28. 'The territories of Kalat, with its tributary areas of Las Bela, Kharan and Mekran, occupied nearly two thirds of the whole of Baluchistan...the influence of the Political Agent provided the cement which held the whole structure together. Terence Keyes was the Political Agent. He was a brother of Roger Keyes, the famous Zeebrugge V.C., and had his fair share of the family courage. He was also a wonderful raconteur.' Sir Conrad Corfield, *The Princely India I Knew*, 38.

Envoy Court of Nepal 1928. Resident Gwalior 1928-29. Resident Hyderabad 1930-33. '...it made a pleasant change for the Nizam to have a Resident more interested in securing a stable future for Hyderabad than in condemning his personal conduct.' Ashton, *British Policy*, 131. Keyes opposed the Political Department 'obsession' with the division between an Indian India and a British India: 'To me this is the madness that the gods send before destruction...What Butler calls British India is just that part of India that is trying to repudiate all that is British...What he calls Indian India is that part that wants to retain the British connection.' Keyes to Bray, 21 July 1930 in IOL:Keyes Collection, No.28, qtd. *Ibid.*, 132. Such partisanship did not win him friends: 'The Resident was not liked in official circles. Irwin's successor [as Viceroy], Lord Willingdon, described him as "one of those people who rather like spreading themselves and has to be watched pretty closely",' *Ibid.*, 133. (For origin of the Willingdon remark see Willingdon to Hoare, 19 March 1934, IOL:Templewood Collection, No.7. Samuel Hoare was Secretary of State for India, 1931-1935. Created Viscount Templewood, 1944. *Cf.* Trench, *Viceroy's Agent*, 188-90, 197.) He 'took with equal zest to contract bridge and pig sticking'. Trench, *Viceroy's Agent*, 198. Retired 1932. CIE 1917. CMG 1920. CSI 1928 (Haileybury *Register* has 1922). KCIE 1933. FRGS 1906. Proposed by Molesworth Sykes and Herbert Sykes. FRZS (see Percy Cox). Freemason. Cocoa Tree Club. IOL:*Papers*, 17 vols. His time as Political Agent in Kalat is described in Trench's *Viceroy's Agent*, 87-88; as Resident in Hyderabad, 188-90, 198, 201-2; and his views on the Indian states, 205. d. 26 February 1939 Bexhill. Executor Sir A.H. McMahon, brother-in-law, IPS and Masonic superior, and fellow Old Haileyburian.

KNOX, STUART GEORGE Political Agent Kuwait 1904-09. Political Agent Bahrain 1910-11. Acting Gulf Resident 1923. b. 7 October 1869, Allahabad, India. Eldest son of Sir G.E. Knox, Allahabad High Court, prolific legal author (see *WW*), and Catherine Anne Louise Loch. Elizabeth College Guernsey 1880-83. His brother Ernest Francis Knox, b. 1871, was at Elizabeth 1880-83, then Westminster 1885-88, becoming Colonel IA. Other brother Robert W. Knox, b. 1873, Elizabeth 1880-83, Westminster 1887-90, Colonel Indian Medical Service. REPTON SCHOOL 1883-86. William M. Furneaux head 1882-1900. Hall House. Under Furneaux there was tremendous building activity. Knox slept in Big School while the Hall dormitories were rebuilt. On Speech Day in 1886 Pears Hall was opened, a large assembly room. O.R. newsletter started. Careers of boys entering with Knox in 1883: lemon farmer in California, missionary in Alaska, Army officer in the Sudan, planter in India, District Commissioner in Nigeria. Contemporaries: Sir Arthur Wauchope, High Commissioner in Palestine 1931-8; war correspondent Edmund Candler, who served in Mesopotamia. Sandhurst 1887-88. Army 1888. Wilts. Regiment. World War I. Despatches 3 times. Married 1893 Ethel OBE 1918 d.1934; eldest daughter of Rt. Hon. Sir John Edge PC, Chief Justice of Northwest Province, Member Council of India and Judicial Committee of Privy Council. Two sons. Ethel Knox operated a library for the British in Basra during WWI. Married 1934 2nd Ethel Rose OBE, RRC and Bar; daughter of James Collins. Entered IPS 1894. Acting Consul Basra 1894-95. Served Sehore, Neemuch, Quetta 1895-97. Political Agent Kalat 1897-1900. Special Duty Coronation Durbar 1902-1903. Political Agent Thal-Chotiali 1903. Quetta 1903-1904. 1st Assistant to Gulf Resident 1904. Political Agent Kuwait 1904-1909. Political Agent Bahrain, 1910-11. Political Agent Muscat 1911-14. Gulf Resident *i/c* 1914. Sr. Judicial Officer Indian Expeditionary Force Basra 1914-15. Sr. Judicial Officer Indian Expeditionary Force 1915-19. President Court of Appeals Mesopotamia 1918-19. Resident Mysore 1921. Resident Hyderabad 1921-2. In 1920 the Viceroy, Chelmsford, imposed an Executive Council and Chief Minister. The Nizam simply isolated himself. In March 1922, Knox complained that he had not been able to see the Nizam alone for five minutes. The Department replied: '...if a Prince chooses to bury himself in his palace the Political Agent cannot dig him out merely for the purpose of cultivating his acquaintance, and however tactful and untiring he may be in his efforts, they will not always be crowned with success'. Ashton, *British Policy*, 85. Acting Gulf Resident 1923. Retired 1924. IA pension. David Lorimer's *qv* wife nicknamed Knox 'The Professor'. Emily Lorimer to Judge and Mrs. T.G. Overend, 11 October 1911, IOR:MSS EUR D922 Lorimer Papers. When he was Political Agent in Kuwait he collected desert shrubs for the Botanical Survey of India. Results were published in *Records Botanical Survey of India*, VI, 1912. He made a 160 mile trip from Kuwait to the archaeological site at Hafar. CIE 1909. CSI 1917. Middle Temple 1910. d. 11 December 1956.

LOCH, PERCY GORDON Political Agent Bahrain 1916-18, 1932-37. Political Agent Kuwait, 1918. Acting Gulf Resident, 1930s. Assumed name Dalyell of the Binns 1938 by permission of the Lord Lyon. b. 16 January 1887. Son of Lt-Col. William Loch CIE, ADC to six Viceroys 1876-1903, Principal Mayo College Ajmer 1878-1903; and of Edith, daughter of James Gibbs CB CCI CIE, Col. Duke of Wellington's Regiment. CHELTENHAM COLLEGE 1901-1904. In Cheltondale House. Contemporary: A.G. Cunningham (Gen. Sir. A.G. Cunningham), C-in-C 8th Army Middle East 1941; High Commissioner Palestine 1945-48. A year before Loch's entry, wearing of *collegers* (mortarboards) restricted. This reached the press and as a compromise straw boaters with House Ribbons were worn daily and *collegers* on Sundays. Morgan, *Cheltenham College*, 88. Sandhurst. Army 1905. North Staffordshire Regiment. 97th Deccan Infantry (Indian) Army. Intelligence 1914-16. Married 1st 1915 Isabel Wynne Vincent 1915. Divorced 12 September 1928. See IOR:L/AG/23/16/17 no. 3076. Married 2nd 12 September 1928 Eleanor Isabel Wilkie-Dalyell; only child of Sir James Bruce Wilkie-Dalyell, 9th Bt.. Two sons. Eldest, Tam Dalyell b. 9 August 1932, educated Eton and King's Cambridge; Director of Studies, India Ship-School *Dunera*; Labour MP 1962-; Chairman Parliamentary Labour Party Education Committee; columnist *New Scientist*; author *The Case of Ship Schools* and *The Ship School Dunera*. 'For about a quarter of a century the Scottish constituency of West Lothian (now Linlithgow), has been represented by the irrepressible Labour MP, Tam Dalyell, whose accent and other vocal features make his voice virtually indistinguishable on the radio from that of a long-serving Tory Lord Chancellor, Lord Hailsham. This is not really surprising since both went to Eton (many years apart), and to aristocratic Oxbridge colleges (Dalyell to King's, Cambridge, Hailsham to Christ Church, Oxford).' John Honey, *Does Accent Matter?*,147.

Assistant to Gulf Resident 1908. Secretary to Sir William Willcocks, Mesopotamia, 1910. Formally entered IPS 1913. 2nd Assistant to Gulf Resident 1913-14. Political Agent Bahrain 1916-18. Political Agent Kuwait 1918. Assistant, Under, and Deputy Secretary Foreign and Political Department 1919-23. Assistant to Resident Kashmir 1924. Political Agent Gilgit 1924-27. Chief Commissioner Coorg and Resident Mysore 1930-31. Political Agent Wadhwan 1931. Political Agent Bahrain 1932-37. Acting Gulf Resident 1933, 1934, 1935, 1936. Retired 1938. Royal Company of Archers, Edinburgh. 'Very dimly the ghost of Lord Curzon, who visited Kuwait in 1902, lingered on among the framed photographs of my predecessors which lined the corridor between the entrance hall and the Chancery...One of them on retirement had been appointed to the Queen's Bodyguard for Scotland and had been photographed in his full regalia of feathered bonnet and so on, and armed with bow and quiver. I was once showing an Arab notable this gallery, which included a number of his earlier acquaintances, when he stopped astonished at the sight of this bowman. "Good God", he said, "I never realised there were Political Agents in Kuwait before the time of firearms".' Bell, *Shadows on the Sand*, 227. Unicorn Pursuivant 1939. The Unicorn wore 'a special variety of the uniform of the Royal Household' with tabard and blue service uniform for less formal occasions. Sir Thomas Innes of Learney, *Scots Heraldry*, revised by Malcolm Innes of Edingighot, Johnson & Bacon, Edinburgh, 1978, 6-7. CIE 1935. FRGS 1910. Proposer Sir William Willcocks KCMG FRCA. Scottish Historical Society. Society of Antiquaries (Scotland). Freemason. United Service Club. New Club. Royal Celtic Club. Wrote *The Family of Loch*. 'My wife and I have presented my father's early and unique film of 1930s Bahrain to the Scottish Film Archive in Glasgow. At the Binns, we have a good many photographs of my father, not least those taken during the visit of the Shaikh of Bahrain to Scotland in the late 1930s.' Tam Dalyell to P.J. Rich 18 August 1987. d. 15 September 1953.

LORIMER, DAVID LOCKHART ROBERTSON Political Agent Bahrain, 1911-12. b. 24 December 1876. Son of Rev. Robert Lorimer. Brothers John *qv*, William (Fettes 1897-1904; head of school, 1903-1904; BA 1908 Trinity Oxford; Professor of Greek, St.Andrews; FBA); Robert (Fettes 1898-1905, Edinburgh University 1905-06; Indian Police 1907-20, Indian Education Department 1920; Anglo-Arabic College New Delhi 1929-42; St. Stephens College New Delhi 1942-46). DUNDEE INSTITUTION. *Times* obituary lists him at Fettes and Trinity Oxford, but he appears in no Fettes register. Oxford archives have no record of his being at Trinity. Army 1896. IA 1896. Commissioned 2nd Lt. Unattached 1896. 8th Rajputs, 1897. Lt. 1898. Corps of Guides 1898. Quartermaster Khyber

Rifles 1900. Special Duty in Delhi Coronation Durbar 1902-1903. Captain 1905. Major 1914. Lt-Colonel 1922. Married Emily OBE; daughter of Judge T.G. Overend K.C., Recorder of Londonderry. She tutored Germanic Philology at Somerville College, Oxford 1907-10; directed Red Cross Mission Egypt 1915; edited *Basrah Times* 1916-17; d. 1949. One adopted daughter living in South Africa. Entered IPS 1903. Personal file includes letter from his brother J.G. Lorimer recommending him. IOR:R/1/4/1337. Assistant Commissioner Umballa and Hazara 1903. Assistant, later Vice Consul, for Arabistan, at Ahwaz, 1904-1909. Political Agent Bahrain 1911-12. Consul Kerman and Persian Baluchistan, and Assistant to Gulf Resident 1912-14. Assistant Political Agent Chitral 1915. Political Agent and Consul Kerman and Persian Baluchistan, and Assistant to Gulf Resident, 1916-20. Political Agent Gilgit 1920-24. Retired 1927. IA pension. CIE 1917. FRGS 1903. Proposed by Sir James Sadler, father of James Sadler *qv*. RAS. He received the Persian volume *Tarikh i Bakhtiari* from Sir Arnold Wilson *qv* and per Wilson's request willed it on his own death to the RAS. Leverhulme Fellow, 1933-35. Hon. Fellow, SOAS, 1953. RAS Burton Medal 1948. Wrote with his wife *Persian Tales*, a children's book, 1919. Authored linguistic studies, including *The Phonology of the Bakhtiari* which won the Royal Asiatic Society prize. There is an extensive Lorimer Collection in IOR:MSS.Eur.D.922. The *Times* obituary in the collection has been annotated in red ink, possibly by Mrs. Lorimer. The *Times* report that he had been educated at Fettes and Trinity College is crossed through, as is the error that his wife taught at Somerville College, *Cambridge*. The cutting is further annotated and where it states that the Lorimers spent their closing years in Welwyn, there is a note 'about 30' and when it states Mrs. Lorimer was District Commissioner for the Girl Guides there is a terse 'No'. The Collection includes essays by Lorimer: *Three Months of Privilege Leave or the Recreations of a Subaltern, Our N.W. Frontier*, and *Essay on Modern Education – Criticisms and Proposals*. The education essay is dated 9 February 1895 and may have been written in preparation for an Army entrance examination. Mrs. Lorimer was a prolific author and her titles include a popular work, *What Hitler Wants*. Some papers SOAS. His will (Somerset House) makes a detailed distribution of his and his wife's papers. The SOAS received linguistic materials and photographs. d. 26 February 1962.

LORIMER, JOHN GORDON Gulf Resident 1913-14. b. 14 June 1870, Glasgow; eldest son of Rev. Robert Lorimer, United Free Church, Strathmartine, Dundee. Brother of David *qv*. DUNDEE INSTITUTION. ICS application papers state he was educated privately, then at Dundee Institution & High School. IOR:L/PJ/6/257, files 1182, 1221/89. Edinburgh University and 'Special preparation' (crammers) at Wren and Gurney. See *Ibid.* 3rd in ICS Open Competition, 1889. Christ Church Oxford as 'ICS selected candidate'. Matriculated 1889. lst in ICS Final 1891. Lorimer 'by inadvertance of the Civil Service Commissioners' sat examinations in two classical languages, Persian and Arabic, when regulations allowed one. He won the prize for both and prizes for Hindustani and Political Economy papers. IOR:L/PJ/6/307, files 1783, 1759/91. September 1891 went to St. Petersburg to 'continue' studies in Russian. Wrote India Office 21 September 1891: 'It is my earnest wish to be set apart sooner or later for political employment.' IOR:L/PJ/6/306, file 1555: 308, file 1874/91. Married Marian Agnes, daughter of G.C. Maclean, Edinburgh. Entered ICS 1891. Entered IPS 1898. Assistant Secretary Foreign Department 1900. Deputation to Persian Gulf 1904-1908. Resident and Consul-General Baghdad 1909-12. Special Duty Foreign Department 1912-13. Resident and Consul-General Baghdad 1913. Acting Gulf Resident December 1913 – February 1914. CIE 1902. Freemason. East India Club. His celebrated *Gazetteer of the Persian Gulf* in two volumes was published at Calcutta in 1908 and 1915. d. 9 February 1914. Self-inflicted gun shot. The circumstances of his death while cleaning his gun remain a mystery. Cox was forced to return to the Gulf to take his place.

McCOLLUM, DANIEL VINCENT Political Agent Kuwait, 1918-20. The surname is frequently misspelled. Some IOL records have 'Mac'. *Thacker's Indian Directory, 1915* has 'McCallum'. He was an assistant master at St.Anthony's School (Roman Catholic), Lahore. Spent 13 months in the Yeomanry and was commissioned 2nd Lt. 1914. Trained with the Somersets. Attached to 1st Battalion, 43rd Erinpura Infantry Brigade. Mesopotamia 1915. Adjunct Indian Base Depot, 1915-16. Staff Lt. GHQ 1916. McCollum took a prominent part in the administration of Basra. Supervisor of Imperial Ottoman Bank and Blockade Officer, Basrah, 1917. Assistant Political Officer Zubair 1917-18 as well as Editor *Basrah Times* and Assistant Military Governor Basrah. Blockade Office Kuwait 1918. Captain 1918. Released 1921. He did not hold a 'substantive' appointment. His contract was with the Mesopotamian Civil Administration. Assistant Political Agent Kuwait 1918. Political Agent Kuwait 1918-20. McCollum was on leave in England in October 1919 at the same time that Arab groups were visiting from the Nejd and Kuwait. There was friction between them, and Shaikh Ahmed of Kuwait demanded to go home. McCollum assumed charge of the Kuwaitis on 27 October and presented the party to King George V on 30 October, continuing in charge when the group went to Glasgow,

Alexandria, and Cairo. IOR:L/PS/10/843.
In 1920 he was briefly the wazir to Sultan of Muscat: 'Even though the establishment of a local military organisation was an essential keystone of British policy, a solid financial and administrative base to support the military was necessary for the over all policy to succeed. Accordingly, a British adviser, locally known as a wazir, was sent to Muscat in April 1920.' Peterson, *Oman in the Twentieth Century*, 76. 'Major decisions were made by McCollum during the six months he spent in Muscat...'. *Ibid.*, 77. 'One of the major effects of the modest 1920s reforms was the institution of regular budgets, beginning with the one prepared by McCollum in 1921...'. *Ibid.*, 89. Papers relating to McCollum's appointment to Muscat are in IOR: L/PS/10/427, including a minute by J.A. Simpson, 27 April 1921 that 'The Government of India in paying tribute to Mr. Wingate and Major Haworth somewhat ostentatiously ignore Capt. McCollum. I suppose this may be accepted, we have certainly had very little information about McCollum's doings as Wazir.' In March 1922 the Gulf Resident, A.P. Trevor, wrote to the Foreign and Political Department: '...as regards British officer, not certain it is necessary for the State to go to such expense and I think the Political Agent can do a good deal to advise in affairs with which the Wazir would deal. Further it is difficult to get the right man as Wazir and the last appointment was not an unqualified success.' Freemason.

MACKENZIE, CHARLES FRASER Political Agent Bahrain 1909-10. b. 21 September 1880. The *Malvern College Register 1865-1924* has 1882, but IOR pension files confirm 1880. See IOR:L/AG/9/19/1. Son of G.K. Mackenzie, West Brighton. MALVERN COLLEGE 1895-97. In School House. '...information about McKenzie is curiously lacking...we spell it *McK* in our 1924 register...there is no entry for him in the 1934 register, which is curious.' Norman Rosser, Archivist, Malvern College, to P.J. Rich, 2 August 1987. IA 1899. Native Mountain Artillery Indore 1899-1903. 8th Rajputs Indore 1903-1905. Special duty for Viceroy's visit to Indore 1905. Boundary Settlement Central India 1905. World War I. Croix de Guerre. Married 1919 Nelly Jeanne Suzanne Martinet. One child. Entered IPS 1906. Assistant Commissioner Hoshiapur and Mianwali, 1906. Assistant to AGG Central India 1907-1909. Assistant to Gulf Resident 1909. Political Agent Bahrain 1909-10. IOR:R/1/4/1129 has a memorial by Arabs of Bahrain bemoaning his leaving. Assistant to Resident Kashmir 1912-14. Guardian of Raj Kumar Hari Singh 1914. Jr. Judicial Officer Basra 1915. Sick Leave 1919-21. Retired 1921. IA pension. CIE 1918. Wrote *Persian Wonder Tales*. d. 5 September 1955.

MALLAM, GEORGE LESLIE Acting Political Agent Bahrain 1925. b. 13 December 1895. MALVERN COLLEGE 1910-13. S.R. James headmaster 1897-1914. 'There is no doubt that some parents were withdrawing their sons as the result of discovering that the moral tone was suffering from what one writer about the period calls "the evils of a monastic institution". C.S. Lewis has described...how gossip about who had connections with whom took second place only to talk about games. Entries in the school prefects' minute book for 1910, 1911, and 1912 bear this out...'. Blumenau, *A History of Malvern College*, 71. In School House. Scholar. RMC, Wellington, India. IA 1919. 2nd Lancers. Married 1926 Constance (awarded Silver Kaisar-i-Hind), daughter of doctor. Married 2nd Sophronia, daughter of a canon. Entered IPS 1921. Probation Peshawar 1921. Assistant Commissioner Bannu 1921-22. Undersecretary to Gulf Resident 1923-24. In training Moradabad 1924-25. Assistant to Political Agent and Acting Political Agent Bahrain 1925. District Judge Abbotabad 1926-27. Assistant Commissioner Tank 1927-28 and Mardan 1928-29. Undersecretary to AGG NWFP 1929. Census Superintendent NWFP 1930-32. Counsellor Legation Kabul 1932-34. Deputy Commissioner Kohat 1934-38. Sr. Sub-Judge Peshawar 1938. Financial Secretary to Government NWFP 1939. Political Agent Swat 1939-41. Chief Secretary, NWFP, 1941-4, Commissioner Post-War Planning, NWFP, 1944-7, Revenue & Development Commissioner NWFP 1947. Retired 1949. IPS pension. Ordained Church of England 1950. Vicar of Eckington 1952-65. CIE 1943. CSI 1947. Grays Inn 1926. Papers in Cambridge University South Asian Archives. d. 17 October 1978.

MEADE, MALCOLM JOHN Gulf Resident 1897-1900. b. 4 February 1854. Son of Lt-Gen. Sir R.J. Meade KCSI CIE, Lewis Pelly's *qv* successor as Resident Baroda. Later Resident Hyderabad. d. 1894. CHELTENHAM COLLEGE 1867-71. In Christowe House. Entering with Meade in January 1867. Walter Lawrence, private secretary to Curzon while Viceroy 1899-1903, and member Council of India 1907-09, author *The India We Served*. IA 1873. Lt. 89th Foot 1873. Bengal Staff Corps 1876. Lt. Attached to Foreign Department for Imperial Assemblage Delhi 1876-77. Married 1st Florence Maria, daughter of Lt. Heder Stedt RN, d. 1928. Twin sons: Richard Stanley de Courcy and Malcolm Morton de Courcy. Married 2nd Dorothy; daughter of H.G. Keene, Judge, Agra High Court. Entered IPS 1878. Assistant to Resident Hyderabad 1878. Assistant to AGG Central India 1880-84. Superintendent for the Control of the Moghias, Ajmer, 1885-87. Agent Bhopal 1891-97. Gulf Resident 1897-1900. Granted Special Duty in England 1900 to defend the suit against him, a gun running and confiscation case.

Meade seized a consignment of weapons and it was argued that in doing so he had violated Persian sovereignty. See *Francis, Times, and Co. v. Meade*, Law Reports, *Times*, 26 and 27 March 1901. Meade's defence was that he was enforcing Persian and Bahrain law rather than the policies of the Resident. 'The Attorney-General shortly opened the case for the defendant...the seizure of arms could only be defended if made in accordance with the law of Persia. In that country the law was the will of the Shah...Was it to be suggested that there was some law in Persia overriding the act of the supreme power? Objection might just as well be made to an Act of Parliament, on the ground that it overrode the common law.' *Ibid.*, 27 March 1901. The case was decided in Meade's favour and illustrates how the Resident could intervene almost at will but maintain a rationale of non-interventionism. IPS confidence in Meade was displayed when, on his return to India, he was immediately assigned as the Resident Indore 1901. A perhaps sentimental promotion made him Resident Baroda 1901-1909, where his father was Special Commissioner in 1875. Retired 1911. CIE 1900. FRGS 1901. Proposed by his father, who was elected FRGS 1885. See Thomas Henry Thornton, *General Sir Richard Meade and the Feudatory States of Central and South India, A Record of Forty-three Years Service as Soldier, Political Officer, and Administrator*, Longmans Green 1899. Thornton, who was Foreign Secretary of the Government of India, acknowledges fully that the book's basis was an earlier sketch by Malcolm Meade. d. 5 September 1933 at Dilkusha, Beauvallon, France.

METCALFE, ROY DOUGLAS Political Officer Trucial Coast 1940-41. b. 9 February 1909, India. Son of Capt. D.H. Metcalfe RNR, of Muswell Hill. HIGHGATE SCHOOL 1922-27. Foundationer. XI Football 1925-26. Sandhurst. IA 1929. 3/15th Punjab Regiment. Entered IPS 1934. Assistant to Gulf Resident 1934-35. Assistant Political Agent Bahrain 1935. Probationer Rawalpindi 1935-38. Undersecretary to Resident Central India and Deputy Opium Agent 1938-40. Publicity Officer for Gulf 1940. Political Officer Trucial Coast 1940-41. Publicity Officer for Gulf 1941. Undersecretary to Resident Eastern States 1942. Assistant Political Agent Raipur 1942-43. Secretary to Resident Eastern States 1943. Political Agent Muscat 1943-44. Political Agent Sibi 1945. Political Agent Chagai 1945-46. Consul Zahidan 1946. Retired 1948. IPS pension.

MILES, SAMUEL BARRETT Gulf Resident 1885-86. b. 2 October 1838. Son of Maj. Gen. M.G. Miles, Bombay Infantry. Elstree Preparatory School, established 18th century, run by a Rev. Rowsell from 1842, and taken over in 1848 by Dr. Leopold Bernays. 'According to the late Commander Ian Sanderson, ex-headmaster of Elstree School, Dr. C.J. Vaughan (1816-97) Headmaster of Harrow from 1844 to 1859, used to visit Bernays at Elstree.' Leinster-Mackay, *Rise of the English Prep School*, 33. Dr. Bernay was 'an extremely savage headmaster who, it has been alleged, foamed at the mouth when in a rage'. *Ibid.*, 38. Refounded in 1869 by Lancelot Sanderson who continued ties with Harrow; moved to Woolhampton in 1939, where it continues to flourish. Montague Rendall, the headmaster of Winchester and relative of Olaf Caroe *qv* went to Elstree and Harrow. HARROW SCHOOL 1853-55. IA 1857. Aden 1866. Married Ellen Marie, eldest daughter of Sir Brooke Kay, Bt. One son, Major H.W. Miles MML, killed HMS Vanguard 1917. Second Assistant Resident Aden 1868-69. Special duty East Coast of Africa 1870. Acting Second Assistant Resident Aden 1871. Entered IPS 1872. Service record reads '...services placed at disposal of Foreign Department' indicating informality of IPS entrance hurdles at the time. See IOL:V/12/28. Muscat 1872-79 and 1880-81. Political Agent Zanzibar 1881-83. Political Agent Muscat 1883-86. Gulf Resident 1886. Dates are at variance with Tuson, but see IOL:V/12/28. Resident Meywar 1890. FRGS 1872. RAS. Miles' application to the RGS gave as an address 'c/o Col. J. Miles, Oriental Club'. Wrote *The Countries and Tribes of the Persian Gulf*, Vols.I & II, Harrisons, 1919. 'Some remarks upon the Country to the south-west of Hoshungabad', *Asiatic Journal*, Vol.III, 61. 'Translation of extracts from an Arabic work relating to Aden', *Asiatic Proceedings* 1875, 218. 'On the Route between Shoar and el-Bereymi in Oman, with a Note on the Zatt, or gypsies, in Arabia', *Asiatic Journal*, Vol.XLVI Pt.1, 41. RGS: Manuscripts and letters; see Joseph Thomson, Corr. Block 1881-1910 (a); also G.H. Grosvenor Corr. 1911-20. Miles presented 50 Arabic manuscripts to British Museum between 1875 and 1891. d. 1914.

MORE, JAMES CARMICHAEL Political Agent Kuwait 1920-29. b. 13 February 1883. Son of J. More of Rothwell, Northants. Efforts to establish his schooling have been unsuccessful. Army 1902. 2nd Lt. Royal Scot Fusiliers. Lt. 1904. IA 1904. 51st Sikhs (Frontier Force). Captain 1911. Major 1917. DSO 1917. Married 1923 Helen Vera Biernacks; daughter of H.S. Harington, Indian State Railways. One son. Entered IPS under contract 1920. Political Agent Kuwait 1920-29. According to Neil Donaldson in *The Postal Agencies in Eastern Arabia and the Gulf*, it was More who in 1927 surveyed and made the first motorable road to Basra, going via Mutla and Safwan. Retired 1930. IA pension. CIE 1930. Junior United Service Club. d. 17 December 1959.

MURPHY, RAYMOND CLIVE Political Officer Trucial Coast 1945-46. b. 4 May 1912. Son of F.A.E. Murphy, schoolmaster. DOVER COLLEGE 3 yrs. Military College of Science 3 yrs. Sandhurst. IA 1932. Entered IPS 1938. 'H.E. the Viceroy will see Lieutenant R.C. Murphy on July 6th and he will be invited to lunch on that day.' IOR: Personal File, Viceregal Lodge to Political Department, 2 July 1936. 'I found that he has very sensible ideas on matters like the admission of Indians to Club.' *Ibid.*, Notation, 15 August 1938. Assistant to Resident Hyderabad 1938-39. Assistant Collector Bareilly 1939. Military duty Gilgit Corps of Scouts 1939-43. Undersecretry to Resident Eastern States 1943. Assistant Political Agent Orissa 1943-45. Political Officer Trucial Coast 1945-46. Undersecretary to AGG Baluchistan 1946-47. Opted for Pakistan 1947.

PELLY, CORNELIUS JAMES Political Officer Trucial Coast 1941-42. Political Agent Kuwait 1943-44. Political Agent Bahrain 1947-51. b. 8 April 1908. Eldest son of Hyacinth Albert Pelly and Charity Mary Pelly, Benmore, Rushbrooke, Cork, Eire. Always known as 'Neil'. (A.C. Galloway.) CLONGOWES WOOD COLLEGE. IOR:IPS personal file, 15 July 1937: 'Confidential...He was apparently at school in a Nationalist part of Ireland at the time of the Irish troubles, as he is a Roman Catholic.' Trinity College Dublin. Married 1949 Una O'Shea; youngest daughter of Patrick Seaborn O'Shea, Lismore, Co. Waterford. One son. One daughter. ICS 1930. Entered IPS 1937. Pelly had difficulty getting released from his ICS post in the Punjab: '...there are at the moment 17 officers of the Punjab cadre holding posts in the Foreign and Political Department...calls of the Foreign and Political Department upon the services of Punjab officers must be moderated.' IOR: Personal File, Chief Secretary to the Government of Punjab, to the Political Secretary, Government of India. Assistant Commissioner Sialkot, Murree, Gurdaspur, Pakputtan, D.G. Khan 1931-36. Undersecretary Punjab Government 1936-37. Colonization Officer Bahawal 1937-41. Political Officer Trucial Coast 1941-42. Assistant Agent Muscat 1942. Political Agent Muscat 1942. Political Agent Kuwait 1943-44. Secretary to Gulf Resident 1945-47. Political Agent Bahrain 1947. Political Agent for Commonwealth Office and then FO Bahrain 1947-51. Acting Gulf Resident 1950 and 1952. Political Agent Kuwait 1951-55. Secretary Financial Affairs Muscat 1968-70. 'He entertains well and keeps a good table.' IOR:Personal File, Arnold Galloway, 31 October 1945. Somewhat paranoid about the intrusion of outside political influences: 'I have had the list of books (enclosed) examined, but it is a very large one, and without the books themselves, I am unable to say more than that those marked with a pencil cross are politically undesirable.' C.J. Pelly (Agent, Bahrain), to F.J. Wakelin, Director of Education (Bahrain and Kuwait), 25 November 1943, IOR:R/15/5/197. In 1947 he applied to all three services: Foreign, Home, and Colonial. Rupert Hay, 10 February 1947, *Ibid.* OBE 1944. CMG 1952. United Service Club. His application to the IPS accompanied by the recommendation of a friend who knew him through the United Service. See the IOR personal files. d. 26 March 1985.

PELLY, LEWIS Gulf Resident 1862-72. b. 14 November 1825 at Hyde Hove. Son of John Hinde Pelly, of Bristol and Hyde House, Cotswold Hills, Gloucestershire; and Elizabeth Lewis of Brinscombe, Glos. Strong family ties with EIC. Lewis's brother Saville Marriott Pelly (1819-1895), educated Winchester and Guys, Indian Medical Service, Inspector-General hospitals, Bombay Presidency. RUGBY SCHOOL. Entered August 1838. Thomas Arnold head 1828-1842. Bird House. Contemporaries included Charles Hobhouse (Sir Charles Hobhouse, Judge of the High Court, Calcutta), Matthew Arnold, Henry Walford (head of Lancing), George Bradley (head of Marlborough), Thomas Hughes (author of *Tom Brown's Schooldays*), Walter Karr (Foreign Secretary, Government of India), Edward Arnold (another son of Dr. Arnold, became HM Inspector of Schools), and Augustus Orlebar, the boy on whom Hughes modelled Tom Brown. In Bird with Pelly was Edmund Hallewell, later commandant of Sandhurst. A total of 1320 boys studied at Rugby under Arnold. *Rugby School Register*, Vol.I, for 1875 to 1879 Inclusive, Rivingtons, 1881. Married 1878 Amy H., daughter of Rev. John Lowder. No children. See IOR:L/AG/23/12/4, no.119. Ensign 1841. Served with Sir John Frere in Sind. In 1860 travelled from Tehran via Herat, Furrah, Kandahar, and Kelat, to Calcutta: 'a most perilous journey, and which he performed, without assuming any disguise, in his British uniform'. Martineau, *Sir Bartle Frere*, Vol.I, 484. This impressed Frere, who got Pelly a roving commission as PA on East Coast of Africa, where (September 1861) he was shipwrecked on Johanna, Comorro Islands. Agent Zanzibar 1861-62. Gulf Resident 1862-72 (Buckland has incorrectly '1871'). Kelly and Bidwell both suggest favouritism by Frere in making the appointment: '...an immensely ambitious and active man, anxious to make a name for himself. Pelly felt that positive measures should be taken to develop the area, almost as if it had been a normal British colony.' Bidwell, *Arabian Gulf Intelligence*, v. John Martineau puts a different cast to Pelly's aggressiveness: 'Frank, straightforward, ardent, fond of adventure, and fearless, Pelly was ready for any service, the more novel and hazardous the better. His shrewdness, tact, and ready wit generally carried him safely and successfully through the various dangers and difficulties he had to encounter.' Martineau, *Frere*, Vol.I, 503. Whatever, Frere and Pelly favoured

intervention in the Gulf, and the bond between them was close, that of father and son. *Ibid.*, 507-10. (See discussion in Chapter V.) Pelly wrote Lady Frere: 'You say truly that I *loved* Sir Bartle, and that I always felt, when I had the privilege – as I often had – of being received under his and your roof, that I was at home...Had I been his son I could not have loved and respected him more than I did, and all possible considerations have been as nothing to me compared with the pleasure I felt in being admitted to his personal friendship.' *Ibid.*, 503. It was during Pelly's administration that control of the Gulf and the IPS, which under the EIC and initially in Government of India administration had been through the Bombay Governorate, was taken over directly by the Viceroy in Calcutta. This Bombay connection accounts for the large number of Gulf records that are in Bombay.
'The other exploration of Nejd which followed immediately on Palgrave's was undertaken in another interest by a very different man. In certain respects it is unique in the history of Arabian exploration. On this occasion only has the official representative of a European power ventured in virtue of his office into the centre of the peninsula without concealment of his nationality, his creed, or the nature of his mission. Colonel Lewis Pelly, British Resident at Bushire and virtual controller of the Persian Gulf, determined on his own motion in 1864 to go up to Riad [*sic*] and have a personal interview with the Wahabi Emir.' Hogarth, *The Penetration of Arabia*, 308. This interest in travelling was lifelong: in 1872, Pelly accompanied Frere to Zanzibar to remonstrate with Sultan about slave-trade. Frere in fact recommended that Pelly head the mission. *Ibid.*, Vol.II, 69-70, 80-89. Offered Governorship of Congo by King of Belgians, 1883. Conservative MP, North Hackney, 1885-92. Director of British East Africa Company, and criticized for being its advocate. *Hansard*, 8 March 1892, 321. CSI 1868. KCSI 1874. KCB 1877. FRGS 1875. FRAS. Freemason. Athenaeum. Pelly was one of eight elected in 1876, including Sir Barrow Ellis (1823-1887), one of the few Jews to enter the ICS and the Chief Secretary of the Bombay Government and member Viceroy's Council; and Field Marshal Viscount Wolsley, head of the Egyptian Expedition 1882 and Commander in Chief British Army. See Humphry Ward, *History of the Athenaeum, 1924-1925*, Athenaeum, 1926. United Service Club. Pelly wrote *The Views and Opinions of Brig-General John Jacob, C.B.*, 1858; *North-West Frontier of India*, 1858; *The Miracle Play of Husan and Husain*, 1879; 'Accounts of a recent tour around the northern portion of the Persian Gulf', *Transactions*, Bombay Geographical Society, 1863, XVIII; 'The Persian Gulf as an area of trade', *Proceedings of the Royal Geographical Society*, 1863-4, VIII; 'Remarks on the pearl oyster beds in the Persian Gulf', *Transactions*, Bombay Geographical Society 1967, XVIII; 'Remarks on the tribes, trade and resources around the shore line of the Persian Gulf', *Transactions*, Bombay Geographical Society, 1863, XVIII. IOL: Papers, 8 boxes. RGS: manuscripts, letters. The RGS has a cranky letter of W.S. Blunt (16 January 1880), protesting 'Pelly no authority at all.' d. 23 April 1892. Promoted General the day of his death. (See Plate 40.)

PRIDEAUX, FRANCIS BEVILLE Political Agent Bahrain 1904-1909. Gulf Resident 1924-27. b. 26 November 1871. Son of William Prideaux, Gulf Resident 1876-77. Marlborough Jr. School. MARLBOROUGH COLLEGE 1885-1888. IA 1890. 2nd Lt. 2nd Middlesex. Arrived India 1891. 2nd Lt. 1892. 31st Pathan Infantry. 1892-94. Married 1910 Constance Mary Clibborn. Entered IPS 1894. (*Marlborough Register* has 1895.) Assistant to Resident Hyderabad 1895. Boundary Settlement Officer Bhopawar 1895. Assignments Sirdarpur, Indore, Nasirabad 1895-96. 1st Assistant Political Resident Gulf 1897-1900. Assistant to Governor-General Rajputana 1900-1901. Political Agent Haraoti and Tonk 1901-1903. Political Agent Bahrain 1904-1909. In 1906 he excavated a number of the Bahrain grave mounds. 'His were really the first professional excavations to be carried out in Bahrain, and he recorded carefully what he found. His report "The Sepulchral Tumuli of Bahrain" published in 1908/9 in the Archaeological Survey of India is a serious study: it is notable for a handsome and detailed plan of the Aali area, which was subsequently to be plagiarised by many writers after him...Prideaux also provides excellent photographs of the mounds, of the pottery including fragments of ivory which led various investigators to believe that they were of Phoenician origin. His report is also remarkable for the note of deep exasperation in which much of it is written. Colonel Prideaux was greatly shocked by the high cost of excavation in Bahrain and the rates which his workers demanded.' Michael Rice, 'Dilmun Discovered' – The Archaeology of Bahrain to the Second Millennium BC', Asian Affairs, Vol.XVII, Part III, October 1986, 254. See discussion of 1990 Bahrain discoveries in Chapter IV.
Political Agent Southern Rajputana 1911. Political Agent Eastern Raputana 1912. Political Officer Nasirabad and Consul, Scistan & Kain, 1912-1920. Consul-General Meshed 1920-24. Gulf Resident 1924-27. 'He was a large, rather pink-complexioned person, who reminded me of a bishop, interested in horses, archaeology, and genealogy.' Belgrave, Personal Column, 9. Retired 1927. CIE 1911. CSI 1917. Freemason. East India Club. Prideaux collected cemetery inscriptions (131 slips) of European graves around the Gulf which were used in H.K. Percy-Smith, Deaths in India, Vol.2, Society of Genealogists, 1942. See IOR:MSS EUR F 146/21. d. 6 September 1938 London.

PRIDEAUX, WILLIAM FRANCIS Gulf Resident 1876-77. b. 30 April 1840, London. Son of F.W. Prideaux, secretary Revenue Department India Office. ALDENHAM 1852-58. Lived with the headmaster, Alfred Leeman, who recommended him for Indian service: '...was a pupil in the Endowed Grammar School and also for the same time an inmate of my house.' Alfred Leeman, 24 September 1859, IOR: L/ML/9/250-628. Aldenham brothers: Robert 1855-60 (Colonel IA); Charles 1857-62 (JP, Clerk Bank of England); Walter 1860-65. See the print of the school in Prideaux's years in Evans, *The Register of Aldenham School*, 9th ed., 49-50. 'The numbers grew slowly. From twenty-seven in 1843, they rose to forty-three in 1851, when the Court remonstrated with the Head Master for taking private pupils, and after some discussion allowed him to have eight private pupils in addition to...foundationers...in 1853 there was a waiting list...In 1857...110.' Beevor, *The History and Register of Aldenham School*, 8th ed., vi. Exhibitioner. Captain of School 1856-58. Clerk India Office 1859. Bombay Army 1860. Ensign 1860. Lt. 1862. Captain 1872. Lt-Colonel 'while serving in Persian Gulf' 1876. Major 1880. Lt-Colonel 1886. Colonel 1890. See IOR:L/AG/23/12/4 no.398. Married 1869 Mary Frances, daughter of A.C. MacLeod, Surgeon/Major Indian Medical Service. She d. 1877, age 33 years. See IOL:V/12/28. Monument, Bushire Armenian Church. Three sons. 2nd was Francis Beville Prideaux *qv*. Married second 1882 Mary Catherine Macleod, daughter of S. Townsend Philpot. Two sons. Assistant Resident Aden, 1864. Expedition against King Theodore II of Ethiopia 1865. Prisoner, Magdala, July 1866 – April 1868. Abyssinian Expedition Medal 1868. Assistant Resident Aden 1870-73. Only then did Prideaux have 'services placed at disposal of Foreign Department'. IOL:V/12/28. Consul-General Zanzibar 1873. Assistant Resident Aden 1875. Officiating Gulf Resident 1876-77. Assigned to ex-King of Oudh 1880-88. Resident Jaipur 1888-90. Resident Kashmir 1890-92. CSI 1895. Fellow, Bombay University 1873. FRGS 1868. Prideaux surveyed the area of the new Kensington Gore clubhouse. Mill, *The Record of the Royal Geographical Society*, 226. Asiatic Society. Wrote *The Lay of the Himarites, Notes for a Biography of Edward Fitzgerald, A Biography of Robert Louis Stevenson*, 'On the Coins of Charibael, King of the Himerites and Sabeans', *Asiatic Society Journal*, 1, pt.i., 95. RGS: See Corr. Blocks 1871-80, 1881-1910. 5 Dec 1914, St. Peter's, Thanet. WW has 6 December.

PRIOR, CHARLES GEOFFREY Political Agent Bahrain, 1929-32. Gulf Resident 1939-46. b. 9 December 1896. Only son of Richard Delabere Prior, Indian Education Department. In IPS application he also lists a relative in the Indian Forestry Service, G.R. Long. SHREWSBURY 1912-14. W.D. Haydon's House. Folliot Sandford English Prize, 1913, 1914. Sandhurst 1914 (Kelly has RMA Woolwich). Prize Cadetship. Army 1915. East Lancashire Regiment. IA 1915. 127th Baluchistan Light Infantry. Quarter Master 127th Baluchistan 1916-19. Company Commander and Battalion Commander South Persian Rifles 1919-21. Entered IPS 1923. Probationer Mysore 1923-24. Undersecretary to AGG Rajputana 1924-26. Undersecretary to Gulf Resident 1926-27. Leave, including study leave, 1927-29. Political Agent Bahrain 1929-32. 'Received the appreciation of the Government of India for services rendered in connection with the Bahrain Riots, 1932'. Deputy Secretary Foreign Department 1933-36. Prime Minister of Alwar 1936-38. Gulf Resident 1939-46. Government of India's representative Middle East War Council Cairo 1941-42. Headed Gulf Spitfire Fund, raising funds for 10 Spitfires. Governor Baluchistan 1946-47.
Prior was master of the *pasquinade* and Caroe *qv* censored him (21 January 1944), for 'overgenerous use of explosives on paper. These defects give the impression of a certain immaturity...They are important in that his position as Resident in the Gulf necessarily brings his work to the direct notice of the Secretary of State and of various high authorities in the Middle East.' IOR:R/1/4, Prior's personal file. Caroe warned: 'His Excellency has observed that you are inclined to be too lavish with explosives in your telegrams, which often spoils a good case.' *Ibid.*, 21 January 1944. Opted for Pakistan. Retired 1949. Resident Director British Bank of Middle East. Donated building Church of Epiphany Bushire. Gave window St. Christopher's Bahrain, and donated to other Middle Eastern churches. CIE 1936. KCIE 1943. President South African Equestrian Federation 1964-67. Royal Aero Club. Travellers Club. A.C. Galloway, *qv*, stated Prior was active in the Travellers. Interview with P.J. Rich, 23 August 1987. United Service. Civil Service (Capetown). Sind (Karachi). d. 11 October 1972 Rhodesia.

RANCE, HUGH DUNSTAN HOLWELL Political Officer Trucial Coast 1946-47. b. 19 May 1912. 'His father was a parson in an East End parish and died in 1923...'. IOR:Personal File, Olaf Caroe, 27 February 1936. CHRIST'S HOSPITAL 1921-30. Grecian. Sandhurst. IA 1932. A reference was W.H. Hamilton Fyffe, former headmaster of Christ's Hospital. Entered IPS 1936. Caroe *qv* wrote: '...the family have had to struggle hard...anxieties have to some extent militated against the attainment of poise...'. Caroe feared 'the straited circumstances of his youth' had given him an inferiority complex. IOR: Personal File, Olaf Caroe, 27 February 1936. Undersecretary to AGG, Gujarat, 1936-37.

Probationer Simla 1937. Assistant Magistrate Agra, then Aligarh, 1937-39. Assistant to Resident Western India 1939. Undersecretary to Resident 1939-40. Reverted IA 1940-43. Assistant Political Agent Quetta 1943-44. Assistant Political Agent Mekran 1944-45. Assistant Political Agent Bahrain 1946-47, as well as Political Officer Trucial Coast 1946. Retired 1949. IPS pension. Colonial Administrative Service Northern Rhodesia 1948-50. Diocesan Secretary Diocese of Chichester 1961-76.

ROSS, EDWARD CHARLES Gulf Resident 1872-1891. b. 23 September 1836 Rosstrevor, Co. Down. Son of David Robert Ross, MP and Governor of Tobago; and of Harriett Knox, daughter of the Bishop of Limerick. EDINBURGH ACADEMY 1845-52. Boys were in one group throughout school career under supervision of one master. Entered 1845 in Dr. Cumming's class, which became Dr. Robert Maclure's class. Cumming taught at the Academy 1826-46, becoming Rector of Glasgow Academy 1846-50, and HMIS 1851-74. His old students formed a club which published *Chronicles* in 1887. Maclure was at the Academy identical years as Ross, left to become Professor of Humanities, Aberdeen University. Contemporaries included planter in Antigua, doctor in the Indian Army, ICS member who wrote papers for the Royal Asiatic, ICS member who served in the Andamans, doctor on the *HMS Euryalus* expedition around the world with Duke of Edinburgh, sheep farmer in Australia, officer in Bombay Artillery, businessman in Minnesota, officer in India Cavalry, judge in Jamaica, journalist in Canada, businessman in Toronto, clergyman in Michigan, tea planter in Ceylon, and the treasurer of Sarawak. See *The Edinburgh Academy Register: A Record of All Those Who Have Entered the School Since Its Foundation in 1824*, Edinburgh Academical Club, Edinburgh, 1924. Scottish Naval and Military Academy 1851-53. Ensign 1855. 3rd Bombay European Regiment Poona. Indian Mutiny 1857-58. Quartermaster and Interpreter. At Siege of Ratgarh, Capture of Garhakota, Forcing of Madanpur Pass, storming of Jhansi. Lt. 1857. Captain 1867. Local Major Mekran Coast 1869. Local Lt-Colonel 'in Persian Gulf' 1872. Major 1875. Lt-Colonel 1881. Colonel 1885. Married 1862 Sarah May Caroline Whitehill; daughter of Col. C.S. Whitehill. Four sons. Five daughters. Passed High Proficiency in Arabic 1869. Political Agent Muskat 1871. Gulf Resident 1872. Tuson lists him as Acting Resident until 1877. The Service Record (V/12/1) lists him as Resident 2nd Class, from 7 February 1874. IOL:V/12/1, 203. Also V/12/28. CSI 1882. KCB 1892. FRGS 1876. Asiatic Society. Several golf clubs. Member St. Paul's Episcopal Church, Edinburgh. See IOL:L/MIL/9/234. Wrote 'An Account of tenets of the Ibadhi sect of Oman', *Asiatic Proceedings* 1873. 'Annals of Oman, from early times to the year 1728. From an Arabic MS.' *Asiatic Journal*, Vol.XLIII, Pt.I, 111. See IOR Service Records for list of reports and memorandum by Ross. RGS: manuscript and Corr. Block 1871-80. d. 2 February 1913.

SADLER, JAMES HAYES Acting Gulf Resident 1893-94. b. 11 October 1851, London. Son of Sir James Hayes Sadler KCMG FRGS who was educated at Eton and Oxford; Hon. Col. Sussex Artillery Militia; Consul, Panama 1885; Chicago 1886; Consul-General Valparaiso, 1895; in charge Legation Santiago 1896; retired 1897; member Jr. Carlton Club; d. 9 January 1910; and of Sophia Jane, daughter of James Taylor HEIC. Grandson of Rev. J. Hayes Sadler. *Who Was Who 1897-1915* confuses father and son, corrected in edition for 1916-1928. Despite Sadler's prominence, his school – if any – is unknown. Possibly privately educated. Sandhurst. Cornet/Ensign 61st Foot (S.Gloucs.), 1870 'without purchase'. Embarked for Nova Scotia 1870. Halifax 1871-72. Lt. 1871. Joined 40th Foot (2nd Somersets) 1873. Arrived India 1873. Bengal Staff Corps 1874. 33rd Native Infantry. Married 1875 Rita Annie Smith (1856-1918); daughter of Wemyss Smith, Colonel IA. Three sons. *Who's Who* 1908 has 4 sons. Indian Military Service Family Pension Funds confirms three: James Hayes b. 1877, killed in action 1914. Ernest Reginald Hayes b. 1878. Edwin John Berkeley b. 1887. See IOR:L/AG/23/16/5 no. 680. Entered IPS 1877. Acting Political Agent Mabikantha 1877-79. Acting Political Agent Cutch 1879-80. Acting Political Agent and Assistant to Governor-General Baroda 1881-90. Secretary to Board of Examiners Calcutta 1886, 1888, and 1889. Tutor to Nawab of Jaora. Tutor Maharaja of Mysore. Political Agent with Ex-Amir of Afghanistan 1891. Political Agent Kotah 1891-92. Political Agent Jhaillawar 1892. Special duty Prince Damrang of Siam 1892. Political Agent Muscat 1892-93. Acting Gulf Resident 1893-94. (Tuson lists 'Salder'.) Political Agent Muscat 1894-95. See Saldhana, *Precis of Maskat Affairs 1892-1905*, esp. 18. Assistant Secretary Foreign Department 1895. Political Agent Muscat 1895-96. Political Agent Kotah 1896. Political Agent Somali Coast 1897. Retired 1899. Continued as Consul-General Somailand until 1902. Commissioner Uganda 1904-1905.

Governor British East Africa 1907-1909. Sought to implement labour laws. Acclaimed by those pro-native but denounced by white settlers under Lord Delamere. Dilley, *British Policy in Kenya Colony*, 216-19. '...its first Governor. He was widely felt, however, to be weak and ineffective.' Harlow, *History of East Africa*, 22. 'Sadler, a weak governor known to the settlers as "Flannelfoot"...The Colonial Office had become tired of his weakness and failure to deal with the problems of the

Protectorate.' *Ibid.*, 280. He had an 'absence of drive'. Barber, *Imperial Frontier*. However, that is not the whole story. Sadler stood up to the settlers over their treatment of the natives, provoking Delamere to shout 'We are not schoolboys...'. Clayton, *Government and Labour in Kenya*, 36. He supported the missionaries despite settler opposition. Hansen, *Mission, Church and State in a Colonial Setting*, 267. While 'a charming old gentleman' (Mungeam, *British Rule in Kenya 1895-1912*, 152. *Cf.* Lord Cranworth, *Kenya Chronicles*), 'Sadler had failed to face up to the fundamental question of whether the country was to be developed in the interests of the settler community or of the local African population'. Mungeam, *British Rule in Kenya, 207.* Governor, Windward Islands, 1909-1914. Retired 1914. CB 1902. KCMG 1907. FRGS 1901. Resigned 1921. Nominated by his father, who was elected to RGS in 1896 as Hayes-Sadler. His bro. W. Hayes Sadler, Director of Customs, Sudan, was nominated by Sir Reginald Wingate and elected 1905. Junior United Service Club. St. James Club. East India Club. d. 21 April 1922, Hotel Britannia, St. Briac nr. St. Malo, France.

SHAKESPEAR, WILLIAM HENRY IRVINE Political Agent Kuwait, 1909-14. b. 29 October 1878, Oudh, NWFP (Winston has Multant, Punjab). Son of William Henry Sullivan Shakespear, Indian Forestry Service, ed. Bromsgrove); and Anne Caroline Davidson, daughter of Jamaican planter. Preparatory education with Misses Lacell, Portsmouth 1887-88. Portsmouth Grammar School 1888-94. Boarder in Mr. Pare's House, 'Prescote'. 1st Football XI and cricket colours. KING WILLIAM'S COLLEGE 1894-96. Brothers at King William's: George and Henry (IA). '...here in the College Chapel there is a splendid brass plaque commemorating him.' L. Earnshaw, Hon. Secretary, King William's College Society, to P.J. Rich. See *King William's College*, June 1915, 77. Sandhurst 1896-97. Left in 11th place. Joined Army 1898. 2nd Lt. unattached. 11th Devonshires. 16th Queen's Lancers. 17th Bengal Lancers. Plaque duty, Bombay 1901. Entered IPS 1904. Assistant to Gulf Political Resident and Consul Bandar Abbas 1904. Political Agent Muscat 1906. Assistant Hyderbad. Motored from Bushire to Paris 1907. CIE 1915 posthumously. FRGS 1914. He died before signing the membership book.

Shakespear had considerable panache. He entertained Ibn Saud & Kuwait's Shaikh Mubaraq to 'an English dinner of roast lamb, mint sauce and roast potatoes'. Brent, *Far Arabia*, 188. '...when he travelled in the desert this Englishman always took his camp table and chair and dressed for dinner.' Harrison, *A Tool in His Hand*, 54. When recording Sabaean inscriptions in the desert he dined as 'a gentleman' on 'salmon, mutton pilaf, blancmange, preceded by vermouth, accompanied by Moselle and closed by port'. Brent, *Far Arabia*, 193. See H.V.F. Winstone's *Captain Shakespear*. Papers at St. Antony's, Oxford. RGS: Notebook, 'Kuwait Tours', 1909-13; other notebooks; letters and letters from father and brother. Winstone has in his personal possession Shakespear's diary for 1914. d. 5 January 1915 in a battle between Ibn Saud and Rashids. The mythology surrounding his demise is an involved one. Either he was shot while firing his revolver in a heroic stand or cut down while busily taking photographs, and either conspicuous in topee or hatless. The India Office recorded his as WWI casualty. See IOR:L/Ag/23/16/13 no. 1119.

STEWART, ANDREW CHARLES Acting Political Agent Kuwait, 1937. b. 22 April 1907. Son of Frederick Naylor K. Stewart, physician. Prepared Hymer's College 1918-1920. SCARBOROUGH COLLEGE 1921-1925. Private Tutor 1922-25. Sandhurst. IA 1927. Married 1935 Emily Caroline Martin. Two sons. One daughter. Entered IPS 1933. 'H.E. considers Mr. Stewart – who lunched at Viceregal Lodge today – a suitable candidate.' IOR: Personal File, 9 August 1932. Undersecretary to Gulf Resident 1933. Probationer Rawalpindi, then Murree, Simla, Mashed, 1934-36. Undersecretary to Gulf Resident 1936. Assistant Political Agent Bahrain 1936-37. Political Agent Kuwait 1937. Political Officer Khorramshahr 1937. Undersecretary to Resident Hyderabad 1938-39. Secretary to Gulf Political Resident 1939-42. Consul Khorramshahr 1943-46. Political Agent Muscat 1946-47. Retired 1949. IPS pension. Joined Foreign Service 1947. Minister Korea 1954-56. Consul-General Jerusalem 1957-59. Ambassador Iceland 1959-61. Libya 1962-63. OBE 1942. CMG 1955. D.L. Ross and Cromarth 1976. East India Club. 'He is extraordinarily modest, a quality rare amongst Political Officers as it is refreshing. His wife...is the granddaughter of the Caledonians who invest these parts.' *Ibid.*, Charles Prior, 1940. 'This officer's heart is in the Gulf...But I rather think he needs to be put through his paces a bit before he returns there.' *Ibid*, Olaf Caroe, 20 January 1943. d. 1 January 1979.

STEWART, HUGH Political Agent Bahrain, 1916. b. 5 November 1872. Only son of Col. C.J.B. Stewart, 78th Seaford Highlanders, Lochgoil, Argyllshire. CHARSLEY HALL Oxford. Statute of 1855 permitted Convocation of members to open private halls licensed by the Vice Chancellor. In 1889-90 there were two: Charsley's with 47 undergraduates, and Turrell's with 8. Charsley's Licensed Master was William Henry Charsley of Christchurch college. *Kelly's Directory of Oxford*, 1889-90. 'It is my guess that W.H. Charsley, the licensed master, in addition to teaching undergraduates as in a College, also taught younger boys, *i.e.* he ran a school. There was at least one other 14 year old from Charsley's matriculating at the same time as Stewart. The Hall itself had ceased to operate by the end of 1891.' Information supplied by Maggie Macdonald, Assistant Archivist, Oxford University Archives, 8 September 1987. Sandhurst. IA 1893. Queen's Own Royal West Kent Regiment. Duty Meerut, Peshawar, Bellary, Hingoli, 1893-1899. Famine duty 1899-1900. Boundary duty 1900-1901. Married 1897 Mabel, daughter of Joseph Rushton of Calcutta. She died 21 May 1899 in giving birth to a son. Married second 1905 Dora May; daughter of Frederick Dallas Barnes DL JP. One son. One daughter. Entered IPS 1901. Famine duty Central India 1901. Special duty Coronation Durbar 1902-1903. Served Swat, Merwar, 1903-1905. Reprimanded for detention and abuse of a native barrister 1904. Tutor and Guardian Raja of Dawas 1905-1906. Stewart removed as tutor: '...disposed to mix himself up in an undesirable manner in local politics'. He made accusations against another IPS officer which were regarded as unfounded: 'One can now feel no confidence as to what he may or may not say to the Raja and a man so wanting in self command cannot possibly exercise a wholesome [influence].' IOR file mentions 'extraordinary ebullition of temper...the most charitable view seems to be that he must have been suffering from some form of temporary insanity'. IOR: Personal File R/1/4/1343. C/F/ Mackenzie *qv* was suggested as replacement. District Judge Peshawar 1908-10. D.I. Khan 1910. Deputy Commissioner Bannu 1910-11. Deputy Commissioner Hazara 1913-15. Political Agent Muscat 1915-16. Political Agent Bahrain 1916, where Cox found him 'an effective and business-like officer of good ability and I should be glad to have him again if he were fit'. *Ibid.*, 3 November 1916. Special duty, orders of the Gulf Political Resident, 1917. Political Officer Zhjob 1919. Military Governor Basra 1917. Political Agent Quetta 1919-22. In 1919 the Department was reluctant to promote him Lt. Colonel, 'he is one of our bad bargains'. Political Agent Malakand 1922-24. In 1922 files, reference to breakdowns, including during Gulf service 'owing largely to alcoholic excess in Basra five years ago'. Noted was 'evil temper and tendency to solitude' that might be public danger. Agent Swat 1922-24. In 1923 protested being passed over for promotion. His political judgement being questioned, he was given a year's leave from 22 October 1924, extended for 16 months. Quotes and information *ibid.* Retired 1927 to Isola di San Giulio, Lago D'Orta, Italy. CIE 1913. Silver Kaisar-i-Hind. Society of Authors, Freemason, United Service Club 1922. Queens Club. Author: *Station Polo, The Web.* d. 26 June 1931 at Bath.

TALBOT, ADELBERT CECIL Gulf Resident 1891-93. b. 3 June 1845. Eldest son of Rev. Hon W.W.C. Talbot, Rector of Hatfield; and Eleongra Julia, daughter of William Coventry. Grandson of Earl Talbot KG, Lord Lieutenant of Ireland 1817-21. Queen Adelaide was sponsor in person at baptism. Adelbert's cousin, Mary Talbot married Lionel Ford, Head of Harrow 1910-28. ETON COLLEGE 1852-62. RMA Woolwich. Lt. 20th Brigade Royal Artillery 1867. Squadron Subaltern 4th Cavalry, Hyderabad Contingent, 1869. Special duty with Afghan Commissioner for Seistan arbitration 1872-73. Married 1870 Agnes Mary; daughter of Rev. W. Clarke. One son: Adelbert William, b. 1876, in ICS. Three daughters: oldest Gwendolen married Stuart Hill Godfrey *qv.* 2nd daughter Muriel married Percy Brown, Indian Education Service. 3rd, Esme married Captain A.B. Dew, Chief Commissioner of Baluchistan. Entered IPS 1873. Political Assistant Mount Abu 1873-74. Attached Foreign Department 1875. Secretary to Board of Examiners Fort William 1875. Assistant to Resident Jalma 1878. Assistant Political Secretary to AGG Rajputana 1878-81. Political Agent Jeypore 1881-82. Political Agent Bhurtpur 1882-83. Political Agent Baghdad 1888-89. Political Agent Bikanir 1889-91. Gulf Resident 1891-93. He suggested in November 1891 that the Government of India offer a formal agreement to the Trucial shaikhs and this (known as the Exclusive Treaty) was sent in March 1892. 'This treaty became the main pillar of British authority on the Trucial Coast and was to serve as a model for agreements signed in due course by the Shaikhs of Bahrain, Kuwait and Qatar.' Abdullah, *The United Arab Emirates*, 26. Deputy Secretary Foreign Department 1894-95. Special duty with Sardar Nasrulla Khan, 2nd son, King of Afghanistan, on visit to England 1895. Deputy Secretary Foreign Department 1895-96. Resident Kashmir 1896. CIE 1885. KCIE 1895. United Service Club. Papers in Godfrey Collection, IOL. Edited and revised *Aitchison's Treaties*, 1876. d. 28 December 1920, Effingham, Surrey.

TANDY, MAURICE PATRICK O'CONNOR Political Officer Trucial Coast 1943-44 Political Agent Kuwait 1945-47. b. 14 May 1912. Eldest son of Col. Maurice Tandy DSO OBE RE, who served India 1898-1928 (in Aden hinterland 1902-1904), Director Survey of India, surveying lecturer, Oxford 1927-40; and Mabel, daughter of James Dillon of Kingston, Co. Dublin. Grandson of Col. E.O. Tandy, Indian Medical Service. Nephew of Brig. Sir Edward Tandy, Surveyor-General of India and author. WINCHESTER COLLEGE 1928-30. Sergent's House. His housemaster Rev. W.D. Monro was 'a large square-cut man, a strict disciplinarian never known to smile; though he himself had been a Winchester scholar...India, the country of his birth, had first call on his affections, and his time as a don was only an interval between two spells in the missionary field. He had a wide understanding of oriental languages and religions...' Sabben-Clare, *Winchester*, 86-87. Herbert Smith Prize. RMA Woolwich. Married 1946 Pamela May; daughter of Charles R. Rice. Their son entered Winchester 1970 and became Lloyds Underwriter. IA 1932 'Does not want to transfer to the Indian Army if he cannot get in to the Foreign and Political Depart.' IOR: Personal File. Entered IPS 1937. Probationer, Mount Abu, then Sind, then Quetta, Sailkot, Dalhousie, Multan, 1936-39. Vice-Consul Zabul 1939-40. Assistant Commissioner Kohat 1940-41. Vice-Consul Bushire 1941. 'He is in the Arnold Wilson tradition.' *Ibid.*, Charles Prior, 8 November 1941. '...though he has curbed his inclinations to live on hilltops with ruffians he still does not take very kindly to an office chair for prolonged periods.' *Ibid.*, T. Hickinbotham, 13 March 1945. Military service 1941-43. Political Officer Trucial Coast 1943-44. 'The party was a very merry one, with a great deal of singing (particularly from the jovial Irish officer, Captain Pat. Tandy, who was to replace Bird as Political Officer)...'. O'Shea, *Sand Kings of Oman*, 26. Assistant Political Agent Bahrain 1944-45. Political Agent Kuwait 1945-47. MBE. Tandy's father belonged to the United Service Club and was FRGS. Opted for Pakistan.

TREVOR, ARTHUR PRESCOTT Political Agent Bahrain 1912-14. Gulf Resident 1920-24. b. 17 March 1872. Eldest son of Lt-Col Sir Arthur Trevor IA KCSI, Supreme Council of India 1895-1901. Grandson of Captain R.S. Trevor, Bengal Cavalry, murdered at Kabul 1841. Nephew of Major-General William Trevor, Director-General of Railways and Secretary Government of India. MARLBOROUGH COLLEGE 1886-. W.H. Madden, housemaster. RMA Woolwich, Army 1891. IA 1891. 22nd West Division 1894. 20th Bombay Infantry 1896. Tirah Expeditionary Force 1897. Married 1918 Lucy May Eleni; daughter of Lt-Colonel H. Peers Dimmock. One son. One daughter. Entered IPS 1899. Served Punjab 1899. Loralai 1899-1901. Assistant Political Agent Thal Chotiali 1901. Assistant Political Agent Fort Sandeman 1901-1902. Assistant to AGG Central India 1903-1904. Assistant to Gulf Resident 1904-1909. Acting Gulf Resident i/c 1909-10. Political Agent Muscat 1910-11. Political Agent Bahrain 1912-14. Consul Mohammerah 1914-15. Deputy Gulf Resident 1915-17 and 1919-20. Gulf Resident 1920-24. He became involved in oil negotiations, and in 1922 extracted from each of the Trucial shaikhs a promise that they would not give a concession to anyone not approved by the British Government. This did not sit well, and in 1924 he admitted that 'At present any ill-wishers of the British of the Anglo-Persian Oil Company never lose an opportunity of impressing upon their hearers that the Anglo-Persian Oil Company is a Government concern and that to grant a concession to this company is tantamount to giving it to the Government: that they have hitherto always looked to the Government to deal impartially with Arab matters, that they cannot hope for Government to do so when the interests of the Anglo-Persian Oil Company come up against those of the Arabs.' IOR:L/PS&S/989, Political Resident to SSC, 28 March 1924. Listed as Gulf Resident 1915-18 in *Marlborough School Register*. CIE 1911. CSI 1918. United Service Club 1919. Ranelagh Club. d. 4 April 1930 Marylebone.

WAKEFIELD, EDWARD BIRBECK Political Agent Bahrain, 1942-43. b. 24 July 1903. Third son of Roger William Wakefield MB JP, Kendal, Westmorland. HAILEYBURY 1917-22. In Edmonstone House, named after Sir George Edmonstone, Lt-Governor NWFP. R. Hornby, housemaster. Head of School. Captain of XV. 2nd Cricket XI. Fives V. School Prefect. In 1920, 30 OHs living in Cairo donated the Allenby Cup to the school. Trinity College Cambridge BA 1925. Married Constance Lalage Thompson; daughter of Sir John Thompson KCSI KCIE ICS, Chief Commissioner Delhi. Two sons: 1st and heir, Sir Edward Humphrey Wakefield; b. 1936, educated Gordonstoun and Trinity Cambridge; Member Standing Council of Baronetage. Two daughters. Entered ICS (Punjab) 1927. Assistant Commissioner Lyaalapur 1927-28, then Simla, Lahore, Palwal, Dehra Dun, 1928-29. First crossing of Laja La Western Tibet 1929. Officer-in-charge, British Trade Agency Gartok 1929-30. Judicial training Delhi 1930. Entered IPS 1930. Undersecretary to AGG Punjab States 1930. Assistant Commissioner Ajmer 1930-32. Assistant Political Agent Quetta 1933. Chief Minister Kelat 1933-36. Wakefield, Weightman *qv* and Hay *qv* were in Quetta during the great earthquake 30 May 1935. The three had been at dinner, and later that evening Wakefield's little daughter was killed and his wife injured. See *Past Imperative*. Also Jackson, *Thirty Seconds at Quetta*, 24-29. Political Officer Sadra 1937. Secretary to Resident Punjab States 1937-39. Service in Nabha 1939-41. Political Agent Kuwait 1941-42. With Tom Hickinbotham *qv* on circumnavigation of Warbah 1942. Political Agent Bahrain 1942-43. 'Mr. Wakefield at Bahrain was a first class square peg in a very important hexagonal hole. [See Chapter VIII.] He had no qualification for the post nor any liking for it, and realising this I opposed his appointment by every means in my power short of my resignation...He did not care for Arabs...Arabs who are a proud and sensitive race soon found how the land lay and let the Agency severely alone.' Charles Prior was admonished for this criticism by Caroe (11 January 1945), who with the Viceroy's approval suppressed it. IOR:R/1/4, Personal File. Chief Minister Rawa 1943-45. Deputy Secretary

Political Department 1946-47. CIE 1945. Baronet 1962. Medal Royal Humane Society for saving drowning man Chattokh Gorge, Kelat, 1935. Conservative MP West Derbyshire 1950-62. Assistant Whip 1954. Controller Royal Household 1958-59. Vice-Chamberlain 1959-60. Treasurer 1960-62. Commissioner and High Commissioner Malta 1962-65. Bath Club. Farmers Club. Wrote *Past Imperative: My Life in India 1927-47*, a fine account of life in the IPS. d. 14 January 1969.

WATTS, RALPH PONSONBY Acting Political Agent Kuwait 1934. b. 24 September 1892, Bareilly, India. Fourth surviving son and seventh of eight children of Col. John Briscoe Watts of Kingston nr. Taunton; Bengal Staff Corps. and 5th Reg. Bengal Cavalry, retired 17 December 1896; and Antoinette Helen Jackson. TAUNTON SCHOOL. Sandhurst. King's India Cadet 1910. Brother Edward Ponsonby Watts was also KIC. Oxford. Matriculated as 'non-collegiate student' 1912. 'Migrated' to Pembroke College 1913. Studied Persian. Exempted from further examinations under Military Decree and awarded BA 1916. His IPS application states he studied Persian 'as has always been my wish to enter the Political Department'. IOR:R/1/4/1313.1930 Pt.1. Hampshire Regiment. 2nd Lt. 1914. IA 1918. Assistant Instructor Machine Gun Corps Training Centre 1916-18. Watts served three years in the Gulf as Head of Intelligence. Applied to the IPS in 1918 and again in 1919. Entered IPS 1925. Assistant Magistrate Allahabad 1925. Political Officer Moradfabad 1925-26. First Assistant to Resident Baroda 1926-27. Secretary to Gulf Political Resident 1927-28. Vice-Consul Ahwaz 1928. Undersecretary to Resident Hyderabad 1930. Vice-Consul Kahgar 1930-31. Undersecretary to Gulf Resident 1933. Secretary to Gulf Resident 1934. Acting Political Agent Kuwait 1934. Secretary to Gulf Resident 1934-35. Political Agent Muscat 1935-38. Census Superintendent Indore 1939. Vice Consul Zahidan 1941. Consul-General Khorasan, Agent Nushki, and Commandant Chagai Levy Corps 1943-4. Retired 1944. IA pension.

WEIGHTMAN, HUGH Political Agent Bahrain, 1937-40. b. 29 November 1898. Son of William S. Weightman (broker). HYMER'S COLLEGE. RAF 1917-19. Corpus Christi College Cambridge BA. Entered ICS 1922. Assistant Commissioner Sibsagar, Jorhat, Golaghat, 1922-25. President of the Manikpur State Durbar 1925-26. Assistant Commissioner Golaghat 1926-27. Undersecretary Government of Assam 1927-29. Undersecretary to AGG Indore 1929. Married Margaret Elizabeth Agnes, daughter of R. Storry Dean, barrister and author. Entered IPS 1929. 'He shoots, but cannot play polo...'. IOR:Personal File, 2 January 1929. 'I should say he is not a bad fellow, but if we had anything like the old competition for the I.C.S. he would hardly catch the judge's eye. Hard up as we are, we might do worse.' *Ibid.*, 24 January 1929. Undersecretary to AGG Central India 1929-30. Assistant Political Agent Quetta 1930-32. Secretary to AGG Baluchistan 1932-35. Political Agent Kalat and Agent-in-charge the Bolan Pass 1935-37. Political Agent Bahrain 1937-40. 'He was also unpopular with the local British community who did not appreciate his de-haut-en-bas manner...He recommended a worthless creature as Defence Officer, who turned out to be not merely a drunkard but probably a pervert as well...I hope he will consider the award [CIE] as payment in advance and justify it by continued interest in Gulf affairs.' *Ibid.*, Geoffrey Prior. To this 'L' has written underneath (13 August 1941): 'I do not propose to waste my time in an attempt to purge Mr. Prior of his bumptiousness. I agree that the victims should be protected.' *Ibid.*, 13 August 1941. Acting Gulf Resident 1938. Deputy Secretary and Joint Secretary External Affairs Department 1940-44. Revenue and Judicial Commissioner Baluchistan 1944-46. Secretary External Affairs Department 1946-47. As Secretary for External Affairs in 1946-47, Hickinbotham worked with Wavell and Nehru and earned from Wavell the commendation: '...a clear head and much intelligence, ability and character.' *Ibid.*, 22 February 1947. Gold Kaisar-i-Hind 1935. CIE 1941. CSI 1946. Kt. 1947. RAF Club. Flyfishers Club. d. 28 October 1949.

WILSON, ARNOLD TALBOT Principal assistant to Percy Cox for many years. b. 18 July 1884. Son of Canon J.M. Wilson, second headmaster of Clifton, 1879-90. Mostyn House preparatory school. '...when A.G. Grenfell assumed control of Mostyn House in 1890 he was the fourth headmaster of a school of only twenty-eight boys. Within six years he had increased the number of pupils to 103...of the 115 boys who went to public schools from Mostyn House between 1890 and 1899, forty-four went to Shrewsbury, with the next highest number of only nine going to Clifton.' Leinster-Mackay, *Rise of the English Prep School*, 137. See *Ibid.*, 160-61. CLIFTON COLLEGE 1898-1902. Clifton brothers: Edward, Native Affairs Department, Rhodesia. Hugh, Assistant Master Rugby, killed in war 1915. Trenchard Fowle *qv* was in Brown's House with Wilson. Entering September 1898 with Wilson: Colin Sharp, Headmaster Abbotsholme (1927-46), and Bishop Gobat School Jerusalem. Contemporary (entered April 1898): Owen Tweedy, Assistant Oriental Secretary Cairo 1918-24. Sandhurst. King's Medal. Sword of Honour. Army 1903. 32nd Sikh Pioneers. Special duty Bakhtiari Oil Fields S. Persia 1907-1909. In March 1907 Wilson spent part of his leave visiting the Gulf, where he stayed with C.H.

Gabriel *qv* at Bandar Abbas: 'I already harboured the half-formed ambition to be one of their number: Sir Louis Dane, then Foreign Secretary [of GOI] had encouraged...if I could win my spurs in the field before and not after I joined the Department. I had no family connections, and very few relatives had ever served, in India: I could not hope, he said, to be nominated unless I had first done something which would give me a very strong claim.' *S.W. Persia: Letters and Diary of a Young Political Officer, 1907-1914*, 3.
Entered IPS 1910. Consul Arabistan 1909-11. Periods of special duty under orders of the Gulf Resident 1911. Special duty projected Mohammerah-Khurrambad Railway 1911. Special duty 39th (King George's Own) Central India Horse in Persia 1911-12. Second Assistant to Gulf Resident 1912-13. Special duty Kurdistan 1913. Deputy British Commissioner Turko-Persian Frontier Boundary Commission 1913-14 and Commissioner 1914. Assistant Political Officer Indian Expeditionary Force 1915-16. A turning point in Wilson's career was Birdwood's *qv* death in action while acting as Cox's assistant. Deputy Chief Political Officer Basra 1916-17. Deputy Civil Commissioner Baghdad and Officiating Civil Commissioner and Officiating Political Resident in the Persian Gulf 1918-20. Officiating Gulf Resident 1920.
Retired 1921. Married 1922 Rose Caroline, daughter of C.H. Ashton of Ellesmere and widow of Lt. Robin Carver RAF. One son. One daughter. Anglo-Persian Oil Co. 1921-32. Conservative MP for Hitchin 1933-40. Editor *19th Century & After* 1935-38. DSO 1916. CMG 1912. CIE 1917. CSI 1919. Kt. of Grace, Order of St. John of Jerusalem 1919. KCIE 1920. FRGS 1907. Proposed by G.E. Leachman. RCAS. RSA: Council, Burton Medal. Girls' Public Day School Trust. Rhodes Scholarship Trust. East India Club. 'I enjoyed being at the Club and meeting men from every part of the East. It was possible for a young officer like myself to meet there men who had served in the Indian Mutiny just fifty years earlier.' Marlowe, *Late Victorian*, 75. Athenaeum. United Service Club. Papers, major deposit, London Library. RGS: Journal S.W. Persia, 1911-12; papers relating to his *The Persian Gulf* (OUP 1928), misc. corr. Biography: John Marlowe, *Late Victorian*, Cresset Press, 1967. Marlowe has lengthy bibliography including Wilson's *Times* letters, 399-406. d. 31 May 1940, in combat as tail gunner, RAF.

WILSON, FREDERICK ALEXANDER Gulf Resident 1894-97. b. 12 June 1842. Son of A. Wilson, 'surgeon on Bengal establishment'. KING WILLIAM'S COLLEGE 1854-58. Cricket XI 1858. Wilson's application to Addiscombe (IOR:L/MIL/9/248, 'Cadet Papers') includes a recommendation signed by R. Dison, principal of King William's, stating he was a day pupil since August 1854. Addiscombe. Lt. Bengal Artillery 1860. Served Peshawar 1862. Bhutan Campaign 1864-65. Capture of Bala Stockade. ADC Lt-Governor Bengal 1866. Hazara Campaign 1868. Extra ADC Viceroy 1869. Guardian and Tutor Nawab of Jaora 1870. Tutor Maharaja of Mysore 1876-78. Acting Resident Hyderabad 1880. Agent and Superintendent Nizam of Hyderabad's Education 1881. Special duty Maharaja of Jeypore on tour 1881-82. Assigned ex-King of Oudh 1882-83. Political Agent Nepal 1883-84. Gulf Resident 1894-97. 'Better quarters were obtained for a mission house [in Bahrain]...through the kindly help of Colonel Wilson, of Bushire.' SLRCA: S.M. Zwemer, *Quarterly Field Report of the Arabian Mission*, January-March 1896, 6. Retired 1899.

WORTH, MEREDITH Political Agent Bahrain 1934. b. 3 December 1905. Son of W.C. Worth, Dillingshurst (tea planter, Ceylon). REPTON 1920. Corpus Christi College Cambridge. ICS 1928. Assistant Magistrate Chittagong, Hooghly, Darjeeling, 1928-30. Joint Magistrate Pargnas 1931-33. Entered IPS 1933. Used as reference G.F. Fisher, formerly headmaster of Repton and later Archbishop of Canterbury. Trade Agent Gyantse 1933. Gyantse is in Tibet halfway between Lhasa and Sikkim border. Following Lhasa Treaty of 1904 between Tibet and Britain, an IPS agent was stationed there. Assistant Political Agent Bahrain 1934-35. Officiating Agent Bahrain 1934. Assistant Political Agent Sibi 1935-36. Political Agent Sibi 1936. Assistant Commissioner Hazara 1937. Counsellor British Legation Kabul 1937. Assistant Commissioner Hazara 1937-38. Secretary to Resident Baroda 1938-39. Secretary to Resident West Indian States 1939-41. Secretary to Resident Rajputana 1941-44. Agent Orissa States 1944-45. Development Officer Baluchistan 1945-47. Subsequently in Department of External Affairs Australian Government. See Trench, *Viceroy's Agent*, 163-64.

A major purpose of this book is to create concern about saving the papers of the IPS officers. Anyone with papers should consider placing them in the collection of St. Antony's College at Oxford or in the India Office Library. It is also hoped that the book will create an interest in research in various aspects of Gulf history. As frequently mentioned in these pages, there are many directions in which further inquiries could be made. A priority is to do further research into family backgrounds. This is in hopes of locating papers. It also tests out the observation that 'The Victorians used the public schools to remove the sons of tradesmen from the taint of trade: and it is still often true,' as G.K. Chesterton put it, that 'the public schools are not for the sons of gentlemen, they're for the fathers of gentlemen.'[20]

There is almost no limit to investigations that can be carried out into the connections that were forged at school and in the club, and of the peculiar *fuglemen* that appear as mentors in more than one Gulf officer's life. For example, Lord Lloyd was a hovering presence in the Gulf, first visiting in 1907 and being involved at a distance in the late 1930s when as head of the British Council he supported the establishment of a public school in Bahrain.[21] *Felix opportunitate mortis suae.* Headmasters, housemasters, and peripatetic masters are a good example. What the biographies suggest by repeated instances of the cross-infections of family, club, and school, is that the IPS in the Gulf were a community. This raises as many questions as it solves:

> We know very little about how ideas are formed in a community. We do not know why something that has often been said before will suddenly catch on, or why both events and opinions seem to remain static for a long time, and suddenly begin to move, and keep on moving. Most mysterious of all is how a consensus of opinion forms, and why it takes the shape it does. We observe the process, but its aetiology escapes us, and prediction is wholly beyond our powers.[22]

Arnold Galloway's remark that 'I was thought of as a Gulfite, both by myself and the Government of India' rings true. The typical Gulfite had relatives who had served in India, was educated at public school, belonged to a London club, had served in an Indian regiment, and possibly was a Mason. What being ruled by a member of this coterie meant for the Arabs is fundamental to Gulf history. The distractions of the recent invasions of the Gulf by Iraqis and Americans should not take away attention from the more profound and more important effects of the invasion by the British Empire.[23]

> *Who's Who started in 1849 as a sparse list of eminent people – judges, peers, archbishops, generals, members of the House of Commons – revealing only their names, date of birth, rank, title, and heir. In 1896 it was bought by its current publisher, A & C Black. In 1897, details of education, publications and recreations were added, a format which has remained unchanged for nearly a century...However, recreations are subject to the influences of time and fashion and have changed enormously over the years. Whereas Mary Archer self-consciously writes in the 1990 edition that her favourite recreation is 'picking up litter,' in 1897 Sir James Frankfort Manners Browne spoke of enjoying 'all kind of field sports' and wrote with pride that he 'hunted the buffalo on the plain of North America.' It would take a brave man to write that now. – The Financial Times*, 1990.

NOTES

1. Kipling, *Kim*, 191.
2. See Rehbock, 'Prosopography?', 117.
3. 'To escape this ennui – prosopographical paralysis, if a clinical term is needed – the prosopographer is best advised to alternate between his central project, and the numerous smaller tasks that spin off from the centre.' *Ibid.*, 120.
4. Bruce Mazlish, *James and John Stuart Mill: Father and Son in the Nineteenth Century*, Hutchinson, 1975, 144.
5. Spangenberg, *British Bureaucracy in India*, 17.
6. *Ibid.*, 20-21.
7. *Ibid.*, 21.
8. A.A. Mains, 'The Expansion of the Infantry of the Indian Army During World War I', *Journal of the Society for Army Historical Research*, Vol.LXVII, No.271, 203-206.
9. Harold E. Raugh, 'Wavell in the Middle East: A Study in Magnanimity', *Indo-British Review*, Vol.XIII, No.2, July-December 1987, 33.
10. Hugh Tinker, 'The Diary of a Military and Civil Nobody', *Indo-British Review*, Vol.XIII, No.2, July-December 1987, 23.
11. Anerjee, *Calcutta 200 Years*, 155.
12. Arlen Harris, 'Duels in the Crown', *Tatler*, Vol.284, No.3, March 1989, 132.
13. *Ibid.*
14. *Medal News*, March 1990, 19-21.
15. Corfield, *The Princely India I Knew*, 88.
16. J.H.B. Bedells, *The British Honours System*, The Heraldry Society, 1974, 8-9.
17. *Ibid.*, 11-12.
18. See *Ibid.*, 21-22.
19. Spangenberg, *British Bureaucracy in India*, 257.
20. Anthony Sampson, *The New Anatomy of Britain*, rev. ed., Hodder and Stoughton, 1983, 132.
21. See John Charmley, *Lord Lloyd and the Decline of the British Empire*, Weidenfeld and Nicolson, 1987.
22. Daniel, *The Cultural Barrier*, 88.
23. This is notwithstanding the detective work necessary to find out what happened behind the scenes, a problem similarly true today. 'Shortly after World War I began in 1914, Britain dispatched its 12th Division from India to occupy Iraq's southern port of Basra...To gain Arab support, as Lawrence wrote, "our cabinet had offered, through (British diplomat) Sir Henry McMahon, to support the establishment of native governments in parts of Syria and Mesopotamia"...Actually, as Lawrence and others recorded, France, Britain, and Russia agreed to annex some areas promised to the Arabs or Jews (Palestine, Lebanon, Syria, Iraq) and to set up their respective spheres of influence throughout the region...In the present war, the United States has pasted together an anti-Saddam coalition. What promises, or in other cases what cash payments have induced as mixed a group as Israel, Egypt, Syria, Turkey, Morocco, and Saudi Arabia to co-operate are only partly known.' *Guardian Weekly*, 3 March 1991.

X

'THAT WAS THAT'

There was no doubt that the Resident considered himself, and was considered, the grandest of all grand people in the Gulf. – John Bulloch, *The Persian Gulf Unveiled*, 1984.

Those revered gentlemen...were as much creatures of their times as we are. They firmly believed that what was good enough for them was the best for those in their charge. – Hugh Gantzer, on the founders, 125th *Anniversary of The Lawrence School*, Lovedale, India, 1984.

It was like having reasonably well-disposed caretakers in the house. It was kept in order, not because it was particularly cherished, but because if neglected a squatter might move in. The owners were allowed the use of the basement, and occasionally invited upstairs to tea, but for the most part they were left alone to live their own lives, provided they did not make a row, or interfere in any way with the caretakers' arrangements. – Molly Izzard, *The Gulf*, 1979.

The Arabs, disposed to be ultra-suspicious about Western intentions, will find much in the history of the British in the Gulf to be suspicious about. The archives provide plenty of ammunition for those who would question Imperial motives. Worried about Shaikh Abdullah of Qatar, who was suspected of wanting an Iraqi 'adviser', Charles Prior wrote to Olaf Caroe in August 1941:

> Our position in these waters depends, however, not so much on our Treaties as upon the good-will of the Arab Rulers and prestige and power of our Political Officers. Daly [*Clive Kirkpatrick Daly, Bahrain Agent 1921-6*], for example, was able in a few years to turn Bahrain into more of a British protectorate than the average Indian State without much assistance from the Treaty position or the Residency or anyone else. Similarly, an incompetent officer ignorant of Arab ways and mentality could lose us our position with almost equal rapidity, in fact I have very often wondered how far we should be able to maintain our position if it was seriously challenged by any State which desired, for example, an *Anschluss* with Saudi Arabia or Iraq.[1]

The British in the Gulf concentrated their attention on those they fancied were the élite. Although this was proved a successful short term strategy, evidence has mounted that the durbars and decorations were not an adequate preparation for the responsibilities of independence. Even during World War II, American espionage reports gave a less happy impression of the political situation than did British reports.

The Americans by then had established intelligence operations at Aden, Bahrain, and Basra. The British were suspicious of the explanations offered for this presence. In Bahrain the operation was part of a procurement agency for American Navy ships. Declassification and study of the despatches now can give a different picture of the Gulf from what the IPS reported. In 1944 the American intelligence officer at Basra visited Kuwait and wrote:

> An audience was had with Shaikh Ahmed Al-Jabir As-Subah [*sic*], Ruler of Kuwait, who responded, through an interpreter, to some pleasantry about his attractive country that 'It was not his country but belonged to the British and Americans.' This was said without any apparent bitterness and a few minutes later during the conversation, he added in what seemed to be a serious manner, that the 'door of Kuwait was always open to the Americans' and, with a glance toward a British Captain among the visitors, he further stated that 'he did not say that [about] the British because it was unnecessary for one to open the door when the party was already in the house.'[2]

Prior, who was Resident from 1939 to 1946, nursed dark opinions of invading Yankees. He was embarrassed at having to work with them because of the war, and complained, '...Bahrain has already become far too Americanised, and if we start introducing them into the Bahrain Administration there will be nothing left but to invite them to assume a Mandate over Bahrain.'[3] His prejudices were confirmed when he hosted a lawn party to raise money for purchasing fighter aircraft for Britain and the American guests stole his forks and spoons for souvenirs.[4]

Given Prior's implacably Imperial stance, it is not surprising that during his administration the plans for a proper public school serving the Gulf élite came to a head. The idea had arisen in 1938 at the end of Trenchard Fowle's regime as Resident, but the pot boiled when in February 1941 the British Council sent their Cairo-based educational representative, C.A.F. Dundas, on a tour of the Gulf. Dundas reported on the reasons for his visit:

> For several years past the Political Resident in the Persian Gulf has felt increasing uneasiness at the extent to which boys from the Gulf area have been absorbing anti-British political theories by attending education institutions in Iraq and Syria. There is no doubt that the Government of Iraq is alive to the possibilities of 'infecting' students from the Gulf (particularly Kuwait) and in many cases free places have been found in Iraqi institutions for boys from the Arab coast between Kuwait and Muscat.[5]

What Dundas wanted was a public school on thoroughly English lines, with entry controlled by the Resident. The Gulf's numerous local schools, mostly meeting in mosques, were of no interest to him. Instead of trying to build up the already existing system, he opted for an elaborate scheme whereby a sizable portion of the Gulf's tiny education budget would have been devoted to a school for shaikhs.

The effect would have been similar to what has occurred in England, where public schools enjoyed endowments diverted to them that were earmarked for local education. The English public schools never were completely financed privately. They received hidden subsidies because of their charitable and tax exempt status, and direct subsidies for specific building projects and activities like the cadet corps. The government paid tuitions of children whose parents were in the colonial service and diplomatic corps. The whole of the British population supported, albeit involuntarily and unknowingly, schools that their children had no chance of attending. A reminder of the diversion of endowments are the 'conscience' schools that were started by governors when complaints about the class pretensions of the public schools grew too loud. In Harrow, local people complained so much about being excluded that in 1874 the governors felt obliged to found the Lower School of John Lyon. Dulwich, Rugby, Tonbridge, and other foundations took similar action. (Ironically, schools such as John Lyon became in time public schools, and so in a number of instances the working class found itself *twice* denied the education that benefactors had intended that they have.)

Rejecting pleas to upgrade the existing mosque schools, which were open to everybody, Dundas pushed for a public school for the Gulf that would take a substantial part of the region's meagre resources: 'The whole could be housed in fine buildings with adequate grounds and playing fields which would not only be a draw for boys from outside, but a cause of satisfaction and pride to Bahrainis.'[6] The school was to have boarding accommodation for more than 195 boys and classrooms for 500. The senior staff of course would be British.[7] Dundas wanted the school called the *Shaikh Hamad School*, in honour of the Bahraini Amir...and in anticipation of the financial contribution that could be expected in pleasure over such an honour. There was to be a house system and emphasis would be on the boarding side, because in Dundas' opinion: 'It might be considered advisable to allow Bahraini boys to attend the junior school as day boys, *but their character training and probably the standard of work would suffer.*'[8]

Prior was deeply involved in these discussions, which concentrated on the school's potential from both an educational and political position. He explained to Dundas:

> As you know, we are greatly concerned with the strategic advantages of a quiet pied-à-terre here, and anything that disturbed the political atmosphere would be contrary to our interests. We therefore have to consider any proposals from the political as well as the educational point of view...It appears to be a universal law in the East that the unemployed student is the normal focus for political agitation, and there have already been signs of this in Bahrain and Kuwait. We should therefore consider closely the probable sources of employment open to these students and make our plans accordingly...[9]

In reply, Dundas reassured him of the positive political results to be expected of starting 'Gulf College'. It would be, he suggested, a welcome alternative to Iraqi schools that planted anti-British ideas, and 'Boys who have spent 3 to 8 years at the Gulf College would be much less prone to unfavourable influences in Iraq or elsewhere than they are at present.'

Furthermore, a real public school '...would help in extending British influence and ideas amongst the sons of important residents in the Persian Gulf area.' Dundas was convinced that the school would be a good investment for the Residency. The obvious route for education in the Gulf in his opinion was to establish an institution which '...would provide a sound, liberal education under British influence'.[10]

Dundas then pressured Alban, the Bahrain Political Agent, to get a 'royal' charter from Shaikh Hamad. For the school's constitution he put forward an agreement similar to one that the British Council had attempted to negotiate with the Government of Iraq in establishing King Faisal College in Baghdad. Unfortunately the war was intruding more and more into Gulf affairs. The Italians had carried out a daring bombing raid on Bahrain in 1940, and Axis submarine attacks were creating supply problems. Prior began to have second thoughts about priorities, and in May 1941 he decided to postpone action indefinitely.[11] The incident illustrates how the British sought to encourage the development of a shaikhy class, and feared Iraqi 'radicalism'.

Revived hopes for the school at the end of the war came to naught, because with the independence of India in August 1947, the Indian Political Service itself came to an abrupt end. The necessity of a transition found the Gulf with no ready plan of action, not just as far as education but as far as continuing British administration. The Gulf Resident at the time, Rupert Hay, had indicated his sense of what came first on the agenda when he wrote to the India Office in May 1947 about preserving the accoutrements of his status after the change. 'The Political Resident with his charge ranks senior to a full General' he fretfully reminded London, and added that the Political Agents were senior to Lt. Colonels. Would this seniority be maintained? There was the worrisome matter of what flag to fly: 'I do not think the Union Viceroy should continue to be flown after 1st April 1948.'[12]

The Resident's flag was the same flag flown by the Viceroy, prominently displaying the badge of Order of the Star of India in the centre of the Union Jack. Hay observed regretfully that it would have to go. There would be no more Knights Grand Cross of the Star of India, and indeed no more Viceroys. Inevitably being jettisoned as well was the guide to the Viceregal social ladder, the cherished *Warrant of Precedence* which guaranteed that lighthouse superintendents, Political Residents, and shaikhs would be properly ordered at any function. 'The refinements of this hierarchical order, the groupings and classifications, ' it was noted by a critic, 'proliferate to the point of Gilbertian incredibility...'.[13]

What did not disappear in 1947 were the divisions which the IPS had produced amongst the Arabs. These remained apparent in 1990 when the Iraqis entered Kuwait. The Gulf was far poorer in opportunities for Western cultural hegemony than Egypt, but Hill shared in the divisiveness induced by Orientalism: 'The absolute opposition between the order of the modern West and the awkwardness and disorder of the East was not only found in Europe, but began to repeat itself in Egyptian scholarship and popular literature, just as it was replicated in colonial cities. Through its textbooks, school teachers, universities, newspapers, novels and magazines, the colonial order was able to penetrate and colonise local discourse.'[14] The Gulf was no exception.

If the shaikhdoms had been short on opportunities for cultural invasion compared with Egypt or India, the IPS nevertheless kept to the very end a hold over which newspapers and magazines were read and what transpired in the classroom. Officers agreed with the view that the British throughout the Middle East held to, that schools were where revolt might start – noting that the Muslim Brotherhood leaders opposed to British rule in Egypt 'were almost invariably school teachers.'[15] Present inhabitants of the Gulf, expatriate or Arab, who find the censorship irritating and complain about the books and journals that the postal services sequester should reflect that this is a tradition inherited from the British. Arnold P. Kaminsky has summarized the situation in an *Indo-British Review* article (Vol.XV, No.1), entitled 'Managing the News Under the Raj', offering evidence of the 'guidance' that the British exercised over films. *King of the Khyber Pass* was banned from the Indian Empire until references to 'hilarious tight Britons' were eliminated. *Charge of the Light Brigade* was prohibited because of scenes of British soldiers dying, and *The Relief of Lucknow* proscribed for sympathetically portraying mutineers. The pettiness that characterized this recalls J.A. Hobson's strident opinion in *Imperialism*:

> Imperialism is a depraved choice of national life, imposed by self-seeking interests which appeal to the lusts of quantitative acquisitiveness and of forceful domination surviving in a nation from early centuries of animal struggle for existence. Its adoption as a policy implies a deliberate renunciation of the cultivation of the higher inner qualities which for a nation as for an individual constitutes the ascendancy of reason over brute impulse. It is the besetting sin of all successful States, and its penalty is unalterable in the order of nature.[16]

On the Other Hand

On the other hand, the IPS did keep the peace in the Gulf for generations, and by that alone must be reckoned successful. This was no small achievement, and looks impressive in the light of the region's present problems. The Residents were not subject to the nervous solecisms of American diplomacy that have replaced the Imperial confidence. They provided order and discipline. Part of their success can be attributed to the ability they learned at public school to exact respect through ritualism.

To understand the Gulf today, it is necessary to understand the British era. Much research remains to be done. The problem must partly be approached by following the lives of the IPS officers after they retired and were able to speak more candidly. Those in Parliament, as MPs in the case of Lewis Pelly, Edward Wakefield, and Arnold Wilson, or in the Lords in the case of Robert Hamilton, are an excellent example. Describing Arnold Wilson, J.H. Grainger writes:

> Arnold Wilson, schooled in the Indian Army and then the Political Service in India, Persia and Mesopotamia, became, as a Member of Parliament in the 1930s, a notable public patriot, Milnerite and Miltonic, yet an Erastian Anglican, a dedicated Imperialist, strongly averse to Continental entanglements. He was an advocate of concentrated national authority in

all spheres, of national self-sufficiency, of a National Political party, of compulsory National Service and of national insurance and welfare – to improve the human resources of the young *patria* which he considered he knew at first hand by virtue of the 'Cobbett-like peregrinations and conversations' throughout the country record in his *Walks and Talks* books.[17]

Big Frogs and a Small Pond

The Gulf and its Residents is also the story of big frogs in a small pond. Sparsely populated and desperately poor until the oil bonanza, it could hardly contain the ambitions of such as Cox or Wilson. The shaikhdoms were not large enough looms on which to weave the intricate patterns that their IPS colleagues did in India – hence the Mesopotamian incursions.

Still, the IPS imposed their patterns wherever they went, and thanks to the Residents the public school was part of the *mysterium magnum* of Gulf administration no less than elsewhere. The Arabs had to put up with the way old boys went through life immersed in a miasma of unreality, men whose tribalism originated in Westminster or Winchester cloisters:

> The virtues and characteristics of the Imperial archetype are the virtues and characteristics bred into him by his public school. The male camaraderie and the subordinate role of women reflects the all-male environment of the public schools. Most significant of all, all the relationships in the Imperial structure, between masters and servants, officers and men, Imperial administrators and naïve subjects, can be paraphrased into an identical headmaster-pupil relationship along the lines of the public school. In the last resort, the Empire was Eton and Harrow writ large.[18]

Curiously, this old school tie élite who were so proud of never shirking *responsibility* could be guilty of what Gramsci called *ponziopilatismo,* the attitude of Pontius Pilate. Social development in the Gulf got short shrift in what can be called the Billy Bunter period, between 1920 and 1947. The region was ill-prepared for the post-war period partly because the IPS put much effort into the maintenance of ritual illusions, and less into practical matters.

Though criticism must be made, the aim in these pages is not to poke fun at the Raj, but to scrutinize manifestations of its rule and generate discussion about its lasting effects. This has been a discussion of ambiguities rather than a savaging of a phenomenology, one made in light of the recent Gulf war.

There have been claims about the similarities between public school men and shaikhs, and they may be attributed to the influence that the IPS had on the Arabs – not to inherent affinities. Professor Donald Leinster-Mackay remarked in *The Educational World of Edward Thring* how myopic it was to take a limited historical or political view of public school influence, because it was an influence felt throughout the English-speaking world. So it was.

The old boys can be remembered as masters of the *coup de théâtre*. This book has only offered a *tour d'horizon* of the influence rather than a *tour du monde,* but the IPS cannot be dismissed without acknowledging that it included remarkable men. The squire hoped that Rugby would make Tom Brown a gentleman. In ways we still only partly understand, it did.

The Foreign Office Takes Over

The reader may be unfamiliar with the events following World War II, and so, briefly to bring the account from the end of the Indian Empire to the very present, it is useful to recall the career of Rupert Hay. Hay was not only the last IPS Resident (1946-47), but he was the only Commonwealth Office Resident and first Foreign Office Resident (1948-53). His was the unenviable job of handling confusing signals from India and Whitehall, but as a young man he had been an assistant to Arnold Wilson and so there was a continuity to administration. His relationship to the Foreign Office was happier than that of Arthur Galloway's; and Galloway was bitterly disappointed in his expectations of being appointed Resident.

For the IPS itself, there was absolutely no prospect of continuation after Indian independence. Its bridges had been burnt long before. In 1934, after a few Indians acquired seniority in the IPS, J.C. Walton of the India Office had written in concern to H.A.F. Metcalfe, the Foreign Secretary of the Government of India: 'We appreciate the delicacy of the position and the fact that there cannot be any firm *official* understanding to the effect. But we shall quite appreciate the co-operation of the Government of India in ensuring that postings to the Gulf continue to be from the European members of the Department only.'[19] A free India would have its own diplomatic corps, and the British could hardly leave the Gulf in Indian hands. The IPS was not like the ICS, a service which had managed to change with the times and was sufficiently Indianized to make the transition to serving a free India. The IPS, as the Viceregal élite, were viewed by friend and foe as arch Imperialists. Sir John Glubb had compared Percy Cox to Cecil Rhodes, David Livingstone, and Rajah Brooke – hardly names likely to inspire confidence in native nationalists.

Yet as late as 1946, recruitment for the Indian services continued.[20] Although the sword of Damocles was descending, the IPS persisted in its last hours to exercise a firm and petty hand over details in the shaikhdoms. Hay was interested in such niceties as whether in the future the Agents would have their gun salutes reduced to seven, which regrettably would be the same as the shaikhs of Kuwait and Bahrain. Nor was any wayward Arab youth going to take advantage of the confusion and go off to a school which did not meet Hay's standards. Only a month after becoming Resident, in November 1946, he characteristically wrote to M.O. Tandy, the Kuwait Political Agent (1945-46): 'I consider it most desirable that if any young man from the Gulf Shaikhdoms wishes to go to the United Kingdom for education he or his parents should consult the Political Agent first...'[21]

The IPS nurtured until the bitter end doubts about the Americans, whom generations of Gulf Residents had regarded suspiciously. When an American doctor wanted a visa for the Emirates, Hay procrastinated for months: 'My idea was to try to get some hold over him.'[22] He thought he might find ways to 'enable us to work ourselves into a position of controlling to some extent the activities of the Mission.'[23] Though he conceded the effectiveness of American hospitals and schools and acknowledged the humanitarianism which brought them to the Gulf, they represented to him (in a phrase that other Residents had also used) the 'thin end of the wedge'.[24]

The point to be emphasized is that Rupert Hay did not envisage the British leaving the Gulf when the IPS did. Nor did they. The Gulf after 1947 became the Indian Empire's last redoubt, just as Goa was Portuguese India's solitary vestige, or Pondicherry was the tag-end of French India. British control continued for a remarkably long time considering the nationalist ferment elsewhere in the world. Kuwait gained independence in 1961, and Bahrain, the Emirates and Qatar only in 1971. Something of the Raj remained until then, although the atmosphere was hardly the same as under the IPS. Something remains to this day, and in respects the Gulf shaikhs are the last maharajahs. The British during the 1980s did their best to cultivate relationships based on the affinities between this Gulf élite and themselves. Visits by the British royal family were an important part of this effort at restoring an influence which for a time had ebbed.

For post-war administrators, a significant problem was that the fabled aplomb was missing from British domestic life. Home problems preoccupied post-war Britain. The arguments that had been made by men such as Arnold Wilson for the socio-political necessity of Imperialism were not so much defeated as temporarily replaced by preoccupations with internal British social issues. This was reflected in a conciliatory colonial 'do-goodism'. Arabs were no longer to be treated 'as if they were naughty boys at a British public school'.[25]

The efforts at reform cannot be regretted, but the loss of panache can be. Nor did the new emphasis on 'development' succeed in building a democratic and lasting political order. The IPS's Foreign Office successors were no more successful in resolving the vexing questions of social justice and political legitimacy in Arabia than was officialdom in England in coping with intramural problems during the same time. In the Gulf, the years after the war were not used judiciously. This owed something to the abruptness of the IPS departure. Mountbatten became Viceroy in February 1947 and hastily announced British withdrawal from India in August. It was only on July 16th that Galloway, who was acting Resident while Hay was away, received the short telegram[26] that Foreign Office contracts would be offered to Hay, and to Pelly at Bahrain, Tandy (who was acting as Hay's secretary in the Residency), and to Rance, the Bahrain Assistant PA. The end was signalled in August when the Resident's Indian troops quietly disappeared, replaced by British soldiers.[27] At midnight on August 14, 1947, the IPS was disbanded.[28]

The Foreign Office men, an old Gulf hand later complained, spent their time 'wondering whether after a year or two they would be sent to Paris, Prague or Nicaragua'.[29] With no sense of irony, Sir Charles Belgrave testily complained that the Foreign Office chaps were '...interfering in internal affairs only when it suits them, without giving the people of the Gulf any of the real advantages of *British* rule.'[30]

There was never any affection between the IPS and the Foreign Office, which had begrudged the IPS its Viceregal perquisites and resented competing with it in Persia. In retrospect, Arnold Galloway recalled this longstanding dispute between the two services and the muddle in post war administration, and thought that there was '...a strong feeling in the F.O. that P.R.S were a thorn in the flesh.' About the unceremonious exit of the IPS, he remarked that he and the other IPS officers had a phase-out plan 'on the tapis' but that in the rush it was brushed aside by Mountbatten – 'A fine sailor but bound by the clock.' He felt strongly that if Wavell had continued as Viceroy, and if Olaf Caroe had not been shifted from his job as Foreign Secretary and head of the Political Department to being the Governor of the North-West Frontier Province, '...things might have been different. Though one must face facts, the Home Government decided on a date and that was nearly kept, despite anything British or Indian individuals might say.'[31] (Caroe might have agreed, because his tenure as Governor brought him into collision with Nehru, who during an October 1946 visit to the Province blamed Caroe's hostility towards Hinduism and pro-Islamic feelings for stonings and demonstrations against the Congress Party. The consequence, according to Philip Ziegler in his biography *Mountbatten*, was that the Viceroy had to let Caroe go.)

As mentioned, Galloway was slated to be Resident, but realized he was suspect in the Foreign Office as a man known as a real 'Gulfite'. He had already been Acting Resident on several occasions. He recalled: 'I was at least fully qualified and had two first interpreterships in Persian and Arabic and Hay was blank of such knowledge.' Hay was regarded as more amenable to the Foreign Office takeover, and the British Ambassador in Tehran became strangely unco-operative about getting Galloway the Persian *exequator* or accreditation as Consul General which went with the job of being Resident. His Gulf appointment was abruptly terminated while he was in England on leave: 'I received a letter with a cheque and that was that.' Forty-one years later, he looked back with humour: 'I am still alive while all the other chief actors are having to keep going with a pair of wings or be frizzed up!!!'[32] He continued until his death in 1988 to be remarkably active and insightful, a Gulfite born during the reign of Queen Victoria who lived to see the oil boom, but thankfully not Kuwait's destruction.

The Faces of Inequality

The IPS in the Gulf was neither the first nor would be the last example of the legitimizing of a not-so-ancient *ancien régime* with ritual. Nor was the Gulf the only place where ritual was becoming a power unto itself, cherished as much for its own sake as for any ulterior goals. The ritual phenomenon, however, has often gone neglected as far as the connection between the public schools and the Empire. In fact, for many years the British Left accepted ritualism docilely and included fervent monarchists and Imperialists as did the Right. Ritualism, whether in England or the Gulf sustained various presumptions. One was that people were content with the *status quo* and that there was an underclass that enjoyed being 'cheerful servants'. Another presumption held was that the 'natives' didn't care about development. As far as the Gulf, while at the time that may have had an element of truth, it is hardly the whole story. The Arab expectations before 1947 were far different from later ones, and Residents were given little reason to doubt the romantic views that they cherished about Arabia. In consequence, they produced stirring accounts of bedouin life, but few social initiatives. This was true particularly in education.

For Britain, the period 1858-1947 saw the formalization of values, taboos, and beliefs on Imperial lines: in short, ritualization. As far as the Gulf was concerned, this process depended for its implementation on a handful of IPS officers who frequently made statements about non-interference,[33] but actually interfered as they wished. Their views on leadership were 'by rote and with rod',[34] *and* with *ritual*. They coroneted shaikhy dynasties of varying legitimacy, and in so doing ignored the Gulf's pluralism. They did the job well. In 1947 the maharajahs, nawabs and nizams lost their power and eventually became plain misters, but the shaikhs to this day remain shaikhs. That they owe to the Indian Political Service. Kuwait's amir is a closet Indian rajah.

British policy in the Middle East after World War II is the more understandable when the emotional importance of the area to a select coterie of old boys is taken into account. The Suez debacle should be seen in that perspective. The public school old boys in Eden's cabinet had sentimental feelings about the region that others did not have, and which obviously President Eisenhower lacked. For the Arabs, the replacement of the IPS did not mean that after 1947 there was less interference in their affairs. Far from it, and between 1947 and 1971 the story is as interesting and contentious as during 1858-1947. That must be another story.

Professor Donald Leinster-Mackay remarks that, 'It is one of the ironies of the history of the English public school that Haileybury, founded to provide recruits for service in India four years after the East India College closed in 1858, should have as one of its most famous old boys, if not *the* most famous old boy, Earl Attlee. As Prime Minister in 1947, Attlee presided over (*pace* Lord Mountbatten) the granting of independence to India and Pakistan.'[35] The IPS, which had put tremendous emphasis on ceremonious arrivals and departures, hastily packed its bags and unceremoniously disappeared. The service's tradition had sprung from the rituals of Empire, and could not survive the end of that mythology.[36] The 'Gulfite' was the quintessential Raj. When the Raj's day ended, his did.

The legacy of the Raj in the Gulf has not been prominently incorporated into contemporary Gulf history. Final judgement is many monographs away, but no amount of burrowing in the records is likely to change the conclusion that the British bequest was a strange and contradictory one as far as political maturity was concerned. There is ample evidence in the IPS record of what has been called the unconscious deceit of the average British gentleman, a failure to connect the abstract principle with the tangible act, to see what is truly real in human affairs'.[37] Writing about Sir Charles Belgrave, an observer noted that 'Belgrave is one of the old school and at heart does not like to see the Bahreines [*sic*] become educated. It is very doubtful, so long as he is Financial Adviser, whether the Shaikh's expenditures on education will be increased.'[39] Belgrave himself reflected at the end of a lifetime of advising the

Bahraini 'royal family': 'I suppose I expected too much from the schools and was inclined to compare them with public schools in England, for I must confess that I found the results were disappointing.'[39] He had not built many schools in Bahrain with which any comparison could be made, but he was right about the disappointing results of his labours. In time the visible signs of British rule faded. In Bahrain the streets were renamed. Prior Road became Kahlifa Road. Belgrave Road is Shaikh Isa. But it would take more than renaming streets to erase the British influence on the Gulf.[40]

It will be recalled how in Rudyard Kipling's story 'The Man Who Would Be King', two men by virtue of their Masonic jewellery and secret recognition signs are able to bamboozle a tribe into accepting them as gods, descendants of Alexander the Great. Inevitably the subterfuge is revealed, and perhaps Kipling shows less concern with the fraudulence than the ineptitude.[41] The hasty departure of the IPS from the Gulf is a similar case of a rather gauche end to a long ceremonial reign. The consequences still reign.

Vestiges of the Raj

Why did so little happen in the way of social progress in the Gulf during the period from 1945 to the 1970s? As the oil money began to come in, why was there so little done in the way of social development? This is a question that those who have worked in the Gulf in later years have often asked, because the lack of education and other necessities made the task of building a society all the more difficult in the 1980s. An explanation, though not the only explanation, is that the Gulf after World War II should be considered as the final gasp of British India. The rituals of the Raj linger yet. As already mentioned, post-war visitors noted that the Foreign Office Residents and Agents still held durbars and had garden parties to mark the proclamation of Queen Victoria as Empress of India.

With India free, the *raison d'être* of the British presence was gone. Protecting supply lines had been the dominant rationale. Now, with domestic problems preoccupying Whitehall and a major purpose rendered moot, the last Residents and Agents had a frustrated air. They did not preside over a beehive of development. The peculiar treaty situation which cut the Gulf states off from the rest of the world fossilized Gulf society as it was when Pelly and Ross encountered it. *This was not altogether unwelcome to the shaikhs.*

In other parts of Asia and Africa, larger areas had been annexed as colonies, been given legislative councils and constitutions, and seen those toppled who in their day were more powerful than the Gulf rulers. The long hiatus of British rule encouraged absolute monarchies, and the shaikhs knew this.

The purported IPS policy of *laissez faire* towards internal Gulf affairs was actually a policy of selective intervention and left the Gulf states less prepared to meet the future than possessions for which Britain claimed direct responsibility. Dennis Hawley concluded: 'If interest in internal affairs could have been shown earlier, the task of reconciling twentieth-century technology with patriarchal social structures would not have been so great.'[42]

The English public schools played a part in all of this,[43] for because of their schooling the British always had feelings about Arabia that other nations did

Plate 27: (previous page) Folk musicians in the Gulf. Indian and African influences on the Gulf are enormous.

Plate 28: (above) The proposed Royal Panopticon, Leicester Square, London (from *The Illustrated London News*, 1852). Originally an institute of popular education, it became a music hall and was pulled down in 1936 for the Odeon Cinema.

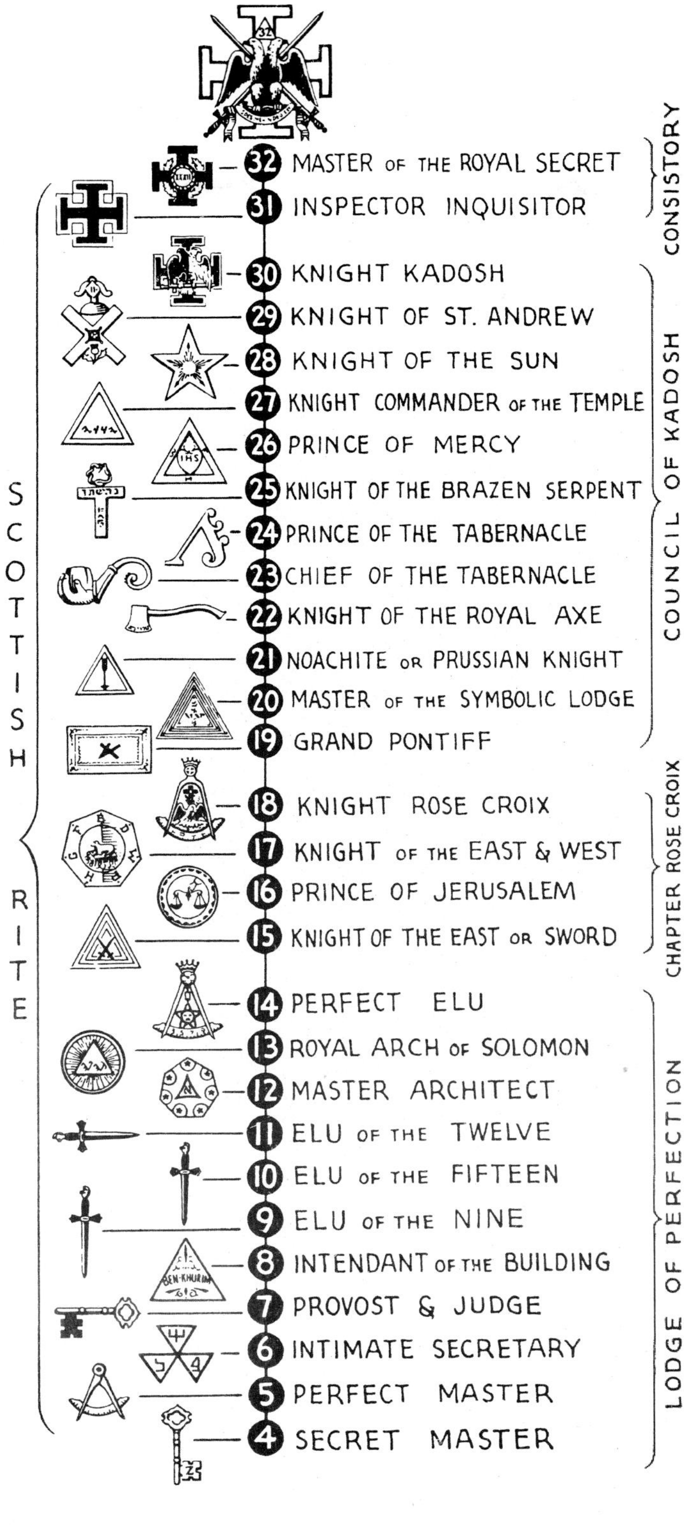

Plate 29: The Masonic Thirty-three Degrees. The first three are Entered Apprentice, Fellowcraft, and Master Mason.

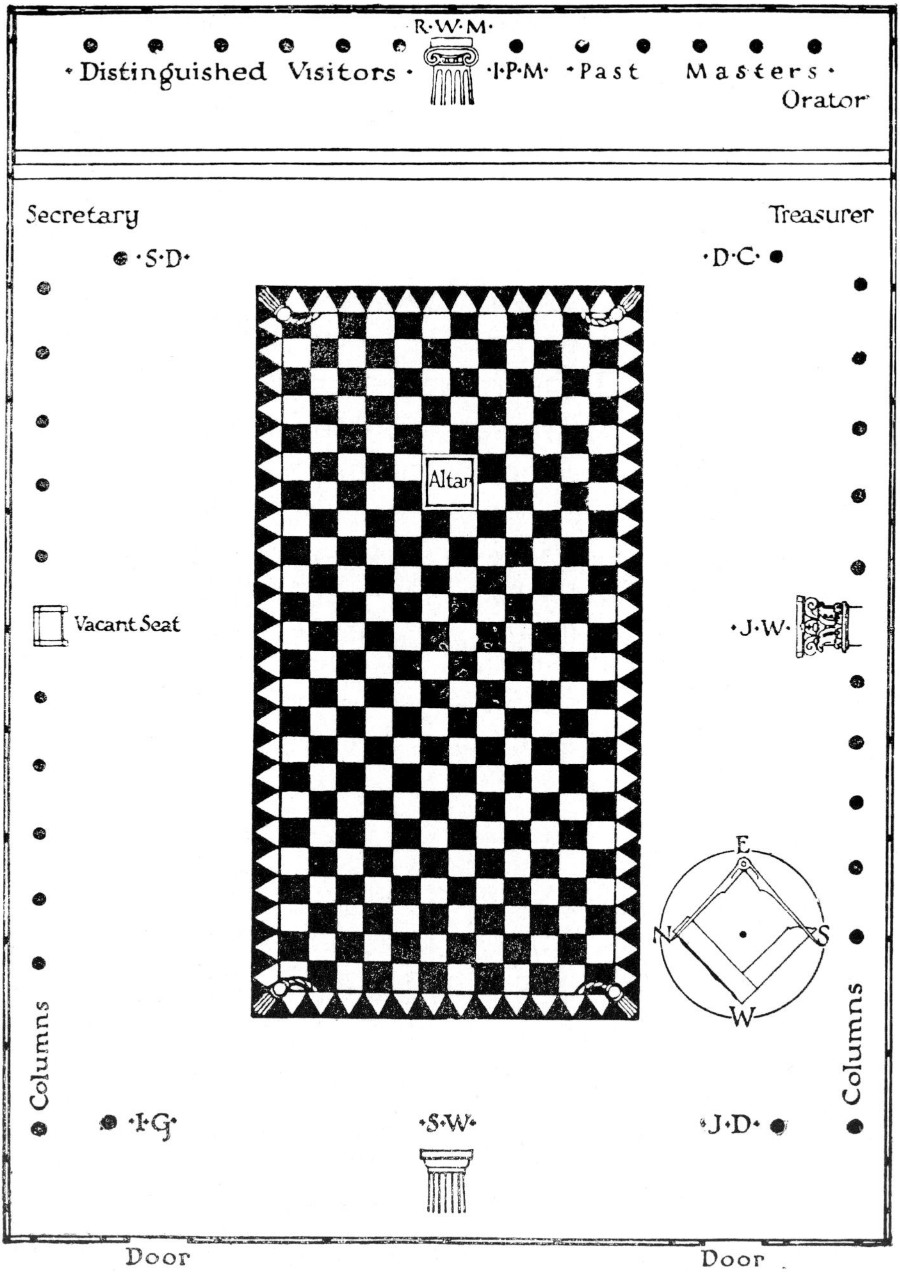

Plate 30: Plan of a Masonic Lodge, c. 1880. This is the arrangement for a 'blue' lodge working the first three degrees. R.W.M. – Right Worshipful Master.

Plate 31: (above) His Excellency, Lord Kitchener, Commander-in-Chief, India, 1902–1909.
Plate 32: (below) Detail, Invitation to Moira Festival, 1813, marking the Earl of Moira's departure for India as Governor of Bengal.

Plate 33: (above) The bazaar, Quetta, 1906. Southernmost of the posts guarding the North West Frontier. Site of Himalayan Brotherhood Lodge.

Plate 34: (below) Haileybury College, completed 1806. Designed by William Wilkins R.A., who also designed the National Gallery.

Plate 35: (left) The clock tower in front of the Grand Mosque and Palace, Doha.

Plate 36: (below) Indian troops entering Baghdad, 1917. A permanent British mission in the city dated from 1798.

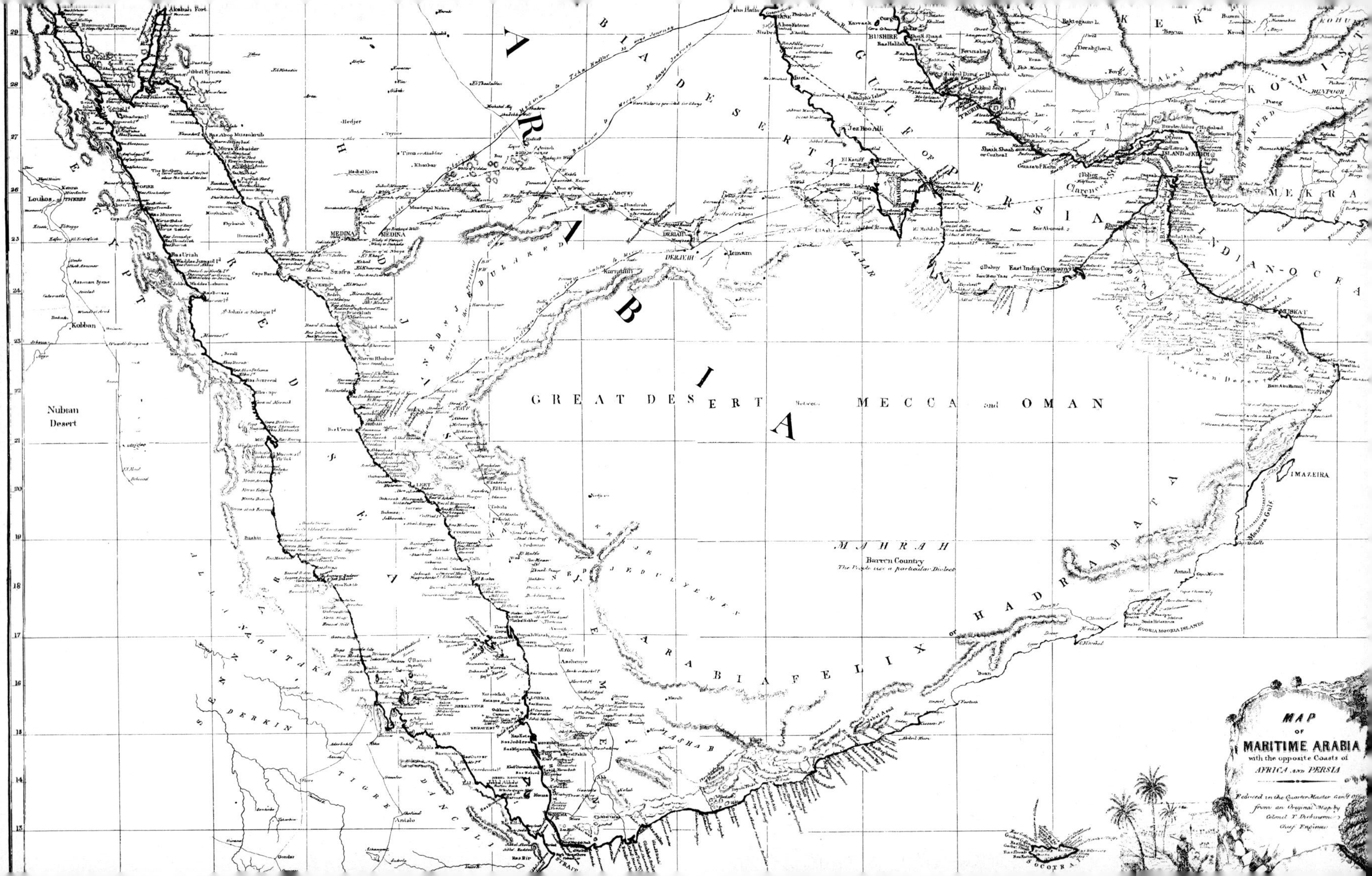
MAP OF MARITIME ARABIA with the opposite Coasts of AFRICA and PERSIA
Reduced in the Quarter Master Genl's Office from an Original Map by Colonel T. Dickinson, Chief Engineer
ARABIA
GREAT DESERT between MECCA and OMAN
ARABIA FELIX or HADRAMAT
MAHRAH
Barren Country
The People use a particular Dialect
GULF OF PERSIA
INDIAN OCEAN
EGYPT
RED SEA
Nubian Desert
MEDINA
BUSHIRE
MUSKAT
SOCOTRA
IMAZEIRA
Mazeira Gulf
KOORIA MOORIA ISLANDS
DERAYEH
BAHREIN
ISLAND OF KISHM
Clarence's Str.
MEKRAN
KOHISTAN
DANCALI
TIGRE
Nejd
Hedjaz

Plate 37: (previous page) Map of Maritime Arabia, 1843.

Plate 38: (above) The United Service Club, London, 1858. Now the Institute of Directors.

Plate 39: (below) Whiteley Bridge, Basra. Postcard c.1919. Iraq's second largest city, from which Sinbad sailed in *The Thousand and One Nights*.

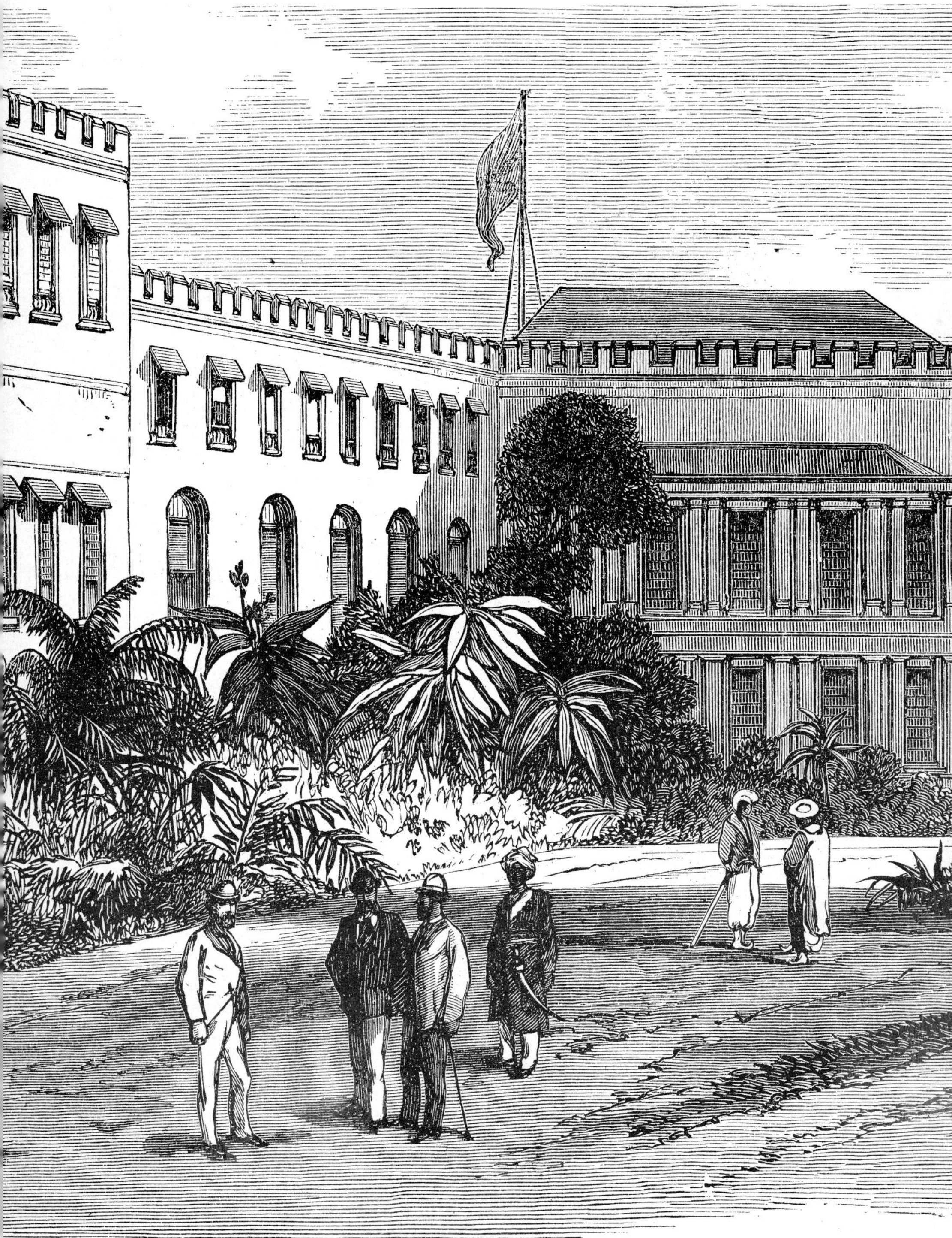

Plate 40: The Bombay Residency. The Government of Bombay remained responsible for the Gulf until control was transferred to the Government of India in 1873.

Plate 41: Lady Curzon. Mary Leiter, the American heiress who married Curzon in 1895 and accompanied him on his visit to the Gulf in 1903. She died in 1904, leaving him with three young daughters.

Plate 42: (above) The British Residency at Bushire (called Persis during the reign of Cyrus the Great, c.559 B.C.).

Plate 43: (below) Bushire on the Persian Gulf. From Lord Curzon's *Persia and the Persian Question*, 1892.

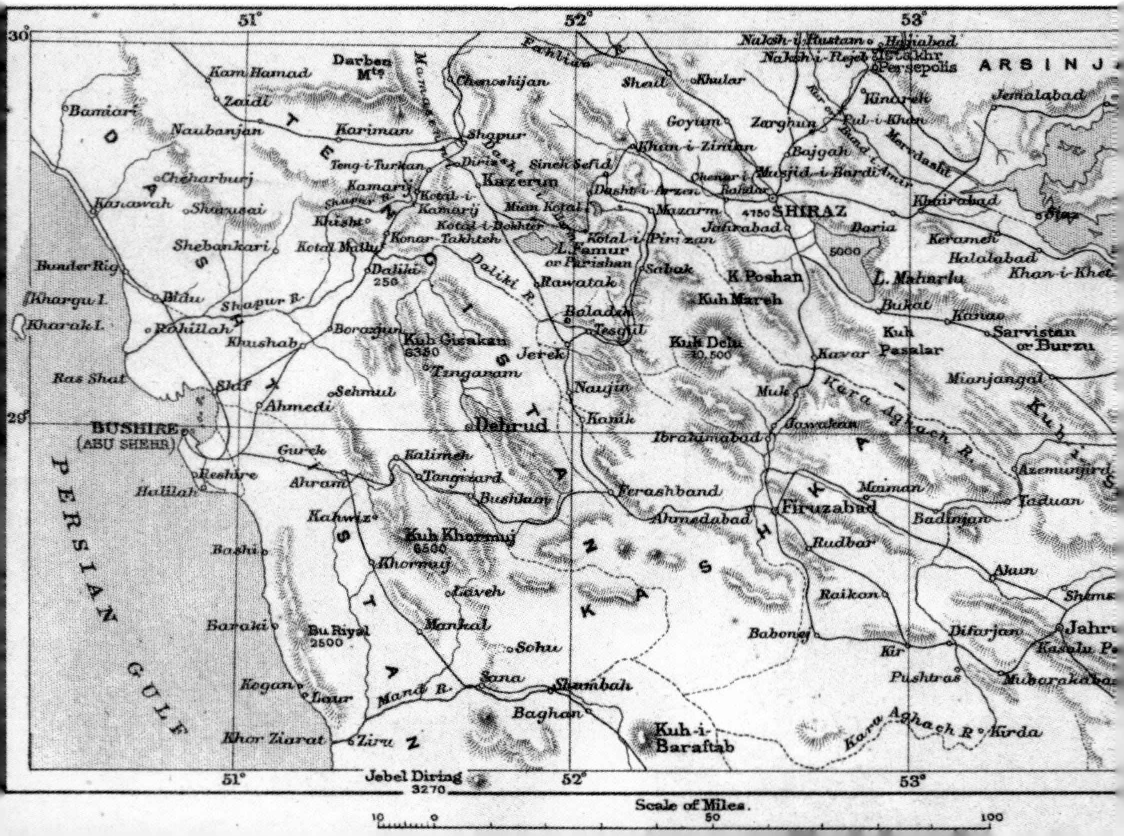

not have. The special attitude towards the Arabs was unique in Imperial annals,[44] but the sentimentality with which the British regime in Arabia has been invested should not get in the way of an honest evaluation of what the consequences have been. Evaluation of the Indian Political Service period hinges on whether or not enough was done for enough people within the limitations of the period, *i.e.* whether judged *not* by present day standards but by the standards of the time.[45]

Old, New, and Indian Arabia

The British were never altogether happy about the effects of the oil money even when it was a comparative trickle, as it spelled the death of the mozarabic old ways, of the sailing ships and the souks with their treasures for sale. Later was only worse. Romantics found nothing appealing about a cargo plane unloading iceberg lettuce or a concrete block store selling Kelvinator refrigerators. The mentality that deplored the passing of crofters' cottages and rickshaws found the lack of bedouin raiders equally regrettable. This writer has always maintained that before bemoaning this loss of atmosphere, thought should be given to the despair that existed in old Arabia:

> Are poverty and hardship, danger and the constant possibility of sudden death a price people should pay for the code of honour, the freedom, the peculiar courage they give rise to? Is it a price any of us would pay? Yet the wilderness vanishes and the ancient fortitude is eroded. The arenas shrink and vanish and the heroes, bereft, stumble into memory. Time, like a sandstorm, obliterates their tracks.[46]

The 'royal' families of the Gulf have appreciated and *encouraged* the values of a ritualistic élitism served up with a soupçon of pearl diving and dhows. This selective history serves a shaikhy upper class that has everything to gain from keeping attention from more prosaic matters like the franchise. The interest the shaikhs show in an illusionary past has much to do with earlier IPS infatuations. *More important than whether the British built enough schools or clinics in the Gulf is whether they encouraged servile deference, a cult of shaikhs which paralleled the cult of Windsordom.*

This was and has continued to be a nasty *noblesse* without *oblige*. It well suited British policy in keeping control.[47] It suits present-day shaikhs. A rebuttal often made to accusations about the lack of democracy is that there was always some sort of *majlis* or consultative political system in the Gulf, one which the British left intact. Dubious as any historical evidence of this is, there does remain an issue as to whether Western style democracy is the only acceptable political system. Arabs resent the idea that their *majlis* and other traditions are unworthy alternatives to the hustling of election campaigns. Fair enough, but that there was an indigenous political structure of any significance that the British left intact seems unlikely.[48]

The end result of having old boys running the Gulf was the immobilization of society for a hundred years and the Arabs becoming enamoured, as had some Indians, of the Raj's totems. The cultural syneresis was disastrous. A visitor to India in the 1970s caught the inherent confusion:

> I went into a coffee-shop; inside were a handful of very old Anglo-Indian survivors, dressed in khaki-drill and the sola topis of a vanished age. The café had made the mistake of printing a quotation from Ruskin on its plastic-covered bill of fare. 'Quality is never the result of an accident. It is always the result of intelligent effort. There must be the will to produce a superior thing.' The thick white cup was cracked. The coffee was cold. This was the permanent Indian confusion of the symbol with the fact. Because someone had discovered Ruskin's words, his principle was obviously fulfilled. 'There must be the will to produce a superior thing.' Should not there also be the ability, or even the intention, to do so? This was not necessary: having proclaimed the truism, that was enough.[49]

Following on the initial decisions about which dynasties deserved to be elevated and which were to be ignored or murdered, the Imperial interference in Gulf affairs put a stop to political evolution. Nevertheless, the lack of political progress during the period and thereafter cannot be put entirely on the Raj's doorstep. Today's difficulties have been created by a multiplicity of causes. On any list would be the pathological fears of criticism on the part of the Gulf ruling families:

> Much of the reason why Arab development strategies have in part failed has been the prevailing illusion that economic and financial development can be accelerated in the absence of clear movement toward political modernization. Thus the absence of fully developed political institutions deprived broad sectors of the population of participation in (as distinct from benefit from) the development process and pre-empted the emergence of the minimal forms of public discourse and accountability essential to the prevention of waste and corruption. The absence of minimal guarantees of basic civil rights and individual freedoms led to a steady and substantial brain drain from the region. Major development decisions taken by autocratic regimes in a political environment filled with fear, indifference, corruption, or some combination thereof have resulted in the initiation of disastrously bad programmes and projects.[50]

Acknowledging that there are many reasons for the failure of the Gulf states to take advantage of their opportunities, considerable work remains to be done in understanding why the Gulf Arabs are so childish when it comes to responsible government, and so frightened of it. Contributing is their failure to acknowledge that their society now combines some of the very worst features of Indo-British and Arab 'tradition'.

That the Gulf was long one of the world's most backward places seems uncontestable. A University of Durham study in Qatar in 1970 showed that 90.6 per cent of those born between 1895 and 1910 were illiterate, 85.2 per cent of those born between 1910 and 1920, 86 per cent of those born between 1920 and 1930, and 81 per cent of those born between 1930 and 1940. Similar figures exist for the other Gulf states. After independence, all four countries launched massive adult literacy programmes which have only been partly successful. The shaikhdoms paid for the failure of the British to develop education. In assigning responsibility it should be recalled that none of the mosque schools got British help and neither did any of the schools established in the early twentieth century by individuals, such as Shaikh Abdulla's school in Manama or Shaikh Mubarak's school in Kuwait. The mosque schools declined steadily and were dealt a lethal blow by the economic depression of the 1930s, despite arguments for using what rudimentary educational system was at hand.

If there is little evidence of an indigenous political structure that could have been supported, at least there was an indigenous educational structure. Its loss is felt politically, because it was as much a possible source of symbolic structure as the public schools proved to be for the English. Some Arabs have appreciated that what education *could* contribute is not only literacy but an egalitarian ethos.[51]

The Residents would have been hard put to understand this. They had shown considerable incongruities in the stress that they placed on their own education and their children's education in contrast to their inattention to abysmal local situations. The patience the Gulf Arabs displayed with this and with other aspects of British behaviour was remarkable. The British themselves were the ones who had the doubts in the end,[52] and plainly lost their nerve.[53] The reasons that they did so were less economic and more psychological, and reflect as much as anything a change in the attitudes nurtured by the public schools. The post World War II Imperial administrators were educated at public schools, but as noted they did not emerge from them with the same self-confidence that their predecessors had.[54]

In the 1990s, the decline in oil revenues has brought the wheel full circle. The shaikhdoms are now abandoning earlier commitments to superior social services for all. Privatization is the clever catch word, but masks parsimony. Discerning that the leadership has abandoned the earlier promises to share the largesse, now that the largesse is limited, the ordinary citizens face little choice if they want excellence but to seek out and pay for private facilities...or change the regimes. Despite much nonsense about high per capita incomes, the poor are returning to the Gulf. They never entirely went away except in journalists' fancies. The radicals have a constituency which is much bigger than realized. The Iraqi defeat has not changed that.

L'envoi

The isolation of the British in the Gulf, cut off from the familiarities of daily life at home, magnified the importance of their school days.[55] In the far-off Gulf a wistfulness developed, the nostalgia Sir Henry Newbolt encapsulated in his school poetry. This nostalgia might tempt the recreation of Clifton, or seeing echoes of Clifton in local customs. Regrettably, mirages are the products of deserts. Although the importance in people's lives of schooling varies, it is a factor in their decision-making when they are adults. The self-imposed social isolation of many of the Gulf's current élite has had similarly unfortunate results for decision-making.

When educators like myself in the Gulf states tried to repudiate in the 1970s and 1980s the British legacy of élitism, we thought we would have enough money to implement universal education. Certainly the contrast in revenues over the past was dramatic. In 1945 the Shaikh of Sharjah was meticulously collecting five rupees for each landing at the airport and averaging £27 a week in takings. He was extremely pleased, and anxious that the bonanza continue. At the time, aviation authorities were sceptical that the Gulf would support an airport. One wrote, 'It is, of course, impossible to prophesize [*sic*] accurately the future of anything, but judging by present-day trends in aviation I do not think it is unduly pessimistic to foretell a day, perhaps in five or ten years' time, when Sharjah will be virtually closed down as a civil airport.'[56] What luck!, thought innocent Westerners in the late 1970s. The Gulf will have enough money to have everything for everyone.

Perhaps it did, but the bulk of the money went into the pockets of the ruling families for nonsense, and still does. Compared to what could have been done, what was done was not impressive. The schools are terrible, the standard of medical treatment is awful except for the privileged, and the cities behind the few token boulevards were depressing even before the recent war.

Of course, Britain has not been any more successful than the shaikhdoms in providing a comprehensive secondary school system that could unite its classes or produce the integrated society of which education is such a significant bell-wether. As late as 1981, only 19% of the United Kingdom's seventeen year olds were full-time in school – compared with 82% in the United States and 87% in Japan. In the age group of sixteen, seventeen, and eighteen year olds, the United Kingdom was the last in percentage of youngsters of that age enrolled as either full or part-time students compared with France, Germany, Italy, Japan, the Netherlands, and the United States.[57]

As far as the significance of education in Gulf history is concerned, what else could have been so decisive in shaping the personalities and attitudes of men like Pelly, Cox, or Wilson? Birth in Scotland or the home counties? Religion? Marriage? It need only be asked concerning the importance of being an old boy: What if the Residents had all gone to grammar schools? *In years to come, those considering the Gulf's instability may ask what could have been if the shaikhs had bought themselves good schools rather than race horses.*

What the rulers of the Gulf learned from the British they reduced to the banality of paste Crown Jewels on display. Like shells on the beach, silently testifying to former occupants, something of the Viceregal past has lingered after Britain's 'moment'.[58] Now the Gulf Arabs have discovered that the ambitions of independence have collapsed, and that the money has not been distributed fairly enough to give everyone a fair chance. This is not amazing. After all, even state school pupils in Britain have considerable privilege in terms of schooling by the 'virtue' of their geographical location.[59] Perhaps it is too much to expect *any* social system to confer equality.[60] Competing imperial powers did no better with their empires and sometimes did much worse.[61]

Whatever else the Residents and Agents will be remembered for, they had sang-froid. This owed much to the public schools and its absence would be later regretted: 'You see, instead of the British Raj you've got the Oil Raj. And honestly, Queen Victoria was better than Shell.'[62]

The Sovereign's representatives in the Middle East were more colourful than today's bureaucrats. In 1932, the traveller Robert Byron had survived the terrors of Abbascabad, and exhausted by his adventures reached Meshed and 'staggered up the steps of the Consulate'. He was greeted by a hearty 'Just in time for the ball!' shouted by the wife of Everald Gastrell, an Old Cheltonian who at the time was secretary to the Gulf Resident. (See his biography in Chapter IX.) Byron had happened upon a costume party organized by Gastrell:

> Does the whole Indian Political Service travel about Asia with dress-up boxes? Mrs. Gastrell was a Negress in black skin-tights and a top hat; Gastrell, who is seven feet high, danced a Scottish reel as Bluebeard, wearing cloth of gold and a caerulean beaver. Rose, of the same service, appeared as a Kate Greenaway schoolboy...Before I could say how pleased I was to see them again, they were transforming me into a charwoman; while Christoper [his companion], pinioned by the Gastrells, was whisked into the regalia of an Arab shaikh.[63]

The Gulfites were remarkable in a variety of ways. From their experiences and writings we might hope to get a better idea of why the Gulf now is such a complicated place. *Pace*, although the notion initially seems most curious, part of Arabia's history is that of the rise of the English public schools.

> *The Empire left behind it a great deal more than a few stragglers.* – Bernard Porter, *The Lion's Share*, 1985.

NOTES

1. IOR:L/P&S/12/3943: Prior to Caroe, 20 August 1941.
2. National Archives, Washington, Intelligence Report 109-44, Alusnob, Basra, 11 August 1944, W.M. Benkart, NND 785050, Declassified 7/30/85.
3. IOR:R/15/1/374, 'Education at Bahrain', Prior to Weightman, 9 July 1940.
4. Geoffrey Prior, 'Review', 'Administrative Reports of the Persian Gulf for the Year 1943', *The Persian Gulf Administration Reports, 1873-1947*, Vol.X, 1941-1947, Archive Editions, 1986, 3-4. Administration Reports in the 1940s were typed rather than printed, and they are not listed in Tuson. The American presence in Bahrain that annoyed Prior increased dramatically during the war, enough so that an American post office was opened at Muharraq from June 1944 to late in 1945 to handle U.S. Air Force personnel mail as well as mail from vessels operating in the Gulf. There were also American workers connected with the construction of the Fluid Catalytic Unit for the Sitra Refinery for the Bahrain Petroleum Company, an American government project. Donaldson, *The Postal Agencies in Eastern Arabia and the Gulf*, 67.
5. IOR:R/15/2/210, 'British Council: Expansion of Activities in Bahrain, Quarterly Reports', C.A.F. Dundas, 'Proposed Gulf College', 35.
6. *Ibid.*
7. *Ibid.*, 38.
8. *Ibid.*, 'Memorandum', 8.
9. *Ibid.*, C.S. Prior to C.A.F. Dundas, 22 February 1941, 4.
10. *Ibid.*, 'Draft Agreement', 40.
11. *Ibid.*, Prior to Weightman, 1 May 1941, 33.
12. IOR:L/P&S/121/3760, Rupert Hay to E.P. Donaldson, 14 May 1947.
13. John Bradley, in John Bradley ed., *Lady Curzon's India: Letters of a Vicerine*, Weidenfeld and Nicolson, 1985, ii.

14. Mitchell, *Colonising Egypt*, 171.

15. *Ibid.*

16. J.A. Hobson, *Imperialism*, University of Michigan Press, 1965 [1902], 368. 'The real trouble as Hobson saw it was that the imperialists – well organized in small but interlocking groups, wielding influence not in political theory only but in social life, in sport, in the public schools, in the cadet forces, in the scouting movement, in the Press, in the pulpit – believed in what they said and in what they were doing, and he knew he could not convince them by any words or by any pages of closely-reasoned argument that "every enlargement of Great Britain in the tropics is a distinct enfeeblement".' A.P. Thornton, *The Imperial Idea and Its Enemies: A Study in British Power*, 2nd ed., Macmillan, 1985 [1959], 73.

17. J.H. Grainger, *Patriotisms*, 355. As Wilson's biographer, John Marlowe, remarked, 'There was something in his "credo" to repel almost everyone.' qtd. *Ibid.* The credo was not only at times repulsive but convoluted, and an anthropologist of Imperial iconography will have to learn something about public school customs if he wants to enter this strange territory.

18. Jeffrey Richards, *Visions of Yesterday*, Routledge & Kegan Paul, 1973, 220.

19. IOR:L/P&S/10/1273, J.C. Walton to H.A.F. Metcalfe, 1934, n.d., 'Personal and Very Confidential'.

20. A candidate for the ICS in the spring of 1946 wrote, 'From time to time I visited the India Office to inquire if there was any definite news. The officials I saw were uncommunicative, uninterested almost. I also visited India House in Aldwych to fix up about my pay. They seemed uncertain whether I was on leave, or what I was doing. Week followed week, month followed month. I tried the hard line: were we really going back? Oh yes, we would be hearing...Eventually the last letter came: they regretted that it had been decided to discontinue recruitment from UK into the ICS. It was all over. The record shows that a decision to suspend ICS recruitment was taken on 17 July 1946 but the Secretary of State was still pondering on 25 July whether or not to cancel offers of appointment already made; the matter was discussed in Cabinet on 31 July and referred to Wavell. I received a letter date 1 August telling me "a further communication will be sent to you as soon as it is possible to decide whether or not an appointment can be offered to you". On 13 September a terse communication from Wavell signified "no further recruitment".' Tinker, 'The Diary of a Military and Civil Nobody', 25. See John Glubb, *Britain and the Arabs: A Study of Fifty Years*, Hodder and Stoughton, 1959, 168.

21. IOR:R/15/2/838, Hay to Tandy, 16 November 1946, 201.

22. IOR:R/15/2/853, 36/1 (1 A77), 'American Mission in Bahrain: Missionary Work', 31.

23. *Ibid.*

24. *Ibid.*

25. Colin Cross, *The Fall of the British Empire*, Hodder and Stoughton, 1968, 151.

26. IOR:L/P&S/12/3645, Secretary of State for India to Political Resident in the Persian Gulf, 16 July 1947. See Nicolas Mansergh ed., *India: The Transfer of Power, 1942-7*, Vol XII, HMSO, 1983, 363.

27. John Marlowe, *The Persian Gulf in the Twentieth Century*, Cresset Press, 1962, 138.

28. Trench, *Viceroy's Agent*, 349.

29. Belgrave, *Personal Column*, 223.

30. *Ibid.*, 237.

31. Arnold Galloway to P.J. Rich, 16 March 1988.

32. *Ibid.*

33. See *e.g.* H.G. Balfour Paul, 'Recent Developments in the Persian Gulf', *Journal of the Royal Central Asiatic Society*, Vol. LVI, Part I, February 1969, 12-13.

34. Hawley, *Trucial Coast*, 234. *Cf.* 260.

35. Donald Leinster-Mackay, 'The Nineteenth-century English Preparatory School: Cradle and Crêche of Empire?', Mangan ed., *Benefits Bestowed?*, 57.

36. See Mangan, 'The Grit of Our Forefathers', Mackenzie ed., *Imperialism and Popular Culture*, 135.

37. Reed, *Old School Ties*, 124.

38. 'Education at Bahrain 1/12/41-31/8/45', IOR:R/15/1/375, A.H.B. Schofield, Foreign Office, to Martin Blake, British Council, 13 June 1944.

39. Belgrave, *Personal Column*, 166.

40. Information supplied by Robert Jarman, 15 January 1987.

41. Phillip Mallett, 'Kipling and the Hoax', Mallett ed., *Kipling Considered*, 103.

42. Donald Hawley, *The Trucial States*, Allen and Unwin, 1971, 262.

43. Some historians, notably Correlli Barnett in *The Collapse of British Power*, claim to have detected a direct relationship between the changes in the schools' influence and the Empire's decline. Whether this is true or not, the schools' importance in maintaining divisions in British society has

been increasingly appreciated. *Pari passu* the British were right in their fears about the influence of Egyptian or Iraqi education – my teacher at Harvard, Rupert Emerson, observed that the agitation for independence comes not from the products of indigenous educational systems but from those, 'who had been exposed to a Western Type of Education and Experience', and it was Egypt and Iraq that were the most Westernized of the Middle East countries. Rupert Emerson, *From Empire to Nation: The Rise of Self-Assertion of Asian and African Peoples*, 3rd ed., Boston, 1964, 199. Control of education was one way the British determined Gulf political development. The schools had been so closely linked with the Empire and had been part of the reason why British involvement with overseas possessions was not only economic and political but intellectual, changing both the rulers and the ruled. The decline in Empire affected not only the British exchequer but the British psyche. The Americans were not appreciably changed by their occupation of the Philippines, nor the Germans by their short empire in Africa – but the British *were* profoundly changed by their colonial experience.

44. 'Historically and culturally there is a quantitative as well as a qualitative difference between the Franco-British involvement in the Orient and – until the period of American ascendancy after World War II – the involvement of every other European and Atlantic power. To speak of Orientalism therefore was to speak mainly, although not exclusively, of a British and French cultural enterprise...'. Said, *Orientalism*, 4.

45. If there was little criticism in the Gulf *at the time*, it remains to be added in fairness that there was comparatively little criticism *at the time* of the educational establishment in Britain. Although there were educators who opposed the public schools and felt that comprehensive schools were the answer to social problems, they were not influential. The people who should have been critical were uneducated and hence had no voice, and those who were educated and could have articulated their ideas were compromised by the very education that made them articulate.

46. Peter Brent, *Far Arabia*, Quartet Books, 1979, 228.

47. Baden-Powell remarked about scouting: 'It will be the highest form of brotherhood and service for Public School men ultimately to take up and impart this training to their less well to do brothers.' qtd. Michael Rosenthal, *The Character Factory: Baden-Powell and the Origins of the Boy Scout Movement*, Collins, 1986, 91. Public schoolism was two-edged: it taught both self-confidence *and* deference, depending on who you were. H. Bompas Smith, headmaster of King Edward VII School, Lytham, emphasized that the public schools '...aim at training their boys to become worthy members of the social group of which the function is the control and guidance of the work and thought of others.' *Ibid.*

48. An argument is that, by concentrating attention on the education, albeit mostly of an informal nature and largely unsuccessful, of shaikhs – and by ignoring the system of local schools – the British created a hierarchical political system. Whatever else, an élite school is a mechanism for preserving and creating élitism: 'The élite boarding schools act as what the sociologist Erving Goffman has defined as a "total institution" – one where..."(1) all activities are conducted in the same place under a single authority; (2) daily life is carried out in the immediate company of others; (3) life is tightly scheduled and fixed by a set of formal rules; and (4) all activities are designed to fulfil the official aims of the institution." The schools strip students of their individuality and sense of privacy, instilling instead a group identity of "web of affiliation" that does not end with graduation but "continues to grow, becoming more interwoven, entangled, and in the end, the basis of status group and class solidarity".' Christopher Lehmann-Haupt, 'Preparing for Power', *International Herald Tribune*, 24-25 December 1985, 3.

49. Cameron, *An Indian Summer*, 32-33. Without fully accepting Barnett's thesis that the English public school spirit and the schools' traditionalist ethos halted economic and technological advance, it does seem likely that a culture such as 'high British Imperial', where symbolism replaces reality, inhibits entrepreneurship. T.J.H. Bishop, who with Rupert Wilkinson studied the Wykehamists in *Winchester and the Public School Élite*, could write to the *Guardian* as late as 1985: 'My judgment, for what it may be worth, is that "gentrification" has damaged and continues to damage our economy...[because] Winchester and public schools like Winchester still function as mechanisms of "social immobility", continuing to make it much less likely that others, not to the manner born – and many women inside as well as outside the charmed circle – will reach their well-merited places in our decision-making élites, right across our steadily declining economy.' T.J.H. Bishop, 'How a Gentrifying Diet Leads to Constipation', *The Guardian Weekly*, Vol.133, No.24, 15 December 1985, 2. *Pari passu* India and the Gulf.

50. George T. Abed, 'The Lean Years: The Political Economy of Arab Oil in the Coming Decade', Sharabi, *The Next Arab Decade*, 102. '...the Muslims have not produced any permanent values and most regrettably, have not made any positive and significant contribution to modern civilization. Since the 15th century, the religious seminaries in the Muslim world became the repositories of such knowledge as was existent then. In these seminaries the emphasis was on convention and tradition.

Originality and innovation were not only discouraged; but were treated with hostility. Hundreds of years later, some Muslim leaders did realize the importance of science and technology, but even they failed to grasp the basic relationship between science and technology and a nation's general advancement. In 1799 Sultan Selim III of Turkey introduced algebra, trigonometry, mechanics, ballistics and metallurgy in some schools in Turkey. He imported French and Swedish teachers to teach these subjects to Turkish students. But...[the] sad and bitter truth is that even today we have not learned there are no short cuts...'. Dawud Assad, 'The Islamisation of Knowledge', *The Muslim World*, Vol.23 No.25, 28 December 1985, 6.

51. There is a resisting national *spirit* in the humblest country, and, despite the efforts of Imperial administrators, it is doubtful whether the full blown *spirit* of English tradition was preserved in any former colony. The incongruities of retaining the husk or shell of course remain. Arab leaders are greeted at their own airports by kilted Arab bands playing *Scotland the Brave*, but Doha is not Dundee.

52. In Britain, public schools went through a period of 'maximum insecurity' when the Labour Party was openly considering how to nationalize them. John Rae, 'New Life for the Old School', *The Times*, 14 December 1985, 8. Dr. Rae, headmaster of Westminster, explained: 'I joined the Headmasters Conference at this time and I recall the mood of defeatism. It was like finding yourself in a besieged town on the point of surrender: public talk about the need to collaborate with the enemy and private plans for *sauve qui peut.*' *Ibid.* Then opinion swung the other way and in the last part of the twentieth century the public schools have flourished. In fact, John Rae said: 'In the new political climate, the independent schools pulled off a notable coup. They persuaded the Conservatives to launch the assisted places scheme to give some poorer children an independent education. The scheme did extend choice but only in the sense that two extra lifeboats would have extended choice aboard the Titanic. A few more children were enabled to escape the sinking ship, but what happened to those left behind did not appear to concern the independent sector...'. *Ibid.*

53. '...when we examine the last stages of British colonial rule and the failure of nerve it exhibits, we must not forget to make due allowance for these vague but powerful and pervasive feelings of guilt.' The famous public school sang-froid faltered. Barnett has few reservations about putting the blame squarely on the schools, and further claims that the rot set in when pragmatism in British policy was replaced by principle: '..the Church of England public school, which by 1900 had re-made the crudely arriviste middle classes and the old upper classes alike according to its ideal of a Christian gentleman. The evolution of the English public school has a crucial bearing on the British plight in 1940, for most of the administrators of the British Empire at home and overseas in the 1920s and 1930s, as well as many British business leaders and MPs, were products of the period of its ripest development between 1870 and 1900. Except for young Nazis or Communists no class of leaders in modern times has been so subjected to prolonged moulding of character, personality and outlook as British public school boys in this era.' Barnett, *The Collapse of British Power*, 24. England's loss of the Gulf reflected the change in social patterns in England. 'England and its allies defeated the Axis powers, but the Churchillians lost the empire. Its knell had tolled from time to time during the war, and Colville reveals that Churchill had not been deaf to it...On August 30, 1941, Churchill learned that the Spitfires and Hawker Hurricanes that had won the Battle of Britain were piloted by students from state schools, not schoolboys from the élite private schools, [and] he said: "They have saved this country; they have the right to rule it." ' William Manchester, 'Downing Street Diarist: An Insider's Portrait of Churchill' review of John Colville, *The Fringes of Power*, Norton, in *International Herald Tribune*, 22 October 1985, 18.

The realization of the fears of the Residents that the Americans would supplant the British came to pass not because of any American initiative but because of the failure of British nerve. On this subject, Winstone wrote: 'And an American president repeated almost word for word the warning of Lord Landsdowne of 1903, "An attempt by any outside force to gain control of the Persian Gulf region will be regarded as an assault on the vital interests of the United States. It will be repelled by the use of any means necessary, including military force." Only the name of the protecting power had changed.' H.V.F. Winstone, *The Illicit Adventure, The Story of Political and Military Intelligence in the Middle East from 1898 to 1926*, Jonathan Cape, 1982, 363. The *British* paratroopers and 'Desert Rats' who were flown to the Gulf in August 1990 immediately after Iraq invaded Kuwait are the proof of Winstone's statement.

The rejection of the 'worldly' atmosphere of the grammar school and glorification of the public school mentality is the root of the decay in Barnett's view. Harrow's Cyril Norwood, who himself went to a grammar school rejected it: 'I do not think that there was any clear presentation to us of the ideal of service so much as a call not to let the other schools or other people beat us. We were trained to face the full rigours of competition, and left for the most part with a real determination to get on in the world. That this was so, was due to the fact that the religious appeal was largely absent from our lives...'. Cyril Norwood, *The English Tradition in Education*, John Murray, 1929, 19, qtd. Barnett, *Collapse of British Power*, 27. Barnett laid a full measure of the blame on Edward Thring, Uppingham's headmaster from 1853 until 1887, and his much reprinted *Theory and Practice of Teaching*, detecting in Thring's writings a sentimentality that he felt took the backbone out of British Imperial administration. He quoted Thring: '...what is a nation doing which calmly stands up and says, "We will only regard in our schools the breeding of the strong head; and we will give all power and honour to the wielders of strength"? This is but the Vandal all over again...glory to the strong on the reverse side of the shield is oppression to the weak...Alas for the many, alas for the pith, and working fibre of the nation; alas for all the gentler, and finer qualities by which society lives...All tender influences, all prevailing, patient, unpretending good may pack and be gone. There is no room for them in the heart of the modern world...the pride of intellect is to be unchained, and with the break-up of humility, reverence, holiness and genius the child of love, the Dark Age will set in...'. Edward Thring, *Theory and Practice of Teaching*, CUP, 1910, 36, qtd, Barnett, *Collapse of British Power*, 29. Barnett in effect echoes the East India Company veterans who were appalled at the new wave of 'competition wallahs' in the 1860s.

54. 'The British colonial servants saw their task as one of efficient, fair public administration, of providing justice, law and order: the Roman imperial virtues. They tended to neglect...the modern importance of science and economics, subjects they understandably found alien and somewhat uncomfortable. Thus, although the British showed a far more tender regard for native culture than other colonial nations, British colonies were often backward in research and technical services, for the staffing of which British education in any case made small provision.' Barnett, *Collapse of British Power*, 127. Norwood wrote, 'Agriculture and production in the Dominions, and particularly the tropical dependencies, require the services of many trained biologists, botanists and zoologists, but they are not to be had...'. Norwood, *The English Tradition in Education*, 256, qtd. Barnett, *Collapse of British Power*, 127-128.

55. Curzon felt lonely in India, and if a man so self-possessed as Curzon felt cut off in his palace how much more isolated would those in the Gulf feel? He kept a room at his Kedleston estate as a replica of his Eton room and maintained a photograph album of school contemporaries, penning in their progress towards honours. He went off to India with crocodile tears of self-pity because it would isolate him from his Eton chums. Old boyism was a chronic ailment.

56. O'Shea, *Sand Kings of Oman*, 76-77. Edward Said was unimpressed by post independence progress in the Arab world: 'In the one part of the Orient that I can speak about with some direct knowledge, the accommodation between the intellectual class and the new imperialism might very well be accounted one of the special triumphs of Orientalism. The Arab world today is an intellectual, political, and cultural satellite of the United States. This is not in itself to be lamented; the specific form of the satellite relationship, however, is. Consider first of all that universities in the Arab world are generally run according to some pattern inherited from, or once directly imposed by, a former colonial power. New circumstances make the curricular actualities almost grotesque; classes populated with hundreds of students, badly trained, overworked, and underpaid faculty, political appointments, the almost total absence of advanced research and of research facilities, and most important, the lack of a single decent library in the entire region. Whereas Britain and France once dominated intellectual horizons in the East by virtue of their prominence and wealth, it is now the United States that occupies that place...'. Said, *Orientalism*, 323. Said, for whom I have the most profound admiration, has been grievously misused by Arab academics. He is not an apologist for the miserable political climate.

57. *Statistical Bulletin*, Department of Education and Science, United Kingdom, 1/85, September 1985.

58. A reminder appeared in the *Guardian*: 'But now a certain breed of Briton that used to be pervasive is seen only rarely in such watering holes as the Nell Gwynne Pub at the Al Falaj Hotel [in Muscat]. Walter Helfer, a German who ran Omani television for two years after it started up in 1974, remembers the walrus-moustached former functionaries from British colonies long since granted independence. 'These guys were in their mid-forties, with no chance to go back to England and make a new life there,' Helfer recalled. 'You found people who defended, silently, the empire. They were like a secret society. They were something straight from Kipling or Somerset Maugham'.' Christopher Dickey, 'UK's Changing Role in Oman', *The Guardian Weekly*, Vol.133, No.21, 24 November 1985, 16.

59. E.G. West, *Education and the State: A Study in Political Economy*, Institute of Economic Affairs, 1965, 68.

60. It must be added as a caveat that the schools themselves have changed drastically in their long history. Lytton Strachey's prophecy in *Eminent Victorians* that regimentation and athleticism might again wane has proved true: '...upon those two poles our public schools have turned for so long that we have almost come to believe that such is their essential nature, and that an English public

schoolboy who wears the wrong clothes and takes no interest in football is a contradiction in terms. Yet it was not so before Dr. Arnold; will it always be so after him? We shall see.' Strachey, *Eminent Victorians*, 187-88.

61. In 1911, in *all of Indonesia* there were 56 middle school graduates – 49 Europeans, 4 Indonesians, and 3 Chinese. In 1939, after 38 years of Dutch educational improvisations, there were 457 European graduates, 204 Indonesian graduates, and 116 Chinese graduates. In a few years Indonesia, the fifth most populous nation in the world, would get her independence – but with only 204 university graduates. Rudolf Von Albertini, *European Colonial Rule, 1880-1940: The Impact of the West on India, Southeast Asia, and Africa*, Clio Press, Oxford, 1982, 181.

62. Kenneth Halliwell qtd. Joe Orton, *The Orton Diaries*, edited by John Lahr, Methuen, Minerva ed. 1989 [1986], 102. To Orton's intense irritation, Halliwell displayed the British working class fascination with upper class school rituals by buying and brazenly wearing an Old Etonian tie. *Ibid.*, 19, 246, 248-49.

63. Robert Byron, *The Road to Oxiana*, Pictor, 1981, 201-203. Lord Curzon enjoyed fancy dress balls – at one of them Lady Curzon appeared as Berengaria, and other guests included Napoleon, Charles II, and 'Nellie'. Patrick Grant, *The Good Old Days*, Thames and Hudson, 1956, 58-59.

EPILOGUE

THE IRAQI INVASION OF KUWAIT

Since the Iraqi invasion of Kuwait did not occur in a vacuum, it cannot be solved in a vacuum. – King Hussein of Jordan, September 1990.

The fusion of the older gentry with the parvenus was completed before the Boer-war. – Roy Lewis and Angus Maude, *The English Middle Classes*, 1949.

I find it hard to believe that there is such a thing as a humble culture. I cannot think of any instance where men believe that their society is seriously inferior to another. – Norman Daniel, *The Cultural Barrier*, 1975.

An immediate consequence of the 1990-91 Iraqi invasion of Kuwait was the destruction of the fledgling Kuwaiti media. More than forty different publications were closed down, including five daily newspapers. According to the president of the Council of Third World Newspapers, H.B. Khokhar, the latest equipment was taken to Baghdad. (*Guardian Weekly*, 30 September 1990.) Kuwait had the best developed publications in the Gulf, including several journals that at least held the promise of scholarship. Given the condition of Gulf studies, the Iraqi vandalism was a particular tragedy.

The destruction illustrates once again that it is outside the Gulf that much of the research into the Gulf will have to be done – unless the Arabs suddenly convert to freedom of the press and classroom. This is not written in any sense of colonial condescension, but only to emphasize that the region's history has been extraordinarily subject to attack and manipulation for political reasons.

Less dramatic than Iraqi troops carting off their spoils is the continuing loss of Gulf history through the ignorance of its value. In all likelihood in attics in South Africa and New Zealand as well as in English villages there are papers and photographs important to the shaikhdoms' past. Implicit to the *coup d'oeil* of these chapters about the Residents and Agents and a chief purpose is an appeal that manuscripts and memorabilia be placed in a secure repository such as St. Antony's College, Oxford or the India Office Library. Few if any regions of the world are more in need of a vigorous programme of search and preservation as far as original documents are concerned.

Search into the antecedents and descendants of the IPS officers by all odds should unearth unknown sources, which is completely to the good since more knowledge about the personal side of the British in the Gulf can contribute to a reappraisal of the official record. For example, when the criticisms of Charles Prior's tart tongue (as reported in his mini biography in Chapter IX) are taken into account, his comments on other officers take on a different complexion. As another illustration, in discussing the career of Samuel Manesty, an eighteenth-century EIC Resident, Shaikh Sultan Muhammad Al-Qasimi seeks to disparage Manesty's reports by referring to his shady personality:

> It was not beyond Manesty's scruples to invent a story, indeed he was a rather unscrupulous man. Saldhana mentioned him as the restless and fussy Resident at Basra. Kelly explained how he resorted to mysterious ways to promote his personal interests. These interests were intricate and widespread over India, the Gulf, Persia and Iraq. It was difficult to differentiate his personal interests from those of the Company. In fact, it was more than likely that he believed that what was good for Manesty was good for the Company. The Basra Diaries reveal a great deal about his vast operations and devious dealings. His seniors, his colleagues, his subordinates and his acquaintances and enemies had nothing good to say about him and a great deal to say about his dishonest, deceitful and underhand dealings. His contemporary, Sir Harford Jones, the Resident at Baghdad, had a great deal to complain about in respect of his intrigues, meddling and pomposity.[1]

Should Manesty's descendants or anyone else disgorge a trove of his papers, the Shaikh's harsh opinion of him might be revised. As central to Gulf historiography as deciding whether an individual Resident such as Manesty was the dismal fellow that Shaikh Muhammad believes he was (a view serving the shaikh's thesis about the British *vis-à-vis* alleged Arab piracy) is the problem of how such judgements are sustained. They cannot be made or refuted without documentation, which is why the claxon needs now to be sounded about finding and preserving the record to be found in letters, diaries, and sketch books of the Residents. These will inevitably continue to constitute a major portion of first-hand observations for the period.

There is little question that further inquiry into the lives of the Residents and Agents is bound to offer the bonus of saving endangered documents about the Gulf. Involved in the success of such investigation, discovery, and preservation is nothing less than the Gulf's cultural identity. Whether there is a quintessential 'Gulfness' remains to be resolved. It would be risky to predict what future paradigms will arise, but my presumption is that a small investment in 'sociological archaeology' will reveal more Indo-British cultural connections. A number of examples of this come to mind – the continued popularity of henna is a case in point and suggests that much more investigation is needed into the origins of Gulf tastes in grooming. Indian visitors are bemused by the way Arab women use this plant (*lawsonia inermis*), to decorate their bodies with elaborate designs, a custom which originated in Rajastan.[2] Cooking is another thriving domestic example of Indianness. Language already has been mentioned.

The Iraqi invasion of Kuwait had been justified on the grounds that Kuwait *historically* was part of Iraq. That is absolutely not true, and the Western press had been guilty of vaguely acknowledging that the notion has some validity. An Indian invasion would have made more sense. What *is* true is that Kuwait and the other Gulf states have a complicated past which sets them apart from the rest of the Arab world. They have to an extent harmed their aspirations to legitimacy by not allowing their own academics to pursue an investigation of that past.

Ignorance of the Indo-British influence on the Gulf can also obscure political possibilities looming in the future. *From the Gulf Arab perspective, prospects of stronger Indo-Arab ties have been more affected by social snobbishness than by logic.* India is not where Gulf Arabs have wanted their perfumes or watches to come from, although India makes fine perfumes and good watches.

A possibility that has not been explored by Gulf educationists has been the use of Indian educational institutions. The Indian public schools have many Indian old boys in the Gulf, and this exerts an influence. The Indian schools themselves are flourishing, and by no means do they have to apologize for their post-1947 progress. Doon School for one has regular exchanges with the English public schools and its staff have recently taught at Berkhamsted and Uppingham, with teachers from English schools coming to Doon in return. The Charles Wallace Trust and the League for the Exchange of Commonwealth Teachers help with such programmes. Given the inadequacy of secondary education in the Gulf, these Indian schools represent excellent value. They would provide a more international and democratic environment than the private schools being proposed for the shaikhdoms. It can be added that India has fine polytechnics and universities that could serve the Gulf.

Moreover, India has one of the world's largest standing armies and could play a helpful part in planning longterm efforts to stabilize the region. Most important, it was not involved in the February war. The shaikhdoms might find that India would make an excellent guarantor of the existing boundaries if American and Western support proves fickle or if Western leaders find that pressure at home prevents the endless involvement in the Gulf that now threatens. The Indian card deserves to be played. Closer ties between the Gulf and India should be pressed by Gulf rulers, if they are allowed to continue ruling. Recent communal strife between Muslims and Hindus in India is probably less significant than the way India has been able to stay out of the current Gulf crisis. This gives India an advantage that should be used.

Dynasties and Legitimacy

A topic related to the Gulf's roots now coming to the fore because of the Iraqi invasion is the status of the Gulf's dynasties. As seen, their legitimacy owes much to the IPS. 'The dominant argument that looms over the Arab world,' wrote Youssef Ibrahim in the *International Herald Tribune* (13 March 1990), 'is that Arab governments, revolutionary or hereditary, have lost their legitimacy in the eyes of their people.' The crux of the political crisis in the Gulf during the 1990s is the effectiveness of rulers who are a legacy of British dynasty-making days. At issue is whether they will be able to respond to the challenge of Arab radicalism.[3]

Just how long the ordinary Gulf Arabs will be willing to accept parturient fictions laid down by the IPS about these ersatz monarchs is not of antiquarian concern. Unfettered monarchy is untenable in the present world political and economic climate, and it is inimical to progress. The unpromising praetorian game plan of the shaikhs is to continue seeking support for unsupportable lasciviousness and legitimacy for illegitimate power by a masquerade of a historical illusion. *By oversimplification they seek, to borrow a phrase of Robert Jervis's, to decrease the burden of cognition.*

'Because they are rich,' *The Economist* (18 May 1990) observed about the Gulf rulers, 'they have granted their citizens a contract that is unsustainably generous.' During the crunch caused by declining oil prices, labyrinthine intra-family quarrels over the booty have largely drowned out problems such as the fact that the population of the shaikhdoms is expected to double from ten million to twenty million people in the next twenty years. The water supply problem is alone enough trouble to deny planners any sleep.

Nor do the uncertainties about the price of oil indicate that conventional wisdom about an eventual second boom can be relied upon. The green revolution combined with desperate pumping by those countries that are perennially short of cash may mean that a price recovery will never come. The increased prices because of Iraq's belligerence do not change the longterm prospects. Even without Iraq and Kuwait, there is no real oil shortage.

Independence so far has been a euphemism for simony. However, this is not a call to the barricades. Both the radical and dynastic alternatives to the present 'royal' policy-makers are depressing. There were other contenders for the Gulf thrones that the IPS created, and for each of the Gulf satraps the shaikhy versions of the Stewart pretenders wait balefully over the water. Like the Stewarts, they appear to offer little alternative in brains or ability. After talking to one 'shaikh without a kingdom' who had a claim to the Nejd, O'Shea, in *The Sand Kings of Oman,* dryly commented that he thought the danger 'about as real as the Jacobite claim to the English throne'. The royal families of the Gulf, incumbent or in waiting, are a sorry crew.

When published, piquant comments in the archives made by the Residents and Agents about foibles of the present reigning houses will not enhance the incumbents' genealogical pretensions. The world's last remaining absolutists resemble the Vicar of Bray, resolute only about incumbents and incomes. Absorption with internecine trivia promises that they will end by having neither.

Having stated that, let it be added that the Gulf monarchs represent a potentially valuable resource to their countries. They have been a principal reason why the shaikhdoms are independent and have not been gobbled up by bigger neighbours. Reaching an accommodation with their restless subjects, they *could* continue to embody the autonomy of Bahrain, Kuwait, Qatar, and the Emirates. Without them, the survival of the satraps is unlikely. With them, unless they change their performance, the situation is precarious.

The prospect is bleak if speculation about solutions to the Gulf's Augean stables remains a pursuit for Westerners and not for Gulf Arabs. So far they are denied the climate that makes reasoned debate possible. There are definite political reasons for the lack of alacrity with which Gulf-based scholars consider the past. They wish to retain their homes and to be able to feed their families. For that reason, there are no serious historians of the Gulf in Gulf 'universities'. There is an appalling lack of history about the Gulf written by Gulf nationals. Young academics returning with Western educations are soon house broken, forced to submit by censorious governments that rely on oversimplification and suppression to maintain authority.

In the spring of 1990 some Gulf shops, with notable entrepreneurial enthusiasm, were selling bricks from the Berlin Wall. An aggressive Dubai commercial photographer brought a section back for his studio, hoping that customers would want to be photographed in front of the pieces. There is an irony to people living in the world's least free societies queuing up to be photographed in front of such a symbolic backdrop. In time they may wish to import more than bricks.

Whatever the Gulf did import in the past in the way of politics was not democracy. The British brought élitism and snobbery and taught the shaikhs about hegemony. Imperialism was hegemony *par excellence.* The IPS sought not only political goals but cultural ones, and in the process substantiated Gramsci's contention that ceremony was hegemony's hallmark. The search for the inspiration of the Imperial ceremonial leads to the nineteenth-century public schools. While the Imperials sometimes represented themselves as a squirearchy accustomed to being educated in old England's ancient schools, they were a new hierarchy educated in a new way. The shaikhs are a similarly recent phenomenon.

Taking the Raj Seriously

The Raj was a conjurer, but there was nothing lightweight about the results of his magic. The consequences were real and substantial. We face them now. A stultifying hegemony of court ritual is a principal obstacle to a Gulf of political maturity in the aftermath of the Iraq-Kuwait conflict.

Gramsci himself enjoyed Kipling's books and wanted his sons to read them.[4] Possibly he found besides being exciting stories that the texts confirmed his notions of cultural hegemony – a *how so* to be learned from *Just So*. The fact is that literary texts *do* have a causal effect, and the texts of Imperialism undoubtedly *did* influence the Imperialists.[5] Discussing the authority of Kipling's *Kim* and of the different classes of British at work in India, Paffard writes, 'The "real" sahibs, however, are experts on Indian languages and customs. Such a sahib is Creighton, the [IPS] spymaster who recruits Kim to the service: "No man could be a fool who knew the language so intimately, who moved so gently and silently, and whose eyes were so different from the dull fat eyes of other sahibs." Among such men ignorance is a cardinal sin.'[6]

We need Colonel Creightons. The current ignorance about the Gulf is enormous. This is partly because of the way the Arabs have treated scholars. An expatriate doctor in Qatar circulated the 'law of the Gulf' that should be handed down to arriving professionals by humourless shaikhs (a list which owes much to A. Sandemose's *A Fugitive Crosses His Track*, Knopf, New York, 1936):

1. **Thou Westerner shalt not believe thou *art* something.**
2. **Thou shalt not believe thou art as good as *we*.**
3. **Thou shalt not believe thou art as wise as *we*.**
4. **Thou shalt not fancy thyself as good as *we*.**
5. **Thou shalt not believe thou knowest better than *we*.**
6. **Thou shalt not believe thou are greater than *we*.**

7. **Thou shalt not believe *thou* amountest to anything.**
8. **Thou shalt not laugh at *us*.**
9. **Thou shalt not believe that anyone is concerned with *thee*.**
10. **Thou shalt not believe thou canst teach *us* anything.**

The Raj's bequest to Arabia has included a ceremonial Ruritanian ludicrousness which seems to have had *something* to do with the present-day political life in the shaikhdoms. The Great Days such as the King's birthday that occasioned a showing of Viceregal splendour are unsuitable in the 1990s; during the IPS administration those were the ones that were marked by gun salutes and flag displays. Despite the jettisoning of Indo-British ceremonialism, the visit of a relatively minor royal such as HRH Duke of Gloucester GCVO gets buildings spruced up and malls planted with far more fervour than the visits of less blue-blooded dignitaries. Neither the ILO nor UNO have the pre-nominal connotations of His Royal Highness, or the post-nominal cachet of Knight Grand Cross of the Royal Victorian Order.

The Gordian knot in the 1990s is that the shaikhdoms sorely need an identity, but pictures of the Amirs have not been an altogether successful substitute for the Viceregal ceremonial: 'A modern *nation* (as distinct from a collection of localities and interests) requires a "cultural" counterpart of this kind to function, however indifferent (or even hostile) some of its inhabitants may appear to the prescribed idiom, some of the time.'[7] Gulf Arabs cannot successfully recycle the symbols of an *ancien régime*.

They have tried rather pitifully to make rituals up, improvising or sometimes scratching far back into fancies about the pre-British era for inspiration. The up-market *kitsch* of Princess Di will not do, but neither, despite strenuous efforts, have tents and coffee pots. The Raj only succeeded in indoctrinating a tiny circle of Arabs with the particular variety of Imperialism that characterized the Indian Empire and the Indian Political Service. At heart, many of these shaikhs remain Anglophiles. When the Queen visited Eton in May of 1990 to mark its 550th anniversary, the boys who greeted her included 'Lord Ulster, son of the Duke of Gloucester, now in his second year, and princes of the royal houses of Nepal and Kuwait.' *The Times* (30 May 1990) added that after those gathered did justice to a smoked salmon luncheon, the sermon at the thanksgiving service was preached by the Archbishop of York. He told a congregation, which included Mr. Douglas Hurd (Old Etonian and present Foreign Secretary), that 'the best part of being an Etonian was that you did not have to worry about being an Etonian or not'.

Whether the Kuwaiti Etonians were getting an education appropriate to ruling their country in the twenty-first century, or whether they will be allowed to do so, remains to be seen. In the Indian Public Schools Conference files kept at Mayo College, there is a revealing interview that a principal of Rajkumar College, T.L. Smith-Pearse, had with M.K. Gandhi in 1939: 'It was obvious during our conversation that he regards the English Public School as the recruiting ground of "Imperialism" and that he is very suspicious of any expensive school in India lest it produce Indians even a little like English Public School products who will be out of sympathy with the Indian masses.'[8] Still, Gandhi's great disciple was Jawaharlal Nehru, an Old Harrovian.

Caveats

The IPS exported the social problems that they had at home. The deleterious effects of the old school tie remain evident in Kuwait *and* England: '...a 1988 report showed that English 14 year olds scored lower than the same age group in all other 17 countries examined in science. The UK is the only major nation where a majority of pupils leave full-time education or training at the age of sixteen. The result is that a much larger proportion of the UK labour force have less upper secondary education than in other major economies.'[9]

Political scientists trying to understand the Middle East should be wary of dismissing education and ritualism as peripheral. The Gulf states are not democracies or republics or commonwealths but tiny *shaikhdoms,* and a shaikhdom is a ritualistic society *par excellence*: '...ritual derives its efficacy and power from its performance and it is in its performance that its work of transformation fails or succeeds.'[10] Currently the performance is not going well. The public schoolboy rulers would have done things better. 'What a sight it is,' remarks a master in *Tom Brown's Schooldays,* 'the Doctor as a ruler! Perhaps ours is the only little corner of the British Empire which is thoroughly, wisely, and strongly ruled just now...'.[11]

The Gulf's Future

When the present hysteria over Kuwait has passed, the decline in superpower rivalry and the opening of Eastern Europe to Western influence may mean a decline in the American, Soviet, and European competition which has been a factor in Gulf history. Long-term priorities are being rearranged and the day is over when every United States senator felt it necessary to visit Doha and Manama.

Surprisingly, none of the pundits who worry about the longterm effects of the war on Gulf affairs have speculated about whether India may play a bigger role than she has so far. Possessed of the world's second largest land army and an admirable navy, she could become the predominant regional influence. In this writer's opinion, that will be an ingredient in any plan for lasting Gulf peace. America and her allies cannot be expected to take direct responsibility for Gulf stability indefinitely, and neither Iran nor Iraq are candidates for the role of honest broker and umpire. India's moment will come.

That the Gulf was part of the Indian Empire may not be as much of a historical footnote as a factor in its future. For years the Gulf has skirted its Indianness. The Arabs need to realize that not all the Indians in the world are houseboys. The *sursum corda* of anyone familiar with the present situation is that the ruling families take some crash lessons in history, pluralism, and constitutionalism. A little *actual* piety rather than the vulgar pretensions would not be out of place. There are alternatives to disaster.

Riposte

British success in Arabia relied on 'rituals with powerful persuasive force; rituals at times theatrical, at times mundane' .[12] The Arabs have found this less successful as a substitute for constitutionalism. Nevertheless, the Gulf cannot be understood without considerable reference to the way politics still are cast in an Anglo-Indian ritualistic idiom.[13] This helps to explain a source of current uneasiness, an anger attributable to the keenly felt lack of an *illud tempus*, a prior time. 'The movie,' a Qatari friend told me, 'is being made without any script'.

The pseudo-history officially purveyed has been disingenuously configured to provide a sort of legitimacy to the present rulers, who are surrounded by tawdry flags and bunting and protocol. The inadequacy of this as a substitute for parliaments is reflected in the increasingly desperate expenditures on security: Qatar in one year spent 46.9 per cent of its Gross National Product on the military.[14] Such armed forces are not primarily to protect against external challenges, and proved ludicrously inadequate when the Iraqi tanks came south. *They are armed forces devoted to maintaining internal authority.*

Effectively silenced by droves of Pakistani and Yemeni mercenaries, the majority of the indigenous population has found itself marginalized in its own homeland. Often the majority's tribe, gender, skin colour, and variety of Islam does not fit the prescribed pattern set down by the rulers. Amir, state, political society, and official history are, for the moment, synonymous. Production of history is a monopoly manifest in fawning museum displays, timorous universities, and a servile media. Scholarship as Western academics understand it is *haram*. What there is must serve narrow goals, and a comparison with Germany can be made:

> In the nineteenth and early twentieth centuries, patriotic German archaeologists sought to project far back into prehistoric times the ethnic continuity that historians emphasised had characterised their homeland throughout the historic period. Gustaf Kossinna sought to demonstrate archaeologically that Germany was the homeland of the Indo-European peoples and the centre of cultural creativity in prehistoric times. While the other Indo-European-speaking peoples had moved off and interbred with allegedly inferior races, the Germans alone had preserved their racial purity and hence their full powers of creativity.[15]

Similarly, the ruling families' fake genealogies and their highly selective archaeology are bent in the service of will-of-the-wisp efforts to sustain dynastic claims. An unfettered university and scholarly community would not be as great a challenge to their suzerainty as they think,[16] but the dilemma as they see it is that to search back for a history from which symbols of unity and patriotism could be drawn would be to stir doubts about their right to rule:

> There may be some legitimization success stories to be told in the Arab countries in the years ahead, but there are also powerful tendencies that may generate an 'era of turbulence'. The issue of political legitimacy, with all its conceptual difficulties, will have to remain the central issue for analytic attention.[17]

The Gulf states are torn between secularism, bolstered as it is by rapacious consumerism which would make Madison Avenue chortle, and the seemingly contradictory but reactive and ominous growth of religio-political movements. The portents are for more symbolic royalist politics in an effort to cope with rising social unrest and protest. The voteless masses will, as Iraq shows, take solace in the promises and the sense of belonging that radical slogans offer. The challenge to regimes posed by this radical revivalism lies in its alleged moral purity and its promise to strike back against the hostility of the West.[18]

For the moment though, the attitude throughout the Gulf remains similar to that of Kuwait just before it was invaded, where 'Few of the pro-democracy activists challenge the right of the al-Sabah to rule Kuwait, but they believe that freedom of speech is essential for the running of a modern state.'[19] If the tragedy of Kuwait finally brings the Gulf monarchs to their senses, it will have done some good – they could be an asset, a source of pride rather than despair to their people.

Prospects are unpromising for the survival of Arab regimes which do not address the problem of legitimacy. Solving the Gulf's problems will require honesty in reaching back and understanding what social historians metaphorically describe as 'the masonic grips of a secret fraternity'.[20] The danger is not one that arises entirely out of the present but arising too out of the perceptions of the past.[21] The long-term threat to the existence of the Gulf states is not from military invasion but from their posture towards past cultural invasions. The loss of the past in the Gulf is the loss of the proverbial nail by which the kingdom was lost.

In all the crises in authoritarianism there is a fundamental clash between the culture of modernization (what I have called the world culture) and the various national political cultures. This is always a psychologically disturbing clash because it brings into confrontation universal standards and parochial values. The former are essential for economic performance and effectiveness, and the latter are critical for creating national loyalties and distinctive national political styles. Arrayed on one side are the technocratic considerations imposed by the combined imperatives of economics, technology, and the principles of efficiency associated with rational public policy. Confronting these impersonal forces there stands the basic need of every polity for a sense of self-identity, for the dignity that comes from a fundamental belief in the collective uniqueness of the national entity and its spirit of community. – Lucian W. Pye, *Political Science and the Crisis of Authoritarianism,* Presidential Address to the American Political Science Association, 1989.

NOTES

1. Al-Qasimi, *The Myth of Arab Piracy* , 49. See Daniel, *The Cultural Barrier*, 121.
2. Sana Bagersh, 'Henna Popularity Still Unchanged', *Gulf News*, 1 February 1990, 3.
3. 'When Saddam Hussein wrapped himself in the flag of Arab radicalism and revolution, he gained considerable support by criticising the corruption and venality of the sheikhs. As an example of insensitivity, the big news in Qatar (*Middle East Economic Digest*, 16 November 1990) was that the

Heir Apparent had decided to spend $9,800,000 to improve his palace in Wajbah. The problem has been not just Iraq but the entire corrupt system of rule in the region. Not everyone in the Gulf is a shaikh – there are poor Qataris and Bahrainis who cannot afford gas masks'. 'Remarks' by Paul J. Rich to a gathering of allied officers, Doha, Qatar, 19 November 1990.

4. Patrick Williams, 'Kim and Orientalism', Mallett, *Kipling Considered,* 33.

5. 'Another reason for continuing to scrutinise works such as *Kim* is that, although clearly neither Kipling the author nor the range of positions offered by his texts is reducible to the merely imperialist, it is nevertheless important to achieve as precise a notion as possible of the ways in which the texts were involved in the process of Empire. As Said reminds us, texts may have very substantial material effects, be they social, political or economic, and nowhere, one might argue, is this more the case than within imperialism.' *Ibid.*, 34.

6. Paffard, *Kipling's Indian Fiction,* 73.

7. Nairn, *The Enchanted Glass,* 93.

8. T.L. Smith-Pearse, 'Report of Interview with Gandhi', Rapiur, 4 December 1939, located in I.P.S.C. Archives, File 2, qtd. Pollitt, 'A History of Mayo College', 174.

9. *Lloyds Bank Economic Bulletin,* No.134, February 1990.

10. Bruce Kapferer, 'Ritual Process and the Transformation of Context', Bruce Kapferer ed., *The Power of Ritual: Transition, Transformation and Transcendence in Ritual Practice,* Special Issue Series, *Social Analysis,* No.1, February 1979, 6.

11. Much has been made of the Empire's decline because of industrial backwardness and technical inferiority, but as Aaron Friedberg notes: 'Shifts in the distribution of power within an international system may be "real" in some sense, but they may fail to have any impact unless and until they are perceived.' Aaron L. Friedberg, *The Weary Titan: Britain and the Experience of Relative Decline, 1895-1905,* Princeton University Press, Princeton (New Jersey), 1988, 6. Ritualism helped to maintain the illusion of British power, whatever the reality. Friedberg quotes the arch priest of ritualism, Kenneth Boulding, about ways in which mythology sustains national images. *Ibid.*, 15.

12. Jean and John Comaroff, 'Through the Looking Glass: Colonial Encounters of the First Kind', *Journal of Historical Sociology,* Vol.1, No.1, March 1988, 8. The quintessential gift of Imperialism was the mirror, in which the transformed 'native' could behold his new self. *Ibid.*, 19, 21.

13. Ibid.

14. Thomas R. Dye and Harmon Ziegler, 'Socialism and Militarism', *PS: Political Science & Politics,* Vol.XXII, No.4, December 1989, 804.

15. Bruce G. Trigger, 'Alternative Archaeologies: Nationalist, Colonialist, Imperialist', *Man,* Vol.19, No.3, September 1984, 360. In the Imperial heyday, 'The achievements of ancient Near Eastern civilisations were appropriated for western Europe by claiming that western Europeans rather than the people who lived in the Near East today were their true spiritual heirs. British archaeologists also stressed that Britain was located where several streams of cultural influence from the Near East had converged; hence Britain, and especially England, had been able to develop more rapidly than its neighbours.' *Ibid.*, 365.

16. An unfettered scholarly community will not assault every Gulf icon. Although the direction that investigations take will be unanticipated there is no reason to think that investigation will produce entirely negative results. An example of what happens when the chips are allowed to fall where they may is the change in opinion brought about by current (1990) archaeological digs in Bahrain. The London-Bahrain Archaeological Expedition work at Sar has upset long-held theories that Bahrain was a Gulf centre for burials. This had been thought to be the case because of Bahrain's 100,000 burial mounds. Now that villages are being uncovered, the thinking is that Bahrain itself had a large enough population to have supported the cemeteries. *So a thesis which made Bahrain important has been replaced by another which makes it equally important.* What is *not* viable is suppression of scholarship in order to preserve legitimacy and self-importance. National symbolism and ritualism must rely on a defensible past, not fakery. See Michael C. Hudson, 'State, Society, and Legitimacy: An Essay on Arab Political Prospects in the 1990s', Sharabi ed., *The Next Arab Future,* 37. 'The liminal symbol operates culturally as a mnemonic, a reminder of cosmologies, values, and cultural axioms, whereby a society's knowledge is transmitted from one generation to another. [*eg.*] French political symbols, such as the barricades, and red and black flags, became meaningful in a time of social crisis, the Commune of 1871 for example, when they may have had (like the barricades themselves) an instrumental as well as symbolic value. These symbols tend to re-emerge in ritual re-enactments of the original event, which serve to reinforce a society's identification with its past...Or, as Durkheim has pointed out: "There is no society which does not feel the need of upholding and reaffirming at regular intervals the collective sentiments and the collective ideas which make up its unity and its personality." ' Turkle, *'Symbol and Festival'*, 93.

17. Hudson, 'State, Society, and Legitimacy', Sharabi ed., *The Next Arab Future* , 35. '...as early as 1928, with the founding in Egypt of the Muslim Brethren, the Middle East began to witness the political potential of Muslim religio-political movements based in the cities, using modern methods of organization and grafting alien, modern political ideas to fundamentalist, anti-establishment programs. In the last few years the importance of such Muslim fundamentalist religio-political groups has increased. So, too, has the nervous concern of most Middle Eastern governments.' Brown, *International Politics and the Middle East*, 261.

18. See Mohamed G. Rumahihi, 'The Mode of Production in the Arab Gulf Before the Discovery of Oil', Tim Niblock ed., *Social and Economic Development in the Arab Gulf*, Croom Helm, 1980, 49-60. Rumahihi's thesis is that social relations in the Gulf are still influenced by the pre-oil boom past.

19. Mallet, 'Eight Kuwaiti Pro-democracy Activists Arrested', 5.

20. George Wyndham qtd. David Trotter, 'Kipling's England: the Edwardian Years', Mallett, *Kipling Considered*, 56. *However* 'The problem is that we no longer understand the code of these masonic communications. The specific terms of Edwardian Imperialism have evaporated, leaving us with what they helped to produce: a myth of rural England already nostalgic at its inception, and now the focus of our own massed nostalgias.' *Ibid.*

21. G. Hossein Razi, 'Legitimacy, Religion, and Nationalism in the Middle East', *American Political Science Review*, Vol.84, No.1, March 1990, 70-72, 84.

APPENDIX I

No event that took place in the Gulf during IPS administration was as splendid as Curzon's visit.

Lord Curzon's Address at Sharjah to the Chiefs of the Arab Coast, 21 November, 1903

I have come here as the representative in the great Empire of India of the British authority which you and your fathers and forefathers have known and dealt with for more than a hundred years; and my object is to show you, that though you live at some distance from the shores of India, you are not forgotten by the Government, but that they adhere to the policy of guardianship and protection which has given you peace and guaranteed your rights for the best part of a century; and that the first Viceroy of India who has ever visited these waters does not quit them without seeking the opportunity of meeting you in person, and of renewing the assurances and engagements by which we have been so long united.

Chiefs, your fathers and grandfathers before you have doubtless told you of the history of the past. You know that a hundred years ago there were constant trouble and fighting in the Gulf; almost every man was a marauder or a pirate; kidnapping and slave-trading flourished; fighting and bloodshed went on without stint or respite; no ship could put out to sea without fear of attack; the pearl fishery was a scene of annual conflict; and security of trade or peace there was none. Then it was that the British Government intervened and said that, in the interests of its own subjects and traders, and of its legitimate influence in the seas that wash the Indian coasts, this state of affairs must not continue. British flotillas appeared in these waters. British forces occupied the forts and towns on the coast that we see from this deck. The struggle was severe while it lasted, but it was not long sustained. In 1820 the first general Treaty was signed between the British Government and the Chiefs; and of these or similar agreements there have been in all no fewer than eight. In 1838 the Maritime Truce was concluded, and was renewed from time to time until the year 1853, when it was succeeded by the Treaty of Perpetual Peace that has lasted ever since. Under that Treaty it was provided that there should be a complete cessation of hostilities at sea between the subjects of the signatory Chiefs, and a 'perfect maritime truce' – to use the words that were employed – 'for evermore'; that in the event of aggressions on any one by sea, the injured parties should not retaliate, but should refer the matter to the British Resident in the Persian gulf; and that the British Government should watch over the peace of the gulf and ensure at all times the observance of the Treaty. Chiefs, that Treaty has not, of course, prevented occasional trouble and conflict; it has sometimes been neglected or infringed; but on the whole it has well deserved its name; and under it has grown up a condition of affairs so peaceful and secure that the oldest among you can only remember as a dim story the events of the past, while the younger have never seen warfare or bloodshed on the seas. It is now eleven years since the last disturbance of the peace occurred.

Chiefs, out of the relations that were thus created, and which by your own consent constituted the British Government the guardian of inter-tribal peace, there grew up political ties between the Government of India and yourselves, whereby the British Government became your overlords and protectors, and you have relations with no other Power. Every one of the States known as the Trucial States has bound itself, as you know, not to enter into any agreement or correspondence with any other Power, not to admit the agent of any other government, and not to part with any portion of its territories. These engagements are binding on every one of you, and you have faithfully adhered to them. They are also binding in their reciprocal effect upon the British Government, and as long as they are faithfully observed by the chiefs there is no fear that any one else will be allowed to tamper with your rights or liberties.

Sometimes I think that the record of the past is in danger of being forgotten, and there are persons who ask – Why should Great Britain continue to exercise these powers?: The history of your states and of your families, and the present condition of the Gulf, are the answer. We were here before any other Power, in modern times, had shown its face in these waters. We found strife and we have created order. It was our commerce as well as your security that was threatened and called for protection. At every port along these coasts the subjects of the King of England still reside and trade. The great Empire of India, which it is our duty to defend, lies almost at your gates. We saved you from extinction at the hands of your neighbours. We opened these seas to the ships of all nations, and enabled their flags to fly in peace. We have not seized or held your territory. We have not destroyed your independence, but have preserved it. We are not now going to throw away this century of costly and triumphant enterprise; we shall not wipe out the most unselfish page in history. The peace of these waters must still be maintained; your independence will continue to be upheld; and the influence of the British Government must remain supreme.

There is one respect in which the chiefs themselves can avert any renewal of trouble in the future. The British Government have no desire to interfere, and have never interfered, in your internal affairs, provided that the chiefs govern their territories with justice, and respect the rights of the foreign traders residing therein. If any internal disputes occur, you will always find a friend in the British Resident, who will use his influence, as he has frequently done in the past, to prevent these dissensions from coming to a head, and to maintain the *status quo*; for we could not approve of one independent chief attacking another chief by land, simply because he was not permitted to do it by sea, and thus evading the spirt of his Treaty obligations. I will mention a case that seems to lend itself to friendly settlement of the character that I have described. You are all of you aware that the strip of coast known as the Batineh Coast, on the opposite side of the Oman peninsula, is under the authority of the Jowasmis. Nevertheless his authority is contested in some quarters. It is desirable that these disputes should cease, and that the peace should remain undisturbed.

Chiefs, these are the relations that subsist between the British Government and yourselves. The Sovereign of the British Empire lives so far away that none of you has ever seen or will ever see his face; but his orders are carried out everywhere throughout his vast domains by the officers of his Government, and it is as his representative in India, who is responsible to him for your welfare, that I am here today to exchange greetings with you, to renew old assurances, and to wish you prosperity in the future.

Lady Curzon, the Vicereine, accompanied her husband on his voyage to the Gulf. Her letters and journal provide a unique picture of the Gulf. On November 26th, she recorded the visit to Bahrain: 'The island is under British protection, but ruled by a Sheikh who is in the hands of a few Indian moneylenders, and these control the wealth of his priceless island, as he leases out the fisheries. The Sheikh came onto the Hardinge to see George, and was received in Durbar. He is a pure Arab, and looks just like a Bible prophet. George returned his visit on shore, but as we are anchored 5 miles out and the tide was low, his launch stuck on a reef. The landing in the surf was very funny, as the party had to transfer themselves from the launch to donkeys' backs and ride through the waves. A good many fell off...'. (See Plate 41.)

APPENDIX II

Address by Lord Curzon to the British Residents at Bushire, 2 December 1903

I am very glad to see you here, and to receive your friendly Address. I am sorry to have been prevented from receiving you on shore, when I might have been introduced to an even larger number of British residents and merchants at this important place.

A Viceroy of India coming to Bushire in the year 1903, though he be the first occupant of that position to visit these waters during his term of Office, is irresistibly reminded of his precursors a century gone by. He is, indeed, the logical as well as the historical successor of Sir John Malcolm, who came here more than once just a hundred years ago; and he is the latest link in an unbroken sequence of political officers who have been deputed from India to represent British and Indian political interests, and to protect their corresponding commercial interests, in this neighbourhood since the appointment of the first political agent as far back as 1812. Even then British interests had been represented here for as much as half a century; since it was in 1763 that the East India Company first opened a factory at Bushire. At that time one vessel a year from India was sufficient to accommodate the whole of British trade. In 1902, 136 steamers entered the port, and of these 133 were British. In the last twenty years the imports have increased from 135 lakhs, of which 117½ were from Great Britain and India to 201¾ lakhs in 1901, of which 152½ lakhs were British and Indian. In the same period the imports of tea from India have risen from a value of Rs.65,000 to a value of close upon 10 lakhs. These figures do not leave much doubt as to where the preponderance of trade lies.

This history of 140 years is without a parallel to the connection of any other foreign nation with these coasts; under it have grown up connections with the local Governments and peoples of close friendships and confidence; it is a chapter of history upon which we have every right to look back with pride; and it imposes upon us obligations which it is impossible that we should overlook, and which no Government, either of Great Britain or India, is likely to ignore.

Bushire is the headquarters of this long-standing connection. From here the British Resident exerts that mild control over the waters of the Gulf, and over the tribes upon its opposite shore, the results of which I have enjoyed so many opportunities of observing during my present cruise. From this place the principal caravan route strikes into the interior of Persia, tapping its chief cities in succession, and ultimately reaching the capital; here the wires of the Indo-European telegraph, which in their earlier stages have brought Persia into connection with Europe, which have done so much to strengthen the authority of the Shah in his won dominions, and which carry the vast majority of the messages from India to England, dip into the sea; here is the residence of the Persian official who is charged with the Governorship of the Persian Gulf ports by his Government, and with whom our relations are invariably those of the friendliest nature; and under these combined auspices – the British bringing the bulk of the trade and policing the maritime highway, and the Persians gradually consolidating an authority which, though once precarious, is now assured – this place has grown from a small fishing village into a flourishing town of 20,000 inhabitants; it has become the residence of foreign Consuls and Consular officers; the leading mercantile communities who trade in Southern Persia and Turkey have their offices and representatives here; there is seldom a day in which steamers are not lying off the port, and Bushire has acquired a name which it is safe to say is known in every part of the world.

This development is the more remarkable because, as you have pointed out, no one could contend that trade is conducted here under favourable conditions; on the contrary there are few, if any, of the conditions that naturally make out a place as an emporium or channel of commerce. Bushire can hardly be said, even by the wildest stretch of imagination, to possess a harbour. Landing is difficult and often impracticable. The trade-route that penetrates into the interior is one of the most difficult in Asia; and inland you do not find a people enjoying great wealth or a high standard of comfort or civilization, but instead you encounter tribes leading a nomadic form of existence; and even when you come to the settled parts of the country and the larger cities, the purchasing power of the people does not appear to be great. The fact that a large and flourishing trade has grown up in spite of these drawbacks is an irrefutable proof of the dependence of Persia upon outside supply for many of the necessities and most of the luxuries of life. Since I first visited Bushire fourteen years ago I have always indulged the hope that, as time passed on, progress would be made in all these directions, and I agree with you in thinking that the Persian Government could embark upon no more remunerative form of expenditure than the improvement both of the maritime and the inland approaches to this place.

During the time in which I have filled my present office in India, I have done my best to facilitate the progress of trade, and to ensure the adequate protection of British interests in the Gulf and in the adjoining provinces and territories. His Majesty's Government at home have also been warmly interested in the matter. The result of these efforts has been that we have gradually developed the Nushki-Seistan trade-route, which is now a recognized channel of commerce to Eastern Persia. We have appointed a Consul at Kerman, and a Vice-Consul at Bunder Abbas, where we are about to build a consular residence; we have connected Muscat too by cable with Jask, and we hope for further telegraphic extensions in the interests of trade. We have established a political agent at Bahrein: and we now have a Consul at Mohammera and a Vice-Consul at Abwaz. The Karun trade-route has made substantial progress, and has been supplemented by the newly opened road, with caravanserais and bridges through the Bakhtiari country to Ispahan. A British Consul has also been appointed to Shiraz. We have improved and accelerated the mail service to all the Gulf ports. British India steamers now call at Kuwait as well. During the same period British medical officers have been lent by us to the Persian Government to conduct the quarantine arrangements in the Gulf. Simultaneously, British interests have found a most vigilant spokesman at Teheran in His Majesty's Minister, Sir Arthur Hardinge, who has been good enough to accompany me throughout my present journey, and with whom I have enjoyed many opportunities of discussing the common interests of the Home and Indian Government in Persia. I hope that our discussions may be fraught with advantage to the interests that we jointly represent.

Altogether I think it may be said that in Bushire you receive an amount of attention that is not always extended in similar measure to places so remote from headquarters, while the fact that a British Resident lives in your midst and is able personally to look after your concerns, which I am glad to learn from your address that he does entirely to your satisfaction, is a further guarantee for their protection. I hope that the position which British interests thus enjoy, and which is neither artificial in origin nor recent in growth, since it is the result of nearly a century and a half of patient and laborious effort both by Government and by private enterprise, may long be maintained, and that Bushire may continue in the future, as it has done in the past, to be the centre from which this benign and peaceful influence radiates throughout Southern Persia and the Persian Gulf.

BIBLIOGRAPHICAL ESSAY

The history of the Victorian Age will never be written: we know too much about it. For ignorance is the first requisite of the historian – ignorance, which simplifies and clarifies, which selects and omits, with a placid perfection unattainable by the highest art. Concerning the Age which has just passed, our fathers and our grandfathers have poured forth and accumulated so vast a quantity of information that the industry of a Ranke would be submerged by it, and the perspicacity of a Gibbon would quail before it. – Lytton Strachey, *Eminent Victorians*, 1918.

At Leysin, in 1945, in order to perform an extrapleural pneumothorax operation, a piece of one of my ribs was removed, and subsequently given back to me, quite formally, wrapped up in a piece of medical gauze...For a long time I kept this fragment of myself in a drawer, a kind of body penis analgous to the end of rib chop, not knowing quite what to do with it, not daring to get rid of it least I do some harm to my person, though it was utterly useless to me shut up in a desk among such 'precious' objects as old keys, a schoolboy report card, my grandmother B.'s mother-of-pearl dance program and pink taffeta card case. And then, one day, realizing that the function of any drawer is to ease, to acclimate the death of objects by causing them to pass through a sort of pious site, a dusty chapel where, in the guise of keeping them alive, we allow them a decent interval of dim agony, but not going so far as to dare cast this bit of myself into the common refuse bin of my building, I flung the rib chop and its gauze from my balcony, as if I were romantically scattering my own ashes, into the rue Servandoni, where some dog would come and sniff them out. – Roland Barthes, *Roland Barthes*, 1975.

Obviously the formation of the modern state of Iraq and its subsequent relationships with Kuwait will be a focus of Gulf studies in the 1990s. This will in turn result in interest in the lives of the Residents such as Percy Cox and Arnold Wilson. However, the old problems of bibliography about the region will remain. The brazen nature of Imperialism is that it imposes a bold bibliographical hegemony, as well as a political one. Reconstruction or deconstruction starts with a review of bibliographical strategies. The 'new history' of the Gulf will be based on 'hybridity, impurity, intermingling, the transformation that comes of new and unexpected combinations of human beings, cultures, ideas, politics, movies, songs'. The quote, expressing a view of history, is taken from Salman Rushdie's *In Good Faith* (Granta, 1990). He adds, 'Mélange, hotch-potch, a bit of this and a bit of that is *how newness enters the world*...Like many millions of people, I am a bastard child of history. Perhaps we all are, black and brown and white, leaking into one another, as a character of mine once said, *like flavours when you cook*'. Amen to that.

A development in Gulf bibliography in the 1990s is likely to be the opening up of hitherto secret archives in the Soviet Union. For practical purposes those relating to the Middle East have been completely closed to Western scholars. It then should be possible to reappraise activities of Russophobes such as Cox and Curzon, and to re-evaluate the alleged Russian threats which were a strong motivation to British policy. Dr. Aaron L. Friedberg in *The Weary Titan: Britain and the Experience of Relative Decline, 1895-1905* quotes a 1905 letter of George Clarke to Arthur Balfour: 'The story of our proceedings dictated by fear of Russia is an amazing one. It will have to be written someday.' Dr. Friedberg emphasizes that the feeling was that 'Britain might not be able to get at Russia' but 'Russia could most certainly get at Britain.'

Another inevitable result of the 1990-91 Iraqi invasion of Kuwait will be an interest in the origins of Kuwait. For that task, a useful starting point is Ahmad Mustafa Abu-Hakima's *The Modern History of Kuwait, 1750-1965* (Luzac, 1983). Abu-Hakima worked for the Kuwait Ministry of Education in the 1950s and subsequently was at the School of Oriental & African Studies in London, then taking up the chair of Arabian history at McGill. His book has an excellent bibliography and is objective in its conclusions about Kuwaiti history. Also useful for a Kuwaiti background is Jennifer M. Scarce's *The Evolving Culture of Kuwait* (Royal Scottish Museum and HMSO, 1985), which draws on extensive field research and is magnificently illustrated. The two books should convince readers that Kuwait has its own identity, notwithstanding Iraqi propaganda.

An anticipated development as far as Gulf historiography in general is concerned will be the move of the Indian Office Library and Archives into new buildings of the British Library, c.1995. Another change may be the construction of an international library at Alexandria, Egypt, although it remains to be seen if enthusiasm for creating a building will carry over to creating a collection. The portents for this have been unfavourable. The effect of the scheme may be harmful in that it will divert energies and monies that should have gone into the conservation of neglected materials in existing Middle Eastern collections. The attention Arab leaders have given to the project could better have gone into lifting the censorship which makes their countries so backward.

On the other hand, recently, access to the Ottoman archives in Istanbul has been greatly facilitated, with numerous guides being published and considerable reorganization going on. The next few decades should bring considerable revisions to the hitherto stereotypical portrait of the Turks. The Ottomans took seriously their responsibilities to history. The ongoing restoration of the Topkapi Seraglio or palace of the rulers is indicative of Turkish concern to preserve Ottoman history. The Topkapi Seraglio preserves such artifacts as a tooth of Mohammad, as well as his cloak, bow, and swords. There is also a letter which he wrote in 627, rescued by a French adventurer in 1850 from a monastery in Egypt where he found it between the pages of a New Testament. Because of this pack rat mentality through the centuries, it may well be that Istanbul has as much about the Gulf as London does.

The negative aspects of the bibliographical situation as far as Middle Eastern studies are concerned have been noted in Chapter IV. They include not only the poor conditions under which existing libraries work but the failure of Gulf states to have taken advantage of petrodollar prosperity to build national or university collections of consequence. The destruction of Beirut, which was the centre of the Arab world for publishing, is representative of a generally impoverished situation as far as books in the Arab world are concerned.

Not only do Gulf countries lack substantial archival holdings about the Gulf, but Gulf studies are notable for the absence of helpful contributions by Arab bibliographers. In 1976 the research committee of the Middle East Studies Association published *The Study of the Middle East* (Leonard Binder ed., John Wiley & Sons, New York). Chapters were written by acknowledged authorities and the topics included Islamic religious tradition, history, anthropology, Islamic art and architecture, political science, philosophy, linguistics, literature, sociology and economics. The report, which has been a foundation of Middle East bibliography since its first appearance, tolerantly remarked that 'For the most part, in Middle Eastern university systems, the premium labour lies in the translation of Western (including, where permitted, Marxist) works and in surveys of general disciplinary literature rather than in specific and applied study.' What could have been added was that plagiarism of Western scholarship was rampant among Arab academics. *That situation has not changed at all.*

The Winter 1990 issue of *MELA Notes*, a publication of the Middle East Librarians Association, carried an article by David H. Partington of the Harvard University Library's Middle East department on the Binder project. Partington notes that none of the contributors discussed libraries as such and inquires 'Could this silence signal a tacit recognition that American libraries have successfully met the post-war challenge of building up research collections for non-Western studies? Are the shelves of American libraries so well stocked and organized for Middle Eastern studies that librarians can be taken for granted by the practitioners and theoreticians of Middle Eastern area studies?' He believes that the failure to mention libraries is not because they have been successful, but because Middle East specialists take them for granted.

Subjective Mediations

Not only do scholars take collections of Middle Eastern material in Western libraries for granted, but they often miss the significance of the subjectivity of the collecting process that has formed those collections. As mentioned in Chapter IV, at a University of Essex conference 'Europe and Its Others' in 1985, Gayatri Chakravorty Spivak delivered a germinal paper entitled 'The Rani of Sirmur: An Essay in Reading the Archives' that serves too as a warning about the bibliography of the Gulf. Dr. Spivak, tongue-in-cheek, quoted from Hayden White's book *Metahistory* (1973) about historians being unaware that language is an *instrument of meditation* rather than *factual* and added:

> In that a hegemonic nineteenth century European historiography has designated the archives as a repository of 'facts,' and I propose that they should be 'read,' my position can be consonant with White's. The records I read show the soldiers and administrators of the East India Company constructing the object of representations that becomes the reality of India. On a somewhat precious register of literary theory, it is possible to say that this was the construction of a fiction whose task was to produce a whole collection of 'effects of the real', and that the 'misreading' of this 'fiction' produced the proper name 'India'.

Essentially any library is a subjective instrument of mediation between the scholar and the subject. The history of the collecting process and the use to which the collections have been put thus is as much a part of Gulf historiography as the books themselves. So far Gulf scholars have not wandered far from the India Office Library and Records in their employment of original materials – and that says something about the region's historians.

A collection which gives the India Office a run for its money as far as unpublished papers is that of the Middle East Centre at St. Antony's College, Oxford. Thirty years have passed since Elizabeth Monroe, Albert Hourani, and others began to urge the deposit of material by those who had spent time in the Middle East. The results in one area, as well as holdings elsewhere in the United Kingdom, are described in a new book (1989) by Gillian Grant, *Middle Eastern Photographic Collections in the United Kingdom*. What is surprising is how much has survived, although there should be no illusions about the fact that considerable documentation, documentation that would alter perceptions of Indian and Gulf history, was destroyed long ago. In Chapter IV this 'vetting' process was mentioned. Sir Conrad Corfield in *The Princely India I Knew* provides additional evidence that it was gone about with vigour. In 1947, he noted, 'Wakefield [onetime Gulf Political Agent *qv*] had prepared a memorandum suggesting how these records should be dealt with, and his proposals were approved. They were briefly that records of historical value or interest were to be retained and sent via the U.K. High Commissioner in Delhi to the India Office in London, but that records which referred to any incident of a personal nature or a Ruler's family should be destroyed, unless they were of potential historic interest. Political Officers were told to take action accordingly.'

Unusual Approaches

The manuscript material surviving from the early days of the Gulf may have been underestimated. According to Donaldson in *The Postal Agencies in Eastern Arabia and the Gulf*, Captain Shakespear in 1910 produced figures on the outgoing mail from Kuwait for Percy Cox. He was attempting to convince Cox that a post office should be opened, and he stated that the Agency in 1909 had despatched 7310 letters. This he felt was on the low side '...for a considerable number of letters are carried personally by passengers for posting on board to obtain the benefit of a lower rate, and also frequently for want of stamps.' When he tried once more in 1912, the outgoing letters were over 12,000 per year. Some must have survived. This author's personal conviction is that one of the best places to look for a cache of letters reporting on the early Gulf will be the archives of Bombay commercial establishments that handled trade with Gulf entrepôts. Moreover, the fact that Kuwait was included in the East India Company's operations, partly because of the usefulness of its location for mail forwarding, suggests that the postal history approach would yield results in even earlier times.

Ideas about creative bibliographical approaches may be had from several other organizations that in addition to the Middle East Librarians Association display an interest in the Gulf and which publish newsletters. These are of limited circulation and are hard to locate unless one subscribes. The India Study Circle, which is for philatelists, often includes articles about the Gulf in the quarterly *India Post* (11 Boston Court, Brownhill Road, Eastleigh, Hampshire). The Society for Arabian Studies is connected with the British Academy. The Anglo-Omani Society in London not only has mailings and sponsors talks on the sultanate, but conducts trips to Oman.

The Sage Library of the Reformed Church in America (cited SLRCA) holds a number of titles that are photocopies of typescripts. American missionaries produced volumes of reminiscences, some of which have been referred to in the text. The American presence in the Gulf provides an interesting gloss on the far more significant British one. Considerable material in the library of the United Grand Lodge of England has a similar typed format to that in the Sage: it is obvious from their condition that they were produced in a non-commercial and informal way. The same is true of unpublished papers circulated, which were presented at the 'Bahrain Through the Ages Conference' held under the auspices of the Emir of Bahrain in Manama, Bahrain, 3-9 December 1983. (In different format most appeared in *Bahrain Through the Ages*, edited by Michael Rice and published in 1986 by Kegan Paul.)

The Clio Press bibliographies of Bahrain and the Emirates by Frank A. Clements and of Kuwait and Qatar by P.T.H. Unwin suggest publications which might otherwise not be investigated. The Kuwait bibliography will be enormously enlarged by the events of 1990. The four books follow the standard format of the World Bibliographical Series of which they are a part, and this format requires separate sections for topics such as the arts and sports which a Gulf bibliographer would normally eschew. Messrs. Clements and Unwin have been forced to scratch to fill out these sections, but effectively.

The India Office and India

The fact remains that the bulk of easily accessible original materials are in the India Office Library and Records of the British Library. While the India Office Library publishes a number of excellent guides, some further cautions are in order. The East India Company Board of Directors and later the India Office corresponded with the Government of India through the Secret and Political Committees and Departments. Naturally they also corresponded with other government departments and with individuals and organizations outside of government. Frequently there would be enclosures with letters such as copies of letters received or sent, tables, or maps. There was only a loose distinction drawn between what was considered secret and what was considered political. Secrecy seems to have included frontier problems and relations with other countries. The correspondence between London and India did *not* mean that there was no direct correspondence between London and the Gulf. The L/P&S/9 series which has been cited occasionally in this volume includes such direct correspondence. In short, there is no single place in the India Office cache where all relevant Gulf materials on a topic will be found.

So far there has been no comprehensive study of the publishing activities of the Imperial Government of India and successor publishing activities of the Republic, *hiatus valde deflendus*. At least six official government presses were established by the British, and the heir of those operations, the Directorate of Printing, today has 21 presses and employs over 13,000 persons. Thus considerable bibliographical work remains to be done, complicated by the shuffling of records in 1911 when the capital was relocated, when a portion of the activities remained at the Calcutta Central Press and much shifted to Delhi and the new Minto Road Press.

Archival material remaining in India itself relating to the Gulf is extensive. Shaikh Muhammad Al-Qasim's forays into the Bombay archives were mentioned in Chapter IV. The Centre for Arab Gulf Studies at the University of Exeter has provided a help to scholars by copying over 11,000 pages from the records held in Bombay. These records include the Bombay Secret and Political Department Diaries. Bombay had its own political service until it was merged with the IPS in the 1920s. Unresolved is the question whether what was left behind in India in 1947 reflects a different bias from what was shipped to London. There is a suspicion on the part of some that throwing open the unused documents will challenge existing views. In the preface to *British Bureaucracy in India: Status, Policy and the I.C.S. in the Late 19th Century,* Bradford Spangenberg writes, 'Until recently historiography of British bureaucracy in India (often called the Covenanted Civil Service or simply the Indian Civil Service) had been permeated by an aura of romantic mythology. This mythology emerged around the turn of the century as part of the defence against criticism of British imperialism in India. Autobiographical literature by officials themselves (especially the memoirs of John Beames, Robert Carstairs, G.R. Elsmie, and Bampfylde Fuller) often reads more candidly and pungently than the analyses of twentieth century historians.' Spangenberg singles out L.S.S. O'Malley's *The Indian Civil Service, 1601-1930* and Philip M. Woodruff's *The Men Who Ruled India* as examples of the nostalgia which he believes confounds the record.

As an introduction to Indian libraries, there is no better guide than the five-volume *Handbook of Libraries, Archives & Information Centres in India* (Information Industry Publications, New Delhi, 1985). Volumes I and II deal with libraries and archives, while Volumes III and IV consider information systems and Volume V looks at professional information organizations in India. Topics that relate to Gulf studies are covered. For example, in Volume I there is an entire chapter on government libraries and another entire chapter on Islamic studies libraries. Volume II has a chapter on the Indian Historical Records Commission. The entire set is a necessity in any serious Gulf library.

Reappraisals

After granting that archival reappraisal is overdue and should start with a bibliographical reconnoitring, a reaction to the mounds to be reviewed is that such accumulations can never be completely mastered. No student of the Gulf will claim to have reviewed the entirety of the India Office collections. The other side of the coin is that an incident can be looked at from several perspectives. Through the India Office documents it often is possible to compare what London, India, and the man on the spot in the Gulf thought, although this will not be as easy as it sounds. For one thing, the India Office Records have been renumbered on several occasions. Moreover, within a file (as anyone knows who has placed photocopy orders), there are as many as five different pencil paginations, presumably done over the years by various clerks. Therefore, unless the pagination in a file is unambiguous, it can be dangerous to follow the convention that some writers have (for example, Khuri in *Tribe and State in Bahrain*) of simply citing the file and a page, *e.g.* IOR:R/15/2/1/51, p.61. On the other hand, if an entire file has relevant material, as is often the case, the citation of the file can stand as a *passim* reference. As noted, they have also been 'edited'. Mark Bence-Jones relates in *The Viceroys of India* how Corfield, the last head of the Political Department, made a bonfire of incriminating files that included unflattering material about the Princes with whom the IPS had dealt. When Nehru protested, Mountbatten told Corfield, 'I will not stop you burning papers, but don't do it so obviously.' This is at variance from his own account mentioned above.

Some dilemmas arise in citing file numbers when it is desired to check one author's citations against another's. By way of illustration, Ismael found the Persian Gulf Administration Report for 1918 in Dickson's papers in the archives at St. Antony's College, Oxford, and cites it as if it were a unique document. (Ismael, *Kuwait*, 18 n.18.) In fact it is a copy of IOR:15/6/519. This is why when Archive Editions reproduced the IOR:R/15/6/473-541 series of Residents' reports, it was unfortunate that a cross-index of the old IOR numbers was not provided. That would have made it possible to correlate the so-called *PGAR* series with citations in the past. In this book's footnotes, the old IOR numbers are given because otherwise references by all the earlier authors to the *PGAR* files cannot be readily identified and compared. It is this author's opinion that IOR numbers should be given if any substantial use is made of authors using the old numbering system, regardless of the later reproduction of the file or files.

A 'file' is not necessarily one folder and can indeed be several bulky folders and envelopes. The contents can be straightforward, *e.g.* letters that can be cited with the correspondents and date. But there are also memoranda, notes, circulars, maps and photographs, printed papers bound in, and other material that must be given a title by the researcher. The discussion of the contents of each file examined might be helpful, but here it would stretch the bibliography to an inordinate length. In the notes, some discussion of this has been offered. The file will often have additional references which were scribbled by officials, suggesting other files that at the time were pertinent. Thus a sort of 'IPS hypertext' was in operation which will be difficult to follow.

Besides the substantial contributions by Penelope Tuson, India Office Library guides referred to above which are relevant include *Printed Books in European Languages, Prints and Drawings, The Map Collections, The European Manuscripts, Periodicals and Newspapers, Official Publications, Select List of Private Collections in the European Manuscripts, Arabic Language Collections in the British Library,* and *Sources for Middle East Studies.* The annual *Report* of the India Office Library and Records comments on acquisitions, and these frequently are pre-1947 items. An introduction to early material is *Arabian Gulf Intelligence: Selections from the Records of the Bombay Government, New Series, No. XXIV, 1856, concerning Arabia, Bahrain, Kuwait, Muscat and Oman, Qatar, United Arab Emirates and the Islands of the Gulf.* This was edited by R. Hughes Thomas and republished by Oleander Press, Cambridge, in 1985.

As mentioned, India Office holdings are being reprinted by Archive Editions. Titles so far include *The Persian Gulf Administration Reports, 1873-1947,* and the *Persian Gulf Précis, 1903-1908.* The *Administration Reports* were compiled by the Resident for the Government of India. They run to over 6600 pages of text. They should not be confused with the series known as the *Bahrain Government Annual Reports,* which were begun in 1924 by the then PA, Clive Daly, and carried on by Charles Belgrave when he became Personal Adviser to the shaikh in 1926. The originals are in the R/15/1/350-355 series. They are not 'unknown' as far as origin and particulars, as mistakenly stated by Littlefield and others. It is important to note that Belgrave prepared a report for the PA (found in the series R/15/2/296-305) which is quite apart from the *Annual Reports* issued in Bahrain. Belgrave's report to the PA then was used by the PA for his own report which eventually appeared, edited, in the R/15/6/473-541 series. Belgrave was not an IPS member, having been recruited to act as the Bahrain shaikh's adviser. He exercised considerable independence and was a thorn in the side of Residents and Agents. His unique situation as the only such adviser in the Gulf (the post was more common in India) makes his writings especially valuable. Of Belgrave's various publications, possibly the most self-revealing is his book about the oasis of Jupiter Ammon in Egypt, *Siwa* (John Lane, The Bodley Head, 1923). This curious book is illustrated with his own watercolours and photographs.

When employing the official reports, consideration should be given to *who originally used them* as that points to possible further sources of archives. The distribution lists give an inkling of who was involved in the decision-making progress. For example, in 1945 the following were receiving the fortnightly intelligence summaries of the Bahrain Political Agent: Secretary of State for India, India Office (5 copies); Secretary to the Government of India in the External Affairs Department (2 copies); Gulf Resident; PA Kuwait; PA Muscat; Consul, Bandar Abbas; PO, Sharjah; Ambassador, Baghdad; Middle East Intelligence Centre, Cairo; Chief of General Staff, New Delhi; Minister, Jedda; Adviser, Aden; Governor, Aden; Intelligence Centre, Baghdad; Naval Officer, Bahrain; Senior Naval Officer, Gulf; Naval Intelligence Centre, Colombo (2 copies); Air Liaison Officer, Bahrain; Staff Intelligence Officer, Basra. (See IOR:R/15/2/316, 'Intelligence Summary of the Political Agency, Bahrain, for the period lst to 15th January, 1945'.) Presumably the archives of those individuals would have material on the Gulf – possibly something unique on the Gulf. In this respect, Coen's account in *Indian Political Service* of the 'sorting' of IPS records in 1947 by Major W.P. Cranston, and their transfer to the Commonwealth Relations Office, deserves consideration.

Judge Saldanha

The number of references to Saldanha call for further explanation. The introduction to the notes to Chapter I called attention to the 3100 pages and 18 volumes of J.A. Saldanha, *The Persian Gulf Précis*, Government Printer, Calcutta and Simla, 1903-1908. The Saldanha series summarized the records of the Bombay Government in the Secretariat Record Office and other archives. The documents were assembled in 1903-1906 by an Indian judge, Jerome Antony Saldanha of the Bombay Provincial Civil Service. He was assisted by Cecil Gabriel, who was Deputy Political Resident briefly in 1919 and whose biography appears in Chapter IX. Judge Saldanha had access to papers which are not in the India Office in London, and which may now be unavailable in the Indian archives. He and Gabriel were able to consult the archives both in Bombay and Calcutta, and their summaries were used by Lorimer in writing his Gazetteer.

Saldanha's titles are listed below. A reprint which consolidates the individual volumes appeared in 1986, condensing them into eight volumes. Information can be had from Archive Editions, Gerrards Cross, Buckinghamshire. It is generally conceded that Lorimer relied heavily on Saldanha for his famous *magnum opus*. Saldanha discusses his own sources in the preface to the volume *Selections from State Papers, Bombay*.

The *Saldanha Précis* listed in order of publication:

Précis of Persian Arabistan Affairs, Government Printer, Simla, 1903.
Précis on Arms Trade in the Persian Gulf (mainly compiled by C.H. Gabriel), Government Printer, Simla, 1904.
Précis of Bahrein Affairs, 1854-1904, Government Printer, Simla, 1904.
Précis of Katar Affairs, 1873-1904, Government Printer, Simla, 1904.
Précis of Kowait Affairs, 1896-1904, Government Printer, Simla, 1904.
Précis of Nejd Affairs, 1804-1904, Government Printer, Simla, 1904.
Précis of Mekran Affairs, Office of the Superintendent of Government Printing, Calcutta, 1905.
Précis on Commerce and Communication in the Persian Gulf, 1801-1905, Office of the Superintendent of Government Printing, Calcutta, 1906.
Précis of Correspondence on International Rivalry and British Policy in the Persian Gulf, 1872-1905, Government Printer, Simla, 1906.

Précis on Naval Arrangements in the Persian Gulf, 1862-1905, Government Printer, Simla, 1906.

Précis of the Affairs of the Persian Coast and Islands, 1854-1905, Government Printer, Simla, 1906.

Précis of Correspondence regarding the Affairs of the Persian Gulf, 1801-1853, Office of the Superintendent of Government Printing, Calcutta, 1906.

Précis of Correspondence regarding Trucial Chiefs, 1854-1905, Office of the Superintendent of Government Printing, Calcutta, 1906.

Précis of Maskat Affairs, 1892-1905, Government Printer, Simla, 1906.

Précis on Slave Trade in the Gulf of Oman and the Persian Gulf, 1873-1905, with a Retrospect into previous history from 1852, Government Printer, Simla, 1906.

Précis of Turkish Arabian Affairs, 1801-1905, Government Printer, Simla, 1906.

Selections from State Papers, Bombay, regarding the East India Company's Connection with the Persian Gulf, with a Summary of Events, 1600-1800, Superintendent of Government Printing, Calcutta, 1908.

Using the Imagination

When attention is given to journals and books on subjects other than the political, use of the imagination will prove rewarding. An instance is the history of medicine in the Gulf. *Pharmacy in History* carried an excellent account of a girl from Qatar who was admitted to Hammersmith hospital in London. She had suffered a *grand mal* attack and was in steady decline. The attending nurse noticed that 'the child's symptoms were remarkably similar and equally as bizarre as those of the series of cases of thallium poisoning described by Agatha Christie in *The Pale Horse*', which the nurse was then reading. Tests showed the hunch to be correct. The child had been consuming thallium in a rat poison that was common in Qatar. (See Eunice Bonow Bardell, 'Literary Reflections of Pharmacy – XI: Thallium As An Untraceable Poison', *Pharmacy in History*, Vol.30, No.4, 1988, 189-90.) The topic and the source hardly are ones that would come to mind immediately, but the article brings to mind that the Residency records are detailed enough to support a study of the various paints and oils imported into the Gulf over the decades, which in this age of consciousness about additives would yield valuable information about illness.

An additional argument for ranging rather widely in sources is to avoid the charge of laziness laid against biographical history. Arthur Marwick was much taken with Sir Lewis Namier's strictures about the blindness of biographers and summarizes this in *The Nature of History*:

> Sir Lewis Namier, it will be recalled, pioneered a 'biographical approach' to history whereby a complete picture of a particular political structure was built up on the basis of a vast number of individual biographies of individual politicians...Namier, though he did leave a biography of Charles Townsend, expressed in classic terms the objections which can be raised against the conventional biography as a form of history. It was, he suggested, a lazy and easy form, having an obvious shape based on the birth, development, and death of the subject of the biography. The biographer, Namier argued, could, without necessarily observing the critical standards of the scholarly editor, simply serve up the information contained in the private papers of his subject, while relying on secondary sources for 'background'.

There can be no doubt that many prosopographies do not rate very highly as history. Too often a single type of material dominates, such as legal papers. The eclectic nature of the following selective bibliography will allay such doubts about the variety of sources in the case of the Residents and Agents. The omissions are of peripheral titles, the particulars of which occur in the notes.

SELECTED BIBLIOGRAPHY

Publication in London unless otherwise specified. n.a., no author. n.d., no date. n.p., no publisher.

Abduyllah, Muhammad Morsy, *The United Arab Emirates: A Modern History*. Croom Helm. 1978.

Abed, George T. 'The Lean Years: The Political Economy of Arab Oil in the Coming Decade'. Sharabi ed. *The Next Arab Decade*.

Abir, Mordechai. *Oil, Power and Politics: Conflict in Arabia, the Red Sea and the Gulf*. Frank Cass. 1974.

Abu-Deeb, Kamal. 'Cultural Creation in a Fragmented Society'. Sharabi ed. *The Next Arab Decade*.

Abu Hakima, Ahmad Mustafa. *History of Eastern Arabia, 1750-1800*. Khayats. Beirut. 1965.

Abu-Hakima, Ahmad Mustafa. *The Modern History of Kuwait, 1750-1965*. Luzac. 1983.

Ackroyd, Peter. *First Light*. Hamish Hamilton. 1989.

Adorono, T. *et al. The Authoritarian Personality*. Harper. New York. 1950.

Ahmad, Jalal Al-i. *Occidentosis: A Plague From the West*. Mizan Press. Berkeley (California). 1984.

Albaharna, Husain M. *The Arabian Gulf States: Their Legal and Political Status and Their International Problems*. 2nd rev. ed. n.p. 1975.

Al-Baharana, Husain M. [Albaharna.] 'The Consequences of Britain's Exclusive Treaties: A Gulf View'. Pridham ed. *The Arab Gulf and the West*.

Al Far, Darwish Mostafa. (Director, Qatar National Museum.) 'Qatar: An Historical Review'. *This is Qatar*. December 1987.

Al-Maamiry, Ahmed Hamoud. *Oman and Ibadhism*. 2nd rev. ed. New Delhi. 1989.

Al-Nahari, Abdulaziz Mohamed. *The Role of National Libraries in Developing Countries: With Special Reference to Saudi Arabia*. Mansell. 1984.

Al-Qasimi, Shaikh Sultan Muhammad. *The Myth of Arab Piracy in the Gulf*. Croom Helm. 1986.

Al-Rashid, Zamil Muhammad. *Saudi Relations With Eastern Arabia and Uman (1800-1871)*. Luzac. 1981.

Anderson, Robert. 'A Higher and Wider Road'. *Times Higher Education Supplement*. 3 February 1989.

Anthony, John Duke. 'The Gulf States and Iraq'. *The Political Economy of the Middle East: 1973-78*. A Compendium of Papers submitted to the Joint Economic Committee, Congress of the United States. Government Printing Office. Washington. 1980.

'The Arab World'. n.a. *The Economist*. 12 May 1990.

Arberry, A.J. *The India Office Library: A Historical Sketch*. Commonwealth Office. 1967 [1938].

Ascherson, Neal. 'Dracula Lives and Thrives in Britain'. *The Observer*. 31 August 1986.

Ashton, S.R. *British Policy Towards the Indian States, 1905-1939*. Curzon Press. 1982.

Ashton, S.R. 'The Indian National Congress 1888-1985'. British Library notes for an exhibition to mark the centenary of the first meeting of the Indian National Congress at Bombay in December 1985, 30 November 1985 to 1 February 1986.

Assad, Dawud. 'The Islamisation of Knowledge'. *The Muslim World*. Vol.23 No.25. 28 December 1985.

Assiri, Abdul-Reda, and Kamal Al-Monoufi, 'Kuwait's Political Élite: The Cabinet'. *Middle East Journal*. Vol.42 No.1. Winter 1988.

Avery, Gillian. 'New Realists for Old'. *Times Literary Supplement*. 11 April 1986.

Bagersh, Sana. 'Henna Popularity Still Unchanged'. *Gulf News*. 1 February 1990.

Banerjee, Samik. *Calcutta 200 Years: A Tollygunge Club Prospective*. Tollygunge Club. Calcutta. 1981.

Barber, John. *Imperial Frontier: A Study of Relations Between the British and Pastoral Tribes of North East Uganda*, East African Publishing House. 1968.

Barnett, Correlli. *The Collapse of British Power*. Alan Sutton. Gloucester. 1984.

Barr, Pat. *The Memsahibs: In Praise of the Women of Victorian India*. Century. 1976.

Barthes, Roland. *Mythologies*. Paladin Grafton. 1987 [1973].

Barthes, Roland. *Roland Barthes*. Macmillan. 1977 [1975].

Batham, Cyril N. ed. *The Collected Prestonian Lectures 1961-1974*. Lewis Masonic. 1983.

Battye, Evelyn. *Costumes and Characters of the British Raj*. Webb & Bower. Exeter. 1982.

Bedells, J.H.B. *The British Honours System*. The Heraldry Society. 1974.

Beevor, Edward. *et al. The History and Register of Aldenham School*. 8th ed. Aldenham School. Worcester. 1948.

Begam, H.H. The Nawab Sultan Jahan. *The Story of a Pilgrimage to Hijaz*. Thacker, Spink & Co. Calcutta. 1913.

Belgrave, Charles. *The Pirate Coast*. Librarie du Liban. Beirut. 1972.

Belhaven, Lord. *The Uneven Road*. John Murray. 1955.

Bell, Gawain. *Shadows on the Sands*. C.Hurst. 1983.

Bence-Jones, Mark. *The Viceroys of India*. Constable. 1982.

Benge, Ronald Charles. *Cultural Crisis and Libraries in the Third World*. Clive Bingley. 1979.

Bernheim, Alain. 'The Dating of Masonic Records'. *Ars Quatuor Coronatorium*. Vol.99. 1986.

Bertram, Sir Anton. *The Colonial Service*. Cambridge University Press. 1930.

Bidwell, Robin. ed. *Arabian Gulf Intelligence: Selections from the Records of the Bombay Government*. New Series. No.XXIV. 1856. reptd. 1985. Oleander Press.

Birdwood of Anzaz, Field Marshal Lord. *In My Time*. Skeffington. 2nd ed. 1946.

Birdwood of Anzaz, Field Marshal Lord. *Khaki and Gown: An Autobiography*. Ward & Lock. 1941.

Bishop, T.J.H. 'How a Gentrifying Diet Leads to Constipation'. *The Guardian Weekly*. Vol.133 No.24. 15 December 1985.

Bloch, Marc. *The Royal Touch: Sacred Monarchy and Scrofula in England and France*. Routledge & Kegan Paul. 1973 [1961].

Bloomfield, B.C. ed. *Middle East Studies and Libraries: A Felicitation Volume for Professor J.D. Pearson*. Mansell. 1980.

Blumenau, Ralph. *A History of Malvern College, 1865 to 1965*. Macmillan. 1965.

Blunt, Wilfrid. *Slow on the Feather: Further Autobiography, 1938-1959*. Michael Russell. 1986.

Blythe, Ronald. 'That Men Died for an Ethos Does Not Mean That the Ethos was Worth Dying For'. *The Listener*, 12 March 1987.

Boulding, Kenneth E. *The Image: Knowledge in Life and Society*. University of Michigan Press. Ann Arbor. 1961 [1956].

Boullata, Issa J. 'Challenges to Arab Cultural Authenticity'. Sharabi ed. *The Next Arab Decade*.

Boustead, J.E.H. 'Abu Dhabi, 1761-1963'. *Journal of the Royal Central Asiatic Society*. Vol.L Parts III & IV. July/October 1963.

Boxhall, Peter. 'Arabian Seafarers in the Indian Ocean'. *Asian Affairs*. Vol.XX, Part III. October 1989.

Bradley, John. ed. *Lady Curzon's India: Letters of a Vicereine*. Weidenfeld and Nicolson. 1985.

Bray, Norman N.E. *Paladin of Arabia*. John Heritage. 1936.

Bray, Norman N.E. *Shifting Sands*. Unicorn. 1934.

Brander, Michael. *The Perfect Victorian Hero*. Mainstream. Edinburgh. 1982.

Brent, Peter. *Far Arabia*. Quartet Books. 1979.

Brett, J.H. 'Fettes and the Great War'. Pyatt ed. *Fettes*.

Brett, Simon. *Marlborough College*. Essex Reprographics. Brentwood. 1971.

SELECTED BIBLIOGRAPHY

Brown, Aggrey. *Colour, Class, and Politics in Jamaica*. Transaction Books. New Brunswick (New Jersey). 1979.

Brown, L. Carl. *International Politics and the Middle East: Old Rules, Dangerous Game*. I.B. Tauris. 1984.

Bullard, Sir Reader. *Britain and the Middle East: From the Earliest Times to 1950*. Hutchinson. 1951.

Bunney, Walter J. 'Freemasonry and Contemplative Art'. Carr ed. *The Collected Prestonian Lectures 1925-1960*.

Busch, Briton Cooper. *Britain and the Persian Gulf, 1897-1914*. University of California Press. Berkeley. 1967.

Byron, Robert. *The Road to Oxiana*. Picador. 1981.

Callan, Hilary. 'The Imagery of Choice in Sociobiology'. *Man*. Vol.19 No.3. September 1984.

Callinicos, Alex. *Making History: Agency, Structure and Change in Social Theory*. Polity Press, 1989.

Cameron, James. *An Indian Summer*. Penguin. Harmondsworth. 1987.

Canetti, Elias. *The Human Province*. Picador. 1986 [1973].

Carey, W.H. *The Good Old Days of Honourable John Company, being Reminiscences Illustrating Manners and Customs of the British in India During the Rule of the East India Company from 1600 to 1856*. Vol.I. R. Cambray. Calcutta. 1906.

Carman, W.Y. ed. *Dress Regulations (India) 1931*. Ray Westlake – Military Books. Newport. 1987.

Caroe, Olaf. *Wells of Power: The Oilfields of South-Western Asia*. Macmillan. 1951.

Carr, H. *The Collected Prestonian Lectures 1925-1960*. Lewis Masonic. rev. ed. 1984 [1965].

Carse, James P. *Finite and Infinite Games*. Ballantine. New York. 1987.

Charmley, John. *Lord Lloyd and the Decline of the British Empire*. Weidenfeld and Nicolson. 1987.

Chilver, E.M. and Vincent Harlow. eds. *History of East Africa*. Oxford University Press. 1965.

Christie, John. *Morning Drum*. British Association for Cemeteries in South Asia. 1983.

Churchward, Hedley. (Mohamad Mobarek.) *From Drury Lane to Mecca*. As told to Eric Rosenthal. Sampson, Low & Co. 1931.

Clayton, Anthony and Donald Savage. *Government and Labour in Kenya*. Frank Cass. 1974.

Clements, Frank A. *Kuwait*. World Bibliographical Series. Clio Press. Oxford. 1985.

Clements, Frank A. *United Arab Emirates*. World Bibliographical Series. Clio Press. Oxford. 1983.

Coates, P.D. 'The China Consuls'. *Asian Affairs*. Vol.XXI, Part I, February 1990.

Coelho, Denise. *Orchids and Algebra: The Story of Dow Hill School*. Maidstone Publications. Maidstone (Kent). 1986.

Cohn, Bernard S. 'Representing Authority in Victorian India'. Hobsbawm. *Inventing Tradition*.

Cole, Donald Powell. *Nomad of the Nomads: The Al Murrah Bedouin of the Empty Quarter*. AHM Publishing. Arlington Heights (Illinois). 1975.

Collini, Stefan. 'What is Intellectual History...?'. Gardiner. *What is History Today?*

Collinson, Patrick. 'Fundamental Objections'. *Times Literary Supplement*. 17 February 1989.

Comaroff, Jean and John. 'Through the Looking Glass: Colonial Encounters of the First Kind'. *Journal of Historical Sociology*. Vol.1 No.1. March 1988.

Constitution and Regulations for the Government of The Order of Mark Master Masons and The Degree of Royal Ark Mariner. Grand Lodge of Mark Master Masons. 1955.

Cook, Stephen. *Empire Born*. Hodder & Stoughton. 1986.

Cordesman, Anthony H. *The Gulf and the Search for Strategic Stability: Saudi Arabia, the Military Balance in the Gulf, and Trends in the Arab-Israeli Military Balance*. Mansell. 1984.

Corfield, Sir Conrad. *The Princely India I Knew: From Reading to Mountbatten*. Indo British Historical Society. Madras. 1975.

Costello, John. *Mask of Treachery*. Pan Books. Rev. ed. 1989 [1988].

Cottrell, Alvin J. ed. *The Persian Gulf States: A General Survey*. Johns Hopkins University Press. Baltimore. 1980.

Coupland, Reginald. *East Africa and Its Invaders From the Earliest Times to the Death of Seyyid Said in 1856*. Russell. 1965 [1938].

Cox, Michael. *M.R. James: An Informal Portrait*. Oxford University Press. 1983.

Cranworth, Lord. *Kenya Chronicles*. Macmillan. 1939.

Cross, Colin. *The Fall of the British Empire*. Hodder and Stoughton. 1968.

Cryer, N. Barker. 'Drama and Craft'. Batham ed. *The Collected Prestonian Lectures 1961-1974*.

Curtis, Michael. ed. *Religion and Politics in the Middle East*. Westview Press. Boulder (Colorado). 1981.

Curzon, George N. *Persia and the Persian Question*. Vol.II. Longmans Green. 1892.

Daly, Hugh. *Memoirs of General Sir Henry Dermot Daly GCB CIE*. John Murray. 1905.

Daniel, Norman. *The Cultural Barrier: Problems in the Exchange of Ideas*. Edinburgh University Press. 1975.

Datta-Ray, Basudeb. *Assam Secretariat, 1874-1947: An Administrative History of North-East India*. K.P. Bagghi. Calcutta. 1978.

David, Natalie Zemon. 'A Modern Hero'. *New York Review of Books*, Vol.XXXVII No.7. 26 April 1990.

Davidoff, Leonore. *The Best Circles: Social Etiquette and the Season*. Cresset. 1986 [1973].

Davies, Andrew. 'Primary and Secondary Sources'. *Times Educational Supplement*. 30 December 1988.

Davies, Robertson. *World of Wonders. The Deptford Trilogy*. Penguin. Harmondsworth. 1983 [1975].

Dawkins, Richard. *The Blind Watchmaker*. Penguin. Harmondsworth. 1988 [1986].

de Gaury, Gerald. *The Grand Captain: Gonzalo de Cordoba*. Longmans Green. 1955.

Dewar, James. *The Unlocked Secret: Freemasonry Examined*. William Kimber. 1986.

Dickey, Christopher. 'UK's Changing Role in Oman'. *The Guardian Weekly*. Vol.133 No.21. 24 November 1985.

Dickson, Violet. *Forty Years in Kuwait*. George Allen & Unwin. 1971.

Dilley, Marjorie Ruth. *British Policy in Kenya Colony*. Thomas Nelson. New York. 1932.

Dodgeon, H. and A.M. Findlay. *Ports of the Arabian Peninsula: A Guide to the Literature*. Centre for Middle Eastern and Islamic Studies. University of Durham. Occasional Papers Series No.7. n.d.

Donaldson, Neil. *The Postal Agencies in Eastern Arabia and the Gulf*. Harry Hayes. Batley. 1975.

Downside School Entries, 1967-1982, First Supplement to the List of Boys at St Gregory's From 1614. Downside Abbey. Bath. 1983.

Draffen, George S. 'The Making of a Mason'. Carr ed. *The Collected Prestonian Lectures 1925-1960*.

Dratten, George. ed. *Yearbook of the Grand Lodge of Ancient Free and Accepted Masons of Scotland*. Edinburgh. 1968.

Dresch, P. 'The Position of Shaykhs Among the Northern Tribes of Yemen'. *Man*. Vol.19 No.1. March 1984.

Dress Regulations for Officers of the Indian Political Service. Government of India Press. New Delhi. 1937.

Drysdale, Alasdair, and Gerald H. Blake. *The Middle East and North Africa: A Political Geography*. Oxford University Press. 1985.

Dunlap, Leslie W. *Readings in Library History*. R.R. Bowker. New York. 1972.

Dye, Thomas R. and Harmon Ziegler. 'Socialism and Militarism'. *PS: Political Science & Politics*. Vol.XXII No.4. December 1989.

Eastwood, G.F. *'Queen Elizabeth's': A New History of the Ancient Grammar School of Blackburn*. Published by the Governors of the School. 1967.

SELECTED BIBLIOGRAPHY

Eco, Umberto. *Foucault's Pendulum*. Trs. William Weaver. Ballantine. New York. 1989.

Edwardes, Michael. *British India, 1772-1947*. Taplinger. New York. 1968.

Edwardes, Michael. *East-West Passage: The Travel of Ideas, Arts and Inventions between Asia and the Western World*. Taplinger. New York. 1971.

Eliade, Mircea. 'A Conversation with Mircea Eliade'. *Parabola*. Vol.1 No.3. Spring 1976. Reptd. 1988.

Emerson, Rupert. *From Empire to Nation: The Rise of Self-Assertion of Asian and African Peoples*. 3rd ed. Boston. 1964.

Evans, R.J. *et al.* eds. *The Register of Aldenham School*. 9th ed. Aldenham School. 1959.

Farrington, Anthony. *The Records of the East India College Haileybury and Other Institutions*. H. Majesty's Stationery Office. 1976.

Field, Michael. *The Merchants: The Big Business Families of Saudi Arabia and the Gulf States*. Overlook Press. Woodstock (New York). 1985.

Fieldhouse, D.K. *Colonialism, 1870-1945*. Weidenfeld and Nicolson. 1981.

Finan, A. *History of the Grand Lodge of All Scottish Freemasonry in India, 1837-1924*. Thacker. Bombay. 1928.

Fisher, H.A.L. *An Unfinished Autobiography*. Oxford University Press. 1941.

Fordham, Frieda. *An Introduction to Jung's Psychology*. Penguin. Harmondsworth. 1987 [1953]. Introduction by Jung.

Foster, Roy. 'What is Political History?'. Gardiner ed. *What is History Today...?*.

Foster, William. *The East India House, Its History and Associations*. Bodley Head. 1924.

Fowle, T.C. *Travels in The Middle East*. Smith, Elder, & Co. 1916.

Fraser, Lovat. *India Under Curzon & After*. William Heinemann. 1912.

Friedberg, Aaron L. *The Weary Titan: Britain and the Experience of Relative Decline, 1895-1905*. Princeton University Press. Princeton (New Jersey). 1988.

Fromm, Erich. *Beyond the Chains of Illusion: My Encounter With Marx and Freud*. Abacus. 1980 [1962].

Gaddis, John Lewis. 'A Time of Confrontation and Confusion'. *Times Literary Supplement*. 8 May 1987.

Gardiner, Juliet. ed. *What is History Today....?*. Macmillan. 1988.

Gardner, Brian. *The Public Schools: An Historical Survey*. Hamish Hamilton. 1973.

Gilmour, Robin. '*Stalky & Co.*: Revising the Code'. Mallett. *Kipling Considered*.

Glubb, John. *Britain and the Arabs: A Study of Fifty Years*. Hodder and Stoughton. 1959.

Goertzel, Ted George. *Political Society*. Rand McNally. 1976.

Gordon, Ian. *The Craft and the Cross*. Kingsway. Eastbourne. 1989.

Gould, Jim. 'Isaac Emmerton, Thomas Hogg and Their Composts'. *Garden History*. Vol.17 No.2. Autumn 1989.

Grabowski, Richard. 'The Theory of Induced Institutional Innovation: A Critique'. *World Development*. Vol.16 No.3. March 1988.

Grainger, J.H. *Patriotisms: Britain 1900-1939*. Routledge & Kegan Paul. 1986.

Grant, Gillian. *Middle Eastern Photographic Collections in the United Kingdom*. Middle East Libraries Committee. Durham. 1989.

Grant, Patrick. *The Good Old Days*. Thames and Hudson. 1956.

Graves, Phillip. *The Life of Sir Percy Cox*. Hutchinson. 1941.

Graves, Robert. *Goodbye to All That*. Penguin. Harmondsworth. 1986 [1929].

Grosvenor, Ian D. 'Review'. *Archives*. Vol.XVII No.74. October 1985.

Haag, Michael. 'Preface'. Lawrence. *Crusader Castles*.

Haffner, Christopher. *Workman Unashamed: The Testimony of a Christian Freemason*. Lewis Masonic. Shepperton. 1989.

Hansen, Holger Bernt. *Church and State in a Colonial Setting, Uganda 1890-1925*. Heinemann. 1984.

Hardy, P. *The Muslims of British India*. Cambridge University Press. 1972.

Harlan, David. 'Intellectual History and the Return of Literature'. *The American Historical Review*. Vol.94 No.3. June 1989.

Harlow, Vincent and E.M. Chilver eds. *History of East Africa*. Oxford University Press. 1965.

Harris, Arlen. 'Duels in the Crown'. *Tatler*. Vol.284 No.3. March 1989.

Harrison, Ann M. *A Tool in His Hand*. Friendship Press. New York. 1958.

Harwood, Dean F. 'Cornerstones: Real and Symbolic'. *The New Age*. Vol.XCVII No.3. March 1989.

Hastings, D.J. ed. *Bombay Buccaneers: Memories and Remembrances of the Royal Indian Navy*. British Association for Cemeteries in South Asia. 1986.

Hawley, Donald. *The Trucial States*. Allen and Unwin. 1971.

Hay, Rupert. 'The Persian Gulf States and Their Boundary Problems'. *Geographic Journal*. Vol.CXX Part 4. December 1954.

Henderson, K.W. *Masonic World Guide*. Lewis Masonic. 1984.

Heywood, Colin. 'Wittek and the Austrian Tradition'. *Journal of the Royal Asiatic Society*. No.1. 1988.

Hilton, James. *Goodbye Mr Chips*. Hodder and Stoughton. 1986 [1934].

Himsworth, Sheila. Compiler. *Winchester College Muniments*. Vol.I. Warden and Fellows of Winchester College. 1976.

Hobsbawm, Eric, and Terence Ranger. eds. *The Invention of Tradition*. Cambridge University Press. 1983.

Hobson, J.A. *Imperialism: A Study*. George Allen & Unwin. 3rd ed. 1961 [1902].

Hogarth, David George. *The Penetration of Arabia*. Hyperion Press. Westport (Connecticut). 1981 [1904].

Holden, David. *Farewell to Arabia*. Faber and Faber. 1966.

Honey, John. *Does Accent Matter? The Pygmalion Factor*. Faber and Faber. 1989.

Honey, John R. de S. *Tom Brown's Universe*. Millington. 1977.

Hoover, Dwight W. 'The Return of the Narrative?'. *Organization of American Historians Newsletter*. Vol.17 No.4. November 1989.

Hopewell, S. *Royal Russell School*. Hutchinson Benham. 1978.

Hopwood, Derek. 'Servants of Empire: Sidelights on the British in Egypt'. Bloomfield ed. *Middle East Studies and Libraries*.

Hopwood, Derek. 'Some Western Studies of Saudi Arabia, Yemen and Aden'. Hopwood. *The Arabian Peninsula*.

Hopwood, Derek. ed. *The Arabian Peninsula: Society and Politics*. George Allen and Unwin. 1972.

Hudson, Michael C. *Arab Politics: The Search for Legitimacy*. Yale University Press. New Haven. 1977.

Hudson, Michael C. 'State, Society, and Legitimacy: An Essay on Arab Political Prospects in the 1990s'. Sharabi ed. *The Next Arab Future*.

Icenogle, David. 'The Romantic Adventurer As Explorer? The Case of Charles Chaille-Long'. *Terrae Icognitae*. Vol.20. 1988.

Islam, Shamsul. *Chronicles of the Raj: A Study of Literary Reaction to the Imperial Idea*. Macmillan. 1979.

Ismael, Jacqueline S. *Kuwait*. Syracuse University Press. Syracuse. 1982.

Izzard, Molly. *The Gulf: Arabia's Western Approaches*. John Murray. 1979.

Jackson, A.C.F. *Rose Croix: The History of the Ancient and Accepted Rite for England and Wales*. Rev. ed. Lewis Masonic. 1987.

Jackson, Brian, and Dennis Marsden. *Education and the Working Class*. Monthly Review Press. 1962.

Jackson, Robert. *Thirty Seconds at Quetta*. Evans Brothers. 1960.

Johnson, Gordon. 'What is Third World History?'. Gardiner ed. *What is History Today...?*.

Jung, C.G. 'Foreword'. Fordham. *An Introduction to Jung's Psychology*.

Kaminsky, Arnold P. *The India Office, 1880-1910*. Mansell. 1986.

Kapferer, Bruce. 'Ritual Process and the Transformation of Context'. Kapferer ed. *The Power of Ritual*.

Kapferer, Bruce. ed. *The Power of Ritual: Transition, Transformation and Transcendence in Ritual Practice*. Special Issue Series. *Social Analysis*. No.1. February 1979.

Kavanagh, Dennis. *Political Culture*. Macmillan. 1972.

Kedourie, Elie. *In the Anglo-Arab Labyrinth: The McMahon-Husayn Correspondence and Its Interpretations, 1914-1939*. Cambridge University Press. 1976.

Kelly, J.B. *Britain and the Persian Gulf*. Oxford University Press. 1968. [new ed. 1991.]

Kennion, R.L. *Diversions of an Indian Political*. William Blackwood & Sons. Edinburgh. 1932.

Kesavan B.S. and C.R. Banerji. 'Library Resources in Oriental Studies in India'. Pearson ed. *Papers on Oriental Library Collections*.

Keyster, Paul. 'The Origin of the Latin Numerals 1 to 1000'. *American Journal of Archaeology*. Vol.92 No.4. October 1988.

Khadduri, Majid. 'Iran's Claim to the Sovereignty of Bahrayn'. *American Journal of International Law*. Vol.45. 1951.

Khalifa, Ali Mohammed. *The United Arab Emirates: Unity in Fragmentation*. Croom Helm. 1979.

Khuri, Fuad I. *Tribe and State in Bahrain: The Transformation of Social and Political Authority in an Arab State*. University of Chicago Press. 1980.

Kipling, Rudyard. *Kim*. Macmillan. 1978 [1901].

Kirk-Greene, Anthony. *A Biographical Dictionary of the British Colonial Governor*. Vol.I: Africa. Harvester Press. Brighton. 1980.

Klieman, Aaron S. *Foundations of British Policy in the Arab World: The Cairo Conference of 1921*. Johns Hopkins Press. Baltimore. 1970.

Kluckhohn, Clyde. '*From Mirror for Man*'. Ross ed. *Perspectives on the Social Order*.

Koestler, Arthur. *Janus: A Summing Up*. Picador. 1983.

Korany, Baghat. 'Unwelcome Guests: The Political Economy of Arab Relations with the Superpowers'. Sharabi ed. *The Next Arab Decade*.

Kour, Z.H. *The History of Aden*. Frank Cass. 1981.

Lane, J.E. and S. Ersson. 'Unpacking the Political Development Concept', *Political Geography Quarterly*. Vol.8 No.2. April 1989.

Lawrence, T.E. *Crusader Castles*. Michael Haag Press. 1986 [1936].

Lawton, Henry. *The Psychohistorian's Handbook*. The Psychohistory Press. 1988.

Leadbeater, C.W. *The Hidden Life in Freemasonry*. Theosophical Publishing House. Madras (India). 1926.

Le Goff, Jacques. 'After *Annales*: The Life as History'. *Times Literary Supplement*. 14 April 1989.

Lehmann-Haupt, Christopher. 'Preparing for Power'. *International Herald Tribune*. 24-25 December 1985.

Leinster-Mackay, Donald. 'The Changing Fortunes and Functions of the English Preparatory Boarding School'. McClelland. *Private and Independent Education*.

Leinster-Mackay, Donald. 'The Nineteenth Century English Preparatory School: Cradle and Creche of Empire?'. Mangan ed. *'Benefits Bestowed'?*

Leinster-Mackay, Donald. *The Rise of the English Prep School*. Falmer Press. 1984.

Leiser, Garry. 'Notes on the Madrasa in Medieval Islamic Society'. *Muslim World*. Vol.LXXVI No.1. January 1986.

Le Quesne, A.L. 'Educational Aspects'. *Times Educational Supplement*. 11 April 1986.

Lewis, Bernard. ed. *The World of Islam*. Thames and Hudson. 1976.

Lewis, Thomas. 'Authoritarian Attitudes and Personalities: A Psychohistorical Perspective'. *The Psychohistory Review*. Vol.18 No.2. Winter 1990.

Liebesny, Herbert J. 'Administration and Legal Development in Arabia: The Persian Gulf Principalities'. *Middle East Journal*. Vol.X No.2. Winter 1956.

Lienhardt, Peter. 'The Authority of Shaykhs in the Gulf: An Essay in Nineteenth Century History'. Serjeant ed. *Arabian Studies II*.

Linabury, George. 'The Creation of Saudi Arabia and the Erosion of Wahhabi Conservatism'. Curtis ed. *Religion and Politics in the Middle East*.

Lindt, A.R. 'Politics in the Persian Gulf'. *Journal of the Royal Central Asian Society*. Vol.XXVI (Old Series). 1939.

Littlefield, '*Bahrain as a Persian Gulf State*'.

Longrigg, Stephen H. *The Middle East: A Social Geography*. 2nd ed.

Lorimer, J.G. *Gazetteer of the Persian Gulf*. 2 vols. Government Printer. Calcutta. 1908.

Lyall, Gavin. *The Wrong Side of the Sky*. Pan. 1983 [1961].

Lynch, H.F.B. 'The Persian Gulf'. *The Imperial and Asiatic Quarterly Review and Oriental and Colonial Record*. Third Series. Vol.XIII Nos.25 & 26. January/April 1902.

McClelland, Vincent Alan. ed., *Private and Independent Education. Aspects of Education Journal*. The University of Hull. No.35. 1986.

McClure, W.K. 'Memories'. Pyatt ed. *Fifty Years of Fettes*.

McCrum, Michael. *Thomas Arnold, Headmaster: A Reassessment*. Oxford University Press. 1989.

McEwan, Neil. *Perspective in British Historical Fiction Today*. Macmillan. 1987.

Mack, Edward C. *Public Schools and British Opinion Since 1860: The Relationship Between Contemporary Ideas and the Evolution of an English Institution*. Greenwood Press. Westport (Connecticut). 1971 [1941].

Mack, John E. 'T.E. Lawrence and the Use of Psychology in the Biography of Historical Figures'. Brown ed. *Psychological Dimensions of Near East Studies*.

Mackenzie, John M. ed. *Imperialism and Popular Culture*. Manchester University Press. 1986.

Macmunn, George. *The Romance of the Indian Frontiers*. Jonathan Cape. 1931.

Mains, A.A. 'The Expansion of the Infantry of the Indian Army During World War I'. *Journal of the Society for Army Historical Research*. Vol.LXVII No.271.

Malim, F.B. *Almae Matres: Recollections of Some Schools at Home and Abroad*. Cambridge University Press. 1948.

Mallett, Phillip. 'Kipling and the Hoax'. Mallett ed. *Kipling Considered*.

Mallett, Phillip. ed. *Kipling Considered*. Macmillan. 1989.

Manchester, William. 'Downing Street Diarist: An Insider's Portrait of Churchill'. Review of John Colville's *The Fringes of Power*. *International Herald Tribune*. 22 October 1985.

Mangan, J.A. 'Athleticism: A Case Study of the Evolution of an Educational Ideology'. Simon and Bradley eds. *Victorian Public Schools*.

Mangan, J.A. ed. '*Benefits Bestowed?: Education and British Imperialism*'. Manchester University Press. 1988.

Mangan, J.A. 'Eton in India: The Imperial Diffusion of a Victorian Educational Ethic'. *History of Education*. Vol.7 No.2. 1978.

Mangan, J.A. 'The Grit of Our Forefathers: Invented Traditions, Propaganda and Imperialism'. Mackenzie. *Imperialism and Popular Culture*.

Mangan, J.A. 'The School Magazine as a Primary Source'. Appendix III. *Athleticism*.

Mansergh, Nicholas. *India: The Transfer of Power, 1942-1947*. Vol.XII. H. Majesty's Stationery Office. 1983.

Mansfield, Peter. *The Arabs*. Allen Lane. 1977.

Maquet, Jacques. *The Aesthetic Experience: An Anthropologist Looks at the Visual Arts*. Yale University Press. New Haven. 1986.

Marlowe, John. *Late Victorian*. Cresset Press. 1967.

Marlowe, Philip. *The Persian Gulf in the Twentieth Century*. Cresset Press. 1962.

Martineau, John. *The Life and Correspondence of the Right Hon. Sir Bartle Frere, Bart., GCB, FRS, Etc.*, Vols. I & II. John Murray. 1895.

Marvick, Elizabeth W. 'Introduction', 'Case Studies in Psychopolitics' issue of *International Political Science Review*. Vol.10 No.1. January 1989.

Marwick, Arthur. *The Nature of History*. 2nd ed. Macmillan. 1981 [1970].

Masanie, Zareer. *Indian Tales of the Raj*. BBC Books. 1987.

Mason, Philip. (Philip Woodruff.) *The Men Who Ruled India: Vol.II, The Guardians*. Jonathan Cape. 1954.

Mason, Philip. *The Men Who Ruled India*. Jonathan Cape. 1985.

Mazlish, Bruce. *James and John Stuart Mill: Father and Son in the Nineteenth Century*. Hutchinson. 1975.

Melikian, Levon H. *Jassim: A Study in the Psychosocial Development of a Young Man in Qatar*. Longman. 1981.

Mill, Hugh Robert. *The Record of the Royal Geographical Society, 1830-1930*. Royal Geographical Society. 1930.

Millgate, Jane. *Macaulay*. Routledge & Kegan Paul. 1973.

Mitchell, Timothy. *Colonising Egypt*. Cambridge University Press. 1988.

Moore, Gloria Jean. *The Anglo-Indian Vision*. Australasian Educa [*sic*] Press. Melbourne. 1986.

Moore, Sally Falk, and Barbara G. Myerhoff eds. *Symbol and Politics in Communal Ideology*. Cornell University Press. Ithaca (New York). 1975.

Moorhead, Lucy. ed. *Letters: The Open Door, 1930-35*. Vol.II. Compton Russell. 1975.

Morehead, John. *In Defiance of The Elements: A Personal View of Qatar*. Quartet. 1977.

Morgan, Lewis Henry. *Ancient Society*. Charles H. Kerr. Chicago. 1877.

Morgan, M.C. *Cheltenham College: The First Hundred Years*. Richard Sadler. Chalfont St. Giles. 1968.

Morgan, Prys. 'From a Death to a View: The Hunt for the Welsh Past in the Romantic Period'. Hobsbawm. *Inventing Tradition*.

Morris, James. *Pax Britannia*. Faber & Faber. 1986.

Morris, Jan. 'Explorer Who Couldn't Change a Wheel'. *The Independent*. 7 May 1987.

Morrow, Ann. *Highness: The Maharajahs of India*. Grafton. 1986.

Mukhopadhyay, Subodh Kumar. *Evolution of Historiography in Modern India: 1900-1960*. K.P. Bagchi. Calcutta. 1981.

Musgrave, Peter. *From Brown to Bunter*. Routledge. 1985.

Nairn, David. *Nairn in Darkness and Light*. Arena ed. 1988.

Nairn, Tom. *The Enchanted Glass: Britain and Its Monarchy*. Hutchinson Radius. 1988.

Newsome, David. *A History of Wellington College*. John Murray. 1959.

Nicolson, Nigel. *Mary Curzon*. Harper & Row. 1977.

Norwich, John Julius. 'The Englishman and the Sons of the Desert'. *UR: The International Magazine of Arab Culture*. No.1. 1982.

Norwood, Cyril. *The English Tradition in Education*. John Murray. 1929.

Oakes, Philip. *From Middle England*. André Deutsch. 1980.

Oaten, Edward Farley. *My Memories of India*. Janaki Prakashan. Patna (India). 1984.

Ohdedar, A.K. *The Growth of the Library in Modern India: 1498-1836*. World Press. Calcutta. 1966.

Orton, Joe. *The Orton Diaries*. John Lahr ed. Methuen. Minerva ed. 1989 [1986].

Orwell, George. 'Boys' Weeklies'. *George Orwell*. Collected ed. Vol.II. Secker & Warburg. 1980.

O'Shea, Raymond. *The Sand Kings of Oman, being the experiences of an R.A.F. officer in the little known regions of Trucial Oman Arabia*. Methuen. 1947.

Ottaway, A.K.C. *Education and Society*. Humanities. 1964.

Paffard, Mark. *Kipling's Indian Fiction*. Macmillan, 1989.

Parsons, Edward Alexander. *The Alexandrian Library: Glory of the Hellenic World*. Cleaver-Hume. 1952.

Pati, Raphael. *The Arab Mind*. rev. ed. Charles Scribner's Sons. 1983 [1973].

Paul, H.G. Balfour. 'Recent Developments in the Persian Gulf'. *Journal of the Royal Central Asiatic Society*. Vol.LVI Part I. February 1969.

Pearson, J.D. ed. *Papers on Oriental Library Collections*. Inter Documentation. Zug (Switzerland). 1971.

Peel, J.D.Y. 'Making History: The Past in the Ijesha Present'. *Man*. Vol.19 No.1. March 1984.

Percy-Smith, H.K. *Deaths in India*. Vol.2. Society of Genealogists. 1942.

Perlman, Michael. 'Memory, Soul, and the Place of Hiroshima'. *The Psychohistory Review*. Vol.16 No.1. Autumn 1987.

Peterson, J.E. *Oman in the Twentieth Century*. Croom Helm. 1978.

Philby, H. St. J.B. *Arabia of the Wahhabis*. Frank Cass. 1977 [1928].

Pois, Robert A. 'The Case for Clinical Training and Challenges to Psychohistory'. *The Psychohistory Review*. Vol.18 No.2. Winter 1990.

Polk, William R. *The Arab World*. Harvard University Press. Cambridge (Massachusetts). 1980.

Porter, Bernard. *The Lion's Share: A Short History of British Imperialism, 1850-1983*. 2nd ed. Longman. 1985.

Potter, David C. *India's Political Administrators, 1919-1983*. Oxford University Press. 1986.

Pridham, B.R. ed. *The Arab Gulf and the West*. Croom Helm. 1985.

Puddester, Robert P. 'Rajkumar College and Its Medals'. *Coin & Medals News*. July 1988.

Purves, Libby. 'And Why Can't the Little Hero Swoon, Too?'. *The Times*. 20 June 1990.

Pyatt, H.R. ed. *Fifty Years of Fettes: Memories of Old Fettesians, 1870-1920*. T. & A. Constable. Edinburgh. 1931.

Qubain, Fahim I. 'Social Classes and Tensions in Bahrain', *Middle East Journal*. Vol.9, No.3. Autumn 1955.

Quigley, Caroll. *The Anglo-American Establishment: From Rhodes to Cliveden*. Books in Focus. New York. 1981.

Quigly, Isabel. *The Heirs of Tom Brown: The English School Story*. Oxford University Press. 1984.

Rae, John. 'New Life for the Old School'. *The Times*. 14 December 1985.

Rai, Jam Rai Bahadur Jamiat. *A Brief History of Freemasonry in Quetta, with a Preface by The Honourable Sir Henry McMahon, KCIE, GSI*. The Times Press. Bombay. 1908.

Raugh, Harold E. 'Wavell in the Middle East: A Study in Magnanimity'. *Indo-British Review*. Vol.XIII No.2. July-December 1987.

Rawlinson, H.G. *The British Achievement in India*. Prabha Publications. New Delhi. 1985 [1948].

Razi, G. Hossein. 'Legitimacy, Religion, and Nationalism in the Middle East'. *American Political Science Review*. Vol.84 No.1. March 1990.

Reed, John R. *Old School Ties: The Public Schools in British Literature*. Syracuse University Press. Syracuse (New York). 1964.

Rehbock, Philip F. 'Prosopography?'. *Ideas and Production*. Issue VI. 1987.

Rich, Paul B. *Race and Empire in British Politics*. Cambridge University Press. 1986.

Rich, Paul John. 'The Bahrain Public School Scheme, 1941'. *Education Research and Perspectives*. Vol.14 No.2. December 1987.

Rich, Paul John. *Chains of Empire: English Public Schools, Masonic Cabalism, Historical Causality, and Imperial Clubdom*. Regency Press. 1991.

Rich, Paul John. *Elixir of Empire: The English Public Schools, Ritualism, Freemasonry, and Imperialism*. Regency Press. 1989.

Rich, Paul John. *Rituals of Empire: English Public Schools, Imperial Baubles, Masonic Magicians, and Morphic Resonances*. Regency Press. 1991.

Richards, Jeffrey. *Visions of Yesterday*. Routledge & Kegan Paul. 1973.

Rihani, Ameen. *Around the Coasts of Arabia*. Caravan. Delmar (New York). 1983 [1930].

Rizvi, S.A.A. 'Muslim India'. Lewis ed. *The World of Islam*.

Roach, Mary Ellen, and Joanne Bubolz Eicher. 'The Language of Personal Adornment'. Cordwell ed. *The Fabrics of Culture*.

Roberts, David. 'The Exclusive Treaties – A British View'. Pridham ed. *The Arab Gulf and the West*.

Roberts, J.M. *The Triumph of the West*. British Broadcasting Corporation. 1985.

Robinson-Horley, E.W. *Last Post: An Indian Army Memoir*. Secker & Warburg. 1985.

Rodinson, Maxine. *The Arabs*. University of Chicago Press. 1981.

Rosenthal, Michael. *The Character Factory: Baden-Powell and the Origins of the Boy Scout Movement*. Collins. 1986.

Ross, H. Laurence. ed. *Perspectives on the Social Order*. McGraw-Hill. New York. 1968.

Ross, Kenneth. *Curzon: A Most Superior Person*. Macmillan. 1985.

Roy, Asim. 'The Politics of Education: The British Raj and Bengal Education, 1871-1884'. *History of Education Review*. Vol.17 No.1. 1988.

Rules and Regulations for the Government of Degrees From the 4 to 32 Inclusive Under the Supreme Council 33 of the Ancient Accepted Scottish Rite in England, Wales, the Dominions and Dependencies of the British Crown. January 1923.

Rumahihi, M.G. *Bahrain: Social and Political Change Since the First World War*. Bowker. 1976.

Rushdie, Salman. *In Good Faith*. Granta. 1990.

Rushdie, Salman. *The Satanic Verses*. Viking. 1988.

Russell, Bertrand. *Education and the Social Order*. Unwin. 1977.

Sabben-Clare, James P. *Winchester College: After 600 Years, 1382-1982*. Paul Cave Publications. Southampton. 1981.

Sack, Robert David. *Human Territoriality: Its Theory and History*. Cambridge University Press. 1986.

Said, Edward W. *Orientalism*. Routledge & Kegan Paul. 1978.

Saldanha, J.A. *Précis of the Affairs of the Persian Coast and Islands, 1854-1905*. Government Printer. Simla. 1906.

Saldanha, J.A. *Précis of Maskat Affairs, 1892-1905*. Government Printer. Simla. 1906.

Saldanha, J.A. 'Preface'. *Précis of Bahrein Affairs, 1854-1904*. Government Printer. Simla. 1904.

Sampson, Anthony. *The New Anatomy of Britain*. rev. ed. Hodder and Stoughton. 1983 [1971].

Sampson, Anthony. *The Seven Sisters: The Great Oil Companies and the World They Made*. Hodder and Stoughton. 1975.

Sanderson, William. *Two Hundred Years of Freemasonry: A History of the Britannic Lodge No.33, Annis Domini 1730-1930*. George Kenning. 1930.

Scarce, Jennifer M. *The Evolving Culture of Kuwait*. Royal Scottish Museum and H. Majesty's Stationery Office. 1985.

Schofield, Richard and Gerald Blake. *Arabian Boundaries: Primary Documents 1853-1957*. Archive Editions. Slough. 1988. 25 volumes.

Schumand, Howard, and Jacqueline Scott. 'Generations and Collective Memories'. *American Sociological Review*. Vol.54 No.3. June 1989.

Selborne, Earl of. *et al. Winchester College, 1393-1893*. Edward Arnold. 1893.

Sergeant, R.B. and R.L. Bidwell eds. *Arabian Studies, II*. C. Hurst for The Middle East Centre of Cambridge University. 1975.

Sergeant, R.B. and R.L. Bidwell. eds. *Arabian Studies*. Vol.IX. C. Hurst. 1979.

Seton, Sir Malcolm C.C. *The India Office*. G.P. Putnam. 1926.

Shah, Idries. *The Natives are Restless*. Octagon Press. 1988.

Sharabi, Hisham. ed. *The Next Arab Decade: Alternative Futures*. Mansell. 1988.

Sharp, H. ed. *Selections from Education Records*. Part I. Bureau of Education, India. Superintendent of Government Printing. Calcutta. 1920.

Sherring, Herbert. *History of Mayo College*. Vol.I. Thacker, Spink & Co. Calcutta. 1897.

Short, Martin. *Inside the Brotherhood: Further Secrets of the Freemasons*. Grafton. 1989.

Siddiqi, Iqtidar Hushin. 'Writings on Muslim Educational Movements in Modern India'. *Studies in Islam*. Vol.IX No.2. January 1972.

Siddiqui, M.K.A. *Educating a Backward Minority*. Abadi Publications. Calcutta. 1984.

Silver, Harold. *Education as History: Interpreting Nineteenth and Twentieth Century Education*. Methuen. 1983.

Simon, B. and I. Bradley eds. *Victorian Public Schools*. Gill & Macmillan. Dublin. 1975.

Singh, Nihar Nindan. *British Historiography on British Rule in India: The Life and Writings of Sir John William Kayes, 1814-1876*. Janaki Prakashan. New Delhi. 1986.

Singh, R.P. *Education in an Imperial Colony*. National. New Delhi. 1979.

Sinha, D.P. *The Educational Policy of the East India Company in Bengal to 1854*. Punthi Pustak. Calcutta. 1964.

Sirkin, Gerald and Natalie Robinson Sirkin. 'The Battle of Indian Education: Macaulay's Opening Salvo Newly Discovered'. *Victorian Studies*. Vol.14. June 1971.

Skocpol, Theda. 'Sociology's Historical Imagination'. Skocpol ed. *Vision and Method in Historical Sociology*.

Skocpol, Theda. ed. *Vision and Method in Historical Sociology*. Cambridge University Press. 1984.

Sleeman, W.H. *Rambles and Recollections of an Indian Official*. rev. ed. Vincent A. Smith ed. Oxford University Press. 1915.

Smith, G. Rex. Review of Ian Richard Netton ed. *Arabia and the Gulf: From Traditional Society to Modern States*. *Journal of the Royal Asiatic Society*. No.1. 1988.

Smith, Whitney. 'New Flags: State of Cambodia'. *The Flag Bulletin*. Vol.XXIX No.1. January-February 1990.

Spangenberg, Bradford. *British Bureaucracy in India: Status, Policy and the I.C.S., in the Late 19th Century*. South Asia Books. Columbia (Missouri). 1986.

Spivak, Gayatri Chakravorty. 'The Rami of Sirmur: An Essay in Reading the Archives'. *History and Theory*. Vol.XXIV No.3. 1985.

Stark, Freya. *The Journey's Echo*. John Murray. 1963.

Statistical Bulletin. Department of Education and Science. United Kingdom. 1/85. September 1985.

Statutes of The Great Priory of the United Religious, Military and Masonic Orders of the Temple and of St. John of Jerusalem, Palestine, Rhodes and Malta of England and Wales and Its Provinces Overseas. Grand Priory. 1986.

Stearns, Peter N. 'Social History Update: Sociology of Emotion'. *Journal of Social History*. Vol.22 No.3. Spring 1989.

'Stephen Austin'. n.a. *The Haileyburian and I.S.C. Chronicle*. November 1957.

Stevenson, David. *The Origins of Freemasonry: Scotland's Century, 1590-1710*. Cambridge University Press. 1988.

Stevenson-Hamilton, V.E.O. *Yes, Your Excellency*. Thomas Harmsworth, 1985.

Stoakes, Frank. 'Social and Political Change in the Third World: Some Peculiarities of Oil-Producing Principalities of the Persian Gulf'. Hopwood ed. *The Arabian Peninsula*.

Stone, Richard. *Information Resources in Australia on the Middle East*. National Library of Australia. Canberra. 1986.

Strachey, John. *The End of Empire*. Victor Gollancz. 1959.

Strachey, Lytton. *Eminent Victorians*. Penguin. Harmondsworth. 1918 [1986].

Strecker, Ivo. *The Social Practice of Symbolization: An Anthropological Analysis*. Athlone Press. 1988.

Suleiman, Michael W. 'Survey Research in the Islamic World: Challenges and Rewards'. *MESTAB*. Vol.19 No.2. December 1985.

Summary of the Proceedings of the Government of India in the Foreign Department during the Viceroyalty of Lord Curzon, January 1899 – November 1905: Native States. Superintendent of Government Printing. Calcutta. 1908.

Taylor, Laurie. 'Inter-course Intercourse', *Times Literary Supplement*, 17-23 November 1989.

Taylor, Peter J. 'Editorial Comment: Geographical Dialogue', *Political Geography Quarterly*. Vol.8 No.2. April 1989.

Thornton, A.P. *The Imperial Idea and Its Enemies: A Study in British Power*. 2nd ed. Macmillan. 1985 [1959].

Thring, Edward. *Theory and Practice of Teaching*. Cambridge University Press. 1910.

Tinker, Hugh. 'The Diary of a Military and Civil Nobody'. *Indo-British Review*. Vol.XIII No.2. July-December 1987.

Tirmizi, S.A. 'Record Management in British India'. *The Indian Archives*. Vol.XXIX No.2. 1980.

Toynbee, Arnold J. ed. *Survey of International Affairs 1934*. Oxford University Press. 1935

Trench, Charles Chenevix. *Viceroy's Agent*. Jonathan Cape. 1987.

Trevelyan, Humphrey. *The India We Left*. Macmillan. 1972.

Trevor-Roper, Hugh. 'The Invention of Tradition: The Highland Tradition of Scotland'. Hobsbawm ed. *Inventing Tradition*.

Trigger, Bruce G. 'Alternative Archaeologies: Nationalist, Colonialist, Imperialist'. *Man*. Vol.19 No.3. September 1984.

Trollope, Anthony. *Dr. Wortle's School*. Introduction by Dr. John Rae. The Trollope Society. 1989.

Trotter, David. 'Kipling's England: the Edwardian Years'. Mallett ed. *Kipling Considered*.

Turkle, Sherry Roxanne. 'Symbol and Festival in the French Student Uprising (May-June 1968)'. Moore ed. *Symbol and Politics in Communal Ideology*.

Turner, Bryan S. 'From Orientalism to Global Sociology'. *Sociology*. Vol.23 No.4. November 1989.

Turner, Victor. *Dramas, Fields, and Metaphors: Symbolic Action in Human Society*. Cornell University Press, Ithaca (New York). 1987 [1974].

Turner, Victor. *The Drums of Affliction*. Clarendon Press. Oxford. 1968.

Turner, Victor. *The Forest of Symbols*. Cornell University Press. Ithaca (New York). 1967.

Turner, Victor. *The Ritual Process: Structure and Anti-Structure*. Cornell University Press. Ithaca (New York). 1977 [1969].

Tuson, Penelope. 'Lieutenant Wyburd's Journal of an Excursion Into Arabia'. Sergeant and Bidwell eds. *Arabian Studies*. Vol.IX.

Tuson, Penelope. *The Records of the British Residency and Agencies in the Persian Gulf*. India Office Library, 1979.

Tuson, Penelope. 'Some British Views of Bahrain: The Work of the Bombay Marine and Indian Navy, 1785-1863'. Typescript provided by author. Paper given at 'Bahrain Through the Ages Conference'. Manama. 3-9 December 1983.

Tyack, David B. 'Foreword'. Silver. *Education as History*.

Tyagi, M.S. *British Administrative Policy in India (June 1895-September 1903)*. S.S. Publishers. Delhi. 1982.

Unwin, P.T.H. *Bahrain*. World Bibliographical Series. Clio Press. Oxford. 1984.

Unwin, P.T.H. *Qatar*. World Bibliographical Series. Clio Press. Oxford. 1982.

Usher, H.J.K. *An Angel Without Wings: The History of University College School*. Chancebest. Harrow. 1981.

van Wolferen, Karel. *The Enigma of Japanese Power: People and Politics in a Stateless Nation*. Macmillan. 1989.

Vaughan, David W.M. *The Diary of a Freed Mason*. Sovereign World. Chichester. n.d.

Visram, Rozina. *Ayahs, Lascars and Princes: Indians in Britain 1700-1947.* Pluto Press. 1986.

von Albertini, Rudolf. *European Colonial Rule, 1880-1940: The Impact of the West on India, Southeast Asia, and Africa.* Clio Press. Oxford. 1982.

von Wright, George Henrick. *Norms and Actions.* Routledge & Kegan Paul. 1963.

Wakefield, Edward. *Past Imperative: My Life in India, 1927-1947.* Chatto & Windus. 1966.

Walford, G.F. *Arabian Locust Hunter.* Robert Hale. 1963.

Ward, Humphry. *History of the Athenaeum, 1924-1925.* Athenaeum. 1926.

Waterbury, John. 'Social Science Research and Arab Studies'. Sharabi ed. *The Next Arab Decade.*

West, E.G. *Education and the State: A Study in Political Economy.* Institute of Economic Affairs. 1965.

Westcott, William Wynn. *The Magical Masons: Forgotten Hermetic Writings of William Wynn Westcott, Physician and Magus.* Aquarian Press. Wellingborough. 1983.

Wilkinson, Rupert. *The Prefects: Ritual Leadership and the Public School Tradition, A Comparative Study in the Making of Rulers.* Oxford University Press. 1964.

Williams, Patrick. '*Kim* and Orientalism'. Mallett ed. *Kipling Considered.*

Willis, Raymond. *Culture.* Fontana Press. 1986 [1981].

Willock, Tim. ed. *Social and Economic Development in the Arab Gulf.* Croom Helm. 1980.

Wilson, Arnold. *S.W. Persia: Letters and Diary of a Young Political Officer, 1907-1914.* Reader's Union. 1942.

Wilson, Arnold. *Thought and Talks.* Right Book Club. 1938.

Winder, R. Bayly. *Saudi Arabia in the Nineteenth Century.* Octagon. 1980 [1965].

Winstone, H.V.F. *Captain Shakespear.* Quartet Books. 1980.

Winstone, H.V.F. *The Illicit Adventure: The Story of Political and Military Intelligence in the Middle East from 1898 to 1926.* Jonathan Cape. 1982.

Winstone, H.V.F. and Zahra Freeth. *Kuwait: Prospect and Reality.* George Allen & Unwin. 1972.

Wissa, Karim. 'Freemasonry in Egypt 1798-1921: A Study in Cultural and Political Encounters'. *British Society for Middle Eastern Studies Bulletin.* Vol.16 No.2. 1989.

Wood, Anthony. *Nineteenth Century Britain, 1815-1914.* 2nd ed. Longman. 1982.

Woolacott, J.E. *British Rule in India.* Anmol Publications. Delhi. Reptd. 1986.

Yates, Nigel. *The Oxford Movement and Anglican Ritualism.* The Historical Association. 1984.

Yodfat, A. and M. Abir. *In the Direction of the Gulf: The Soviet Union and the Persian Gulf.* Cass. 1977.

Young, T. Cuyler. *Middle East Focus: The Persian Gulf.* Princeton University Conference. Princeton (New Jersey). 1969.

Zahlan, Rosemary Said. 'Hegemony, Dependence and Development in the Gulf'. Willock ed. *Social and Economic Development in the Arab Gulf.*

Zahlan, Rosemary Said. *The Making of the Modern Gulf States: Kuwait, Bahrain, Qatar, The United Arab Emirates and Oman.* Unwin Hyman. 1989.

Zinkin, Maurice and Taya. *Britain and India: Requiem for Empire.* Chatto & Windus. 1964.

Zwemer, S.M. *Arabia: The Cradle of Islam.* 2nd ed. Fleming H. Revell. New York. 1900.

Journals and Newspapers

The American Historical Review, American Journal of Archaeology, American Sociological Review, Archives, Ars Quatuor Coronatorium, Aspects of Education Journal.

British Society for Middle Eastern Studies Bulletin, The Bulletin (Sydney).

Coins and Medals News.

Economist.

Financial Times, Financial Review (Sydney), Flag Bulletin.

Garden History, Geographic Journal, The Guardian, The Guardian Weekly, Gulf Times.

The Haileyburian and I.S.C. Chronicle, Hansard, History of Education, History of Education Review, History & Theory, Horizons.

Ideas and Production, The Imperial and Asiatic Quarterly Review and Oriental and Colonial Record, Indian Archives, The Indian Freemason, Institute for Social Research Newsletter, International Herald Tribune.

The Journal of Comparative Education, Journal of Historical Sociology, Journal of the Royal Asiatic Society, Journal of Social History.

Khaleej Times.

Lloyds Bank Economic Bulletin.

Man, Medal News, MESTAB, Middle East Journal, The Muslim World.

The New Age.

The Observer, Organization of American Historians Newsletter.

Parabola, Political Geography Quarterly, PS: Political Science & Politics.

Science, Sociology, Studies in Islam.

This is Qatar, The Times, Times Educational Supplement, Times Higher Educational Supplement, Times Literary Supplement.

UR: The International Magazine of Arab Culture.

Victorian Studies.

World Development.

Dissertations

Littlefield, Richard E. 'Bahrain as a Persian Gulf State: With Reference to Its Relations with Great Britain and the Province of Al-Hasa'. M.A. thesis. American University of Beirut. 1964.

McGreal, Shirley Pollitt. 'A History of Mayo College, Ajmer, India, 1875-1971'. Ph.D. dissertation. University of Cincinnati. 1971.

Moir, Ian. 'A Study of the History and Organization of the Political and Secret Department of the East India Company, the Board of Control, and the India Office, 1784-1919, With a Summary List of Records'. University of London Diploma in Archive Administration thesis. 1966.

Rich, Paul John. 'The Rule of Ritual in the Arabian Gulf, 1858-1947: The Influence of the English Public Schools'. Ph.D. dissertation. The University of Western Australia. 1989.

Archives

Archives of the Reformed Church of America, Sage Library, New Brunswick (New Jersey). See H. Conway Ziegler, 'A Brief Flowering in the Desert: Protestant Missionary Activity in the Arabian Gulf, 1889-1973', M.A. dissertation, Princeton University, 1977. In the archive see esp. Stanley G. Mylrea, 'Kuwait Before Oil: Memoirs of Dr. C. Stanley G. Mylrea, Pioneer Medical Missionary of The Arabian Mission, Reformed Church in America', written between 1945 and 1951, bound typescript, 'produced privately by Mrs. John Van Ess and Mrs. A.L. Warnshuis'. Also 'Minutes of the Annual Meeting of the American Mission', November 1912, manuscript.

India Office Library and Records. Besides the book-length contributions of Tuson and others, the IOLR produces a variety of short guides to specific parts of its collections whose information will not be reproduced here. As already mentioned, some India Office holdings have been photographed and published by Archives Editions, including *The Persian Gulf Administration Reports, 1873-1947*. The *Administration Reports* should not be confused with the *Bahrain Government Annual Reports*, begun in 1925 by the Political Agent, Clive Daly, and carried on by Charles Belgrave after he became adviser to the shaikh in 1926. The originals are in the R/15/1/350-355 series. Belgrave also prepared reports for the Political Agent, found in the series R/15/2/296-305. These are distinct from the Annual Reports and after being edited appeared along with other reports from around the Gulf in the series R/15/6/473-541, which Archives has published as *The Persian Gulf Administration Reports*. Not understanding this process leads to confusion, *i.e.* Jacqueline Ismael in *Kuwait* (Syracuse University Press, 1982, page 18, note 18) found a Gulf Administration Report for 1918 in Dickson's papers at St. Antony's College, Oxford, and cited it as if it were a unique document. It is a copy of IOR:15/6/519.

National Archives. Washington, D.C. Intelligence Reports. Persian Gulf. Declassified 7/30/85. The author has placed a representative selection in the India Office Library and Records. He has given a selection of letters that relate to the Royal Geographical Society to the Society's archives. The Royal Geographical Society archives are cited RGS.

INDEX

ALLBOROUGH MIDDLE EAST CLASSICS

With introductions by Paul Rich.

In the wake of current troubles in the Gulf, an understanding of the area's convoluted history has become invaluable for those who wish to assess the present situation. Many of the border conflicts and disputes surrounding the legitimacy of the ruling families and governments have their foundations in the period of, and immediately after, the First World War. The effects of the British Empire's involvement in the area (analysed in *The Invasions of the Gulf*) were widespread, causing cultural and political upheavals that are still at the heart of the area's problems. The Allborough Middle East Classics provide a great insight into the events of that period by presenting first-hand accounts of the Gulf at that time, from a variety of authors and viewpoints. Long since out of print and unavailable even to the most ardent enthusiast, these valuable texts are now republished and updated by Allborough Press in association with Paul Rich, who provides in-depth explanatory introductions to all the books. These volumes now once more provide both essential reference material for the Middle East specialist and enlightening reading for those wishing to learn more about the history of one of the world's most dangerous flashpoints.

The Allborough Middle East Classics series comprises:

IRAQ AND IMPERIALISM: Thomas Lyell's *Mesopotamia*
A SOLDIER IN KURDISTAN: Rupert Hay's *Two Years in Kurdistan*
UNHAPPY KUWAIT, UNFORTUNATE IRAQ: C.M. Cursetjee's *Land of the Date*
WARTIME IN BAGHDAD 1914-1922: Eleanor Egan's *War in the Cradle of the World*
CHAOS IN IRAQ: Aylmer Haldane's *The Insurrection in Mesopotamia, 1920*
THE IRAQI MIND: Henry Foster's *The Making of Modern Iraq*
ARAB WAR LORDS AND IRAQI STARGAZERS: Gertrude Bell's *The Secret Basra Papers*
IRAQ, IRAN AND RITUAL MURDER: T.C. Fowle's *Travels in the Middle East*

ALLBOROUGH ELECTRONIC BOOKS